Confederate Fort Fisher
A Roster, 1864-1865

By

Richard H. Triebe

First Edition published by Smokey River Publishing.

ISBN-13: 978-0-9798965-4-5

ISBN-10: 0-9798965-4-1

Cover Painting: "Charge of the Marines on the Traverse" by Julian O. Davidson

Front and Back Cover Design by Richard H. Triebe.

Other books by this author:

Fort Fisher to Elmira, ISBN 978-1453687369
Point Lookout Prison Camp and Hospital, ISBN 978-0-9798965-3-8
Port Royal, ISBN 0-9798-9650-9
On A Rising Tide, ISBN 1-4208-7849-2

Printed in the United States of America

This book is printed on acid-free paper.

Contact Information:
Email: richtriebe@aol.com
Web Address: richardsbooks.net

Printed in the United States of America.

Smokey River Publishing

Table of Contents

Dedication

This book was written to honor all the soldiers who fought and died during the battles of Fort Fisher, North Carolina. It is hoped that in some small way this text will help to keep alive the memory of all the men who perished at Fort Fisher.

Introduction

Like all good war stories the battle of Fort Fisher has all the elements needed to make a great tale. The fort's hopelessly outnumbered Confederate defenders made a heroic Alamo-like stand against the invincible Union juggernaut. Like the Texans before them, they also called for help but were largely ignored by General Braxton Bragg. Undeterred, the Confederate soldiers stood to their guns and fought gallantly until they were overwhelmed by superior numbers. Both sides fought well but thanks to the lack of support from Bragg, the fort, and ultimately Wilmington was lost.

Visiting the remains of the fort, I can't help but think of all the history those traverses and gun chambers have seen. Nearly one hundred and fifty years ago soldiers in blue and gray met here in mortal combat. The carnage was horrible. After the battle solders stated that it was difficult to walk without stepping on bodies of the dead and wounded. This is indeed hallowed ground because it was made sacred by the blood of soldiers who fought and died here.

I began researching the Fort Fisher's battles about twenty-five years ago. This was not done with the intention of writing a book, but merely because I was fascinated with Fort Fisher's history. I also wondered about the Confederate soldiers who were stationed here. What were they feeling when the vast Union armada sailed into sight? Fifty-six warships, bristling with huge cannon, had to be an awe-inspiring sight because the fleet stretched from horizon to horizon. Soon dozens of Union transports landed an immense invasion force north of the fort. Certainly the Confederate soldiers must have had doubts about their ability to withstand such a formidable assault. Fortunately they were led by capable men like Major General William H. C. Whiting and Colonel William Lamb. These men fought gallantly and made what appeared an impossible task seem fairly doable if they had had cooperation from General Bragg. This was not to be. Bragg's inactivity sealed the fate of the men at Fort Fisher.

Thanks to the plethora of information on the internet, what began as a hobby so long ago has developed into this book. I have included soldiers accounts of the battle which gives us a perspective of what it was like. I can't think of a better person to write about the battles than the commanding officer of Fort Fisher; Colonel William Lamb has written a gripping account of that life and death struggle. We are indeed fortunate to have an author who was aware of the many facts surrounding this battle. A few of the soldier's accounts tell where their company was during the fight, so I have included a special section that lists those locations. I added this information into the roster at the back of the book as well.

I have also consulted over 2,400 soldiers' records at the National Archives and made a roster of all the Confederate troops who were involved in the second battle. This list includes North Carolina Troops as well as South Carolina Volunteers, Confederate States sailors and marines. Many times these records indicated the nature of the wound a soldier received, often specifying whether it was caused by a rifle bullet or a shell fragment.

Lastly is included a statistics section which breaks down the number of killed, wounded and captured for each regiment. This is helpful to determine which units were involved in the heaviest fighting.

With Fort Fisher captured, the Federal Army turned its sights on Wilmington. After all, closing the "Port City" to blockade-running had been the objective of the Wilmington Campaign all along. Now with Fort Fisher out of the way, all that stood between Union General Terry and Wilmington was General Hoke's 6,000 Confederate troops. After five-weeks of skirmishing with Confederate forces, the city was abandoned and the Union Army marched triumphantly into Wilmington. Forty-five days later the war ended when General Robert E. Lee surrendered at Appomattox, Virginia.

Richard H. Triebe
Wilmington, N. C., May 2013

Chapter 1

Abraham Lincoln Takes Office and the South Secedes

History of battle is reprinted from *Fort Fisher to Elmira*

Abraham Lincoln in 1860

When Abraham Lincoln ascended to the presidency on March 4, 1861, he was faced with the worst nightmare a president could have. South Carolina and six other states had announced their intention to secede and it appeared the nation was headed toward open rebellion and armed conflict. Lincoln, who wanted to preserve the Union at all costs, tried to calm the anxieties of the Southern states by assuring them their property and personal security would not be endangered because a Republican administration was taking office. In his inaugural address Lincoln vowed that he had no intention of interfering with the institution of slavery and he would enforce the Fugitive Slave Act. This controversial law declared that all runaway slaves be returned to their masters.

However, Lincoln also declared secession to be illegal and announced he would "hold, occupy and possess the property and places belonging to the government and collect the duties and imposts." South Carolina reacted to Lincoln's promises by bombarding Fort Sumter in Charleston Harbor on April 12, 1861. A discouraged but determined President Lincoln called for 75,000 volunteers to help put down the Southern insurrection.[1]

On April 19th President Abraham Lincoln declared a blockade of Confederate ports. Lincoln was aware the Confederacy did not have the weapons of war to sustain a rebellion past six months. He also knew that because the Southern states lacked the manufacturing necessary to produce these weapons, they would be forced to rely on trade with Europe. Therefore, the United States Navy must blockade the Confederacy. However, Lincoln's peacetime navy had only ninety warships to enforce a blockade of 3,549 miles of Southern coastline. Unfortunately, half of these vessels were obsolete sailing craft used mainly as training vessels.

When the Federal blockade began it was largely a blockade in name only because the United States lacked enough warships ships to enforce it.[2]

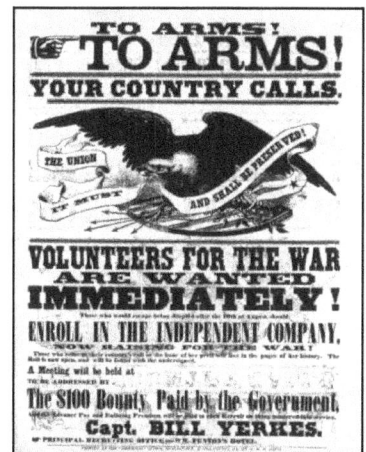
1861 Union recruitment poster

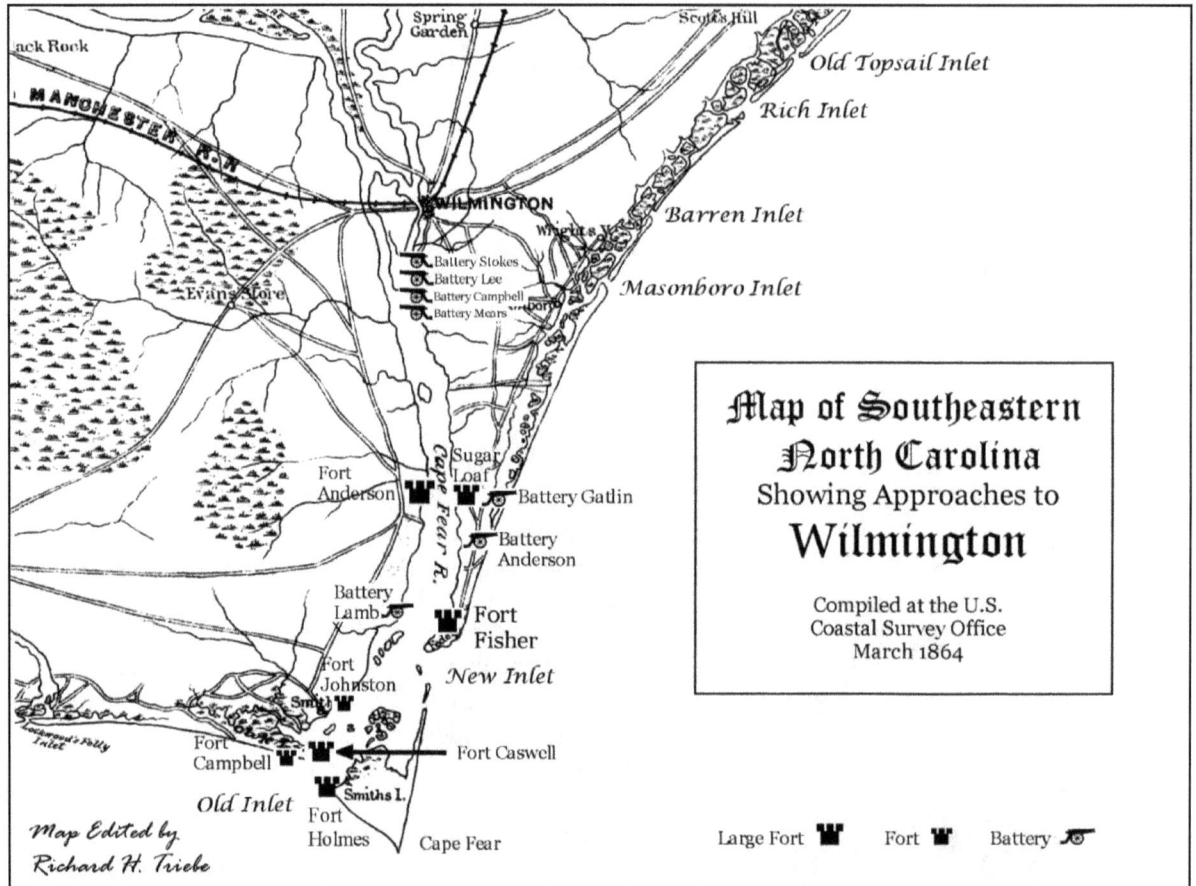

Map of the approaches to Wilmington, North Carolina, showing the Confederate forts and batteries guarding the Cape Fear River.

As the war progressed, and more navy ships became available, the blockade became more effective. One by one the Confederate ports were closed by the Federal Navy until only the port of Wilmington, North Carolina, remained open. By the summer of 1864 Wilmington literally became the *Lifeline of the Confederacy* since it was the only seaport still able to supply the South with the materials it needed to survive. A large factor in making Wilmington ideal for blockade-runners and commerce raiders was its advantageous geography. The city lay twenty-eight miles up the Cape Fear River, well protected from the Federal fleet offshore. Blockade-runners could choose from two inlets to enter the Cape Fear River. Old Inlet and New Inlet were only six miles apart but due to the treacherous Frying Pan Shoals, this distance was extended to an arc of fifty miles. This meant the Federal Navy would have to blockade both entrances. Such an undertaking would require twice the men and ships. Perhaps the biggest factor in creating a superior blockade-running port was due to the presence of Fort Fisher. This mighty fort was the largest and most powerful earthwork fort in the Confederacy and guarded the entrances to the Cape Fear River and the crucial port of Wilmington.

Excellent transportation also made Wilmington a desirable destination for blockade-runners. Once the vessel's cargo was on the Wilmington docks it was relatively easy to ship these items to where they were needed. The city was served by three railroad lines that went to different parts of the South. The Wilmington & Weldon Railroad was the city's most important line because it became the main supply route for Robert E. Lee's Army of Northern Virginia. Another important line was the Wilmington & Manchester Railroad because it traveled into South Carolina and connected the port city with Charleston. Charleston was a major blockade-running port herself until the Federal Navy tightened its blockade and made it virtually impossible to run into or out of the city. A third line was the Wilmington, Charlotte & Rutherford Railroad which traversed the North Carolina Piedmont and was an important route into the interior. The Cape Fear River also served as a highway for the goods brought in through the blockade. This river flowed to the northwest and was navigable for 100 miles for small to medium-sized vessels.

Unlike most fortifications, Fort Fisher was only a two-sided structure. Since the fort was built near the end of Confederate Point peninsula, the mile-wide Cape Fear River acted as its third and final side. The fort resembled an enormous number seven with the long side facing the sea and the short, upper side crossing the peninsula. The woods had been cleared for a half-mile north of the land-face to provide a clear field of fire for the Confederate defenders. To discourage an infantry attack, an electrically detonated mine field and a nine-foot palisade fence of sharpened stakes was erected fifty feet in front of the fort. Its twenty-five foot high land-face stretched from the Cape Fear River on the west to the Atlantic Ocean on its right, a distance of one third mile.

Fort Fisher mounted a total of forty-four heavy cannon, not counting the field artillery and mortars. The land-face contained sixteen gun chambers, mounting twenty-three heavy seacoast artillery pieces, which were separated by fifteen-foot high mounds of sand called traverses. These traverses protected the gun chambers from enfilading fire and also gave Fort Fisher its characteristic bumpy appearance. Inside the hollowed-out traverse was a bombproof where the men could take refuge and an ordinance magazine. The land-face gun chambers were

Colonel William Lamb, the commander of Fort Fisher.

accessible from the rear by wooden stairs and a long interior passage connected all the bombproofs. The fort's gate, located in the western-most corner, was barricaded with sandbags and guarded by two field artillery pieces.

Halfway down the land-face was a tunnel through the earthen wall that ended in a raised gun platform for field artillery. In military jargon of the day this was known as a sally-port. Since these cannon were mobile, the gunners could push the artillery pieces inside the mound to seek shelter during a bombardment. Then, when the shelling ceased, the cannon could be run out to fire on an enemy approaching from the north. Since the sally-port extended outside the walls of the fort it was possible for the artillery pieces to have flanking fire on an enemy to the east or west of its position.[3]

The earthwork continued at a right angle where the land-face meets the sea-face. Here a forty-three foot mound of sand known as the Northeast Bastion provided the commander, Colonel William Lamb, with a sweeping view of the Atlantic Ocean and the entire fort. Just to the south lay the Pulpit Battery, or Lamb's combat headquarters. Below the crescent-shaped Pulpit Battery lay the fort's field hospital. This structure extended twenty-eight feet into the mound of sand. The hospital's sides and roof were reinforced with huge oak timbers to hold the enormous weight of the Pulpit Battery. Surgeons Joseph C. Shepard and Spiers Singleton, along with a half-dozen assistant surgeons, would perform their operations by lantern light in the one-hundred foot long hospital. A semi-circular mound of sand lay nearly parallel to the hospital's entrance, protecting it from shell explosions in the fort's interior. As massive as the hospital was, it was still not roomy enough to house all the soldiers wounded during the second battle. Dozens of stretchers would be lined up outside the building while only the most seriously injured men were brought inside for surgery.[4]

Most of the sea-face was almost a duplicate of the land-face but it was only half as high and much longer in length. About midway down its rampart was the fort's heaviest gun, a monstrous 150-pounder Armstrong rifled cannon. The gun was a gift for the Confederacy from Sir W. G. Armstrong at Armstrong & Co. of London in 1864. This artillery piece was known for its accuracy and tremendous range. It came mounted on a beautiful mahogany and rosewood carriage fitted with brass hardware. It was said the gun crew took great pride in keeping the enormous cannon cleaned and polished.[5]

The sixty-foot Mound Battery anchored the south end of the fort and dominated the surrounding area armed with two heavy seacoast artillery pieces. The Mound kept Federal ships a respectable distance from the fort, and its gunners could direct a plunging fire onto the decks of enemy ships attempting to enter New Inlet. Since it was the tallest structure on Confederate Point, its summit was fitted with a beacon to signal blockade-runners. One of the most successful blockade-runner captains, John Wilkinson called the Mound Battery, "an excellent landmark. Joined by a long low isthmus of sand with the higher main land, its regular conical shape enabled the blockade-runner easily to identify it from the offing and in clear weather; it showed plain and distinct against the sky at night."[6]

On the tip of the peninsula, two-thirds of a mile southwest of the Mound Battery, Lamb constructed his final defensive work. Battery Buchanan was an elliptically-shaped earthwork designed to protect New Inlet and the fort's rear. Buchanan extended 320 feet and was enclosed with fifteen-foot sloping walls which mounted two 11-inch Brooke smoothbores and two 10-inch Columbiad cannons. Lamb later wrote, "Battery Buchanan was a citadel to which an overpowered garrison might retreat and with proper transportation be carried off at night, and to which reinforcements could be safely sent under the cover of darkness."[7]

Fortunately for the Confederacy, capturing the port of Wilmington remained low on the Federal list of priorities during the first years of the war. Northern generals focused their attention on the immediate threat posed by the Southern armies. The Federal armies of the Potomac and the James had been trying to defeat Robert E. Lee's Army of Northern Virginia and capture Richmond since the beginning of the war. Closing the port of Wilmington would have to wait until more men became available. The error with this thinking was that it gave the South a viable seaport that allowed supplies to flow uninterrupted to the Confederate Army. It also provided the Confederates with the opportunity to strengthen Fort Fisher and the other defenses around the mouth of the Cape Fear River.

The sixty-foot high Mound Battery served as a landmark for blockade-runners. Image Timothy O'Sullivan, *Photograph courtesy of the National Archives.*

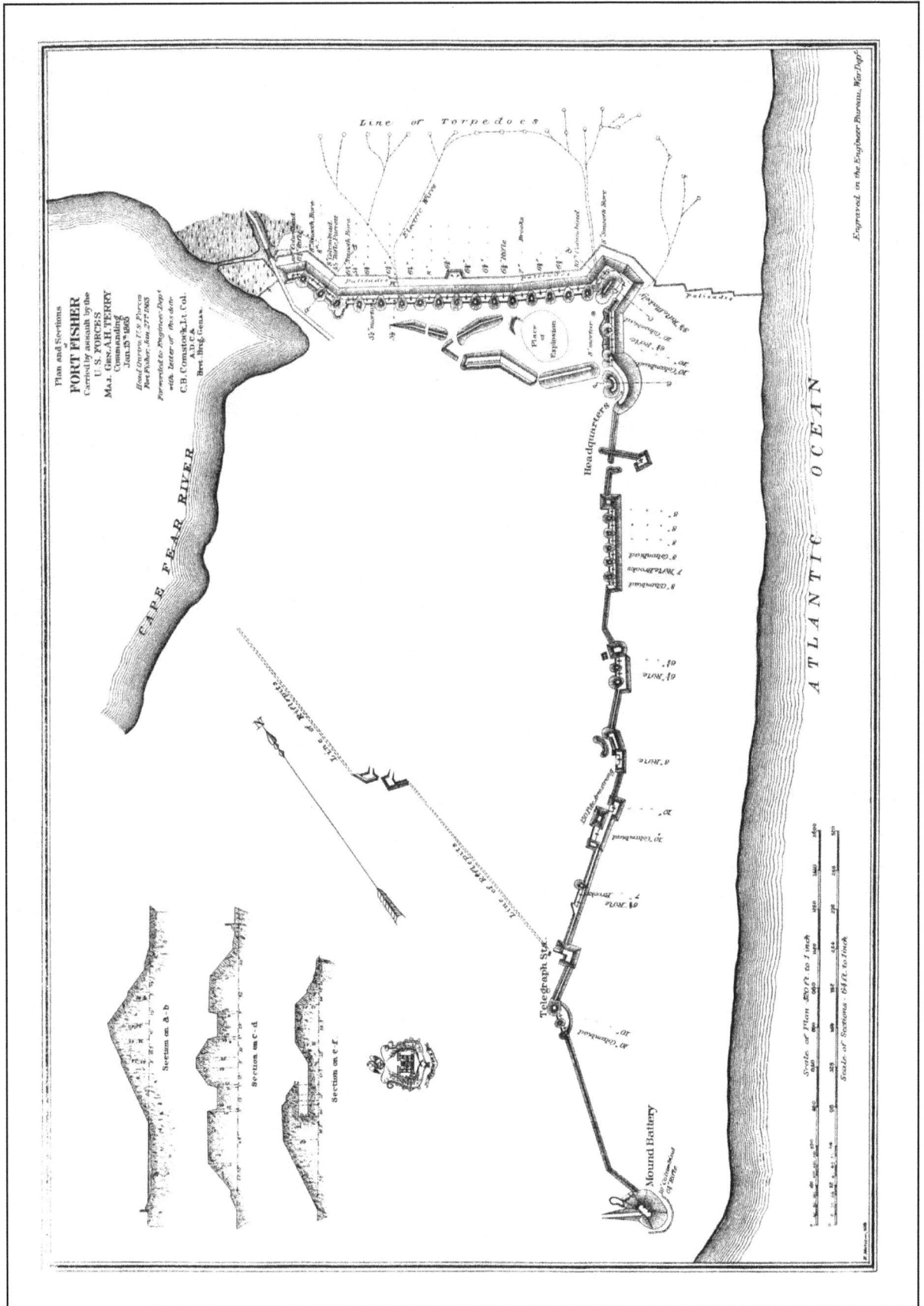

Map of Fort Fisher drawn by Lieutenant Colonel Cyrus B. Comstock in 1865

Firing at a blockade-runner off Wilmington, North Carolina, drawing from *Harper's Weekly*.

Chapter 2

Wilmington Takes On New Importance

"The importance of closing Wilmington and cutting off Rebel communication is paramount to all other questions—more important practically than the capture of Richmond." Gideon Wells, United States Secretary of the Navy, September 15, 1864

Capturing the port of Wilmington became more attractive to Lieutenant General Ulysses S. Grant in the fall of 1864. Union General William T. Sherman's army had nearly completed its March to the Sea and was nearing the Georgia coast. After capturing Savannah, Sherman then planned to drive north through the Carolinas, and he would need a seaport to resupply his army and reinforce it with more troops if necessary. Grant saw Wilmington as the perfect place to accomplish this. On September 12, 1864, he wrote to Sherman saying, "I want to send a force of from six to ten thousand men against Wilmington. This will give us the same control of the harbor of Wilmington that we now have of the harbor of Mobile."[1]

Federal War and Navy Departments organized a joint movement to insure the Fort Fisher expedition's success. Secretary of the Navy Gideon Welles chose Rear-Admiral David D. Porter to lead the naval assault against Fort Fisher, while General Grant selected Major General Godfrey Weitzel to command the army expedition. Weitzel's superior, Major General Benjamin F. Butler, felt that Weitzel was too young

Major General Benjamin Butler

and inexperienced to handle such a complicated operation so he assumed command instead. In fact, Butler was looking for a way to redeem himself after his miserable failures at New Orleans and Bermuda Hundred.

Because of his infamous proclamation Butler's image decorates the bottom of thousands of chamber pots.

Bitterly resentful of the Union occupation of New Orleans, the ladies of that city took pleasure in heaping insults on the occupying soldiers. Whenever any of Butler's men were present they would contemptuously gather in their skirts, cross streets, flee rooms, cast hateful glances, or make disrespectful comments. Some sang spirited renditions of "The Bonnie Blue Flag" and other Confederate songs. Naval commander David G. Farragut became a target of the women's wrath when the contents of a chamber pot was emptied on his head by a Confederate woman in an upstairs window as he walked down a street. Butler, infuriated by these insults, issued his notorious General Order Number 28 that declared any woman who was disrespectful to a Federal officer would be arrested as a prostitute plying her trade. Benjamin Butler's image decorated chamber pots throughout the South. President Jeff Davis also declared Butler a criminal to be hanged if captured. Butler's reputation took another serious hit in June of that year when he had a New Orleans man hanged for tearing down a United States flag.[2]

7

BUTLER'S PROCLAMATION

An outrageous insult to the Women of New Orleans!

Southern Men, avenge their wrongs ! ! !

Head-Quarters, Department of the Gulf,
New Orleans, May 15, 1862.

General Orders, No. 28.

As the Officers and Soldiers of the United States have been subject to repeated insults from the women calling themselves ladies of New Orleans, in return for the most scrupulous non-interference and courtesy on our part, it is ordered that hereafter when any Female shall, by word, gesture, or movement, insult or show contempt for any officer or soldier of the United States, she shall be regarded and held liable to be treated as a woman of the town plying her avocation.

By command of Maj.-Gen. BUTLER,
GEORGE C. STRONG,
A. A. G. Chief of Stables.

General Butler's Proclamation infuriated Southerners and prompted Confederate President Jefferson Davis to order Butler to be hanged if captured.

General Butler was known for his fanciful ideas regarding new weapons of warfare. He had once suggested that fire engines could be used to destroy Confederate earthworks by shooting jets of water at them, and for a while he had promoted a plan to tunnel under Richmond and launch a surprise attack from beneath the city. The latest brainstorm of the infamous general concerned a floating bomb. Butler was fascinated by this idea ever since a tremendous explosion of a munitions barge on the James River entirely destroyed a wharf, killing forty-three people and wounding one hundred twenty-six. It was later determined that Confederate agents had planted an explosive device on the barge.[3]

Butler concocted an ambitious scheme to blow down the walls of Fort Fisher and stun its garrison into submission with a giant floating bomb. Admiral Porter was skeptical of the plan at first, but after talking with Butler he reluctantly agreed to supply the sacrificial vessel that would be used. The *USS Louisiana* was a 295-ton, 143-foot long iron hulled steamer that only drew eight and a half feet of water when fully loaded. This shallow draft was important because the *Louisiana* would have to be towed into shore and run aground for the explosion to have the desired effect on the fort. She was stripped of her boiler and machinery and a fake smokestack was erected near the ship's single stack and the vessel painted a dull gray. On a dark night the ship could easily pass for a blockade-runner and get close to Fort Fisher without being fired upon. Once her disguise was complete, the *Louisiana* was towed a safe distance away from the federal fleet at Hampton Roads, Virginia, and loaded with 215 tons of gunpowder.

Admiral Porter gathered a variety of warships to pound Fort Fisher into submission. Sixty-four armed vessels with 635 guns took part in the bombardment in December 1864. This flotilla included four ironclad monitors propelled by either side-wheels or screw propellers, and wooden-hulled steam frigates. Porter's largest steam frigate was the *Colorado*, with fifty-two guns, followed by the *Minnesota* and *Wabash*, with forty-six and forty-four respectively. The pride of Porter's fleet was the *New Ironsides*, whose hull was sheathed with four inches of iron. This warship carried fourteen 11-inch guns, two 150-pounders, and two 60-pounders. The monitor *Monadnock* boasted four 15-inch guns whose shells weighed three hundred pounds each.[4]

Admiral Porter's armada left Hampton Roads on December 13, 1864. Porter asked Butler to allow the navy at least twelve hours lead time because his heavily armed warships were weighty and slow, and the unseaworthy monitors and the *Louisiana* would have to be towed. He also needed to stop at Beaufort, North Carolina, to take on more fuel and ammunition for the monitors and more gunpowder for the *Louisiana*. Butler agreed with the admiral.

At Petersburg, Virginia, Confederate General Robert E. Lee received a report that the Federal armada had sailed from Hampton Roads. He knew the fleet could be bound for either Charleston, South

Carolina, or Wilmington, North Carolina. As it happened, Lee was brooding over reports that his Army of Northern Virginia had less than a month's worth of rations. If Fort Fisher fell, Lee's most important artery of supply would be severed. Lee could not afford this, so he withdrew General Robert F. Hoke's Division of 6,150 men from the trenches around Petersburg, and ordered them to help defend Wilmington.[5]

When General Butler arrived twenty-five miles east of Cape Fear, North Carolina, on December 15th, he was surprised to find only a few naval vessels on station. He was told that Admiral Porter was in Beaufort with most of the fleet getting supplies. While Butler waited for Porter to arrive the weather was perfect with spring-like temperatures and calm seas. Unfortunately, the pleasant weather began to deteriorate after three days. Somehow the communication between General Butler and Admiral Porter was disrupted. Butler steamed north to Beaufort to seek shelter from the gale while Porter's fleet put out to sea and braced itself for the coming storm. Despite high seas and gale-force winds the naval fleet rode out the storm without loss of life or vessel. Unable to meet up with Butler or his army, Porter decided to explode the powder boat near Fort Fisher. When Butler's aide arrived on the morning of December 23rd, Porter informed him of his plans to tow the *Louisiana* toward shore that night and explode it. The aide returned to Beaufort to report Porter's intentions to General Butler.

The Federal armada sent to capture Fort Fisher contained powerful ships such as the forty-four gun frigate *USS Wabash*. Painting by artist Clary Ray. *Photograph courtesy of the Naval Historical Foundation.*

Butler was furious when he heard the news. He felt that Porter wanted to destroy Fort Fisher in the army's absence so he could claim all the credit for himself. "The Admiral supposed he would blow the fort all to pieces, and be able to land with his marines and take possession of it," Butler seethed. His officers agreed with their superior that Porter was seeking all the glory.[6]

Admiral Porter's fleet assembling at Hampton Roads, Virginia, for the Wilmington expedition. *Photograph courtesy of the Naval Historical Foundation.*

Chapter 3

The First Attack

The steamer *USS Louisiana* was disguised to look like a blockade-runner, loaded with 215 tons of gunpowder and towed to Fort Fisher as a floating bomb. Drawing from *Harper's Weekly*.

Commander Alexander Rhind of the *USS Wilderness* put a crew aboard the *Louisiana* to detonate the ship when she grounded on the shallows near Fort Fisher. It was 10:30 PM when the *Wilderness* towed the floating bomb toward shore, cast it loose in the darkness and then picked up the crew after they had set the fuses.

Admiral Porter took the fleet to an anchorage twelve miles off shore and ordered all the ships to release the steam from their boilers so they would not rupture from the gigantic explosion that was sure to light up the night. Shortly after midnight sailors of the Federal fleet spotted several rockets in the western sky—Rhind's signal that the powder boat was set to detonate. For more than an hour they waited. At 1:40 AM the sailors saw a bright flame on the horizon. Commander Daniel Ammen on board the *Mohican* recalled the explosion resembled distant lightning. Seconds later a low rumble that sounded like an approaching thunderstorm raced across the water. As the rumble increased, the masts and spars on the vessels began to rattle, but the explosion failed to live up to expectations. Disappointed at the feeble explosion, Commander Rhind turned to the men on the *Wilderness*, shook his head and said, "There's a fizzle!" General Butler's idea of using a powder boat to destroy Fort Fisher had proved to be a loud and spectacular failure.[1]

Colonel William Lamb had already gone to bed when the *Louisiana* blew up. Fort Fisher was undamaged, but the fort's sentries immediately sounded the alarm, alerting Lamb and the garrison. When Lamb observed the burning wreckage of an unknown vessel, he wired General Whiting in Wilmington and informed him that, "a blockader got aground near the fort, set fire to herself and blew up."[2]

The first Confederate sentry to spot the Federal Fleet was Private Arthur Muldoon. He was detailed as a lookout upon of Fort Fisher's Pulpit Battery when the Federal warships materialize one by one out of the early morning mist. Muldoon sent for Colonel Lamb at once. Lamb wrote about what he observed in *Colonel Lamb's Story of Fort Fisher*:

A grander sight than the approach of Porter's formidable armada toward the fort was never witnessed on our coast. On the vessels came, growing larger and more imposing as the distance lessened between them and the resolute men who had rallied to defend their homes. The *Minnesota, Colorado* and *Wabash* came grandly on, floating fortresses, each mounting more guns than all the batteries on land, and the first two combined carrying more shot and shell than all the magazines in the fort combined.[3]

Lamb watched the Federal fleet deploy with a mixture of awe and dread. Fort Fisher's garrison had always been undermanned even though General Whiting had pleaded with President Davis to send him more troops. Even after receiving reinforcements from the other Cape Fear defenses Colonel Lamb only commanded 1,371 soldiers, a third of whom were Junior Reservists, mere boys sixteen to eighteen years of age. Lamb was also worried there was too little ammunition for him to allow his gunners to fire at will. For all forty-four of the fort's cannon, Lamb had a total of 3,000 rounds—an average of 68 rounds per gun. Ammunition would have to be rationed and controlled. Lamb ordered that only long-range guns would fight the ships, and no piece would be permitted to fire more than once every half-hour. To spare the men from unnecessary exposure, the gun crews remained inside the bombproofs until the time came to fire their half-hourly shot. Lamb's largest artillery piece, the gigantic 150-pounder Armstrong cannon, had only thirteen rounds of ammunition and he ordered it to be fired only at his command.[4]

The forty-six gun frigate *USS Minnesota* was one of the ships which Colonel Lamb had seen on the morning of January 13, 1865. *Photograph courtesy of the Naval History & Heritage Command.*

Lamb was afraid Porter would use the same naval tactic that was employed by Admiral Farragut in Mobile Bay, Alabama. Farragut had run his fleet past three Confederate forts and captured all of them from behind. If Porter could cross the sandbar at the river's entrance and proceed up river, Fort Fisher could be taken from the rear because its defenses were directed seaward, away from the ships behind them. Lamb was determined that this would not happen here. He ordered his gunners to fire as rapidly as possible if any attempt was made to enter the Cape Fear River.

While still beyond the range of the fort, the wooden ships slowed and the ironclads steamed ahead. The *New Ironsides, Monadnock, Saugus, Canonicus* and *Mahopac* reached their anchorage about three-quarters of a mile off the beach. They came into line, dropped bow and stern anchors so their broadsides could bear on the fort. The gunboats deployed into three adjacent lines of battle forming an arc running north to south with lines of fire directed at specific gun chambers in Fort Fisher.

The honor of opening the battle went to the *USS New Ironsides*. A sudden flash of light and a great cloud of smoke billowed from one of her starboard cannon. An 11-inch shell screamed over the heads of the Confederate defenders and exploded harmlessly in the rear of the fort. The *New Ironsides* first shot started a chain of broadsides down the length of the lines. "It was a magnificent sight," Federal Naval officer B. F. Blair wrote to his mother, "and one never to be forgotten. [The ships'] sides seemed sheets of flame and the roar of their guns like a mighty thunderbolt. . . .Nothing could withstand such a storm of shot and shell as was now poured into this fort."[5]

The *USS New Ironsides* fired the first shot, an 11-inch shell, into Fort Fisher. Painting by artist Clary Ray. *Photograph courtesy of the Naval Historical Foundation.*

From his position atop the Pulpit Battery, Colonel Lamb could see the *New Ironside's* shell as it hurtled over the ocean. When it exploded, he ordered the fort's signal gun fired. The huge Columbiad cannon bellowed a deep roar and sent the fort's first round whizzing toward the fleet. The missile, a 10-inch solid shot cannonball, ricocheted off the sea, bounded over the rail of the *USS Susquehanna* and punched a gaping hole in the ship's smokestack. This was the signal the fort's gunners were waiting for. They sprang into action and the line of batteries on the fort's sea-face belched fire and sulfur-laden smoke. Several of Porter's ships were struck in this opening salvo. The *USS Minnesota* was struck four times, losing her anchor cable and sustaining damage to her rigging and masts.[6]

Anchored at their battle stations, the long line of Federal warships replied with a stunning barrage. A mile-wide storm of shot and shell screamed toward the fort, exploding overhead and sending hot iron fragments to plow up the fort's sandy interior. When the frigates *Minnesota, Colorado* and *Wabash* opened up, Captain Thomas Selfridge wrote:

> The enemy replied briskly, but when these frigates found the range and commenced firing rapidly, nothing could withstand their broadsides of twenty-five 9-inch guns. It was a magnificent sight to see these frigates fairly engaged, and one never to be forgotten. Their sides seemed a sheet of flame and the roar of their guns like a mighty thunderbolt.[7]

Aboard the large warships conditions were almost intolerable for the sailors working the guns. The constant roar, smoke and concussion of cannon fire in tight, confined spaces aboard ship prompted Acting Master's Mate Joseph Simms to comment, "The roar of the cannon was something terrible. Every particle of flesh upon one's bones seemed to be slipping off, eyes stinging, and we were almost blinded by the powder and smoke and refuse. The guns and our clothing were almost white from the saltpeter and several men at my gun bled at the nose."[8]

Colonel Lamb wrote about the federal bombardment in *Colonel Lamb's Story of Fort Fisher*:

> This was the commencement of the most terrific bombardment from the fleet which war had ever witnessed. Ship after ship discharged its broadside, every description of deadly missile, from a 3-inch rifle bolt to a 15-inch shell flying wildly over the fort. In the rear of the flagstaff the wooden quarters of the garrison were situated, and these were soon set on fire by the bursting shells and more than one half of them were consumed. The day being balmy most of the men had left their overcoats and blankets in their bunks and these were consumed.

This lack of overcoats and blankets would play an important role later in promoting disease among the Confederate prisoners in Northern prisoner of war camps during one of the harshest winters in years.[9]

About 4:30 PM that afternoon General William Whiting and his staff arrived at Battery Buchanan to assist in the defense of Fort Fisher. Ordinarily the general and his staff would be met by saddle horses so they could ride to the fort. But the stable was destroyed during the bombardment and the horses were either killed or scattered throughout the fort. Braving the naval bombardment the men hurried across the mile and a half of deep sand to Colonel Lamb's combat headquarters in the Pulpit Battery. Lamb was surprised to see General Whiting and his staff climbing the path to the Pulpit. He offered to relinquish command to Whiting, but the general told Lamb that he had come merely to assist and observe. Whiting also brought with him some badly needed reinforcements and the welcome news that advance elements of General Robert F. Hoke's Division had arrived at Sugar Loaf, a fortified natural earthwork, six miles north of the fort.

Colonel Lamb made an important discovery after the fort's garrison flag was shot away. When Private Christopher C. Bland climbed the shattered staff to reattach the flag, the Federal fleet concentrated a heavy fire on it. Taking a cue from this, Lamb decided to plant a flag where the fleet's cannon fire would do the least damage. He personally planted a company flag on Shepperd's Battery, the westernmost mound in the fort. Here, Lamb figured at least half of the shells aimed at the flag would overshoot their target and fall harmlessly into the Cape Fear River.

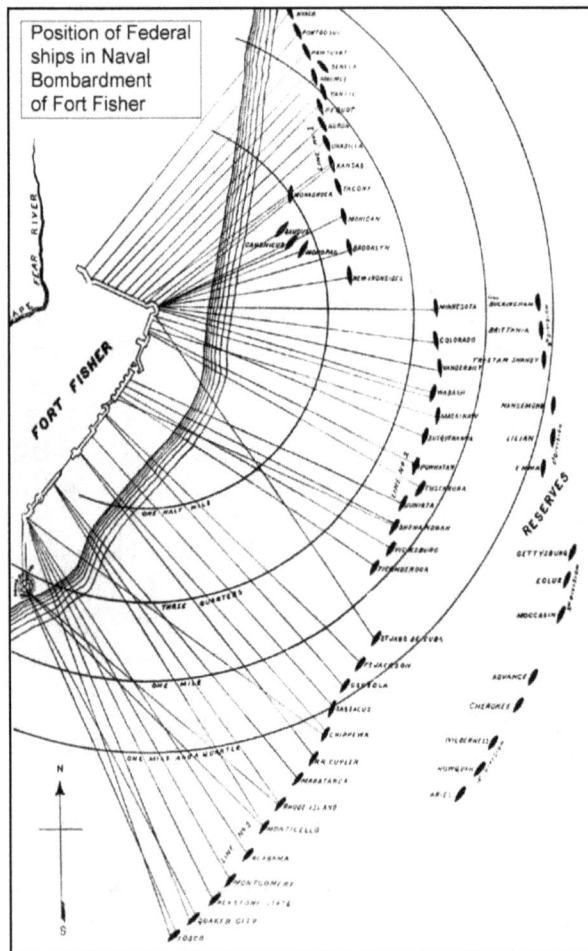

Walter A. Lane's drawing of the position of the Federal Fleet during the bombardment of Fort Fisher. Reprinted from *The Soldier In Our Civil War.*

However, some shots from the Federal fleet found their mark. A Confederate courier dashed across the open plain to deliver a message to the Brooke Battery. Before he could reach his destination a 15-inch shell scored an almost direct hit on him, exploding and blowing him into so many pieces that the soldiers could hardly find enough to bury in the shallow grave they scraped out of the sand. The Brooke Battery itself took a hit some moments later, and a shell fragment tore off the leg of one of the Confederate gunners.[10]

The Federal fleet did not escape unscathed, either. Confederate gunners made their shots count even though they were only allowed to fire their cannon once every half-hour. A shell struck the gunboat *Mackinaw* at the waterline, tearing through a coal bunker and smashing into the port boiler. The engine room was flooded and filled with steam, nearly extinguishing the fires in the furnace and scalding ten men. A similar fate occurred to the *Osceola*. A 10-inch solid shot penetrated the hull below the waterline and pierced a boiler. Six men were scalded and the engine room began to take on so much water that the captain pulled his vessel out of line and signaled that his ship was sinking. The former blockade-runner *A. D. Vance* came to the *Osceola*'s aid and towed the stricken ship to a safe anchorage where emergency repairs could be made. On board the frigate *Wabash* five sailors were injured by shrapnel. The fleet's largest frigate, the *Colorado*, received at least four rebel cannonballs. One shot hit the cut-water, the bow was struck by another, the starboard gangway was hit twice, shattering some deck planks, the main topmast and head of the topgallant mast also received damage. Luckily, only one man was injured on the *Colorado*.[11]

Ironically, most of the damage and casualties suffered by the Federal fleet occurred when five of the Navy's 100-pounder Parrott rifles burst upon firing. Two sailors were mortally wounded when the *Yantic*'s Parrott rifle exploded, damaging the vessel so severely that her commander pulled her out of the battle. The *Ticonderoga* suffered the most from the malfunctioning Parrotts. A cannon exploded killing eight sailors and wounded twelve others. The ship was such a bloody mess that the decks had to be covered with sand to absorb the blood. Seeing the demoralizing effect the mangled bodies were having on his men, Coxswain William Shipman shouted encouragement to his shipmates, "Go ahead, boys, this is only the fortune of war." Under Shipman's guidance his fellow sailors returned to their posts and continued loading and firing. Coxswain Shipman would later receive the Medal of Honor for his coolness under fire.[12]

Another Parrott rifle exploded on the screw sloop *Juanita*, turning her deck into a slaughter house. The blast sprayed pieces of the gun in all directions, killing five and wounding eight. With forty-five casualties on five ships from exploding Parrott rifles, Porter ordered all the 100-pounders retired from the battle.[13]

At 5:50 PM the fire from the Federal fleet sputtered to a stop and the vessels withdrew to their anchorage five miles offshore. Describing the first day's battle Lamb wrote:

> Never since the invention of gun powder was there so much harmlessly expended as in the first day's attack on Fort Fisher. I had about one-half of the quarters burned, three gun carriages disabled, a light artillery caisson exploded, large quantities of the earth work torn and plowed up, with some revetments broken and splintered, but not a single bombproof or magazine injured. Only twenty-three men wounded, one mortally, three seriously and nineteen slightly.

Lamb also noted that the fort had only fired 672 projectiles while the navy expended at least 10,000. At the height of the bombardment on the 24th Admiral Porter estimated the rate of fire at Fort Fisher as 115 shells per minute.[14]

The limited return fire from Fort Fisher was proof enough to Admiral Porter that most of the fort's guns had been rendered useless. This prompted him to send a telegram to Secretary of the Navy Gideon Welles boasting:

> Sir: I have the honor to inform you that I attacked the forts at the mouth of Cape Fear River this morning at 12:30, and after getting the ships in position silenced them in about an hour and a half. There being no troops here to take possession, I am merely firing at it now to keep up practice. The forts are nearly demolished, and as soon as troops come we can take possession. We have set them on fire, blown some of them up, and all that is wanted now is the troops to land to go into them.[15]

Rear Admiral David Dixon Porter

General Butler did not arrive with the army transports until the evening of December 24th, just as the Navy was finishing its bombardment of Fort Fisher. Butler learned of the utter destruction of the fort from the boastful Admiral Porter. Although Butler was angry that he had missed the powder boat explosion, he was hopeful that when his troops landed they would capture the fort with ease.

Shortly after sunrise on the 24th, Confederate General William W. Kirkland had left Wilmington with his brigade and followed Confederate Point Road south toward Fort Fisher. Kirkland's Brigade, which was the vanguard of General Robert F. Hoke's Division, consisted of 1,300 troops from the 17th, 42nd and a portion of the 66th North Carolina Infantry regiments. The general rode ahead of his troops and reached Sugar Loaf about 1 PM. In the distance he could hear the Federal fleet pounding Fort

Fisher. There he was met by a ragtag Confederate force of 1,200 Junior and Senior Reserves. These old men and boys were drafted into service to fill the depleted ranks. On April 16, 1862, the Confederacy began conscription for three years' service of all white males between 18 and 35 who were not legally exempt. The age was raised several times until the Confederacy conscripted nearly everyone from seventeen to fifty who could shoulder a rifle.[16]

Kirkland placed his brigade on a line of defensive works across the peninsula from the Cape Fear River, near Sugar Loaf , to Battery Gatlin on the beach. He also sent a small force of eighty men two miles down the beach to a one-gun earthwork called Battery Anderson.

At 10:30 AM Christmas morning the Federal fleet resumed its bombardment of Fort Fisher. Federal Chaplain Henry Turner described the scene in his diary: "Broadside after broadside was fired, until the reports became so continuous that, in many instances it was one unbroken roar, which seemed to be awful enough to shake the world."[17]

Federal Sergeant Edward K. Wightman observed the bombardment with awe. Only one day later, while the events were fresh in his mind, Wightman wrote a vivid account of the shelling to his brother:

> I can imagine nothing like the bellowing of our fifteen-inch guns. The belching of a volcano with accompanying explosions may suggest a corresponding idea. The din was deafening. Above the fort the countless flashes and puffs of smoke from bursting shells spoke for the accuracy of our guns while columns of sand heaved high in the air suggested that possibly the [fort's] casements were not so safe and cozy after all.[18]

Confederate General William Kirkland's Brigade was the first unit from Hoke's Division to arrive at Wilmington.

On Christmas morning nineteen Federal warships moved into position between Battery Gatlin and Battery Anderson, three miles north of Fort Fisher. These gunboats were ordered to shell the batteries and the woods in preparation for the Federal landing. Admiral Porter, observing the action from the deck of his flagship *Malvern*, thought the gunboats were positioned too far from shore for their gunfire to be effective. Porter signaled the *Brooklyn* to show the others how a beach should be shelled. The *Brooklyn*, the fourth-largest ship-of-the-line in the armada, was a powerful screw sloop with twenty-six big guns. Porter respected the ability of its commander, Captain James Alden. The *Brooklyn* had helped Admiral Farragut capture New Orleans and Alden knew how to bombard a shore installation.

The intense shelling by the Federal gunboats killed and wounded twenty soldiers of Kirkland's Brigade and an undetermined number of reserves. As Kirkland's brigade advanced in line-of-battle through the woods they encountered several dead from the Senior Reserves. Confederate Captain Charles G. Elliott wrote, "It was pitiful to see some gray-haired patriots dead in the woods, killed by shells from the fleet. I saw the ships extending as far as I could see down the beach and rode down through the woods and found a large [Federal] force on the beach and more coming while the woods around us were filled with shrieking shells."[19]

Around 2 PM General Butler's landing force shoved off from the fleet for the shore. The long, blue column snaked through the rolling swells and then fanned out as they came ashore. Before they reached the beach, the men were over the sides of the boats, waist deep in water, and were deploying as skirmishers. To his surprise, General N. Martin Curtis' came ashore unopposed and secured the landing site with a strong skirmish line. Curtis, and a reconnoitering party of five hundred men from the 142nd

Because of his skill in the capture of New Orleans, Captain James Alden of the *USS Brooklyn* led the bombardment three miles north of Fort Fisher prior to the army coming ashore. *Photograph courtesy of the Naval Historical Foundation.*

and the 112th New York, was to push as close as possible to Fort Fisher, ascertain its condition, and report whether the rest of the troops should be landed and an assault made.[20]

Noticing Confederate Battery Anderson was three-quarter of a mile due south, and between him and Fort Fisher, Curtis promptly led a force down the beach to assault the battery. In the distance he saw a white flag appear above the battery. General Butler, noticing the landing was unopposed and allowed the rest of Curtis' brigade to go ashore also.

There has always been a fierce competition between the army and the navy and so it was at Fort Fisher. When Lieutenant Samuel Huse of the *Britannia* saw the white flag and Curtis' brigade approaching the battery, he ordered Ensign W. H. Bryant to take a boat ashore and receive the surrender before the army got there. Boats were also sent out from the *Tristram Shandy, Howquah* and the *Santiago de Cuba*, each eager to receive the battery's surrender. When the army troops noticed the boats racing ashore, they ran as quickly as they could, trying to get there before the navy.

The *Britannia*'s crew arrived there ahead of the army and Ensign Bryant planted a United States flag atop the battery. He was met by the demoralized battery commander, Captain Koonts, holding out his sword in surrender. He and eighty men from the 42nd North Carolina had been badly battered by the navy's intense shelling. When his only cannon exploded and he saw his soldiers were outnumbered six-to-one, he decided to give up.[21]

General Kirkland and his staff had just left Battery Gatlin and were riding south to Battery Anderson when he heard a deafening cheer from the fleet. A courier dashed up to the general and reported the surrender of Battery Anderson. Kirkland's regiment was stretched thin, but he thought if he attacked the Federal-occupied battery it might be possible to release the prisoners. Kirkland needed to know more about the Federal advance so he conducted a closer reconnaissance of the beach. He saw his men were facing at least three Federal brigades with more men coming ashore. The enemy was overlapping his flanks so Kirkland deployed his whole regiment as skirmishers. As soon as Lieutenant Colonel Sharp's 17th North Carolina regiment was deployed, they advanced on Battery Anderson.

In a short while they encountered the enemy and pushed their skirmish line back upon the main body. Once the Confederates left the woods and came out on the beach they found they were covered by the guns of nineteen warships. "It would have been madness to have advanced farther," Kirkland said, "besides I was fearful the enemy would land a force at Gatlin and push up the Wilmington Road which was covered by one regiment."[22]

General Whiting sent numerous telegrams to Confederate Headquarters in Wilmington pleading for help. "A large force of the enemy has landed near the fort, deploying as skirmishers. May be able to carry me by storm." In another telegram Whiting told Bragg, "Our case is critical. The enemy have landed and are now skirmishing with our troops on the parapet. If you send reinforcements for Kirkland to attack in the rear we can hold out." Major General Bragg sent no help to Whiting, in fact, "in an alarming display of pessimism he made arrangements for his wife, Elisa, to flee the city." This single move by the commanding general caused widespread panic in Wilmington.[23]

While the Federal infantry was skirmishing and moving down Confederate Point, Admiral Porter was contemplating an attack on the south end of Fort Fisher. Porter figured if several warships could enter New Inlet, and steam up the Cape Fear River, they could bombard the fort from the rear and perhaps force it to surrender. However, the inlet was hazardous due to the wrecks of blockade-runners and shifting sandbars. Porter needed accurate soundings and the channel marked with buoys before he would commit his ships to such a daring plan. The inlet was well guarded by the Mound Battery and Battery Buchanan which bristled with Confederate cannon. A mission like this was practically suicide and would require a man who was fearless in battle. Admiral Porter knew Lieutenant Commander William B. Cushing was such a man.

Cushing formed his reputation for reckless bravery by leading a small party of volunteers in a commando style raid against the powerful ironclad *CSS Albemarle* in the Roanoke River. Brandishing only a fourteen-foot long spar torpedo and the audacity to try something that everyone else thought was impossible, Cushing set out in a thirty-foot steam launch and destroyed the rebel ship.

Lieutenant Commander William B. Cushing became known as "Lincoln's Commando" after leading several daring missions. *Photograph courtesy of the Naval Historical Foundation.*

Cushing became a national figure in the North for sinking the *CSS Albemarle* and this exploit earned him an audience with President Abraham Lincoln. When the media learned of the story they dubbed him "Lincoln's Commando". Cushing also conducted several small raids into the Cape Fear River the previous year, capturing a number of prisoners and embarrassing the Confederate military.[24]

At Fort Fisher Commander Cushing led a force of ten launches into New Inlet while Commander John Guest of the *USS Iosco* and eight other warships unleashed a heavy, suppressing fire against the Mound Battery and nearby Battery Buchanan. Even though the increased Federal cannon fire made it hazardous for the Confederates to man their guns, they still gave a good account of themselves. Before the battle began Colonel Lamb had specifically ordered the gunners to fire as rapidly as possible if anyone tried to enter New Inlet because the enemy might try to take the fort from the rear. Although countless Rebel shells fell all around the boats, the sailors coolly took soundings and marked the shipping channel. So many shell fragments peppered the water's surface that the sailors had to stop what they were doing and bail out the launches several times.

Ironically, the first casualties from this action occurred when one of the Confederate Brooke rifles exploded. The barrel split, spraying red-hot iron in all directions. Seven gunners were wounded but no one was killed.[25]

One of the Confederate cannon found the range of a Federal launch from the *USS Tacony* and shot the flagstaff from its stern. A sailor picked up the pennant and was busy tying it to the broken staff when another shell smashed into the boat, cutting it in two. One man received several splinters in his backside while seaman Henry Sand's legs were severed at the knees, mortally wounding him. The other boats rescued the men in the water and Cushing ordered a hasty withdrawal. This was the last attempt by the Federals to enter the river.[26]

The Federal fleet also suffered under the Confederate fire. At 3:30 PM the fort's gunners found the range of the *USS Powhatan* and hit the ship with four cannonballs in quick secession. One ball struck below the waterline where it destroyed some copper sheathing and caused the ship to leak badly.[27]

At 4 PM Admiral Porter's flagship signaled the fleet to cease fire and retire to avoid hitting the Federal Army as it approached the fort. For some reason the *USS Colorado* and the *USS Minnesota* ceased fire but remained at anchor. Since the other Federal ships were steaming out of range, the Confederate gunners concentrated their fire on the two largest ships in the Federal fleet. At 4:30 PM a

ten-inch solid shot struck the *Colorado* over the No. 4 gun on the starboard side damaging two guns and killing one man and wounding five more. Commodore Thatcher of the *Colorado* wrote:

> Near the close of the second day's action, we perceived the approach of the advanced skirmishers of our army force when our fire ceased for nearly thirty minutes, and was resumed after we had been hulled several times by a vicious gun which appeared to be fired from the N. E. angle of Fort Fisher. We then reopened heavily, but more to the left than we had preciously fired, to avoid annoying our own troops who were seen approaching the fort.[28]

At 4:40 P.M. the *Colorado* signaled to the *Minnesota*, Enemy are hulling us; fire for your own protection.

But the *USS Minnesota* was struck below the starboard waterline, and another shell struck amidships and lodged in the stern of one of the cutters. Shortly after, a rebel shell exploded on the chain armor, scattering shrapnel on both sides of the ship.[29]

Leading 250 soldiers of the 142nd New York, General Weitzel and Colonel Curtis advanced within 800 yards of the fort's land-face. From there, the officers studied the sprawling fort through binoculars. General Weitzel wrote, "I counted seventeen guns in position, bearing up the beach, and between each pair of guns there was a traverse so thick and so high above the parapet that I have no doubt they were all bombproofs. I saw plainly that the work had not been materially injured by the heavy and very accurate shell fire of the navy." He recalled the Federal slaughter that had occurred in repeated attacks against Battery Wagner near Charleston. Their present situation was virtually the same except the Rebel fort was at least ten times as strong. General Weitzel did not want to make that same mistake here. He returned to the fleet and told General Butler about his findings. He strongly advised against an attack, saying, "it would be butchery to order an assault."[30]

Before General Weitzel left, Colonel Curtis asked for permission to conduct a reconnaissance of the area. Weitzel reluctantly agreed, but insisted Curtis not bring on a general engagement with the enemy. Curtis said he wouldn't, then led a reconnaissance force toward the western part of the fort. Skirmishers located a telegraph pole which linked the fort to Sugar Loaf and Confederate headquarters in Wilmington. Lieutenant George Simpson shinnied up the pole and chopped the wires with a hatchet.

Major General Godfrey Weitzel advised Butler against attacking Fort Fisher. *Photograph courtesy of Library of Congress.*

Curtis' men advanced within 500 yards of the fort and halted at an abandoned Confederate battery. The colonel used this slightly higher ground to get a better view of the fort. Although he saw many serviceable cannon on the fort's wall the guns appeared unmanned. Encouraged by this, Curtis and 40 soldiers from the 142nd New York advanced to within 75 yards of the fort. Some of the more daring men slipped through a jagged hole blown in the palisade fence.

A huge naval shell exploded on the fort's ramparts, throwing a plume of sand into the air and knocking down the Confederate flag staff so it extended past the parapet walls. Captured enemy flags were highly prized and seizing one made a soldier an instant legend. Witnessing what had happened, Lieutenant William Walling scaled the exterior slope of the fort and grabbed the flag along with a twelve-foot section of the pole and brought it back as a trophy. Walling describes the incident in the book *Deeds of Valor*:

> [A] shot from the fleet cut down the Confederate flag on the fort. . . .I said to my men: 'I'll go and get the flag; you keep a sharp lookout for the riflemen on the works. Let every man have his gun in position to fire.' 'We will, Lieutenant; we will!' came the response from my men as with one voice. I started off. I had gone but a few steps when one of the great monitor shells passed in front of me and exploded before reaching the river. I confess I was frightened, and for an instant halted involuntarily, stunned by the fearful crash. But, quickly recovering my wits, I proceeded and came to a place where a shell had cut a hole in the palisade a little to the left of the flag. Through this opening I entered, passed along toward the river, gained the parapet, secured the flag and returned, uninjured as I had gone.

Lieutenant William Walling captures a fallen Confederate flag from Fort Fisher's land-face. Picture Reprinted from *Deeds of Valor*.

This daring deed earned Lieutenant Walling the Medal of Honor.[31]

Several minutes later a Confederate courier on horseback emerged from the fort's gate and clattered over the wooden bridge that crossed the marsh. Nineteen-year-old Private Amos H. Jones carried a dispatch from Major William Saunders to General Hebert's chief of artillery, requesting a battery of light artillery be placed in the fort. As Jones galloped down River Road toward Sugar Loaf, a Federal soldier rose up from his hiding place beneath the bridge and shot him from the saddle, killing him.[32]

The lack of Confederate soldiers on the fort's walls convinced Colonel Curtis that Fort Fisher could easily be taken by assault. He sent a dispatch back to the rear guard and ordered Lieutenant Colonel Barney to bring forward the rest of the First Brigade. Curtis took the captured flag to the beach and began waving it to signal the fleet that the army's assault was about to begin and for them to shift their fire away from his advancing soldiers. The sailors on the ships did not understand Curtis' signal and cheered the plucky Federal officer waving the Confederate flag from the beach.

It had been twenty minutes since Curtis called for reinforcements. Curious why it was taking so long, he looked down the beach and his soldiers appeared to be milling around the landing site instead of moving forward as ordered. Curtis stormed down the beach.

Lieutenant Colonel Barney informed Curtis that he had received orders from General Butler to withdraw and re-embark the troops. Curtis was bewildered by the orders. Clearly Butler did not understand the situation. He scribbled a message, appraising his commanding officer of the conditions at Fort Fisher. "Your order is held in abeyance that you may know the true condition of the fort; the garrison has offered no resistance; the flagstaff of the fort was cut by a naval shot and one of my officers brought from the rampart the garrison flag; another cut the telegraph wire connecting the fort with Wilmington; my skirmishers are now at the parapet."[33]

Colonel N. Martin Curtis was wounded four times in the second battle of Fort Fisher, winning him the Medal of Honor. His last wound was from a shell fragment which carried away his left eye and orbital bone. *Photograph courtesy of Library of Congress.*

About 8 PM Colonel Curtis received another dispatch from General Butler calling off the attack and ordering him to return to the landing site and load his men on the ships. Captain Birney B. Keeler brought the message to his friend and told Curtis, "All the troops which have landed, including the larger part of your brigade, Pennypacker's brigade, and Bell's brigade, have been taken on board the ships, and there is no one on land but your force and the flankers and pickets you have left out, and it will be entirely useless for you to expect any assistance." Saddened, Curtis had no choice but to return to the landing site.

Curtis reached the beach sometime after 9 PM and saw the reembarkation process was well underway. The wind had been increasing all evening and the seas were running so high that boats approaching the beach faced the dangerous prospect of being swamped or overturned. The Federal boats bravely continued coming ashore, tossed about by the wind-driven waves. After they were loaded, the boats ferried the men to the ships while the gale increased in intensity. Six boats were destroyed and one man drown in the rough surf before General Adelbert Ames called a halt to the reembarkation, leaving 600 of Curtis' men and 200 prisoners stranded on the beach.

Regimental Surgeon James A. Mowris of the 117th New York, recalled being left behind:
> The 3rd brigade had already departed, and the 2nd [brigade], despite the increasing sea, had nearly all recovered their places on the transports. Soon after they had all done so, the 1st brigade attempted it, but the violence of the surf promptly arrested the work and emphatically, forbade its renewal. Then followed a gloomy night for the 1st brigade. Darkness was about us—we were destitute of materials for shelter, or tools for entrenching—a heavy and cold rain was upon us—the forbidding sea roared on one side and Hoke's division threatened on the other.[34]

General Butler retired to his cabin aboard the *USS Ben De Ford*. Nothing seemed to be going right for him. Butler's troubles began with the ill-fated powder boat explosion. He was convinced if he had been here to supervise things would have gone as planned and Fort Fisher would have been captured by now.

Now, Butler was faced with another set of problems. Colonel Curtis had captured some prisoners from Confederate General Hoke's army. These prisoners reported that General Lee had ordered their division from the Petersburg trenches to help defend Wilmington and Fort Fisher. Butler had seen evidence of this himself because his troops were already skirmishing with Confederate soldiers moving south from Wilmington and into the Federal rear. This certainly added to Butler's worries, but the bad news didn't stop there. The weather was deteriorating quickly and night was coming on. If Butler left his troops ashore these men would be extremely vulnerable to an assault. To the north was General Hoke's 6,000 man division and to the south was Fort Fisher's garrison. These Confederate forces were numerically superior to the Federal troops ashore. If they coordinated their attacks, his invasion force could very well be captured. With night falling, and the weather blowing a gale, even the navy with its 640 guns would be useless to help the troops ashore.

Butler had also received a report from General Weitzel that Fort Fisher appeared uninjured from the naval bombardment and, in his opinion, it would be butchery to assault the fort now. General Ames agreed with Weitzel that any Federal land assault now would end in failure. Butler trusted Weitzel's assessment of the situation, but he needed to see for himself before he called off the assault.[35]

Butler transferred from his flagship to the *Chamberlain,* a shallow draft vessel, so he could get in close to study the fort. As the *Chamberlain* steamed by the Northeast Bastion, Butler saw that Fort Fisher appeared as formidable as ever after the naval attack. While he scanned the fort with his binoculars, the naval bombardment ceased and the fort's parapets were soon fully manned with Confederate defenders. Apparently General Weitzel had been right about the soldiers seeking shelter in bombproofs, waiting for the naval fire to end. Butler could plainly see his army would be slaughtered in a futile attempt to capture Fort Fisher.

Due to the severe weather even the evacuation did not go right for General Butler. Colonel Curtis' 600 man brigade was stranded ashore for an indefinite period until the storm abated. It didn't seem to matter what course of action Butler took, the situation kept getting worse. Now Curtis' men were surrounded by a vastly superior enemy who outnumbered his men twelve to one. Apparently this news was too much for Butler to handle for he sailed north to Hampton Roads, leaving Colonel Curtis' Brigade to its fate.

The survival of Fort Fisher depended upon a vigorous Confederate defense led by a bold commander. Unfortunately General Braxton Bragg would let the soldiers down. *Photograph courtesy of Library of Congress.*

As history would eventually show, Major General Butler worried needlessly about the Federal brigade stranded on the beach for a day and a half. Confederate Major General Braxton Bragg appeared paralyzed by fear and indecision and thus made no move to capture the enemy. A cold, driving rain fell that evening while the wet and hungry Federal soldiers hunkered down behind their sand breastworks, and waited for an attack that never came. Finally, the weather moderated on the morning of the 27th of December, allowing the fleet to send boats ashore to rescue the men. The choppy water was so turbulent that many of the naval launches had to be hooked to hawsers running from the beach back to the ship. True to his nature, the gallant Colonel Curtis was the last man to leave the beach at two that afternoon.

When Curtis came aboard the *Nereus* both he and his staff complained bitterly about the handling of the invasion force. "Fort Fisher would have been captured if General Butler had properly supported my men," Curtis contended. Lieutenant George Simpson of the 142nd New York seemed to sum up the Wilmington Campaign succinctly by saying, "One of the grandest and most expensive expeditions ever organized in our country has been terminated in a complete farce."[36]

Confederate Major General Bragg's inaction dumbfounded Whiting. "It was a matter of grave charge against [Bragg] that the whole [Federal] force was not captured," Whiting wrote in a letter to General Benjamin Butler while he was a prisoner on Governor's Island, New York. "I agree with General Whiting," wrote Colonel Lamb, "that but for the supineness of General Bragg the 3,500 men who landed would have been captured on Christmas night, and it is incomprehensible why he should have allowed the 700 demoralized troops who were forced to remain on the beach on the night of the 26th of December escape unmolested."[37]

Admiral David D. Porter was aghast at Butler's withdrawal. He sent a telegram to Secretary of the Navy Gideon Wells:

> I can't conceive what the army expected when they came here. [Fort Fisher] was so blown up, burst up, and torn up that the people inside had no intention of fighting any longer. Had the army made a show of surrounding it, it would have been ours, but nothing of the kind was done. I feel ashamed that men calling themselves soldiers should have left this place so ingloriously.

Porter confided privately to Welles, "It was however nothing more than I expected when General Butler got himself mixed up in this expedition."[38]

The unpleasant duty of informing President Lincoln about the failure at Wilmington fell upon General Ulysses S. Grant. *Photograph courtesy of Library of Congress.*

·On December 28, 1864, Lieutenant General Ulysses S. Grant undertook the unpleasant task of informing President Lincoln about the expedition's lack of success. "The Wilmington expedition has proven a gross and culpable failure. Many troops are now back here. Delays and free talk of the object of the expedition enabled the enemy to move troops to Wilmington to defeat it."[39]

General Grant decided the best way to capture Fort Fisher was to immediately select a new commander and renew the attack before the Confederates had a chance to repair the damage from the first assault. Grant was aware that General Butler could use his considerable political influence to absolve himself of any blame in the Wilmington affair. If he did so, Grant wondered if the president would approve of his decision to replace Butler. To his relief Lincoln agreed, but he cautioned Grant that this time he must select a commander who was both aggressive and dependable.

Grant already had a new commander in mind when he spoke to the president. Unlike the quarrelsome Butler, Major General Alfred H. Terry was a mild-mannered officer who got along easily with his superiors. He was a seasoned combat veteran and his proven ability instilled confidence in the men around him. "Although the General was a brave soldier," observed one of Terry's staff officers, "pomposity, arrogance, cowardice and self-conceit seemed to be elements foreign to his character."[40]

As the Federal ships faded into the horizon, General Whiting and Colonel Lamb realized that Fort Fisher was safe for the moment. The Confederates had won a major victory and the casualties were light: The total for the two days inside the fort was three killed, sixty-one wounded, two mortally. General Hoke's forces had five killed, sixteen wounded and 307 missing. The damage to the fort was relatively light and could easily be fixed. Only two guns were dismounted by enemy fire, another two were dismounted by recoil, three Brooke guns had burst and the headquarters and barracks buildings were destroyed.[41]

On January 4th, 1865, the Ladies Soldier's Aid Society travelled to Fort Fisher to show their appreciation to the soldiers by serving them a warm meal. A reporter from the *Wilmington Daily Journal* accompanied the women and wrote about the damage to the fort. "Deep holes are dug in the parapets and many of the traverses are marked and scarred. The outside and top of the ramparts looked as though rooted by gigantic hogs; none of this rooting, however, seemed to do more than roughen the surface."[42]

Confederate Major General Braxton Bragg continued to be Fort Fisher's worst enemy. He erroneously believed the fort and Wilmington were no longer in any danger. General Robert E. Lee even offered to send more ammunition to Fort Fisher but Bragg refused the supplies. In fact, Bragg sent Hoke's troops to Wilmington for a victory parade and then made plans for them to return to Richmond.[43]

The Federal Army suffered one man killed, eleven men wounded and one captured from the 142nd New York, while the navy had twenty killed and sixty-three wounded. The navy's sixty-four warships expended 20,271 projectiles against Fort Fisher, or fifteen shells for every defender.[44]

A drawing of Fort Fisher's interior showing Shepperd's Battery and the main gate. Horrific fighting for possession of the fort would take place in this area. Picture is from *The Seventh Regiment New Hampshire Volunteers in the War of the Rebellion. 1861-1865.*

Chapter 4

The Second Attack

"The country will not forgive us for another failure at Wilmington." Gustavas V. Fox, Assistant Secretary of the United States Navy[1]

In January, 1865, Lieutenant General Ulysses S. Grant had Confederate General Robert E. Lee right where he wanted him. Lee was a brilliant commanding general who had out-fought and embarrassed a much larger, better equipped Federal army. The daring Lee was not opposed to splitting his smaller force in the face of the enemy and boldly marching a portion of his army around an opponent to deliver a devastating blow where it was least expected. Unfortunately, Grant denied Lee the ability to maneuver by pinning him down in the trenches around Richmond and Petersburg. Lee was woefully aware that his smaller, poorly supplied army could not win a battle of attrition. Before his army was in the Petersburg trenches, Lee stated to the Reverend J. William Jones, a former Chaplain in the Army of Northern Virginia, "We must destroy this army of Grant's before he gets to the James River. If he gets there, it will become a siege, and then it will be a mere question of time."[2]

One of Lee's constant worries was feeding his 52,000-man army. Much of the rich farm land of the Southern states was devastated by General William T. Sherman during his march through Georgia and the Carolinas. General Philip Sheridan's cavalry conducted a similar scorched earth policy in the Shenandoah Valley, commonly referred to as "the breadbasket of

General Robert E. Lee knew the assault on Wilmington would be renewed. *Photograph courtesy of Library of Congress.*

the Confederacy." These men systematically tore up the Southern railroads, destroyed crops, burned government buildings and homes of suspected Southern sympathizers.

Blockade-runners provided much of the food for Lee's starving army. By mid-1864 Wilmington, North Carolina, was the only viable blockade-running seaport left in the South. As early as January 1863, Lee told Major General Gustavus Smith the city must be "defended at all hazards." Lee also sent word to Colonel Lamb warning, "if the fort fell he could not maintain his army." This statement had severe implications regarding the Confederacy; Lee was saying he could no longer defend Richmond and would have to evacuate the city if Fisher fell. As outnumbered as he was, Lee could not afford to send any troops to Wilmington. And yet, he realized if he did not defend Wilmington vigorously, the Confederacy's last line of supply might be severed. Lee could not afford to lose Wilmington and so he sent one of his best generals and 6,000 men to the port city.[3]

General Lee at first had been greatly relieved when he heard that the December attack against Fort Fisher had been repulsed. But now he had received alarming information which pointed to a renewal of the attack on Wilmington. Lee sent a telegram to Secretary of War Sedden, warning him about the new campaign and telling him the commander was General Alfred H. Terry. Lee also told Sedden that General Bragg had been notified and had reported "nothing has yet appeared off here."[4]

Colonel Lamb was aware that the Federal fleet had gone to Beaufort, North Carolina, to resupply but he could only guess when Admiral Porter might resume his attack of Fort Fisher. At 10 PM on January 12th, Colonel Thomas J. Lipscomb of the 2nd South Carolina Cavalry reported to headquarters that the enemy fleet of at least thirty vessels was off of Masonboro and steaming south. Later that night, Colonel Lamb was summoned to the Pulpit Battery. He later wrote, "I saw from the ramparts of the fort the lights of the great armada, as one after another appeared above the horizon." Lamb immediately prepared the fort for action. Only 800 soldiers from the 36th North Carolina were inside the fort. This prompted Lamb to telegraph an urgent plea to Wilmington Headquarters for reinforcements and call for the return of General Hoke's division. By January 15th, 700 men arrived from the other forts in the area and a detachment of 50 sailors and marines of the Confederate Navy.[5]

Major General Whiting and his staff traveled to Battery Buchanan on Friday the 13th of January, and walked across the deep sand to the Pulpit Battery at Fort Fisher. Lamb greeted Whiting and offered to turn over command of Fort Fisher's defense. Whiting declined, saying that he had come only as an advisor. Then he said, "Lamb, my boy, I have come to share your fate. You and your garrison are to be sacrificed." Colonel Lamb was shocked that his friend and mentor was so pessimistic after their glorious victory less than a month before. "Don't say so, General! We shall certainly whip the enemy again." Whiting then told him that when he left Wilmington General Bragg was removing his stores and ammunition and was looking for a place to fall back upon.[6]

When Lamb told General Whiting of the Federal landing, he wasn't surprised. Whiting had predicted this was going to happen for some time. Months earlier he had told President Davis and General Lee that this was the location where a Federal landing would take place. Whiting also told them he needed reinforcements so he might station a brigade there to oppose such a landing. It appeared he had been branded an alarmist because no would listen to him. Whiting would never let Fort Fisher slip away without a fight. He immediately sent several urgent messages to General Bragg advising him of the situation. "The enemy have landed in large force. Garrison too weak to resist assault and prevent their advance. You must attack them at once."

Confederate Major General William Whiting was appalled by Braggs inaction against the 700 Federals left on the beach during the December attack.

Whiting expected Bragg to wire him back with some sort of plan but as the minutes turned to hours and there was still no reply he began to wonder if his message had gotten through. Whiting sent another telegraph message, "Enemy have landed a large force. They will assault me tonight, or try to do it. You must attack." Still Bragg was curiously silent, so General Whiting sent a third message at 1:30 PM:

> The game of the enemy is very plain to me. They are now furiously bombarding my land front; they will continue to do that, in order, if possible, to silence my guns until they are satisfied that their land force has securely established itself across the neck and rests on the river; then Porter will attempt to force a passage to co-operate with the force that takes the river-bank. I have received dispatches from you stating that the enemy had extended to the river. This they never should have been allowed to do; and if they are permitted to remain there the reduction of Fort Fisher is but a question of time. I will hold this place till the last extremities; but unless you drive that land force from its position I cannot answer for the security of this harbor. The

fire has been and continues to be exceedingly heavy, surpassing not so much in its volume as in its extraordinary condition even the fire of Christmas.[7]

For some reason Bragg would not telegraph Whiting directly. If he needed to communicate with Whiting, he would send a message to him through Lieutenant Colonel Archer Anderson. Anderson sent Whiting a message at 2 PM saying General Bragg would send a brigade of 1,000 men to Fort Fisher that evening. Still not pacified by this report that promised re-enforcements, Whiting sent Bragg another telegraph at 8 PM. "Enemy are on the beach, where they have been all day. Why are they not attacked?" As he had done all day, Bragg virtually ignored Whiting, and reported to General Lee on the afternoon of the 15th that, "It is believed by the commander of your troops that the (Federal) effort will fail if made, and at a heavy sacrifice. If defended, as I believe it will be, by your veterans and the former garrison, it cannot be taken."[8]

Admiral Porter's plan of battle was similar to that of the first bombardment. Three lines of warships would anchor off the fort while the five ironclads would be positioned in front of the first line. Porter had instructed the captains in the fleet that for the first few hours they were to fire into the woods north of the fort in the vicinity of Battery Anderson and Battery Gatlin.

This would destroy any Confederate resistance to General Terry's landing. After this, the ships were to concentrate their fire on the fort's artillery. Special attention was to be paid to the gun chambers on the land-face because this is where the Federal assault was to be made.

Shepperd's Battery showing dismounted cannon and holes in palisade fence. *Photograph courtesy of Library of Congress.*

Sailors on board the *USS Unadilla. Photograph courtesy of the Naval Historical Foundation.*

At 8:30 AM the *USS New Ironsides* dropped anchor and waited for Fort Fisher to begin the battle. The Federals did not have to wait long. The Columbiad cannon in the Pulpit Battery roared to life, signaling the rest of the fort's gunners to open fire. Waiting for the fort to fire first was not as chivalrous as it sounds. Commodore William Radford wanted to count the fort's guns and see where they were located so very little ammunition would be wasted. One by one the ironclad's guns fired methodically to get the range of their targets. Gunners were instructed to note the elevation required for their cannon because when the bombardment began in earnest, the gun smoke would be so thick it would be impossible to tell where the shots were falling.

Fort Fisher's gun crews took advantage of the Federal's sporadic firing. Apparently the artillerists had honed their marksmanship during the first battle because the *New Ironsides* was struck by a series of shells. A ten-inch shot smashed through a starboard porthole into the ship's sick bay. The ship's iron hull was badly battered, her stern pennant and lightning rod were shot away, and a wooden launch was damaged severely along with sections of her railing.[9]

Federal soldier Augustus Buell wrote about the monitors in action at Fort Fisher in a book called *The Cannoneer:*

> The day was bright and clear, but cold and crisp, which made the smoke light, and the wind from the northwest lifted it quickly seaward, so that the flash of every gun could be seen. I wouldn't have missed seeing that bombardment of Fort Fisher for 10 years of my life. It beat anything in history for weight of ordinance used, even greater than the bombardment of the Sebastopol forts by the English and French fleets, because the guns we used were so much heavier. I cannot describe the discharges of those 13 and 15-inch Rodman guns of the monitors, or the explosion of their great shells in the air over the fort or among its traverses. To me it seemed like firing meteors out of volcanoes. I would watch the turrets of the monitors through my glass. They would turn their iron backs on the enemy to load, and I could distinctly see the big rammer staves come out of the ports. Then they would wheel round on a line with the fort, there would be two puffs of blue smoke about the size of a thunder cloud in June, and then I could see the big shell make a black streak through the air with a tail of white smoke behind it and then it would come over the water, not the quick bark of a field gun, but a slow, quivering, over powering roar like an earthquake, and then, away among the Rebel traverses, there would be another huge ball of mingled smoke and flame as big as a meeting house."[10]

Quartermaster Daniel D. Stevens replaced the flag on the *USS Canonicus* two times after it was shot down by Confederate fire. Drawing from *Deeds of Honor, Volume 2, Photograph courtesy of the Naval Historical Foundation.*

For the first several hours the fort's gunners concentrated on the ironclads because the wooden warships were two miles north, shelling the beach for General Terry's landing. During this time the *Canonicus* was struck thirty-six times, the *New Ironsides* took twenty-five hits and the *Saugus* suffered eleven direct shots. Although the Confederate gunners' aim was excellent the cannonballs merely dented the iron sides of the ships and bounced harmlessly off.

Quartermaster Daniel D. Stevens had one of the most hazardous duties in the Federal fleet. His job was to stand outside on the deck of the *Canonicus* and act as an artillery spotter, watching for the effects of her shots on the fort. He was also required to take soundings so the ironclad would not run aground. The heavy Confederate fire twice shot away the *Canonicus* flag. Stevens, at great risk to his safety, replaced the flag both times, winning the Medal of Honor for his bravery.[11]

At 8:45 AM twenty-two troop transports anchored four miles north of Fort Fisher and began lowering boats of every type. Captain Adrian Terry (General Alfred Terry's brother) described the landing to his wife in a letter dated January 24, 1865:

> The transports had hardly anchored when the water was covered with the small boats of the navy, varying in size from the small cutter to the huge launch, the former pulling six oars and the latter between twenty and thirty, which pulled rapidly up to the transports and were quickly filled with the soldiers who evinced the utmost eagerness to reach shore as soon as possible, more I fear in order to get on solid land once more than from their desire to meet the enemy.[12]

Terry's force of 9,600 men had three day's rations and forty rounds of ammunition in their cartridge boxes. The sea was rough due to a recent gale and the soldiers rarely came ashore dry. Eager to be on land once more, many men jumped over the side as the launches came into shallow water. "Loaded down as they were with ammunition, provisions, blankets, etc," one Union soldier observed, "there was some tall scrambling done on all-fours before they extricated themselves from their involuntary saltwater bath."[13]

Lieutenant Henry F. Little of the 7th New Hampshire recorded in his diary the rough sea conditions during the landing:

> As the boats were rowed up to the beach, the heavy waves would recede, and for an instant the bow of the boat would rest upon the sand, when the order would be given to jump, which order was supposed to be executed on the instant. . . .[to] clear the next wave. The men being in heavy marching order, and judging from the size of their knapsacks, perhaps a little top-heavy, could not all execute the movement promptly at the right moment, and those who were late in the execution of the command would invariably be caught by the next big roll, when they would find themselves in water perhaps ten feet deep. Many came near being drowned, and were very fortunate in getting off with only a thorough drenching.[14]

Major General Alfred H. Terry, Commander of the Wilmington expedition.

The soldiers were not the only thing to get soaking wet that day. Provisions and ammunition got drenched as well. General Terry ordered 300,000 cartridges and six days' rations to replace the ruined supplies.[15]

Lieutenant Samuel Little also recalled several humorous incidents that occurred during the landing:

A very broad smile was caused by those who witnessed the misfortune which befell an officer, in a brand new uniform, whose foot slipped just as he was ready to jump, sending him headlong into the water. The sailors pulled him out by the collar, and seemed much pleased at the opportunity to lend a hand at his rescue. Again, two company cooks, who had been closely watching this operation of jumping, were anxiously waiting their chance to land. They were in charge of quite an accumulation of sugar and coffee belonging to their company, and resolved to keep it dry if possible; in order to do so, one fastened the bag of sugar around his neck, and the other secured the bag containing coffee in a like manner around his own. They jumped just quick enough to get caught in one of the largest of the incoming waves. The one having charge of the sugar was fished out just in time to save his life, while the one having the coffee came near being drowned, but was finally rescued in an exhausted condition by one of the sailors belonging to the boat, but the sugar and coffee were spoiled.[16]

Once General Terry's army was on shore, his greatest fear was that Confederate General Robert Hoke would assault him before he was ready. He wanted to construct a defensive line across Federal Point to protect the rear of the force that would advance on the fort. This would isolate Fort Fisher and make it more vulnerable to attack. Taking the bulk of his army on the evening of January 14th, General Terry marched south in the darkness through the pines and scrub oaks toward Fort Fisher. Terry found most of the ground was low and swampy with thick underbrush unsuitable for defense. By 2 AM the soldiers reached a point of fairly high ground, two miles north of the fort where Terry ordered his troops to establish a line of entrenchments from the river to the beach.

"All night long the troops labored most vigorously, the tools passing from hand to hand," reported an officer, "until by sunrise we had a line of breastworks across from the river to the sea, behind which our men could easily repel the attack of double their force." The 142nd New York, under Colonel Joseph McDonald, was ordered to establish a skirmish line as close to the fort as possible. The New York regiment pressed on through the dense underbrush in the darkness until they came to a large clearing. Across the moonlit silvery-white sand was an impressive sight. Fort Fisher's immense twenty-five foot wall, dotted by fifteen-foot high traverses, stretched as far as the eye could see. In anticipation of a land assault, Colonel Lamb had ordered the trees and underbrush removed for half a mile north of the fort to provide a clear field of fire for the fort's gunners. Colonel McDonald, knowing he could go no farther without being observed by the enemy, ordered the 142nd New York to deploy their skirmish line here.[17]

Colonel N. Martin Curtis was not satisfied with halting his men at the tree line. He had been on this same ground during the last expedition and his brigade was allowed to approach the fort without a shot being fired. Curtis felt that Fort Fisher's garrison lacked vigilance and that his brigade could have easily captured the fort if only General Butler had given him the opportunity. This time Butler wasn't here to

100-pounder rifled Parrott aboard the *USS Wabash*. Although this cannon did not explode during the battle five other similar guns blewup on Federal ships causing forty-five casualties.

hold Curtis back and the expedition had a bold new commander in General Terry. Because Curtis had knowledge of the enemy and terrain, Terry trusted his opinion on matters concerning the assault. This knowledge gave Curtis the confidence to move his brigade out of the tree line to within 900 yards of Fort Fisher for the assault the next day. Curtis also sent skirmishers even closer to the fort and had men dig a series of rifle pits for sharpshooters so they could clear the fort's parapet of enemy marksmen.[18]

While the Federal army was landing 9,000 troops, General Hoke's division was marching from Wilmington to Sugar Loaf. Kirkland's Brigade, which had been transported downriver on steamers, arrived in time to watch the Federal landing. Hoke's soldiers were confident they could push the Federals back into the sea if only their commander would order an attack. "We did nothing," complained a disgusted Asa King of the 66th North Carolina infantry, "just lay quiet . . . and let the enemy land. We could have repulsed them if we had fired on them as they landed, which we were anxious to do. We received no orders from our officers, just let the Federals assemble a force together, then they commenced firing on us."[19]

Meanwhile, at Fort Fisher, Colonel Lamb was observing the Federal landing with growing alarm. He telegraphed Wilmington headquarters asking, "Where is Hoke? The Yankees are landing a heavy force. I should have a regiment of veterans before sundown. I have plenty of shelter, and the firing is slow. They can come in. I have fewer men than on the 24th (of December)."[20]

Chapter 5

The Final Day of Battle

"Our fleet and the ironclads were doing some beautiful marksmanship, landing their shells between and in the enemy's traverses, throwing up clouds of sand and driving the rebels from their guns." Federal Captain Benjamin Sand

Fort Fisher's land-face takes a pounding prior to the Federal ground assault. Drawing from *Battles and Leaders of the Civil War*.

Colonel Lamb wrote about the severity of January 14th's Federal bombardment:

On the morning of the 15th, the fleet, which had not ceased firing during the night, redoubled its fire on the land-face. The sea was smooth, and the navy having become accurate from practice, by noon had destroyed every gun on that face except one Columbiad, which was somewhat protected by the angle formed by the northeast salient. The palisade had been practically destroyed as a defensive line and was so torn up that it actually afforded cover for the assailants. The harvest of wounded and dead was hourly increasing and at that time I had not 1,200 effective men to defend the long line of works.[1]

Sea-face cannon muzzle broken off from direct hit. Timothy O'Sullivan image, 1865, *Photograph courtesy of the Library of Congress.*

The successful landing by General Terry's troops allowed the wooden warships to join the fight at Fort Fisher by late afternoon. From this point on, Fort Fisher began to take a terrible beating from the increased firepower. The Federal Navy, which had been criticized for their failure to destroy Fort Fisher's defenses in the previous assault, wanted desperately to have another chance to show the navy's destructive power. This time they resolved that nothing was going to prevent them from reducing the fort to a pile of useless rubble. The naval fire was far more accurate and destructive than it had been in the previous battle. The Federal gunners had been instructed to concentrate their fire on the gun chambers of the land-face and not waste any ammunition by shooting at the Confederate flags. Furthermore, each warship had been assigned certain gun chambers to destroy, to avoid repetition. All day and night on the 13th and 14th of January the fleet kept up its relentless bombardment. After the wooden warships withdrew for the evening the ironclads would remain at anchor and continue shelling the fort with their

Fort Fisher gunners return the fire of the Federal fleet during the second bombardment. Drawing from the March 15, 1865 issue of the *Illustrated London News.*

huge 11-inch and 15-inch cannonballs to prevent the Confederate soldiers from retrieving their wounded and making any repairs to the gun chambers. Sergeant Thomas A. McNeill of Company D, First Battalion, North Carolina Artillery, wrote of the intense bombardment:

> The 15-inch shells landed often on the guns, knocking off trunnions, breaking off great pieces of the Columbiad muzzles, wrecking gun carriages, and often bespattering the walls of the gun chambers with blood and brains of the men of the detachments, yet the gunners coolly adjusted the degrees. The men obeyed every order. . . .often mounting the parapet amid a storm of exploding shells when necessary to sponge a gun, the flannel bursting into flame as soon as out of the muzzle.[2]

Colonel Lamb had given orders to the Confederate gun crews they could only fire their artillery pieces once every thirty-minutes, but even then the increased naval fire did not allow his gunners much opportunity to man their cannon. The tremendous hail of iron kept the men in their bombproofs for long periods of time, interrupting the fort's return fire. Nearly all of

Confederate Sergeant Murdock Smith, 36th North Carolina, captured at Fort Fisher.

the fort's artillery pieces would suffer a direct hit that would either destroy or dismount the gun. As the damage to the fort increased, so did the number of casualties. In the first two days of the fight, over two hundred Confederate soldiers had been killed or wounded.[3]

Federal Captain Benjamin Sand of the *Fort Jackson* later wrote about the severity of the bombardment:

> Our fleet and the ironclads were doing some beautiful marksmanship, landing their shells between and in the enemy's traverses, throwing up clouds of sand and driving the rebels from their guns. I saw several alight near a gun, between a couple of traverses, and the men kept loading their gun and were training it on the fleet, when another shell exploded right over them and cleaned them away entirely, that gun not being fired afterwards.[4]

Private James Montgomery of company B, 36th North Carolina, noted, "Shot and shell rained on us. We could not repair our displaced guns, cook or eat or bury our dead lying around us. We were helpless . . . our guns were disabled and our front shot to pieces." Confederate seaman Robert Watson, who was manning the Brooke Battery on the sea-face, wrote in his diary, "Several of us were knocked down with sand bags. We were all nearly buried in sand several times. This was caused by shells bursting in the sand. Whenever one would strike near us, it would throw the sand over us by the cartload." A group of army signal corpsmen assigned to Battery Buchanan had a spectacular view of the bombardment. "[The shells were] exploding so fast that it would seem to be one roaring sound. . . .and the sand and water rising in great clouds—so that you could not see ten feet in any direction and the atmosphere was filled, it seemed, by sulfur," explained one soldier.[5]

35

Despite the fierce Federal bombardment, some Confederate artillery on the fort's sea-face did survive and saw good service. Seaman Robert Watson served as a gunner for a Brooke rifle and saw the effect his shots had on the fleet. Fortunately for us, Watson was one of the few Confederate seamen who kept a journal and wrote of his experiences at Fort Fisher. "Our shot and shell would strike the monitors iron sides and break in pieces and of course did them no injury, but the wooden vessels did not fare so well for several of them had to haul off." Indeed, the *Huron* and the *Unadilla* were forced to retire when they were struck repeatedly by Fort Fisher's cannon. The *Huron* was struck four times and had her mainmast shot away and main shroud cut. The *Unadilla* was hit several times and sailed out of range, leaking badly.[6]

Federal Captain Adrian Terry was so impressed by the bombardment of Fort Fisher's land-face that he described it in a letter to his wife:

> The fleet was throwing into the fort tremendous broadsides of shells and solid shot of all sizes from the 30-pounder Parrott to the huge 15-inch shells, the explosions seeming. . . .to shake the solid earth and throwing huge clouds of sand high in [the] air from every part of the fort.[7]

Confederate Robert Church, Company F, 10th North Carolina, killed at Fort Fisher. Photograph reprinted from *State Troops and Volunteers, Vol I*

Confederate Sergeant Thomas A. McNeill of the 1st Battalion, North Carolina Artillery, was on the receiving end of this bombardment and observed, "All the land-face looked as if wrapped in flame and smoke. The screaming, exploding shells [were] tearing the earthwork, making holes in the traverses, and in all the history of war it is doubtful if a more infernal fire ever fell upon a fort."[8]

Bragg ordered 1,100 men of the 11th, 21st and 25th South Carolina infantry to proceed by steamer to Battery Buchanan and reinforce Fort Fisher, but it was another example of too little too late. The soldiers on the transport *Sampson* did not arrive at Battery Buchanan until the early morning hours of the 15th, the third day of the Federal assault. Unfortunately the two other steamers, *Petteway* and *Harlee*, ran aground on a shoal near the docks at Gander Hall. After unloading her soldiers at Battery Buchanan the *Sampson* returned to the stranded steamers and began the tedious task of transferring the rest of the troops in small boats. By the time the *Sampson* had taken on a load of men and returned to Battery Buchanan, the Federal warships had resumed their bombardment of the fort. Only 482 men from the South Carolina regiments had been put ashore when the severe fire of the fleet forced the *Sampson* to retreat to safer waters.

The South Carolinians had never experienced such a terrific bombardment as the one they were witnessing at Fort Fisher. After a short rest, they had to double-quick a mile and a half to the main fort. Unfortunately, these troops were so traumatized by the shells exploding all around them they were practically useless for the rest of the battle. Lamb wrote, "They were out of breath, disorganized and more or less demoralized. They reached our front about thirty minutes before the attacking columns came like avalanches on our right and left. I sent them to an old commissary bombproof to recover their breath."[9]

Federal Private Simeon Chase, 97th Pennsylvania, died of wounds suffered at Fort Fisher.

General Terry's battle plan called for General Adelbert Ames' division to attack in echelon, with Colonel Curtis' First brigade; the 112th, 117th and 142nd New York infantry regiments, leading the charge and angling toward the area between the second traverse and the main gate. The second brigade, led by Colonel Galusha Pennypacker, would then advance to the line vacated by Curtis' brigade. Colonel Bell's Third Brigade would move forward and occupy the line vacated by Pennypacker's brigade. The second and third brigades would halt their advance and wait for further orders from General Ames. If the assault stalled, Ames could send in a fresh brigade to keep the advance moving forward. Colonel Abbott's 1,400-man brigade would stand by in reserve. The 3,600 black soldiers of Paine's division would hold the Federal rear line against Hoke's Confederates and would not be put into action unless it was absolutely necessary.[10]

By 2 PM, on January 15th, 3,700 Federal soldiers were in position for their assault against Fort Fisher's western land-face. The troops waited inside the tree line, half-a-mile north of the fort, for the signal from General Adelbert Ames to advance. Unlike the largely untried Fort Fisher garrison, these men were veterans of the Army of the James. They had survived difficult combat at places like Malvern Hill, Antietam, Fredericksburg, Chancellorsville, Gettysburg, Cold Harbor and the trenches around Petersburg.[11]

Regimental Surgeon James A. Mowris of the 117th New York was busy setting up the field hospital for the coming battle. There were operating tables to construct, medicine and instruments needed to be unpack and stretcher bearers to assign. As Mowris worked, he was struck by the men's somber behavior before they would charge the fort and described it in his book, *History of the 117th Regiment, New York Volunteers*:

> We again reached a time that "tries men's souls." It was traceable in the faces of those about us. One could read there the silent language of stern determination and high resolve. Men were cheerful, but not mirthful; serious but not solemn. In every eye might be read, not fear, but volumes of thought, too deep for utterance. . . .Not far in advance towered the frowning Fortress. . . .and, though none saw, all knew, that above, in imperial majesty, sat the Angel of Death. It was an awful moment, and, with compressed lips, our troops were breathing a silent petition for home and country.[12]

Interior of Fort Fisher's Hospital. *Frank Leslie's Illustrated Newspaper* February 18, 1865.

Admiral Porter was not satisfied with the navy's limited role in this campaign. According to General Grant's plan the navy was to soften the fort's defenses so Terry's army could march in and accept the Confederate surrender. This subservient role to the army was unacceptable to Porter. He wanted the navy to take a more active part in Fort Fisher's capture. Porter realized with his vast armada that he could easily find 2,000 volunteers to storm the fort and share in the glorious victory. It was possible, he reasoned, that the navy might even show the army a thing or two about storming a fort and forcing it to surrender. His supreme confidence in the navy's fighting ability prompted Admiral Porter to issue General Order 81 to the commanders of the fleet. Upon reading the admiral's order, the sailors volunteered in droves. They thought this would be a grand adventure and likened the assault to the spirited race they had against the army to capture the Confederate batteries on the beach north of Fort Fisher.

General Order 81 stated that each vessel was to provide as many men that could be spared for a landing party. "The sailors will be armed with cutlasses, well sharpened, and with revolvers. When the signal is made to assault. . .[the sailors will] board the fort on the run in a seaman-like way." The admiral had high hopes for the success of the campaign and bragged to Secretary Wells that if the army failed again, the navy would "show the soldiers how to do it. I can do anything with . . . my own good officers and men and you need not be surprised to hear that the webfooters have gone into the forts."[13]

The night before the Federal ground assault, General Terry met with Admiral Porter on the *Malvern* so they could coordinate their attacks for the following day. Terry agreed to signal the flagship right before the army's assault was to begin using a system of semaphore flags, so the fleet could shift its fire away from the land-face to avoid hitting the attacking force. The admiral's flagship would then hoist a signal flag and announce the charge with two long blasts from her steam whistle. This shrill blast was then to be repeated by the rest of the fleet.

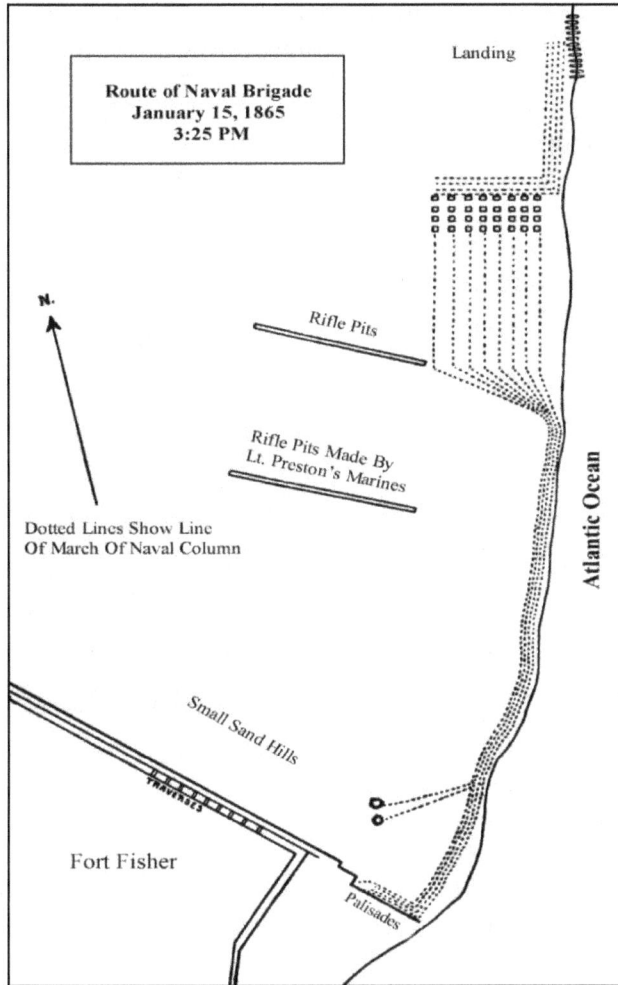

The Naval Brigade's assault targeted Fort Fisher's Northeast Bastion. Drawing from: *The Official Records of the Union and Confederate Navies in the War of the Rebellion*, Series I, Vol. XI.

Although the land assault was scheduled to begin at 3 PM, it appears there was some confusion over the time. In a letter to Gideon Wells, the Secretary of the Navy, Porter states he was under the impression the assault was to begin at 2 PM. "It was arranged between the General and myself that the ships should all go in early and fire rapidly through the day until the time for the assault came off. The hour named was 2 PM." Porter goes on to say, "At 2 o'clock I expected the signal for the vessels to change the direction of their fire, so that the troops might assault. The sailors and marines had worked, by digging ditches or rifle pits, to within 200 yards of the fort, and were all ready. The troops, however, did not get into position until later, and at 3 o'clock the signal came."[14]

Had Porter given his officers the wrong time for the army's assault to begin? If he did, this could help explain why the naval brigade was in position so early and why Lieutenant Commander Breese, after waiting nearly an hour and a half for the army to begin their attack, went ahead with their assault.

Admiral Porter's plan called for three columns of sailors to get into position for the assault a half-mile north of the fort. The sailors were ordered not to charge until they saw the army going over the northwest parapet of the fort. The marines were to act as sharpshooters and keep the fort's wall clear of Confederate defenders while the naval brigade charged. The route of the attack would take the sailors down the beach where they would skirt the end of the palisade fence and continue on to the fort. They were to scale its mounds and kill or capture the Confederate garrison.[15]

The landing party of 1,600 sailors and 400 marines came ashore at 11 AM and was put in charge of Lieutenant Commander K. Randolph Breese. Breese instructed the officers of the naval brigade that it was imperative to coordinate their attack with the army, a half mile to the west. Doing so would divide the fort's defenders and make the fort more vulnerable to the Federal ground assault. The sailors were divided into three divisions or columns. Lieutenant Commander Charles H. Cushman was assigned command of the first column, the second, Lieutenant Commander James Parker, and Lieutenant Commander Thomas O. Selfridge had the third column. The marines were led by Captain Lucien L. Dawson.

Sailors armed with spades had orders to construct a series of entrenchments for the marine sharpshooters as close to the fort as possible. A marine detachment under Lt. Louis Fagan was to provide covering fire for the sailors while they dug. Despite this protection the naval brigade was peppered with grape and canister from Fort Fisher's remaining eight-inch Columbiad on the land-face and from two 12-pounder Napoleon cannons at the main sally-port. The sailors persevered and managed to construct breastworks 600 yards in front of the fort and then gradually advanced them within 200 yards of the fort's northern wall.[16]

Breese marched the naval brigade from their landing site to a half mile north of the fort's land-face. This distance was adequate if the men were to begin the assault within the next few minutes. However, this was far too close if they were to remain there long. The problem was Breese was under the mistaken impression the assault was scheduled for 2 PM instead of 3 PM. This exposed his large column of blue-jackets to Confederate sharpshooters for over an hour while the army moved into position. The sailors, armed only with Remington and Whitney revolvers, were too far away from the fort to return fire. Several men were killed and wounded because of this failure to coordinate the time for the assault. Breese ordered his brigade to move closer to the water so the sloping beach might provide some cover, and instructed them to lie flat on the sand.

Two o'clock passed without any significant movement by the army toward the fort. Two thirty came and went and there was still no signal from the army. The fire from the fort was growing heavier. Besides receiving fire from the Confederate cannon, a few of the artillery rounds from the Federal fleet fell short of the fort and sprayed the naval brigade with red-hot shrapnel. "We were under a galling fire from a hateful gun mounted upon a field carriage at the fort's sally port, as well as musketry along the land face," Acting Master's Mate Joseph Simms recalled. "Together with musketry, canister, and grape fired by the enemy in front of us, fragments of bursting shell

Lieutenant Commander K. Randolph Breese would lead the Navy's ground assault.

fired by our ships at the rear and left of us, entrenching (sic) near the face of Fort Fisher was not a pleasant job." Ensign Ira Harris of the *Powhatan* noted the stray shells of the Federal fleet in a letter, "The shells from fifty-eight men-of-war made a horrible screeching and one eleven-inch gun [said to be the after pivot-gun of the *Vanderbilt*] fired several shells into our column. The wounded had to be carried through our ranks, and it seemed to discourage the men somewhat."[17]

When 3:15 PM came the army was still getting into position. Breese was irritated because his men were being needlessly exposed to hostile fire for over sixty minutes. Gazing anxiously to the west one more time, Breese saw some troop movements and determined the army was preparing to attack. At this point one has to question the movements that Breese saw. Were they meaningful troop movements signaling the army was beginning their assault, or were they merely wishful thinking on Breese's part? It is important to know the answer to this question because the navy suffered terribly during the ground assault. Was this a direct result of Breese launching his assault too early? It would appear some thought it was. This is part of the report Marine Captain Lucien L. Dawson made on January 27, 1865 to Colonel Jacob Zeilin, United States Marine Commandant, in Washington, D.C. Dawson is addressing the criticisms made by Rear-Admiral Porter in which he blames the Marine Corps for failing to support the naval ground assault at Fort Fisher and thus contributing to the severe casualties suffered by the Navy:

> The naval party assaulted before the army instead of after, thereby not only drawing nearly the whole fire of the rebels upon themselves, but acting in direct violation of the admiral's express written order, which was that the naval party should not move to the assault until the army was seen going in over the northwest parapet of the fort.[18]

Ensign Robley Evans also wrote of the naval brigade assaulting before the army in his book, *A Sailor's Log*, saying, "At three o'clock the order to charge was given, and we started for our long run of

twelve hundred yards over the loose sand. . . .The army had not yet assaulted, so the whole garrison concentrated its fire on us."[19]

The fateful 3 PM deadline for the ground assault had long since passed. Tired of waiting for the army, Lieutenant Commander Breese drew his sword and turned to look at the men gathered around him. Dozens of brightly colored United States flags fluttered in the breeze. Beneath these flags, hundreds of men with determination deeply etched on their faces were watching him. Brimming with confidence, he thrust his sword toward the fort, and bellowed, "Charge! Charge!"[20]

Medal of Honor winner Marine Sergeant Richard Binder advances on Fort Fisher during the naval ground assault.

Armed with cutlasses and revolvers, the sailors raced down the beach toward the Northeast Bastion, cheering wildly. The marines, who were instructed to stay in their entrenchments and provide covering fire for the navy, became caught up in the excitement of the charge and joined the sailors. This proved to be a fatal mistake because the lack of the marine support allowed the Confederate defenders to fire at will from the fort's parapet. In Breese's official report of the incident he wrote, "(The naval brigade) assaulted to within 50 yards of the parapet, which was lined with one dense mass of musketeers, who played sad havoc with our men. The marines having failed to occupy their position, gave the enemy an almost unmolested fire upon us."[21]

When the Federal fleet saw the naval brigade running down the beach, they sounded the charge with dozens of steam whistles. Admiral Porter beamed with fatherly pride as he stood on the deck of the *Malvern* and closely followed the progress of his men. He had every reason to be proud. Not only was this charge his idea, but his own seventeen-year-old son, Carlisle P. Porter, was participating in the assault. Porter could understand his son's eagerness to join the attack on the fort. The war was quickly drawing to a close and Carlisle was afraid he would miss the last great battle. Admiral Porter mentioned this to Lieutenant Commander Breese, who had the responsibly of organizing the Navy's ground assault, and now was ordered to keep an eye on the admiral's son. Breese decided the best way to get young Porter involved was to put him to work as a courier delivering dispatches, thus keeping him away from the hazardous assault.

Aboard other ships, crewmen scaled the rigging and crowded the rails to watch their shipmates charging down the beach toward the rebel fort. "We almost held our breath as they charged," reported Seaman John Grattan. "The noise of the guns, whistles, cheers and yells of the sailors and marines was terrific and made the most exciting and indescribable event."[22]

Upon hearing the fleet's steam whistles and the wild cheering from thousands of sailors and marines, the Confederate defenders were aware that the long awaited ground assault had finally begun. When the naval bombardment shifted to another area of the fort, they stormed out of their bombproof and raced to the top of the northeast bastion. Suddenly the fort came to life, bristling with guns. Men clad in a mix of butternut-brown and dirty gray uniforms lined the walls. Colonel Lamb climbed to the crest of the parapet and scanned the beach with his binoculars. Half a mile to the north he detected an undulating blue mass, topped by curious flashes of light. As they drew closer, Lamb discovered the men of the naval brigade were running down the beach and waving their cutlasses. The steel from these cutlasses caught the sunlight and reflect it toward the fort creating the flashes of light Lamb saw.

The Naval Brigade was ordered to charge through the palisade fence and scale the formidable 43-foot-high Northeast Bastion. Image Timothy O'Sullivan, *Photograph courtesy of Library of Congress.*

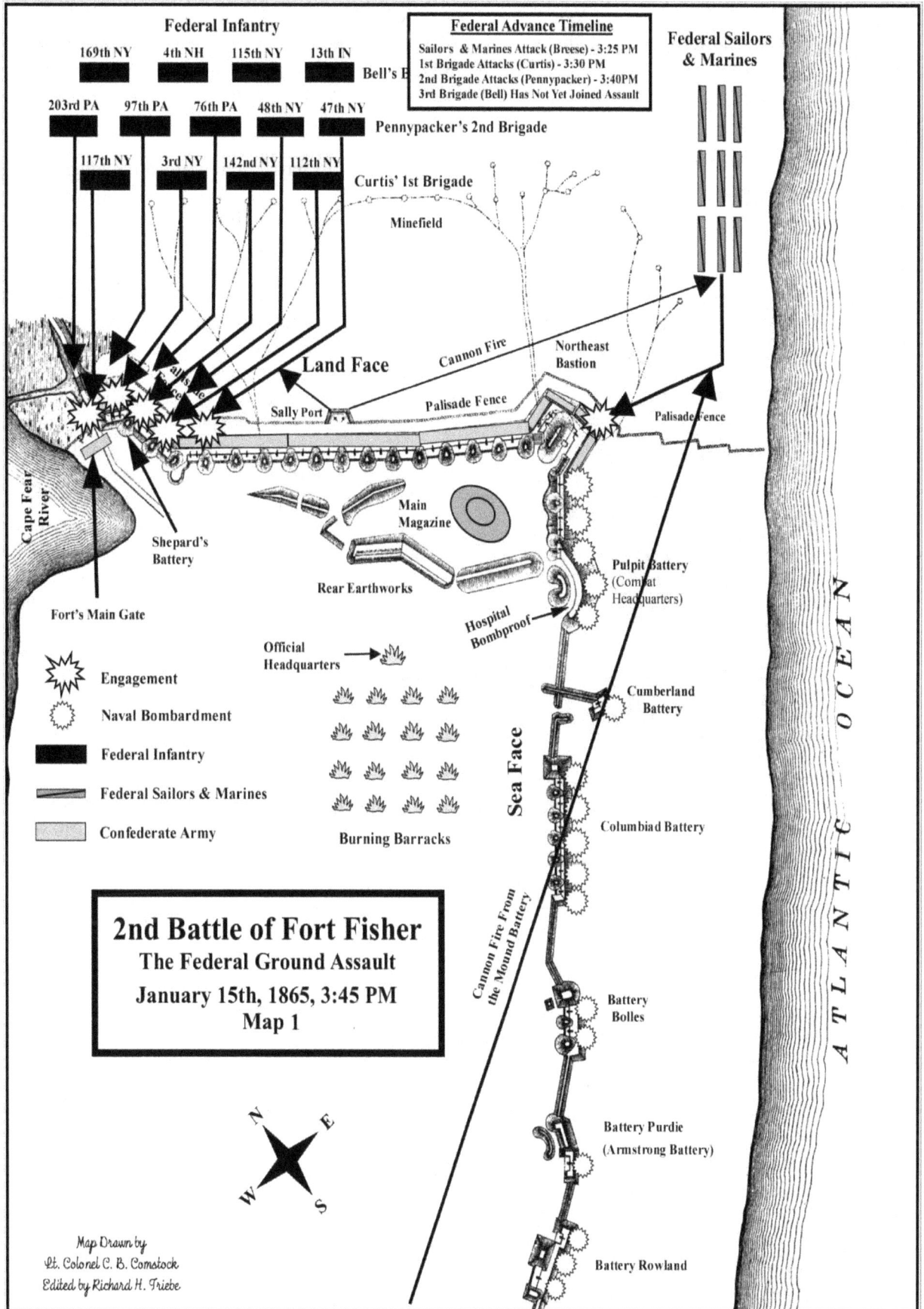

Federal Infantry

169th NY 4th NH 115th NY 13th IN

Bell's B

203rd PA 97th PA 76th PA 48th NY 47th NY

Pennypacker's 2nd Brigade

117th NY 3rd NY 142nd NY 112th NY

Curtis' 1st Brigade

Minefield

Federal Advance Timeline

Sailors & Marines Attack (Breese) - 3:25 PM
1st Brigade Attacks (Curtis) - 3:30 PM
2nd Brigade Attacks (Pennypacker) - 3:40 PM
3rd Brigade (Bell) Has Not Yet Joined Assault

Federal Sailors & Marines

Cannon Fire

Northeast Bastion

Land Face

Palisade Fence

Sally Port

Palisade Fence

Cape Fear River

Shepard's Battery

Fort's Main Gate

Main Magazine

Rear Earthworks

Hospital Bombproof

Pulpit Battery (Combat Headquarters)

Official Headquarters

Cumberland Battery

Engagement

Naval Bombardment

Federal Infantry

Federal Sailors & Marines

Confederate Army

Burning Barracks

Sea Face

Columbiad Battery

Cannon Fire From the Mound Battery

2nd Battle of Fort Fisher
The Federal Ground Assault
January 15th, 1865, 3:45 PM
Map 1

Battery Bolles

Battery Purdie (Armstrong Battery)

N E W S

Map Drawn by
Lt. Colonel C. B. Comstock
Edited by Richard H. Triebe

Battery Rowland

A T L A N T I C   O C E A N

Colonel Lamb planned to withhold the Confederate fire until the naval brigade had come within 150 yards of the fort, then give the order to detonate the underground torpedoes, trapping half of the enemy between the explosion and the fort. Volleys of Confederate gunfire would decimate the soldiers left standing and any remaining sailors would be so thoroughly demoralized that they would retreat in confusion.

Ensign Robley Evans was severely wounded in the assault on Fort Fisher.

To his dismay, Lamb noticed the attacking column was keeping close to the water's edge and would miss the line of buried torpedoes. It became clear that Fort Fisher's fate rested solely on the soldier's ability to throw back the assaulting column. Lamb instructed his men "to pick off the officers in the assaulting columns" but not to fire yet. The sharpshooters and the few remaining artillery crews would continue to fire at targets of opportunity, but Lamb wanted his main troops held in reserve. He needed to draw the enemy closer to the fort before unleashing the first devastating Confederate volley. A sudden blast of gunfire delivered at close range could shatter the enemy's resolve and force them to withdraw.[23]

The Confederate defenders, their rifles at the ready, tensed as they watched the mass of enemy troops surging toward them, unchecked. The two sally-port field pieces, the lone land-face Columbiad and the two cannons at the mound battery fired, reloaded and fired again, but this wasn't enough. Still the blue clad horde ran on, cheering and waving their cutlasses and revolvers. Nothing was going to stop them from reaching the fort. As the naval brigade neared the palisade fence they angled toward the opening where the fence meets the sea. A bottleneck occurred in this small area, cramming the sailors and marines together.

This was the moment Lamb had been waiting for; the enemy was within easy range and densely packed so that his men could not miss. Colonel Lamb commanded his soldiers, "Men of the thirty-sixth North Carolina, prepare to fire!" All along the line hammers clicked as men cocked their guns. He thrust his sword at the Yankees and shouted, "Fire!" The parapet of the Northeast Bastion exploded into a forbidding wall of flame and gun smoke.

Lieutenant Commander Breese led the naval brigade's charge down the beach when suddenly white gun smoke exploded on the fort's parapet along with the roar from hundreds of Confederate rifles. All of the men fell to the sand, either struck by bullets or desperately seeking any sort of shelter they could find. Ensign Robley Evans recalled the incident in his book *A Sailor's Log*, "About five hundred yards from the fort the head of the column suddenly stopped, and, as if by magic, the whole mass of men went down like a row of falling bricks; in a second every man was flat on his stomach," Ensign Robley Evans recalled.[24]

One of the first seamen to be shot was James Flannigan. The night before the assault, Flannigan shared a premonition of his death with fellow *Powhatan* shipmate Ensign Evans. The sailor came to Evan's room with a small box and said, "Mr. Evans, will you be kind enough to take charge of this box for me—it has some little trinkets in it—and give it to my sister in Philadelphia?" Evans asked why he did not deliver it himself. Flannigan replied, "I am going ashore with you tomorrow and will be killed." Evans wrote of the incident later:

Ensign Benjamin Porter was killed in the Naval Brigade's charge while carrying the Admiral's flag.

He showed no nervousness over it, but seemed to regard it as a matter of course. I took the box and, after making a proper memorandum, put it away among my things. On the afternoon of the next day, when we were charging the fort and just as we came under fire, at eight hundred yards, I saw Flannigan reel out to one side and drop, the first man hit, with a bullet through his heart. I stepped up quickly to his side and asked if he were badly hurt; the only reply was a smile as he looked up into my face and rolled over dead.[25]

Several Federal officers got to their feet, urging the men to get up and resume the charge, which they did. The naval brigade raced forward another 50 yards when they encountered a second murderous Confederate volley. The men instantly dropped to the sand and tried to present as small a target as possible. Because the beach was relatively flat with no cover, men began scooping sand in front of them with their bare hands. In a letter to his sisters Lieutenant John Bartlett wrote about his experience:

I began to dig a hole with my hands. You would have laughed to have seen me. It did not take me long to get a pile of sand in front of me high enough to screen me from fire. This was at about half past 3. I kept on digging until I had a hole that I could stand up in. The sand was very soft and dry, so that it was easily thrown up. Every time I threw up a handful of sand on the edge of my pit, a dozen bullets would skip over my head. It was rather unpleasant, as it knocked the sand all down on me.[26]

Once more Lieutenant Commanders Breese, James Parker and Captain Thomas Selfridge encouraged the naval brigade to get to their feet and continue the charge. When the head of the column reached the palisade fence, they were stopped in their tracks by a devastating volley of rifle fire delivered at close range. Commodore Joseph Lanman noted the assault in his report:

The enemy opened a heavy fire upon us of musketry and grape, which soon became very hot. A few of the officers and men pressed beyond the palisades, but the advance along the beach was there checked, and turned along the palisades toward the fort. In the hurry of the advance, the different divisions had somewhat intermingled, and almost every shot from the enemy carried its message of wound or death to some one of our number.[27]

Flag Lieutenant Samuel W. Preston and Ensign Benjamin Porter were killed moments apart. They were the best of friends and shared everything together, even death on the sands of Fort Fisher.

At the head of the column Lieutenant Benjamin Porter was proudly carrying the Admiral's flag. Porter, who was no relation to Admiral David D. Porter, was the 19-year-old commander of the Admiral's flagship, the *Malvern*. Lieutenant Porter had boasted that the admiral's flag would be the first on the fort. Accompanying him was his longtime friend, Flag Lieutenant Samuel W. Preston. The blue banner with two white stars which Porter held aloft made him an irresistible target for the fort's marksmen. It's amazing Porter was able to get as far as he did. When he was only fifty feet from the palisade fence a Confederate bullet struck him square in the chest, killing him instantly. Lieutenant Preston, unaware that Porter had been shot, raced on and moments later he too was fatally shot.

Lieutenant Roswell H. Lamson wrote of this incident in his official report:

> The men pressed forward, and when near the palisades Mr. Preston was struck in the left thigh or groin, the femoral artery being severed. He fell forward, and one of the men stooped to assist him and was shot, falling on Mr. Preston. Someone pulled him off, and Mr. Preston turned over on his back and soon expired. . . . I had got forward some twenty paces more, when I was knocked down by a shot through the left arm and shoulder. I arose again and got up nearer the parapet, when I fell from loss of blood and exhaustion.[28]

True to his calling, assistant Surgeon William Longshaw Jr. selflessly moved from one wounded man to another, carrying medical instruments, tourniquets and canteens of water. Ensign Robley D. Evans was wounded in both legs and remembers Surgeon Longshaw treating him and giving him a sip of water. "We will have you all off the beach tonight," the doctor said, and continued on to the next man. Longshaw's lifeless body was found on the beach the following morning. He had been binding up the wounds of a mortally wounded marine when his skull was shattered by a Confederate bullet.[29]

Terrified by the hail of lead and iron whizzing by them, most men refused to go any farther. Some sought out bomb craters for protection while others hid behind the dead bodies of fallen comrades. The palisade fence, intended as a defensive structure for the Confederates, was now being sought out by the

Charge of the Marines on the Traverse, painting by J. O. Davidson, 1887, print by L. Prang & Co. This picture portrays the climactic moment when the Naval Brigade broke through the palisade fence and stormed Fort Fisher's Northeast Bastion.

enemy for shelter. After catching their breath, a few of the men ran through splintered gaps in the fence and continued on to the fort. Most of the men who ventured beyond the palisade fence were shot down before they reached the fort, but a few managed to elude the storm of minie balls. One man, quarter gunner James Tallentine from *USS Tacony*, scaled the fort's steep slope alone. Apparently he did not realize the other men had been killed or wounded. Up he went, toward the horde of Confederate soldiers trying to shoot him. Bullets plucked at his coat and kicked up the sand around him, but none found their mark. One has to wonder why he got as far as he did. Was he just lucky, or did the Confederate soldiers reward his determination and bravery by allowing him to finish his climb? We will never know. What we do know is that James Tallentine reached the crest of the parapet and was shot by a Confederate soldier, causing him to fall into the ranks of the fort's defenders.[30]

Lamb wrote of this brave charge in his book, *Colonel Lamb's Story of Fort Fisher*:

The sailors and marines reached the berme (sic) and sprang up the slope, but a murderous fire greeted them and swept them down. Volley after volley was poured into their faltering ranks by cool, determined men, and in half an hour several hundred dead and wounded lay at the foot of the bastion.[31]

There were no more Confederate volleys. Now each man fired his rifle-musket as rapidly as possible. Colonel Lamb wisely placed the best marksmen that Fort Fisher had to offer along the fort's walls. After these men had fired their rifles, they would pass their weapons back to the soldiers behind them to be reloaded. In turn, these expert sharpshooters would be handed a loaded rifle so they could keep up a steady, accurate fire. Through the thick smoke General Whiting could be seen scaling the parapet. He boldly stood on the wall with his sword raised, pointing at the Yankees and urging his men to fire. Ramrods rattled and scraped in hot rifle barrels as soldiers reloaded, then fired again. Federal ensign Ira Harris recalled the intense Confederate fire:

From where I lay on the glacis, we could see four rows of [Confederate] soldiers in the fort, two ranks firing, and two loading, and hear their taunts to "come on". . . .At this time there was no distinct sound of bullets, but only a steady rush, and the water close to the beach was lashed to foam. I would not have supposed men could fire so fast.[32]

Seaman William Cobb survived the charge of the Naval Brigade and wrote about the death that surrounded him.

The area in front of the Northeast Bastion became a killing zone. The smoke-filled beach was strewn with dead and wounded seamen, struggling to get out of the line of fire. The moans and cries of the injured along with the rattle of gunfire and the bursting of shells combined to create a cacophony of sounds which seemed to emanate from the bowels of hell.

"I have been in a great number of battles," reported Seaman William Cobb, "but I never saw men fall so fast in my life. There was a shower of canister (that came) through the ranks where I was running up the beach and out of about twenty that stood within eight paces of me, there was but four of us that came out." It was clear to the sailors and marines that they could not advance without being slaughtered, but it was equally clear they could not remain where they were because their only shelter was the shattered remnant of the palisade fence. As things stood right now it was only a matter of time before the rest of the sailors were picked off by Confederate sharpshooters.[33]

As before, Lieutenant Commander Breese was on his feet, waving his sword and his arms, trying to encourage the men to renew the attack. No matter how hard he tried, nobody would budge. The only thing he succeeded in doing was attracting more Confederate gunfire in his direction. Frustrated, Breese turned to the rear thinking maybe he could rally the men back there. What he saw made him sick to his stomach. Dozens of men in the rear of the formation were drifting back up the beach toward the Federal lines. Breese chased after them, shouting, "No, men, charge! Charge the fort! Don't be cowards! Don't retreat!"[34]

Pinned down by an avalanche of Confederate fire, the sailors began to grumble amongst themselves about the hopelessness of their situation. Those men who had heard Breese shouting at the retreating sailors misinterpreted what he was saying. They heard the word retreat, and they repeated it. "Retreat! Retreat!" That was all it took. What began as a few stragglers going to the rear soon escalated into a panicked mob, shoving at each other in a mad dash to get away from the fort. "Flesh and blood could not long endure being killed in this slaughter-pen, and the rear of the sailors broke, followed by the whole body, in spite of all efforts to rally them," Lieutenant Commander Selfridge recalled with bitterness. His sentiments were echoed by Lieutenant John Bartlett, "I shouted and waved my sword for the sailors to come back, but no, off they went down the beach. . . .I could have cried when the blue jackets retreated."[35]

As Lieutenant Commander Breese chased the deserting sailors down the beach, it soon became obvious that the men were ignoring his curses and threats; if anything, his pursuit was making them run even faster. Disheartened, Breese slowed to a stop and returned to the front amid a shower of enemy bullets. "How [Breese] escaped death is a marvel to me," Lieutenant Commander Parker said.[36]

Only sixty sailors remained near the foot of the fort, hiding behind the remains of the palisade fence. A wave of relief and jubilation overcame the Confederate soldiers, and they began tossing their hats into the air and cheering the retreating mob of sailors. Even the normally reserved General Whiting and Colonel Lamb were dancing about and shouting with glee. But the festive mood soon faded when they realized that not all of the sailors had withdrawn. The Confederate defenders began to concentrate their fire on the small band of men who had not fled. In a matter of moments, four Federal officers fell wounded. Seeing the futility of continuing the advance, Lieutenant Commander Parker ordered everyone to stay put until they were able to withdraw under the cover of darkness.[37]

Some of the wounded sailors and marines were unable to move and drowned when the tide came in.

Death for the sailors and marines did not end there. Another tragedy occurred when the tide came in. The assault had been at low tide to allow the naval brigade as much room as possible to slip between the end of the palisade fence and the ocean. Some of the wounded men, either too weak from loss of blood or severely injured, were unable to escape the rushing sea and drowned. Landsman Edward Lindsay was wounded in his right hip and his left leg was broken by grapeshot. Unable to stand, Lindsay was swept out to sea where he disappeared beneath the waves. Lieutenant John Bartlett wrote of his frustration over not being able to help these injured men. "It was low tide when we made the charge and a few fell close to the water. Before dark the tide rose and the waves washed up on the poor fellows, some only wounded. It was hard to look on and not be able to give them any help."[38]

The charge of the naval brigade was considered a failure because it did not achieve its objective and left over three hundred sailors and marines killed or wounded in the twenty-five minute assault. This amounts to twelve men being shot every sixty seconds. One thing the naval ground assault did accomplish, however, was a diversion for the army's attack a half mile to the west. It is questionable if the army would have been successful in their assault had it not been for the navy's sacrificial charge that divided the enemy's attention at such a crucial time. When considered in this light, it would appear that the naval assault was a success of sorts because it did contribute to the expedition's ultimate goal, the capture of Fort Fisher.[39]

Colonel William Lamb and his Confederates leaped upon the parapets, whooping for joy at the retreating naval brigade which was flying down the beach. Men dressed in butternut brown and gray were laughing, dancing and waving their battered hats, shouting, "Come aboard, Billy Yank! Don't run away! Come aboard an' we'll show you some real Southern hospitality!" The cheering Confederates believed they had thrown back the main assault. "The heroic bravery of [the Federal] officers, twenty-one of whom were killed and wounded, could not restrain the men from panic and retreat, and with small loss to ourselves, we witnessed what had never been seen before, a disorderly rout of American sailors and marines," Lamb wrote.[40]

As the cheering began to subside, Lamb's attention was drawn to his left by an ominous swell of gunfire. He stared in stunned disbelief at several Federal battle flags amid a smoky swirl of activity upon the fort's westernmost ramparts. Blue-clad soldiers were clamoring over the parapet and fighting with the gray defenders for possession of the gun chambers. Incensed, General Whiting called for volunteers to "Haul down those flags and drive the enemy from the works!" Flushed with the taste of victory, hundreds of Confederate soldiers rushed to obey. They swarmed down the Northeast Bastion and swept along the fort's land-face until they met the Yankees in mortal combat at the third gun chamber.[41]

General Adelbert Ames, Commander of the Second Division, had the honor of leading the Federal assault.

Federal General Adelbert Ames' Division had been given a daunting task. They were to charge across a half mile of barren, sandy plain while their every movement was being observed by an enemy in an elevated, fortified position. Confederate defenders would be firing a storm of iron and lead projectiles at these soldiers from four sally-port cannons. One of the 8-inch Columbiad artillery pieces next to the Northeast Bastion had miraculously survived the bombardment and would join the assault on the Federal troops. Also firing with these cannons would be hundreds of rifle muskets. Even if the Federals were able to penetrate this barrage, a muddy ditch blocked their approach to the fort's main gate. Although a wooden bridge that spanned the River Road marsh was left in place, the Confederates had removed the planks and left only several grease-coated stringers for the Federals to navigate.[42]

General Terry was aware these men's lives depended on his decisions. This was a grave responsibly and it weighed heavily on his mind all morning. Terry needed to give this assault every opportunity to succeed. After much consideration, he sent 100 sharpshooters forward to entrench within 175 yards of the fort. These men would cover the area with a suppressing fire while the other troops advanced. The sharpshooters were armed with the latest weapon, a lever-action Spencer repeating rifle with a seven-shot magazine, and were instructed to pick off any Confederate riflemen that appeared on the fort's walls. Because the palisade fence on the western side of the fort survived the bombardment largely intact, some of these men also carried axes so they could chop openings for the charging infantry.[43]

General Terry also had Curtis' brigade move out of the woods in a line of battle and rush to within 200 yards of the fort. They dropped to the sand and quickly began to construct crude breastworks with anything they had, scooping up the loose sand with bayonets, swords, tin plates, cups and bare hands. Curtis waited until the naval bombardment drove the Confederates back to their bombproofs, then sent his brigade forward again, one regiment at a time.[44]

Satisfied with the disposition of his army, General Terry issued orders for the fleet to shift their bombardment away from the land-face because the land assault was about to begin. Immediately a huge signal flag was waving back-and-forth above the command-post earthwork, alerting Admiral Porter on the *Malvern*. Lieutenant F. E. Beardsley, the signal officer waving this large flag, became a prime target for Confederate sharpshooters. The rebel marksmen were instructed to pick off the officers, but they were also told to disrupt Federal communications by shooting at the signalmen.[45]

General Terry turned to his division commander, and ordered, "Colonel Ames, the signal agreed upon for the assault has been given. Your division is ready to advance."[46]

As the naval column was being slaughtered a half-mile to his left, Colonel Curtis rose in the center of his line, waved his hat and called out to his men, "Forward!" Each man sprang to his feet, charging the fort without saying a word. Curtis had forbidden cheering because every man would need his breath to charge up the fort's steep parapet.[47]

"The enemy quickly showed themselves upon the ramparts and was pouring into [us] a tremendous fire of musketry while four or five cannon threw showers of grape and canister into [our ranks]," Captain Adrian Terry recalled in a letter. The Federal troops were just beginning their charge, and not yet fully upright, causing the first volley to pass overhead. The second did not miss, however. All along the line men began to fall. Colonel John F. Smith, the commanding officer of the 112th New York, was struck in the bowels shortly after he rose. Bullets furiously kicked up the sand around his body. Several men saw their colonel in the line of fire and dropped their weapons to help him. Under a hail of lead they carried the severely wounded Smith to a depression in the sand, so he would be safe until a surgeon could tend to him. Despite the surgeon's best efforts, Smith would die of his wounds three days later. On the day of his death, the colonel revived for a short time and asked, "Do we still hold the fort?" He was assured they did. Colonel Smith smiled briefly, closed his eyes and passed away.[48]

The same Confederate volley also felled Lieutenants Frank Lay and Paul Horvath. Lay would later rejoin the battle, but Horvath was killed instantly. Federal soldier Leonard Thomas was so impressed by the accurate fire that he wrote:

> It was not a blinding fire whistling and humming overhead. The number of stricken men, increasing from moment to moment, showed how well the veterans on the ramparts could aim. Caps and clothing were pierced, swords and scabbards were hit, belts and canteen straps were cut."[49]

Captain Albert G. Lawrence, Ames' aide-de-camp, was the first man through the palisade fence. He stepped through the jagged opening and turned around to help a color bearer behind him. He grabbed the man's guidon, and was turning to resume the charge when a Confederate shell exploded beside him, tearing off his left arm and fatally wounding him.[50]

Confederate rifle fire along with blasts of grape and canister from the middle sally-port artillery began to take a fearful toll on the left of Curtis' line. Federal Captain George F. Towle recalled the terrible slaughter, "For the first few minutes out of every five [men] who gained the slope of the

Captain Albert Lawrence was killed by an artillery fragment moments after he stepped through the palisade fence.

parapet, three went down dead or wounded." The 112th New York had twice as far to charge as the other regiments because it needed to right oblique from its position on the left and advance toward the far side of the fort. Thus these soldiers were exposed to the withering Confederate fire for a longer period of time.

Federal soldier N. M. Robinson described the hazards of charging Fort Fisher in a letter dated February 27, 1865:

We had to run about 50 rods right under the fire of the rebs sharpshooters & there (sic) grape and canister & I tell you it thinned out our men very bad, going to the fort I could see them fall on every side of me. . . .I considered it more dangerous going up to the fort than it was after we got into it.[51]

Confederate Captain Kinchen Braddy, 36th North Carolina, commanded the River Road battery during the Federal assault.

The most destructive fire came from the two light artillery pieces at the fort's sandbagged River Road entrance. A 12-pounder Napoleon and a 3.2-inch Parrott rifle were pointed menacingly up River Road, blocking the entrance to the main gate. These cannons were manned by gunners from Captain Kinchen Braddy's Company C, 36th North Carolina and men from Captain James McCormic's First Battalion North Carolina Artillery. Lead case-shot spewed from these guns and tore gaping holes in Curtis' charging Federals. Judge Zachary F. Fulmore, who was a Confederate private during the assault at Fort Fisher, wrote Colonel Lamb a letter regarding the battle at the River Road sally-port in 1883:

Company D was [to] the extreme left of the fort, occupying the space on both sides of the Napoleon, and although protected only by a shallow ditch and the remnants of the palisade, successfully repulsed every charge made by Curtis' brigade in front, and compelled the charging columns to abandon this. . . .entrance to the fort and go off to the right, to climb the high parapets in order to get into the fort. . . .There was another piece, however, a Parrott gun. . . .which we used once or twice very effectively in blowing to atoms a bridge on the main road into the fort. At the [Federals] first charge the boys at the Napoleon made a shot which cleared that road and caused many to take refuge under that bridge.[52]

The Federals, who witnessed dozens of their fellow soldiers being blown away by the Confederate artillery, chose wading through the cold, murky water rather than certain death on the bridge. Unfortunately, this route did not provide the shelter the men sought. Chaplain William L. Hyde, a veteran of the 112th New York wrote:

(The men of our regiment) moved forward in the charge, were greeted by a murderous fire from the fort! Many a brave fellow fell. Soon they reached the marsh in front, which some attempting to cross, were mired, and became the easy mark for riflemen in the fort.[53]

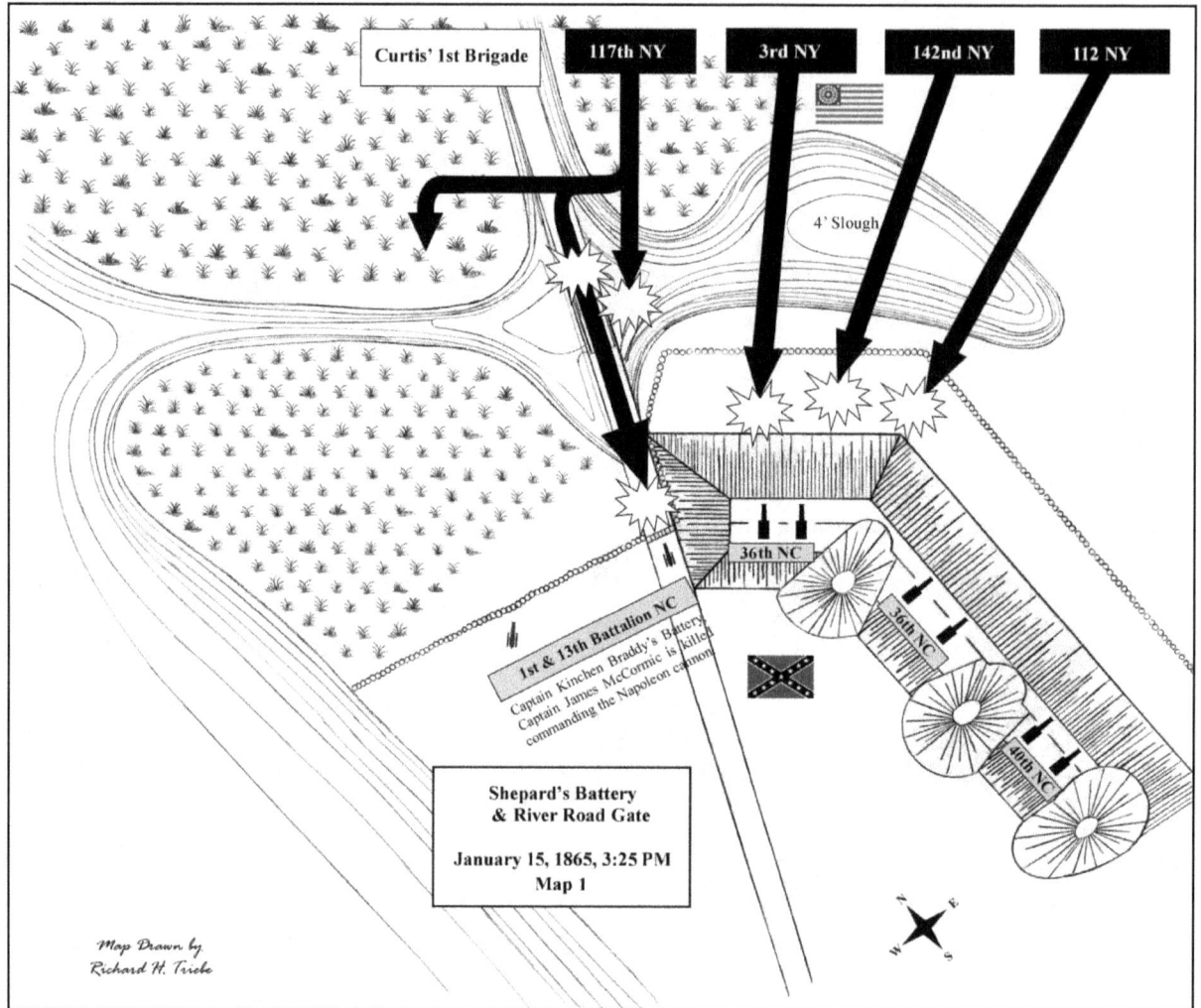

Colonel Curtis' Brigade charged Fort Fisher and met a storm of cannon and rifle fire. Many soldiers decided it was safer to wade through the marsh because of the barrage of Confederate fire on the bridge.

Confederate Captain Kinchen Braddy's small detachment of thirty-five soldiers was in extreme peril at the River Road gate. His men bravely stood their ground against hundreds of charging Federal troops, loading and firing the battery's two cannons. There were not enough men to stem the tide and the battery was in danger of being overrun. Hordes of screaming Federals stormed the sandbagged sally-port gate, trying to force their way through. These men were met by equally determined Rebel defenders, who fired their muskets point-blank into the charging Federals. It seemed like the harder these men fought, the more determined their attackers became. One after another, the Confederates soldiers fell dead and wounded. When it appeared the Northern troops would burst through the entrance, the defenders were reinforced by soldiers from the First North Carolina Heavy Artillery. These men had seen the desperate fight from the gun chamber above and rushed over to keep the Yankees out of the fort.

Confederate Sergeant Thomas A. McNeill recalled the deadly combat at the River Road gate:

> The men of [Company D] rushed to the . . . sally-port [and] at once opened fire on the enemy, and a destructive fire was kept up. . . .After a few rounds from the battery, the detachments, two or three in succession, were all shot down at their guns, and the pieces were not after this served . . . The [Yankee] column advanced to

the right of this company's position, under a heavy fire poured on it from the palisades between the sally-port and the river's edge, moving as if to effect a lodgment on the fort. . . .In the midst of this fire, it was found that the enemy were inside the palisades, to the right of Company D, and then a desperate struggle succeeded almost hand-to-hand, some of [our men] clubbing their muskets and fighting the width of the palisade between them and the enemy.[54]

Confederate Private Zachary Fulmore recalled the terrible bloodbath in a letter to Colonel Lamb, "On the afternoon of the fight my recollection is that there were eleven men killed and seventeen wounded in Company B, during the three charges. . . .[made by] Curtis' Brigade."[55]

As brutal as the fighting was for the Confederates, it was just as hard for the Federal soldiers. It's true that the Northern troops greatly outnumbered the Confederates inside the fort, but the men on the firing line knew no such advantage. To them it was kill or be killed. Shoot the man in the gray uniform aiming his rifle before he gets the chance to shoot you. This was the most brutal combat imaginable. The men were so close, many times only a few feet separated them, that the struggle became personal. Not only could you look your opponent in the eye, but you could hear him scream in pain as you shot him or clubbed him with your musket. The fighting at the gate became so bitter that many veterans of the battle would later refer to this entrance as the "bloody gate". For one Federal veteran this was an unusually apt name. "The fighting at the sally-port was terrific and the carnage the most terrible that I had ever witnessed," recalled Federal 2nd Lieutenant George Simpson of the 142nd New York. "Rivulets of blood ran from the gateway."

Federal Lieutenant George Simpson of the 142nd New York, recalled, "[The fighting] was terrific and the carnage the most terrible that I had ever witnessed . . . rivulets of blood ran from the gateway."

First Lieutenant J. C. Clements of the 21st South Carolina, Company B, saw the advance elements of the 117th New York moving through the marsh attempting to flank the defenders at the River Road gate. He took about 15 men and went to the marshy area to the left of the gate to oppose them. Clements formed his men behind some posts and opened a brisk fire with the Union troops. Several blue-coated soldiers fell to the accurate Confederate shooting and the remainder crouched down, temporarily halting their progress. Soon the Union soldiers resumed moving toward the fort. When the fighting became hand-to-hand Lieutenant Clements said that one of his men performed the coolest and bravest act he had ever witnessed during the war. "Private Ira Register, who was nearest the roadway, stepped into the road and came in contact with a Federal officer who was urging his men on, and after firing his piece into the ranks he then clubbed his musket and no doubt would've brained the officer, but was himself shot instantly and killed."[56]

Colonel Curtis saw the desperate fight for the River Road gate and realized his frontal assault was not working. He was losing too many men and no ground was being gained. Curtis figured the best way to capture the gate was to flank it by taking the elevated gun chamber next to it. Once this had been captured, his men could either fire down on the stubborn Confederate defenders at the gate or move around behind them and attack from the rear.

While Curtis was contemplating the best way to capture the Confederate battery, his men veered to their left to get away from the murderous cannons at the fort's gate. Dozens of Federal soldiers gathered at the base of the fort's sloping walls. Here they found temporary shelter from the Confederate guns. A serious mistake was made by Major Riley's Confederate defenders in the gun chambers. Unlike Colonel Lamb's soldiers at the Northeast Bastion, who stood on top of the fort's parapets, shooting down at the charging Federals, these Confederate defenders waited for the Union soldiers inside the gun chamber thus limiting their field of fire. This inadvertently created a blind spot for the defenders and allowed the enemy a brief respite to catch their breath and regroup before continuing their charge up the steep slope. This error in judgment exacerbated the already small number of Confederate troops available. As a result, the soldiers were unable to see the advancing Federals until they were practically on top of them. By then, it would be too late. Large numbers of Federal troops would swarm over the fort's walls and overwhelm the Confederate defenders.[57]

Colonel Lamb mentioned this grave error in 1893 while addressing the Cape Fear Camp of the United Confederate Veterans in Wilmington, North Carolina:

> I knew my only hope of repelling greatly superior numbers was to man the top of the parapet and fire down upon the assaulting columns. . . .The guns immediately to the right of Shepperd's Battery were manned by some of the bravest officers and men, but the fatal mistake of the commander was fighting from behind the revetment instead of from the top of the parapet, as ordered. Only two of the men mounted the parapet, and they were instantly shot down. One was Bob Harvey, a recklessly brave boy, the last male member of an old family of Bladen County. I have been unable to learn the name of his heroic companion. Had [the soldiers] been on top of the parapet they could have used their bayonets or clubbed their guns, and thus delayed a lodgment until reinforcements came.[58]

The Confederate defenders in Shepperd's Battery watched the area over the sandbagged parapet, anxiously waiting for the Yankees to appear. First the brass eagle of the national flag came into view, then the silver spear point at the top of the blue and gold banner of the 117th New York. The flags were rising higher, billowing gracefully in the smoky, sulfur laden breeze. Below these flags appeared scores of bearded veterans of the Federal Army of the James, determined to be the first to plant their flags on Fort Fisher's parapet.

A sudden explosion of Confederate gunfire shattered the Federal ranks, hurling back the dazed survivors. The color bearer for the 3rd New York was shot and fell down the steep slope. Sergeant Frederick Boden, who was carrying the 117th New York's flag up the sandy hill, had to quickly step out of the way so he would not be bowled over by the dead and wounded soldiers as they tumbled past him. Grim men in brown and gray rushed forward to meet the Yankee charge. These

Private Uriah Scull, 203rd Pa., wounded at Fort Fisher

soldiers became locked in mortal combat, shooting their rifles at point-blank range, swinging muskets, slashing with swords and bowie knives, and stabbing with bayonets. Confederate defenders bit open cartridges, loaded their weapons and rammed the charges down smoking gun barrels. If these men were lucky, and somehow avoided being shot, they raised their rifles and blasted away at the surging blue mob before them. Corporal Henry Clay McQueen of the First North Carolina Artillery Battalion remembered his company lost twelve men in the bloody struggle for the gun chamber. "A comrade next to me on the traverse was shot in his brains and killed," McQueen recalled. "His brains splattered in my face." Another bullet knocked off McQueen's hat, and then he fell wounded in the left thigh.[59]

James A. Mowris, Regimental Surgeon for the 117th New York, recalled the desperate fight:

> (Though) the roar of artillery abated, it was more than supplied by the yelling and the din of deadly musketry. All along on the crest of the parapet, as far to the left as our line extended, might be seen the desperate contest. The national colors and the insurgent rag were seen simultaneously and then alternately, on the same traverse. Hand to hand, foot to foot, the combatants fought.[60]

Colonel Curtis, a guidon from the 117th New York in one hand and a sword in the other, appeared in the midst of this free-for-all. Several men from a Confederate gun crew were desperately trying to fire a huge Columbiad artillery piece into the mass of Yankees swarming over the parapet. A shot had been jammed into the cannon's muzzle, but the crew was overpowered as they were ramming the charge home. The Confederate gunner was still trying to get off a shot even though the rammer's shaft was protruding from the barrel. Curtis called for the man's surrender. Ignoring him, the Confederate gunner inserted a friction primer into the cannon's vent hole. Curtis angrily leaped into the gun chamber and struck the gunners outstretched hand with his sword, forcing him to surrender.[61]

The 3rd Brigade joins the Federal assault. The 1st and 2nd Brigades charge up the earthworks and fight a bloody hand-to-hand struggle with the Confederate defenders.

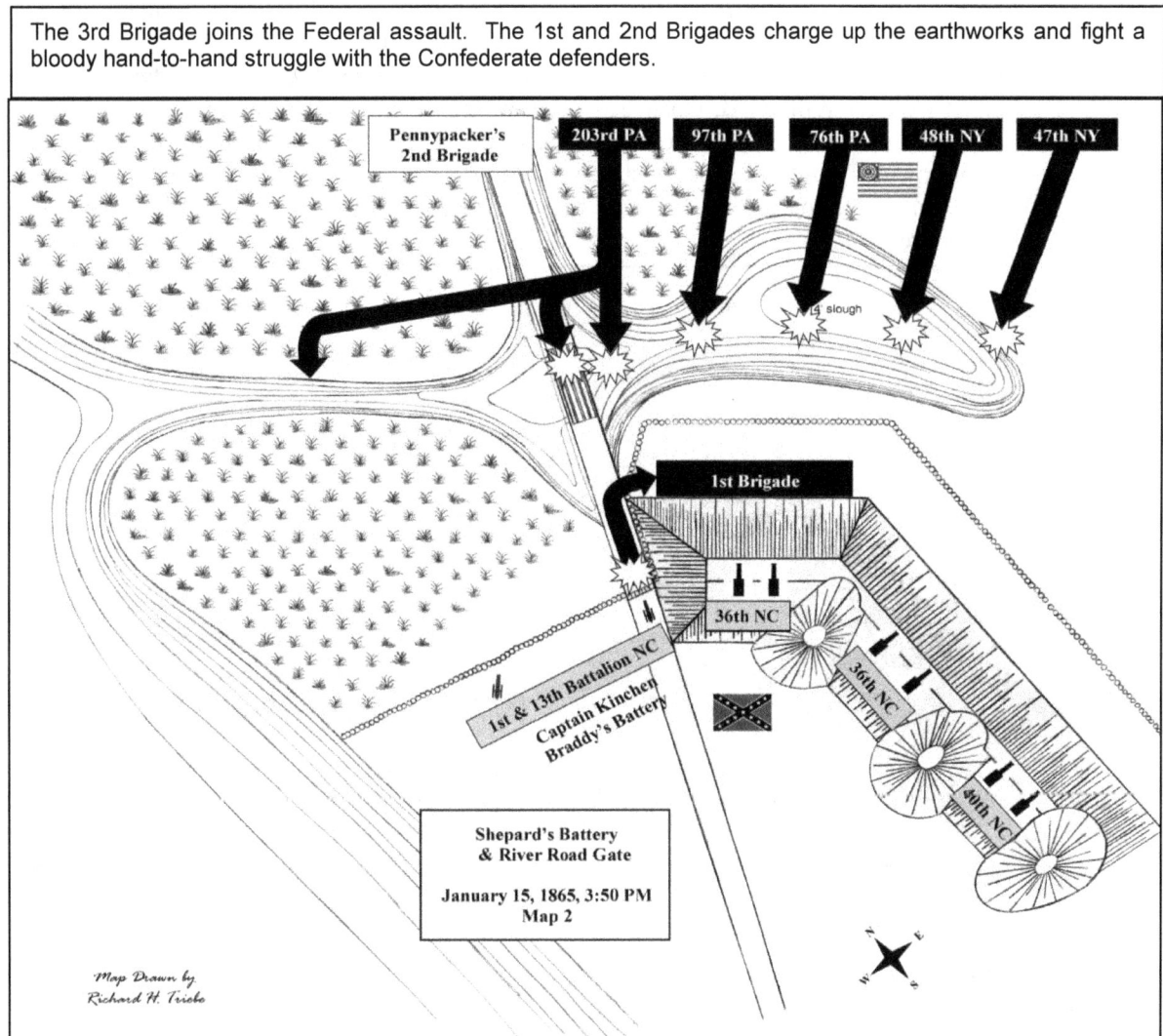

Pennypacker's 2nd Brigade · 203rd PA · 97th PA · 76th PA · 48th NY · 47th NY · slough · 1st Brigade · 36th NC · 36th NC · 40th NC · 1st & 13th Battalion NC · Captain Kinchen Braddy's Battery

Shepard's Battery & River Road Gate

January 15, 1865, 3:50 PM
Map 2

Map Drawn by
Richard H. Triebe

Federal soldiers swarmed over the parapet in such large numbers that halting their advance was near impossible. Hopelessly outnumbered, the Rebels were unable to contain this serious breach of the fort's walls. One-by-one the ranks of the Confederates were being thinned as more men were shot down. With so few men available, there was no one to replace those who had fallen. Such was not the case for the Union army. For every Northern soldier killed, it seemed two appeared to take his place.

However, everything was not fine with the Federal advance. No one knew this better than Colonel Curtis. Curtis was aware they needed to exploit this breach in the Rebel defenses, but how could he possibly do this when his men barely had the strength to hold on. His brigade had done their job well, spearheading the Federal attack, but the soldiers were quickly running out of steam. The unexpected Confederate resistance had fought his men to a standstill. What Curtis needed more than anything was for General Ames to send in the second brigade so he could fill this gap in the Confederate defense with more men. A sudden swell of gunfire and men cheering outside of the fort was a glorious sound to Curtis. Ames had answered his prayers by sending in a fresh brigade!

General Adelbert Ames saw that Colonel Curtis' brigade had stalled and decided to send in Colonel Galusha Pennypacker's brigade to get them moving forward again. Ames planned on accompanying this new attack and commanded his staff, "Gentlemen, we will now go forward." Leaving the relative safety of their earthwork, the large group of officers made an irresistible target for Confederate sharpshooters. Noticing the bullets whizzing around them, Ames warned his staff, "We had better separate somewhat from each other." He had no sooner spoken these words when two of his aides, Captain Richard W. Dawson and Captain Birney Keeler, were both struck by enemy fire. Dawson was severely wounded in the left elbow and would later die from his injuries.[62]

The 2nd brigade began to take casualties even before they began their advance on Fort Fisher. Lieutenant Colonel William B. Coan was severely wounded while forming the 48th New York battle line and carried from the field. Moments later Captain James W. Dunn and Private Ferdinand Walser were shot down. Dunn was killed instantly while Walser was wounded so severely that his right arm had to be amputated to save his life. As the brigade rose to their feet to charge, they were met by a murderous fire.

Color Sergeant William McCarthy, 97th PA, with the regiment's flag he carried at Fort Fisher. McCarthy was wounded in the knee and the flag was snatched up by Colonel Pennypacker. Pennypacker was severely wounded moments later and carried to the rear. Photograph reprinted from *Advance the Colors!* Vol. 2.

The 47th New York, commanded by Colonel Joseph M. McDonald, held the left of the brigade line, north of the center sally-port. The assault route took the regiment close to the Confederate battery commanded by Captain Zachariah Adams. As the 47th New York moved forward, the entire color guard was swept away by a vicious blast from a Napoleon cannon at the sally-port. Although these men had been horribly killed, this didn't halt the Federal advance. Other soldiers quickly snatched up the battered flags and continued the charge. These silk banners were a source of regimental pride, and it was a considered a terrible disgrace to let them fall in battle. These men would rather die than let that happen.[63]

All of the Federal regiments suffered during the battle of Fort Fisher, but none had it worse than the 203rd Pennsylvania. The regiment was on the extreme right of the Federal line, alongside the river. This area was covered by Confederate Captain Kinchen Braddy's battery which guarded the fort's "bloody gate". The 203rd bravely charged the western side of the fort and were slaughtered wholesale. This single regiment would earn the dubious distinction of having the most men killed and wounded at Fort Fisher. This figure was high enough to earn it a place on the list of the most casualties suffered by a single regiment during a Civil War battle. By battle's end the 203rd Pennsylvania would suffer 191 casualties. Colonel Pennypacker's 2nd brigade, to which the 203rd belonged, also suffered 280 casualties in the same charge. One Union officer recalled, "(The 203rd Pennsylvania) was being mowed down in windrows," by the Confederate gunners at the gate. Another soldier from the 203rd Regiment commented, "(It was) Sure death to stop-almost certain destruction to go on."[64]

Pennypacker's brigade came on like a surging blue wave, rushing up the fort's sloping walls and joining the rear of Curtis' soldiers. The regimental flags of the 97th and 203rd Pennsylvania now joined the banner of the 117th New York on the crest of the parapet. Holding the 97th flag aloft, color bearer

William McCarty was leading the way for his regiment when he fell, shot through the knee. Colonel Pennypacker grabbed the fallen banner, inspiring his men to greater efforts by his bravery. A short distance away, Colonel John W. Moore of the 203rd Pennsylvania was climbing the fort's sandy slope and saw color bearer George Deitrich get shot down. Moore picked up the fallen flag. Seeing him, Pennypacker called to him. "Moore," he shouted, holding up the banner, "I want you to take notice that this is the flag of my old regiment." Moore, who had been "waving his colors and commanding his men to follow," glanced up at Pennypacker and then toppled over, taking a bullet through the heart. "The flag of the 97th Pennsylvania was pierced by one hundred and seven bullets and canister shot and its staff cut in two in the action," recalled Major Isaiah Price.[65]

Reinforced with a fresh brigade, Curtis boldly pushed more men into the gap in the Confederate defensive line. The bitter hand-to-hand struggle was reaching a crescendo as more men fought for control of the gun chamber. The Confederate soldiers were fighting with everything they had, but it still wasn't enough. They could not halt the aggressive Federal attack and were being driven back. The defenders were paying dearly for their stubborn resistance by leaving behind a bloody trail of dead and wounded men as they doggedly backed away, firing as they went. It was clear the Southerners were running out of room and needed to take immediate action. They could leave the gun chamber or be killed in a valiant attempt to save that which was probably already lost. At this point there was no officer left alive to order the men to retreat, yet the men instinctively withdrew over and around the traverse to the next gun chamber. Those men, who were not carrying an ounce of lead in their body, fell back and left Shepperd's Battery to the Yankees.

The national flag of the 203rd Pennsylvania displays the battle scars from Fort Fisher. Photograph from *Advance the Colors!*, Vol. 2.

Colonel Curtis now turned his attention to the stubborn Confederates at the River Road gate to his right. Attacking them and holding on to the gun chamber was more difficult than Curtis had imagined. The Federal soldiers now had to fight on three fronts. A few of the Confederates they had been fighting had escaped by retreating over the traverse to the next gun chamber. Curtis urged his soldiers to keep up the pressure on these men by scaling the traverse and firing into the enemy, but he also needed to divert some men to the other side to attack the Rebel right flank at the River Road gate. To make the situation worse, he was receiving hostile fire from the parade ground in back of the gun chamber. Captain George F. Towle recalled, "A foothold was barely obtained, and the brigade here came to a stand [still], holding on by the eyelids, as it were, while men fell fast on every side."

Curtis had learned from his battlefield experience that the longer his men remained in one place the more difficult it was to get them moving again. He knew his best strategy was to stay on the offensive because this would keep the enemy off balance and prevent him from mounting an effective counterattack. That was why he needed to organize a thrust where the Confederates least expected it. He turned his attention to the stubborn enemy battery that was preventing his men from entering the fort through the River Road gate. Curtis knew what he had to do. He would lead a charge down the traverse to smash into the Confederate right flank.

The toll on Confederate officers leading the courageous band of soldiers at the River Road gate was heavy. In a matter of minutes Lieutenant Thomas M. Argo fell wounded and Captain James McCormic was killed. Without these two officers there was no one in authority left to lead the men. The only other officer, Captain Kinchen Braddy, had departed moments before in search of men to reinforce his besieged battery. The South Carolinians that General Hoke had sent to the fort had been ordered to reinforce the riverside battery, but they stayed in their bombproof and refused to come out. A few of the soldiers that did venture forth thought Braddy was the enemy and fired at him, killing men on either side of the captain.

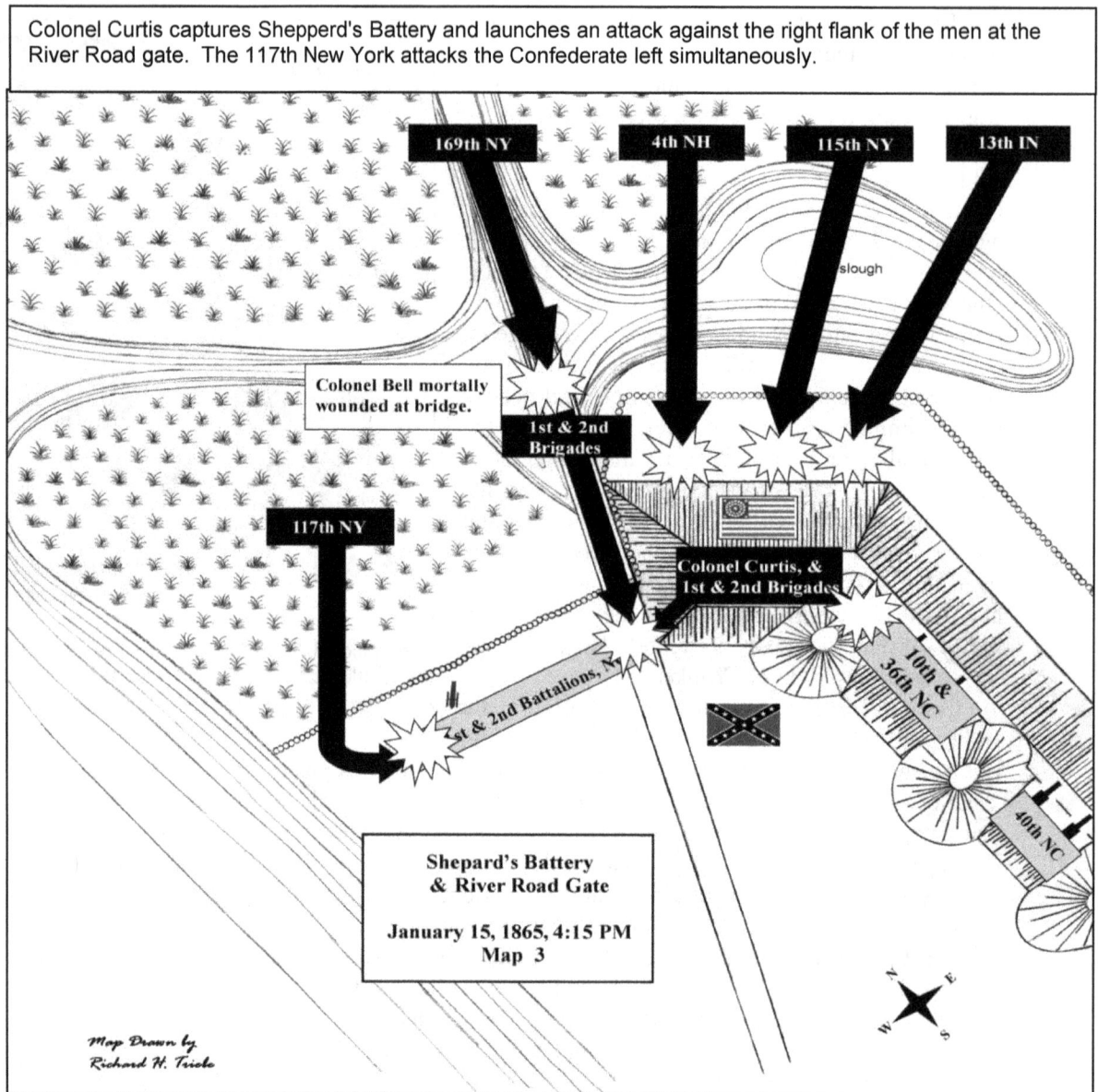

Colonel Curtis captures Shepperd's Battery and launches an attack against the right flank of the men at the River Road gate. The 117th New York attacks the Confederate left simultaneously.

169th NY   4th NH   115th NY   13th IN

slough

Colonel Bell mortally wounded at bridge.

1st & 2nd Brigades

117th NY

Colonel Curtis, & 1st & 2nd Brigades

10th & 36th NC

1st & 2nd Battalions, N.

40th NC

Shepard's Battery & River Road Gate

January 15, 1865, 4:15 PM
Map 3

N E W S

Map Drawn by Richard H. Triele

The bravery of the Confederates at the River Road gate was no match for the overwhelming numbers of Union soldiers. The massive Federal juggernaut seemed invincible. Blue-coated soldiers appeared everywhere. Some of the determined Union troops were even wading through the supposedly impassable swamp to the left. Others were putting incredible pressure on the gun chamber to the right. Private Zachary Fulmore described this desperate action in a letter to Colonel Lamb, dated May of 1897:

Our captain was killed . . . one lieutenant had been shot down, so that we . . . were in charge of a non-commissioned officer. As Adams men were being shot down one by one, our boys took the places of the dead or disabled. Our non-commissioned officer was killed, and four of our force on the left of the gate, within a very few minutes. . . .One of our boys was killed by a shot coming from our rear. I looked around and saw the stars and stripes floating from the top of the parapet, with what seemed to me to be a thousand bluecoats around it—some shooting at us. As soon as I saw this, I jumped to the Napoleon to see if I could spike it when they dashed down on us [from the traverse] and demanded our surrender. . . .I saw they had us completely surrounded—knew we would have to give up the gun, and in that event they would turn it on our men in the fort, hence my determination to spike it if possible. [66]

Seeing that further resistance would cause useless bloodshed, the Confederate defenders at the Bloody Gate dropped their weapons and surrendered.

Cannon fire from Battery Buchanan was targeting the Federal attack at the River Road gate. Unfortunately, the shells were killing friend and foe alike. Federal soldier George G. Spencer of the 117th New York was celebrating his 19th birthday in a very unusual way. He had mentioned to a friend that he thought the battle would be a "great birthday excursion". Spencer had managed to survive the horrific fighting at the fort's entrance only to be killed by a shell that fragment shattered his skull. On the other side, Confederate Privates John Cooper and Angus Blue were struck by shell fragments from their own men. Cooper, who was one of Braddy's best men, was killed instantly while Blue was wounded from behind by a shell that put him out of the fight. [67]

Colonel Galusha Pennypacker had taken the 97th Pennsylvania's flag after color bearer William McCarty was wounded in the knee. As he led his men up to the third traverse, a dozen Rebels rose up and fired a volley. Pennypacker was struck in the hip, the bullet passing close to his spine, doing tremendous damage. He would spend eleven months in the hospital. Forty-six years later, Pennypacker was asked by journalist Philip R. Dillon if he had seen the man who shot him. The Colonel said, "I did see him--a big North Carolinian. I took my flag and planted it on the parapet, which was 20 feet high. There were eight or ten men with me going over. When we got over the top there was the traverse, 10 feet above us, and a whole platoon, 20 men . . . rose up from behind the traverse and fired. I saw the man who shot me. I saw him aim his gun, and I felt his bullet."

Seeing they were outnumbered, the Confederates surrendered. While they were being led away, Pennypacker's orderly saw a Confederate soldier with a blanket wrapped around him, trying to stay warm. "Take off that blanket and give it to us to carry away this wounded officer!" he demanded.

The soldier refused to give up his blanket, saying, "I'm a prisoner and I'm entitled to my blanket!"

Colonel Galusha Pennypacker, commander of the 2nd Brigade, was severely wounded in the hip at Fort Fisher. What his soldiers did next would stay with him forever.

Pennypacker remembered what happened immediately after. "The next instant my men, with clubbed muskets, dashed out his brains; he died instantly. For the blood of my men was up, and they were as savage as the Carolinian. I closed my eyes and they carried me away in that blanket, but the horror of it has never gone out of my mind to this day!"[68]

General Whiting led 500 Confederate soldiers in a wild counterattack that slammed into the Yankees at the fourth gun chamber. "The Rebels attacked our men like savage dogs," exclaimed E. D. Williams of the 117th New York. "Give and take was the watchword on both sides, face to face and gun to gun." The Confederates would, "jump up on the top of a traverse and shoot down upon our men, and if that failed, they would attempt their slaughter with clubbed muskets," wrote a Federal soldier. "A few instances were found in which our men and theirs had pinned each other with their bayonets, and died together." There was little room for the opponents to maneuver. Men fired their muskets point-blank into the enemy, then plunged into brutal hand-to-hand combat—grappling with each other and killing their attacker any way they could.

"It was a soldier's fight now," recalled Confederate Private James A. Montgomery, Company B, 36th North Carolina. "As a man would fall, another sprang up to take his place, our officers loading and firing with us." The combatants trampled on the dead and wounded, stumbling over bodies, all the while keeping their eyes focused on the enemy. "Our killed and wounded on the parapet impeded our advance to the fourth traverse so that we were scarcely able to go forward without treading upon them," explained Colonel Curtis. "The struggle was the hottest and most prolonged single contest of the day. The loss of life was great on both sides."

Colonel Zent, of the 13th Indiana, had a close call during the fight for the fourth traverse. Zent climbed to the top of the mound of sand and peered over the crest. "All I remember seeing was a flash and feeling a sensation similar to an electric shock," the officer recalled. "The fellow had pulled the trigger a little too soon and the ball passed through my hat just grazing the top of my head."[69]

Colonel Louis Bell suffered a fatal wound crossing the River Road bridge.

A big man with a drooping mustache and wild, brown hair spilling out from beneath his cap, moved in front of the Third Brigade and observed the battle, intently. Colonel Louis Bell had picked up a soldier's discarded rifle ramrod to use as a walking stick. Right now the long metal rod was being bent by powerful hands, revealing his frustration at being left behind while his army was fighting for its life. Bell was a man of action. He could not sit idly by and watch his army being destroyed without doing everything in his power to help. Each time the United States flag fell to the ground he took it as a personal insult and wanted to rush over and raise it up again. When the banner went down for the fifth time, Bell anxiously turned his gaze to the abandoned Confederate earthwork where General Terry had his combat headquarters. He was hoping to see a runner coming toward him with an order from the general to advance.[70]

At that moment, General Terry had received an urgent dispatch from General Ames inside the fort reporting that the Federal assault was stalled. His troops were holding their own, but they needed help. Send in the Third Brigade and he could take the fort. Terry quickly wrote the order for the 3rd Brigade to join the assault in his notebook, tore off the sheet and gave it to Captain George F. Towle to deliver.[71]

Captain Towle, General Terry's aide, hand carried the order to Colonel Bell. Bell jammed his ramrod into the sand and read the order. He gave Towle a brief smile, then went to the front of his brigade. Bell nodded to Colonel Alonzo Alden to proceed with the advance. Alden shouted the preparatory command, "Third Brigade!"

The regimental commanders from the four regiments that made up the Third Brigade drew their swords and echoed the command to their men. Colonel Alden then gave the command of execution, "Forward! Double-quick!"

The men shifted their rifles to a loose form of port-arms and began to trot toward the fort. Bell raced out ahead, leading his troops into battle. The same devastating Confederate fire which greeted the two previous brigades now fell upon Bell's men.

Some of Pennypacker's soldiers had replaced several of the planks on the bridge and the Third Brigade angled to the right so they could cross it.

"How well the brigade is coming on under so severe a fire," Bell told one of his staff officers as they raced to the fort.[72]

The men began to bunch up on the north side of the bridge as they funneled over it. A Confederate marksman singled out Bell because a high ranking officer was leading the brigade. A bullet slammed into Bell's chest, exiting his lower back and knocking him to the ground. At first Bell did not realize how seriously he was wounded. He said to Lieutenant Hugh Sanford, his aide, "My arm is broken."

The aide knew better. He had heard the sickening thud of a body wound and saw the growing stain of blood on his colonel's left chest. A crowd had gathered around the prostrate officer, picked up their wounded colonel and carried him to the rear.

Surgeon David Dearborn hurried to Bell's side and began cutting off the colonel's bloody clothing so he could examine the wound. "Is the wound mortal?" Bell asked. "I am fearful it is, Colonel," Dearborn replied. "Well," Bell said in a calm, matter of fact voice, "I thought as much myself."

Someone told Bell his men had planted their flags on the enemy ramparts. Bell struggled to raise himself a little, saying, "I want to see my colors on the parapet." He spied a distant flag and smiled because his dying wish had been granted.[73]

Whiting and his Confederates drove the Federals from the fourth gun chamber, then climbed up the traverse to continue the fight. "Much hand-to-hand fighting of a desperate character ensued upon these huge traverses," recalled Captain Edson J. Harkness. "Our men would make a charge to the summit of a traverse, to be met by Confederates coming from the other side, where these hand-to-hand struggles occurred. One or two of these traverses were retaken, and held for a short time by the Confederates, but they were soon driven out for the last time."

Atop the traverse General Whiting grabbed a Federal flagstaff. He was instantly surrounded by Northern troops, demanding his surrender. "Go to hell, you Yankee bastards!" he shouted. They fired and Whiting fell with two wounds in his right thigh. Some of his men saw him go down, rushed to his side and carried him to the fort's hospital.[74]

The fire of the Federal fleet was largely responsible for halting the Confederate counterattack on the fort's parapets. Colonel Curtis had communicated with Terry, who in turn signaled the fleet to shift their fire back to the land-face and stay ahead of the attacking Federal army. This is the earliest incident the author is aware of in which artillery fire was adjusted by the attacking commander to provide close-ground-support for his

Confederate Major James Stevenson lived through the battle only to die of pneumonia at Fort Columbus Prison in New York Harbor.

troops.

Colonel Lamb credited the Federal fleet's accurate artillery fire for stopping the Confederate attack:

We had retaken one of these [gun chambers] in the charge led by Whiting, and since we had opened on their flank we had shot down their standard bearers and the Federal battle flags had disappeared from our ramparts; we had become assailants and the enemy were on the defensive, and I felt confident that we would soon drive them out of the fort. Just as the tide of battle seemed to have turned in our favor, the remorseless fleet came to the rescue of the faltering Federals. Suddenly the bombardment which had been consigned to the sea-face during the assaults turned again on our land front and with deadly precision. They swept the recaptured gun chamber of its defenders, and their 11 and 15 inch shells rolled down into the interior of the work, carrying death and destruction in their pathways. They drove from the parapets in front of the enemy all of my men except those so near that to have fired on them would have been slaughter to their own troops.[75]

Back at Sugar Loaf, Confederate General Braxton Bragg ordered Hoke to probe the Federal's northern defensive line. At 4 PM Hoke sent the brigades of Kirkland and Clingman forward to make a reconnaissance of the enemy position. According to Captain Elliott of Kirkland's Brigade, "We easily drove in the enemy's skirmish line, occupied their rifle pits, and our skirmishers were making their main line keep their heads down behind their entrenchments."

Captain John T. Thomas, Company F, 117th New York. Thomas would be killed trying to take the 3rd traverse. *Photograph courtesy of Chris Fonvielle Jr.*

Hoke rode down from his headquarters at Sugar Loaf to observe the action. He later reported to General Bragg that his men were involved in a sharp firefight in which he had gotten, "two balls in his clothes, between the left arm and breast." Should he proceed with the attack? Hoke asked Bragg.

Captain Elliott later recalled the anticipation of many of the soldiers: "We confidently expected to run over the troops in our front and drive them in confusion upon Terry's attacking column." But Bragg was not of that opinion. He considered the Federal entrenchments too formidable for Hoke. "Their line was impracticable for his small command," Bragg said, "and I did not hesitate to recall him. [Hoke] could not have succeeded." Captain Elliott was dismayed. "When we all expected an order to charge a courier came to Hoke from Bragg advising him to withdraw to Sugar Loaf." Bragg had made the grim decision that Fort Fisher would stand or fall on its own.[76]

Federal Colonel John W. Ames of the 6th U.S. Colored Troops commented on Hoke's so-called attack, saying, "It was little more than a weak attempt to carry the picket line. It's feebleness was so striking that it did us good service in showing how little we had to fear from that quarter." Federal General Charles J. Paine agreed with Colonel Ames and confessed, "If [Hoke] had made an attack, and if he had carried my line and they held out in the fort, we should have been in a tight place."

Years later, Captain Edson J. Harkness wrote:

It is difficult to understand why General Hoke, with his splendid record as a fighting Confederate, and with the magnificent troops which he brought with him from Richmond, should have allowed himself to remain at Sugarloaf, seven miles above Fort Fisher, without making any attempt to relieve Whiting or to attack Paine's defensive line. There has never been any question in my mind, either from the reports made of these operations, or from my own observation, that the landing of our forces at Masonborough Sound, or, at any rate, the establishment of a line across the peninsula from the ocean to the river, could have been prevented by a resolute and determined enemy. Neither has there been any doubt that after the line was established, an attack by Hoke upon the north line would have been so serious a diversion as to have withdrawn a large portion of the assaulting force from Fort Fisher, and rendered that assault impracticable.[77]

Unlike General Braxton Bragg, Colonel Lamb was the correct officer to defend Fort Fisher. Lamb was both resourceful, could think clearly in time of great stress. Like any good field commander, Colonel Lamb was flexible. He could appraise the combat situation immediately and adapt to the ever changing tide of battle. This ability led Lamb to do the unthinkable in his search for information on how to defeat his enemy. Lamb describes this in Walter Clark's book the *Histories of North Carolina Regiments and Battalions*:

> I doubt if ever before the commander of a work went outside the fort and looked upon the conflict for its possession, but from the construction of the fort it was absolutely necessary for me to do so in order to quickly comprehend the position of affairs. . . . I rushed through the sally-port, and outside the work and witnessed a fierce hand-to-hand conflict for the possession of the fourth gun chamber. The men led by the fearless Whiting had driven the standard bearer from the top of the traverse and the enemy from the parapet in front. They had recovered one gun chamber with great slaughter, and on the parapet and on the long traverse of the next gun chamber the contestants were savagely firing into each other's faces, and in some cases clubbing their guns.[78]

Seeing his men savagely fighting the enemy convinced Colonel Lamb a determined assault would drive the enemy from the fort. Lamb rushed to the various gun chambers and bombproofs to appeal to his men to come with him and defeat the Yankees. He was saddened to see the magnificent fort which he had helped build reduced to smoldering wreckage. He described the grisly death and destruction in an address to the Cape Fear Camp, United Confederate Veterans of Wilmington. "As I passed through portions of the work, the scene was indescribably horrible. Great cannon broken in two, their carriages wrecked and among their ruins the mutilated bodies of my dead and dying comrades."[79]

Confederate Surgeon Joseph Shepard treated both General Whiting and Colonel Lamb.

Lamb returned around 4:30 PM with several hundred soldiers and placed them behind a breastwork on the parade ground. The Confederates were within one-hundred feet of the enemy, close enough to see their faces distinctly. Lamb asked the officers and men if they would follow him in a charge against the Yankees, and they all agreed. Encouraged by the overwhelming support of his men, Lamb jumped upon the breastwork, waving his sword. "Charge, bayonets! Forward, double quick, march!"

The moment Lamb uttered the command, a rifle bullet slammed into his hip, knocking him off the breastwork. The same volley that wounded Lamb also fatally wounded Lieutenant Daniel R. Perry. The Confederate soldiers were starting over the breastworks when they met a storm of Federal gunfire. The men ducked back behind their mounds of sand and returned fire.

Lamb turned over defense of the breastwork to Captain Daniel Munn, telling him he would return after he had his wound bandaged. Before reaching the hospital Lamb became so weak from loss of blood that he knew he could not return to the battle. Surgeon Joseph Shepard had Lamb's litter set down next to General Whiting. Whiting told Lamb that General Bragg had ignored his messages and they could expect no help from him.

Lamb ordered his adjutant, Lieutenant John Kelly, to find Major Reilly because he was the next senior officer in line to take command of Fort Fisher. When Major Reilly arrived at the hospital, he was given command of the fort from Lamb and Whiting, and promised he would keep fighting, "as long as a man or a shot was left."[80]

General Whiting sent a message to General Bragg at 6:30 PM, downplaying his severe wounds and appealing for help. "The enemy are assaulting us by land and sea," he reported. "Their infantry outnumber us. Can't you help us? I am slightly wounded." Whiting never received a direct response to his dispatch from General Bragg. Instead, Colonel Archer Anderson, Bragg's assistant adjutant, sent a dispatch about 7:40 PM, telling Whiting General Colquitt was coming to the fort to relieve him and take immediate command. Whiting was also ordered to report to General Bragg at his headquarters.[81]

Confederate Major James Reilly assembled some of the men from the earlier charge Colonel Lamb had led. Reilly managed to deploy a force of 150 men behind the huge main magazine. With a color bearer from Captain Izlar's South Carolinians, the small band of Confederate soldiers advanced to do battle with the Federal troops massed behind Shepperd's Battery.

Shepperd's Battery with the Bloody gate to the left. Some of the most fierce fighting occurred there. Timothy O'Sullivan image, 1865. *Photograph courtesy of the Library of Congress*

"As soon as the enemy observed our object, they opened a very destructive fire on our advancing column," Reilly later reported. "Under such a fire our men began to waver and fall back." The color bearer was shot dead and Reilly's troops dispersed in confusion. "By the time I reached near the [Northeast Bastion] I had not sixty men with me." The major withdrew to a position near the main magazine and "kept up as heavy and destructive a fire as [his] small command would allow." Nearly two-thirds of his men had become casualties.[82]

While Curtis' men were capturing the traverses, other Federal soldiers were keeping pace with the advance on the floor of the fort. The going was difficult because these troops were battling Confederates hiding behind debris from the burned-out buildings, shell craters and any other obstruction that afforded any sort of cover. It was during this action that Lieutenant Colonel Jonas W. Lyman of the 203rd Pennsylvania was killed while urging his troops forward. Captain Heber B. Essington described what happened after his regiment entered the fort:

> After having assisted in capturing the first two mounds, a portion of the regiment went with the first Brigade over the traverses, and the remainder went to the right and stationed themselves behind a bank [of sand] in the open field south of the fort. The latter portion then charged across the plain, until opposite the seventh or eighth traverse, where they threw up an embankment with their tin plates and shovels, keeping up a steady fire upon the enemy.[83]

Photographer Timothy O'Sullivan poses next to a land-face cannon with a broken muzzle. *Image Timothy O'Sullivan, 1865.*

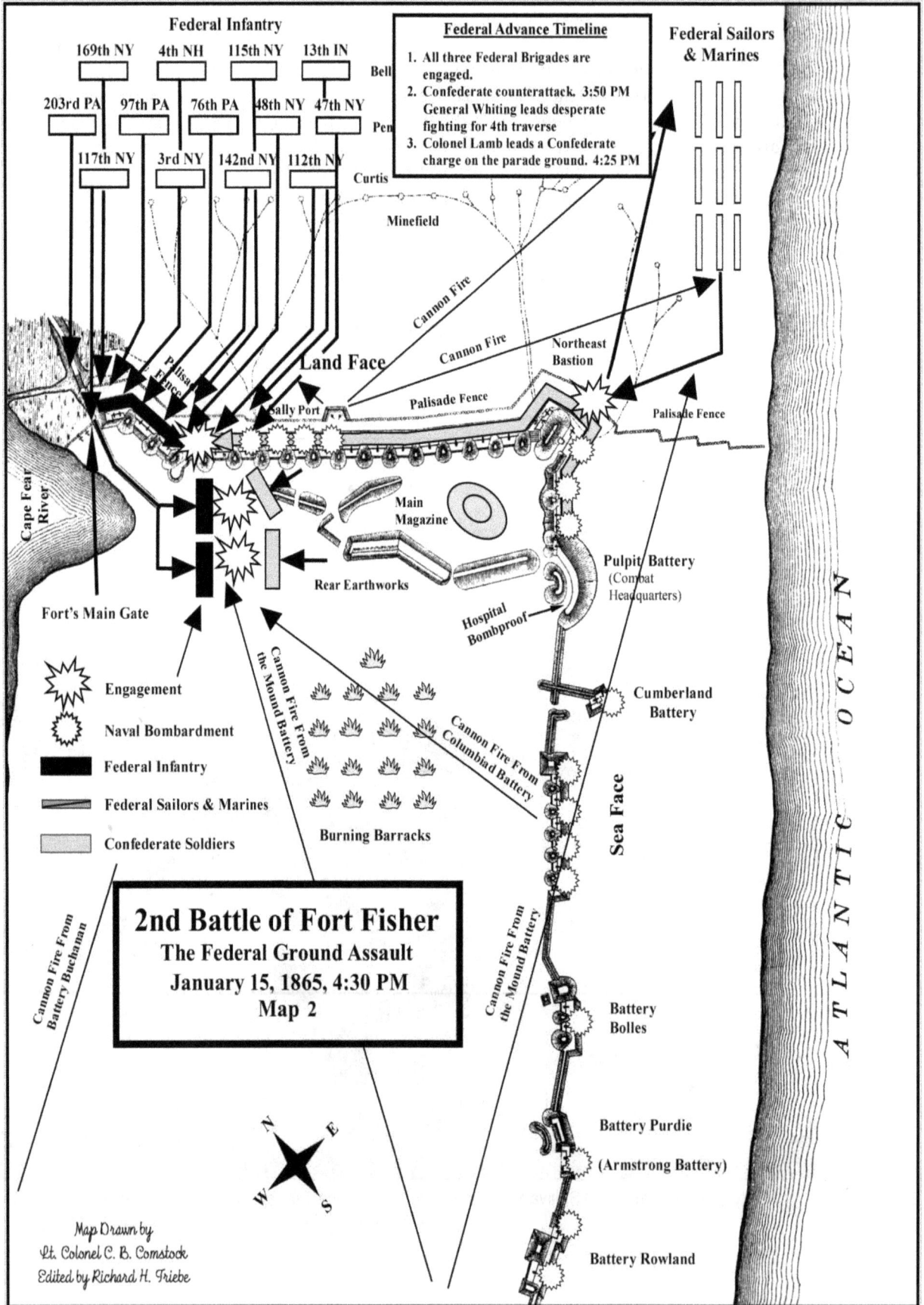

Federal Infantry

169th NY   4th NH   115th NY   13th IN

203rd PA   97th PA   76th PA   48th NY   47th NY

117th NY   3rd NY   142nd NY   112th NY

Bell

Pen

Curtis

Minefield

Federal Sailors & Marines

Federal Advance Timeline

1. All three Federal Brigades are engaged.
2. Confederate counterattack. 3:50 PM General Whiting leads desperate fighting for 4th traverse
3. Colonel Lamb leads a Confederate charge on the parade ground. 4:25 PM

Cannon Fire

Cannon Fire

Land Face

Palisade Fence

Northeast Bastion

Sally Port

Palisade Fence

Cape Fear River

Palisade Fence

Main Magazine

Rear Earthworks

Pulpit Battery
(Combat Headquarters)

Hospital Bombproof

Fort's Main Gate

Cannon Fire From the Mound Battery

Cannon Fire From Columbiad Battery

☀ Engagement

☼ Naval Bombardment

▬ Federal Infantry

▨ Federal Sailors & Marines

▨ Confederate Soldiers

Burning Barracks

Cumberland Battery

Sea Face

Cannon Fire From Battery Buchanan

Cannon Fire From the Mound Battery

2nd Battle of Fort Fisher
The Federal Ground Assault
January 15, 1865, 4:30 PM
Map 2

Battery Bolles

Battery Purdie
(Armstrong Battery)

N E W S

Map Drawn by
Lt. Colonel C. B. Comstock
Edited by Richard H. Triebe

Battery Rowland

A T L A N T I C   O C E A N

The Federal fleet kept up its accurate bombardment of the fort firing three shots per second amid the Confederates on the parapet. Colonel Curtis describes the action when one of these shells went astray:

> At the fifth traverse a shot went wide of its mark and killed or disabled all but four men in our front line. Fearing that a slackening of our fire would invite a countercharge, I myself discharged the guns of the killed and disabled men until reinforcements were brought forward. A sudden emergency compelled this action. It was not done to encourage the soldiers—no such efforts were needed to quicken their zeal. Men unable to stand and fire their pieces handed up the guns of their dead and helpless comrades, and when given back reloaded them again and again, exhibiting an unselfish devotion that seemingly nothing but death could chill. Within twenty minutes I found wounded men dead who had handed me their guns.[84]

From the seventh traverse, Colonel Curtis noticed that a troublesome Columbiad Battery on the sea-face could be silenced by some expert marksmen. He sent Corporal John Jones, of the 117th New York, to the west end of the fort to bring back some Union sharpshooters. When Jones returned, he told Curtis that General Ames refused to send these men forward. Ames also told him he would issue spades so the soldiers could entrench for the night. Curtis then sent his orderly, Captain Arthur O. Knight to explain to General Ames why these men were needed.

Confederate Captain Daniel Munn, 36th North Carolina, captured at Fisher.

Knight returned shortly and told Colonel Curtis that Ames said the men were exhausted and no further advance would be attempted until morning. He also ordered Knight to tell Curtis to hold onto the ground now occupied and he would send forward entrenching tools. Curtis ordered Knight to go back and request officers under his rank to come to the front, so that an attack could be made before dark. If Ames would not provide him with soldiers, Curtis would attack with his own men.

Knight came back with an armful of spades from General Ames. Curtis, a huge man six-feet-six inches in height, grabbed the spades and threw them over the traverse to the Confederates. Curtis went over General Ames head by sending Seaman Silas W. Kempton to Major General Terry, urging Terry to have the troops then engaged in digging entrenchments join in an advance and take possession of the fort before reinforcements could be sent by the Confederate army.[85]

Curtis ordered Captain David B. Magill of the 117th New York to keep pressing the next traverse while he went to the west end of the fort to obtain some men. While Curtis was assembling some soldiers, he was met by General Ames, who said, "I have two or three times sent you word to fortify your position and hold it until reinforcements can be sent to aid us, the men are exhausted, and I will not order them to go forward."

Curtis reminded Ames that the Confederates had two steamboats in the river loaded with troops waiting for darkness so they could put them ashore. "Should they succeed in landing, they may be able to drive us out," he said. "Therefore, the fort should be captured before fresh troops come to the enemy." Curtis had no sooner said this when he was struck in the face by two shell fragments. One destroyed his left eye while the other carried away portions of the front orbital bone. Unconscious and believed by his men to be fatally wounded, Colonel Curtis was carried from the battlefield. This was Curtis' fifth wound of the day. Ames promptly informed General Terry that Curtis was mortally wounded.[86]

General Terry was concerned. He had over four thousand troops engaged at Fort Fisher and still the fort had not fallen. Casualties were heavy, especially among the senior officers. Colonels Lyman, and Moore had been killed. Colonels Bell, Coan, Curtis, Littell, Pennypacker and Smith were severely wounded, perhaps mortally. The troops were tired and disorganized. Darkness was coming and the Confederates would probably reinforce the fort. Terry asked his aide, Lieutenant Colonel Cyrus B. Comstock for advice. Comstock had a definite opinion: Bring up Abbott's Brigade and throw it into the fort against the Rebels. Bring up Pain's troops too. Leave just a skeletal force behind to guard the entrenchments against Confederate General Hoke. Overwhelm the Rebels with fresh troops and finish the job.[87]

Terry agreed with Comstock and sent orders to General Abbott to enter the fort with his brigade as soon as possible. Abbott was told to report to General Ames and ask where he should deploy his troops. General Paine was ordered to send his best regiment into the fort and then report to Ames for further orders.

General Abbott withdrew his soldiers from the entrenchments on the northern defensive line and replaced them with sailors and marines who had participated in the assault of the naval brigade. It was about dusk when Abbott's

Federal Lieutenant Colonel Cyrus B. Comstock advised General Terry to throw in Abbott's Brigade and overwhelm the Rebels with fresh troops.

brigade filed through the River Road gate. Abbott located the division command post and reported to General Ames. He was told to replace Ames' tired troops with fresh soldiers.

General Terry had found that the sound of gunfire was a reliable indicator of how the battle was going. When the first three brigades had stalled in their advance, the rifle fire had slackened. It was over an hour since Terry had sent in Abbott's brigade, but the firing had not increased as expected. Curious, General Terry went inside the fort to investigate. What he found alarmed him greatly. Troops were milling around, brigades and regiments intermingled, showing no form of cohesion or purpose.

Federal General Abbott's troops would be the fourth Federal brigade to fight at Fort Fisher.

Instead of rushing Abbott's Brigade to the front, Ames put some of the men to work digging entrenchments and placed one regiment, the 7th Connecticut, on picket duty in his rear. A single regiment, the 3rd New Hampshire, had been sent to the front, but instead of renewing the Federal assault, they were ordered to relieve the weary troops already there.[88]

Ames explained to General Terry he was fortifying his position for the night and would resume the assault in the morning, after his men were rested. Ames then went on to tell Terry his troop losses had been especially heavy. "Ten of my officers had been killed, forty-seven wounded, and about 500 men were killed and wounded." Terry agreed that many a good man had been lost that day. He also agreed the soldiers were tired, but so were the Rebels. Terry pointed out that the Confederate troops had barely survived the nonstop, three-day bombardment and then fought a bloody hand-to-hand struggle all afternoon. One final push was all that was needed to convince them to surrender. Besides, General Terry had noticed the Confederate troop transports in the Cape Fear River,

68

waiting for dark so they could unload thousands of fresh troops. No! General Terry told Ames. The Federal advance would go forward tonight as planned.[89]

Confederate Captain Edward B. Dudley, 36th North Carolina, made sure no Yankee would ever take Colonel Lamb's sword.

The Federal troops had captured two-thirds of the land-face, but the Confederates held the rest. General Abbott ordered his brigade forward around 9 PM. Captain Trickey's regiment, the 3rd New Hampshire, captured all the remaining land-face traverses but one. Abbott surrounded the gun chamber with the 7th New Hampshire and the 6th Connecticut. The Federal soldiers charged up the slope and met a sharp fire from the Confederates waiting for them behind the parapet. The scene had a terrifying, surreal quality. Darkness had fallen and the slopes and traverses were eerily illuminated by the brilliant flashes of gunfire. Abbott's troops, who were armed with Spencer repeating rifles, made short work of the few remaining defenders who were hiding in the gun chamber. Those who were not killed, wounded or captured escaped southward along the sea-face.[90]

Inside the Confederate hospital, Colonel Lamb could hear the sounds of battle drawing closer. Things had gone terribly wrong. Apparently Fort Fisher had been deserted by General Bragg, the minefield had failed to explode because of damage to the wires by the intense naval bombardment. Now Lamb heard more bad news from several of his officers. Major Reilly reported that one of the fort's officers had raised a white flag, let the Yankees into the main sally-port and surrendered a large part of the garrison. That wasn't all. Around 8 PM Lamb's aide returned to the hospital and reported that the troops were almost out of ammunition. Chaplain McKinnon had gathered all he could from the dead and wounded in a blanket and distributed it among the troops. The situation appeared hopeless, the aide lamented. He told Lamb that the Yankees nearly had all the land-face and appeared to be regrouping for another attack. Since it was nearly impossible to hold out much longer, he asked, wouldn't it be wise to surrender to prevent further bloodshed?[91]

"I replied that while I lived I would not surrender as Bragg would surely come to our rescue in time to save us," Colonel Lamb later wrote. "General Whiting declared if I died he would assume command and would not surrender." Lamb also had promised the women of Wilmington who had visited the fort after the first battle that their homes would be protected by his garrison. Lamb had an even more substantial reason for refusing to surrender. General Lee had sent word that if Fort Fisher fell, he could not maintain his army. This meant the South would lose the war. All the sacrifices they had made for four long years would have gone for nothing. Lamb refused to be the man who had lost the war for the South. "Is it to be

Confederate Private Thomas Yarborough and his wife Martha. Yarborough, a private in the 21st South Carolina, was captured at Fort Fisher but later died of pneumonia at Elmira Prisoner of War Camp.

wondered that I felt it my sacred duty, even after I was shot down," Lamb asked, "to appeal to officers and men to fight in defense of the last gateway to the South?"[92]

After the land-face had fallen the fighting for the sea-face intensified. The gunfire moved steadily closer to the hospital and prompted an evacuation of the structure. General Whiting and Colonel Lamb were hurriedly removed on stretchers to Battery Buchanan, while Major Reilly's troops covered their retreat. "When we left the hospital the men were fighting over the adjoining traverse, and the spent balls fell like hailstones around us," Lamb recalled. "The remnant of the garrison then fell back in an orderly retreat along the sea-face, the rear guard keeping the enemy engaged as they advanced slowly and cautiously in the darkness as far as the Mound Battery."

As Lamb was being carried away, Captain Edward B. Dudley, 36th North Carolina, took the colonel's saber and sword belt. "No damned Yankee shall ever have the sword!" he exclaimed as he tossed it into the Atlantic Ocean.[93]

Colonel Lamb had designed Battery Buchanan as a citadel where the Fort Fisher garrison could retreat if they were under great pressure from a Federal assault. The earthwork had four large artillery pieces and was served by a dock on the Cape Fear River. Here the garrison could join forces with Lieutenant Robert T. Chapman's Naval detachment and continue their defense of Confederate Point. Should it become necessary, the embattled troops could either be reinforced by soldiers from the mainland or evacuated under the cover of darkness.[94]

Major Reilly planned on reforming his scattered command once they reached Battery Buchanan. If the Confederates could put up a stubborn defense for only two hours it was believed substantial numbers of troops could be ferried across the river before the Federals captured them.[95]

When Reilly's column of refugees arrived at Battery Buchanan, he and his men were shocked. The sailors and marines had fled. They had spiked the guns, and worst of all, they had taken the boats that the garrison was relying on to take them to safety. About 600 soldiers had fallen back from Fort Fisher and were milling about the battery, at least three-fourths were without weapons and could offer no defense against the pursuing Federal troops.[96]

Colonel Lamb and General Whiting would have passed these sea-face gun chambers when the hospital was evacuated. Note that two of the cannon have been turned around to fire at the Federal troops near Shepperd's Battery. Timothy O'Sullivan image, 1865. *Photograph courtesy of the Library of Congress.*

Reilly was furious. First Fort Fisher had been deserted by General Bragg; but the final, devastating blow was delivered by Lieutenant Chapman when he fled Battery Buchanan and left the garrison to be captured by the Yankees.

Reilly later recalled that he had sent Captain Zachariah Adams to Battery Buchanan around 4 PM with orders for the naval commander to hold the battery and be ready to fight the enemy. Reilly further stated, "not to abandon the Battery for when I was forced out of Fort Fisher I would fall back on Buchanan and fight the enemy there." Captain Adams reported back with Chapman's cryptic reply. "Very well." Major Reilly "was confident Chapman was still in the battery for I thought him too good a soldier to abandon us." Major Reilly was gravely mistaken about Chapman.

"We had a splendid opportunity to retrieve our defeat and get away," Reilly recalled about the Confederates ability to defend Battery Buchanan. "If the armament of the battery was serviceable. . . .Our men were free from the destructive and demoralizing effect of the fire from the fleet. . . .The whole mode of fighting was changed. We would have regained courage and the enemy would not have captured us."[97]

Seaman Robert Watson kept a diary of the events of the battle including Lieutenant Chapman's decision to abandon his post at Battery Buchanan:

CDV of First Lieutenant Robert T. Chapman taken Cherbourg, France, 1863

> As soon as we saw that the enemy had gained a footing and planted their hateful flag on the left of the works we knew that the fort was lost and Captain [Robert T.] Chapman had all hands mustered, the roll called, and he then informed us that the fort was lost and that it was useless for him to keep us here to be taken prisoners or slaughtered, that we could fight the battery for some time and probably do the enemy some damage but that we could not hold it for any length of time. He then ordered us in the boats.[98]

It appeared to Major Reilly no one was in command of the Confederate soldiers that crowded Battery Buchanan because all discipline had vanished. Men wandered about aimlessly or huddled into despondent groups to await the Yankees. Reilly was worried the Federal troops would assault the battery before they had a chance to surrender. If that happened, the unarmed men inside wouldn't stand a chance.

The only safe thing to do was to go out and meet the Yankees and surrender before they reached the battery. Major Reilly, accompanied by Major James H. Hill, General Whiting's chief-of-staff, and Captain Alfred C. Van Benthuysen of the Confederate States Marine Corps, went toward Fort Fisher to meet the enemy commander. After they had gone 300 hundred yards from Battery Buchanan, Reilly halted and tied a white handkerchief to his sword. "It was a distressing time to me and the brave officers and men under my command," Reilly admitted.[99]

By 9 PM Federal troops had occupied so much of Fort Fisher that further bombardment was dangerous. General Terry signaled the fleet to cease-fire so his soldiers would have a clear path to Battery Buchanan. Regiments of General Abbott's brigade cautiously advanced in skirmish formation, securing the deserted Confederate batteries. Abbott's troops were joined by Colonel Albert M. Blackman's 27th Colored Troops in the mopping-up operation. The gunfire ceased and for the first

time in many hours the soldiers could hear the crash of the surf on the beach nearby over the low moans of the wounded.

As Abbott's troops closed in on the Mound Battery, Captain J. Homer Edgerly of the 3rd New Hampshire spied the Confederate flag flying on the crest of the battery. He raced up the huge sand hill, cut down the banner and rejoined his regiment. This was the same flag that Confederate Private Christopher Bland had replaced twice when it was shot down by the Federal Fleet.

The 7th Connecticut, commanded by Captain E. Lewis Moore, continued their cautious advance. As the line of skirmishers approached Battery Buchanan, Moore noticed a small group of Confederate officers holding a white flag. He halted his soldiers, selected a few men to accompany him, and went out to meet the Confederates.

Asked about the incident years later, Major Reilly recalled what he had said to Captain Moore. "I told that officer we surrendered and requested him to halt and retire his line and not let them fire on our defenseless troops. Capt. [Moore] with the instinct of a true soldier . . . complied with my request and reported, I think, to Genl. Abbott."[100]

Three Unoin soldiers pose alongside a 10-inch Columbiad heavy artillery piece. A Union Navy projectile broke off its muzzle. Photograph by Timothy O'Sullivan.

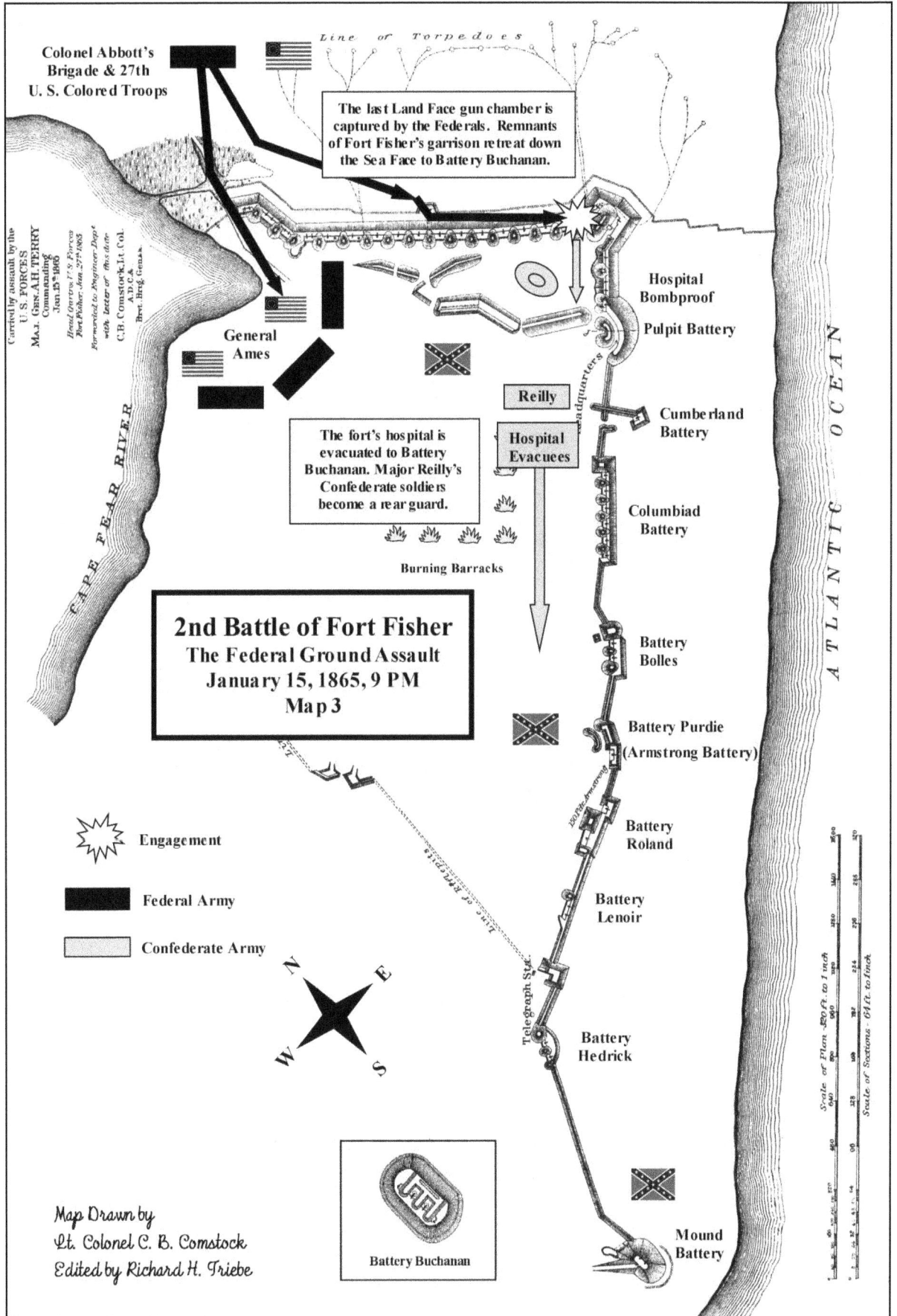

Line of Torpedoes

Colonel Abbott's
Brigade & 27th
U. S. Colored Troops

The last Land Face gun chamber is
captured by the Federals. Remnants
of Fort Fisher's garrison retreat down
the Sea Face to Battery Buchanan.

Carried by assault by the
U. S. FORCES
Maj. Gen. A.H. TERRY
Commanding
Jan. 15th 1865

Head Quarters U. S. Forces
Fort Fisher. Jan. 27th 1865
Forwarded to Engineer Dept.
with letter of this date
C. B. Comstock. Lt. Col.
A.D.C.A.
Bvt. Brig. Genrs.

Hospital
Bombproof

General
Ames

Pulpit Battery

Reilly

Cumberland
Battery

The fort's hospital is
evacuated to Battery
Buchanan. Major Reilly's
Confederate soldiers
become a rear guard.

Hospital
Evacuees

Columbiad
Battery

CAPE FEAR RIVER

ATLANTIC OCEAN

Burning Barracks

Battery
Bolles

2nd Battle of Fort Fisher
The Federal Ground Assault
January 15, 1865, 9 PM
Map 3

Battery Purdie
(Armstrong Battery)

Battery
Roland

Engagement

Battery
Lenoir

Federal Army

Confederate Army

N
E
W
S

Battery
Hedrick

Scale of Plan 320 ft. to 1 inch

Scale of Sections - 64 ft. to inch

Map Drawn by
Lt. Colonel C. B. Comstock
Edited by Richard H. Triebe

Mound
Battery

Battery Buchanan

The Confederate soldiers retreated from Fort Fisher to Battery Buchanan where they planned to renew their defensive struggle. Image Timothy O'Sullivan. *Photograph courtesy of the National Archives.*

Shortly before James Reilly's surrender, Confederate General Alfred H. Colquitt took a row boat downriver from Sugar Loaf to Battery Buchanan. Colquitt was ordered to take command of Fort Fisher and replace General Whiting. He was appalled by what he found at the battery. "[The] men were without guns, without accoutrements, some of them without hats, and all in a very bad state of demoralization," he reported to General Bragg.

Colquitt found General Whiting and Colonel Lamb on stretchers and told them Bragg had given him command of Fort Fisher. Lamb said that a fresh brigade of Confederate troops might retake Fort Fisher from the battle-weary Federals. Colquitt told Lamb that he could not help because he brought no troops. Lamb asked if he would take the seriously wounded General Whiting with him. "It was suggested that the general should take me with him as I was probably fatally wounded," Lamb recalled, "but I refused to leave, wishing to share the fate of the garrison, and desiring that my precious wife anxiously awaiting tidings across the river, where she watched the battle, should not be alarmed, spoke lightly of my wound." Suddenly, one of Colquitt's staff officers appeared, urging him to leave at once because it was reported that the Yankees were advancing on the battery. General Colquitt left abruptly, leaving Lamb and Whiting behind.[101]

General Terry was summoned to Battery Buchanan to receive the formal surrender of Fort Fisher from its commanding officer. Captain Adrian Terry, the general's brother, recalled what happened as they approached Battery Buchanan. "We saw a thin line of men standing by the shore several hundred in number . . . utterly cast down and helpless. Lying upon a stretcher . . . was Major General Whiting and near him was Colonel Lamb."

Confederate General Alfred H. Colquitt was sent to Battery Buchanan to relieve General Whiting of command.

Seeing several blue-coated officers around him, General Whiting asked for the commanding officer. Major General Alfred H. Terry stepped forward and identified himself. "Alfred walked up to him and stated his name and rank," Captain Terry recalled. "Gen. Whiting said, 'I surrender, sir, to you the forces under my command. I care not what becomes of myself.'" General Terry promised Whiting that he and his solders would receive kind treatment.[102]

During the early morning hours of January 16th, the Confederates were taken under guard to the beach two miles north of the fort. Federal Colonel Alfred P. Rockwell wrote in his report:

The prisoners . . . were marched out of the work. My regiment [sixth Connecticut], with the Seventh New Hampshire, formed the guard to these prisoners, and marched them back through Fort Fisher, collecting others on the way, to the beach about two miles north of the fort, where they bivouacked. . . .My regiment was detailed to guard the camp of prisoners (about 1,800 in number) until about noon, when I was relieved.[103]

General Terry was presented with the Confederate flag that Captain Jonathan H. Edgerly had cut down from the Mound Battery. Eager to inform General Grant of the victory at Fort Fisher, Terry commandeered a horse from the battery. In a highly controversial act, General Terry then wrapped himself in the captured Confederate banner and rode to his headquarters. Captain Elridge remembered Terry's triumphant appearance. "Gen. Terry rode into the fort with the flag of [the Mound Battery] wound around his body. We gave him three cheers, when he made this remark: 'Boys, rather than that you should cheer for me, I ought to cheer for you.'"[104]

About 10 PM a rocket was fired from atop Fort Fisher's Northeast Bastion. This was the prearranged signal announcing the army's capture of the fort. Admiral Porter ordered three cheers to celebrate the fall of Fort Fisher. Ensign John Gratten wrote about this memorable night in his book, *Under the Blue Pennant*:

The Admiral never before gave an order which was so heartily obeyed. Everyone appeared to be wild with joy. . . .The flag ship signaled the fleet and repeated the Admiral's order, and in a few seconds thousand of voices were united in tremendous cheering. All the vessels were quickly illuminated, rockets and signal lights were flashing in the air, bells were rung and steam whistles were screaming forth the glad tidings.[105]

"My very heart went up in thanksgiving," reported Lieutenant Frank Lay of the 117th New York, who realized he was the only officer in his regiment not dead or wounded. "Never did I feel as I felt then," he wrote his wife. "Men grasped each other's hands and wept as brave men can in the hour of victory."[106]

75

General Hoke's headquarters flag. Fort Fisher's garrison flag would have been similar but much larger. *Photograph courtesy of the North Carolina Museum of History.*

"The fall of this fort was one of the greatest disasters which had befallen our cause from the beginning of the war," Alexander H. Stevens, Vice-President of the Confederacy

Chapter 6

The Aftermath

A Union soldier stands before a sea-face gun chamber. Note the blood on the dismounted cannon barrel to the left. Image Timothy O'Sullivan, *Photograph courtesy National Archives.*

Exhausted by the fierce combat the day before, many of the soldiers of both armies literally dropped where they were and slept. A few men were surprised when they awoke and found themselves sleeping next to the enemy or possibly a corpse. As the men slowly came awake the first thing they noticed was the smell. The pervasive odors of burnt sulfur, charred wood and the horrible stench of death were in the air. While some of the soldiers were visiting the latrine others were building campfires to cook their breakfast. Some men were early risers and as soon as it was light enough to see, they explored the fort. One *New York Tribune* correspondent aptly wrote these men were "breakfasting on horrors." The gruesome sights were everywhere:

> Within the fallen fort were sights sickening and dreadful. Guns dismounted, guns split, guns broken; caps, clothes, bayonets, swords, muskets, rifles, scattered, battered, blood-stained; knapsacks, powder in bags, cartridges, dead horses, broken bottles, shells exploded, bullets, scabbards, bedding. And then the dead! Men in all postures,

mangled in the head and body, with brains out, but with perfect features, covered with sand and grimed with powder. Arms, legs, hands, faces distorted, swollen, in all the traverses, in the trenches, in green water pools, in the bombproofs, upon the parapet, down in the embankments, here, there, everywhere. . . .The carrying past of the wounded, the groans of the dying, and the smell of blood and powder.[1]

Sailor James Cleer of the *Maratanza* was so frightened by the horrible things he saw inside Fort Fisher that he took a few swallows of whiskey to calm his nerves. "I never saw such a sight in all my life," he wrote his parents. "There was soldiers and sailors laying around me dead, some with arms and legs and heads off. I [found] a demijohn of whiskey. I filled a quart bottle with the whiskey, took a drink of it and I tell you it did not come amiss. I never wanted it more in my life than I did then."[2]

SCENE AFTER THE BOMBARDMENT OF FORT FISHER—LAYING OUT DEAD U. S. SOLDIERS FOR BURIAL.

This picture from *Frank Leslie's Illustrated* shows the Federal troops preparing to bury the dead from the battle. One soldier is carrying a bundle of wooden stakes to use as grave markers while another stirs a can of paint to write the men's names.

Another soldier wrote a letter to his brother describing the carnage inside the fort:
The scenes. . .were indescribably horrible. Great cannon lay in ruins, surrounded by the bodies of the defenders; men were found partly buried in graves dug by the shells which had slain them. . . .Some lay face downward in the sand, and others who had been close together when struck by an exploding shell had fallen in a confused mass, forming a mingled heap of broken limbs and mangled bodies.[3]

After breakfast some of the more hearty men climbed the sixty-foot Mound Battery to get a view of the fort and to see the battery that had given them so much trouble during the battle. Federal Ensign John W. Grattan wrote of these experiences in his book *Under the Blue Pennant*:

[The Mound Battery] mounted two heavy guns which were in good order, the enemy having neglected to spike them before the surrender. The ground was thickly covered with the iron fragments of our shells, and one of the guns was splattered with the blood and brains of a rebel gunner who must have been engaged in training the gun--which was loaded--on our soldiers . . . when a fragment of a shell from the [fleet] struck him down."[4]

Paymaster Henry M. Rogers of the *Gettysburg* recalled the sights in Fort Fisher would "horrify even the stoutest heart. Devastation, ruin, [and] death in every attitude and every form, these are the things we lose sight of when the pride, pomp and circumstance of 'Glorious War' are mentioned."[5]

Visiting a wounded friend in a field hospital could also be a traumatic experience. The three Union hospitals were filled with so many patients that there was a shortage of surgeons to tend them. Regimental Chaplain T. D. Jones wrote:

> The wounds are terrible on both sides and in the hospitals a heart of stone would have bled to see such sights. It was very cold by this time and many had to lie on the ground without covering while others lay in their blood for hours outside the fort where they had fallen. We were short of doctors and there was only one chaplain in Ames' command to help them. Everyone did their best. We were on our feet for three days and nights with little food or sleep, cleaning and binding up wounds.[6]

Chaplain Henry M. Turner also spent much of his time in the hospitals comforting the dying and the wounded:

> It would be impossible to describe what I witnessed among the wounded. But one thing I must mention as a fact. I found twice the number of rebels calling upon God for mercy to what I found among our own wounded soldiers. One rebel particularly, whom I passed, was saying in a most pathetic tone, "O, Lord God, have mercy on me! Please have tender compassion on one who is a sinner, and comfort me in this hour of trial! O Lord, have mercy on me this one time more." When I commenced talking with him, and he discovered I was a chaplain, his countenance seemed to be illuminated with joy. But the prayer that went up from the rebel wounded bought off my prejudice, and I rendered them every comfort in my power.[7]

The explosion of the main powder magazine occurred on the morning after the fort's surrender. *Harpers Weekly.*

Shortly after the surrender of Fort Fisher General Ames ordered Lt. Colonel Zent to place guards on thirty-one bombproofs and magazines. Weary from the long night of battle, Zent made a deadly mistake by not any posting sentries on the main magazine. Apparently he was unaware the large mound of sand in the northeast corner of the fort was a powder magazine. It didn't seem to matter if he had posted guards or not because troops were allowed inside despite orders. Many Union soldiers, sailors and marines went from bombproof to bombproof searching for liquor, souvenirs and the spoils of war. "The soldiers were ransacking every nook and corner," Chaplain Henry M. Turner claimed, "in search of trophies and other memorials, such as tobacco, segars [sic], clothes, pistols, etc." Some of the soldiers found a large quantity of liquor used for medicinal purposes and became intoxicated.[8]

In the early morning hours of January 16th a tremendous explosion rocked the fort. The fort's large reserve magazine, which contained 13,000 pounds of gunpowder, blew up. Unfortunately, the top of this magazine was an inviting area for weary soldiers to bed down for the night. The 4th New Hampshire, 115th and 169th New York regiments were among those who chose this grassy mound for their camp. A *New York Tribune* correspondent wrote:

> This morning about 8 o'clock, as I had just entered and was walking leisurely through Fort Fisher, studying the record of horror before me, torn traverse by traverse, dismounted gun by gun, ghastly corpse by corpse, death and destruction all around that I might know of what I speak, I was suddenly startled by a terrific explosion and the sight of an immense column going high into the air. Following the instincts of nature and the example of those around me . . . I put myself under the best cover within reach.[9]

Surgeon James A. Mowris was searching for the dead of his regiment near the crest of a gun chamber when he heard a deep explosive sound. The violent explosion hurled him to the ground and buried him with falling sand and debris. Mowris wrote about his near death experience:

> I beheld an immense shaft of earth and rubbish . . . rising to the very clouds. . . . I found myself the victim of the most intense violence . . . Then came a distressing sense of suffocation with a clear conviction that my immediate death was inevitable. I felt the grave rudely closing around me, and realized the horrors of being buried alive. Then a temporary lull in the descent of the debris. Instinctively I thrust out a hand . . . [and] gained the air. Again was I . . . overwhelmed by a fresh fall of sand and rubbish . . . another struggle for life and I gained the atmosphere. The danger had passed, and I was still alive.[10]

Men from all over the fort rushed to the scene of the explosion to help rescue the victims. The huge magazine had disappeared leaving only a large crater. The victims of the disaster were seen here and there amid shattered pieces of timber. "On my right, lay a quivering face, all that was visible of a victim," Mowris recalled. "All the bodies [from the battle] that lay along the [slope], before the

The temporary graveyard for the Federal dead was about 250 feet north of the center of the landface. This photograph also shows the middle sally-port and tunnel through the landface. *Photograph courtesy of the National Archives.*

explosion had been suddenly buried in many nameless unmarked graves, while the surface of that general grave-yard was already dotted with the mutilated members of scores of new victims."[11]

There would never be an exact count of the casualties from the magazine explosion. Estimates of the dead and wounded ranged from 130 to 265 with most historians agreeing there were at least 200. However, the 3rd brigade reported that the 115th New York had 110 casualties; the 169th New York had 105 casualties; and the 4th New Hampshire had 50 casualties. This would place the army's casualties at 265. To complicate matters further, both the Federal Navy and Colonel Lamb also claimed to have lost men in the explosion.[12]

Confederate Private James Wright Farmer of the 3rd Battalion, North Carolina Light Artillery was captured and sent to Point Lookout Prison, Maryland. *Photograph courtesy of Pat Hoggard.*

Many of the Federal soldiers blamed the magazine explosion on rebel saboteurs. They knew about the Confederate minefield in front of the fort, so it was not beyond comprehension that the rebels would rig the powder magazine also. Lt. Colonel Nathan J. Johnson found some suspicious copper wires among the debris of the magazine. These wires were concealed underground and led to the Cape Fear River. Some Northern soldiers believed the copper wire was proof that this tragedy was no accident.

"I heard that the Yankees thought we blew the magazine up," Confederate Private John M. Johnston said, "and they were going to kill as many Confederates as the explosion had killed in Yankees. I felt sure if the report was true, I would be among the number killed."[13]

"This circumstance cast a serious gloom over our army than all the casualties which had happened on the previous day and caused more oaths to be uttered than I ever heard before," said Chaplain Henry M. Turner. "Many were for killing all the rebel prisoners, while others were for blowing them up too."[14]

On January 20th the Union Army held a "court of inquiry" to determine the cause of the magazine explosion. Following the testimony of many witnesses it was concluded "that the explosion was the result of carelessness" on the part of Federal soldiers, sailors and marines who were running about with burning torches in the fort and entering bombproofs while intoxicated.[15]

Lieutenant George Quimby of the 4th New Hampshire testified that as he was walking past the main magazine he saw several soldiers standing around the entrance, examining something that had been carried out:

> One man said, 'Have you got it all out?' The other replied, 'I have--perhaps not; they've got a light in there now,' (meaning the magazine). I then stepped to the entrance and inquired what it contained. Someone inside said, 'Boxes of powder.' I then ordered if they had a light to put it out, and cautioned them not to have any more, as it was very careless and dangerous. I then left the fort, and ten or fifteen minutes afterward the explosion took place.[16]

The number of casualties from the second battle of Fort Fisher is difficult to determine. The Union army records showed 184 killed and 749 wounded with 22 missing. This figure, however, does not include the casualties suffered by the navy. The Federal navy had 82 men killed, 269 wounded and 35 missing. This makes the combined total casualties for the Federal armed forces in the second battle of Fort Fisher, 266 men killed and 1,018 wounded and 57 missing.[17]

The Confederate casualties are difficult to determine since we have no official figures. Typically after a battle both the Union and Confederate officers would submit a written report to their superiors explaining their regiment's activities and casualties. Because the Confederate officers at Fort Fisher were sent to prison no report was ever submitted. Any Confederate histories written about the battle of Fort Fisher were done years later and usually appear in regimental histories and contain no useful information as to numbers. This being the case, we can only piece together the facts that we have. We know from General Terry's report that 1,546 Confederate soldiers were captured at Fort Fisher. Of these 286 were wounded. We could perhaps determine the Confederate dead by subtracting 1,546 men from the size of the garrison. Colonel Lamb had reported this to be about 1,900. But was this the true size of the garrison on January 15th?

When Colonel Lamb was asked how many South Carolina soldiers were inside Fort Fisher on the 15th of January, his response was there were 350 men from the 11th, 21st and 25th South Carolina. It is difficult to tell how many men landed since only part of Hagood's 1,100 man brigade had been allowed to come ashore before

Federal Sergeant Henry Odiorne, 97th Pennsylvania, died of wounds suffered at Fort Fisher.

the Federal bombardment drove the Confederate troopship away from Battery Buchanan. The only sure way to achieve an accurate account would be to examine each soldier's record at the National Archives to see if he had been killed or captured at Fort Fisher. This was no small task since Hagood's entire Brigade numbered several thousand. However, every man in this brigade was checked to see if he had been at Fort Fisher. Of this group 466 South Carolina troops were reported inside the walls of the Fort. This new information would add 116 more soldiers to the fort's garrison than previously thought. Lamb's force would now total 2,016. However, I have checked the soldier's records and found 2,476 men were present at Fort Fisher. I believe the reason only 1,546 Confederate soldiers were captured is because some men left the fort before it fell. The largest group of soldiers escaped with Captain Robert T. Chapman when he evacuated Battery Buchanan during the evening of the 15th. During the two days previous to the fort's capture some men also left the fort such as Lieutenant Colonel George T. Gordon and some of the wounded soldiers so they could go to the hospital in Smithville. Gordon, who was a staff officer to General Whiting, was ordered by Whiting to meet with General Bragg and request that his support was urgently needed at the fort.[18]

The Federal dead were buried in two temporary cemeteries in front of the land-face. One graveyard for Federal officers was located 250 feet north of the center of the middle sally-port. The other much larger cemetery for the enlisted men was in front of Shepperd's Battery at the western end of the land-face. The Confederate dead were buried in the post cemetery. These men were later reinterred at Wilmington's Oakdale Cemetery and Wilmington National Cemetery.[19]

Federal Colonel Alfred P. Rockwell and the 6th Connecticut were assigned to guard the Fort Fisher prisoners two miles north of the fort. The Confederate soldiers were separated into manageable 150 man groups and spent a miserable night on the exposed seashore. "We slept on the cold beach," Private William Haigh remembered, "the screaming winter blast blowing unobstructed fresh from the ocean, and the damp ground, (always colder and damper near salt water) chilling us through our blankets."[20]

The morning of the 16th brought many changes for the prisoners. As the Confederates awoke they were reminded that life would never be the same. Above the fort a large Federal flag had replaced the Confederate banner on the post's flagpole. Evidence of the terrible struggle was everywhere. The dead were strewn along the Federal navy's route where they had charged the Northeast Bastion. The

Confederates comfortable barracks had been destroyed and replaced by the bitterly cold, windswept beach. "The morning found us strongly guarded," William Haigh remembered. "A line of sentinels surrounded us, and gunboats & frigates lay off [the fort]." The Confederate prisoners were saddened by the loss of so many of their friends, but they were also relieved that the bloody fighting was finally over. As the haggard men looked around and saw the strong Union guard watching them, the reality of their uncertain future seeped in. If they were sent to prison, who would care for their families? The men's anxiety was heightened when the fort's powder magazine exploded, causing the guards to cast vengeful glances at the prisoners.[21]

Confederate First Lieutenant William Drew was wounded and captured at Fort Fisher. Photograph reprinted *from State Troops and Volunteers*

Fortunately, not all the guards saw their captives as the despicable enemy, but fighting men just like themselves. These rugged men were basically of the same mold. The Confederates had the same complaints that soldiers have griped about for ages; the quality of their rations, the officers, and the foolish orders they were forced to obey. Like any devoted husband or father they also talked lovingly of their families. Although it remained unspoken, the Federal soldiers knew if things had gone badly for them during the battle they could be the ones being guarded instead of the Confederates. It wasn't long before the Federal and Confederate soldiers began freely talking to one another and a few of the guards began to share what food they had in their haversacks.

"They appreciated those Union rations," remembered Captain Leonard R. Thomas, "for those of the Confederacy in January 1865 were poor in quality and meager in quantity . . . composed mostly of coarse corn and not an ounce of sugar or coffee. It was almost pathetic to see how those iron-sided veterans took to the Union coffee. As they drank it, they were heard to say, 'This is the first we've tasted since early in 1862.' Those men had marched, toiled and fought during the last year of the war on rations which might have caused a mutiny had they been served to the Union army. . . There was not a man among the victors who did not thereby get an access (sic) of admiration for the gallant men whom the fortunes of war had made our prisoners."[22]

"Glad enough were we to get anything to eat, and thanks to the Masonic Order, I found friends among my enemies," said William H. Haigh. "I shall ever remember with grateful heart Captain Wm. S. Marble, 7th Conn. Vols, and Rev. Mr. Eaton, Chaplain of the same Regt. who not only ministered to my then present necessities, but gave me money to aid me as a prisoner."[23]

On Wednesday morning the Confederate prisoners were marched back through the fort to the wharf near Battery Buchanan. Here they were loaded onto the transports *California, DeMolay, General Lyon* and *North Point* to begin the arduous five-day voyage north to their respective prisons.

Private Haigh describes his journey aboard the *North Point* in a letter to his wife Kate:

> You know that the prisoners from Fort Fisher arrived here [Point Lookout, Md.] on Sunday the 22nd of January, 1865, but you do not know, for no pen could describe, or tongue tell the awful horrors of that terrible sea voyage from Fort Fisher to this place. . . .From Wednesday the 18th until Sunday the 22nd, late in the evening, six hundred of us were in the hold of the ship *North Point*. I will not attempt to describe the scene. Memory sometimes sickens me with a retrospective view of that motley medley of men, almost stifled and crushed to death. There poor McNeill fell a victim to "Black Hole in

Calcutta" cruelty [prisoners dying from suffocation and crushing]; and others had sown the fatal seed of these terrible maladies that made them inmates of Point Lookout Grave Yard. Cooped up in that 'cattle transport" (for such it literally was) midst the darkness of night, the hatches down, men writhing in agony, many blaspheming, cursing and quarrelling, it made one feel that he was next door neighbor to the damned spirits of the infernal regions.

Morning after morning came, but still the endless waste of waters, tossed and heaving with a winter's storm. I was one of those whose duty it was to give out the rations--and this enabled me to move about a little on deck, and thus get a little fresh air, though bitter cold with drifting snow.[24]

Private John M. Johnston also wrote of his experience:

After remaining [on the beach at Fort Fisher] for about two days, [we] were marched back to the fort . . . and put into small boats and carried to a large steamer. After being put on the steamer, we were put in charge of a Negro guard. We had been guarded by white men up to this time. I had never seen a Negro soldier before so you can imagine how we Confederate prisoners felt. We didn't know what they were going to [do] with us or where they were going to cary (sic) us. And right then, I felt like I didn't care where they carried us or what became of us. I was reckless, felt like I had rather be dead than alive. Anyway the vessel with about 800 prisoners put out to sea, I stood on its stern and looked and watched as long as I could see a sight of land. When I could no longer see land I felt that all hope was lost. [Where] I was going I knew not . . . but found out after a while that we were bound for Point Lookout, a Yankee prison situated on the Chesapeak (sic) Bay.

After being on the ocean for about five days about 10 o'clock on 22 of January. We anchored in sight of the prison. It was my first and last sea voyage and rough one it was. The vessel came very near being broken to pieces by striking a rock as we passed Cape Lookout. One of the prisoners died on the way and was buried after we arrived at prison.[25]

Confederate President Jefferson Davis tried to negotiate a peace settlement with the Federal government.

The fall of Fort Fisher sent shock waves racing throughout the world. Like all disasters it was felt hardest in the area closest to the epicenter. The Confederacy was already reeling from one calamity after another and now this terrible news seemed to seal her fate as surely as the port of Wilmington had been sealed from the outside world. Not only had the Confederacy lost their last major seaport, but it also lost its ability to supply General Lee's army with food and equipment. By late February Lee was already feeling the pinch of not enough provisions and reported that his men were deserting by the hundreds every night.

Confederate President Jefferson Davis sent Congressman Duncan F. Kenner to Europe a week after the fall of Fort Fisher. Kenner was to advise the governments of Great Britain and France of the Confederacy's willingness to emancipate its slaves if either nation would recognize the sovereignty of the Confederate States. Both governments declined to do so, seeing the fall of Fort Fisher as the death knell of the Confederacy.

President Davis realized the Confederacy was sinking and tried to salvage what he could. He appointed a three-man team to travel to Hampton Roads, Virginia, to discuss a peace settlement with United States officials. These men met with President Abraham Lincoln and Secretary of State William Seward aboard the ship *River Queen* on February 3, 1865. Historian Rod Gragg wrote:

"The meeting failed to produce a settlement. Lincoln offered amnesty to Confederate leaders and indicated slave owners might receive some Federal compensation for their freed slaves, but rejected the suggestion of an armistice. Instead, he insisted the Southern states surrender, return to the Union and comply with some form of compensated emancipation. Lincoln was unyielding on the question of an armistice--the South *had* to surrender and rejoin the Union. The peace conference was a failure. Lincoln was no longer interested in negotiating a peace settlement, Davis said, and instead now insisted on a 'humiliating surrender.' The Confederate President attributed Lincoln's change in attitude to the fall of Fort Fisher: the loss of the Confederacy's last major port and the resulting isolation of the South had convinced Lincoln that the death of the Confederacy was only a matter of time."[26]

No one seemed more shocked about the fall of Fort Fisher than General Bragg. After learning of the fort's surrender from General Colquitt, Bragg telegraphed General Lee at 1 AM on January 16, 1865:

"I am mortified at having to report the unexpected capture of Fort Fisher, with most of its garrison, at about 10 o'clock tonight. Particulars not known."[27]

Bragg's reputation was on shaky ground after his defeats at Murfreesboro, Missionary Ridge, and at Chattanooga, Tennessee. Bragg, knowing his critics would relish the opportunity to blame him for the loss of Fort Fisher, began a search for a scapegoat to divert attention from himself. The most logical choice would be to find fault with General Whiting's or Colonel Lamb's leadership. Bragg was unable do this since both men had been severely wounded during the battle and were considered heroes. The citizens would never allow these patriotic men to be attacked. However, the fort's garrison was another story.

In his official report Bragg wrote: "The (Federal) army column, preceded by a single regiment, approached along the river and entered the work on that flank almost unopposed."[28] This must have been news to the men who fought a life and death struggle at the River Road gate. Private Zachery T. Fulmore, who was captured at the gate, would have to live with the shame of General Bragg's lies the rest of his life. In 1883 he wrote to Colonel Lamb about an experience he had returning home:

Confederate General Braxton Bragg tried to save his reputation by shifting the blame for Fort Fisher's surrender to someone else.

On my way home from prison in the later part of May, 1865, I was put off the boat up at Meares' Bluff and walked the ties up to Lumberton. At the end of the first day's journey we stopped at the farm house of Colonel Joe Green, a prominent citizen of Bladen County, to get something to eat. We received excellent treatment, as he knew some of my family connection, but he said he was very much mortified to know that we had acted so cowardly as to let the enemy come in at that gate unopposed. I protested that we had done all that we could; told how many men we had killed and wounded right there, etc, etc. He said General Bragg was an experienced fighter--saw the whole affair, and his statement would outweigh the statement of anybody else, but seeing our ragged and starved condition and knowing of our sufferings subsequently, he expressed a kindly sympathy, and gave us food. I assured him he would learn the truth someday, and hoped it would be soon. I have never seen him since, but presume he died under the impression that General Bragg had given us our just deserts.   Many years afterwards, however, I left the State of Virginia on a big disgust over the war reminiscences . . . I despaired of ever overcoming the impression created by General Bragg and dropped the whole subject.[29]

General Whiting was extremely vocal in their criticism of Bragg. Whiting wrote to General Lee from his death bed at Governors Island in New York Harbor:

> I think that the result might have been avoided, and Fort Fisher held, if the commanding general had done his duty. I charge him with this loss; with neglect of duty in this, that he either refused or neglected to carry out every suggestion made to him in official communications by me for the disposition of the troops. . . . I charge him further with making no effort whatever to create a diversion in favor of the beleaguered garrison during the three days' battle, by attacking the enemy. . . . I desire that a full investigation be had of this matter and these charges which I make; they will be fully borne out by the official records. . . . I demand in justice to the country, to the army, and to myself, that the course of this officer be investigated.[30]

No investigation of Bragg's conduct was ever done. Some say it was too late in the war to do anything. Others said it was because General Bragg and President Jefferson Davis were friends.

General Whiting was healing from his wounds and appeared to be doing better, but died unexpectedly of chronic diarrhea on March 10, 1865. Known as the soldier's disease, this illness claimed more lives than any other disease in the Civil War.

Fort Fisher's importance to the Confederate war effort was largely ignored by historians until fairly recently. Even Ken Burns' lengthy Civil War documentary failed to mention Fort Fisher. Perhaps the battle's significance was overshadowed by President Lincoln's assassination and then by the end of the war itself. In either case, Fort Fisher was mostly forgotten by everyone except the people in southeastern North Carolina.

Colonel Lamb could not forget the sacrifice made by those brave men who defended the fort against all comers. At a reunion in 1875, Lamb addressed the gallant veterans of Fort Fisher and paid them the ultimate compliment:

> I stand here a witness to the heroic bravery of that small body of North Carolina troops, assisted by a mere handful of Confederate sailors and marines, who after the fort was entered and its citadel captured, and they might have surrendered with honors, refused to submit, but withstood for hours the fierce assaults of three splendid brigades of Federal soldiers led by gallant officers. They disputed hand-to-hand every inch of ground until pushed by the force of irresistible numbers to the very brink of the sea, and then surrendered only when their ammunition was expended and all hope lost.
> North Carolina need cross no ocean to search amid Roman and Grecian stories for examples of self-sacrifice in defense of home and country, for here among her own sons, upon her own soil, the valor of Pharsalia and of Thermopylae were reproduced, and no correct history of this grand old State can be written unless the defense of Fort Fisher by North Carolinians in January, 1865, be placed among the most heroic deeds in the drama of our Civil War.[31]

Chapter 7

Fort Fisher Regiment Placement During the Second Battle

The battle at Fort Fisher was a dynamic, flowing fight. When the marine brigade made its charge on the Northeast Bastion most of the Confederate soldiers were defending the right against the assault. After the repulse of the marine brigade, the Confederate soldiers discovered there were Federal flags on the fort's parapets. Led by Major General Whiting, the soldiers rushed to the left to fight the Federal Infantry which had made a lodgment of the western side of the fort. For a while this battle had an ebb and flow nature as the Confederates would push the Federal troops back; the Federal soldiers would be reinforced by a fresh brigade and counterattack, pushing the Confederate defenders back. This makes placement of troops difficult. Because a regiment is mentioned as defending a certain gun chamber only means that it has been documented as being there. This is not to say that other companies or regiments were not standing beside these soldiers.

The soldier's accounts of the battle give several clues to where the regiments where located during the second battle. For instance Sergeant Thomas A. McNeill states that Company D, 1st Battalion North Carolina Heavy Artillery on January 15th was at the middle sally-port until about 2 p. m.[1] Colonel Lamb, concerned that there were not enough soldiers at the River Road gate, ordered that company to reinforce Captain Zachariah Adams Battery, Company D, 13th Battalion,[2] North Carolina Light Artillery. Private Zachariah T. Fulmore confirmed this movement in his letter to Colonel Lamb. Captain Adams also had a battery at the center sally-port. We also know that when Sergeant Thaddeus C. Davis, of 3rd Company G, 40th Regiment North Carolina Light Artillery, moved up to the land face and helped defend the gun chamber to the left of the North East Bastion.[3] Davis later states that his company followed General Whiting during his charge to the fourth gun chamber. Private Buckner Lanier Blackmore states in his letter in the July 2, 1893 issue of the *Wilmington Messenger* that Company A, 36th Regiment North Carolina Artillery, under the command of Captain Edward L. Faison, helped defend the Mound Battery.[4]

There were also subtle hints such as Colonel Lamb saying Private Robert Harvey was killed on Shepperd's Battery parapet.[5] This was before the Confederate soldiers rushed over to defend the left. This seems to indicate that Harvey's Company I, 36th Regiment North Carolina, Heavy Artillery was assigned to defend Shepherd's Battery. Major William J. Saunders mentions Lieutenant William Swain was in the gun chamber with the last serviceable columbiad.[6] This was located to the left of the Northeast Bastion on the land face. The reason this cannon survived is because it was somewhat sheltered by the higher bastion on the right. Lieutenant Swain commanded 3rd Company G, 36th Regiment North Carolina, Heavy Artillery. According to Seaman Robert Watson the Confederate States Navy manned several batteries on the sea face. Watson mentions being assigned to a battery with three Brooke rifles.[7] I examined the Fort Fisher map and found that Batteries Pudie and Bolles fit that description. We know from Colonel Lamb's and Lieutenant Colonel George T. Gordon's reports that a detachment of the C. S. Navy also defended Battery Buchanan.[8]

87

Chapter 8

Colonel Lamb's Story of Fort Fisher

The following article appeared in the *Wilmington Messenger,* June 15, 1893

Colonel William Lamb

About noon on the 4th of July, 1862, while in command of Fort St. Philip, near Orton on the Cape Fear River, I received a most unexpected order to proceed to Fort Fisher and take command. I went immediately, assumed command, and before sunset of that day had thoroughly inspected the works. They then consisted of, first, a recently erected work, with two guns, called Shepperd's Battery. It was on the extreme left and faced the sea, its rear being close to the river shore. Next, towards the sea, came a quadrilateral field work known as Fort Fisher. It was a small work, part of it constructed of perishable sand bags and its longest face was about one hundred yards. Out of its half dozen large guns, only the two eight-inch Columbiads were suitable for seacoast defense. One of the Federal frigates could have cleaned it out with a few broad-sides. Next to this on its right, facing the sea and opposite the bar, came a very handsome and creditable casemated battery of four eight-inch Columbiads, called after Capt. Meade. It was constructed of turfed sand over a heavy timber framework, the embrasures of palmetto. Col. Fremont has informed me since the war that he designed the work. A one gun battery stood to the right of this, well out on the seashore. It was called Cumberland's battery and contained a long ranged

rifle gun, the only piece of modern ordnance on Confederate Point. (This gun exploded subsequently when fired at a blockader without loss of life, and was replaced with a ten inch Columbiad.) To the right and rear of this and some two hundred yards apart, were two batteries, each having two barbette guns of modern caliber, one called Bolles and the other I called Hedrick battery, after the former gallant commander of the Fort. There was besides these batteries a large commissary bomb proof. There were only seventeen guns of respectable caliber, including thirty-two pounders. There was on Zeke's Island a small two gun battery, subsequently washed away by the sea. I thought on assuming command, and experience afterwards demonstrated, that as a defense of New Inlet against a Federal fleet, our works amounted to nothing.

I determined at once to build a work of much magnitude that it could withstand the heaviest fire of any guns in the American Navy. I had seen the effect of eleven inch shell, and had read about the force of the fifteen inch shell, and believed that their penetrating power was well ascertained and could be provided against. I obtained permission of Maj. Gen. French, who had placed me in command of Confederate Point to commence such a fortification, although he did not altogether concur with me as to the value of elevated batteries nor the necessity of such unprecedentedly heavy works. Shortly after obtaining permission, I commenced the new Fort Fisher, and from that time, the summer of 1862, until the morning of 24th of December, 1864, I never ceased to work, sometimes working on Sundays when rumors of an attack reached me, having at times over one thousand men, white and colored, hard at work. In the construction of the mound on the extreme right of the sea-face, which occupied six months, two inclined railways worked by steam supplemented the labor of men. Although Fort Fisher was far from completed when attacked by the Federal fleet, it was the largest seacoast fortification in the Confederate States. The plans were my own, and as the work progressed were approved by French, Raines, Longstreet, Beauregard, and Whiting. It was styled by Federal engineers after the capture, the Malakoff of the South. It was built solely with the view of resisting the fire of a fleet, and it stood uninjured, except as to armament, two of the fiercest bombardments the world has ever witnessed.

The morning after I took command of the fort, I noticed a blockader lying a little over a mile from the bar, not two miles from the work. I asked if she was not unusually close in, and was answered no. I then remarked that she could have thrown a shot into the fort without warning, and was informed that the enemy sometimes fired on our working parties unexpectedly and drove them from their work, and that the fort never fired on the enemy unless they fired first. I replied that it should never occur again, and ordering a detachment to man the rifle in the Cumberland battery, opened fire on the blockader. The astonished enemy slipped his cable and retreated as fast as possible, and from that day to the final attack no blockader anchored within range of our guns and no working party was ever molested, not even when hundreds were congregated together in constructing the mounds.

When the Federal fleet appeared off the Fort in December, 1864, I had built two faces to the works; these were two thousand five-hundred and eighty yards long or about one and a half miles. The land-face mounted twenty of the heaviest seacoast guns and was about 682 yards long; the sea-face, with twenty-four equally heavy guns (including a 170 pounder Blakeley rifle and 130 pounder Armstrong rifle, both imported from England) was 1,898 yards in length.

The land-face commenced about 100 feet from the river with a half bastion, originally Shepperd's Battery, which I had doubled in strength, and extended with a heavy curtain to a full bastion on the ocean side, where it joined the sea-face. The work was built to withstand the heaviest artillery fire. There was no moat with scarp and counter-scarp, so essential for defense against storming parties, the shifting sands rendering its construction impossible with the material available. The outer slope was twenty feet high from the berme to the top of the parapet, at an angle of 45 degrees, and was sodded with marsh grass, which grew luxuriantly. The parapet was not less than twenty-five feet thick, with an inclination of only one foot. The revetment was five feet nine inches high from the floor of the gun chambers, and these were some twelve feet or more from the interior plane. The guns were all mounted in barbette or Columbiad carriages; there was not a single casemated gun in the fort. Experience has taught that casemates of timber and sand bags were a delusion and a snare against heavy projectiles, and there was no iron to construct others with. Between the gun chambers, containing one or two guns each, there were heavy traverses, exceeding in size any heretofore constructed, to protect from an enfilading fire. They extended out some twelve feet on the parapet, and were twelve feet or more in height above the parapet, running back thirty feet or more. The gun chambers were reached from the rear by steps. In each traverse was an alternate magazine or bomb proof, the latter ventilated by an air chamber. Passageways penetrated the traverses in the interior of the work forming additional bomb proofs for the reliefs for the guns.

The sea-face for 100 yards from the northeast bastion was of the same massive character as of the land-face. A crescent battery built for four casemated guns joined this. It had been originally constructed of palmetto logs and tarred sand bags and sand revetted with sod; but the logs had decayed and it was converted into a hospital bomb proof. In its rear a heavy curtain was thrown up to protect the chambers from fragments of shells. From this bomb proof a series of batteries extended for three quarters of a mile along the sea, connected by an infantry curtain. These batteries had heavy traverses, but were not more than ten or twelve feet high to the top of the parapets and were built for ricochet firing. On this line was a bomb proof electric battery connected with a system of submarine torpedoes. Further along, where the channel ran close to the beach, inside the bar, a mound battery, sixty feet high was erected, with two heavy guns, which had a plunging fire into the channel; this was connected with the battery north of it by a light curtain. Following the line of the works it was over one mile from the mound to the redan at the angle of the sea and the land-faces. From the mound for nearly a mile to the end of the point was a level sand plain, scarcely three feet above high tide, and much of it was submerged during the gales. At the point was battery Buchanan with four guns, in the shape of an ellipse, commanding the inlet, its two eleven inch guns covering the approach by land.

It was constructed after a plan furnished me by Reddin Pittman, an accomplished young engineer officer from Edgecombe County, and for its purpose was perfect in design. I remember when he gave me the plan he named it "Augusta Battery" after his sweetheart, but Gen. Whiting wishing to compliment the gallant hero of Mobile directed me to call it Battery Buchanan. When completed it was garrisoned by a detachment from the Confederate States Navy. An advanced redoubt with a twenty-four pounder was added after the repulse of Butler and Porter, Christmas 1864. A wharf for large steamers was in close proximity to this work. Battery Buchanan was a citadel to which an overpowered garrison might retreat and with proper transportation be carried off at night, and to which reinforcements could be safely sent under the cover of darkness.

Returning to the land-face or northern front of Fort Fisher, as a defense against infantry there was a system of sub-terra torpedoes extending across the peninsula five to six hundred feet from the land-face and so disconnected that the explosion of one would not affect the others; inside the torpedoes, about fifty feet from the berme of the work, extending from river banks to seashore, was a heavy palisade of sharpened logs nine feet high, pierced for musketry, and so laid out as to have an enfilading fire on the centre, where there was a redoubt guarding a sally port, from which two Napoleons were run out as occasion required. At the river end of the palisade was a deep and muddy slough, across which was a bridge, the entrance of the river road into the fort; commanding this bridge was a Napoleon gun.

There were three mortars in the rear of the land-face. Having described Fort Fisher as I found it on the 4th of July 1862, and as it was on the eve of the great battles, I will now take a cursory glance of events on Confederate Point during these two and a half years. Just previous to my going there the British steamer "Modern Greece," laden with provisions, clothing, liquors and four pieces of artillery, with ammunition, attempted to run in New Inlet. Her draft being too great to enter the commander of the fort, fearing capture, sunk her outside the bar and proceeded to save her cargo. I completed this work, rescuing four twelve pounder Whitworth rifle guns which afterwards bore a conspicuous part in the operations in the war, not only in my command but elsewhere. They were the longest range guns then constructed, throwing a shot five miles when at an angle of twenty-five degrees. After mounting them, the blockaders were obliged to move their anchorage still further from the fort.

Blockade running into Wilmington had just commenced. It was first carried on by any light draft seagoing steamer that could be procured and even by small sailing craft, but this was of short duration. The blockade became so effective that to run it successfully was quite a science. The fastest steamers were built for the purpose, side wheelers or double screws, long, low and narrow, usually nine times as long as wide and from four hundred to seven hundred tons burthen. They were all painted a light gray, making them as nearly invisible as possible; light lower masts without yards, with a small lookout on the foremast. Funnels could be lowered close to the deck in case of need and when possible smokeless coal was used. No light was permitted to be visible. No animal likely to make a noise was allowed on board, the only exception to the rule being a splendid Arabian steed brought in for President Davis. No precaution was omitted to prevent discovery. During my stay on Confederate Point at least one hundred different steamers were engaged in running the blockade in the Cape Fear River, and very few were captured before making one round trip. The squadron off Wilmington reported sixty-five steam blockade runners captured or destroyed during the war. The most skillful sailors were secured as commanders, and Confederate and British naval officers were engaged when practicable, the latter being on leave under assumed names. One thousand pounds was paid to a captain for a successful trip. The pilots, who were most essential to success, received as high as 750 pounds for the round trip. It was usual to pay half the sum in advance. The most fortunate of the commanders of my acquaintance was Capt. John M. Wilkinson of the C.S.N., who, in ten months, made twenty-one trips in the British side-wheel steamer "Giraffe" which was purchased by the Confederate Government and named the R. E. Lee. Capt. Roberts whose name was Hon. Augustus C. Hobart Hampden, and who afterwards as Hobart Pasha commanded the Turkish Navy until his death, was also most successful running the "Don" between Nassau and Wilmington, and with the regularity of a packet boat. Capt. Murray, who was C. Murray Aynsley, now a retired admiral in the British Navy, who received rapid promotion for distinguished and gallant service from the government, after our war, was not only successful, but forced to show more skill pluck than the others, having to run the gauntlet of the blockade by daylight on two occasions, receiving shot in his vessel each time.

As blockade running was of such vital interest to the Southern cause, I did everything to foster it, and New Inlet protected by Fort Fisher, became the most popular entrance to the South. Wilmington was the last gateway closed, and during the last year I commanded the fort, there was scarcely a dark night I was not called upon the ramparts to admit a friendly vessel. Had I time, I would dwell on some of the many interesting events on blockade running at Fort Fisher, but it is quite impossible to in the limit necessarily put upon this narrative. The running through the squadron and safely over the bar in daylight of the power laden "Cornubia" in 1862, and the "A. D. Vance" with a party of ladies and Dr. Hoge of Richmond, with Bibles for the soldiers, in 1864, the latter steamer rescued by a timely shot from a ten inch Columbiad, in the fort were incidents never to be forgotten. The recapture of the "Kate of London" and the "Nighthawk," the wreck of the "Condor" under the guns of the Fort, and the sad drowning of Mrs. Greenhough, the famous Confederate spy, the fights over the "Venus"; and the "Hebe" on the beach of Masonboro Sound where one of the garrison was killed and a Whitworth gun captured from a detachment of men guarding the wrecks August 23rd, 1863, by the United States frigate "Minnesota" carrying forth four guns, which came close to shore and rendered a retreat with the gun impossible, were thrilling events in our camp life.

We had a visit from President Davis; he landed at the end of the point and rode on horseback with Gen. Whiting to the mound. As soon as he reached the top, giving him a complete view of the works, the sea-face guns being manned for the purpose, gave him the Presidential salute of twenty-one guns. We doubt whether many of the forts in the South could claim the distinction of having fired this salute. I would mention in this connection that I never failed on the 4th of July and the 22nd of February to fire at noon the national salutes of thirteen guns, although not required by the Confederate States army regulations.

I shall never forget a most interesting discussion between the President and Gen. Whiting at my headquarters in regard to their preference as to the mode of trial they would prefer; the President preferred the usual trial by jury, while Gen. Whiting preferred the court-martial.

Among the saddest events which occurred previous to the battles were the execution of deserters. On one occasion one soldier was shot, and on another two were executed at the same time. It is a solemn sight to see a command draw up to witness the death of fellow soldiers, and it is made as impressive as possible as a warning against desertion. The condemned ride to the stake upon their coffins, the band playing the dead march, are blindfolded when shot, and are usually tied to the stake unless they request otherwise. The weapons are loaded by the ordnance sergeant, one with a blank cartridge so that no soldier detailed is positive that his gun is loaded with a ball when he fires.

All three shot at Fort Fisher had been farmers, and were married, and doubtless the condition of their families at home had much to do with their crime. They had not deserted from my command but when captured their companies were stationed at Fort Fisher, and it was my painful duty to see the sentences of the court-martial enforced. They all died fearlessly.

Monday, October 24th, 1864, was a day of excitement on Confederate Point. Information was received that Fort Fisher was to be attacked and Porter was to command the fleet. Intelligence was also received through an anonymous letter at headquarters at Wilmington that our men were expected to spike the guns, cut telegraph wires and pilot the enemy to the city. This was conveyed to me confidentially, but I repudiated it so far as my garrison was concerned, having implicit faith in their loyalty, and subsequent events sustained my convictions. The same day Gen. Braxton Bragg assumed command of the defenses of Wilmington, superseding but not removing Gen. Whiting, who remained second in command. This was a bitter disappointment to my command who felt that no one was so capable of defending the Cape Fear as the brilliant officer who had given so much of his time and ability for its defense. When a few days after a Virginia paper announced, "Braxton Bragg has been ordered to Wilmington. Goodbye Wilmington," to many it seemed as prophetic as the Wizard's warning to Lochiel on the eve of Culloden. I did not so regard it but was as sanguine of success as that unfortunate

Highland chieftain. The patriotic Whiting showed no feeling at being superseded, but went to work with redoubled energy to prepare for the impending attack. He visited Confederate Point repeatedly, riding over the ground with me and selecting points for batteries and covered ways, so as to keep up communication after the arrival of the enemy, between the fort and the entrenched camp which I commenced constructing at Sugar Loaf. He pointed out to me where the enemy would land on the beach beyond the range of our guns, and on both occasions the enemy landed at that place without opposition, although Whiting had prepared ample shelter for troops to seriously retard if not prevent a landing. It seems incomprehensible that Gen. Bragg should have allowed the Federal troops on both attacks to have made frolic of their landing on the soil of North Carolina. Six thousand soldiers from Lee's army within call and not one sent to meet the invader and drive him from the shore. Sub-terra batteries were planted in front of the Fort and a strong palisade line erected from river to sea. A number of heavy rifles and Columbiads were put on the land and sea-faces to strengthen Fort Fisher and the armament of Battery Buchanan was completed. In the sixty days before the attack our threatened works were so materially strengthened that we felt with proper cooperation on the part of the army under Whiting we would certainly defeat the enemy. On the morning of December 20th the expected fleet was seen off Fort Fisher hulls down. A stiff gale was blowing from the northeast. Only half of my garrison, five companies of the Thirty-sixth North Carolina were with me, and the other half having been sent to Georgia under the gallant Maj. James M. Stevenson to assist in resisting Sherman's advance to the sea. My effective force was not over 500. I immediately sent the slaves who were at work on the defenses to town and put everything in readiness for action, expecting a fleet at a high tide. Gen. Whiting visited me for a short time, promising to send reinforcements. Commodore Pinckney was with him, and gravely informed me that the heavy frigates would drive my men from the guns on the sea-face with a broadside of grape and canister. I respectfully disagreed with him. The gale increased in severity and continued through the night. The fleet remained at their anchorage during the 21st, the wind shifting to the southwest. During the day a detachment of three officers and twenty-five sailors of the Confederate States Navy reported. During the next day the fleet remained at anchor, their hulls still below the horizon. Gen. Herbert, my immediate commander, visited me; he was very blue, having really no men to spare from the reduced garrison of the other forts. On the 23rd there was no demonstration by the enemy, but I was reinforced by Major James Reilly with two companies of his regiment, the Fortieth, 110 men, accompanied these, tenth battery Junior reserves, boys between 16 and 18 years of age, 140 in number, making a total in the Fort of 900 men and boys. The new arrivals were assigned the quarters of the absent company, and the regulars among them were soon at home. The old garrison had ceased to speculate on the impending attack, and in the evening hours before taps a visitor among them would never have supposed a battle was imminent. The violin and accordion could be heard from different groups and a quartette was singing "Lorena," "My Maryland," and other camp fire melodies. The usual games were being played around the tallow dips with as much zest as if a more serious game were not impending; here and there a few were reading their Bibles before retiring, but only such as were accustomed to end the day in such devotions. The formidable fleet had no terror for such stout hearts. The regulars who had come from the other forts were naturally discussing the situation and after their comparative inactivity seemed pleased with the opportunity to see some active service in behalf of the cause. The brave little boys torn from their firesides by the cruel necessities of the struggle were as bright and manly as if anticipating a parade. They should never have been called out for service, it was robbing the cradle.

What nobler women can be found in all history, than the matrons of the Old North State, who, with their prayers and tears sent forth their darlings in a cause they had believed in to be right and in the defense of their homes. Self-sacrificing courage seems indigenous to North Carolina. No breast is too tender for this heroic virtue. Since the ten year old son of the Regulator begged the truant Tryon, after the Battle of Alamance, to hang him and let his father live, lest his mother die and the children perish, even the boys of this sturdy Commonwealth have been ever ready to rally in her defense. The first life blood that stained the sand of the Confederate Point was from one of these youthful patriots.

The sun set in a cloudless sky on December 23rd, and with its parting rays the gale subsided. At midnight the blockade runner "Little Hattie" came in, Captain Lebby came ashore to report his narrow escape from capture. He had passed safely through the formidable fleet and thought he had been followed in by one of the enemy's ships, but she had not molested him. He was about leaving when the officer of the day reported a vessel on fire at the beach about a mile from the fort. I went on the rampart and saw what looked like a blockade runner on fire. Captain Lebby thought it must be the "Agnes Fry," which steamer had left Nassau with him for Wilmington, and I so telegraphed Gen. Whiting. I watched the burning vessel for half an hour and ordered the mounted pickets to be careful not to fire on any approaching boats. I had a good opportunity to note the position of the vessel and considered her a mile from the fort. Gen. Butler some years after the war informed me that the wreck was found and her exact position known, but I think the remains of the "Modern Greece" were mistaken for her and that nothing was left of this vessel. Returning to my quarters I laid down on my lounge to get a rest before the anticipated engagement the next day, but I had hardly lain down before I felt a gently rocking of the small brick house (formerly the light-keepers) which I would have attributed to imagination or to vertigo, but it was instantly followed by an explosion sounding very little louder than the report of a ten inch Columbiad. The corporal of the guard was called for in every direction by the sentinels, and the officer of the day reported the blowing up of the magazine of the vessel which had been on fire. I telegraphed Gen. Whiting at Wilmington of the explosion and retired to rest. In the morning the explosion was the subject of conversation among the officers, and some had not even been aroused by the commotion it created. I thought so little of it that the only entry I made in my diary was "a blockader got aground near the fort, set fire to herself and blew up." I was surprised to learn from prisoners captured Christmas night, that the explosion was that of a greater floating magazine, the steamer "Louisiana," with more than 250 tons of powder, intended to demolish the work and paralyze the garrison. The vessel was doubtless afloat when the explosion occurred, or the result might have been very serious. The shock was distinctly felt in Wilmington.

Saturday, December 24th, was one of those perfect winter days that occasionally are experienced in the latitude of the Cape Fear. The gale which had backed around from the northeast to the southwest had subsided the day before, and was followed by a dead calm. The air was balmy for winter, and the sun shone with almost Indian summer warmth, and the deep blue sea was as calm as a lake and broke lazily on the bar and beach.

A grander sight than the approach of Porter's formidable Armada towards the fort was never witnessed on our coast. With the rising sun out of old ocean there came upon the horizon one after another, the vessels of the fleet, the grand frigate leading the van, followed by the iron clads. More than fifty men-of-war heading for the Confederate stronghold. At 9 o'clock the men were beat to quarters and silently the detachments stood by their guns. On the vessels came, growing larger and more imposing as the distance lessened between them and the resolute men who had rallied to defend their homes. The "Minnesota," "Colorado," and "Wabash" came grandly on, floating fortresses, each mounting more guns than all the batteries on the land, and the two first combined carrying more shot and shell than all the magazines in the fort combined. From the left salient to the mound Fort Fisher had forty-four guns, and not over 3,000 shot and shell, exclusive of grape and shrapnel. The Armstrong gun had only one dozen rounds of fixed ammunition, and no other projectile could be used in its delicate grooves. The order was given to fire no shot until the Columbiad at headquarters fired, and that each gun that bore on a vessel should be fired every thirty minutes, and not oftener except by special order, unless an attempt was made to cross the bar, when every gun bearing on it should be fired as rapidly as accuracy would permit, the smooth bores at ricochet.

Before coming within range, the wooden ships slowed down and the great ironsides and three monitors forged ahead, coming within less than a mile of the northeast salient, the other ships taking position to the right and left, the line extending more than a mile. As the Ironsides took her position she ran out her starboard guns, a flash was seen from the forward one, then a puff of white smoke a deep boom was heard and over our heads came an eleven inch shell which I saw distinctly in its passage towards our flagstaff, passed, and exploded harmlessly with a sharp report. The signal gun had been trailed to bear on an approaching frigate, so I gave the command, the lanyard was jerked and a ten inch shot went howling along, ricocheted and bounded through the smoke stack of the "Susquehanna."

This was the commencement of the most terrific bombardment from the fleet which war had ever witnessed. Ship after ship discharged its broadside, every description of deadly missile, from a three inch rifle bolt to a fifteen inch shell flying wildly into and over the fort, until the garrison flagstaff was shattered. Most of the firing seemed directed towards it and as it stood in the center of the parade, all these bolts fell harmless as to human life, many of the shells, especially rifle shots, going over the fort and into the river in the rear. The dead calm which prevailed in nature caused the smoke to hang around the hulls of the vessels, so enveloping them as to prevent the effect of the shots our gunners were allowed to fire from being seen. It was two hours after the bombardment commenced before the flag was shot away, and in that time although thousands of shot and shell were hurled at us, I had heard of no casualty in the works. For these two hours I had remained on the parapet of the sea watching intently for any effort to cross the bar, and in all that time only one shell had exploded near enough to endanger my life. In the rear of the flagstaff the wooden quarters of the garrison were situated, and these were soon set on fire by the bursting shells and more than one half of them were consumed. The day being balmy most of the men had left their overcoats and blankets in their bunks and these were consumed. There was quite a quantity of naval stores, tar and pitch, near these quarters and they took fire and made an imposing bonfire in sympathy with the occasion.

As soon as the garrison flag was shot away, finding the shaft so split and slivered that it could not be raised, I sent word to Captain Munn to raise the flag on the mound. It seems that the halyards had gotten unreeled and it was necessary to climb the staff to fasten the flag. Private Christopher C. Bland of Company K, Thirty-six North Carolina Regiment, volunteered for the service and climbed the staff under heavy fire and secured the battle flag to the masthead. At once a terrific fire was poured on the mound and the lower end of the flag having been cut loose, again that heroic soldier repeated the daring act amid the cheers of the garrison and securely fastened the flag where it floated in triumph although torn and rent by fragments of shells, until the victory was won. While this was being done I went to the left salient and planted a company battle flag on the extreme left. My two hours experience had taught me that the fleet would concentrate a heavy fire on it and I wanted to put it where it would do the most good by causing the least harm.

For five hours this tremendous hail of shot and shell was poured upon the devoted works, but with little effect. At 5:50 p.m. the fleet withdrew.

The fleet to our surprise made no effort to cross the bar and run by our guns. One vessel inside would have ended the fight. Our guns and work would have been taken in reverse. The fort was built to prevent the passage of the bar and remembering Mobile and New Orleans we did not regard the battle as seriously begun, until the American Navy, with its accustomed dash, attempted a passage of the fort. It was this that made me reserve my fire, for nothing tempted me to waste my short supply of ammunition, not even the glory of sinking one of the hostile fleet. I rigidly carried out the thirty minute rule, except when some vessel would be unusually impudent and spiteful, and I would personally direct several guns to bear on her and fire until she had apparently received a merited punishment. During the whole day in answer to at least 10,000 shots, I only fired 672 projectiles. It was this deliberation which gave the fleet the false idea that they had silenced our guns, and the fact on this day I came to fire the last shot as they were withdrawing did not disabuse their minds of this erroneous idea. Not a detachment was driven from the gun chamber.

In the first day's fight I had about one-half of the quarters burned, three gun carriages disabled, a light artillery caisson exploded, large quantities of the earth work torn and plowed up, with some revetments broken and splintered, but not a single bomb proof or a magazine injured. Only 23 men wounded, one mortally, three seriously and 19 slightly.

Never since the invention of gun powder was there so much harmlessly expended, as in the first day's attack on Fort Fisher. All was quiet during the night, but next morning, Christmas day, at about 10 o'clock the great fleet again moved in towards the fort, being reinforced by another monitor and some additional wooden ships of war. At half past 10 o'clock the Ironsides opened and the fleet commenced an incessant bombardment, if possible more noisy and furious than that of the preceding day. About 2 o'clock several of the frigates came up to the bar and lowered boats, apparently to sound the entrance, but a heavy fire was immediately directed against them and they were promptly driven out. At 3:30 a very gallant attempt was made by a number of barges to sound the Carolina shoals, south of the mound. A few shots from Battery Buchanan, the naval battery in my command, first cut the flag from a barge and then cut the barge in two, causing the remainder after rescuing their comrades, to retreat rapidly.

My two seven inch Brooke rifles both exploded in the afternoon of this day. Being manned by a detachment of sailors and situated opposite to the bar I had given the officer in charge discretion to fire upon the vessels which had approached the bar, and his fire had been more rapid than from any other guns, and with this disastrous result, the explosion wounding a number of men.

Strange as it may appear no attempt to pass the fort was made by any of the fleet, and none except the armored vessels came within a mile of our heaviest guns. Whether the smoke obscured the fort or the gunners were untrained, it is hard to account for the wild firing of these two days. If they had tried to miss the guns on the sea-face they could not have succeeded better, no gun or carriage on that face being injured by the fire of the fleet, the only guns disabled were the two Brooke rifles which exploded. All the disabled guns were on the land-face, which was enfiladed by the fleet as well as subjected to the direct fire of the armored ships which came within a half mile of the fort. With the exception of the Brooke battery and some special firing on some vessels the firing of the fort was slower and more deliberate than on the previous day, only six hundred shot and shell being expended. The temptation to concentrate the whole of the available fire of the fort on a single frigate and drive her out and destroy her was very great, as I found that the garrison were disappointed at having so much trophy for the first days engagement, but I had a limited supply of ammunition and did not know when it could be replenished. Already on the first day I had expended nearly one-sixth of my supply in merely keeping the men in heart by an occasional shot. I could easily have fired every shot and shell away the first day. Admiral Porter expended all of his ammunition in the two days bombardment. The "Minnesota" fired 1,982 shots and the "Colorado" 1,569 shots, a total for these two frigates of 3,551, about as many as we had in all the batteries of Fort Fisher. On both days I fired the last gun to let our naval visitors know that we had another shot left in the locker. In the bombardment the second day the most of the remaining quarters were destroyed, more of the earth works were displaced, but none seriously damaged, and five guns were disabled by the enemy. The greatest penetration noticed (from fifteen inch shell) was five feet perpendicularly. During the day a large fleet of transports were seen up the beach and the enemy landed a large force at Battery Anderson, three miles up the beach. At half past four p.m., sharpshooters were seen on our left flank and they fired upon our gunners from the old quarters across the causeway and killed a young courier who had been, without my knowledge, sent out of the fort, capturing his horse. I had two pieces of artillery run out of the sally port and a few discharges of the canister stopped the annoyance. At this time, on the 25th, my effective force had been increased to 921 regulars and 450 junior reserves, total 1,371.

At 5:30 p.m. a most furious enfilading fire against the landface and palisade line commenced certainly never surpassed in warfare, a 130 shot and shell per minute, more than two every second. I ordered my men to protect themselves behind the traverses, and removed all extra men from the chambers, with the order, the moment the firing stopped to rally to the ramparts without further orders.

Fort Fisher gunners return the fire of the Federal fleet. Drawing printed in the March 15, 1865 issue of the Illustrates London News.

As soon as this commenced I saw a heavy line of skirmishers advancing on our works. Just as the naval fire ceased the guns were manned and I opened with grape and canister, and as it was becoming too dark to see the advance from the ramparts, threw 800 men and boys behind the palisades, which had been scarcely injured. I never shall forget the gallant youths which I rallied that night to meet the enemy. I had ordered all to man the parapets as soon as the naval fire ceased, as I supposed it would be followed by an assault. I thought the junior reserves were coming up too slowly and I called out rather impatiently "Don't be cowards, boys," when one manly little officer rushed over the work followed by his companions, shouting "We are no cowards, Colonel," and manned the palisades. I ordered them not to fire until the enemy was within a few feet of the palisades, but the whistle of bullets from Butler's skirmish line so excited them that in spite of my orders they kept up a fusillade until the enemy retired.

I was determined to meet the enemy at the palisade, feeling confident that the few who reached it would easily be captured or repulsed. I had the land guns, heavy and light, manned, with orders to fire grape and canister whenever they saw an advance in force, and the operators stood ready upon my orders to explode some of the sub-terra torpedoes. I stood upon the parapet to the left of the center sally port after giving directions in person to the officers on the land-front. The fleet had ceased except for an occasional shell from the ironclads down this face. The Federal sharpshooters were firing wildly in the darkness at our ramparts, but the bullets which were few and far between went harmless over our heads. My plan was to open with grape and canister on the assaulting column, and when its front reached the palisade, to open the infantry fire, and explode a line of torpedoes in their rear to stop the reinforcing line. I am confident that this would have resulted in a repulse of the main body and the capture of the first line. But Butler with wise discretion determined not to assault. There were not enough Federal troops landed to have stormed our palisade that Christmas night. If the assaulted column could have reached the comparatively uninjured palisades through the fire of canister and grape, the explosion and infantry fire would have resulted in their capture or destruction. My own uneasiness was from a boat attack in the rear between the mound and battery Buchanan, where a thousand sailors and marines could have landed with little opposition at that time and attack us in the rear. About 3 o'clock a.m. it was reported that such an advance was being made, and I sent Maj. Reilly with two companies to repulse them, following shortly after in person with a third company to reinforce him. A heavy rain and windstorm had arisen at midnight, and if such a movement was contemplated it was abandoned. Two prisoners from the One Hundred and Forty Second New York were captured in our front at night, and the next morning a number of new graves were seen on the beach and an officer's sword and some small arms were found. Our casualties for the second day were: Killed 3; wounded mortally 2; severely 7; slightly 26; Total for the two days 3 killed and 61 wounded.

Just before the close of the first day's bombardment Gen. Whiting and staff came into the fort and remained until the enemy departed. His presence was encouraging to the officers and men, who were devoted to him, and his disregard of danger inspired the men with courage to stand by their guns under the terrific fire of the fleet.

It is remarkable what a mistaken idea Admiral Porter and many of the commanders in his fleet had of conditions of the fort after the first attack. They claimed to have silenced the guns of the fort and that a few hundred men could have taken it on Christmas night. Capt. Alden, of the "Brooklyn," voiced this impression when, in his official report, he said: "The rebels I am satisfied considered from the moment

Major General William H. C. Whiting

that our troops obtained a footing on the shore, the work, (battered as it was) was untenable and were merely waiting for some one to come and take it," and that if the troops had not been recalled 'they would have been in it before dark and in quiet possession without firing a shot."

I know that they could not have captured Fort Fisher, and I agree with Gen. Whiting that but for the supineness of Gen. Bragg, the 3,500 men who were landed would have been captured on Christmas night, and it is incomprehensible why he should have allowed the 700 demoralized troops who were forced to remain on the beach on the night of the 26th of December escape unmolested.

Gen. Butler was severely criticized and retired from active service, because he failed to capture the works. For this he had himself to blame to a great extent. On the evening of December the 25th, without waiting for official reports, he listened to camp gossip and wrote as follows to Admiral Porter:

"Gen. Weitzel advanced his skirmish line within fifty yards of the Fort, while the garrison was kept in their bomb proofs by the fire of the navy, and so closely that three or four men of the picket line ventured upon the parapet and through the sally port of the work, capturing a horse which they brought off, killing the orderly, who was a bearer of a dispatch from the Chief of Artillery of Gen. Whiting, to bring a light battery within the fort, and also brought away from the para*pet* the flag of the fort."

This absurd statement was sent North and has gotten a lodgment in current history and is repeated in Gen. Grant's "Memoirs," although Gen. Butler corrected the error in his official report. No Federal soldier entered Fort Fisher during this attack except as a prisoner. The courier was sent out of the fort without my knowledge and was killed and the horse captured within the enemy's lines and the flag captured was a company flag which I had placed on the extreme left of the work and which was carried away and thrown off the parapet by an enfilading mine shot from the navy.

The garrison of Fort Fisher was composed altogether of North Carolinians. After the repulse of the enemy, although some important guns were destroyed by the bombardment and by the explosion, very little was done to repair damages. Requisitions were made for additional ammunition especially for hand grenades to repulse assaults, but it was impossible to obtain what was needed. Application was made for the placing of marine torpedoes where the ironclads had anchored and whither they returned, but nothing was done. Although it was known that the fleet would return, Gen. Bragg withdrew the supporting army from Sugar Loaf and marched it to a camp sixteen miles distant, and there had a grand review. The fort was not even advised of the approach of the fleet, but its arrival was reported from Fort Fisher to headquarters in Wilmington.

At night on January 12th, 1865, I saw from the ramparts of the fort the lights of the great armada, as one after another appeared above the horizon. I commenced at once to prepare for action. I had in the works but 800 men, the Thirty-sixth North Carolina regiment, at least 100 of whom were unfit for duty. Daylight disclosed the return of the most formidable fleet that ever floated on the sea, supplemented by transports carrying 8,500 men, and soon there rained upon fort and beach a storm of shot and shell which caused both earth and sea to tremble.

I had telegraphed for reinforcements and during the day and night following about 700 men arrived, companies of North Carolina, light and heavy artillery, and a detachment of 50 sailors and marines of the Confederates States Navy, giving me 1,500 men all told up to the morning of January 15th, including sick and slightly wounded. Friday the 13th, in the midst of the bombardment, Gen. Whiting and his staff arrived. They walked from Battery Buchanan, and the General came to me and said, "Lamb, my boy, I have come to share your fate. You and your garrison are to be sacrificed." I replied, "Don't say so, General; we shall certainly whip the enemy again." He then told me that when he left Wilmington Gen. Bragg was hastily removing his stores and ammunition and was looking for a place to fall back upon. I offered him the command which he refused, saying he would counsel and advise, but leave me to conduct the defense.

In the former bombardment the fire of the fleet had been diffuse, at least one third of the missiles fell in the river beyond the fort, but now the fire was concentrated, the object being the destruction of the land-face by enfilade and direct fire. When attacked in December I had for the forty-four guns and three mortars in the works, about 3,600 shot and shell, and in that fight we had fired 1,272 shot and shell leaving about 2,328, exclusive of grape and shrapnel, to resist the assaults by sea and land.

The same slow and deliberate firing was ordered as in the previous battle, as no attempt was made by the ships to run past the fort and into the river. Occasionally a vessel would come close in towards the bar, when the guns of the several batteries would be concentrated upon her and she would quickly withdraw before being seriously injured. All day and night on 13th and 14th of January the fleet kept up a ceaseless and terrific bombardment. It was impossible to repair damages on the land-face at night, for the ironsides and monitors bowled their eleven and fifteen-inch shells along its parapet, scattering shrapnel in the darkness. No meals could be prepared for the exhausted garrison; we could scarcely bury our dead without fresh casualties. Fully 200 of my men had been killed and wounded, in the first two days of the fight. Not more than three or four of my land guns were serviceable. The Federal army had been slowly approaching on the river side during the day, but they were so covered by the river bank that we could only surmise their number. They had passed my cottage at Craig's Landing and occupied the redoubt about half a mile from our left salient. We fired occasionally at their approaching columns, but at fearful cost as it drew upon the gunners the fury of the fleet. Early in the afternoon of the 14th I saw the "Isaac Wells," a steam transport loaded with stores, approach Craig's Landing, which was in the enemy's lines. We fired at her to warn her off, but on she came, falling an easy captive to the foe. The Confederate steamer "Chickamauga" seeing her stupid surrender fired into and sunk her. This incident gave me the first intimation that Gen. Bragg was shamefully ignorant and indifferent to the situation of affairs.

From the conformation of the Cape Fear river, Gen. Bragg could have passed safely from his headquarters at Sugar Loaf towards Smithville, and with a field glass have seen everything transpiring on the beach and in the fort, and in person or through an aide, with the steamers at his command, could have watched every movement of the enemy, and yet thirty-six hours after the battle had begun, and long after Craig's Landing had been in the possession of the enemy, he sends into the enemy's lines a steamer filled with needed stores that could have gone at night to Battery Buchanan unseen, and in the day with comparative safety. There was a telegraphic and signal communication between Fort Fisher and Bragg's headquarters and I got Gen. Whiting to telegraph him to attack the enemy under cover of night when the fleet could not co-operate, and that we would do the same from the fort, and as our combined force nearly equaled them in numbers, and my garrison was familiar with the beach at night, we could capture a portion if not the whole of the force. Strange to say, no response of any kind came. I had ten companies ready for a sortie, and through skirmishers had discovered the position of the enemy in our front.

We waited in vain: for Gen. Bragg to avail himself of this opportunity to demoralize if not capture the besieging forces, and just before daylight our skirmishers returned to the fort.

On the morning of the 15th, the fleet which had not ceased firing during the night, redoubled its fire on the land-face. The sea was smooth, and the navy having become accurate from practice, by noon had destroyed every gun on that face except one Columbiad, which was somewhat protected by the angle formed by the northeast salient. The palisade had been practically destroyed as a defensive line and was so torn up that it actually afforded cover for the assailants. The harvest of wounded and dead was hourly increasing and at that time I had not 1,200 effective men to defend the long line of works. The enemy were now preparing to assault, their skirmish lines were digging rifle pits close to our torpedo lines on the left, and their columns on the river shore were massing for the attack, while sharpshooters were firing upon every head that showed itself upon our front. Despite the imminent danger to the gunners, I ordered the two Napoleons at the central sally port and the Napoleon on the left to fire grape and canister upon the advancing skirmish line. They fearlessly obeyed, but at a sad sacrifice in killed and wounded. At the same time on the ocean side a column of sailors and marines, two thousand strong, were approaching, throwing up slight trenches to protect their advance. On these we brought to bear our single heavy gun on the land-face and the two guns on the mound.

Shortly after noon Gen. Bragg sent Hagood's South Carolina brigade, consisting of four regiments and one battalion, about one thousand strong, under Col. Graham, from Sugar Loaf by the river to reinforce the fort landing them near Battery Buchanan. The fleet, seeing the steamer landing troops, directed a portion of their fire towards her and although she was not struck and we believe no casualties occurred, after landing a portion of the men, (two of the regiments) ingloriously steamed off with the remainder. Never was there a more stupid blunder committed by a commanding general. If this fresh brigade had been sent to this point the night before they could have reached the fort unobserved, could have been protected until needed, and could have easily repulsed the assault by the army on our left; but landed in view of the fleet they had to double quick over an open beach to the mound under a heavy fire. When they reached the fort, 350 in number, they were out of breath, disorganized, and more or less demoralized. They reached our front about thirty minutes before the attacking columns came like avalanches on our right and left. I sent them into an old commissary bomb proof to recover breath.

My headquarters during the fight were at the Pulpit battery on the sea-face, 100 yards from the northeast salient, which commanded the best view of the works and their approaches by sea and land. At 2:30, as I was returning from another battery, one of my lookouts called to me, "Colonel, the enemy are about to charge!" I informed Gen. Whiting, who was near, and at my request he immediately telegraphed Gen. Bragg at Sugar Loaf as follows:

"The enemy is about to assault; they outnumber us heavily. We are just manning our parapets. Fleet have extended down the sea-front outside and are firing very heavily. Enemy on the beach in front of us in very heavy force, not more than 700 yards from us. Nearly all land guns disabled. Attack! Attack! It is all I can say and all you can do!"

I passed hurriedly down in rear of the land-face and through the galleries, and although the fire of the fleet was still terrific, I knew it would soon cease, and I ordered additional sharpshooters to the gun chambers to pick off the officers in the assaulting columns and directed the battery commanders to rush with their men upon the parapets as soon as the firing stopped and drive the assailants back. I determined to allow the assailants to reach the berme of the work before exploding a line of torpedoes, believing it would enable us to kill or capture their first line, while destroying or demoralizing their supports.

I had not reached Headquarters when the naval bombardment ceased, and instantly the steam whistles of the vast fleet sounded a charge. It was a soul stirring signal both to the besiegers and the besieged.

I ordered by aide, Lieut. Charles H. Blocker, to double quick the Twenty-first and Twenty-fifth South Carolina to reinforce Maj. Reilly who was in command of the left, while I rallied to the right of the land-face some 500 of the garrison, placing the larger portion of them on top of the parapet adjoining the northeast salient. There were at least 250 men defending the left, and with the 350 South Carolinians ordered there and the Napoleon and torpedoes, I had no fears about the successful defense of that portion of the work.

The assaulting line on the right, consisting of 2,000 sailors and marines, was directed at the northeast salient at the intersection of the land and sea-faces, and the greater proportion had flanked the torpedoes by keeping close to the sea. Ordering the two Napoleons at the sally port to join the Columbiad in pouring grape and canister into their ranks, I held in reserve the infantry fire. Whiting stood upon the parapet inspiring those around him. The sailors and marines reached the berme and sprang up the slope, but a murderous fire greeted them and swept them down. Volley after volley was poured into their faltering ranks by cool, determined men, and in half an hour several hundred dead and wounded lay at the foot of the bastion. The heroic bravery of their officers, twenty-one of whom were killed and wounded, could not restrain the men from panic and retreat, and with small loss to ourselves, we witnessed what had never been seen before, a disorderly rout of American sailors and marines. But it was a Pyrrhic victory. That magnificent charge of the American navy upon the center of our works, enabled the army to effect a lodgment on our left with comparatively small loss.

As our shouts of triumph went up at the retreat of the naval forces; I turned to look at our left and saw to my amazement several Federal battle flags upon our ramparts. Gen. Whiting saw them at the same moment, and calling on those around him to pull down those flags and drive the enemy from the works, rushed towards them followed by the men on the parapet. It was in this charge that the fearless Lieut. Williford was slain.

In order to make an immediate reconnaissance of the position of the enemy, I rushed through the sally port, and outside the work and witnessed a fierce hand to hand conflict for the possession of the fourth gun chamber from the left bastion. The men led by the fearless Whiting had driven the standard bearer from the top of the traverse and the enemy from the parapet in front. They had recovered one gun chamber with great slaughter, and on the parapet and on the long traverse of the next gun chamber the contestants were savagely firing into each other's faces, and in some cases clubbing their guns, being too close to load and fire. Whiting was quickly wounded by two shots and had to be carried to the hospital. I saw that my men were not only exposed to the fire from the front, but to a galling infantry fire from the left salient which had been captured. I saw the enemy pouring in it by the river road apparently without resistance. I doubt if ever before the commander of a work went outside and looked upon the conflict for its possession, but from the construction of the fort it was absolutely necessary for me to do so in order to quickly comprehend the position of affairs, and I was concealed from that portion of the army not too hotly engaged to notice me, by remnants of the palisade. Ordering Capt. Adams, who was at the entrance of the sally port, to turn his Napoleons on the column moving into the fort, I re-entered the work and rallying the men, placed them behind every cover that could be found, and poured at close range a deadlier fire into the flank of the enemy occupying the gun chambers and traverses than they were able to deliver upon my men from the left salient.

While thus engaged I was informed by my Aide Cpt. Blocker that the South Carolinians had failed to obey my order, although their officers pleaded with them, and only a few had followed their flag and gone to the front; that the assaulting column had made two charges upon the extreme left, and had been repulsed, that the torpedo wires had been destroyed by the fire of the fleet and the electrician had tried in vain to execute my orders to explode the mines when the enemy reached the foot of the works; that driven from the extreme left the enemy had found a weak defense between the left bastion and the sally port in their third charge, and had gained the parapet, and capturing two gun chambers, had attacked the force on the left on their flank simultaneously with a direct charge of another brigade and that our men after great slaughter had been compelled to surrender just as we had repulsed the naval column; that to add to the discomfiture of the Confederates, as soon as the Federal battle flags appeared on the ramparts Battery Buchanan had opened with its two heavy guns on the left of the work, killing and wounding friend and foe alike. This was rather disheartening, but I replied if we could hold the enemy in check until dark, I could drive them out, and I sent a telegram by him to Gen. Bragg imploring him to attack, and that I could still save the fort.

While I shall ever believe, that if my order to man the parapet had been obeyed all along the line on the left, the assaulting column would have been repulsed until I could have reinforced my men, and I would have been able to hold the fort on that fatal Sunday afternoon, yet Gen. Bragg in his official report does gross injustice when he says: "The army column preceded by a single regiment approached along the river and entered the work on that flank almost unopposed." Gen. Terry says in his report that 100 sharpshooters with Spencer repeating Carbines were sent forward to within seventy-five yards of the work and dug pits for their shelter, and "as soon as this movement commenced the parapet of the fort was manned and the enemy's fire both musketry and artillery opened." The assaulting column consisted not of a regiment, but of Curtis' brigade, supported closely by two other brigades, a total of not less than 5,000 troops.

The enemy was unable to enter by the river road, and some of the most desperate fighting done in the work was in the space between the left bastion and the river shore.

Judge Z. E. Fulmore, of Austin, Tex., who proved himself a young hero in the fight, wrote me in 1883:

"Company D, First Battalion North Carolina artillery, Capt. McCormic, was the company in the extreme left of the fort, occupying the space on both sides of the Napoleon, and although protected only by a shallow ditch and the remnants of a palisade, successfully repulsed every charge made by Curtis' brigade in front and compelled the charging columns to abandon this usually traveled but unprotected entrance to the fort and to go off to the right to climb the high parapets in order to get into the fort, some fifty yards to the right and back of us. The portion of Company D, which was stationed to the right of the Napoleon saw the breaking of our lines to the right in time to retreat behind the parapet, but that portion of the company on the left some fifteen or twenty in number, stood their ground until Pennypacker's charging columns commenced their slaughter from the rear. Four of this company were killed at the Napoleon. There was another piece, however, a Parrott gun, just on the edge of the river which we used once or twice very effectively in blowing to atoms a bridge on the main road into the fort, some 200 feet in the front of the gate. At the first charge the boys at the Napoleon made a shot which cleared that road and caused many to take refuge under that bridge, and I was told by the officers in charge of us after our capture, that the destruction of that bridge impressed the Federals that that was one of the many mines exploded and to be exploded under them, and the officers couldn't charge the soldiers any further down that road on account of it. On the afternoon of the day of the last fight my recollection is that there were eleven men killed and seventeen wounded in Company B, during the three charges, and if successfully defending the most defenseless spot in all Fort Fisher against Curtis' Brigade and early surrendering after being completely surrounded by another brigade, isn't pretty good evidence of true soldiery, I would be glad to see a specimen of it."

Judge Fulmore did not mention that before his company took charge of this Napoleon, the original detachment from Adams' battery had lost three of its gunners killed and two seriously wounded, not leaving men enough to man it. Seven men killed at one field piece by sharpshooters in thirty minutes, and many wounded, and the gun had not surrendered until after surrounded by the brigade, should have paralyzed the arm of that North Carolinian, who in the "last ninety days of the war," said "that no resistance was made and the conduct of the garrison had been disgraceful." A number of those who were captured on the left have told me that when they were marched out of the fort as prisoners they saw their front thickly strewn with dead and wounded Federals.

Gen. N. M. Curtis, the fearless hero who led the assaulting columns of the army, informed me in 1888 that he saw a portion of the parapet joining the left salient unmanned, and it was at this point he succeeded in making a lodgment and that if he had been stoutly resisted from the top of the parapet, he could not have then succeeded. The guns immediately to the right of Shepperd's battery were manned by some of my bravest officers and men, but the fatal mistake of the Commander was fighting from behind the revetment instead of from the top of the parapet, as ordered. Only two of the men mounted the parapet and they were instantly shot down. One was Bob Harvey, a recklessly brave boy, the last male member of an old family of Bladen county. I have been unable to learn of the name of his heroic companion. From behind the revetments these gallant men poured a destructive fire on the assailants as they reached the parapet and the enemy fell thick and fast in their front, but they were too few to load and fire in time to stop the ever increasing column, and soon the assailants were firing down upon them, and they were forced to surrender, although refusing at first to do so. Had they been on top of the parapet they could have used their bayonets or clubbed their guns, and thus delayed a lodgment until reinforcements came.

In justice to Maj. Reilly and the officers on the left, it must be remembered, that as is usual in the defense of a fort and breastworks to cover the men and fire upon the assailants from behind the works, but Fort Fisher was built to stand a naval bombardment and the magnitude of the work and great width of parapet gave opportunity for an assaulting column to protect itself under cover of its outer slope, and I knew my only hope of repelling greatly superior numbers was to man the palisades, as in the first battle, or in their absence, being destroyed by the fleet, to man the top of the parapet and fire down upon the assaulting columns.

Notwithstanding the capture of a portion of the work and several hundred of the garrison, the Confederates were still undaunted and seemed determined to recover the captured salient and gun chambers. We had retaken one of these in the charge led by Whiting, and since we had opened on their flank we had shot down their standard bearers and the Federal battle flags had disappeared from our ramparts; we had become assailants and the enemy were on the defensive, and I felt confident that we would soon drive them out of the fort. Just as the tide of battle seemed to have turned in our favor, the remorseless fleet came to the rescue of the faltering Federals. Suddenly the bombardment which had been consigned to the sea-face during the assaults turned again on our land front and with deadly precision. The ironclads and frigates drove in our two Napoleons, killing and wounding nearly all the men at these guns, which had been doing effective service at the entrance to the sally port. They swept the recaptured gun chamber of its defenders, and their 11 and 15 inch shells rolled down into the interior of the work, carrying death and destruction in their pathways. They drove from the parapets in front of the enemy all of my men except those so near that to have fired on them would have been slaughter to their own troops.

Nor was this all. We had now to contend with a column advancing around the rear of the left bastion by the river into the interior plane of the fort. It moved slowly and cautiously, apparently in column of companies and in close order. I met it with an effective infantry fire, my men using the remains of an old work as a breastwork and taking advantage of every object that would offer cover, for we were now greatly outnumbered. The fire was so unexpected and so destructive, combined with the shells from Battery Buchanan, on the massed columns of the Federals, that they halted, when a quick advance would have overwhelmed us. Giving orders to dispute stubbornly any advance, I went rapidly down the sea-face and turned the two mound guns and two Columbiads on this column in the fort. Unfortunately these were the only ones available. I brought back with me to the front every man except a single, detachment for each gun. On my return I found the fighting still continuing over the same traverse for the possession of that gun chamber, despite the fire of the fleet. As the men would fall, others would take their places. It was a soldiers fight at the point, for there could be no organization; the officers on both sides were loading and firing with their men. If there ever was a longer or more desperate hand to hand fight during the war, I have never heard of it. The Federal column inside had not advanced a foot, and seemed demoralized by the fire of the artillery and the determined resistance of the garrison. More than a hundred of my men had come with me and I threw them in front with those already engaged. Going to the South Carolinians who were in a position to flank the enemy, I appealed to them to rally and help save the fort. I went to the sally port and had Adams' two Napoleons brought out and manned, and opened on the enemy. I went along the galleries and begged the sick and slightly wounded to come out and make one supreme effort to dislodge the enemy; as I passed through portions of the work, the scene was indescribably horrible. Great cannon broken in two, their carriages wrecked and among their ruins the mutilated bodies of my dead and dying comrades. Still no tidings from Bragg! The enemy's advance had ceased entirely, protected by the fleet they still held the parapet and gun chambers on the left, but their massed columns refused to move while those in the rear, near the river, commenced entrenching against any assault from us. I believed a determined assault with the bayonet would drive them out. I had sent word to our gunners not to fire on our men if we become closely engaged with the enemy. The head of their column was not over a hundred feet from the portion of our breastwork where I stood, and I could see their faces distinctly, while my men were falling on either side of me.

I passed quickly down the rear of the line and asked officers and men if they would follow me; they all responded fearlessly that they would. I returned to my position and giving the order "charge bayonets," sprang upon the breastwork, waved my sword, and as I gave the command "forward, double quick, march!" fell on my knees, a rifle ball having entered my hip. The brave Lieut. Daniel R. Perry fell mortally wounded by my side. We were met by a heavy volley aimed too high to be very effective, but our column wavered and fell back behind the breastworks. A soldier raised me up and I turned the command over to Capt. Munn, who was near me, and told him to keep the enemy in check and that as soon as my wound was bandaged I would return. Before reaching the hospital I was so weak from the loss of blood that I realized I could never lead my men again. In the hospital 1 met Gen. Whiting, suffering uncomplainingly from his wounds. He told me that Gen. Bragg had ignored his presence in the fort and had not noticed his messages.

Perceiving the fire of the garrison had slackened, I sent my adjutant, John N. Kelly, for Maj. James Reilly, next in command, (Maj. Stevenson, who died shortly after in prison, being too ill for duty). Reilly came and promised me that he would continue the fight as long as it was possible and nobly did he keep his promise. I again sent a message to Bragg begging him to come to the rescue. Shortly after my fall the Federals made an advance, and capturing several more of the gun chambers reached the sally port. The column in the work advanced and was rapidly gaining ground when Maj. Reilly, rallying the men including the South Carolinians, drove them back with heavy loss. About 8 o'clock my Aide came to me and said the supply of ammunition was exhausted and that Chaplain McKinnon had gathered all from the dead and wounded and distributed it; that the enemy had possession of nearly all the land-face, and it was impossible to hold out much longer and suggested that it would be wise to surrender, as a further struggle would be a useless sacrifice of life. I replied that while I lived I would not surrender as Bragg would surely come to our rescue in time to save us. Gen. Whiting declared if I died he would assume command and would not surrender.

I have been blamed for unnecessarily prolonging the fight, but when it is remembered that I had promised the noble women of Wilmington who had visited the fort after our Christmas victory, that their homes should be protected by my garrison, and that Gen. Lee had sent word that if the fort fell he could not maintain his army, (and that meant the loss of our cause) is it to be wondered that I felt it my sacred duty, even after I was shot down, to appeal to officers and men to fight in defense of the last gateway to the South, as there was a ray of hope?

I had a right to believe that the troops which Gen. Lee sent to our assistance would rescue us, and if Bragg had ordered Hoke to assault with his divisions late that afternoon we would have recovered the works. I have positive information that so positive was our resistance that Gen. Terry sent word to Gen. Ame's, commanding the three brigades assaulting us to make one more effort, and if unsuccessful to retire. Gen. Abbott, who commanded a brigade, and who lived in North Carolina after the war, told Capt. Braddy that at one time during our fight, only one colored brigade held Bragg's army in check, and they were so demoralized that 500 veteran troops could have captured them. But an all wise Providence decreed that our gallant garrison should be overwhelmed.

In less than an hour after I refused to surrender, a fourth brigade (three were already in the fort), entered the sally port and swept the defenders from the remainder of the land-face. Maj. Reilly had Gen. Whiting and myself hurriedly removed on stretchers to Battery Buchanan where he proposed to cover his retreat. When we left the hospital the men were fighting over the adjoining traverse and the spent balls fell like hailstones around us. The remnant of the garrison then fell back in an orderly retreat along the sea-face, the rear guard keeping the enemy engaged as they advanced slowly and cautiously in the darkness as far as the Mound Battery, where they halted. Some of the men, cut off from the main body, had to retreat as best they could over the river marsh, while some few unarmed artillerists barely eluded the enemy by following the seashore.

When we reached Battery Buchanan there was a mile of level beach between us and our pursuers, swept by two 11-inch guns and a 24-pounder, and in close proximity to the battery, a commodious wharf where transports could have come at night in safety to carry us off.

We expected with this battery to cover the retreat of our troops, but we found the guns spiked and every means of transportation taken by Capt. R. F. Chapman of our navy, who, following the example of Gen. Bragg, had abandoned us to our fate. The enemy threw out a heavy skirmish line and sent their Fourth brigade to Battery Buchanan, where it arrived about 10 p.m. and received the surrender of the garrison from Maj. James H. Hill and Lieut. George D. Parker. Some fifteen minutes before the surrender, while lying on a stretcher near Gen. Whiting, outside of the battery, witnessing the grand pyrotechnic display of the fleet over the capture of Fort Fisher, I was accosted by Gen. A. H. Colquitt, who had been ordered to the fort to take command. I had a few minutes hurried conversation with him, informed him of the assault, of the early loss of a portion of the work and garrison, and that when I fell it had been for a time demoralized by our unexpected resistance, and I assured him that if Bragg would even then attack, a fresh brigade landed at Battery Buchanan could retake the work. It was suggested that the General should take me with him as I was probably fatally wounded, but I refused to leave, wishing to share the fate of my garrison, and desiring that my precious wife anxiously awaiting tidings across the river, where she had watched the battle, should not be alarmed, spoke lightly of my wound. I asked him to carry Gen. Whiting to a place of safety as he came as a volunteer to the fort. Just then the near approach of the enemy was reported and Colquitt made a precipitate retreat leaving our beloved Whiting a captive to die in a Northern prison.

One more distressing scene remains to be chronicled. The next morning after sunrise a frightful explosion occurred. My large reserve magazine which my ordnance officer, Capt. J. C. Little, informed me contained some 13,000 pounds of powder, blew up, killing and wounding more than a hundred of the enemy and some of my own wounded officers and men. It was an artificial mound, covered with luxuriant turf, a most inviting bivouac for wearied soldiers. Upon it were resting Col. Alden's 169 New York regiment, and in its galleries were some of my suffering soldiers. Two sailors from the fleet, stupefied with liquor, looking for plunder, were seen to enter the structure with lights, and a few minutes after the explosion occurred. The telegraph wires, between a bomb proof near this magazine across the river to Battery Lamb, gave rise to the impression that the Confederates had caused the explosion, but an official investigation traced it to those drunken sailors.

So stoutly did our works resist the 50,000 shot and shell thrown against them in the two bombardments that not a magazine or bomb proof was injured, and after the land armament with palisades and torpedoes had been destroyed, no assault could have succeeded in the presence of Bragg's force, had it been under a competent officer. Had there been no fleet to assist the Army, at Fort Fisher, the Federal infantry could not have assaulted it until its land defenses had been destroyed by gradual approaches.

For the first time in the history of sieges, the land defenses of the work were destroyed, not by any act of the besieging party, which looked on in safety, but by the concentrated fire, direct and enfilading, of an immense fleet, poured upon them for three days and two nights without intermission until the guns were dismounted, torpedo wires cut, palisades breached, so that they afforded cover for assailants, and the slopes of the work rendered practicable for assault.

I had half a mile of land-face and one mile of sea-face to defend 1,900 men, for that is all I had from first to last in the last battle. I have in my possession papers to prove this statement; I know every company present and its strength. This number included the killed, wounded and sick. If the Federal reports claim that our killed, wounded and prisoners showed more, it is because they credited my force with those captured outside the works who were never under my command. To capture Fort Fisher the enemy lost, by their own statement, 1,445 killed, wounded and missing. Nineteen hundred Confederates with forty-four guns, contending against 10,000 men on shore and 600 heavy guns afloat, killing and wounding almost as many of the enemy as there were soldiers in the fort, and not surrendering until the last shot was expended.

When I recall this magnificent struggle, unsurpassed in ancient or modern warfare, and remember the devoted patriotism and heroic courage of my garrison, I feel proud to know that I have North

Carolina blood coursing through my veins, and I confidently believe that the time will come with the Old North State, when her people will regard her defense of Fort Fisher as the grandest event in her historic past.

Colonel William Lamb
June 15, 1893

Chapter 9

Soldier's Accounts of Battle

Private Albert Marion Baldwin

Company K., 40th North Carolina heavy artillery

The following letter appeared in the *Wilmington Morning Star News*, December 4, 1927

Dr. Albert Marion Baldwin, Confederate veteran, was born in Columbus County, February 9, 1845. He enlisted from Wilmington, Company K., 40th North Carolina heavy artillery, at the age of 18. "I was sent to Fort Fisher where I served one year and was then sent to Bald Head Island, where ten companies were stationed. Here I witnessed the first bombardment of Fort Fisher. I remained one year at Bald Head and was sent back with four other companies to the second bombardment. The coast from Carolina Beach was lined with gunboats about 50. The ironclads came near in shore. We could make no impression on them with our small guns. In front of Fort Fisher there was a channel called the New Channel. It has since filled in by building the wall from the lower end of Fort Fisher to Zeke's Island. This channel was valuable to the blockade runners. I saw the wreck Modern Greece. She was attacked by the Yankees and ran in near shore and was wrecked. She can still be seen off the seas beach at low tide—24 sister blockade runners shared her fate along our coast.

The fort faced the ocean a mile. About every 200 yards a 64-pound gun was mounted and manned by eight to ten men. The largest gun we had was the Armstrong gun. We only had it at the last. I was instructed to stand on tiptoe when the gun went off; I did, and was alright. The bombardment was too terrible to describe. It was a rain of fire, shot and shell over us three days and two nights. Our barracks were all burned. The bomb proofs saved some of us, when we could crawl in at night. When the firing ceased and we were captured, we were exhausted, but the Yankees marched us up the beach a mile. Here we camped, with a strong guard around us. They were kind. A soldier gave me something to eat from his haversack. We had no time to eat during the bombardment. We spent two nights on the beach. I had two blankets and the sand was soft. We were marched back and through the fort and put on two transports where the prisoners were taken through the New Channel into the ocean. There were 800 prisoners on the transport I was on.

Our captors were kind and kept the companies together. We put to sea, steaming due north. We entered the Delaware River, cutting through the ice. It was about the 20th of January, and the ice being so heavy our transport was ordered back and we put into New York harbor where we awaited orders from Washington, which was to proceed to Elmira. Our friends on the other transports were taken to Point Lookout. We were to have been sent to Fort Delaware, but our transport could not get through the ice we encountered. From New York we went by train to Elmira. Everything was covered in snow. Crowds came to look at us but no one said anything. We got off in the snow and marched a mile and a half to prison, but it seemed like 10 to me, leaving our southern climate, where I had been put to sleep with the rustling of the palm trees and the warm ocean winds from the Gulf Stream, it was a bitter exchange for this ice and snow—but so I entered my prison January 31, 1865. The officers and guards had icicles hanging from their moustaches. They paid no attention to it, but it was new to me, being from the South, where gentlemen wore no such ornaments.

My bed was a board—we slept in tiers of three along the wall, two to each tier. I occupied a center with a friend, James Lesesne, a member of my company and a comrade at Fort Fisher. I had held on to my two army blankets, and he had two, so we encountered the zero weather. We had two meals a day. We were marched by barracks, 100 to be fed at a time. We ate with our fingers, no plate, knife, fork or spoon. A thin slice of bread—with a thinner slice of meat—pork or corned beef—on it served as a plate. This was breakfast. The next meal and the last of the day was a cup of bean soup and a slice of bread, I was always glad to get the end slice, because it was a little thicker. I was so hungry I felt worse after eating than before. It was just a teaser what they gave me. One day James Lesesne received five dollars from a friend in Vermont, and then we felt as if we had come into a fortune, and so we had. We used it little by little, never more than 75 cents at the time for something to eat, cheese and crackers, which were bought from the sutler, the prison merchant. When money came it was posted on the bulletin board, and what glad news it was; some friend would tell us if we did not see it. I was so thin and weak and hungry that I felt like I was starving to death, and I was. I knew with the fall of Fort Fisher the South could not hold out much longer, and now the question was, would I hold out.

When a prisoner broke a rule he was marched around, up and down through the barracks with a barrel shirt on. The barrel shirt was a barrel with the heads knocked out and a place for the prisoner to put his arms through. The weather was getting better, snow and ice were melting and I could walk outside some days.

The news came, "Lee had surrendered!" Mr. C. C. Covington's uncle was the means of my getting released as soon as I did; he sent my name to Washington. At last the day came when we were ordered to the dining room under strong guard and on the way Lesesne saw on the bulletin board another five was waiting for him. We were so happy release was near. Lesesne was eager to hurry on, but I knew what the money had done for us and would do now, so I had consent to try and get it. I asked permission to see the treasurer, and a guard was given me, and I got the money and again laid in a supply of cheese and crackers. We had to take the oath, then we were marched through a large gate and on to the station.

I was in prison in Elmira four and a half months. I was released June 13, 1865. When I entered I was weighed and measured and a description taken of me. I was six feet and two inches tall and light in weight, 120 pounds, and far less now. From Elmira we went to Baltimore and took a boat to Old Point, changed to a smaller boat and went up the James River to Richmond, from there to Danville, in boxcars to Greensboro, Raleigh, Goldsboro and Wilmington, where I boarded the steamer A.P. Hurt, to Fayetteville, which was my home. My parents were not living, but my sister was there to welcome me—she did not recognize me when I appeared—I was so emaciated and had grown a long black beard. I spent my 20th birthday in prison."

Private Buckner Lanier Blackmore

2nd Co. A, 36th Regiment North Carolina Artillery

The following letter was published in the *Wilmington Messenger*, July 2, 1898

Warsaw, N. C. June 30th.

Editor Messenger:

I have read Col. William Lamb's address on Fort Fisher with a great deal of interest, and, having been engaged in the same memorable combat and an eye witness to the terrible scenes there enacted, I write this letter to add my testimonies to the truthfulness of Col. Lamb's statements and to bring out some new facts that the colonel unintentionally left out.

We being survivors of that sanguinary struggle, what we write may go down the ages into history. Therefore, it is very important that the reports should be full and the whole truth.

One of the new points I wish to bring out is the gallant and heroic defense made from the Mound Battery after the fleet had dismounted nearly all the big guns on the land face and the assault was about to be made by the enemy's infantry, as stated by Col. Lamb. The Mound Battery was manned by Company A, thirty-sixth regiment, North Carolina troops, commanded by Capt. Edward L. Faison, of Sampson, and better known as Maj. J. M. Stevenson's King Artillery. But I will mention right here that when it was seen that the enemy was going to assault the land face fully one-half of Company A under Lieut. Joshua Sawles (Sowles), of Columbus, was sent to join Col. Lamb and Gen. Whiting's infantry force. They were collecting to assist and repel the assaulting columns of the enemy, which they did so nobly, as described by Col. Lamb. But just before the assault was made the fleet withdrew its fire from the land face and concentrated its whole aim and fire on the Mound Battery and the works nearby, striking the Mound with fully 500 shot and shell to the minute. This was the most terrific and rapid fire of heavy artillery ever directed at so small a space of fort or earthworks in the history of the known world. Nothing could be heard but the roar of cannon, the bursting of shells and the peculiar screams of broken fragments of shell and shot. We were surrounded by whole acres of smoke reddened with flame and all Federal Point seemed to rock as if caused by an earthquake.

It was during this frightful bombardment that Capt. Edward L. Faison, Ordinance Officer Harold E. Blackmore and the brave men of old Company A distinguished themselves by daring deeds and bravery that ought to have won for them a place in fame, as well as song and glory. It was during this fearful bombardment that the enemy succeeded in landing one fifteen inch shell and the only one they ever did land, inside the Mound Battery. The shell exploded, killing the gallant Sergeant B. F. Buffkin (William B. Bufkin), of Columbus County, and wounding nearly every man of the two detachments who were working the guns of the Mound Battery, some dangerously, others only slightly. But Capt. Faison immediately rallied his men and put a fresh detachment at the guns and continued the fight. In this particular combat we were fighting Porter's whole fleet, of 100 ships mounting 600 guns, with 50 men and 2 guns.

About this same time word reached the Mound that the fort had surrendered and Capt. Faison ordered the Confederate flag taken down, and some of the men cut the flag pole down with an axe. But it was soon discovered that the fort had not surrendered, as it was seen that Col. Lamb was leading his last charge on the enemy infantry, who were then coming in large numbers. This was the time the Colonel was wounded and carried to the hospital. As soon as this was discovered, Capt. Faison and Serg. Tim Strickland, of Duplin, With the help of others (I cannot recall their names now) re-erected the flag amidst that ruinous shower of shot and shell. It was then discovered that the Confederates were falling back toward the hospital battery, followed by the Federals, led by Gen. Curtis, I afterward learned. Major Reilly had then assumed command and was slowly but sullenly retiring along the sea face, disputing every inch of ground as he came, but, pressed by superior numbers continued to fall back. The fleet had withdrawn its fire from the Mound was again firing on some part of the land face.

It was seen that the enemy were pouring in at the bridge near the river beach in large numbers, and we trailed the Mound guns to them, one mile distant, with shell and spherical case. We kept up a steady fire on them until near sundown. This was on Sunday; the last day of the fight, January 15, 1865. I saw the effects of our shell about the bridge while marching out of the garrison as prisoners of war. We, like brave men, fought long and well; we piled that ground with foemen felled. But Maj. Reilly and his brave men continued to fall back, followed by the enemy in large numbers. When we saw all hope was lost we, too, fell back to the point or Battery Buchanan, and, finding the guns of the battery spiked and the fort or battery deserted by the marines, who manned those guns earlier in the day, there was nothing left to be done but surrender, which was did [sic], as stated by Col. Lamb.

While I would not detract one iota of the fame and good name of Col. Lamb, nor pluck a single laurel from his brow, as he was a good commander, and brave indeed and well beliked [sic] by all his men, and my feelings towards him are of the kindest, yet whether it could have been best to surrender the fort after all the guns on the land face were dismounted and his ammunition nearly exhausted and all chances of repulsing the enemy were lost, and there by save the lives of a large number of men, who afterward died in Northern prisons. (Out of thirty-six men of Company A who went to Elmira, N. Y. only four returned to North Carolina. I suppose those who went to Point Lookout shared the same fate) I will leave to future impartial historians and generations unborn to answer.

Sergeant Thaddeus C. Davis

Co. G, 40th Regiment, 3rd North Carolina Light Artillery

This article reprinted from *Histories of Several Regiments and Battalions From North Carolina,* Volume II, written by Walter Clark

At the first attack on Fort Fisher, and during the bombardment, 24 and 25 December, 1864, Companies E and K, of this regiment, reinforced that command, after which the enemy's land force re-embarked, and withdrew, leaving Fort Fisher slightly injured.

On 13 January, 1865, we were ordered to reinforce Fort Fisher, Companies D, E, G, K of the Fortieth Regiment, embarked on the steamer *Pettaway*, and arrived at Confederate Point about dark, where we landed by wading waist deep in water to reach the beach, under fire from the fleet, and took our position at the guns and palisades on the land face of the fort, where firing was kept up at short intervals, until daylight, when the whole fleet drew up in line and opened fire on the fort which returned fire. This was kept up all day; at night we formed a picket line on the beach, where we kept up a fire with the enemy until about 4 o'clock a. m. A most furious enfilading fire of shot and shell from the fleet caused us to fall back inside the fort. The bombardment continued to increase, and about 8 o'clock Sunday morning the 15th, the whole fleet opened a more terrific fire upon the fort. From about 11 a. m. antil 3 p. m. the booming of cannon and bursting of shells was like the roar of heavy peals of thunder. All the guns on the land face were disabled, but two, and the palisades were demolished, which left our garrison almost helpless when the assault was made on the fort. This occurred about 3 o'clock Sunday afternoon on the right and left both, at the same time. We were on the right where the marines and sailors, 2,000 strong, charged, who were repulsed with heavy loss, after which we were ordered to the left to drive back the enemy, who had made lodgment on the fort. We rushed in that direction, led by General Whiting and drove the enemy from the traverse and parapet in front and recaptured one gun chamber with great loss. On the parapet and traverse of the next gun chamber, the contestants were firing into each other's faces, and in some cases clubbing their guns, being too near to load and fire. It was in this charge that General Whiting was wounded. The fight continued after the enemy entered the fort until about 10 o'clock p. m., when the last traverse was taken and firing ceased. Thus ended the greatest bombardment ever known in modern warfare. It was the largest hand-to-hand fight during our civil war, and the struggle inside the fort was unsurpassed in stubbornness. Our casualties were not known as the roll was never again called.

The enemy's killed and wounded lay thick upon the battlefield, especially in the front of the Fortieth Regiment, which was in the hardest of the fight. Surely the valor displayed by North Carolinians in that effort to hold the last gateway of the South against such overwhelming numbers, both on land and sea, is glory enough to perpetuate in the annuals of this state for all time. After the battle was over, seeing so many of our comrades alive and able for duty, was a cause of deep gratitude to Almighty God.

The next morning the magazine in the fort exploded and killed about two hundred of the enemy, which was a scene of inexpressible horror. That evening we were put on board the steamships *De Mollay* and *General Lyon*, and carried to Northern prisons, the sick and wounded to Point Lookout, and those able for duty to New York City, thence transported by railroad to Elmira, N. Y., where they remained until after the war. The officers were carried to Governor's Island, N. Y., and released on parole there. During our stay in prison many of our men died from starvation and exposure.

Sergeant Thaddeus C. Davis

THE FALL OF FORT FISHER

By Mrs. Thaddeus C. Davis, Morehead City, North Carolina
Reprinted from *The Confederate Veteran Magazine*, March, 1905, Volume XIII, No. 3

This is the 15th of January and the fortieth anniversary of the fall of Fort Fisher. Every year since then this day has brought back vividly to my mind that heroic struggle. It was the last fort in the Confederacy through which we could communicate, even by blockade runners, with the outside world; and, although then in her death throes, the Confederate government made a desperate effort to hold it. It was a useless sacrifice of life, but what loyal man or woman counted the cost of life in those days, so long as the flag of the Confederacy was unfurled?

I lived directly on the coast, and could see the powerful Atlantic Squadron, under Admiral Porter, assembling for the attack. The bombardment by the fleet began Friday morning, the 13th, and continued day and night until Sunday evening, the 15th. In his official report, Admiral Porter says he threw fifty thousand shells in and around the fort within that time. It is estimated that for several hours Sunday, preceding the attack by the army under General Terry, three hundred shells per minute were thrown into the fort. It was the most powerful armament of war vessels ever assembled up to that time, and perhaps the most dreadful bombardment.

"I, with several other ladies, went out to a point on the west side of the Cape Fear River, where we could see the entire field of action. My husband was a member of the garrison in the fort, and none but a wife could experience the awful agony of my suspense as I stood that Sunday and watched the fearful shower of shell fall upon the doomed but devoted little garrison. At times my imagination would tell me that my anxious eyes were resting upon him in the little group of heroic defenders that we could see distinctly; the next instant a monster shell would explode in their midst, enveloping everything in smoke and dust. At such moments I would feel as if my heart would burst; but when the wind would lift the shroud of battle and I could see our flag still there, and the thin gray line still in action, I would feel that exultant joy that I imagine the old veterans felt when they rushed forward with the Rebel yell.

About three o'clock the bombardment suddenly ceased, but it was only a lull in the storm. The ships had dismounted or rendered useless by their terrific fire all of our guns on the sides of the fort most exposed to them; and now the land forces, under General Terry, assisted by the marines from the fleet, making a total force of nearly fifteen thousand, were preparing to assault the fort, and we could see our men. Oh, how few they looked compared to the vast army of Federals!

We could count our heart beats as, with silent prayers and eyes too dry for tears, we watched the storm gather in great masses of dark columns of men moving on the helpless, but still defiant Confederates. Praying that my husband was yet alive, seeing the overwhelming odds against him, and realizing that victory was utterly hopeless, can I be blamed that courage failed me and that a white flag over the wrecked fort would have been grateful to my sight? But before I could give expression to the feeling a red sheet of fire screamed along the front lines of the advancing hosts, and the death struggle had begun.

I could not, if I would, describe the fearful scenes that followed, for even at this late day it makes my heart sick to think of it; how foot by foot our men were forced back from one traverse to another, often fighting with clubbed muskets, and marking every foot of the way with the dead bodies of their foes. When the smoke would lift, we could see distinctly the lines engaged often in hand-to-hand fighting; but oh, we could see so distinctly that the thin gray line was growing thinner and the dark, heavy masses were growing heavier. The gallant General Whiting had fallen, desperately wounded, in the midst of his men; but the battle continued to rage until night had shut out the dreadful sight. Even then we could hear the roar and see the flash of guns.

The fighting continued until about ten o'clock that night when the fort surrendered. I could learn nothing of the fate of my husband, whether living or dead, and it was a month afterward that I received a letter from him, saying he was a prisoner at Elmira, New York. He was released after the close of the war, and returned home on the 1st of June, 1865, but the 15th of January always brings back to me a remembrance of that awful Sunday evening forty years ago.

Report of Captain Charles G. Elliott

Staff Officer, Kirkland's Brigade, Hoke's Division

Report reprinted from *Histories of Several Regiment and Battalions From North Carolina,*
Volume IV, Page 538-543

During the fall and winter of 1864 Longstreet's Corps, composed of the divisions of Field, Kershaw and Hoke, defended the lines on the north side of James River confronted by General B. F. Butler's "Army of the James."

Late in December Butler's army was sent on its expedition against Fort Fisher, N. C., and Hoke's Division was ordered to proceed to Wilmington to meet Butler. Kirkland's Brigade, the Seventeenth, Forty-second and Sixty-ninth North Carolina Troops, was moved first to Richmond. Having been recruited in winter quarters, the command made a fine appearance marching through the streets of the capital, with three brass bands and three fife and drum corps, its steady step and fine bearing eliciting cheers from the people. Officers and men felt the thrill which comes to the young soldier's heart from "the pomp and circumstance of war" and the approving smiles of women. The troops were very enthusiastic when told they were going to defend the soil of their native state.

As the railroad from Petersburg to Weldon was closed to us our only route was via Danville, Greensboro and Raleigh.

Leaving Richmond by the Richmond & Danville Railroad, Kirkland's Brigade reached Wilmington, N. C., after a long and fatiguing ride on the cars in extremely cold weather, and Kirkland marched at once with the two regiments which arrived first, viz: the Seventeenth, under Lieutenant Colonel Thomas Sharpe, and Forty-second, under Colonel Brown, for Sugar Loaf, a point a few miles above Fort Fisher. Our horses and wagons had not come, so all of the mounted officers were on foot (as an Irishman would say). On the march at night we heard a loud explosion and saw the bursting of a magazine on one of the Federal ships, and the men gave three cheers. But we afterwards learned it was the explosion of Butler's famous "Powder Boat," which he thought would scare the poor rebels away.

First Bombardment of Fort Fisher

In the morning we halted at Sugar Loaf. The fleet had been bombarding Fort Fisher, but the enemy had not landed. The Confederate forces under Bragg, outside of Fort Fisher, consisted of a small body of Senior Reserves, aged from 45 to 50, and some little cavalry. It was pitiful to see some of those gray-haired patriots dead in the woods, killed by shells from the Federal fleet. Among those that carried a musket was Mr. William Pettigrew, brother of the heroic general—since a venerable minister of the Gospel.

Kirkland placed one company from the Forty-second, under Captain Koontz, in Battery Gatlin, a small fort on the sea beach at the southern end of Masonboro Sound, and held the rest of his command on the road covered by the thick woods and dense undergrowth.

I had found a pony at an abandoned farm house and mounted him, so as to convey orders, but he was new to the business and did not like my spurs. Kirkland ordered me to ride down to the beach to see if there were any signs of landing troops from transports. I did so, and saw the ships extending as far as I could see down the beach, but no indication of landing. Returning, I reported this to the General, but in a few minutes a soldier came running up, almost breathless, and told us that the enemy had lowered his boats on the side opposite the shore, pulled rapidly to the land and captured Captain Koontz and his company, but few escaping. We rode down through the woods and found a large force on the beach and more coming, while the woods around us were filled with shrieking shells. General Kirkland promptly ordered his small command forward to the edge of the woods which skirted the shore and deployed both regiments as skirmishers. By his direction I rode down the line and told the men to keep up the fire upon the enemy and cheer as much as they could, but if they were hard pressed to fall back from pine to pine in the direction of Wilmington, and not let the enemy cut us off.

General Butler's forces, being thus very promptly checked, began at once to throw up breastworks on the sand shore. As they consisted of at least six times our numbers we could not have prevented their advance. But General Butler greatly exaggerated our force, and I have always believed that his examination of Captain Koontz had something to do with his false impression. As it was these two regiments held his army at bay the entire day, which was Christmas, 1864. By pushing our line close to his we escaped much injury from the ships' guns, their shells passing over our heads. We had the help of Southerland's battery of artillery (Company I, Tenth North Carolina) and Lipscomb's South Carolina Cavalry. During the night the troops began to come in from our division. But a reconnaissance the next morning showed that General Butler had taken advantage of the darkness, re-embarked his army and abandoned his expedition.

The navy had bombarded Fort Fisher for two days, but inflicted slight loss. Kirkland's bold and spirited defense must have convinced Butler that we had a large force, as Koontz had told him that Longstreet was there with his three divisions—Hoke, Field and Kershaw.

The fact is that we did not have 2,000 men of all arms to oppose him, and so no infantry except two regiments of Kirkland's Brigade. Why Butler was considered fit to be a general I don't know, unless his tyranny and oppression of non-combatants qualified him for "crushing out the rebellion."

Capture of Fort Fisher

Soon after this a battle General Bragg, the Department Commander, ordered Hoke's Division to Wilmington—not expecting a renewal of the attack on Fort Fisher. We marched, with colors flying and band playing, into the city and were enthusiastically received by the people as their victorious defenders. General Bragg reviewed the division and made preparations for a new campaign—and the capture of New Bern, N. C. This was kept a secret, but it came to my knowledge. Our brigade had orders to prepare three days' rations, and all got ready for a march—destination unknown. But during the very night previous to this intended movement we were suddenly ordered to move to the wharf and take boats down the river to Sugar Loaf, Kirkland's Brigade again in the advance, as the enemy had reappeared in front if Fort Fisher, the army this time being commanded by an able Federal soldier, General Terry. When we reached Sugar Loaf we found that Terry had landed his forces without opposition, and we began skirmishing with them at once. But the enemy had entrenched his line from the ocean across the narrow peninsula to the Cape Fear River, between Sugar Loaf and Fort Fisher. We threw up a line in his front, Sugar Loaf being our base, but were enfilade by fire from the enemy's fleet.

Terry's command consisted of two divisions. One of our brigades (Hagood's South Carolina) was detached to the south side of the river to assist Fort Caswell. During the action Colquitt's (brigade) was sent too late to reinforce the garrison of Fort Fisher, leaving Hoke the two brigades of Kirkland and Clingman, with some artillery and Lipscomb's cavalry regiment, which were confronted by Paine's Division of colored troops and Abbott's white brigade behind intrenchments and protected by the grand Federal fleet to rake the intervening space with shot and shell, grape and canister, while Terry with the white forces stormed Fort Fisher. Bragg moved Hoke's two brigades forward to attack. We easily drove in the enemy's skirmish line, occupied their rifle pits, and our skirmishers were making their main line keep their heads down behind the intrenchments. When we all expected the order to charge a courier came to Hoke from Bragg ordering him to withdraw to Sugar Loaf. My recollection is that we confidently expected to run over the troops in our front and drive them in confusion upon Terry's attacking column. But we obeyed orders and fell back to the line at Sugar Loaf, about 3 o'clock in the afternoon, and there we laid down, shelled by the ships, and heard musketry fire at Fisher until its brave garrison was overcome at 11 o'clock that night. The rockets from the fort said, "Come and help us," but we were not moved; and sad was the sight when rockets from the ships and display of colored lights and blowing of whistles announced the surrender of the fort. I felt that all had not been done to save it.

Private Zachery T. Fulmore's Letter to Colonel Lamb

Company D, First Battalion North Carolina Heavy Artillery

May, 1887

My Dear Sir:

I have just had the pleasure of receiving a letter from General Curtis, in which he encloses an extract from a lecture delivered by him on the—instant on Fort Fisher. He informs me that he has recently enjoyed your hospitality and compared notes on that fight. His statement is incorrect in one particular. He says, "they (the men at the gate) were so intent on serving their gun that they were seized by the 117th New York, etc." There was no seizure of our men. We surrendered voluntarily. Since I first wrote you some years ago, I have made it a point to see as many of that little squad who stood with me at the gate until surrounded, as I could, but I have seen only two of them. We have compared notes, but our memories scarcely differ in any detail. The detachment of Adam's Battery in charge of the gun at the gate, were supported by our company D, McCormick's. As we ran out from the bomb-proof to meet the charge we were arranged on both sides of that gate, and the river. Our captain was killed before that; one lieutenant had been shot down, so that we, on that side of the gate, were in charge of a non-commissioned officer. As Adams' men were being shot down one by one, our boys took the places of the dead and disabled. Our non-commissioned officer was killed, and four of our force on the left of the gate, within a very few minutes, several disabled. The two charges were repulsed, immediately after the first charge, and when a force of the enemy had taken refuge under a bridge and embank the Parrot gun, right at the water's edge, was turned loose, and that bridge blown away, for some reason or another, not remembered by any of us, we couldn't get that gun to work anymore. We then kept ourselves as a reserve for the Napoleon. The enemy in front seeing that it was useless to enter there, dashed around to our right, and as they did, all our company on the right of the gate, together with Braddy's, retreated around and behind the parapet, as we supposed to fight from the top of the parapet. We couldn't fire the gun, or rather did not, for the reason that there was nothing in front to fire at. Curtis' brigade had gotten out of range. We expected every moment to see them flying back and were ready to rake them on their retreat as soon as they came within range of the gun. We picked up our small arms in the meantime to keep back a small detachment we were watching for a chance to run through the gate, we thought. All shooting into the gate which was at that moment closed. We laid down on our stomachs within a few feet of the Napoleon, ready to jump to the Napoleon as soon as Curtis' Brigade should begin their retreat.

A half minute did not elapse before one of our boys was killed by a shot coming from the rear. I looked around and saw the stars and stripes floating from the top of the parapet, with, what seemed to me to be a thousand "blue coats" around it—some shooting at us.

As soon as I saw this, I jumped to the Napoleon to see if I could spike it, when they dashed down on us and demanded our surrender. We had no officer there, and I held up both hands as a signal of surrender, and our little crowd was marched to the rear. I saw they had us completely surrounded— knew we would have to give up the gun, and in that event they would turn it on our men in the fort, hence my determination to spike it if possible. At that very moment, the guns in the fort, Battery Buchanan, I think, turned loose on that end of the fort, and we were rushed away from there in a hurry. The circumstances were such that you couldn't know these facts.

On my way home from prison in the later part of May, 1865, I was put off the boat up at Meares' Bluff and walked the ties up to Lumberton. At the end of the first day's journey we stopped at the farm house of Colonel Joe Green, a prominent citizen of Bladen County, to get something to eat. We received excellent treatment, as he knew some of my family connection, but he said he was very much mortified to know that we had acted so cowardly as to let the enemy come in at that gate unopposed. I protested that we had done all that we could; told how many men we had killed and wounded right there, etc, etc. He said General Bragg was an experienced fighter—saw the whole affair, and his statement would outweigh the statement of anybody else, but seeing our ragged and starved condition and knowing of our sufferings subsequently, he expressed a kindly sympathy, and gave us food. I assured him he would learn the truth someday, and hoped it would be soon. I have never seen him since, but presume he died under the impression that General Bragg had given us our just deserts.

Many years afterwards, however, I left the State of Virginia on a big disgust over the war reminiscences in view of my obscure position in the army. I despaired of ever overcoming the impression created by General Bragg and dropped the whole subject, until I saw your reply in the Southern Historical Society Papers some years ago. You can imagine what pleasure the reply gave me, and now that General Curtis has corroborated every material statement I have ever made in regard to it, and time which makes all things even, has at last shed its kindly beams over the truth of history, and justice has come. To have a Union general vindicate the character of an ex-rebel, aspersed by his commanding general, is one of those paradoxes, which illustrates the absurdity of attempts to teach the present generation the details of our war in school histories.

I reiterate my assurances of the mostly profound esteem for yourself, and owe gratitude for your efforts to set all things right. Though an 18-year-old boy then, I am now in my 55th year and as the shadows begin to lengthen the men and events of that ordeal range themselves closer and closer around the tenderest memories of life. With most grateful and kindly assurances, I am, cordially yours.

Z. T. Fulmore

Report of Lieutenant Colonel George T. Gordon

General Whiting's Staff

O. R. Volume XLVI, Part I, pages 435-436

Headquarters Third Military District,

January 17, 1865

Sir: I have the honor to transmit the following report of the attack on Fort Fisher:

On the morning of the 13th instant, at about 8 o'clock, the enemy opened on the fort with the Ironsides, one double and three single turreted iron-clad monitors, concentrating their whole fire on the land face, keeping up a regular fire till 5 p. m. At this hour three frigates—Colorado, Minnesota and Wabash—came into action and continued a terrific fire until 6 p. m. Colonel Lamb, anticipating an assault, made repeated applications to Major-General Whiting for re-enforcements. The only forces available were those of the navy manning Fort Buchanan, sixty in all, which were willingly furnished by Captain Chapman, C. S. Navy. Six companies were brought from the forts below at 8 p. m., and 150 men, under Major James Reilly, arrived at 3 o'clock on the morning of the 14th instant. During this night the gunners and troops of the garrison were manning the palisades, a general attack being anticipated, our guns keeping up a fire, covering the land approach, at intervals during the entire night. Major-General Whiting, accompanied by myself, was also on the works and beach during the greater portion of the night, keeping watch on the enemy's movements.

On the morning of the 14th instant the enemy again opened on the land face, the rest of the fleet (seventy-two in all) forming two lines of battle; fifteen of these moved into position and joined in the action, keeping up a terrific fire during the whole day and succeeding night, dismantling every gun on the land face, one 8-inch columbiad alone excepted. Our guns replied with great accuracy, but with little effect, the wooden vessels remaining out of range of our shot, making but slight impression on the iron-clads, as far as we could judge. The gunners displayed the greatest gallantry under this most terrific fire. The enemy had also advanced a line of sharpshooters, who had sunk rifle pits, and annoyed the men serving the guns by keeping up a constant fire. The dismantled guns could not be remounted during the night, nor could the works be repaired, owing to the constant and heavy fire kept up by the enemy's fleet during the entire night. A telegram having been received from the commanding general that Brigadier-General Hagood's brigade had been sent to re-enforce us, and was ordered to await their arrival at Fort Buchanan.

About 4:30 on the 15th the first of these regiments (the Twenty-first) arrived, and shortly afterward the Twenty-fifth, under the command of Captain Du Bose and Carson, respectively. The twenty-first Regiment at once moved up to Fort Fisher; the other was moved to the rear of the Mound Battery for shelter from the enemy's fire, which at this time was awful; it moved up to Fort Fisher later in the day. About fifty-two ships having joined the monitors at 8 o'clock, they concentrated their fire, without any cessation, on different portions of the works. During this morning of the day (the 15th) and the preceding night the enemy landed the assaulting column, supposed, and as confirmed by a prisoner, to number 10,000 men. They were formed in three lines across the entire neck of land, covered by a heavy

line of skirmishers about 400 yards in front of the main body, and at a distance of about 1,000 yards from the fort. On this force we brought to bear our one available gun and three mortars, which had been mounted during the night, and these repeatedly broke their line and temporarily checked the advance. As the attacking column advanced a part of the fleet moved in single line in succession ahead of the skirmish line, thus enfilading the entire land face of the work, whilst the remainder of the fleet, in their original position, kept up a murderous fire on nearly every part of the whole fort. Under cover of the dense smoke a brigade was moved from the enemy's left along the beach, the tide being low, and succeeded in getting within the palisade line before they were seen, but were instantly repulsed twice and driven from their position with heavy loss. Corresponding with this movement a heavy force of the enemy, under cover of the woods, moved up on our left and got possession of the first gun chamber.

Lieutenant Latham, of Captain Adams' light battery, was stationed with two guns at a point commanding the causeway leading to the palisade line (the palisade line itself having been destroyed by the enemy's fire), with orders to run his guns into position as soon as the fire of the fleet had slackened. What occurred at this period on the left of the line I am unable to state, being myself engaged on the right, and the first intimation I had of the enemy's approach was by seeing their flag planted on the third traverse. As soon as discovered all the available force was led to repulse this attack, by Major-General Whiting in person, but it failed in dislodging the enemy from the position occupied, and at this point I have, with much regret, to state Major-General Whiting was seriously wounded and was carried from the field. Major Hill, chief of the general's staff, had dispatched couriers to Battery Buchanan to bring up the three remaining regiments of Hagood's brigade, who had been ordered to remain there till sent for (the fire from the fleet rendering it almost impossible for any troops to move), when it was discovered that this force had never reached Battery Buchanan (a circumstance much indeed to be regretted). I was then ordered by Major-General Whiting to communicate with the commanding general, which I immediately attempted to do, as he is aware. What occurred, therefore, subsequently to my leaving the field I only know form hearsay; but I consider it my duty to state that I was informed, as I was on the point of leaving, that a flag of truce had been hoisted by the enemy and answered by some officer, who then surrendered himself and 300 men to the enemy, and that a regiment of the enemy had been marched into the gallery of the sally-port. I have also to add that the garrison, though in good heart, was sadly worn out by the hard work they were called upon to perform by day and night, but that a feeling of much disappointment existed that the long-looked-for co-operation from the forces outside, which they expected would have been rendered, failed to assist them in their hour of need.

G. T. Gordon,
Lieutenant Colonel and Assistant Inspector General

Private William Robert Greer

Co. B, 25th South Carolina Volunteers

Reprinted from "Recollection of a Private Soldier in the Army of the Confederate States."
Manuscript Department, William R. Perkins Library, Duke University

At 3:30 A. M. there rang out through the bitterly cold air, it was sleeting heavily, the bugle call of "To the Colors" and our brigade started in heavy marching order, southward, destination not divulged. After toiling wearily through heavy mud for ten miles that night, it appeared to be fifty miles, we reached Richmond early in the morning. We received no welcome there and no coffee or anything else, although we were bitterly cold and suffering greatly. We were then packed, like cattle, into box cars with no seats therein and so closely packed that we could not move. The redeeming qualities of this arrangement being the warmth of such intimacy saved us from freezing to death. We traveled in this fashion all night, reaching Danville, Virginia, the next morning. Upon disembarking one comrade was discovered dead from cold and exposure, a dozen more were hustled to the hospital.

Later on we continued our journey south but with improved transportation facilities, but owing to the condition of the roads, the rolling stock, and careless or treacherous human assistance, everything pertaining to the transportation department was then beginning to disintegrate, we did not reach Wilmington, North Carolina, until December 26th. Rations were not, at that period, superabundant as I recollect while enroute Christmas day. I enjoyed for dinner a large uncooked sweet potato. On reaching Wilmington we embarked for the neighborhood of Fort Fischer [sic] situated at the mouth of the Cape Fear River. Before our arrival, however, at this destination an expedition for the reduction of the fort, the land forces under B. F. Butler and a large naval force commanded by Admiral Porter had appeared, but although Porter inaugurated a determined attack, Butler failed in his support and the expedition sailed away December 31st. We were then ordered back to Wilmington and there held in reserve.

January 13th a second attack on the fort was imminent, the expedition this time being under command of General Terry supplanting old Butler. Terry's land force of 8,000 men was auxiliary to Porter's fleet officially numbering 58 vessels of various grades. The garrison of the fort being deemed insufficient our regiment and one other was ordered to proceed with all haste to the point of attack. This journey, my last under Confederate rule, was noteworthy as to the unwillingness or treachery of the captains of the river steamers to risk their precious lives in close proximity to the bombardment now in progress. My recollection is that the application of a loaded weapon near the head of the recalcitrant sailors proved a persuasive argument, and on to our fatal destination we sailed. It was a clear, cold morning, Sunday January 15th, when our force disembarked at the extreme inner end of the landing under cover of a high battery, although we were witness of the progress of this continuous and terrific bombardment (up to this time there had been no demonstration from Terry). Porter evidently wished to reduce the fort first; we were soon in a position to realize the magnitude of this unceasing torrent of iron missiles which were being hurled at us. Finding a barrel of hardtack flavored with worms, our last rations from Dixie, and thus being prepared for the adventure, we wore ordered to proceed singly, keeping a reasonable distance apart, into the main fort, under this enfilade fire, and ordered to protect ourselves "as well as possible", this was somewhat possible, from gun projectiles as we hugged the intervening batteries and bomb-proofs closely on our hazardous journey to the ramparts of our 1700 yards but mortar shells are deadly missiles which are difficult to elude. The result of this maneuver which was absolutely correct insofar as necessity demanded, was not quite successful, inasmuch as many men perished or were disabled, and many more in consequence partly of the disorganization of the different companies, officers and men being widely apart, and furthermore, many tired out and utterly disheartened men took shelter in the bombproofs on the route and refused to budge, so that only a portion of our force joined the organized garrison on the front who themselves had been of necessity in the bombproofs nearby.

A determined attack by sailors from the fleet who marched up the beach with drawn cutlasses was quickly defeated by our force who manned the breastworks. The loss to the attacking party was reported very heavy. Shortly after this incident, a squad of Union soldiers appeared in the fort at the extreme left, the sallyport not only unprotected but left wide open. [Untrue. The most fierce fighting at Fort Fisher happened at the River Road gate.] A larger force appearing there ensued a struggle between the contestants fighting from each bastion when it became useless to resist any further, and Fort Fischer [sic] surrendered.

It was recalled to the memory of the writer that one of the members of our command had in his rapid movement while dodging shells witnessed my complete entombment in the sand from the explosion of a nearby shell and as he stated "only one foot sticking out." Thirty years after the close of the war, he was convinced that the fact of my having one foot out encouraged my extrication.

After a time squads of Federal soldiers marched through the fort gathering up prisoners saying "fall in"—"Johnny got any tobacco?" We were marched out of the fort in a body and placed on the beach, cold, wet, and hungry, sentinels closely guarded us. The only diversion being the pyrotechnic display from the fleet celebrating the victory.

The following morning there occurred a heavy explosion in the magazine of the fort in which it was reported the Confederates who fired the fuse perished as did a number unknown to us of the Union force. As I have no memory of any food being given us I presume we were still hungry, living on the memory of the last Confederate ration mentioned above.

The weather was clear but quite cold, but we were ordered to wade knee deep in the surf and were then hauled in launches, and after boarding a tug, were loaded into a "Greyhound" named the *General Lyon* said craft being noted as having only one live boiler, its companion having perished as a result of the high rate of speed characterizing the ship, this was confirmed by the fact of its taking ten days to speed from Cape Fear, North Carolina to Jersey city. The memory of this sea voyage lingers like a sinister dream. I re-visualize the situation in the whole as comparable only to an enlarged box of sardines, the temperature ranging in the 90's and when it is remembered that on deck the yard arms as well as the deck were coated with ice, there could have been only one result, which was speedily achieved by the mortality list shortly after our incarceration in the prison camp, Elmira, N. Y. Rations for the prisoners appeared to be of the least consequence to our guardians. One day we had, I distinctly recollect, four soda biscuits and some rice gruel. I desire here to emphasize the thought, that what is written about my captivity, that may appear censorious, is related and has always lain in memory without sectional prejudice, if any statement of hardship or suffering is emphasized it is with the view of picturing the horrors of war to some extent with the hope, that even this slight contribution, may assist in producing a situation as outlined by Tennyson—"Till the war drums throbbed no longer and the battle flags furl'd".

On the landing at Jersey city we were at once transferred to a train of cars in waiting and then, under guard, commenced our Journey to a prison camp on the outskirts of the city of Elmira in New York state. The journey was long and uncomfortable and on landing at the depot we were marched through the streets, almost waist deep in snow, and being gazed at from the dwellings as if we were wild animals. As the sinister walls of the camp, which proved to be my home for the next six months, or might, as it was in the case of thousands whose graves lie nearby, in mute evidence of their suffering and endurance, have resulted in my relief from earthly existence, I recall while the gates swung back for our admittance, the familiar quotation from Dante which I had memorized in early youth—"All hope abandon ye who enter here."

Private James B. Hunter Letters

These letters were found by Federal Colonel Albert M. Blackman's officers while searching Battery Buchanan. They were among letters written by soldiers at Fort Fisher, but were never delivered because of the fall of the fort. Private James B. Hunter, the author of the letters below, was killed during the battle. Unfortunately Sue was probably never aware of James final letter to her. These appeared in the *New York Herald-Tribune, January 26, 1865.*

Fort Fisher, Jan. 15th, 1865,

My Dearest Sue:

Night is about to close one of the most terrific bombardments that have ever happened on the continent. For 48 hours the enemy have shelled us most furiously, commencing Friday morning at 8:15. They have landed many troops, and we are looking for an assault any moment by land. Dear one, I can alone attribute my safety to a merciful Providence. I volunteered as courier on the morning of the engagement, and have been exposed to the hottest of the shelling. Several times I have escaped most miraculously, and if it is the Lord's will, I hope to endure all and come home safe. I have no time to write anymore. May God bless you; and if I never see you again, believe that I loved you, and have died fighting for my country and my all. Good bye my dear Sue. Yours forever.

James B. Hunter

Fort Fisher, Jan. 15th, 1865,

Dear Father:

I am safe thus far but have suffered one of the most terrific bombardments that the world has ever known. No material damage is done the fort. The Confederate flag still floats triumphantly over old Fort Fisher. There is nothing left but her works; all the barracks are demolished. We are attacked by four monitors, eleven iron sides and fifty-six other vessels. The enemy has landed a very heavy force, and we are looking for an assault every moment from that direction. May God bless our arms with victory. I volunteered as courier and have been exposed in the hottest of the shelling most of the time. It is now 11 o'clock. I have been to the land front. Our pickets are firing into each other. Gen. Whiting and staff are down, all the boys are in fine spirits, and as long as we can fire a gun this fort will never show the white flag. May God bless you all and give us victory.

James B. Hunter

Private John M. Johnston

Company H, 36th Regiment, North Carolina Heavy Artillery

Papers From the Lower Cape Fear Historical Society

At the earnest request and many solicitations of my children to write a record of my life during the three years that I served as a Confederate soldier. These lines are penned:

About the middle of July 1862, I bid farewell to home and friends and boarded a steamboat at Johnston's Landing bound for the war. I arrived in Wilmington sometime during the night and the next morning proceeded on my way to Fort Anderson, situated about 15 or 20 miles below Wilmington arriving safely. I applied for permission to join Company H, 36th Regiment, North Carolina Heavy Artillery. After some few days, I was sworn in for three years or the during [sic] of the war. Mr. Arthur Melvin, of Bladen County, who at the time was visiting his brothers, who were members of the same company, administering the oath. From the time I left home until I arrived at Fort Anderson, I was accompanied by Lt. M. W. Pridgen, who was an officer in the company, and was at home at the time on furlough. Capt. D. Patterson was in command of the company. I was assigned to the same tent that the Melvin brothers were in and was kindly treated by them. Thus began my life as a Confederate soldier.

I was given a uniform and a gun and assigned the duties that fall to the lot of all soldiers; such as standing guard, working fortifications, drilling, etc., for we had no fighting to do at that time. Our company remained at Fort Anderson about one year after I joined and while we were stationed there. I was sick with a very severe case of pneumonia. The doctors and nurses had no idea that I would recover. My brother was making a visit and I was taken sick while he was there. He went home and told my mother how sick I was. She came right away and by good nursing, kind attention brought me back to life and health. One of the sad events on my life comes in connection with this spell of sickness. Mother stayed with me until all danger had passed. When she left for home, the doctor promised her that, as soon as I was able to travel, he would send me home on a thirty day furlough. In a short time, I was able to go. The doctor had the furlough properly drawn and signed by himself and Capt. Patterson. It then had to go to the Colonel; he was drunk and refused to sign it. I had written mother that I would be up on the boat on a certain night. Lt. Pridgen was to go with me. Mother was so sure I would come, she had a wagon and feather bed at the landing with torches all along the road, the gates all open and everything ready to drive the wagon up to the house door. You can imagine your Grandma's surprise and disappointment when the wagon drove up and I was not there. Lt. Pridgen got his furlough, but I did not. Your grandma could not speak of that time while she lived without shedding tears. I do not think I have ever fully forgiven old Colonel Hedrick for the way he treated me on that occasion.

It was nearly two years after this that I went home on a ten days furlough, the only time I was away during my stay of three years. When we left Fort Anderson, we went to Smithville where we remained for about a year. Nothing of interest transpired while we were there. From Smithville, we went to Fort Fisher where we joined our regiment and were under the command of our own Colonel Lamb. Life here was about like it had been at other places, not very much to do. We had good comfortable quarters and a good deal of leisure; true guard duty was harder here especially in the winter on account of the cold winds from the ocean but in summer we had delightful times bathing in the surf. Not long after we moved to Fort Fisher, I was promoted to corporal which relieved me from guard duty, as officers either commissioned or non-commissioned did not have to perform guard duty.

Near the first of this paper, I said we did not have any fighting to do but that changed fast. Twas my first experience in a battle and to tell how I felt would be impossible. I don't think I felt like a coward or that I wanted to run away but I imagined I would have felt more comfortable somewhere else but anyway we whipped the Yankees for the next morning they left. General Butler, who commanded, reported to headquarters that the fort was impregnable. Of course we felt good. When the Yankee fleet started off, the band played Yankee Doodle, we gave them Dixie and a true rebel yell. Of course our quarters, including clothing, and everything we had was destroyed by fire from the Yankee shells. Colonel Lamb put us to work repairing the damaged fort for you know that the guns many of them were dismounted, the works torn, etc. We repaired as best we could and about the time we began to feel easy, that is to say on the 12th of January, 1865, the fleet reappeared reinforced and with a new commander. I think it was on Friday that the second fight began and for three days the most terrific bombardment that history records was carried on between the contending forces. It was on the evening of the third day of the fight that I was struck on the left arm by a piece of timber knocking my gun from my hand almost completely covering me up with dirt and taking the skin from my arm. At the same time, a piece of shell struck me on the head while it was not serious, I was painfully hurt so much so that I could take no further part in the fight.

I went at once to Dr. Willis, who had a temporary hospital and was caring for the wounded. He was an officer in our company. He told me alright he needed someone to assist him so I stayed and helped him until I surrendered that night about 10 o'clock. I stayed there for the rest of the night; slept very little. Next morning about sunrise a powder magazine exploded. It was a short distance from the place I was and I was sure that I was killed. I had been asleep and just waked up when I heard the report. The bombproof that I was in began to rock and reel. I thought sure that it was falling and expected to be buried alive, but it did not fall and I got out as quick as possible. After going out, I heard that the Yankees thought we blew the magazine up, and they were going to kill as many Confederates as the explosion had killed in Yankees. I felt sure if the report was true, I would be among the number killed.

After remaining [on the beach at Fort Fisher] for about two days, [we] were marched back to the fort . . . and put into small boats and carried to a large steamer. After being put on the steamer, we were put in charge of a Negro guard. We had been guarded by white men up to this time. I had never seen a Negro soldier before so you can imagine how we Confederate prisoners felt. We didn't know what they were going to [do] with us or where they were going to cary (sic) us. And right then, I felt like I didn't care where they carried us or what became of us. I was reckless, felt like I had rather be dead than alive. Anyway the vessel with about 800 prisoners put out to sea, I stood on its stern and looked and watched as long as I could see a sight of land. When I could no longer see land I felt that all hope was lost. [Where] I was going I knew not . . . but found out after a while that we were bound for Point Lookout, a Yankee prison situated on the Chesapeak (sic) Bay.

After being on the ocean for about five days about 10 o'clock on 22 of January. We anchored in sight of the prison. It was my first and last sea voyage and rough one it was. The vessel came very near being broken to pieces by striking a rock as we passed Cape Lookout. One of the prisoners died on the way and was buried after we arrived at prison.

Report of Lieutenant Augustus A. McKethan

Company B, 51st Regiment, North Carolina Troops

Reprinted from *Histories of Several Regiments and Battalions From North Carolina,*
Volume 3, Walter Clark, page 215

On 24 December we received marching orders and proceeded to Richmond on our way to North Carolina, having been called on account of Butler's threatening Fort Fisher. On reaching Wilmington we went into camp at Camp Lamb, spending about one week, when we changed our camp to a point near Green's Mill Pond, where we remained until the final attack on Fort Fisher. On 12 January, 1865, our division (General Robert F. Hoke's) was mustered at camp for division review for the benefit of a large number from the city, and after marching and counter marching for the greater portion of the day we returned to our quarters for rest, but were not given this, as the "long roll" called us to arms during the night and we were hurried towards Fisher. A march however, had been stolen on our people, as a heavy force had been landed by the enemy and cut us off from the fort.

Why we should have been stopped in Wilmington, thirty miles from Fort Fisher. I have never understood. Had General Hoke and his division been put in supporting distance of Fisher, the enemy could not have made their landing, and without this the capture of Fisher was, in my opinion impossible.

After the fall of Fort Fisher we made a line across the peninsula and threw up works, our right resting on the Cape Fear River near Sugar Loaf, and our left on the ocean near what is now known as Carolina Beach. From this point we fell back to within a few miles of Wilmington, skirmishing with the enemy as they followed. We then evacuated Wilmington, crossing North East River and marching to Rockfish in Duplin County.

Report of Sergeant Thomas A. McNeill

Company D, First Battalion North Carolina Heavy Artillery

Reprinted from *Histories of Several Regiments and Battalions From North Carolina,*
Volume 3, Walter Clark, pages 306-311

First Attack On Fort Fisher

On the morning of 24 December, 1864, the huge Federal fleet composed of iron-clads, the new *Ironsides* and a large number of frigates and gun boats, accompanied by transports, was seen in crescent-shaped order of battle off Fort Fisher, and soon thereafter orders came directing Captain James L. McCormick to move Company D, First Battalion Heavy Artillery, to Fort Fisher. Boarding the transport at Fort Caswell wharf and taking on other troops at Smithville, the men landed late in the afternoon of the same day at Craig's Landing, about one mile above Fort Fisher. There they were formed and marched towards the fort, then being heavily bombarded, till within a few hundred yards of the works and under fire, the command was ordered under cover of a sand bank till nightfall. They then entered the works and at once were put on guard and picket duty, mounting guns and replacing carriages dismounted or destroyed during the day.

Early on the morning of 25 December, Bowles' and Rollins' Batteries on the sea face of the fort or curtain extending towards Battery Buchanan, at the extreme point on the river, which, with the "Mound Battery," and others guarded the entrance to New Inlet bar, were manned by Company D. On the resumption of Porter's attack this day the guns were served well and steadily, with coolness and precision, by the detachments under the terrific fire to which they were subjected, the enemy, under the rain of shot and shell, desiring to take soundings of the bar and run the batteries to gain the river if possible. Late in the evening, while the pieces were being served, the company was ordered to the left, to repel an attack of infantry advanced on the fort by General Butler, in command of the land forces, and took position in the palisading in the marsh to the right of Shepperd's Battery, and opened upon the enemy's sharpshooters till they retired. Afterward, with two other companies under Major Reilly, they marched to the point as infantry to resist a supposed landing of the enemy, but no landing had been made. The loss of the company was slight, only a few of the men being dangerously wounded in this action, and none killed. The men were complimented by Colonel Lamb for their coolness and gallantry under fire, and Lieutenant Rankin was specially mentioned for gallantry. General Whiting, who in the midst of the hottest fire passed the guns, spoke words of commendation to the detachments.

General Grant, disappointed at the failure of December, now sent General Terry with about 8,500 men, supported by a formidable fleet with more than 600 heavy guns under Admiral Porter, to reduce this place and both appeared near Fort Fisher about 11 or 12 January, 1865.

Second Attack On Fort Fisher

On this being known Company D, of the First Battalion, then in garrison at Fort Caswell, was ordered to Fisher on 13 January, the bombardment beginning on that day. At once boarding the transport it landed near Battery Buchanan after dark that night and was ordered by Colonel Lamb to move at once to the land face to meet an expected assault. It double-quicked to its position near the west end of the land face, but the enemy did not then approach.

On the 14th, men of this company under a heavy fire, manned guns on the land face, unflinching amid the accurate aim of the monitors and iron-clads. The 15-inch shells landed often on the guns, knocking off trunnions breaking off great pieces of the Columbiad muzzles, wrecking gun carriages, and often bespattering the walls of the gun chambers with the blood and brains of the men of the detachments, yet the gunners coolly adjusted the degrees. The men obeyed every order till in turn relieved, often mounting the parapet amid a storm of exploding shells when necessary to sponge a gun, the flannel bursting into flame as soon as out of the muzzle, and continuing in this way the contest throughout the day. At night one-half of the picket on the land face was composed of men from this company. Advancing until the enemy's pickets were discovered, they fought by the light of the enemy's guns on the line until near midnight, when they were drawn in close to the fort.

On the morning of 15 January, the attack was renewed with unabated fury and daylight, as near as the writer recalls, showed only two guns on the land face in condition for service, and one of these was manned by detachment from the navy. A line of rifle pits having now been established by the enemy within range, the men at the guns were shot as they attempted to serve them, but this fire was returned from the parapets with effect.

With the exception of some detachments at the guns, which participated gallantly in the repulse of the naval brigade in the assault on the land face, Company D was stationed on this day at a sallyport about midway on the land face of the fort, until between 1 and 2 o'clock p. m., when Colonel Lamb ordered the company to the extreme left, with instructions to keep cover as well as possible under the fort until the enemy, now apparently massing for an assault, should approach within the range of musketry, and then, rushing to the palisades, man them and contest their nearer approach. Instantly the company cleared the gallery and bomb-proof, the fleet at this time turning their whole fire on the land face to cover the assault and drive the men to shelter, Captain McCormick moving at the base of the works. All the land face now looked as if wrapped in flame and smoke—the screaming, exploding shells tearing the earthwork, making holes in the traverses, and in all the history of war it is doubtful if a more infernal fire ever fell upon a fort. The company reaching the sallyport (River Road gate) at the extreme end of the work next to the river, halted under cover, when in a few minutes there was a sudden cessation of the fire, and on the instant the vidette reported the advance of the enemy's column. The men of this company rushed to the palisades, and a section of a battery at the sallyport at once opened fire on the enemy, and a destructive fire was kept up by the battery and Company D on the enemy now within a short distance of the slough, and this was kept up until the enemy veered, or could not be seen from the palisades at all. In this time, after a few rounds from the battery, the detachments, two or three in succession, were all shot down at their guns, apparently by sharpshooters, and the pieces were not after this served. In a very short time the enemy again showed himself in our front. This time the column advanced to the right of this company's position, under a heavy fire poured on it from the palisades between the sallyport and the river's edge, moving as if to effect a lodgment on the fort to the right of the position held by Company D, but to some extent exposed to its fire now being delivered in volleys. In the midst of this fire, it was found that the enemy were inside the palisades, to the right of Company D, and then a desperate struggle succeeded almost hand-to-hand, some of Company D to the left of the sallyport clubbing their muskets and fighting with the width of the palisades only between them and the enemy. But to the right of the sallyport and on that angle of the fort, the enemy in this assault for possession of the exterior slope, a lodgment was effected, the parapet gained, and the men were surrounded. A large number of the company were taken at the palisade, a few retreated down the lines of the fort, others to slight entrenchments near the river at right angles to the land face, and there fought and held possession until overpowered. Those who retreated joined the other commands in resisting the enemy from the traverses to the west of the middle sallyport, the enemy's line now enveloping the land face on both sides. At length the enemy reached a traverse defended by detachments of Company D, which had been left serving the guns when the company went to the left. Here these men made a deadly struggle with the foe for the traverses, the enemy and they firing into each other's faces at a few paces distance. Our men yielded the traverse only when all or nearly so, were killed or disabled. Some of the men joined Colonel Lamb, who conducted the charge on the enemy shortly afterwards, and were close to that gallant officer when he was shot down, and continued to resist until the works were occupied.

In the assault on the palisading on the extreme left extending from the left angle of the fort to the river's edge, Company D, together with the section of a light battery, repelled the enemy, their line on the second rush apparently obliquing to the right of this position, moving over the Wilmington road, and from a redoubt above the fort. General Whiting in referring to the assault in a dispatch after the battle and while a prisoner, said: "A portion of the troops on the left had also repelled the first rush to the left of the works." This Company D, of the First Heavy Artillery Battalion, carried into the action seventy to seventy-five men, and in the three days' fight lost forty men killed and wounded, and those left were prisoners. It is not intended in any way to say that other commands in this action did not act as gallantly in this terrible fight, but only to state the facts in connection with the part borne in it by one of the companies of the First Battalion.

A TYPICAL CONFEDERATE SOLDIER.

Private Henry Clay McQueen

Company D, First Battalion North Carolina Heavy Artillery

Reprinted From *The Veteran Talks,*
compiled by Ida Brooks Kellam, Historian of
Cape Fear Chapter No. 3, United Daughters Of the Confederacy

I enlisted in the service of the Confederacy in 1863, Company D, First Battalion, North Carolina Heavy Artillery, under Captain McCormick, Major Alexander MacRae, father of our townsman, Captain Walter McRae. I was then 17. I first saw active service at Fort Caswell. I had not been in service long before I was secretary of ordinance officer and then corporal. We were ordered from Fort Caswell to Fort Fisher for the first bombardment. The enemy's fleet began to assemble December 20, 1864.

On Christmas Eve, December 24, 1864, a rain of shot and shell was poured over us continuously for five hours. I afterwards learned 10,000 shot were fired by the fleet. While we were obliged to use ours sparingly and only returned 672 shots. Many of the soldier's quarters were burned, gun carriages disabled, one artillery caisson struck and revetments torn down, but our loss was light considering the rain of fire we endured. The fleet retired, our fort firing the last gun.

Next day the fleet returned with other ships, and a terrible charge of 150 shot and shell a minute fell upon us. People in church in Wilmington were nearly jarred off their feet by the bombardment 20 miles distant. It was the Sabbath day and also Christmas day. The shelling was furious, but we again forced the fleet to retreat and again we fired the last gun. After this battle I was returned to Fort Campbell.

The fleet returned January 12, and we were ordered back to Fort Fisher. Three days and two nights they kept up ceaseless firing. The ocean seemed covered with gun boats and transports bearing veteran soldiers. We had no time to eat, or be relieved from duty, or bury our dead. The earth was in a continuous tremor from the fire of the ships which formed a semi-circle around two fronts, tearing our fort to pieces and making the white sands of the sea beach red with the blood of soldiers. After practically disabling all our guns, the enemy 10,000 strong, having been landed in sight of the fort on the beach, we had about eight men to meet them. Twelve of my company were killed. A comrade next to me on the traverse was shot in his brains and killed. His brains splattered in my face. Our gun was displaced and disabled. My hat was shot off and I was wounded in the leg.

I was taken prisoner and put in a temporary hospital for two weeks. My captors were kind. When I was lying in the hospital they came and emptied their haversacks for us. They knew we had nothing to eat for days and no rest, being under continuous fire of their guns. We were put on hospital ships and laid on low cots close together on deck. During one night, the soldiers on each side of me died. In the morning, the hospital steward brought breakfast for us and I ate mine and one of the others also. My comrades were rolled in their blankets, a weight attached to their feet and then they were cast into the ocean. We were well out to sea.

Private James Alexander Montgomery

Company B, 36th North Carolina Heavy Artillery

Reprinted From *The Veteran Talks,*
compiled by Ida Brooks Kellam, Historian of
Cape Fear Chapter No. 3, United Daughters Of the Confederacy

I volunteered and enlisted for service in 1862 at the age of 17 years, in Company B, 36th N. C. Regiment, with Captain Daniel Munn, Colonel William Lamb and Lt. Colonel John D. Taylor.

I was sent to Fort Fisher, where I saw three years service. It was there I saw my boyhood friends and companions fall. I saw their blood dye crimson the white sea sands. I was home on a short furlough during the first attack on December 25th 1864, but the second—I was there. I can still hear the call at night: "Post number one all's well" from the parapet ring out around the fort every hour.

The assault on our fort commenced with heavy and ceaseless firing day and night. How any of us escaped I do not know. There were 600 guns against our 44; 10,000 men on shore against our 1,900. Shot and shell rained on us three days and two nights. We could not repair our displaced guns, cook or eat or bury our dead lying around us. We were helpless when the attack was made on our fort by land. Our guns were disabled and our front shot to pieces. Thousands rushed upon us—we met them led by our brave General Whiting who commanded in person. We drove the enemy from traverse and parapet. It was a soldier's fight now, as a man would fall another sprang forward to his place. Our officers were loading and firing with us. Then it became a hand to hand fight. We were too close to fire, but we continued to beat them back until our last traverse was taken and firing ceased.

General Whiting was mortally wounded in his last charge, he fell leading his men. I helped to carry him from the field. We fell into the hands of the enemy and I was sent to Point Lookout and he to Governor's Island. I never saw him again, he died of his wounds March 10th 1865.

Private John Covert Plowden

Company I, 25th South Carolina Volunteers

This is a copy of a letter written by Private John Covert Plowden to his wife Caroline. John was assigned to Company I, 25th South Carolina Volunteers. He was a dutiful husband and wrote his wife nearly every week for nearly three years. This particular letter is important because it describes the hardships that General Robert F. Hoke's Brigade suffered during its journey to Wilmington, North Carolina, in December of 1864. Private Plowden was captured when Fort Fisher fell and sent north to Elmira Prisoner of War Camp. Like many of his fellow prisoners John became sick and died of disease May 3, 1865. He was buried at Woodlawn Cemetery near Elmira, New York.

> On the peninsular 15 miles from
> Wilmington NC
> Dec 29th 1864

To My Beloved Wife,

Dear C I feel thankful that it is again my privilege to drop you a few lines. It has been longer than usual since I wrote to you. I commenced once on the 27th but we were ordered to move before I got through so I have not had a chance since until now. My Dear I am thankful although to my great surprise to tell you that I am quite well & hearty. When I left the lines & suffered what I did before I reached this place, I had no idea that I or any of the company could stand what we have without being sick. We left the lines the 21st at too (sic) o'clock at night. It had been sleeting from dark & just as we started it commenced to rain. We had 7 miles to march to Richmond before we took the cars the mud & water being over our shoes & the ground so slippery that I think 1/3 of the men fell down on the march in the mud. I was lucky enough to keep myself from falling though with great difficulty. When we got to the cars we were wet to the skin & our clothes were frozen on us. The trees too were all frozen & the tops bending down with the ice. Oh I never felt the weather so cold. Were then put on the cars in that condition & the cars were all open on the top so that it leeked (sic) as bad as if they had no covering. The car that I rode in was actually half way my shoes in mud & water & we were so crowded that we had not room to sit on the floor for there were no seats, but if I had had room I would have sat down in the water I was so tired. We were kept in this condition 24 hours & that with scarcely anything to eat as our rations had all got wet & spoilt on the march. When we got to Danville it was still as cold as ever but after a time we got fire & dried & after that time it was some better but still it was so bad all the way I can't tell you half. If you see Mr. McDowel he can tell you what a fix we were in when he saw us. I sent you word by him & Ted Hodge how I was. Three of the men from our brigade froze to death & 4 others got off the cars when they stopt (sic) on the road & in attempting to get in they were so numb with the cold fell & the cars run over them & killed them. Others got off & were left & it is supposed some of them are dead also. A great many were left at the different hospitals. 17 of our company were left on the road. I can't tell you no more now.

The enemy's fleet had collected here I suppose was the cause of our being brought here. They had landed a force here but when we got here they took to their gunboats again so we have had no fight. Their fleet has gone again & it is generally believed they are gone to Georgetown or Charleston. Part of our division it is said has gone on to one of those too places & if the fleet has gone we too may soon follow. I don't think we will stay here long. I am very well satisfied here as we are again under our old native pines & on sandy soil & have been getting plenty to eat since we came here. You may be surprised at it but I had rather have staid (sic) in Virginia than to leave there. The reason is because the fighting had ceased there till next spring & now we are sent out here where we can fight all the winter &

next spring go back to Virginia & fight all the summer but you must not fret about me. I trust the Lord will still deliver me & hope we will meet again. I believe the war is near a close but I believe slavery is among the things that were.

Give my love to Lizie & the children, ma & all the girls & Whit if he has not left. If you hear no more direct your next to Wilmington, NC.

J. C. Plowden

This is the last piece of paper I have & it is borrowed. I left my knapsack in Wilmington. Don't know if I will get it again. I could tell you lots if I could see you again now. If you have not sent anything to me yet you must wait till we get stationary.

Yours as Ever
J. C. Plowden

Union soldiers pose in front of the hospital bombproof. *Image Timothy O'Sullivan, 1865.*

Major James Reilly

Field & Staff, 10th Regiment North Carolina Artillery

James Reilly
Late Maj. Regt. Arty. N. C. S. T.

I saw it stated that Col. Lamb was in command of Fort Fisher when it was captured. Such is not the case. Please make this correction. I was in command of the fort after the chivalrous Whiting, and the brave Lamb were wounded. Both of these officers were wounded about the same time, Whiting first and Lamb shortly after. This sad occurrence happened about 3 in the afternoon. I being the Senior Officer then for duty—the command devolved to me, and under the circumstances I was placed in a very disagreeable situation, but I assumed it with all its responsibility and with a small number of brave men kept the heavy assaulting column of the enemy in check all that memorable afternoon. The men that did fight, fought as well as any men ever fought.

Shortly after the enemy got possession of the western angle of the work the fleet slackened its fire to a very great extent. This encouraged our men and I revived considerable enthusiasm and determination amongst them and it showed plainly that they meant business and the few that did come out of the chambers, where they were seeking protection from the destructive and murderous fire of the enemy fleet all day, fought as men ought to fight for the protection of Hearths and Homes. I availed myself of this cessation of shot and formed about one hundred and fifty men in the open space near the sally-port. As soon as the formation was complete, I advanced on a body of the enemy that established themselves in the open space between the western angle of the fort and the river. This body annoyed us very much all afternoon. I put one of the S. C. Regt. colors by my side and in front of the column. As soon as the enemy observed our object they opened a very destructive fire on our advance column. Under such a fire our men began to waver and fall back, and by the time I reached near the angle of the work I had not sixty men with me, the balance who were not killed or wounded took shelter behind the traverses and in the sally-port. In this last effort to expel the enemy I lost heavily and that brave and gallant soldier who carried the colors was killed by my side. His loss created some confusion in the attack and I was compelled to fall back to the sand bank in front of the main magazine. I reformed and kept up as heavy and destructive a fire on the enemy as my small command would admit throughout the whole fight. In this effort I was ably assisted by Capts. Baker & Brady, (the former belonged to a S. C. Regt.) and my orderly. They acted as brave soldiers and some other officers who I regret I do not know, Lt. Arendell, and my adj. Lt. Fuller of the tenth N. C. S. T., and act. Segt Madell, Dill and Pvt. C. Will have done good service during the whole afternoon. The former took his musket and used it very effectively, besides encouraging several of his own company pvts. Pate, Hobbs and others who rallied about him. His conduct had good effect on the troops and kept them to their work pretty well. The fighting was very close and severe with shot and shell, and had a very demoralizing effect on the men that were fighting behind the sand bank and exposed to quite a terrible fire. The enemy were not able to dislodge us until after dark and the moon raised when I found myself nearly surrounded, this little band was completely broke down after fighting nearly all day but there was no surrender written on their faces.

After I reform my line with my left well up the old [illegible] breast work so as to enable me to give a direct fire on the works. Capt. McCormick, that gallant officer, was killed at his post. Peace be to his ashes. He displayed courage and ability and kept his men well in hand up to the time of his death, about this time a white flag was displayed from the sally-port. I could not understand what it meant, as I knew the enemy did not get that far down the work. At the solicitation of the officers I ceased firing and took my handkerchief and gave it to Capt. Brady, who put it on the point of his sword. I ordered him to advance towards the sally-port (and see what was wanted) as soon as the firing ceased, and everything was quiet. To my surprise our men came out and instead of coming toward us they ran towards the enemy. As soon as I observed their object I recalled Capt. Brady and commenced firing. I knew I gained considerable advantage by keeping up a constant and as steady a fire on the enemy as I could. It kept them from making any formation whatever for the continuation of the assault, and they were content to keep behind the captured works. And the men fought with more determination than ever, and my gallant troops were greatly incensed at the dastardly conduct of their comrades.

I maintained my position until about seven P. M.. Under cover of darkness the enemy made their formation and made the attack simultaneously at several points. Genl. Whiting & Col. Lamb were sent to Battery Buchanan with the expectation that they would be able to get over the river, as I was under the impression that Capt. Ghapman had everything in readiness to render what assistance he could (for he & a portion of his command was not employed during the day that I am aware of) in getting our wounded officers & men away from the battery. After allowing sufficient time to elapse for the officers before mentioned to get away, I formed my brave little command of thirty-two into a column of fours, and the brave men who did the last fighting near head quarters at Fort Fisher with the cool & brave Capt. Powell, the gallant Arendell & Lieut. Murdoch of the marines with saddened hearts marched away from the fort we defended with all our might. In fact from the superior force & fire we had to contend against the whole afternoon I consider the defense one of the most determined of the war. It was from traverse to traverse, from traverse to main magazine, from there to the breastwork where the last and most determined stand was made, and I did not leave until we were attacked on both flank & front. I wish I could know the names of the thirty-two men who stood by me that evening. Well might their names be put on the Roll of Honor of the N. C. Troops, for none fought more gallantly or with more determination or valor.

Our march was directed to Battery Buchanan, where I expected to reform our shattered ranks, and to be in a position to engage the enemy under more favorable circumstance. The command was badly disorganized from the position they were placed in and the mode of fighting we had to resort to, then were subject to the demoralizing effect of the destructive fire of the enemies fleet and the land forces I was fully confident I would be able to reorganize when I came within sight of the battery. I halted my little column for two objectives, first to see if we were pursued, second to inform Capt. Chapman, as I presumed he was in a position to render me what assistance I needed by having his men and armament ready for action, and on my approach to the battery not to fire on us. For this reason when I halted I sent Capt. Powell to the battery with a verbal message to Capt. Chapman not to fire on any organized body approaching the work. I was confident Chapman was still in the battery for I thought him too good a soldier to abandon us, for we were sailing in the same ship and let us all go down together.

I sent Capt. Adams, a gallant officer, to him about 4 P. M. with a verbal message to this effect not to abandon the battery for when I was forced out of Fort Fisher I would fall back on Buchanan and fight the enemy there. Capt. Adams returned to me and said he saw Capt. Chapman and gave me as a reply 'very well'. But what surprise and mortification came upon me when Capt. Powell returned and informed me that Capt. Chapman & command was gone with few exception, the battery was abandoned and the guns spiked, and on my advance I found about six hundred officers & men perfectly disorganized. With considerable effort of myself and several officers we succeeded in getting their battery re-organized but three fourths of them had no arms & we had no means at that hour of the night of procuring any or of defending our position against an organized and victorious enemy.

We had a splendid opportunity to retrieve our defeat and get away. If the armament of the battery had been serviceable. It was as bright as day the enemy advancing on the two fronts of the battery, with our guns pouring shell and canister on them as they advanced down the sandy plain. Our men free from the destructive and demoralizing effect of the fire from the fleet, with the officers in charge of their respective commands and that their men kept a well directed fire of musketry on the lines as they came within range and advanced. The whole mode of fighting was changed. We would have regained courage and the enemy would not have captured us, not that night for the position was very strong. And I always have been confident we were able to hold it. I could have communicated with Genl. Hebert and got some boats for there was plenty at his disposal at Fort Pender, for to get all the troops across the river.

I knew from the activity the enemy displayed in the latter part of the attack on the fort that they would soon advance upon and attack Buchanan and as soon as they would come within range they would open fire on a defenseless mass. When I saw there was not a possible chance of defending ourselves, I took Maj. Hill and Capt. Van Benthusen [sic], of the marine corps, and went some distance in advance of the battery and awaited their coming. We had a white flag with us and met the enemies skirmish line under the command of Capt. Eldridge and I told that officer we surrendered and requested him to halt and retire his line and not to let them fire on our defenseless troops. Capt. Elridge, with the instinct of a true soldier, he complied with my request and reported I think to Genl. Abbott who came up and was conducted by Maj. Hill to Genl. Whiting.

This is a mere detail account for the time I was in command of the fort during the assault of the enemy, the operations and surrender of Fort Fisher. It was immaterial to me who commanded. I went there with my battalion to fight knowing there was a trusted leader, the gallant Whiting, in command. I saw him tried on a hard fought field. History wants a true record of this event of our late struggle, and I give it impartial so that hereafter it may be correctly known who was in command on that memorable afternoon and who surrendered Fort Fisher. I did it not from any cause or act of my own, but for the want of fighting material to defend the most important of our sea coast defenses. It is not my desire to detract one iota from the reputation Col. Lamb made for himself whilst in command of Fort Fisher, for so far as I know, he was a good officer. But it has been so often repeated by the press that he was in command at the time, I think it proper to give a correct statement of the fact by Maj. Hill and directed as Senior Officer for duty to assume command of the fort.

There were several acts of bravery performed by both officers and men during the day. For instance, Lt. Hazell (1st Lieutenant William Hassell) in command of a detachment of men in one of the gun platforms, took his musket during the assault and, by his conduct and behavior, encouraged his men & they fought during the time very well as he inspired confidence in them by his gallantry. Another instance came to my knowledge of a marine, an Irishman by the name of Fitz. Patrick, observed a crowd of about fifteen that were in the act of removing Genl. Galusha Pennypacker who was wounded during the assault. I called the Ord. Segt. and got a lanyard & some free men for him and told him to go and select one of the guns between where we were standing & the salient angle of the works. That was not badly disabled, double shot it with canister and report to me and we would fire at the crowd. He quickly went as ordered. He worked the gun and I pointed it. As soon as it was ready to be discharged, I went to the windward side to observe the effect of the fire. It was very good and it done him so much good to see the crowd scatter and some of them wounded. He forgot everything else and the risk he was running for both transom and the carriage were shattered by an envalade [sic] shot. The right transom being the shortest and from the recoil of the gun, carriage and gun went over the platform. Ah may if it was not for the gun going over we would have got some of them, as it was we got a few. They left their genl. there. They were careful how they crossed the plateau the whole evening afterwards. It was the last heavy gun fired from the fort. There were several more acts of bravery the names of the gallant officers and men who performed them I do not know. At the last traverse we fought the enemy on one side and we the other. I directed my men to stand firm. I was on the ground between two traverses, pistol in hand. I heard the officer in command on the other side encourage his men by directing them to move forward. As soon as they appeared above the top of the traverse, I discharged my six shots at them (& from what I could learn wounded the officer), drove them back then I formed my little column and doubled quick to the main magazine. I took a position and opened a well directed fire on the assaulting column that was approaching me from the sally-port and made them take shelter behind the traverses.

Jas. Reilly

Report of Adjutant George M. Rose

66th North Carolina State Troops

Reprinted from *Histories of Several Regiments and Battalions From North Carolina,*
Volume 3, Walter Clark, pages 693-694

Our regiment reached Wilmington during the night of the 24th, and on the morning of the 25th, Christmas Day, took up its weary march along the sandy road below Wilmington in the direction of Sugar Loaf Hill. As it went along and drew nearer and nearer to Fort Fisher, the sound of the shelling from the gunboats assembled there could be more and more distinctly heard, and as we reached a point just below Sugar Loaf Hill and near where "Carolina Beach" now is, the shelling from the gunboats became terrific, but as it was impossible to land troop with transports and keep up the shelling at the same time, we were very soon engaged in quite a strong skirmish with those of the enemy who had landed and were about to land and they were soon driven back. Immediately after this first shelling was over, the division commenced to build a line of breastworks from the top of Sugar Loaf Hill diagonally across the strip of land between it and the ocean and in the direction of a battery which was located on the beach.

Here we remained for some days, throwing up the fortifications which we made strong, to us, seemed impregnable for any land attack that could be made by land forces; but we were not long allowed to remain. General Bragg having been assigned to the command in this locality, we were ordered back to Wilmington and went into camp a mile or two east of Wilmington for the purpose of holding a grand review.

Why Fort Fisher Fell

We remained in that camp some days, and while on review the enemy again made his appearance in front of Fort Fisher; this time not in command of "Beast Butler," but General Terry. We were ordered back to our old line, but before we were able to make the weary march from Wilmington down, the enemy had succeeded in making a lodgment upon the shore, and had thrown up a line of breastworks which General Hoke considered it was impracticable for his men to attack, as his division would be exposed to an enfilade fire from the enemy's gunboats. It has always been the opinion of most of the officers connected with Hoke's division, so far as I have been able to ascertain those opinions, that if his division had been allowed to remain at Sugar Loaf and not have been carried to Wilmington for the purposes of review, that the troops of the enemy could never have made a landing and Fort Fisher would never have fallen into their hands. It is well known that it fell by reason of the land attack and not by reason of the fire from the gunboats. If Hoke's division had been where, it seemed to the officers, it ought to have been, this landing of troops could never have been made and there never would have been a land attack upon Fort Fisher. It is useless, however, to speculate upon what might have been and what might not have been, under such circumstances. General Sherman was going in the direction of the center of North Carolina and if he had kept on his march, his army would have been in the rear of Fisher and it would necessarily have been abandoned anyway, but we would have been saved the loss of the gallant soldiers who met their death at Fisher and would have been spared the humiliation of having had that fort, even after a gallant defense, taken from us.

On the night after its fall, the scene was brilliant; rockets and roman candles were thrown in every direction from the gunboats in its front, and the soldiers of Hokes Division had to grind their teeth and bear the humiliation of not having "been there" to prevent the fall of Fisher, and to listen in silence to the shouts and huzzas of the enemy over their victory.

Report of Major William J. Saunders, Confederate States Army, Chief of Artillery Operations January 13-15, 1865

O. R. Volume XLVI, Part I, pages 437-439

Colonel Archer Anderson,
Assistant Adjutant General

Wilmington, N. C. January 18, 1865

Colonel:

In obedience to verbal instructions, I have the honor, respectfully, to report that on Friday, the 13th instant, I was ordered by Brigadier-General Hebert to proceed to Fort Fisher, then menaced by a powerful fleet of the enemy. Upon my arrival I reported at once to the post commandant, who requested that I would perform my duties as chief of artillery. The action began at 8 a. m. by the *Ironsides* and four monitors, one a double turreted and the other three single turreted. Their firing was slow and deliberate and directed upon the land face of the fort, evidently with a view to dismounting our guns and breaking down the palisades in front of the work. Our guns, under my immediate command, replied steadily and with accuracy, but I am unable to state with what effect.

In the afternoon several frigates, having formed a second line of battle on our sea face, opened a tremendous bombardment upon our works. As soon as the fire of the enemy ceased, the troops were taken to the palisade line, upon which I posted (by order of the major-general commanding) six light guns. During the entire night (at intervals of half an hour) I fired from different portions of the land face, as also with my light guns, up the beach, having previously (at dark) opened with all of them upon the woods covering the approach to the fort, to dislodge, if possible, any of the enemy who might seek to throw up works at that point, as also to open the road for the re-enforcements expected from that direction. During the night the *Ironsides* and monitors occupied their relative positions of the day before, all being quiet in that direction.

On the morning of Saturday, the 14th instant, the enemy again opened from the ironclads, directing their fire as the day before. A number of sharpshooters had likewise effected a lodgment on the road leading to the fort, and annoyed our gunners at their work. During this day the enemy dismounted all of our guns on the land face, with the exception of one 8-inch columbiad, three 32-pounders (smooth-bores), and one 30-pounder Parrott. These, however, kept a steady fire. During the whole of this night the enemy kept up a steady fire on the fort, rendering it impossible for us to remount the guns, excepting one 10-inch mortar, two 24-pounder Coehorn mortars having been placed in the gun chambers of the land face. The enemy's fire was very effective, killing and wounding many of our men on the palisade line, and still further increasing their already exhausted condition, which from want of rest and food, was very great.

The troops were withdrawn at daylight and held in readiness to resist the assaulting column, which during the day (Sunday, the 15th instant) were being landed and formed in three lines across the neck of land upon which the works were built, a line of skirmishers being thrown some 400 yards to their front, and at about 1,000 yards from the fort. Meanwhile (from an early hour in the morning) a tremendous fire was kept up from the entire fleet, numbering seventy-two vessels of all classes. From a number of these (I am unable to state how many, but should think a sufficient number to bring 300 guns to bear on the works) a concentrated fire was directed at different portions of the works, which was kept up at intervals of ten and twenty minutes. Its effect was terrible, the works being torn to pieces and every gun on the land face (except one 8-inch columbiad) dismounted. Our mortars, with this gun, however, kept up a steady fire upon the enemy's line of infantry, whilst our sea face batteries replied with steadiness and coolness to the fire of the fleet, but as I was engaged entirely on the land face, for want of data not now to be had, I am unable to report with what effect. The exhausted condition of our men, now greatly decimated by fifty-six hours of hard fighting, the major-general commanding being unable to relieve them without, in effect, evacuating the works at the mouth of the river, from which he had drawn as heavily (in re-enforcing Colonel Lamb) as he could, rendered it necessary to fire at the fleet seldom and at long intervals. This may in some measure account for their being able to keep up their fire, as none of their ships were withdrawn from action. Under cover of the smoke of this terrific fire the enemy threw forward a column (supposed to be a brigade) from the left of their line along the sea beach (the tide being low), who succeeded in gaining the right of our palisade line before they were discovered. This advance was quickly and gallantly repulsed by our troops with heavy loss. The attack on the flank of the work would now seem to have been only a feint, to be converted into a real attack as circumstances might determine, since a heavier column had approached under cover of the hill and woods on the river side (our left) and succeeded in gaining a foothold on our works.

It was whilst this attack was going on on our sea front that Colonel Lamb (as I was confidently informed) reported to Major-General Whiting the fact of the repulse of the enemy at all points. The enemy, in his hurried retreat, were destroyed in large numbers. Such guns on the sea face as would bear, together with our only remaining gun (an 8-inch columbiad), opened on them with canister at short range. It was while engaged in bringing this last gun to bear on them that I discovered that their assaulting column had gained a position on the left of our works, when I immediately ordered the officer in charge (Lieutenant Swain) to traverse his gun and open on them, the gun having a flanking fire, and at once led in person the troops collected at this point (as the only field officer present) to attack them down the parapet of the work. The fire of the heavy force of sharpshooters on the enemy's right, together with the torn up condition of the work, rendered it necessary to take them down within the work, where I joined Major-General Whiting, who was leading his men in person with the entire disposable force, hurrying on to drive the enemy from his position. I had been previously wounded in the attack on the right; I fell at the foot of the fifth traverse from the left of the work, the enemy having possession of and firing from the third, when I was taken up and carried into a magazine. As soon as I recovered sufficiently I rejoined Major-General Whiting, whom, I was informed, was wounded in the bombproof.

At this juncture Colonel Lamb entered, wounded, and told the general that his men, whom he had endeavored to lead from the works on the sea front to drive the enemy from his lodgment on our left, would not follow him. General Whiting, although wounded, was still directing as far as possible the movements of his small force, when Major Reilly rushed in and reported the astounding fact that an officer, having put his handkerchief on a ramrod whilst he was temporarily in another portion of his command, had surrendered 300 of his men and admitted a regiment of the enemy into the galleries of the sally-port on the land face. The general, who had repeatedly ordered Colonel Graham, with the remainder of Hagood's Brigade, whom he supposed at the Mound Battery, directed me to bring him up without delay. I need not add that the troops were not there, and the want of them lost us the fort. On attempting to rejoin the general I found that the enemy, in overwhelming force, covered the land and sea face, and were firing from the parapet of the work, in the bombproof of which I had left the general. I returned to Battery Buchanan and advised the immediate withdrawal of the force at this point, as the enemy had the fort and were marching on the battery, the troops for whose defense were reduced to the gun detachments in re-enforcing the fort, the guns having been spiked. The bombproof being full of wounded, the commanding officer was unable to blow up the magazine. This command was safely brought off, but, owing to the want of a steamer, numbers of our poor fellows who were retreating before the enemy were left on the beach. I came off with the naval officer commanding Battery Buchanan at 10:40 p. m.

I have the honor to be, colonel, very respectfully, your obedient servant.

WM. J. Saunders,
Major and Chief of Artillery

Dr. Joseph C. Shepard's Letter To His Wife

I received a copy of this letter from Tom Morrison. Tom is the great, great grandson of Dr. Joseph Christopher Shepard. This letter was written to his wife, Henrietta Foy Shepard, before the first battle. Shepard was one of the surgeons at Fort Fisher who would soon be overwhelmed with wounded soldiers.

Fort Fisher Dec. 21st 1864

My Darling,

I have not heard from you now in more than a week but as I may not have the opportunity of writing you again soon I think it's my duty, and I know it is a great pleasure to write you.

We are now on the eve of a battle at this place. The fleet has been assembling off here for the last two days.

There are now about forty sail off here, and they are increasing every day. When the weather clears up we expect the fight to begin which I reckon will be tomorrow. We are all in readiness and I hope & think that we will be successful. If we are overcome and taken prisoners, I beg of you, darling, not to be uneasy about me. You may be assured that I will do the best for myself under the circumstances. I shall stand to my post and go wherever duty calls me. I shall never disgrace my wife and child. If I should fall, however, weep not for me! Your dear brother & uncle have gone before me, and I hope I will be prepared to meet them in a peaceful land.

If I should happen to take a trip North I will let you hear from me as soon as I can. In the meantime teach my little Trudi to love me, if she can't remember me. There is one information that I wish to leave you and it is this—"Never be caught in the lines of the enemy." You know what atrocities they have committed and the violations they have perpetrated on the innocent. I rather that you were in your grave than be subjected to such outrages.

If the attack blows over, and everything becomes quiet I will come to see you as soon as possible.

I want to see you very bad, it seems nearly an age since we were together last.

Tell mother to conduct my family as she thinks best, and tell her that I will write her if I have a chance to do so. My love to your ma and all my connections. Hug Trudi for me darling and remember me as an affectionate & devoted husband.

Joe

Private James Chapman Stevenson

Son of Major James Stevenson, Staff Officer, 36th North Carolina Artillery

Reprinted from a document from the Lower Cape Fear Historical Society

I enlisted in the service, having joined my father's old company commanded by Capt. Robert Murphy who had succeeded my father. I was immediately detailed to serve on the Signal Corps, where I remained until the fall of Fort Fisher. My first station was 8 miles below Fort Caswell, an outpost completely at the mercy of the blockading squadron; at any time they might have seen fit to take us, they could have done so, why they did not, I have never been able to understand. Every morning they would steam by our quarters so close that we might have recognized a friend, had there been one on board the vessels.

I was subsequently moved from there to Fort Fisher; this was decidedly more agreeable to me, my father being there, next in command to Col. Wm. Lamb. During the time I was at Fort Fisher the great powder ship prepared by Gen. B. F. Butler was exploded under the fort, my quarters being nearest the explosion, and while it broke windows in Wilmington, a distance of 25 miles we were not inconvenienced by it in the least, the reverberations being broken by the immense earthworks which formed the fort.

I was in both fights at Fort Fisher, and at the time the assault was made on the fort, and when the enemy's pickets had completely surrounded it, and shooting at everything which showed its head above the parapet. Col. Lamb sent a messenger to get a volunteer who would send a message to Fort Anderson, to the General in command, W. H. C. Whiting. I volunteered to send this message. It was late in the evening, about dark. Signaling was done with flags in the day and with torched at night—balls of cotton were saturated in spirits of turpentine and fastened to a pole, while another ball was placed at the feet of the operator, so that the waving from right to left might be distinguished. I prepared my balls of cotton and started up the ramparts. I was told that it was certain death to go there, in fact, I knew nothing could show above the parapet which was not struck by Yankee shot. However, I had promised, and I fully intended to do it. As soon as my head showed above the parapet the bullets began to whistle around me and I expected every moment to be shot, but just at the opportune moment, before a missile had touched me, Col. Lamb countermanded the order and told me to come down.

The first fight lasted three days, on the last day I was taken violently sick and was carried to the hospital, and from thence to Battery Buchanan, on the extreme point half mile below Fort Fisher; there I remained and was assigned to duty and participated in the second fight at that point.

Just before the first fight at Fort Fisher my father with six of the best companies of the 36th Reg. had been ordered to Georgia to oppose the advance of Sherman in his diabolical march through that state, and so was not in the first battle at Fisher. Father made a fine reputation for cool bravery and military skill in this campaign, he being in command of the rear guard who protected the retreat of the Confederate forces from the city of Savannah.

Between the first and second fights, which were about two weeks apart, my father and his command returned to Fort Fisher. Suring the second bombardment, I would go at night, to visit Pa who was stationed with his command on the right wing of the fort having famous "Mound Battery" in his command. I found him stretched in a bombproof, after two days hard fighting, almost overcome with weariness and anxiety. He called me to him, took my hand in his and told me that the care of the family would devolve on me, and he felt satisfied that I would prove equal to the occasion; he gave me some good advice which I remember to this day. This was the last time I ever saw him.

After the Federal troops had entered the garrison, and it was evident that they had possession, the commander of Battery Buchanan Capt. Chapman, a Confederate Naval officer, ordered the men to get away as best they could. There were a number of fishing boats at the point, some bad, some worse; I got possession of one of these, took three wounded soldiers in with me and carried them to the opposite side of the river. I then went to Battery Lamb, a small battery on the west side of the river, opposite Fort Fisher and reported for duty. Some of the Signal Corps got down to Battery Buchanan and signaled over to send a boat back as Gen. Whiting and staff, Col. Lamb and Maj. Stevenson were there. The commander called for a volunteer crew to undertake the perilous trip—I again volunteered and we succeeded in getting a crew, I was put in charge of the boat and we started back across the river. While in mid-stream, struggling with a strong flood tide, against which we could make scarcely any headway, there went up from the Yankee fleet thousands of rockets of all colors; the ships were illuminated, the heavens were ablaze with light, I had never seen before, nor have I since seen such a display of fireworks. The boat's crew knew this meant surrender, and they refused to go further. I have since learned, had we reached Battery Buchanan, we might have rescued the whole garrison during the night, for this post had not fallen and the forces were not taken prisoner until the following day.

Seaman Robert Watson's Journal

The CSS Savannah's crew was ordered to Fort Fisher after the first battle

Reprinted From *Civil War Times Illustrated*, April 1976, pages 14-16

Friday, December 30th: Very cold day. Washed my clothes and just as I wrung them out we were ordered to pack up to go to the Battery Buchanan. Started at 1 P. M. in a small tugboat and arrived at the battery at 5 P. M., landed in boats and had to wade ashore, water very cold. The quarters are small and badly crowded, scarcely room to turn around. Spread our blankets on the floor and slept very well.

Saturday 31st: Cold and clear. This place is called Confederate Point. It is a low, sandy place, water brackish, sand blowing over everything. The battery is a fine one, it mounts 2 eleven inch Brooke smooth bore and 2 ten inch Columbiards [sic] and 1 six pounder Howitzer. There is a great deal of humbugging in boats, they are noticed off all day and hauled up at night. The water is very shoal about this place and everything that is brought here we have to wade out to the boats and carry it on shore. I went over to Fort Fisher in the afternoon. The men in the fort all busy repairing and strengthening the works. The ground was covered with shell of all sizes, many of them unexploded. On Christmas day the Yankee fleet threw about 30,000 shells at the fort. They burned all the quarters but did not injure the works much. 2 guns bursted and several were dismounted. Our loss was small. Fort Fisher is a large and strong work. Rain all afternoon and night. We have to sleep on the floor and are so crowded that we can scarcely find room to lie. Our food is badly cooked, consequently have not enough food to eat. The bread is made without salt or yeast and is as heavy as a stone, the beef boiled, and the coffee is slops. This day one year ago I was at Dalton, Ga. and felt confident that the war would be over and I (would) be at home today, but alas am sadly disappointed and God only knows when this cruel and unnatural war will end. I am afraid that it will not end during Lincoln's administration. This ends the year 1864 and I pray to Almighty God that I may be at home this time next year.

Sunday, January 1st, 1865: New Years day. Very cold and on guard, 1 iron clad biscuit and a cup of weak coffee for breakfast and 1 iron clad biscuit and a small piece of boiled beef for dinner and 1 biscuit and a cup of slops for supper. Pretty rough fare for New Year's Day. Austin Williams and 5 marines took a boat and went to the Yankees during the night. Some of them were on guard when they deserted. As soon as they were missed the long roll was beat and the roll called to find out who were missing. Williams was one of the Savannah's crew. They got off clear.

Monday, Jany 2nd: Came off guard at 9 ½ AM all hands fell in for drill. Our crew were told to look on and see how the guns were worked, but we gained no information for the men were very poorly trained. They drilled about ¾ hour then fell in and marched to qrs. where we broke ranks. I did not get any sleep last night and was kept busy all day. When a man comes off guard he is not excused from duty that day.

Tuesday, Jany 3rd: I asked Lieut. Arledge to allow the Savannah's crew to mess together as it was very unpleasant for us to mess with a lot of "tar heels." He consented and I went to work and made a mess chest. In afternoon took a lot of beef and vegetables on shore and carried them up to the bomb proof and hauled up the boats. Very cold all night.

Wednesday 4th: Went to work on officer's qrs. The tools consist of 2 old broken saws, 1 hatchet and two hammers. Very cold day.

[This is the beginning of the second attack on Fort Fisher.]

Friday 13th: Have been at work on officer's qrs. since last date. Roll call at 4 AM and ammunition given out for small arms. At sunrise the enemy opened fire on Fort Fisher. At 12 AM we were ordered to Fort Fisher to reinforce it. Double quicked up to the fort, the shell bursting around us in large numbers but did us no damage. We manned 3 guns and commenced firing at 1 PM and continued till dark when both parties ceased fire. The Yankees had been firing at the fort all day with 3 monitors and the iron sides but at 4 PM they brought the whole fleet to bear and kept up a terrific fire until dark. Fortunately none of our men were hurt except Lieut. Hudgins who was slightly wounded in the mouth with a fragment of shell and several of us were knocked down with sand bags. We were all nearly buried in sand several times. This was caused by shell bursting in the sand. Whenever one would strike near us in the sand it would throw the sand over us by the cart load. All quiet through the night and very cold. Got no sleep for we were on lookout all night for an infantry attack. Fired out guns every 15 minutes along the beach with canister. Very dark.

Saturday 14th: At daylight we all fell in and marched back to Battery Buchanan. Marched in quick time and got a drink of whiskey on arrival, got breakfast and turned in and just as I fell asleep we were ordered to fall in and go back to Fort Fisher. The Yankees saw us for they shelled us furiously all the way but did us no injury. We got through safe and manned the same guns we had yesterday. I was at a 64/10 in. Brooke rifle [probably 6.4 inch] and made some excellent shots. We ceased firing at dark but the enemy kept up a severe fire all night. They seemed to direct their whole fire at our 3 guns for we were the only ones that did them any injury. Our shot and shell would strike the monitors and iron sides and break in pieces and of course did them no injury but the wooden vessels did not fare so well for several of them had to haul off. Their shell bursting among us very often but fortunately none of us were injured. After dark a company of soldiers came in our gun chambers and had not been there 15 minutes before two of them were wounded, one mortally. We all suffered very much with cold and want of sleep. Skirmishing on our left between our pickets and the Yankee pickets. They are reported to be in large force up the beach on our left. Our pickets drove theirs back.

Sunday 15th: At daylight we went back to Battery Buchanan, took a drink, got breakfast and turned in, the Yankee fleet keeping up a heavy bombardment all the time and many of their shells exploding near our qrs. One man had a leg cut off and the other broken, he was asleep in the guard tent at the time. At 11 AM turned out and got dinner and all hands were ordered to pack up and go to the battery for the fleet had moved to the right and near us. The shelling was terrific. At 3 ½ PM the Yankee infantry advanced on Fort Fisher and were repulsed three times but on the 4th charge they gained a footing on the left of the works. Unfortunately all the guns were disabled, if this had not been the case they never would have gained a footing, but our men fought them bravely until after dark with musketry and contested every inch of ground. The slaughter was great. As soon as we saw that the enemy had gained a footing and planted their hateful flag on the left of the works we knew that the fort was lost and Captain (Robert T.) Chapman had all hands mustered, the roll called, and he then informed us that the fort was lost and that it was useless for him to keep us here to be taken prisoners or slaughtered, that we could fight the battery for some time and probably do the enemy some damage but that we could not hold onto it for any length of time. He then ordered us into the boats and we had to wade out to them up to our waists in water to get into them and just as we started he ordered us to await orders. Our battery then opened fire on the left of Fort Fisher with one 11 inch and one 10 inch gun, the other two guns would not bear. Continued shelling until 8 PM. At 10 PM we were ordered to go across the river to Battery Lamb. We were very glad to leave for we were nearly frozen as our clothes were wet and it was a very cold night. The shells were bursting very near us all the time. Stopped at Battery Lamb ½ hour and started for Wilmington. I and several of my shipmates marched about four miles, halted, built a fire and turned in after drying our clothes. Slept well. Lieut. Hudgins was captured while trying to get into the boat. The Yankees threw up thousands of rockets when they gained possession of Fort Fisher. The sight was magnificent.

Report of Major General William H. C. Whiting to General Robert E. Lee

O. R. Volume XLVI, Part I, pages 439-441

January 18, 1865

General: I am sorry to have to inform you, as a prisoner of war, of the taking of Fort Fisher on the night of the 15th instant, after an assault of unprecedented fury, both by sea and land, lasting from Friday morning until Sunday night.

On Thursday night the enemy's fleet was reported off the fort. On Friday morning the fleet opened very heavily. On Friday and Saturday, during the furious bombardment on the fort, the enemy were allowed to land without molestation and to throw up a light line of fieldworks from Battery Ramseur to the river, thus securing his position from molestation and making the fate of Fort Fisher, under the circumstances, but a question of time.

On Sunday the fire of the fleet reached a pitch of fury to which no language can do justice. It was concentrated on the land front and fort. In a short time nearly every gun was dismounted or disabled, and the garrison suffered severely from the fire. At 3 o'clock the enemy's land force, which had been gradually and slowly advancing, formed into two columns for assault.

The garrison during the fierce bombardment was not able to stand to the parapets, and many of the re-enforcements were obliged to be kept at a great distance from the fort. As the enemy here slackened his fire to allow the assault to take place, the men hastily manned the ramparts and gallantly repulsed the right column of assault. Portion of the troops on the left had also repelled the first rush to the left of the work. The greater portion of the garrison being, however, engaged on the right, and not being [able] to man the entire work, the enemy succeeded in making a lodgment on the left flank, planting two of his regimental flags in the traverses. From this point we could not dislodge him, though we forced him to take down his flag, from the fire from our most distant guns, our own traverses protecting him from such fire. From this [time] it was a succession of fighting from traverse to traverse, and from line to line, until 9 o'clock at night, when we were overpowered and all resistance ceased.

The fall both of the general and the colonel commanding the fort, one about 4 and the other about 4:30 p. m., had a perceptible effect upon the men, and no doubt hastened greatly the result; but we were overpowered, and no skill or gallantry could have saved the place, after he effected a lodgment, except attack in the rear.

The enemy's loss was very heavy, and so, also, our own. Of the latter, as a prisoner, I have not been able to ascertain.

At 9 p. m. the gallant Major Reilly, who had fought the fort after the fall of his superiors, reported the enemy in possession of the sally-port. The brave Captain Van Benthuysen, of the marines, though himself badly wounded, with a squad of his men picked up the general and colonel and endeavored to make way to Battery Buchanan, followed by Reilly with the remnant of the force.

On reaching there it was found to be evacuated; by whose order, or what authority, I know not. No boats were there. The garrison of Fort Fisher had been coolly abandoned to its fate. Nothing was left but to await the approach of the enemy, who took us about 10 p. m. Thus fell Fort Fisher after three days battle, unparalleled in the history of war. The fleet surpassed its tremendous effort upon the previous attack.

The fort has fallen in precisely the manner indicated so often by myself, and to which your attention has been so frequently called, and in the presence of the ample force provided by you to meet the contingency. The fleet never attempted to enter until after the land force had done its work, and, of course unless the supporting force played its part, Fort Fisher must have fallen. Making every allowance for the extraordinary vigor and force of the enemy's assault, and the terrific effect of the fire of the fleet upon the garrison, and the continual and incessant enfilading of the whole point from Battery Buchanan to the fort, thereby preventing to a great extent the movement of my troops, I think that the result might have been avoided, and Fort Fisher still held, if the commanding general had have done his duty. I charge him with this loss; with neglect of duty in this, that he either refused or neglected to carry out every suggestion made to him in official communications by me for the disposition of the troops, and especially that he, failing to appreciate the lesson to be derived from previous attempt of Butler, instead of keeping his troops in the position to attack the enemy on his appearance, he moves them twenty miles from the point of landing in spite of repeated warnings. He might have learned from his failure to interrupt either the landing or the embarking of Butler for two days with his troops, though disgraceful enough, would indicate to the enemy that he would have the same security for any a future expedition. The previous failure was due to Fort Fisher alone, and not to any supporting troops. I charge him further with making no effort whatever to create a diversion in favor of the beleaguered garrison during the three days' battle, by attacking the enemy, though that was to be expected, since his delay and false disposition allowed the enemy to secure his rear by works, but works of no strength. I desire that a full investigation be had of this matter and these charges which I make; they will be fully borne out by the official records. I have only to add that the commanding general, on learning the approach of the enemy, would give me no orders whatever, and persistently refused from the beginning to allow me to have anything to do with the troops from General Lee's army. I consequently repaired to Fort Fisher as the place where my own sense of duty called me.

I am, general, very respectfully, your obedient servant.

W. H. C. Whiting
Major-General, (prisoner of war)

Chapter 10

Blood-Stained Testament, Fort Fisher Relic, Returned By A Newton Veteran

James E. Reid, Then of New York Troops,
Finds Son of Confederate Soldier in North Carolina
Reprinted from the Boston Journal, April 22, 1905

Treasured for forty years as a memento of the capture of Fort Fisher, James E. Reid of Newton Center, late of Company C, 115th New York Volunteers is about to return to the son of a Confederate soldier a little blood-stained testament found in the fort on the night of its fall.

Prompted by the same spirit that actuated the government to return the captured battle flags to the Southern States, Mr. Reid has, after the lapse of two (sic) decades and through the aid of Governor Robert B. Glenn of North Carolina, located the son of the dead soldier. To him personally Governor Glenn will soon deliver the little volume, lost by his father as he lay wounded in the bombproof casement of the fort on the night of Jan. 15, 1865.

By Drummer Boy

It was on the morning following the surrender of Fort Fisher that the testament was handed to Mr. Reid by a drummer boy from his company. The boy had found it the night before in the bomb-proof hospital casement beneath the works of the fort. The edges bore bloodstains, even now faintly discernible. On the title page was the inscription, "H. A. Sledge. October the 9th, 1864. A present given to H. A. Sledge by McKinnon, Chaplain 36th North Carolina Troops. Fort Fisher, N. C. October 9th, 1864." On the third page was written: "Miss _____ D_____."

For fifteen years Mr. Reid carried the volume, but one of the many souvenirs of the war he has preserved. In 1880 he attempted, through a friend in Wilmington, N. C., to locate the owner of the testament or his heirs, but without result.

Last month he again came across the little book and determined to make a final effort to locate the descendants of Sledge. Accordingly he wrote to Governor Glenn and requested his assistance. Governor Glenn at once promised his cordial co-operation, and during the latter part of March informed Mr. Reid that one, H. M. Sledge, now a resident of Tarboro, N. C., was the son of H. A. Sledge, the owner of the testament. Both

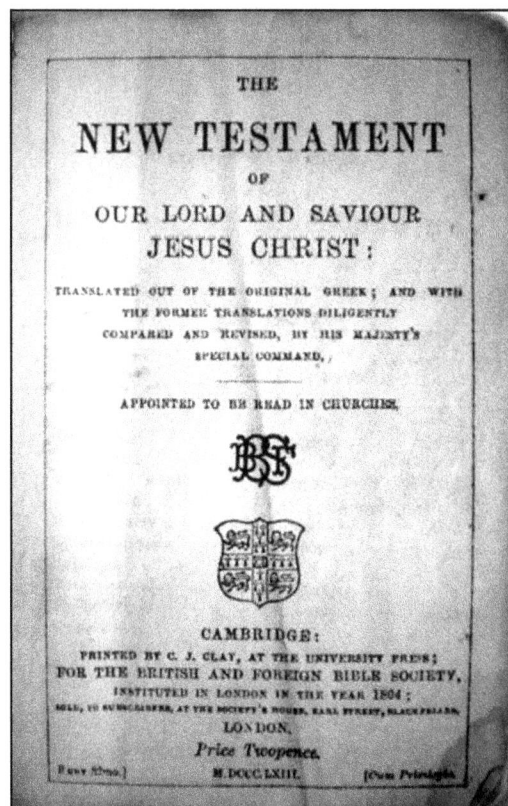

father and son served in the Thirty-sixth North Carolina Regiment. The father was wounded at the storming of Fort Fisher and died after the close of the war. The son was taken prisoner in the same engagement.

Continuing, Governor Glenn said: "I will deliver the testament to H. M. Sledge personally, or someone dully authorized to receive it. You little know how much I appreciate the spirit that has actuated you in this matter. You must have been a brave soldier and show the (illegible) spirit in returning this little testament to the heir of a fallen enemy. If only we had more of this spirit existing in all sections we would hear no more of sectional hate."

Thus after nearly half a century, the testament lost by the father when the latter fell in one of the last great engagements of the Civil War, has been restored to the son, who was captured fighting for the same cause.

Mr. Reid, through whose efforts the testament has been restored to the family of a dead soldier, is 61 years old and a native of New York. He enlisted in Company C, 115th New York Infantry during the second year of the war, and served three years. At present he resides with his daughter on Crescent Avenue, Newton Center.

Eighteen year-old Herbert A. Sledge traveled from his home in Brinkleyville, North Carolina, and volunteered for Company F, 36th N. C. on August 4, 1862 at Fort Caswell in Brunswick County. He was wounded and then captured at the second battle of Fort Fisher. He was sent to Point Lookout Prisner of War Camp in Maryland. Sledge took the oath of allegiance June 20, 1865. His Testament was donated by his son, H. M. Sledge, to The North Carolina Museum of History in Raleigh, North Carolina.

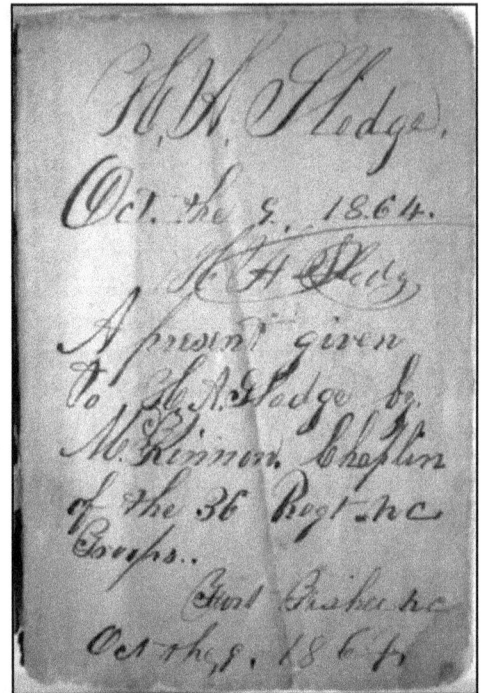

Chapter 11

Confederate Fort Fisher: A Roster, 1864-1865

I have used many resources in compiling this roster. It contains information found in the Confederate soldier's records at the National Archives as well as data obtained from the 1860 United States Census. Various references such as *North Carolina Troops, 1861-1865 A Roster* compiled by Louis H. Manarin, *Service Records of Confederate Enlisted Marines* by Ralph W. Donnelly, numerous letters, soldier's accounts and newspaper articles were also consulted.

NAME & RANK	ENLISTED	RESIDENCE AGE & TRADE	UNIT	RESULT OF BATTLE	PRISON	PRISON RELEASE
Ackey, John, Private	Date and Place Unknown	Unknown	Co. C, Confederate Marine Corp	Captured	Point Lookout Prison, Maryland	Date of release unknown
Adams, A. Private	Charleston, South Carolina, 5/14/1862	Unknown	Co H, 25th Regiment South Carolina Volunteers	Captured	Elmira Prison, Elmira, New York	Died of Chronic Diarrhea, 2/17/1865
Adams, Archibald Seaman	Place Date and Place Unknown, 8/14/1861	Brunswick County, North Carolina, 31 Years Old Fisherman	Galloway Co., Confederate States Coast Guard	Captured	Unknown	Date of release unknown
Adams, John Q. Private	Brunswick County, North Carolina, 2/19/1863, Volunteer	Lumberton, Robeson County, North Carolina, 33 Years Old, Teamster at Fort Fisher Farm Laborer	Co. E, 40th Regiment, 3rd North Carolina Artillery	Captured	Point Lookout Prison, Maryland	Oath of Allegiance 6/23/1865

NAME & RANK	ENLISTED	RESIDENCE AGE & TRADE	UNIT	RESULT OF BATTLE	PRISON	PRISON RELEASE
Adams, Josephus Private	Washington, Beaufort County, North Carolina, 9/23/1861	Unknown, 17 Years Old	Co. D, 13th Battalion, Battery North Carolina Light Artillery	Captured, Defended River Road Gate	Point Lookout Prison, Maryland	Oath of Allegiance 6/3/1865
Adams, William F. Sergeant	Bennettsville, South Carolina 12/25/1861	Marlbourgh District, South Carolina, 23 Years Old	Co. F, 21st South Carolina	Gunshot Wound Right Arm and Shoulder & Captured	Point Lookout Prison, Maryland	Oath of Allegiance 6/23/1865
Adams, Zachariah T. Captain	Beaufort County, North Carolina, 11/4/1863, Volunteer	Beaufort County, North Carolina, 25 Years Old	Co. D, 13th Battalion, North Carolina Light Artillery	Captured, Defended River Road Gate	Fort Columbus Prison, New York Harbor	Exchanged 3/5/1865 Boulware's Wharf, James River, Virginia
Adcock, Ransom J. Private	Holly Springs, Miss., 8/29/1862	Marshall County, Mississippi, 18 Years Old	Co. B, Confederate Marine Corp, Assigned to Guard Duty Aboard CSS *Tallahassee.*	Captured	Point Lookout Prison, Maryland	Oath of Allegiance 6/3/1865
Adkins, Robert J. Private	Enfield, Halifax County, North Carolina, 10/9/1861, Volunteer	Edgecombe County, North Carolina, 21 Years Old	Co. F, 36th Regiment North Carolina, 2nd N. C. Artillery	Captured	Elmira Prison, Elmira, New York	Oath of Allegiance 7/7/1865
Alden, J. Private	Date and Place Unknown	Unknown	Co. K, 36th Regiment North Carolina, 2nd N. C. Artillery	Captured	Unknown	Date of release unknown, No Further Information

NAME & RANK	ENLISTED	RESIDENCE AGE & TRADE	UNIT	RESULT OF BATTLE	PRISON	PRISON RELEASE
Alford, Jacob Evander Private	Robeson County, North Carolina, 2/8/1864, Volunteer	Lumberton, Robeson County, North Carolina, 26 Years Old, Farm Laborer	3rd Co. B, 36th Regiment North Carolina, 2nd North Carolina Artillery	Captured	Point Lookout Prison, Maryland	Oath of Allegiance 6/4/1865
Allen, Caleb Private	Cerro Gordo, Columbus County, North Carolina, 3/5/1862 Volunteer	Columbus County, North Carolina, 25 Years Old Farmer, Teamster	Co. E, 36th Regiment North Carolina, 2nd N. C. Artillery	Killed In Action 1/15/1865		
Allen, Charles G. Private	Moore County, North Carolina, 3/14/1862,	27 Years Old Farmer	Co. F, 36th Regiment North Carolina, 2nd N. C. Artillery	Gunshot Wound Of Left Arm & Captured	Treated At Mansfield Hospital Morehead City, N. C., Sent To Fort Delaware Prison, Del.	No Record Of Allen Being Released
Allen, Daniel J. Private	Fort Holmes, Brunswick County, North Carolina, 2/24/1864, Volunteer	Prospect Hall, Bladen County, North Carolina, 19 Years Old Farmer	2nd Co. K, 40th Regiment North Carolina, 3rd N. C. Artillery	Captured	Elmira Prison, Elmira, New York	Oath of Allegiance 8/7/1865
Allen, David F. Private	Bladen County, North Carolina, 5/6/1862, Volunteer	Robeson County, North Carolina, 33 Years Old Farmer,	2nd Co. K, 40th Regiment, 3rd North Carolina Artillery	Shell Wound Right Leg & Captured	Point Lookout Prison General Hospital, Maryland	Right Leg amputated, Oath of Allegiance 6/26/1865

NAME & RANK	ENLISTED	RESIDENCE AGE & TRADE	UNIT	RESULT OF BATTLE	PRISON	PRISON RELEASE
Allen, Dockery Carver Private	Robeson County, North Carolina, 3/22/1862, Volunteer	Lumberton, Robeson County, North Carolina, 24 Years Old Farmer	Co. H, 36th Regiment North Carolina, 2nd N. C. Artillery	Captured	Point Lookout Prison, Maryland	Oath of Allegiance 6/23/1865
Allen, Drewry A. Private	Battery Island, South Carolina 4/12/1862	Gage Station, South Carolina, 37 Years Old	Co E, 25th Regiment South Carolina Volunteers	Captured	Elmira Prison, Elmira, New York	Died of Pneumonia, 2/20/1865
Allen, George Frank Private	Elizabeth-town, Bladen County, North Carolina, 5/6/1862, Volunteer	Prospect Hall, Bladen County, North Carolina, 20 Years Old, Turpentine	2nd Co. K, 40th Regiment, 3rd North Carolina Artillery	Captured	Elmira Prison, Elmira, New York	Exchanged 3/2/1865 Boulware's Wharf, James River, Virginia
Allen, John Private	Wayne County, North Carolina, 9/9/1863, Volunteer	Green County, North Carolina, 43 Years Old Farmer	Co. K, 40th Regiment, 3rd North Carolina Artillery	Captured	Point Lookout Prison, Maryland	Oath of Allegiance 6/23/1865
Allen, John H. Assistant Surgeon	Unknown	Wythe, Virginia	Confederate States Navy	Captured	Fort Delaware, Del.	Oath of Allegiance 5/15/1865
Allen, Joseph B. Private	Elizabeth-town, Bladen County, North Carolina, 5/6/1862, Mustered in Ft St Philip, Volunteer	Bladenboro, Bladen County, North Carolina, 27 Years Old Farmer, Detailed as Nurse in Hospital	2nd Co. K, 40th Regiment, 3rd North Carolina Artillery	Captured	Elmira Prison, Elmira, New York	Oath of Allegiance 6/12/1865

NAME & RANK	ENLISTED	RESIDENCE AGE & TRADE	UNIT	RESULT OF BATTLE	PRISON	PRISON RELEASE
Allen, Lewis Private	Cerro Gordo, Columbus County, North Carolina, 3/5/1862, Mustered in Wilmington, North Carolina Volunteer	Columbus County, North Carolina, 28 Years Old Laborer, Teamster at Smithville	Co. E, 36th Regiment North Carolina, 2nd N. C. Artillery	Gunshot Wound of Head & Captured	Treated At Mansfield Hospital, Morehead City, North Carolina, Sent To Fort Delaware Prison, Del.	Oath of Allegiance 6/19/1865
Allen, Miles Private	Fort Caswell, Brunswick County, North Carolina, 7/3/1863, Volunteer	Eastern Division, Randolph County, North Carolina, 18 Years Old	2nd Co. D, 36th Regiment North Carolina, 2nd N. C. Artillery	Wounded & Captured	Elmira Prison, Elmira, New York	Exchanged 3/14/1865, Captured in Jackson Hospital, Richmond, Va, Oath of Allegiance 5/25/1865
Allen, Thomas Private	New Berne, Craven County, North Carolina, 1/29/1862, Volunteer	New Berne, Craven County, North Carolina, 27 Years Old Civil Engineer	Co. F, 36th Regiment North Carolina, 2nd N. C. Artillery	Captured	Elmira Prison, Elmira, New York	Died of Pneumonia, 2/19/1865
Allen, William Rufus Private	Elizabeth-town, Bladen County, North Carolina, 5/6/1862, Mustered In At Fort St. Philip, Volunteer	Prospect Hall, Bladen County, North Carolina, 20 Years Old Farmer, Laborer	2nd Co. K, 40th Regiment, 3rd North Carolina Artillery	Captured	Elmira Prison, Elmira, New York	Exchanged On the James River, Va, 2/20/1865
Alsbrook, Benjamin Ira Corporal	Halifax County, North Carolina, 10/9/1861, Volunteer	Halifax County, North Carolina, 18 Years Old	Co. F, 36th Regiment North Carolina, 2nd N. C. Artillery	Captured	Point Lookout Prison, Maryland	Oath of Allegiance 6/23/1865

NAME & RANK	ENLISTED	RESIDENCE AGE & TRADE	UNIT	RESULT OF BATTLE	PRISON	PRISON RELEASE
Altman, John J. Private	Marion District, South Carolina 3/15/1864	Marion District, South Carolina, 23 Years Old	Co. F, 21st South Carolina Volunteers	Captured	Elmira Prison, Elmira, New York	Exchanged On The James River, Virginia 3/10/1865
Altman, Nathan T. Private	Wilmington, New Hanover County, North Carolina, 7/23/1863, Volunteer	New Hanover County, North Carolina, 18 Years Old Extra Duty as Boatman	3rd Co. G, 40th Regiment, 3rd North Carolina Artillery	Captured, Defended Land Face	Elmira Prison, Elmira, New York	Died of Chronic Diarrhea, 4/18/1865
Altman, Owen N. Private	Bay Point, Whippy Swamp, South Carolina, 7/15/1861	Edgefield County, South Carolina, 21 Years Old	Co. F, 11th South Carolina Volunteers	Captured	Elmira Prison, Elmira, New York	Exchanged On The James River, Virginia, 3/14/1865
Ammons, William Henry Private	Brunswick County, North Carolina, 8/24/1863, Volunteer	Macon County, North Carolina 18 Years Old Laborer	Co. E, 40th Regiment, 3rd North Carolina Artillery	Captured	Point Lookout Prison, Maryland	Oath of Allegiance 6/3/1865
Anders, William King Private	Enlistment 12/24/1864, No Further Information	Flat Rock, Henderson County, North Carolina, 17 Years Old Laborer	Co. H, 36th Regiment North Carolina, 2nd N. C. Artillery	Captured	Point Lookout Prison, Maryland	Exchanged 2/13/1865 Boulware's Wharf, James River, Virginia
Anderson, Alexander Private	Bladen County, North Carolina, 4/14/1862, Volunteer	Bladen County, North Carolina, 25 Years Old Teamster at Fort Fisher, North Carolina	3rd Co. B, 36th Regiment North Carolina, 2nd N. C. Artillery	Captured	Point Lookout Prison, Maryland	Oath of Allegiance 6/23/1865
Anderson, David Private	Date and Place Unknown	Fayetteville, Cumberland County, North Carolina, 28 Years Old Merchant	Co. D, 40th Regiment, 3rd North Carolina Artillery	Captured	Unknown	Captured 1/16/1865, Caswell Hospital, Smithville, North Carolina

NAME & RANK	ENLISTED	RESIDENCE AGE & TRADE	UNIT	RESULT OF BATTLE	PRISON	PRISON RELEASE
Anderson, George H. Private	Fort Caswell, Brunswick County, North Carolina, 10/5/1863, Volunteer	Sampson County, North Carolina, 35 Years Old Laborer	2nd Co. D, 36th Regiment North Carolina, 2nd N. C. Artillery	Captured	Elmira Prison, Elmira, New York	Died of Chronic Diarrhea, 4/10/1865
Anderson, Henry Private	Wayne County, North Carolina, 5/10/1864	Goldsboro, Wayne County, North Carolina, 49 Years Old Farmer	Co. D, 40th Regiment, 3rd North Carolina Artillery	Captured	Elmira Prison, Elmira, New York	Oath of Allegiance 7/19/1865
Anderson, Pinckney S. Private	Pee Dee Bridge, South Carolina 4/25/1862	Darlington District, South Carolina, Age Unknown	Co. K, 21st South Carolina Volunteers	Severe Gunshot Wound In Neck & Captured	Treated At Mansfield USA Hospital, Morehead, North Carolina, Transferred 2/16/1865 to Fort Delaware, Del.	Oath of Allegiance 6/10/1865
Anderson, Silas P. Private	Pee Dee, South Carolina 4/25/1862	Darlington District, South Carolina, 30 Years Old Farmer	Co. K, 21st South Carolina Volunteers	Killed In Action 1/15/1865		
Anderson, William J. Private	Duplin County, North Carolina, 10/16/1861, Volunteer	Wayne County, North Carolina, 24 Years Old Laborer	3rd Co. G, 40th Regiment, 3rd North Carolina Artillery	Captured, Defended Land Face	Elmira Prison, Elmira, New York	Exchanged On The James River, Va, 2/20/1865
Anderson, William L. Musician	Craven County, North Carolina, 1/31/1862	Halifax County, North Carolina, 22 Years Old	Co. F, 36th Regiment North Carolina, 2nd N. C. Artillery	Captured	Point Lookout Prison, Maryland	Oath of Allegiance 6/22/1865
Andrews, James W. Private	Brunswick County, North Carolina, 2/19/1862	Brunswick County, North Carolina, 36 Years Old Laborer, Seaman	Co. K, 36th Regiment North Carolina, 2nd N. C. Artillery	Captured	Point Lookout Prison, Maryland	Oath of Allegiance 5/12/1865

NAME & RANK	ENLISTED	RESIDENCE AGE & TRADE	UNIT	RESULT OF BATTLE	PRISON	PRISON RELEASE
Andrews, Robert A. Private	Chatham County, North Carolina, 3/16/1863, Volunteer	Rowan County, North Carolina, 36 Years Old, Extra Duty as Fisherman	3rd Co. G, 40th Regiment, 3rd North Carolina Artillery	Captured, Defended Land Face	Elmira Prison, Elmira, New York	Oath of Allegiance 6/12/1865
Anten, J. Private	No Further Information	New Hanover County, North Carolina, 33 Years Old	Co. K, 36th Regiment North Carolina, 2nd N. C. Artillery	Captured	Point Lookout Prison, Maryland	Oath of Allegiance 5/12/1865
Antley, Furman M. Private	Coles Island, South Carolina 4/11/1862	Orangeburg, South Carolina Overseer of Negro labor	Co. G, 25th South Carolina Volunteers	Captured	Elmira Prison, Elmira, New York	Oath of Allegiance 6/27/1865
Antley, J. B. Private	James Island, South Carolina 3/13/1864	Unknown, 17 Years Old	Co. H, 25th South Carolina Volunteers	Gunshot Wound In Left Arm & Captured	Fort Monroe Hospital, Virginia, Transferred To Point Lookout, Maryland	Oath of Allegiance 6/4/1865
Applewhite Robert B. Private	Craven County, N. C., North Carolina, 1/1/1862, Volunteer	Scotland's Neck, Halifax County, North Carolina, 16 Years Old Farmer	Co. F, 36th Regiment North Carolina, 2nd N. C. Artillery	Wounded Severely Right Shoulder by shell, 12/25/1864	Not Sent to Prison	1/17/1865 Hospitalized Raleigh, Wake County, North Carolina
Ard, Benjamin Private	Williamsburg South Carolina 1/27/1861	Unknown	Co H, 25th Regiment South Carolina Volunteers	Captured	Elmira Prison, Elmira, New York	Died of Pneumonia, 6/1/1865
Ard, E. G. Private	Battery Island, South Carolina 4/12/1864	Kingstree, South Carolina, 23 Years Old	Co B, 25th Regiment South Carolina Volunteers	Captured	Elmira Prison, Elmira, New York	Oath of Allegiance 7/13/1865
Ard, S. R. Private	Battery Island, South Carolina 4/12/1862	Kingstree, South Carolina, 21 Years Old	Co C, 25th Regiment South Carolina Volunteers	Captured	Elmira Prison, Elmira, New York	Oath of Allegiance 7/26/1865

NAME & RANK	ENLISTED	RESIDENCE AGE & TRADE	UNIT	RESULT OF BATTLE	PRISON	PRISON RELEASE
Arendell, Thomas First Lieutenant	Beaufort, Carteret County, North Carolina, 7/5/1861, Volunteer	Carteret County, North Carolina, 30 Years Old Merchant	Co. F, 10th Reg. 1st North Carolina Artillery	Captured	Fort Columbus Prison, New York Harbor	Exchanged 3/5/1865 Captured 4/26/1862 Fort Macon
Argo, Thomas Monroe Second Lieutenant	Orange County, North Carolina, 1/13/1864, Volunteer	Orange County, North Carolina, 19 Years Old Student	Co. D, 1st Battalion North Carolina Heavy Artillery	Wounded & Captured	Fort Columbus Prison, New York Harbor	Exchanged 2/25/1865 Wounded in defense of the River Road Gate.
Arnold, Owen T. Private	Fort Caswell, Brunswick County, North Carolina, 2/28/1863	Town Creek District, Brunswick County, North Carolina, 18 Years Old	3rd Co. G, 36th Regiment North Carolina, 2nd N. C. Artillery	Wounded & Captured, Defended Battery to the Left of Northeast Bastion	Unknown	May Have Died of Wounds at Fort Fisher
Arnold, William Private	Brunswick County, North Carolina, 2/19/1862	37 Years Old Farmer, Guard duty at 24 pounder cannon at Fort Campbell on beach	Co. K, 36th Regiment North Carolina, 2nd N. C. Artillery	Captured	Point Lookout Prison, Maryland	Exchanged 2/20/1865 Boulware's Wharf, James River, Virginia
Arrington, James Lewis Private	New Berne, Craven County, North Carolina, 2/4/1862, Volunteer	Heathsville, Halifax County, North Carolina 25 Years Old Farmer	Co. F, 36th Regiment North Carolina, 2nd N. C. Artillery	Captured	Elmira Prison, Elmira, New York	Exchanged 3/2/1865 Boulware's Wharf, James River, Virginia
Arrowood, David Private	Moore County, North Carolina, 11/4/1863	Moore County, North Carolina, 28 Years Old Farmer	Co. D, 13th Battalion, North Carolina Light Artillery	Captured, Defended River Road Gate	Elmira Prison, Elmira, New York	Died of Chronic Diarrhea, 3/14/1865
Atkinson, J. W. Private	Wake County, North Carolina, Date Unknown	Raleigh, Wake County, North Carolina, 30 Years Old Farmer	Co. D, 1st Battalion, North Carolina Heavy Artillery	Captured, Defended River Road Gate	Elmira Prison, Elmira, New York	Oath of Allegiance 6/30/1865

NAME & RANK	ENLISTED	RESIDENCE AGE & TRADE	UNIT	RESULT OF BATTLE	PRISON	PRISON RELEASE
Atkinson, Thomas W. Private	Sumter, South Carolina 3/1/1863	Unknown	Co G, 21st Regiment South Carolina Volunteers	Captured	Elmira Prison, Elmira, New York	Died of Chronic Diarrhea, 4/6/1865
Atkinson, William Private	Edgecombe County, North Carolina, 1/5/1864, Volunteer	Edgecombe County, North Carolina, 17 Years Old	Co. D, 40th Regiment, 3rd North Carolina Artillery	Captured	Point Lookout Prison, Maryland	Oath of Allegiance 6/22/1865
Atkinson, William E. Private	Wake County, North Carolina, 4/15/1864	Wake County, North Carolina, Age Unknown	Co K, 10th Reg. North Carolina State Troops	Severely Wounded & Captured	Prison Unknown	Release Unknown, May have Died of Wounds at Fort Fisher
Attmore, Sitgreaves Private	Camp Holmes, Wake County, North Carolina, 3/22/1864	Wake County, North Carolina, 34 Years Old, Detailed at Smithville by order General Hebert	Co K, 10th Reg. North Carolina State Troops	Captured	Elmira, New York & Point Lookout Prison, Maryland	Exchanged 2/20/1865 on the James River, Va., Recaptured in Jackson Hospital, Richmond, Va. 4/3/1865, Died of Chronic Diarrhea, 5/22/1865 Point Lookout Hospital, Md.
Ausley, Jesse A. Private	Robeson County, North Carolina, 5/7/1862, Volunteer	Robeson County, North Carolina 22 Years Old, Detailed as guard on Wilmington & Weldon Railroad, 1863	Co. D, 1st Battalion, North Carolina Heavy Artillery	Captured, Defended River Road Gate	Point Lookout Prison, Maryland	Oath of Allegiance 6/22/1865
Austin, Richard Private	Hertford City, North Carolina, 7/20/1864	Hertford County, North Carolina, Age Unknown	Co. C, 40th Regiment, 3rd North Carolina Artillery	Captured	Elmira Prison, Elmira, New York	Died of Chronic Diarrhea, 6/11/1865

NAME & RANK	ENLISTED	RESIDENCE AGE & TRADE	UNIT	RESULT OF BATTLE	PRISON	PRISON RELEASE
Autery, John W. Private	Clinton, Sampson, North Carolina, County, 2/9/1863, Volunteer	Sampson County, North Carolina, 29 Years Old Farmer	2nd Co. C, 36th Regiment North Carolina, 2nd N. C. Artillery	Gunshot Wound In Upper Jaw on Left side, Compound Fracture Of Lower Jawbone	Hammond General Hospital, Point Lookout Prison, Maryland	Oath of Allegiance 6/3/1865, Defended River Road Gate
Autry, Micajah Private	Clinton, Sampson County, North Carolina, 2/9/1863, Volunteer	Owensville, Sampson County, North Carolina, 33 Years Old Timber Cutter	2nd Co. C, 36th Regiment North Carolina, 2nd N. C. Artillery	Captured	Elmira Prison, Elmira, New York	Died of Chronic Diarrhea, 4/9/1865, Defended River Road Gate
Autry, Newsome Private	Sampson County, North Carolina 4/16/1863	26 Years Old Laborer	Co. A, 36th Regiment North Carolina, 2nd N. C. Artillery	Captured	Point Lookout Prison, Maryland	Died of Disease 3/2/1865, Cause Unknown
Avant, James H. Private	Coles Island, South Carolina 4/11/1862	McCantsville, South Carolina, Age Unknown	Co. G, 25th South Carolina Volunteers	Captured	Elmira Prison, Elmira, New York	Exchanged 3/2/1865 Boulware's Wharf, James River, Virginia
Avant, O. R. Private	Camp Harllee, South Carolina 12/20/1861	Kingstree, South Carolina, Age Unknown	Co. I, 21st South Carolina Volunteers	Captured	Elmira Prison, Elmira, New York	Oath of Allegiance 7/11/1865
Avery, D. Private	Wilmington, New Hanover County, North Carolina, 3/4/1862	Unknown, 31 Years Old	2nd Co. I, 36th Regiment North Carolina, 2nd N. C. Artillery	Captured, Defended Shepperd's Battery	Unknown	Date Of Release Unknown,
Avery, J. Private	No Further Information	Unknown	2nd Co. I, 36th Regiment North Carolina, 2nd N. C. Artillery	Captured, Defended Shepperd's Battery	Unknown	Date Of Release Unknown

NAME & RANK	ENLISTED	RESIDENCE AGE & TRADE	UNIT	RESULT OF BATTLE	PRISON	PRISON RELEASE
Avinger, Alexander P. Sergeant	Coles Island, South Carolina 4/11/1862	Vans Ferry, South Carolina, 24 Years Old	Co. F, 25th South Carolina Volunteers	Captured	Elmira Prison, Elmira, New York	Oath of Allegiance 7/7/1865
Aycock, Jesse T. Private	Wayne County, North Carolina, 10/11/1864	Nahunta, Wayne County, North Carolina, 17 Years Old	Co. D, 40th Regiment, 3rd North Carolina Artillery	Captured	Point Lookout Prison, Maryland	Oath of Allegiance 6/22/1865

NAME & RANK	ENLISTED	RESIDENCE AGE & TRADE	UNIT	RESULT OF BATTLE	PRISON	PRISON RELEASE
Bagnal, Isaac J. M. Sergeant	Georgetown South Carolina 1/1/1862	Sumter, South Carolina, 18 Years Old	Co. I, 25th South Carolina Volunteers	Captured	Elmira Prison, New York	Oath of Allegiance 6/27/1865
Bail, J. N. Private	No Further Information	Unknown	Co. D, 1st Battalion, North Carolina Heavy Artillery	Captured, Defended River Road Gate	Unknown	Paroled, Date Of Release Unknown
Bailey, Charles M. Private	Coles Island, South Carolina 4/11/1862	22 Years Old Farm Laborer	Co. G, 25th South Carolina Volunteers	Captured	Elmira Prison, Elmira, New York	Died of Typhoid Fever, 4/19/1865
Bailey, Henry Private	Orangeburg, South Carolina 4/14/1862	Edisto Island, South Carolina, 25 Years Old Merchant	Co. G, 25th South Carolina Volunteers	Captured	Elmira Prison, Elmira, New York	Died of Chronic Diarrhea, 3/13/1865
Bain, Joel W. Private	Cumberland County, North Carolina, 2/15/1864, Volunteer	Cumberland County, North Carolina, 25 Years Old	2nd Co. C, 36th Regiment North Carolina, 2nd N. C. Artillery	Captured, Defended River Road Gate	Point Lookout Prison, Maryland	Oath of Allegiance 6/24/1865

NAME & RANK	ENLISTED	RESIDENCE AGE & TRADE	UNIT	RESULT OF BATTLE	PRISON	PRISON RELEASE
Baisden, Alfred Private	Lenoir County, North Carolina, 6/9/1861, Volunteer	Duplin County, North Carolina, 23 Years Old Detached service in Signal Corps	Co. D, 40th Regiment, 3rd North Carolina Artillery	Captured	Point Lookout Prison, Maryland	Oath of Allegiance 5/12/1865
Baker, Amos L. Private	Wilmington, New Hanover County, North Carolina, 11/4/1861, Volunteer	Bladen County, North Carolina, 31 Years Old Farmer	2nd Co. I, 36th Regiment North Carolina, 2nd N. C. Artillery	Captured, Defended Shepperd's Battery	Point Lookout Prison, Maryland	Oath of Allegiance 6/24/1865
Baker, George S. Corporal	Coles Island, South Carolina 3/28/1862	Unknown, 27 Years Old	Co. B, 25th South Carolina Volunteers	Captured	Elmira Prison, Elmira, New York	Exchanged 2/11/1865
Baker, Henry Private	Brunswick County, North Carolina, 1/9/1864, Volunteer	Mount Olive, Duplin County, North Carolina, 18 Years Old Farmer	Co. A, 36th Regiment North Carolina, 2nd N. C. Artillery	Captured	Point Lookout Prison, Maryland	Died of Inflammation Of Lungs, 4/9/1865,
Baker, Ira D. Private	Chalk Level, North Carolina, Cumberland County, N. C., 3/1/62, Volunteer	Cumberland County, North Carolina, 34 Years Old	2nd Co. C, 36th Regiment North Carolina, 2nd N. C. Artillery	Captured, Defended River Road Gate	Elmira Prison, Elmira, New York	Exchanged 3/14/1865 Boulware's Wharf, James River, Virginia
Baker, James Anderson Private	Chalk Level, Cumberland County, North Carolina, 3/1/62, Volunteer	Cumberland County, North Carolina, 34 Years Old	2nd Co. C, 36th Regiment North Carolina, 2nd N. C. Artillery	Captured, Defended River Road Gate	Elmira Prison, Elmira, New York	Died of Smallpox, 3/14/1865
Baker, James F. Sergeant	Duplin County, North Carolina, 11/4/1861, Volunteer	Mount Olive, Duplin County, North Carolina, 23 Years Old Farmer	Co. A, 36th Regiment North Carolina, 2nd N. C. Artillery	Captured	Point Lookout Prison, Maryland	Oath of Allegiance 6/24/1865 Resided: Sampson County

NAME & RANK	ENLISTED	RESIDENCE AGE & TRADE	UNIT	RESULT OF BATTLE	PRISON	PRISON RELEASE
Baker, Jesse J. Private	Wayne County, North Carolina, 4/7/64	Wayne County, North Carolina, 17 Years Old	Co. D, 1st Battalion, North Carolina Heavy Artillery	Gunshot Wound & Fracture of Left Leg, Captured Defended River Road Gate	Point Lookout Prison General Hospital, Maryland	Died of Disease, Pyemia From Gunshot Wound, 2/7/1865
Baker, John Private	Fort Fisher, New Hanover County, North Carolina, 3/18/1862, Volunteer	White Pine, Gaston County, North Carolina, 36 Years Old Blacksmith	2nd Co. C, 36th Regiment North Carolina, 2nd N. C. Artillery	Captured, Defended River Road Gate	Point Lookout Prison, Maryland	Died of Chronic Diarrhea, 1/31/1865
Baker, Joseph Private	Elizabeth-town, Bladen County, North Carolina 10/19/1864, Volunteer	Elizabethtown North Carolina, 18 Years Old	2nd Co. I, 36th Regiment North Carolina, 2nd N. C. Artillery	Captured, Defended Shepperd's Battery	Point Lookout Prison, Maryland	Exchanged 2/14/1865 Cox's Landing, James River, Virginia,
Baker, M. R. D. Corporal	Battery Island, South Carolina 4/12/1861	Unknown, 17 Years Old	2nd Co. C, 25th Regiment, South Carolina Volunteers	Captured	Elmira Prison, Elmira, New York	Died of Disease, Chronic Diarrhea, 3/31/1865
Baker, Patrick H. Private	Fort Fisher, New Hanover County, North Carolina, 3/22/1862. Volunteer	Chalk Level Harnett County, North Carolina, 19 Years Old	2nd Co. D, 36th Regiment North Carolina, 2nd N. C. Artillery	Captured	Point Lookout Prison, Maryland	Oath of Allegiance 6/23/1865
Baker, William B. Captain	Marion District, South Carolina 1/26/1862	Unknown, 21 Years Old	Co. L, 21st South Carolina Volunteers	Wounded & Captured	Fort Columbus Prison, New York Harbor	Exchanged 2/25/1865

NAME & RANK	ENLISTED	RESIDENCE AGE & TRADE	UNIT	RESULT OF BATTLE	PRISON	PRISON RELEASE
Baldwin, Albert Marion Private	Fort Fisher, New Hanover County, North Carolina, 4/15/1863, Volunteer	Fayetteville, Cumberland County, North Carolina, 18 Years Old	2nd Co. K, 40th Regiment, 3rd North Carolina Artillery	Captured	Elmira Prison, Elmira, New York	Oath of Allegiance 6/12/1865 Resided Columbus County
Baldwin, Warren W. Sergeant	New Hanover County, North Carolina, 2/18/1862, Volunteer	Brunswick County, North Carolina, 28 Years Old Overseer	2nd Co. D, 36th Regiment North Carolina, 2nd N. C. Artillery	Wounded & Captured	Prison Unknown	Date of release unknown
Baldwin, William Turrentine Corporal	Wilmington, New Hanover County, North Carolina, 2/18/1862, Volunteer	Brinkley's Depot, Pender County, North Carolina, 20 Years Old	2nd Co. D, 36th Regiment North Carolina, 2nd N. C. Artillery	Wounded & Captured	Elmira Prison, Elmira, New York	Oath of Allegiance 7/11/1865
Balfour, James Fletcher Private	Washington, Beaufort County, North Carolina 10/14/1861	Beaufort County, North Carolina, 22 Years Old	Co. D, 13th Battalion North Carolina Light Artillery	Wounded & Captured, Defended River Road Gate	Point Lookout Prison, Maryland	Wounded at Fort Fisher, Hospitalized Smithville, Captured 1/18/1865, Oath of Allegiance 6/26/1865
Ballantine, Brobstone Sergeant	Wilmington, New Hanover County, North Carolina 9/27/1861, Volunteer	Bladen County, North Carolina, 28 Years Old	3rd Co. B, 36th Regiment North Carolina, 2nd N. C. Artillery	Wounded 12/25/1864, Concussion From Shell & Captured 1/15/1865	Elmira Prison, Elmira, New York	Exchanged 3/20/1865
Ballantine, George W. Sergeant	Elizabeth-town, Bladen County, North Carolina, 5/6/1862, Volunteer	Baden County, North Carolina, 33 Years Old, Turpentine	2nd Co. K, 40th Regiment, 3rd North Carolina Artillery	Gunshot Wound Right Calf & Captured	Point Lookout Prison General Hospital, Maryland	Died of Erysipelas, 4/10/1865

NAME & RANK	ENLISTED	RESIDENCE AGE & TRADE	UNIT	RESULT OF BATTLE	PRISON	PRISON RELEASE
Banks, John D. Private	Craven County, North Carolina, 1/24/1863	Swift Creek, North Carolina 49 Years Old Cooper	Co. D, 40th Regiment, 3rd North Carolina Artillery	Captured	Point Lookout Prison, Maryland	Exchanged 2/20/1865 Boulware's Wharf, James River, Virginia
Barber, George D. Private	Coles Island, South Carolina 4/11/1862	Orangeburg, South Carolina, 22 Years Old	Co. F, 25th South Carolina Volunteers	Captured	Elmira Prison, Elmira, New York	Died of Chronic Diarrhea, 6/26/1865,
Bardin, J. B. Private	Wilson County, North Carolina, Date of Enlistment Unknown	Wilson, Wilson County, North Carolina, 24 Years Old	Co. D, 40th Regiment, 3rd North Carolina Artillery	Captured	Point Lookout Prison, Maryland	Oath of Allegiance 6/23/1865
Bardsdon, A. Private	No Further Information	Unknown	Co. D, 40th Regiment, 3rd North Carolina Artillery	Captured	Prison Unknown	Date Of Release Unknown
Barham, Samuel P. Private	Goldsboro, Wayne County, North Carolina, 3/20/1864	Goldsboro, Wayne County, North Carolina, Age Unknown	Co. F, 10th Reg. 1st North Carolina Artillery	Captured	Elmira Prison, Elmira, New York	Died of Chronic Diarrhea, 2/24/1865
Barksdale, Sherod Private	Fort Caswell, Brunswick County, North Carolina, 9/5/1863 Volunteer	Sampson County, North Carolina, 18 Years Old Extra Duty setting lights for blockade-runners	Co. A, 36th Regiment North Carolina, 2nd N. C. Artillery	Captured	Point Lookout Prison, Maryland	Oath of Allegiance 6/23/1865 Resided: Sampson County
Barnes, B. Willie Private	Wayne County, North Carolina 10/7/1864	Pikeville, North Carolina, Carpenter, 55 Years Old, Laborer at Fort Campbell & Fort Caswell	Co. D, 40th Regiment, 3rd North Carolina Artillery	Captured	Point Lookout Prison, Maryland	Exchanged 2/20/1865 Boulware's Wharf, James River, Virginia

NAME & RANK	ENLISTED	RESIDENCE AGE & TRADE	UNIT	RESULT OF BATTLE	PRISON	PRISON RELEASE
Barnes, F. H. Private	Manning, South Carolina 2/23/1863	Unknown, Age Unknown	Co. I, 25th South Carolina Volunteers	Captured	Elmira Prison, Elmira, New York	Died of Chronic Diarrhea, 4/1/1865,
Barnes, Haynes L. Seaman	Place of Enlistment Unknown, 12/17/1862	Unknown, Age Unknown	Galloway Company, Confederate States Coast Guard	Captured	Unknown	Date Of Release Unknown
Barnes, John W. Private	Wilmington, New Hanover County, North Carolina, 3/24/1864	Wilmington, New Hanover County, North Carolina, 31 Years Old School Teacher	Co. F, 10th Reg. 1st North Carolina Artillery	Gunshot Wound of Left Thigh & Captured	Point Lookout Prison General Hospital, Maryland	Compound Fracture Of Left Femur, Died Of Pyemia, 2/10/1865
Barnes, William L. Private	Fort Holmes, North Carolina 114/1863	Wilson County, North Carolina, Age Unknown	Co. F, 10th Reg. 1st North Carolina Artillery	Gunshot Wound left leg, Fracturing Femur & Wound of Neck, Captured	Point Lookout Prison General Hospital, Maryland	Oath of Allegiance 6/24/1865
Barnes, William Private	Darlington, South Carolina 5/16/1862	Age Unknown, Mechanic	Co. B, 21st Regiment, South Carolina Volunteers	Gunshot Wound In Back & Captured	Point Lookout Prison General Hospital	Died Of Wounds 2/6/1865
Barnhill, Duncan R. Private	Bladen County, North Carolina 3/9/1862,	Bladen County, North Carolina, 25 Years Old Farmer	Co. H, 36th Regiment North Carolina, 2nd N. C. Artillery	Captured	Elmira Prison, Elmira, New York	Died of Chronic Diarrhea, 3/9/1865
Barrentine, Evander Private	Fort Caswell, North Carolina, 2/25/1863,	Brunswick County, North Carolina, 17 Years Old Extra Duty Cutting Timber	Co. E, 40th Regiment, 3rd North Carolina Artillery	Captured	Elmira Prison, Elmira, New York	Died of Chronic Diarrhea, 3/24/1865

NAME & RANK	ENLISTED	RESIDENCE AGE & TRADE	UNIT	RESULT OF BATTLE	PRISON	PRISON RELEASE
Barrett, Benjamin J. Private	Mt. Tabor, North Carolina, 5/1/1862	Forsyth County, North Carolina, Age Unknown	Co. C, 3rd Battalion, North Carolina Light Artillery	Captured	Elmira Prison, Elmira, New York	Exchanged 3/14/1865 Boulware's Wharf, James River, Virginia
Barrett, James Private	Date and Place Unknown	Rocky Creek, Iredell County, North Carolina, Age Unknown	Co. E, Confederate States Marine Corp, Assigned to Guard Duty Aboard the CSS *Savannah.*	Captured, Defended Sea Face	Point Lookout Prison, Maryland	Oath of Allegiance 6/5/1865
Barrett, James B. Private	Roxobel, North Carolina, 7/1/1864	Person County, North Carolina, 18 Years Old	Co. C, 3rd Battalion, North Carolina Light Artillery	Captured	Elmira Prison, Elmira, New York	Exchanged 3/14/1865
Barrineau, R. H. Private	Battery Island, South Carolina 4/12/1862	30 Years Old, Overseer-Farmer at Castle Pinckney, South Carolina	Co. C, 25th South Carolina Volunteers	Captured	Elmira Prison, Elmira, New York	Exchanged 3/2/1865 Boulware's Wharf, James River, Virginia
Barrineau, Ebenezer M. Private	Battery Island, South Carolina 4/12/1862	Kingstree, South Carolina, 16 Years Old	Co. B, 25th South Carolina Volunteers	Captured	Elmira Prison, Elmira, New York	Oath of Allegiance 7/11/1865
Barrington, Adam First Lieutenant	Craven County, North Carolina, 9/21/1861, Volunteer	Craven County, North Carolina, 26 Years Old Farmer & Miller	Co. D, 40th Regiment, 3rd North Carolina Artillery	Captured	Fort Columbus Prison, New York Harbor	Exchanged 3/5/1865 Boulware's Wharf, James River, Virginia

NAME & RANK	ENLISTED	RESIDENCE AGE & TRADE	UNIT	RESULT OF BATTLE	PRISON	PRISON RELEASE
Barrington, William T. Private	Craven County, North Carolina, 3/4/1863, Substitute for his father, Rich Barrington	Craven County, North Carolina, 17 Years Old	Co. D, 40th Regiment, 3rd North Carolina Artillery	Captured	Elmira Prison, Elmira, New York	Exchanged On the James River 2/20/1865
Barrow, James Private	Wilson County, North Carolina, 8/18/1863, Volunteer	Wilson County, North Carolina, 43 Years Old	Co. D, 40th Regiment, 3rd North Carolina Artillery	Captured	Elmira Prison, Elmira, New York	Died of Chronic Diarrhea, 5/2/1865
Barrow, Joseph W. Private	Fort Johnson, Brunswick County, North Carolina, 4/1/1863. Volunteer	Lenoir County, North Carolina, 16 Years Old	3rd Co. G, 40th Regiment, 3rd North Carolina Artillery	Captured, Defended Land Face	Elmira Prison, Elmira, New York	Exchanged 3/18/1865, Boulware's Wharf, James River, Virginia
Barton, Jefferson Private	Date and Place Unknown	Marietta, Greenville County, South Carolina, 34 Years Old Merchant	Co. B, 11th South Carolina Volunteers	Captured	Point Lookout, Maryland	Oath of Allegiance 6/24/1865
Barwick, George W. Private	Charleston, South Carolina 5/18/1862	Georgia, 18 Years Old	Co. I, 25th South Carolina Volunteers	Captured	Elmira Prison, Elmira, New York	Exchanged 2/20/1865 On James River, Virginia, Died 3/10/1865 from Debility & Frostbite at Howard's Grove General Hospital, Richmond, Va.
Barwick, Richard M. Musician	Lenoir County, North Carolina, 11/7/1861, Volunteer	Mosely Hall, Lenoir County, North Carolina, 18 Years Old	3rd Co. G, 40th Regiment, 3rd North Carolina Artillery	Captured, Defended Land Face	Elmira Prison, Elmira, New York	Exchanged On the James River 2/20/1865, Drummer

NAME & RANK	ENLISTED	RESIDENCE AGE & TRADE	UNIT	RESULT OF BATTLE	PRISON	PRISON RELEASE
Barwick, William Private	Fort Branch, Brunswick County, North Carolina, 7/17/1863, Volunteer	Mosely Hall, Lenoir County, North Carolina, 43 Years Old Farmer	3rd Co. G, 40th Regiment, 3rd North Carolina Artillery	Captured, Defended Land Face	Elmira Prison, Elmira, New York	Exchanged 3/14/1865, Boulware's Wharf, James River, Virginia
Bass, Bright Private	Sampson County, North Carolina, 2/18/1863, Volunteer	Sampson County, North Carolina, Hawley's Store Post Office, 38 Years Old Farmer	2nd Co. A, 36th Regiment, 2nd North Carolina Artillery	Captured, Defended the Mound Battery	Point Lookout Prison, Maryland	Oath of Allegiance 6/24/1865
Bass, Cornelius Private	Union County, North Carolina, 10/14/1861, Volunteer	Red Banks, Robeson County, North Carolina, 21 Years Old	Co. E, 40th Regiment, 3rd North Carolina Artillery	Captured	Elmira Prison, Elmira, New York	Died of Chronic Diarrhea, 5/24/1865
Bass, Edmund D. Private	Union County, North Carolina, 8/27/1861, Volunteer	Robeson County, North Carolina, 22 Years Old Extra Duty as Nurse in Hospital July/August 1864	Co. E, 40th Regiment, 3rd North Carolina Artillery	Captured	Point Lookout Prison, Maryland	Oath of Allegiance 6/24/1865
Bass, Edwin Private	Wilson County, North Carolina, 10/7/1864	Black Creek, Wilson County, North Carolina, 16 Years Old	Co. D, 40th Regiment, 3rd North Carolina Artillery	Captured	Point Lookout Prison, Maryland	Oath of Allegiance 6/23/1865
Bass, Isaac Private	Brunswick County, North Carolina, 4/29/1863, Volunteer	Sampson County, North Carolina, 19 Years Old Laborer	Co. A, 36th Regiment North Carolina, 2nd N. C. Artillery	Captured	Point Lookout Prison, Maryland	Exchanged 2/20/1865 Boulware's Wharf, James River, Virginia
Bass, James Olan Private	Fort Caswell, North Carolina, 4/22/1863 Volunteer	Sampson County, North Carolina, 19 Years Old Farmer	Co. A, 36th Regiment North Carolina, 2nd N. C. Artillery	Captured	Point Lookout Prison, Maryland	Exchanged 2/14/1865 Cox's Landing, James River, Virginia

NAME & RANK	ENLISTED	RESIDENCE AGE & TRADE	UNIT	RESULT OF BATTLE	PRISON	PRISON RELEASE
Bass, Stephan Private	Fort Caswell, North Carolina, 5/6/1862, Volunteer	Robeson County, North Carolina, 21 Years Old Farm Laborer	Co. E, 40th Regiment, 3rd North Carolina Artillery	Captured	Point Lookout Prison, Maryland	Oath of Allegiance 6/24/1865
Bass, William M. Private	Whippy Swamp, South Carolina 7/15/1861	Unknown, 21 Years Old	Co. D, 11th South Carolina Volunteers	Captured	Elmira Prison, Elmira, New York	Exchanged 3/2/1865 Boulware's Wharf, James River, Virginia
Bates, W. T. Corporal	Barnwell Court House, South Carolina 11/7/1862	Greenland, South Carolina Farmer	Co. B, 11th South Carolina Volunteers	Captured	Point Lookout Prison, Maryland	Oath of Allegiance 6/5/1865
Baugh, Lemuel Private	Edgefield, South Carolina 5/15/1862	Edgefield, South Carolina, 22 Years Old	Co. F, 25th South Carolina Volunteers	Gunshot Wound Left Arm, Fracture & Captured	Point Lookout Prison, Maryland	Oath of Allegiance 6/28/1865, Amputation Of Left Arm
Baugh, Pleasant Private	Edgefield, South Carolina 9/24/1864	Edgefield, South Carolina, 17 Years Old	Co. H, 25th South Carolina Volunteers	Captured	Elmira Prison, Elmira, New York	Oath of Allegiance 7/11/1865
Baxley, Dougald Private	Robeson County, North Carolina, 2/9/1863, Volunteer	Robeson County, North Carolina, 37 Years Old	Co. D, 1st Battalion, North Carolina Heavy Artillery	Captured, Defended River Road Gate	Point Lookout Prison, Maryland	Oath of Allegiance 6/24/1865
Baynor, Hyman Private	Martin County, North Carolina, 8/11/62	Martin County, North Carolina, Age Unknown	Co. D, 13th Battalion, North Carolina Light Artillery	Died		Died Fort Fisher, N. C., 1/9/1865 Cause Unknown
Beard, Windsor F. Private	New Hanover County, North Carolina, 8/15/1863 Volunteer	White Oak, Bladen County, North Carolina, 38 Years Old Farmer	2nd Co. C, 36th Regiment North Carolina, 2nd N. C. Artillery	Captured, Defended River Road Gate	Point Lookout Prison, Maryland	Exchanged 6/24/1865

NAME & RANK	ENLISTED	RESIDENCE AGE & TRADE	UNIT	RESULT OF BATTLE	PRISON	PRISON RELEASE
Belch, James Willis Private	New Hanover County, North Carolina 3/221864, Volunteer	Robeson County, North Carolina, 17 Years Old	3rd Co. G, 36th Regiment North Carolina, 2nd N. C. Artillery	Captured, Defended Battery to the Left of Northeast Bastion	Point Lookout Prison, Maryland	Oath of Allegiance 6/24/1865
Bell, Manning A. Private	Georgetown South Carolina 1/1/1862	Sumter, South Carolina, 16 Years Old	Co. I, 25th South Carolina Volunteers	Captured	Elmira Prison, Elmira, New York	Oath of Allegiance 7/3/1865
Bell, Noah Private	Edgecombe County, North Carolina 6/25/1864	Tarboro, Edgecombe County, North Carolina, 16 Years Old	Co. D, 40th Regiment, 3rd North Carolina Artillery	Captured	Point Lookout Prison, Maryland	Exchanged 2/14/1865 Cox's Landing, James River, Virginia
Bell, Thomas Private	Date and Place Unknown	Clinton, Sampson County, North Carolina, 39 Years Old Farmer	Confederate States Coast Guard	Captured	Prison Unknown	Date Of Release Unknown
Bellamy, John C. Private	Fort Caswell, Brunswick County, North Carolina, 11/2/1863, Volunteer	Brunswick County, North Carolina, 17 Years Old, Signal Duty	Co. K, 36th Regiment North Carolina, 2nd N. C. Artillery	Wounded & Captured	Prison Unknown	Date Of Release Unknown
Bennett, Aaron B. Private	Brunswick County, North Carolina, 2/28/1863, Volunteer	Waccamaw, Brunswick County, North Carolina, 18 Years Old Farmer	Co. K, 36th Regiment North Carolina, 2nd N. C. Artillery	Wounded & Captured	Point Lookout Prison, Maryland	Oath of Allegiance 5/15/1865

NAME & RANK	ENLISTED	RESIDENCE AGE & TRADE	UNIT	RESULT OF BATTLE	PRISON	PRISON RELEASE
Bennett, Asa B. Private	Fort St. Philip, Brunswick County, North Carolina, 5/5/1862, Volunteer	Shallotte, Brunswick County, North Carolina, 32 Years Old Farmer	3rd Co. G, 36th Regiment North Carolina, 2nd N. C. Artillery	Wounded & Captured, Defended Battery to the Left of Northeast Bastion	Elmira Prison, Elmira, New York	Died of Chronic Diarrhea, 3/9/1865
Bennett, Benjamin Sergeant	Brunswick County, North Carolina, 3/29/1862	Shallotte, Brunswick County, North Carolina, 22 Years Old Laborer	Co. K, 36th Regiment North Carolina, 2nd N. C. Artillery	Captured	Point Lookout Prison, Maryland	Oath of Allegiance 6/24/1865
Bennett, Hosea Private	Brunswick County, North Carolina, 7/14/1863, Volunteer	Waccamaw, Brunswick County, North Carolina, 39 Years Old Farmer	Co. K, 36th Regiment North Carolina, 2nd N. C. Artillery	Captured	Point Lookout Prison, Maryland	Oath of Allegiance 6/24/1865
Bennett, John N. First Sergeant	Fort St. Philip, Brunswick County, North Carolina, 4/23/1862, Volunteer	Town Creek, Brunswick County, North Carolina, 26 Years Old School Teacher	3rd Co. G, 36th Regiment North Carolina, 2nd N. C. Artillery	Wounded & Captured, Defended Battery to the Left of Northeast Bastion	Fort Delaware, Del.	Release Unknown
Bennett, Noah B. Corporal	Brunswick County, North Carolina, 2/19/1862' Volunteer	Waccamaw, Brunswick County, N. C., 22 Years Old Farmer	Co. K, 36th Regiment North Carolina, 2nd N. C. Artillery	Captured	Point Lookout Prison, Maryland	Oath of Allegiance 5/15/1865
Benson, Daniel J. Private	Fort St. Philip, Brunswick County, North Carolina, 7/23/1862, Volunteer	Wilmington, New Hanover County, North Carolina, 27 Years Old	3rd Co. G, 36th Regiment North Carolina, 2nd N. C. Artillery	Captured, Defended Battery to the Left of Northeast Bastion	Elmira Prison, Elmira, New York	Admitted to Jarvis USA Hospital, Baltimore, Maryland with Chronic Diarrhea, 6/25/1865, Released from Hospital 7/7/1865

NAME & RANK	ENLISTED	RESIDENCE AGE & TRADE	UNIT	RESULT OF BATTLE	PRISON	PRISON RELEASE
Benson, George Washington Private	New Hanover County, North Carolina, 5/12/1864	West Brook, Bladen County, North Carolina, 19 Years Old Farmer	Co. H, 36th Regiment North Carolina, 2nd N. C. Artillery	Captured	Point Lookout Prison, Maryland	Oath of Allegiance 6/24/1865
Benson, J. H. Private	Date and Place Unknown	Unknown	Co. H, 36th Regiment North Carolina, 2nd N. C. Artillery	Captured	Prison Unknown	Date Of Release Unknown
Benson, Jesse J. Private	Bladen County, North Carolina, 1/28/1861, Volunteer	White Creek, Bladen County, North Carolina, 22 Years Old Student	Co. H, 36th Regiment North Carolina, 2nd N. C. Artillery	Captured	Point Lookout Prison, Maryland	Oath of Allegiance 6/23/1865
Benson, John M. First Sergeant	Wilmington, New Hanover County, North Carolina, 11/13/1861, Volunteer	White Hall, Bladen County, North Carolina, 22 Years Old Day Laborer	3rd Co. B, 36th Regiment North Carolina, 2nd N. C. Artillery	Wounded, Concussion of Brain and Contusion Of Right Thigh 12/24/1864, Captured 1/15/1865	Elmira Prison, Elmira, New York	Oath of Allegiance 7/7/1865
Benton, Henry E. First Lieutenant	Fayetteville, Cumberland County, North Carolina, 2/15/1862, Volunteer	Cumberland County, North Carolina, 23 Years Old	Co. C, 36th Regiment North Carolina, 2nd N. C. Artillery	Captured, Defended River Road Gate	Fort Columbus Prison, New York Harbor	Exchanged 3/5/1865 City Point, Virginia
Benton, Kilbee Private	New Hanover County, North Carolina, 5/1/1862, Volunteer	Magnolia, Duplin County, North Carolina, 21 Years Old	Co. D, 1st Battalion, North Carolina Heavy Artillery	Captured, Defended River Road Gate	Prison Unknown	Date Of Release Unknown

NAME & RANK	ENLISTED	RESIDENCE AGE & TRADE	UNIT	RESULT OF BATTLE	PRISON	PRISON RELEASE
Beofford, Wesley Private	Goldsboro, Wayne County, North Carolina, 9/20/1862	Unknown, 15 Years Old	Co H, 10th Regiment North Carolina, 1st North Carolina Artillery	Captured	Elmira Prison, Elmira, New York	Died of Smallpox, 4/10/1865
Best, Isaac Private	Unknown, No Further Information	Kinston, Lenoir County, North Carolina, 16 Years Old	2nd Co. A, 36th Regiment North Carolina, 2nd N. C. Artillery	Captured, Defended the Mound Battery	Prison Unknown	Date Of Release Unknown
Best, Matthew J. Private	Whiteville, Columbus County, North Carolina, 2/6/1863 Conscript	Whiteville, Columbus County, North Carolina, 36 Years Old Farmer	Co. E, 36th Regiment North Carolina, 2nd N. C. Artillery	Captured	Elmira Prison, Elmira, New York	Oath of Allegiance 7/7/1865
Best, Richard W. Corporal	Wayne County, North Carolina, 7/29/1861	Buck Swamp District, Wayne County, North Carolina, 24 Years Old Farmer	Co. F, 10th Reg. 1st North Carolina Artillery	Wounded, Fracture Of Outer Table Of Frontal Facial Bone 12/25/1864 & Captured	Hart's Island Prison, New York Harbor	3/19/1865 at Neuse River Bridge Oath of Allegiance 6/19/1865
Best, Waitman. T. Corporal	Wayne County, North Carolina, 7/29/1861	Stony Creek, Wayne County, North Carolina, 22 Years Old Farmer	Co. F, 10th Reg. 1st North Carolina Artillery	Wounded & Captured	Hart's Island Prison, New York Harbor	Fracture Of Left Arm, Severe, 12/25/1864, Captured at Goldsboro, N. C., 3/19/1865, Oath of Allegiance 6/19/1865
Bevans, John C. Sergeant	New Hanover County, North Carolina, 8/5/1861	28 Years Old Assigned to Captain Samuel Bunting's Wilmington Horse Artillery	2nd Co. I, 10th Reg. 1st North Carolina Artillery	Captured, Deserter came into Federal lines 1/25/1865	Fort Monroe, Virginia	Exchanged 2/4/1865

NAME & RANK	ENLISTED	RESIDENCE AGE & TRADE	UNIT	RESULT OF BATTLE	PRISON	PRISON RELEASE
Beverly, John Private	Unknown, No Further Information	Marion District, South Carolina, 16 Years Old Farm Laborer	Co. D, 25th South Carolina Volunteers	Captured	Elmira Prison, Elmira, New York	Died of Smallpox, 2/27/1865
Biggs, Jefferson Private	Fort St. Philip, North Carolina 5/15/1862, Volunteer	Town Creek, Brunswick County, North Carolina, 18 Years Old, Extra Duty at Fort Campbell and Smithville as a Raftsman	3rd Co. G, 36th Regiment North Carolina, 2nd N. C. Artillery	Captured, Defended Battery to the Left of Northeast Bastion	Elmira Prison, Elmira, New York	Died of "Hospital Gangrene", 3/30/1865
Biggs, Kenneth Murchison Private	Robeson County, North Carolina, 8/27/1861, Volunteer	Lumberton, Robeson County, North Carolina, 20 Years Old	Co. E, 40th Regiment, 3rd North Carolina Artillery	Captured	Point Lookout Prison, Maryland	Died of Pneumonia, 4/29/1865
Biggs, Moses Private	New Hanover County, North Carolina, 8/5/1861	Town Creek, Brunswick County, North Carolina, Black Smith	3rd Co. G, 36th Regiment North Carolina, 2nd N. C. Artillery	Captured, Defended Battery to the Left of Northeast Bastion	Elmira Prison, Elmira, New York	Oath of Allegiance 6/23/1865
Biggs, Washington Private	Fort St. Philips, North Carolina, 5/14/1862	Town Creek, Brunswick County, North Carolina, 20 Years Old	3rd Co. G, 36th Regiment North Carolina, 2nd N. C. Artillery	Gunshot Wound Left Thigh & Captured, Defended Battery to the Left of Northeast Bastion	Point Lookout Prison General Hospital, Maryland	Oath of Allegiance 6/4/1865
Belton, Jacob J. Private	Charleston, South Carolina 2/22/1862 Conscript	Charleston, South Carolina, 31 Years Old Carpenter	Co. E, 25th South Carolina Volunteers	Captured	Elmira Prison, New York	Oath of Allegiance 5/17/1865

NAME & RANK	ENLISTED	RESIDENCE AGE & TRADE	UNIT	RESULT OF BATTLE	PRISON	PRISON RELEASE
Bilton, William H. Private	Charleston, South Carolina 2/22/1862,	Charleston, South Carolina, 31 Years Old, Carpenter	Co. E, 25th South Carolina Volunteers	Captured	Elmira Prison, Elmira, New York	Exchanged 2/20/1865, Died of Chronic Diarrhea 3/3/1865 at Howard's Grove Hospital, Richmond, Virginia
Bishop, John C. Private	Beaufort County, North Carolina, 9/23/1861	Long Street, Moore County, North Carolina, 22 Years Old	Co. D, 13th Battalion North Carolina Light Artillery	Captured. Defended River Road Gate	Point Lookout Prison, Maryland	Oath of Allegiance 6/3/1865
Black, John M. Private	Fort Fisher, New Hanover County, North Carolina, 8/26/1862, Volunteer	Elizabethtown Bladen County, North Carolina, 23 Years Old Student	Co. E, 36th Regiment North Carolina, 2nd N. C. Artillery	Captured	Elmira Prison, Elmira, New York	Exchanged 3/2/1865 Boulware's Wharf, James River, Virginia
Blackburn, Kinnon Private	Fort Fisher, New Hanover County, North Carolina, 4/6/1862, Volunteer	New Hanover County, North Carolina, 34 Years Old	2nd Co. I, 36th Regiment North Carolina, 2nd N. C. Artillery	Captured, Defended Shepperd's Battery	Elmira Prison, Elmira, New York	Died of Smallpox, 2/28/1865
Blackmore, Buckner Lanier Private	Duplin County, North Carolina, 9/15/1861, Volunteer, Mustered In At Fort Caswell	Duplin County, North Carolina, 15 Years Old	2nd Co. A, 36th Regiment North Carolina, 2nd N. C. Artillery	Captured, Defended The Mound Battery	Elmira Prison, Elmira, New York	Exchanged On The James River 2/20/1865 Musician
Blackmore, Harold E. Private	Fort Caswell, North Carolina, 9/15/1861, Volunteer	Warsaw Depot, Duplin County, North Carolina, 21 Years Old	2nd Co. A, 36th Regiment North Carolina, 2nd N. C. Artillery	Captured, Defended The Mound Battery	Elmira Prison, Elmira, New York	Oath of Allegiance 7/7/1865

NAME & RANK	ENLISTED	RESIDENCE AGE & TRADE	UNIT	RESULT OF BATTLE	PRISON	PRISON RELEASE
Blackmore, Romulus A. Private	Duplin County, North Carolina, 5/13/1862, Volunteer	Sampson County, North Carolina, 24 Years Old Farmer, Detailed in Signal Service at Cape Fear River, N. C.	Co. A, 36th Regiment North Carolina, 2nd N. C. Artillery	Captured	Elmira Prison, Elmira, New York	Died of Chronic Diarrhea, 6/3/1865
Blackwell, Patrick K. Private	Bladen County, North Carolina, 10/19/1861, Volunteer	Elizabethtown Bladen County, North Carolina, 31 Years Old	2nd Co. I, 36th Regiment North Carolina, 2nd N. C. Artillery	Killed In Action 1/15/1865, Defended Shepperd's Battery		
Blackwood, G. G. Corporal	Charleston, South Carolina 1/8/1863	Charleston, South Carolina, 30 Years Old	Co. A, 25th South Carolina Volunteers	Captured	Elmira Prison, Elmira, New York	Oath of Allegiance 7/26/1865
Blake, Richard M. Private	Brunswick County, North Carolina, 5/17/1863, Substitute	Whitesville, Columbus County, North Carolina, 16 Years Old	Co. E, 36th Regiment North Carolina, 2nd N. C. Artillery	Captured	Elmira Prison, Elmira, New York	Oath of Allegiance 7/3/1865
Blake, Robert Private	Fort Branch, Brunswick County, North Carolina, 8/6/1863, Volunteer	Montgomery County, North Carolina, 18 Years Old	3rd Co. G, 40th Regiment, 3rd North Carolina Artillery	Captured, Defended Land Face	Elmira Prison, Elmira, New York	Died of Pneumonia, 2/27/1865
Bland, Christopher Columbus Private	Fort Campbell. Brunswick County, North Carolina, 7/15/1864	Shallotte, Brunswick County, North Carolina, 19 Years Old	Co. K, 36th Regiment North Carolina, 2nd N. C. Artillery	Shell Wound to Left Ankle 1/13/1865, & Captured At Smithville Hospital, 1/18/1865	Point Lookout Prison, Maryland	Oath of Allegiance 6/3/1865, Amputated Lower Third of Left Leg, Point Lookout General Hospital, Maryland

NAME & RANK	ENLISTED	RESIDENCE AGE & TRADE	UNIT	RESULT OF BATTLE	PRISON	PRISON RELEASE
Blanton, Blaney Private	Wilmington, New Hanover County, North Carolina, 3/25/1862, Volunteer	Teachers Depot, Duplin County, North Carolina, 19 Years Old	Co. D, 1st Battalion, North Carolina Heavy Artillery	Captured, Defended River Road Gate	Elmira Prison, Elmira, New York	Oath of Allegiance 7/11/1865
Bledsoe, Powhatan Assistant Surgeon	Henrico County, Virginia, 5/14/1862	Richmond, Virginia, 28 Years Old Physician	Field & Staff, 36th Regiment North Carolina, 2nd N. C. Artillery	Captured	Fort Columbus Prison, New York Harbor	Exchanged 3/5/1865 Boulware's Wharf, James River, Virginia
Blocker, Charles H. Captain	Fayetteville, Cumberland County, North Carolina, 6/1/1861	Fayetteville, Cumberland County, North Carolina, 18 Years Old College Student	Field & Staff, 36th Regiment North Carolina, 2nd N. C. Artillery	Captured	Fort Columbus Prison, New York Harbor	Aide DeCamp on Colonel Lamb's Staff, Exchanged 3/5/1865 Boulware's Wharf, James River, Virginia
Blue, Angus Private	Richmond County, North Carolina, 5/15/1863, Volunteer	Laurel Hill, Richmond County, North Carolina, Farmer	Co. D, 1st Battalion, North Carolina Heavy Artillery	Wounded in Back By Explosion Of Shell & Captured, Defended River Road Gate	Point Lookout Prison General Hospital, Maryland	Oath of Allegiance 6/21/1865
Blue, D. Private	Date and Place Unknown	Unknown	Co. C, 3rd Battalion North Carolina Light Artillery	Captured	Fort Monroe, Virginia	Date Of Release Unknown
Blue, Daniel Private	Richmond County, North Carolina, 12/1/1862	Laurinburg, Scotland County, North Carolina, 25 Years Old	Co. D, 1st Battalion, North Carolina Heavy Artillery	Severe Gunshot Wound of Left Leg & Neck, Captured, Defended River Road Gate	Camp Hamilton, Virginia	Wounded, Stunned Oath of Allegiance 6/14/1865

NAME & RANK	ENLISTED	RESIDENCE AGE & TRADE	UNIT	RESULT OF BATTLE	PRISON	PRISON RELEASE
Boggan, James N. Private	Fort Branch, Brunswick County, North Carolina, 8/20/1863, Volunteer	Wadesboro, Anson County, North Carolina, 18 Years Old	3rd Co. G, 40th Regiment, 3rd North Carolina Artillery	Captured, Defended Land Face	Elmira Prison, Elmira, New York	Exchanged On The James River 2/20/1865
Boldt, J. D. Private	Pocotaligo, South Carolina 9/10/1863	Beaufort District, South Carolina, 46 Years Old	Co. F, 11th South Carolina Volunteers	Captured	Point Lookout Prison Hospital, Maryland	Oath of Allegiance 7/19/1865
Bomar, George W. First Sergeant	Charleston, South Carolina 2/24/1862	Spartanburg, South Carolina, 17 Years Old	Co. B, 25th South Carolina Volunteers	Captured	Elmira Prison, Elmira, New York	Oath of Allegiance 6/16/1865
Bond, Ballas H. Private	Enfield, Halifax County, North Carolina, 10/9/1861, Volunteer	Birtee Cay, North Carolina, 31 Years Old, Extra Duty Laborer at Fort Campbell and Smithville	Co. F, 36th Regiment North Carolina, 2nd N. C. Artillery	Captured	Elmira, New York & Point Lookout Prison, Maryland	Exchanged 3/18/1865, Boulware's Wharf, James River, Virginia, Recaptured, Oath of Allegiance 6/26/1865
Bond, John F. Private	Fort Ocrecoke, Hyde County, North Carolina, 4/22/1861	Washington, Beaufort County, North Carolina, 21 Years Old	Co. K, 10th Reg. 1st North Carolina Artillery	Captured	Elmira Prison, Elmira, New York	Died of Chronic Diarrhea, 2/18/1865
Bonnett, D. D. Private	Columbia, South Carolina 3/1/1864	Orangeburg County, South Carolina, 44 Years Old Farmer	Co. D, 25th South Carolina Volunteers	Captured	Elmira Prison, Elmira, New York	Exchanged 2/20/1865, Died 3/7/1865 of Chronic Diarrhea at Wayside Hospital No. 9, Richmond, Virginia

NAME & RANK	ENLISTED	RESIDENCE AGE & TRADE	UNIT	RESULT OF BATTLE	PRISON	PRISON RELEASE
Bordeaux, Enoch Private	Brunswick County, North Carolina, 9/2/1863	Brunswick County, North Carolina, 18 Years Old	Co. H, 36th Regiment North Carolina, 2nd N. C. Artillery	Captured	Elmira Prison, Elmira, New York	Died of Smallpox, 4/10/1865
Bordeaux, Isreal Washington Private	Elizabeth-town, Bladen County, North Carolina, 5/8/1862, Volunteer	Bladen County, North Carolina, 27 Years Old, Farmer, Detailed as ambulance driver at Fort Pender Hospital	Co. H, 36th Regiment North Carolina, 2nd N. C. Artillery	Captured	Point Lookout Prison, Maryland	Captured Smithville Hospital, N. C., 1/16/1865, Oath of Allegiance 6/23/1865
Bourdeaux, John Private	Wilmington, New Hanover County, North Carolina, 8/20/1863, Volunteer	Brunswick County, North Carolina, 40 Years Old Laborer	Co. K, 36th Regiment North Carolina, 2nd N. C. Artillery	Captured	Point Lookout Prison, Maryland	Oath of Allegiance 6/24/1865
Boswell, John C. Sergeant	Elizabeth-town, Bladen County, North Carolina, 10/19/1861, Volunteer	Bladen County, North Carolina, 35 Years Old Cooper	2nd Co. I, 36th Regiment North Carolina, 2nd N. C. Artillery	Captured, Defended Shepperd's Battery	Elmira Prison, Elmira, New York	Exchanged 3/21/1865 Boulware's Wharf, James River, Virginia,
Bout, Thomas F. Private	Unknown, No Further Information	Unknown	Co. F, 36th Regiment North Carolina, 2nd N. C. Artillery	Wounded & Captured	Fort Monroe, Virginia	Exchanged 2/15/1865
Bow, Michael Private	New Orleans, La, 5/3/1861	Unknown	Co B, Confederate States Marine Corp, Assigned to Guard duty Aboard CSS *Richmond* & *Tallahassee,*	Wounded In Breast and Bowels	Not Sent To Prison	Died Of Wounds at Fort Fisher 1/17/1865

NAME & RANK	ENLISTED	RESIDENCE AGE & TRADE	UNIT	RESULT OF BATTLE	PRISON	PRISON RELEASE
Bowden, Joseph N. Private	Wilmington, New Hanover County, North Carolina , 1/17/1863, Volunteer	Wilmington, New Hanover County, North Carolina, 17 Years Old, Clerk	Co. D, 1st Battalion North Carolina Heavy Artillery Battery	Captured, Defended River Road Gate or Middle Sallyport	Elmira Prison, Elmira, New York	Exchanged On The James River 2/20/1865
Bowditch, Nathaniel J. Private	New Hanover County, North Carolina, 3/26/1864 Volunteer	Tarboro, Edgecombe County, North Carolina, 18 Years Old	2nd Co. C, 36th Regiment North Carolina, 2nd N. C. Artillery	Wounded & Captured, Defended River Road Gate	Confined Camp Hamilton Military Prison, Virginia	Oath of Allegiance 4/26/1865
Boyce, John H. Private	Charleston, South Carolina 2/22/1862	Charleston, South Carolina, 19 Years Old	Co. E, 25th South Carolina Volunteers	Captured	Elmira Prison, Elmira, New York	Oath of Allegiance 5/15/1865
Boyett, John A. Private	Brunswick County, North Carolina, 12/4/1863, Volunteer	Warsaw, Duplin County, North Carolina, 17 Years Old	2nd Co. A, 36th Regiment North Carolina, 2nd N. C. Artillery	Captured, Defended The Mound Battery	Point Lookout Prison, Maryland	Died of Pneumonia, 2/9/1865
Boyette, Milton Private	Brunswick County, North Carolina, 2/6/1864, Volunteer	Brunswick County, North Carolina, 16 Years Old Farm Laborer	2nd Co. A, 36th Regiment North Carolina, 2nd N. C. Artillery	Killed In Action 1/15/1865, Defended The Mound Battery		
Bozard, David T. Private	Orangeburg, South Carolina 4/21/1862	Orangeburg, South Carolina Lane, South Carolina, 28 Years Old Overseer	Co. G, 25th South Carolina Volunteers	Captured	Elmira Prison, Elmira, New York	Oath of Allegiance 7/7/1865
Bracey, Archibald Private	Brunswick County, North Carolina, 5/17/1862, Volunteer	Brunswick County, North Carolina, 24 Years Old, Teamster, Fort Caswell	Co. E, 40th Regiment, 3rd North Carolina Artillery	Captured	Point Lookout Prison, Maryland	Oath of Allegiance 6/9/1865

178

NAME & RANK	ENLISTED	RESIDENCE AGE & TRADE	UNIT	RESULT OF BATTLE	PRISON	PRISON RELEASE
Bracey, James A. Private	Union County, North Carolina, 8/27/1861, Volunteer	Lumberton Robeson County, North Carolina, 26 Years Old Laborer	Co. E, 40th Regiment, 3rd North Carolina Artillery	Captured	Point Lookout Prison, Maryland	Oath of Allegiance 6/9/1865
Braddock, Ralph Private	Camp Harllee, South Carolina 1/1/1862	27 Years Old, Carpenter	Co. D, 21st South Carolina Volunteers	Captured	Elmira Prison, Elmira, New York	Exchanged On The James River 2/20/1865
Braddock, Thomas Private	Chesterfield, South Carolina 1/1/1862	Chesterfield, South Carolina, 17 Years Old	Co. D, 21st South Carolina Volunteers	Captured	Elmira Prison, New York	Oath of Allegiance 7/7/1865
Braddy, Kinchen J. Captain	Cumberland County, North Carolina, 2/15/1862, Volunteer	Fayetteville, Cumberland County, North Carolina, 23 Years Old Farmer, Company Commander Co. K, 36th Regiment N. C.	2nd Co. C, 36th Regiment North Carolina, 2nd N. C. Artillery	Captured, Defended River Road Gate	Fort Columbus Prison, New York Harbor	Exchanged 3/5/1865 City Point, Virginia
Bradford, David First Lieutenant	Marine Corps Commission as 2nd Lieutenant, March, 1862	Cedar Creek, Granville County North Carolina, 40 Years Old Farm Laborer	Co. B, Confederate States Marine Corp	Captured, Wounded, Contusion of Left Hip by Shell Fragment	Fort Delaware, Del.	Exchanged at City Point, Virginia, 2/27/1865
Bradley, Augustus Private	Conscripted New Orleans, Louisiana, 6/10/1863	New Orleans, Louisiana, Age Unknown	Co. B, Confederate States Marine Corp	Captured	Elmira Prison, New York	Oath of Allegiance 5/15/1865
Bradley, J. P. Private	Date and Place Unknown	Unknown	Co. B, 40th Regiment, 3rd North Carolina Artillery	Wounded & Captured	Unknown	Date Of Release Unknown

NAME & RANK	ENLISTED	RESIDENCE AGE & TRADE	UNIT	RESULT OF BATTLE	PRISON	PRISON RELEASE
Bradley, J. T. Private	Date and Place Unknown	Tarboro, Edgecombe County, North Carolina, 20 Years Old	Co. D, 40th Regiment, 3rd North Carolina Artillery	Severely Wounded Right Knee and Lower Jaw & Captured	Point Lookout General Hospital, Maryland	No Release On File, Possibly Died Of Wounds
Bradley, James E. Private	Beaufort County, North Carolina, 2/15/1862	Beaufort County, North Carolina, 31 Years Old	Co. H, 36th Regiment North Carolina, 2nd N. C. Artillery	Captured	Point Lookout Prison, Maryland	Exchanged 2/14/1865
Bradley, Joseph J. Private	Craven County, North Carolina, 1/23/1862, Volunteer	Halifax County, North Carolina, 26 Years Old Farm Laborer	Co. F, 36th Regiment North Carolina, 2nd N. C. Artillery	Captured	Point Lookout Prison, Maryland	Oath of Allegiance 6/23/1865
Bradley, William H. Private	Halifax County, North Carolina, 10/9/1861, Volunteer	Gaston, Hampton, North Carolina, 18 Years Old	Co. F, 36th Regiment North Carolina, 2nd N. C. Artillery	Gunshot wound of neck & Captured	Confined David's Island , New York	Oath of Allegiance 6/20/1865
Bradly, John H. Private	Fort Fisher, New Hanover County, North Carolina, 3/15/1864	Enfield, Halifax County, North Carolina, 18 Years Old	Co. F, 36th Regiment North Carolina, 2nd N. C. Artillery	Captured	Elmira Prison, Elmira, New York	Died of Smallpox, 2/21/1865
Brafford, Joshua Private	Wilmington, New Hanover County, North Carolina, 4/9/1864, Conscript	Wayne County, N. C., 51 Years Old, Detailed as Cook at Fort Fisher, N. C., Turpentine	Co. F, 10th Regiment, 1st North Carolina Artillery	Captured	Elmira Prison, Elmira, New York	Died of Smallpox, 4/21/1865
Brafford, Wesley Private	Goldsboro, Wayne County, North Carolina, 9/20/1862, Conscript	Wilmington, New Hanover County, North Carolina, 17 Years Old	Co. F, 10th Regiment, 1st North Carolina Artillery	Captured	Elmira Prison, Elmira, New York	Died of Smallpox, 4/10/1865

NAME & RANK	ENLISTED	RESIDENCE AGE & TRADE	UNIT	RESULT OF BATTLE	PRISON	PRISON RELEASE
Brake, Jesse Private	Enfield, Halifax County, North Carolina, 10/9/1861 Volunteer	Tarboro, Edgecombe County, North Carolina, 19 Years Old	Co. F, 36th Regiment North Carolina, 2nd N. C. Artillery	Captured	Elmira Prison, Elmira, New York	Oath of Allegiance 6/12/1865
Brann, Lewis L. Private	Brunswick County, North Carolina, 8/2/1863, Volunteer	Granville County, North Carolina, 18 Years Old	Co. F, 36th Regiment North Carolina, 2nd N. C. Artillery	Killed In Action 1/15/1865		
Bray, David C. Private	New Hanover County, North Carolina, 3/5/1862, Volunteer	Surry County, North Carolina, 28 Years Old	Co. D, 1st Battalion North Carolina Heavy Artillery Battery	Captured, Defended River Road Gate or Middle Sallyport	Elmira Prison, Elmira, New York	Exchanged 2/20/1865, Admitted To Hospital Richmond, Virginia, Died of Chronic Diarrhea 3/6/1865
Brewer, Terrell Private	Chatham County, North Carolina, 3/26/1863, Volunteer	Chatham County, North Carolina, 33 Years Old Farmer	3rd Co. G, 40th Regiment, 3rd North Carolina Artillery	Severely Wounded Right Hip & Captured, Defended Land Face	Prison Unknown	No Release On File, May Have Died of Wounds at Fort Fisher
Brickett, Joseph H. Sergeant	Summersville Coles Island, South Carolina 4/11/1862	St. Matthew, South Carolina, Age Unknown	Co. H, 25th South Carolina Volunteers	Captured	Elmira Prison, Elmira, New York	Died of Chronic Diarrhea, 6/15/1865
Bridgeman, Lewis J. Private	New Hanover County, North Carolina, 8/20/1864	Wilmington, New Hanover County, North Carolina, Age Unknown	2nd Co. D, 36th Regiment North Carolina, 2nd N. C. Artillery	Captured	Elmira Prison, Elmira, New York	Oath of Allegiance 7/7/1865
Bridgers, John Private	Beaufort County, North Carolina, 7/13/1861	Johnston County, North Carolina 36 Years Old Farmer	Co. F, 10th Regiment, 1st North Carolina Artillery	Wounded & Captured	Fort Delaware, DE	1/15/1865 Oath of Allegiance 6/19/1865

NAME & RANK	ENLISTED	RESIDENCE AGE & TRADE	UNIT	RESULT OF BATTLE	PRISON	PRISON RELEASE
Bridgers, John C. Private	Fort Holmes, North Carolina, 2/7/1864, Volunteer	Brunswick County, North Carolina, 18 Years Old	2nd Co. K, 40th Regiment, 3rd North Carolina Artillery	Captured	Elmira Prison, Elmira, New York	Exchanged 3/14/1865 Boulware's Wharf, James River, Virginia
Briggs, C. C. Private	Unknown, No Further Information	Unknown	Co. D, 40th Regiment, 3rd North Carolina Artillery	Captured	Point Lookout Prison, Maryland	Exchanged 2/14/1865 Cox's Landing, James River, Virginia
Briggs, Joseph S. Seaman	Date and Place Unknown	Madison County, North Carolina, 17 Years Old	Confederate States Navy	Wounded, Contusion Of Knee 12/25/1864 & Captured	Prison Unknown	Served as Ordinary Seaman Aboard *CSS Chattahoochee*, 1864
Briggs, William W. Sergeant	Wayne County, North Carolina, 12/10/1861	Wayne County, North Carolina, 19 Years Old	Co. D, 40th Regiment, 3rd North Carolina Artillery	Captured	Point Lookout Prison, Maryland	Oath of Allegiance 6/23/1865
Bright, George F. Private	Date and Place Unknown	Swift Creek, Craven County, North Carolina, 30 Years Old Farmer	Co. C, Confederate States Marine Corp	Captured	Point Lookout Prison, Maryland	Died of Pneumonia 3/6/1865
Bright, Samuel S. Private	Wilmington, New Hanover County, North Carolina, 12/10/1861, Volunteer	Bladen County, North Carolina, 25 Years Old Turpentine	Co. E, 36th Regiment North Carolina, 2nd N. C. Artillery	Captured	Elmira Prison, Elmira, New York	Died of Chronic Diarrhea, 3/2/1865
Brinkley, James Private	Brunswick County, North Carolina, 2/19/1862, Volunteer	Shallotte, Brunswick County, North Carolina, 35 Years Old	Co. K, 36th Regiment North Carolina, 2nd N. C. Artillery	Captured	Point Lookout Prison, Maryland	Oath of Allegiance 6/24/1865

NAME & RANK	ENLISTED	RESIDENCE AGE & TRADE	UNIT	RESULT OF BATTLE	PRISON	PRISON RELEASE
Brinkley, William H. Private	Brunswick County, North Carolina, 6/28/1863, Volunteer	Halifax County, North Carolina, 18 Years Old	Co. F, 36th Regiment North Carolina, 2nd N. C. Artillery	Wounded in right shoulder blade by shell 1/13/1865& Captured	Point Lookout Prison, Maryland	Hospitalized Smithville, Captured 1/16/1865 Smithville, N. C., Oath of Allegiance 6/3/1865
Brinson, William G. Sergeant	Wilmington, New Hanover County, North Carolina, 7/8/1862	New Berne, Craven County, North Carolina, 30 Years Old Fisherman	Co. F, 10th Regiment, 1st North Carolina Artillery	Captured	Elmira Prison, Elmira, New York	Exchanged on the James River, Va, 2/25/1865
Brisson, Alexander Private	Bladen County, North Carolina, 3/11/1862, Volunteer	Lumberton, Robeson County, North Carolina, 20 Years Old Farmer	Co. H, 36th Regiment North Carolina, 2nd N. C. Artillery	Captured	Point Lookout Prison, Maryland	Oath of Allegiance 6/23/1865
Brisson, Joseph H. Private	New Hanover County, North Carolina, 3/11/1862, Volunteer	Lumberton, Robeson County, North Carolina, 16 Years Old Farmer	Co. H, 36th Regiment North Carolina, 2nd N. C. Artillery	Captured	Point Lookout Prison, Maryland	Oath of Allegiance 6/23/1865
Brisson, Reuben Private	New Hanover County, North Carolina, 3/11/1862, Volunteer	Lumberton, Robeson County, North Carolina, 25 Years Old Turpentine	Co. H, 36th Regiment North Carolina, 2nd N. C. Artillery	Wounded & Captured	Point Lookout Prison, Maryland	Oath of Allegiance 6/23/1865
Brisson, Stephen T. Private	Fort Pender, North Carolina, 12/14/1863 Volunteer	Lumberton, Robeson County, North Carolina, 18 Years Old	Co. H, 36th Regiment North Carolina, 2nd N. C. Artillery	Wounded & Captured	Prison Unknown	No Release On File, Reported Killed at Fort Fisher
Bristow, Daniel M. Private	Bennetts-ville, South Carolina 4/6/1863	Marlboro, South Carolina, Age Unknown	Co. F, 21st South Carolina Volunteers	Captured	Elmira Prison, Elmira, New York	Died of Pneumonia, 3/3/1865

NAME & RANK	ENLISTED	RESIDENCE AGE & TRADE	UNIT	RESULT OF BATTLE	PRISON	PRISON RELEASE
Bristow, Robert N. Private	Bennetts-ville, South Carolina 4/6/1862	Marlboro, South Carolina, 29 Years Old	Co. F, 21st South Carolina Volunteers	Captured	Elmira Prison, Elmira, New York	Died of Typhoid Fever, 3/18/1865
Britt, Elberry Private	Wake County, North Carolina, 5/9/1863	Morrisville, Wake County, North Carolina, 40 Years Old	Co. C, 3rd Battalion North Carolina Light Artillery	Killed In Action		
Britt, George W. Corporal	New Berne, Craven County, North Carolina, 1/13/1862, Volunteer	Buncombe County, North Carolina, 35 Years Old Farmer	Co. F, 36th Regiment North Carolina, 2nd N. C. Artillery	Wounded In Arm, 12/25/1864, Captured 1/15/1865	Elmira Prison, Elmira, New York	1/15/1865, Oath of Allegiance 6/12/1865
Britt, Joseph L. Corporal	Halifax County, North Carolina, 1/15/1862, Volunteer	Lumberton, Robeson County, North Carolina, 19 Years Old	Co. F, 36th Regiment North Carolina, 2nd N. C. Artillery	Gunshot Wound To Thigh & Captured	Fort Delaware Prison, Del.	Oath of Allegiance 6/19/1865
Britt, Lemuel H. Private	Goldsboro, Wayne County, North Carolina, 11/29/1863	Lumberton, Robeson County, North Carolina, 28 Years Old Farmer	Co. F, 10th Regiment, 1st North Carolina Artillery	Captured	Elmira Prison, Elmira, New York	Oath of Allegiance 6/23/1865
Britt, William T. Private	Craven County, North Carolina, 1/1/1862, Volunteer	Enfield, Halifax County, North Carolina, 24 Years Old	Co. F, 36th Regiment, North Carolina, 2nd N. C. Artillery	Killed In Action 1/15/1865		
Broderick, John Private	Mobile, Alabama, 11/3/1863	New Orleans, Louisiana, Age Unknown, Molder	Confederate States Marine Corp	Captured	Point Lookout Prison, Maryland	Oath of Allegiance 5/12/1865
Brooks, Cyrus D. Private	Chatham County, North Carolina, 3/26/1863 Volunteer	Goldston, Chatham County, North Carolina, 37 Years Old Farmer	3rd Co. G, 40th Regiment, 3rd North Carolina Artillery	Captured, Defended Land Face	Point Lookout Prison, Maryland	Died of Chronic Diarrhea 2/3/1865

NAME & RANK	ENLISTED	RESIDENCE AGE & TRADE	UNIT	RESULT OF BATTLE	PRISON	PRISON RELEASE
Brooks, Thomas D. Private	Chatham County, North Carolina, 8/18/1863, Volunteer	Gulf, Chatham County, North Carolina, 42 Years Old	3rd Co. G, 40th Regiment, 3rd North Carolina Artillery	Captured, Defended Land Face	Elmira Prison, Elmira, New York	Died of Chronic Diarrhea 3/8/1865
Brooks, William F. Captain	Brunswick County, North Carolina, 2/19/1862	Shallotte, Brunswick County, North Carolina, 24 Years Old Farmer, Company Commander	Co. K, 36th Regiment North Carolina, 2nd N. C. Artillery Battery	Captured	Fort Columbus, New York Harbor	Exchanged Date Unknown, Wounded At Bentonville, North Carolina, 3/19/1865
Browder, Benjamin R. Private	Williamsburg, South Carolina 12/29/1861	Kingstree, Williamsburg, South Carolina, 16 Years Old	Co. K, 25th South Carolina Volunteers	Captured	Elmira Prison, Elmira, New York	Oath of Allegiance 7/11/1865
Browder, Gadsden W. Private	Gourdings Dept, South Carolina 12/29/1861	Kingstree, Williamsburg District, South Carolina, 36 Years Old Teamster	Co. I, 25th South Carolina Volunteers	Captured	Elmira Prison, Elmira, New York	Oath of Allegiance 6/23/1865
Browder, John J. Private	Charleston, South Carolina 3/6/1862	Kingstree, Williamsburg District, South Carolina, 16 Years Old	Co. G, 21st South Carolina Volunteers	Captured	Elmira Prison, Elmira, New York	Oath of Allegiance 7/7/1865
Browder, William T. Private	Williamsburg, South Carolina 12/29/1862	Kingstree, Williamsburg, South Carolina, 39 Years Old Farmer	Co. K, 25th South Carolina Volunteers	Captured	Elmira Prison, Elmira, New York US General Hospital	Oath of Allegiance 7/19/1865
Brown, Amos J. Private	New Hanover County, North Carolina, 2/6/1862	Wilmington, New Hanover County, North Carolina, 29 Years Old Clerk	2nd Co. D, 36th Regiment North Carolina, 2nd N. C. Artillery	Captured	Point Lookout Prison, Maryland	Died of Chronic Diarrhea 6/14/1865

NAME & RANK	ENLISTED	RESIDENCE AGE & TRADE	UNIT	RESULT OF BATTLE	PRISON	PRISON RELEASE
Brown, Archibald Private	New Hanover County, North Carolina, 3/15/1863	Lumberton, Robeson County, North Carolina, 36 Years Old Farmer	2nd Co. C, 36th Regiment North Carolina, 2nd N. C. Artillery	Captured, Defended River Road Gate	Point Lookout Prison, Maryland	Died of Dropsy, 3/21/1865
Brown, Bryant Private	Wilmington, New Hanover County, North Carolina, 4/22/1862, Volunteer	Duplin County, N. C., Farmer, 22 Years Old, Detached to Work on Gunboat *CSS Raleigh*, February, 1863	Co. D, 1st Battalion North Carolina Heavy Artillery Battery	Captured, Defended River Road Gate or Middle Sallyport	Elmira Prison, Elmira, New York	Died of Chronic Diarrhea, 4/16/1865
Brown, Daniel Private	New Hanover County, North Carolina, 3/15/1863	Fayetteville, Cumberland County, North Carolina, 19 Years Old	2nd Co. C, 36th Regiment North Carolina, 2nd N. C. Artillery	Captured, Defended River Road Gate	Point Lookout Prison, Maryland	Exchanged 2/15/1865
Brown, Daniel B. Private	Robeson County, North Carolina, 9/1/1864	Lumberton, Robeson County, North Carolina, 16 Years Old	Co. D, 1st Battalion North Carolina Heavy Artillery Battery	Killed In Action 1/15/1865, Defended River Road Gate or Middle Sallyport		
Brown, Doctor E. Sergeant	Bladen County, North Carolina, 3/11/1862	Bladen County, North Carolina, 23 Years Old Farmer	Co. H, 36th Regiment North Carolina, 2nd N. C. Artillery	Captured	Point Lookout Prison, Maryland	Oath of Allegiance 6/24/1865
Brown, Frank Private	Wake County, North Carolina, 7/20/1862 Conscripted	Wake County, North Carolina, Age Unknown	Co. D, 13th Battalion, North Carolina Light Artillery	Wounded & Captured, Defended River Road Gate	Prison Unknown	Date Of Release Unknown, No Further Information

NAME & RANK	ENLISTED	RESIDENCE AGE & TRADE	UNIT	RESULT OF BATTLE	PRISON	PRISON RELEASE
Brown, H. J. Private	Battery Island, South Carolina 4/12/1862	Kingstree, South Carolina, 20 Years Old	Co. C, 25th South Carolina Volunteers	Captured	Elmira Prison, Elmira, New York	Oath of Allegiance 6/23/1865
Brown, Henry M. Private	Fort Branch, Brunswick County, North Carolina, 8/19/1862, Volunteer	Fair Bluff, Columbus County, North Carolina, 18 Years Old	Co. E, 36th Regiment North Carolina, 2nd N. C. Artillery	Captured	Elmira Prison, Elmira, New York	Oath of Allegiance 7/11/1865
Brown, James B. Private	Chesterfield, South Carolina 1/8/1862	Newberry, South Carolina, 28 Years Old Master Mechanic	Co. E, 21st South Carolina Volunteers	Wounded & Captured	Prison Unknown,	Wounded In Face From Explosion, Concussion
Brown, James R. Private	Brunswick County, North Carolina, 4/29/1863	Sampson County, North Carolina, 18 Years Old, Farm Laborer	2nd Co. A, 36th Regiment North Carolina, 2nd N. C. Artillery	Captured, Defended The Mound Battery	Point Lookout Prison, Maryland	Exchanged 2/20/1865 Boulware's Wharf, James River, Virginia
Brown, Jesse Private	Duplin County, North Carolina, 3/17/1864, Volunteer	Cypress Creek, Duplin County, North Carolina, 17 Years Old Farmer	Co. D, 1st Battalion North Carolina Heavy Artillery Battery	Captured, Defended River Road Gate or Middle Sallyport	Elmira Prison, Elmira, New York	Exchanged On the James River, Virginia 3/2/1865, Drummer
Brown, John O. Private	Marion Dist, South Carolina 1/8/1862	Marion County, South Carolina, 19 Years Old Farmer	Co. L, 21st South Carolina Volunteers	Captured	Point Lookout Prison, Maryland	Exchanged 2/13/1865 Boulware's Wharf, James River, Virginia
Brown, John R. Corporal	Fayetteville, Cumberland County, North Carolina, 4/4/1862	Fayetteville, Cumberland County, North Carolina, 16 Years Old	2nd Co. C, 36th Regiment North Carolina, 2nd N. C. Artillery	Wounded & Captured, Defended River Road Gate	Prison Unknown	No Release On File, May Have Died of Wounds At Fort Fisher

NAME & RANK	ENLISTED	RESIDENCE AGE & TRADE	UNIT	RESULT OF BATTLE	PRISON	PRISON RELEASE
Brown, Malcom Private	Cumberland County, North Carolina, 11/25/1863	Fayetteville, Cumberland County, North Carolina, 21 Years Old	3rd Co. B, 36th Regiment North Carolina, 2nd N. C. Artillery	Captured	Point Lookout Prison, Maryland	Oath of Allegiance 6/24/1865
Brown, Thomas A. Private	Brunswick County, North Carolina, 5/15/1862	Wilmington, New Hanover County, North Carolina, 24 Years Old	Co. D, 13th Battalion North Carolina Light Artillery	Gunshot Wound Left Thigh & Captured, Defended River Road Gate	Fort Monroe Hospital, Virginia, Fort Delaware Prison, Del.	Oath of Allegiance 6/19/1865
Brown, T. E. Lieutenant	Date and Place Unknown	Unknown	1st North Carolina Reserves	Wounded 12/25/1864		Wounded, Contusion of Hip and Thigh
Brown, William Private	Date and Place Unknown	Unknown	Co. C, Confederate States Marine Corp	Captured	Elmira Prison, Elmira, New York	Died of Chronic Diarrhea, 4/4/1865
Brown, William W. Sergeant	Cerogordo, North Carolina, 3/1/1862, Mustered in Wilmington, N. C., Volunteer	Whiteville, Columbus County, North Carolina, 20 Years Old	Co. E, 36th Regiment North Carolina, 2nd N. C. Artillery	Captured	Elmira Prison, Elmira, New York	Exchanged 3/2/1865 Boulware's Wharf, James River, Virginia
Browning, Thomas Jefferson Corporal	Fort Fisher, New Hanover County North Carolina, 12/20/1862, Volunteer	Elizabethtown Bladen County, North Carolina, 21 Years Old Turpentine Distiller	2nd Co. I, 36th Regiment North Carolina, 2nd N. C. Artillery	Captured, Defended Shepperd's Battery	Elmira Prison, Elmira, New York	Oath of Allegiance 6/12/1865
Bruton, Atlas J. Private	Fort Branch, Brunswick County, North Carolina, 7/22/1863, Volunteer	Zion District, Montgomery County, North Carolina, 36 Years Old	3rd Co. G, 40th Regiment, 3rd North Carolina Light Artillery	Captured, Defended Land Face	Elmira Prison, Elmira, New York	Exchanged On the James River, Va, 2/20/1865

NAME & RANK	ENLISTED	RESIDENCE AGE & TRADE	UNIT	RESULT OF BATTLE	PRISON	PRISON RELEASE
Bruton, Richard N. Private	Fort Branch, Brunswick County, North Carolina, 7/25/1863, Volunteer	Mt. Gilead, Montgomery County, North Carolina, 42 Years Old	3rd Co. G, 40th Regiment, 3rd North Carolina Light Artillery	Captured, Defended Land Face	Elmira Prison, Elmira, New York	Died of Intermittent Fever, 3/20/1865
Bryan, Carney J. Private	Kinston, Lenoir County, North Carolina, 6/28/1862	Washington, Beaufort County, North Carolina, 18 Years Old	Co. D, 13th Battalion North Carolina Light Artillery	Wounded & Captured Defended River Road Gate	Elmira Prison, Elmira, New York	Exchanged 3/2/1865 Boulware's Wharf, James River, Virginia
Bryan, Charles L. First Lieutenant	Bladen County, North Carolina, 4/27/1862	Prospect Hall, Bladen County, North Carolina, 29 Years Old Farmer	2nd Co. K, 40th Regiment, 3rd North Carolina Light Artillery	Captured	Fort Columbus Prison, New York	Exchanged 2/25/1865
Bryan, David Corporal	Fort Fisher, New Hanover County, North Carolina, 6/30/1863	Bladen County, North Carolina, 30 Years Old Turpentine	2nd Co. I, 36th Regiment North Carolina, 2nd N. C. Artillery	Gunshot Wound Fractured Right Humerous & Captured, Defended Shepperd's Battery	Point Lookout General Hospital, Maryland	Right Arm Amputated, Oath of Allegiance 6/29/1865
Bryan, James P. Private	New Hanover County, North Carolina, 2/3/1862	Unknown, 17 Years Old	2nd Co. I, 36th Regiment North Carolina, 2nd N. C. Artillery	Captured, Defended Shepperd's Battery	Point Lookout Prison, Maryland	Oath of Allegiance 6/24/1865
Bryan, Joseph Walter Private	Halifax County, North Carolina, 10/9/1861	Scotland Neck, Halifax County, North Carolina, 18 Years Old	Co. F, 36th Regiment North Carolina, 2nd N. C. Artillery	Killed In Action 1/15/1865		
Bryan, William T. Private	Fort Caswell, Brunswick County, North Carolina, 9/5/1863, Volunteer	Asheboro, Randolph County, North Carolina, 41 Years Old	3rd Co. G, 36th Regiment North Carolina, 2nd N. C. Artillery	Captured, Defended Battery to the Left of Northeast Bastion	Elmira Prison, Elmira, New York	Exchanged 3/2/1865 Boulware's Wharf, James River, Virginia

NAME & RANK	ENLISTED	RESIDENCE AGE & TRADE	UNIT	RESULT OF BATTLE	PRISON	PRISON RELEASE
Bryant, George Private	Enfield, Halifax County, North Carolina, 10/9/1861	Enfield, Halifax County, North Carolina, 20 Years Old Farm Laborer	Co. F, 36th Regiment North Carolina, 2nd N. C. Artillery	Killed In Action 1/15/1865		
Bryant, George T. Private	Fort Branch, Brunswick County, North Carolina, 8/20/1863, Volunteer	Diamond Hill District, Anson County, North Carolina, 18 Years Old	3rd Co. G, 40th Regiment, 3rd North Carolina Light Artillery	Captured, Defended Land Face	Elmira Prison, Elmira, New York	Oath of Allegiance 6/12/1865
Bryant, James S. Private	Halifax County, North Carolina, 10/9/1861	Enfield, Halifax County, North Carolina, 28 Years Old Farm Laborer	Co. F, 36th Regiment North Carolina, 2nd N. C. Artillery	Killed In Action 1/15/1865		
Bryant, Jesse Private	Darlington, South Carolina 5/16/1862	Darlington District, South Carolina, 19 Years Old	Co. B, 21st South Carolina Volunteers	Gunshot and Shell Wounds In Both Ankles & Captured	Treated At Mansfield Hospital, Morehead City, N. C., Transferred to Fort Delaware, Del.	Oath of Allegiance 6/10/1865
Buchan, George C. Captain	Wayne County, North Carolina, 11/7/1861	Indian Springs District, Wayne County, North Carolina, 31 Years Old Farmer	3rd Co. G, 40th Regiment, 3rd North Carolina Light Artillery	Wounded Severely in Neck & Captured, Defended Land Face	Hospital at Point Lookout, Maryland	Oath of Allegiance Johnson's Island Prison, Oh, 6/17/1865
Buchan, Jonathan E. Private	Brunswick County, North Carolina, 3/24/1863	Moore County, North Carolina, 18 Years Old	3rd Co. G, 40th Regiment, 3rd North Carolina Light Artillery	Wounded & Captured, Defended Land Face	Point Lookout Prison, Maryland	Oath of Allegiance 6/23/1865
Buckner, John J. Private	Northhampton County, North Carolina, 3/10/1862, Volunteer	Brunswick County, North Carolina, 18 Years Old Farmer	Co. C, 3rd Battalion, North Carolina Light Artillery	Captured	Elmira Prison, Elmira, New York	Died of Chronic Diarrhea, 4/14/1865

NAME & RANK	ENLISTED	RESIDENCE AGE & TRADE	UNIT	RESULT OF BATTLE	PRISON	PRISON RELEASE
Buffkin, James M. Private	Brunswick County, North Carolina, 11/10/1863	Columbus, North Carolina, 17 Years Old	2nd Co. A, 36th Regiment North Carolina, 2nd N. C. Artillery	Captured, Defended The Mound Battery	Point Lookout Prison, Maryland	Exchanged 2/14/1865 Cox's Landing, James River, Virginia
Bufkin, Bethel H. Private	Brunswick County, North Carolina, 11/14/1861	Columbus County, North Carolina, 18 Years Old	2nd Co. A, 36th Regiment North Carolina, 2nd N. C. Artillery	Captured, Defended The Mound Battery	Point Lookout Prison, Maryland	Oath of Allegiance 6/24/1865
Buffkin, Thomas Private	Brunswick County, North Carolina, 10/20/1863	Horry District, South Carolina, 38 Years Old	2nd Co. D, 36th Regiment North Carolina, 2nd N. C. Artillery	Captured	Point Lookout Prison, Maryland	Oath of Allegiance 6/24/1865
Bufkin, William B. Corporal	Columbus County, North Carolina, 10/21/1861	Columbus County, North Carolina, 22 Years Old	2nd Co. A, 36th Regiment North Carolina, 2nd N. C. Artillery	Killed In Action 1/15/1865, Defended the Mound Battery		Killed by an enemy shell exploding at the Mound Battery
Buie, Daniel C. First Sergeant	Robeson County, North Carolina, 9/19/1861	Robeson County, North Carolina, 26 Years Old	Co. E, 40th Regiment, 3rd North Carolina Light Artillery	Captured	Point Lookout Prison, Maryland	Oath of Allegiance 6/24/1865
Buie, Hayes M. Private	Brunswick County, North Carolina, 5/15/1862	Elizabethtown Bladen County, North Carolina, 16 Years Old Farmer	2nd Co. K, 40th Regiment, 3rd North Carolina Light Artillery	Captured	Point Lookout Prison, Maryland	Exchanged 3/21/1865 Boulware's Wharf, James River, Virginia,
Buie, John Malloy Corporal	Robeson County, North Carolina, 5/5/1862	Robeson County, North Carolina, 24 Years Old	Co. D, 1st Battalion, North Carolina Heavy Artillery	Captured, Defended River Road Gate	Point Lookout Prison, Maryland	Oath of Allegiance 6/24/1865

NAME & RANK	ENLISTED	RESIDENCE AGE & TRADE	UNIT	RESULT OF BATTLE	PRISON	PRISON RELEASE
Buie, William N. Sergeant	Wilmington, New Hanover County North Carolina, 11/5/1861, Volunteer	White Creek, Bladen County, North Carolina, 18 Years Old	3rd Co. B, 36th Regiment North Carolina, 2nd N. C. Artillery	Wounded & Captured	Elmira Prison, Elmira, New York	Exchanged on the James River, Va, 2/20/1865, Died of Smallpox, 4/27/1865, Marine USA Hospital, Baltimore, Maryland
Buie, William R. Second Lieutenant	Wilmington, New Hanover County, North Carolina, 3/11/1862	Bladen County, North Carolina, 25 Years Old Farmer	Co. H, 36th Regiment North Carolina, 2nd N. C. Artillery	Wounded & Captured	Prison Unknown	May Have Died of Wounds at Fort Fisher.
Bullard, Jesse F. Private	Gerogordo, North Carolina, 3/1/1862, Mustered in Wilmington, N. C., Volunteer	Columbus County, North Carolina, 45 Years Old	Co. E, 36th Regiment North Carolina, 2nd N. C. Artillery	Captured	Elmira Prison, Elmira, New York	Died of Pneumonia, 2/15/1865
Bullard, John Isom Private	Columbus County, North Carolina, 3/7/1862, Volunteer	Columbus County, North Carolina, 17 Years Old	Co. E, 36th Regiment North Carolina, 3rd N. C. Artillery	Captured	Elmira Prison, Elmira, New York	Died of Pneumonia, 2/27/1865
Bullard, Malcom Henry Private	Bladen County, North Carolina, 7/7/1862	Ellisville, Bladen County, North Carolina, 22 Years Old Farmer	2nd Co. C, 36th Regiment North Carolina, 2nd N. C. Artillery	Captured, Defended River Road Gate	Point Lookout Prison, Maryland	Oath of Allegiance 6/23/1865
Bullard, William J. Private	Fort St. Philip, Brunswick County, North Carolina, 8/16/1862, Volunteer	White Oak, Bladen County, North Carolina, 18 Years Old Farmer	2nd Co. K, 40th Regiment, 3rd North Carolina Light Artillery	Captured	Elmira Prison, Elmira, New York	Died of Pneumonia, 2/16/1865

NAME & RANK	ENLISTED	RESIDENCE AGE & TRADE	UNIT	RESULT OF BATTLE	PRISON	PRISON RELEASE
Bunce, Walter Private	Unknown, No Further Information	Unknown	Co. D, 13th Battalion North Carolina Light Artillery	Wounded & Captured, Defended River Road Gate	Prison Unknown	Wounded, Amputation Of Right Arm, Date Released Unknown
Bundy, G. W. Private	Bennetts-ville, South Carolina 10/11/1864	Unknown	Co. F, 21st Regiment South Carolina Volunteers	Captured	Elmira Prison, Elmira, New York	Died of Chronic Diarrhea, 3/5/1865
Burke, Levi Corporal	Washington, Beaufort County, North Carolina, 9/23/1861	Beaufort County, North Carolina, 19 Years Old	Co. D, 13th Battalion North Carolina Light Artillery	Captured. Defended River Road Gate	Prison Unknown	Date Released Unknown, No Further Information
Burgess, Joseph C. Corporal	James Island, South Carolina 5/28/1863	Clarendon County, South Carolina, 43 Years Old Farmer	Co. I, 25th Regiment South Carolina Volunteers	Captured	Elmira Prison, Elmira, New York	Died of Chronic Diarrhea, 7/10/1865
Burgess, Shelton H. Private	Camp Harlee, Georgetown South Carolina 1/1/1862	Lightwood Creek, Lexington, South Carolina, 19 Years Old	Co. I, 25th Regiment South Carolina Volunteers	Captured	Elmira Prison, Elmira, New York	Exchanged 3/2/1865 Boulware's Wharf, James River, Virginia
Burkett, John W. Private	Wilmington, New Hanover County, North Carolina, 4/19/1863, Volunteer	Robeson County, North Carolina, 40 Years Old, Extra Duty as Teamster at Smithville	Co. A, 1st Battalion, North Carolina Heavy Artillery	Captured	Elmira Prison, Elmira, New York	Died of Chronic Diarrhea, 2/25/1865
Burnett, William J. Private	Edgecombe County, North Carolina, 4/30/1864	Tarboro, Edgecombe County, North Carolina, 17 Years Old Farmer	Co. D, 40th Regiment, 3rd North Carolina Light Artillery	Captured	Point Lookout Prison, Maryland	Oath of Allegiance 6/23/1865

NAME & RANK	ENLISTED	RESIDENCE AGE & TRADE	UNIT	RESULT OF BATTLE	PRISON	PRISON RELEASE
Burney, Charles J. Private	Wilmington, New Hanover County, North Carolina, 12/28/1861	Unknown	3rd Co. B, 36th Regiment North Carolina, 2nd N. C. Artillery	Wounded & Captured	Prison Unknown	May Have Died of Wounds at Fort Fisher.
Burney, John W. Private	Fort Holmes, North Carolina 10/26/1864	White Creek, Bladen County, North Carolina, 16 Years Old	Co, K, 40th Regiment, 3rd North Carolina Light Artillery	Captured	Elmira Prison, Elmira, New York	Died of Chronic Diarrhea, 4/23/1865
Burney, Shipman B. Private	Brunswick County, North Carolina, 8/31/1862, Enlisted as Substitute for James A. Coleman	Unknown, 42 Years Old	Co. E, 36th Regiment North Carolina, 2nd N. C. Artillery	Wounded Left Shoulder & Captured	Point Lookout Prison, Maryland	Oath of Allegiance 5/14/1865
Burney, William James Private	Elizabeth-town, Bladen County, North Carolina, 3/5/1862, Volunteer	Elizabethtown Bladen County, North Carolina, 23 Years Old Farmer	3rd Co. B, 36th Regiment North Carolina, 2nd N. C. Artillery	Wounded & Captured	Elmira Prison, Elmira, New York	Exchanged on the James River, Va, 3/2/1865, Died Of Debility, 4/3/1865, Charlotte, N. C.
Burr, Ancrum B. First Lieutenant	New Hanover County, North Carolina, 3/3/1862	Wilmington, New Hanover County, North Carolina, 22 Years Old Medical Student	2nd Co. D, 36th Regiment North Carolina, 2nd N. C. Artillery	Captured	Fort Columbus Prison, New York Harbor	Exchanged 3/5/1865 City Point, Virginia
Burt, John J. Corporal	Craven County, North Carolina, 1/1/1862	Grove Hill, Warren County, North Carolina, 22 Years Old Farmer	Co. F, 36th Regiment North Carolina, 2nd N. C. Artillery	Wounded & Captured	Fort Delaware Prison, Del.	Oath of Allegiance 6/19/1865, Resided Halifax County

NAME & RANK	ENLISTED	RESIDENCE AGE & TRADE	UNIT	RESULT OF BATTLE	PRISON	PRISON RELEASE
Butler, Edward Private	Wilmington, New Hanover County, North Carolina, 3/10/1863, Volunteer	Clinton, Sampson County, North Carolina, 20 Years Old	Co. D, 1st Battalion, North Carolina Heavy Artillery	Captured, Defended River Road Gate	Elmira Prison, Elmira, New York	Listed in the National Archives as having died at Elmira, No date is Given
Butler, James L. Private	Clinton, Sampson County, North Carolina, 2/9/1863	Clinton, Sampson County, North Carolina, 31 Years Old School Teacher	2nd Co. D, 36th Regiment North Carolina, 2nd N. C. Artillery	Captured	Point Lookout Prison, Maryland	Sick With Pneumonia, Oath of Allegiance 6/24/1865
Butler, Luke Private	Sampson County, North Carolina, 2/18/1863	Clinton, Sampson County, North Carolina, 30 Years Old Farmer	2nd Co. A, 36th Regiment North Carolina, 2nd N. C. Artillery	Captured, Defended The Mound Battery	Point Lookout Prison, Maryland	Exchanged 2/10/1865, Cox's Landing, James River, Virginia
Butterton, James H. Corporal	Bertie County, North Carolina, 1/23/1862, Mustered in at Camp Mangum	Bertie County, North Carolina, 15 Years Old Farmer	Co. C, 3rd Battalion, North Carolina Light Artillery	Captured	Elmira Prison, Elmira, New York	Oath of Allegiance 6/12/1865
Byrd, John Owen Private	Elizabeth-town, Bladen County, North Carolina, 5/12/1862, Volunteer	Lumberton, Robeson County, North Carolina, 25 Years Old Farmer	2nd Co. K, 40th Regiment, 3rd North Carolina Light Artillery	Captured	Elmira Prison, New York	Oath of Allegiance 7/11/1865
Byrd, Mathew Private	Darlington, South Carolina 1/13/1862	Darlington District, South Carolina, 18 Years Old	Co. G, 21st Regiment South Carolina Volunteers	Captured	Elmira Prison, Elmira, New York	Died of Pneumonia, 3/28/1865

NAME & RANK	ENLISTED	RESIDENCE AGE & TRADE	UNIT	RESULT OF BATTLE	PRISON	PRISON RELEASE
Byrd, Robert Private	Fort Fisher, New Hanover County, North Carolina, 7/4/1863, Volunteer	Duplin County, North Carolina, 39 Years Old	2nd Co. K, 40th Regiment, 3rd North Carolina Light Artillery	Captured	Elmira Prison, Elmira, New York	Died of Chronic Diarrhea, 3/21/1865
Byrd, Wiley Private	Darlington, South Carolina 1/13/1862	Darlington District, South Carolina, 19 Years Old	Co. G, 21st Regiment South Carolina Volunteers	Captured	Elmira Prison, Elmira, New York	Oath of Allegiance 6/23/1865
Byrd, W. C. Private	Charleston, South Carolina 3/22/1863	Charleston, South Carolina, 24 Years Old	Co. A, 25th South Carolina Volunteers	Captured	Elmira Prison, Elmira, New York	Oath of Allegiance 7/7/1865

NAME & RANK	ENLISTED	RESIDENCE AGE & TRADE	UNIT	RESULT OF BATTLE	PRISON	PRISON RELEASE
Cade, John L. Sergeant	Georgetown South Carolina 1/1/1862	Florence, South Carolina, 25 Years Old	Co. K, 21st Regiment South Carolina Volunteers	Captured	Elmira Prison, Elmira, New York	Oath of Allegiance 7/11/1865
Cahoon, George F. Private	Craven County, North Carolina, 8/15/1863	New Berne, Craven County, North Carolina, 16 Years Old Day Laborer	Co. D, 40th Regiment, 3rd North Carolina Light Artillery	Captured	Point Lookout Prison, Maryland	Oath of Allegiance 6/26/1865
Cahoon, Nathan Private	Craven County, North Carolina, 8/20/1861	Craven County, North Carolina, 24 Years Old Farmer	Co. D, 40th Regiment, 3rd North Carolina Light Artillery	Captured	Point Lookout Prison, Maryland	Oath of Allegiance 6/26/1865
Cain, Beaman D. Private	Fort Fisher, North Carolina, 7/15/1863	Elizabethtown Bladen County, North Carolina, 18 Years Old Cooper	2nd Co. I, 36th Regiment North Carolina, 2nd N. C. Artillery	Severely Wounded & Captured, Defended Shepperd's Battery	Prison Unknown	No Release On File, May Have Died of Wounds at Fort Fisher

NAME & RANK	ENLISTED	RESIDENCE AGE & TRADE	UNIT	RESULT OF BATTLE	PRISON	PRISON RELEASE
Cain, Calvin M. Private	New Hanover County, North Carolina, 5/10/1863	Elizabethtown Bladen County, North Carolina, 18 Years Old Farmer	2nd Co. I, 36th Regiment North Carolina, 2nd N. C. Artillery	Captured, Defended Shepperd's Battery	Point Lookout Prison, Maryland	Oath of Allegiance 6/26/1865
Cain, David R. Private	Fort Fisher, New Hanover County, North Carolina, 7/25/1863	Bladen County, North Carolina, 45 Years Old	2nd Co. I, 36th Regiment North Carolina, 2nd N. C. Artillery	Captured, Defended Shepperd's Battery	Point Lookout Prison, Maryland	Oath of Allegiance 6/26/1865
Cain, Isaac J. Second Lieutenant	Bladen County, North Carolina, 10/19/1861	Elizabethtown Bladen County, North Carolina, 27 Years Old Farmer	2nd Co. I, 36th Regiment North Carolina, 2nd N. C. Artillery	Captured, Defended Shepperd's Battery	Fort Columbus Prison, New York	Exchanged 3/5/1865 Boulware's Wharf, James River, Virginia,
Cain, John S. Corporal	Bladen County, North Carolina, 5/6/1862, Mustered in Wilmington, Volunteer	Prospect Hall, North Carolina, 22 Years Old Farmer	Co. H, 36th Regiment North Carolina, 2nd N. C. Artillery	Captured	Elmira Prison, Elmira, New York	Oath of Allegiance 7/7/1865
Cain, Joshua Private	Fort Fisher, New Hanover County, North Carolina, 3/8/1862, Volunteer	White Oak, Bladen County, North Carolina, 20 Years Old Farmer	2nd Co. I, 36th Regiment North Carolina, 2nd N. C. Artillery	Captured, Defended Shepperd's Battery	Elmira Prison, Elmira, New York	Died of Smallpox, 4/20/1865
Cain, Travis H. Private	Elizabeth-town, Bladen County, North Carolina, 5/6/1862, Volunteer	Bladen County, N. C., 34 Years Old Farmer, Absent for 12 days from June 27, 1863 to attend crops, by order of General Whiting	2nd Co. K, 40th Regiment, 3rd North Carolina Light Artillery	Captured	Elmira Prison, Elmira, New York	Exchanged On the James River 2/20/1865

NAME & RANK	ENLISTED	RESIDENCE AGE & TRADE	UNIT	RESULT OF BATTLE	PRISON	PRISON RELEASE
Cain, Wiley Private	Cumberland County, North Carolina, 10/24/1863, Volunteer	Fayetteville, Cumberland County, N. C., 38 Years Old, Hospital Nurse at Camp Wyatt, N. C., July, 1864	Co. E, 36th Regiment North Carolina, 2nd N. C. Artillery	Captured	Elmira Prison, Elmira, New York	Oath of Allegiance 6/30/1865
Caison, Isaac Seaman	Place Unknown, 5/13/1862	Lockwood Folly District, Brunswick County, North Carolina, 26 Years Old, Cooper	Galloway Co. Confederate States Coast Guard	Captured	Prison Unknown	Date Of Release Unknown
Caison, Thomas Seaman	Place Unknown 1/29/1862	Owensville, Sampson County, North Carolina, 17 Years Old	Galloway Co. Confederate States Coast Guard	Captured	Prison Unknown	Date Of Release Unknown
Calder, Edwin Private	Charleston, South Carolina 2/20/1862	Charleston, South Carolina, 27 Years Old	Co. A, 25th Regiment South Carolina Volunteers	Captured	Elmira Prison, Elmira, New York	Oath of Allegiance 5/17/1865
Caldwell, James S. Private	Charleston, South Carolina 2/24/1862	Charleston, South Carolina, 19 Years Old	Co. B, 25th Regiment South Carolina Volunteers	Gunshot Wound In Head And Face & Captured	Fort Delaware Prison Hospital, Del.	Oath of Allegiance 6/10/1865
Cale, William Seaman	St. Louis, Missouri Conscript 10/15/1863	St. Louis, Missouri	Confederate States Navy	Captured	Elmira Prison, Elmira, New York	Oath of Allegiance 5/29/1865
Caler, J. E. Private	Battery Island, South Carolina 4/12/1862	Unknown	Co. B, 25th Regiment South Carolina Volunteers	Captured	Elmira Prison, Elmira, New York	Exchanged 2/20/1865, Died On Route

198

NAME & RANK	ENLISTED	RESIDENCE AGE & TRADE	UNIT	RESULT OF BATTLE	PRISON	PRISON RELEASE
Callihan, Thomas Private	Charleston, South Carolina 5/10/1862	Nashville, Tenn., 34 Years Old	Co. E, 25th Regiment South Carolina Volunteers	Captured	Elmira Prison, Elmira, New York	Oath of Allegiance 8/7/1865
Callihan, William J. Private	Wilmington, New Hanover County, North Carolina, 11/5/1861, Volunteer	White Creek, Bladen County, North Carolina 18 Years Old Farmer	3rd Co. B, 36th Regiment North Carolina, 2nd N. C. Artillery	Captured	Elmira Prison, Elmira, New York	Died of Gangrene of Feet, 3/14/1865
Campbell, Alexander Private	Bladen County, North Carolina, 12/28/1861	White Creek, Bladen County, North Carolina, 16 Years Old Farmer	3rd Co. B, 36th Regiment North Carolina, 2nd N. C. Artillery	Captured	Fort Monroe, Virginia	Exchanged 2/4/1865
Campbell, Archibald Private	Elizabeth-town, Bladen County, North Carolina, 10/19/1861, Volunteer	Elizabethtown Bladen County, North Carolina, 30 Years Old Turpentine	2nd Co. I, 36th Regiment North Carolina, 2nd N. C. Artillery	Captured, Defended Shepperd's Battery	Elmira Prison, Elmira, New York	Exchanged on the James River, Va, 2/20/1865
Campbell, Archibald C. Private	Robeson County, North Carolina, 2/6/1864, Volunteer	Robeson County, North Carolina, 16 Years Old	3rd Co. B, 36th Regiment North Carolina, 2nd N. C. Artillery	Wounded Left Arm, 12/25/1864	Not Sent to Prison	
Campbell, Charles J. Private	Moore County, North Carolina, 3/11/1863, Volunteer	Graham's District, Iredell County, North Carolina, 18 Years Old	3rd Co. B, 36th Regiment North Carolina, 2nd N. C. Artillery	Captured	Elmira Prison, Elmira, New York	Died of Chronic Diarrhea, 2/19/1865

NAME & RANK	ENLISTED	RESIDENCE AGE & TRADE	UNIT	RESULT OF BATTLE	PRISON	PRISON RELEASE
Campbell, Colen Private	Fort Branch, Brunswick County, North Carolina, 8/15/1863, Volunteer	Chesterfield District, South Carolina, 41 Years Old	3rd Co. G, 40th Regiment, 3rd North Carolina Light Artillery	Captured, Defended Land Face	Elmira Prison, Elmira, New York	Died of Chronic Diarrhea, 3/2/1865
Campbell, Daniel H. Private	Bladen County, North Carolina, 11/13/1861	Bladen County, North Carolina, 20 Years Old	3rd Co. B, 36th Regiment North Carolina, 2nd N. C. Artillery	Captured	Point Lookout Prison, Maryland	Oath of Allegiance 6/24/1865
Campbell, David A. Private	Moore County, North Carolina, 3/11/1863	Montgomery County, North Carolina, 18 Years Old Farmer	3rd Co. B, 36th Regiment North Carolina, 2nd N. C. Artillery	Wounded, forearm broken 12/25/1864		
Campbell, Duncan D. Private	Bladen County, North Carolina, 9/25/1862, Volunteer	Robeson County, North Carolina, 18 Years Old Farmer	3rd Co. B, 36th Regiment North Carolina, 2nd N. C. Artillery	Captured	Elmira Prison, Elmira, New York	Died of Chronic Diarrhea, 3/9/1865
Campbell, H. B. Private	Chesterfield, South Carolina 10/10/1863	Cheraw, South Carolina, 20 Years Old	Co. D, 21st Regiment South Carolina Volunteers	Captured	Elmira Prison, Elmira, New York	Oath of Allegiance 7/11/1865
Campbell, J. H. Corporal	James Island, South Carolina 4/23/1864	Anderson County, South Carolina, 23 Years Old	Co. H, 21st South Carolina Volunteers	Killed In Action, 1/15/1865		
Campbell, John C. Sergeant	Camp Harllee, South Carolina 1/1/1862	Cheraw, South Carolina, 17 Years Old	Co. D, 21st Regiment South Carolina Volunteers	Captured	Elmira Prison, Elmira, New York	Oath of Allegiance 7/11/1865

NAME & RANK	ENLISTED	RESIDENCE AGE & TRADE	UNIT	RESULT OF BATTLE	PRISON	PRISON RELEASE
Campbell, William A. Private	Wilmington, New Hanover County, North Carolina, 11/5/1861, Mustered in Wilmington, Volunteer	White Creek, Bladen County, North Carolina, 24 Years Old Cooper	3rd Co. B, 36th Regiment North Carolina, 2nd N. C. Artillery	Captured	Elmira Prison, Elmira, New York	Exchanged on the James River, Va, 3/2/1865, Admitted Hospital, Richmond, Virginia, Died 3/9/1865 Cause Unknown
Campbell, William N. Private	Bladen County, North Carolina, 11/1/1862	Bladen County, North Carolina, 24 Years Old	3rd Co. B, 36th Regiment North Carolina, 2nd N. C. Artillery	Wounded & Captured	Point Lookout Prison, Maryland	Oath of Allegiance 6/24/1865
Campion, Benjamin Franklin Corporal	Chesterfield, South Carolina 1/1/1862	Cheraw, South Carolina, 18 Years Old	Co. D, 21st Regiment South Carolina Volunteers	Captured	Elmira Prison, Elmira, New York	Oath of Allegiance 5/29/1865
Canaday, William J. Private	Fort Fisher, New Hanover County, North Carolina, 3/15/1863, Volunteer	Fayetteville, Cumberland County, North Carolina, 39 Years Old	2nd Co. C, 36th Regiment, North Carolina, 2nd N. C. Artillery	Captured, Defended River Road Gate	Elmira Prison, Elmira, New York	Oath of Allegiance 6/12/1865
Cane, Alvin Private	Fort Fisher, New Hanover County, North Carolina, 5/1/1863	Unknown, 18 Years Old	3rd Co. A, 36th Regiment North Carolina, 2nd N. C. Artillery	Captured	Point Lookout Prison, Maryland	Oath of Allegiance 6/26/1865
Cane, Stephen Private	Unknown	Unknown	Co. B, Confederate States Marine Corp	Captured	Point Lookout Prison, Maryland	Died of Disease 3/8/1865

NAME & RANK	ENLISTED	RESIDENCE AGE & TRADE	UNIT	RESULT OF BATTLE	PRISON	PRISON RELEASE
Cannon, Archibald Private	New Hanover County, North Carolina, 2/27/1862, Volunteer	Pitt County, North Carolina, 26 Years Old, Detailed as Signal Guard at Battery Gatlin, N. C.	2nd Co. D, 36th Regiment North Carolina, 2nd N. C. Artillery	Captured	Elmira Prison, Elmira, New York	Exchanged on the James River, Va, 2/20/1865, Died of Pneumonia, 3/11/1865 Howard Grove Hospital, Richmond, Virginia
Cannon, James Private	Duplin County, North Carolina, 7/21/1863, Volunteer	Mount Olive, Duplin County, North Carolina, 41 Years Old Farmer	3rd Co. G, 40th Regiment, 3rd North Carolina Light Artillery	Captured, Defended Land Face	Elmira Prison, Elmira, New York	Died of Pneumonia, 4/10/1865
Cannon, R. J. Private	Gourdin's Dept., South Carolina 5/11/1862	Clarendon, South Carolina, 26 Years Old	Co. I, 25th Regiment South Carolina Volunteers	Captured	Elmira Prison, Elmira, New York	Died of Chronic Diarrhea, 3/9/1865
Canoy, John H. Private	Randolph County, North Carolina, 3/23/1863	Randolph County, North Carolina, Age Unknown	Co. K, 10th Reg. 1st North Carolina Artillery	Captured	Elmira Prison, Elmira, New York	Oath of Allegiance 8/7/1865
Capel, Jesse A. Private	Fort Fisher, New Hanover County, North Carolina 5/20/1864	Fayetteville, Cumberland County, North Carolina, 18 Years Old	Co. H, 36th Regiment North Carolina, 2nd N. C. Artillery	Captured	Elmira Prison, Elmira, New York	Oath of Allegiance 7/11/1865
Capps, Henry Private	New Hanover County, North Carolina 9/24/1864	Wayne County, North Carolina, Age Unknown	Co. F, 10th Reg. 1st North Carolina Artillery	Wounded Right Thigh 12/24/1864 & Captured	Hart's Island Prison, New York Harbor	Oath of Allegiance 6/18/1865
Card, N. R. Private	Date and Place Unknown	Unknown	Co. K, 36th Regiment North Carolina, 2nd N. C. Artillery	Captured	Prison Unknown	Date Of Release Unknown, No Further Information

NAME & RANK	ENLISTED	RESIDENCE AGE & TRADE	UNIT	RESULT OF BATTLE	PRISON	PRISON RELEASE
Carlyle, Andrew J. Private	Brunswick County, North Carolina, 5/22/1863	Brunswick County, North Carolina, 35 Years Old	Co. E, 40th Regiment, 3rd North Carolina Light Artillery	Captured	Point Lookout Prison, Maryland	Exchanged 2/15/1865 Cox's Landing, James River, Virginia
Carmichael, John D. Private	Marion District, South Carolina 3/28/1862	Marion District, South Carolina, 21 Years Old	Co. L, 21st South Carolina Volunteers	Captured	Elmira Prison, Elmira, New York	Died of Pneumonia, 3/30/1865
Caroon, James M. Private	Craven County, North Carolina, 11/9/1861	Craven County, North Carolina, 17 Years Old	Co. D, 40th Regiment, 3rd North Carolina Light Artillery	Captured	Point Lookout Prison, Maryland	Oath of Allegiance 6/26/1865
Carr, William J. Private	New Hanover County, North Carolina, 7/7/1863	Magnolia, Duplin County, North Carolina, 22 Years Old	Co. D, 1st Battalion, North Carolina Heavy Artillery	Killed In Action, 1/15/1865, Defended River Road Gate		
Carricker, William P. Private	Wake County, North Carolina, 4/8/1863	Mount Pleasant, Cabarrus County, North Carolina, 38 Years Old Farm Laborer	Co. C, 3rd Battalion, North Carolina Light Artillery	Wounded in Hand, Thigh & leg 12/25/1864		
Carrigan, Quincey A. Private	Place Unknown 8/31/1864	District on the Weldon North Carolina Rail-Road, Iredell County, North Carolina, 16 Years Old	Co. D, 1st Battalion, North Carolina Heavy Artillery	Wounded		Wounded In Hand 12/25/1864, Finger Amputated
Carroll, Haywood Private	Old Brunswick Town, North Carolina, 4/16/1862	Robeson, North West District, Brunswick County, North Carolina, 42 Years Old Planter	3rd Co. G, 36th Regiment North Carolina, 2nd N. C. Artillery	Captured, Defended Battery to the Left of Northeast Bastion	Elmira Prison, Elmira, New York	Died of Smallpox, 3/25/1865

NAME & RANK	ENLISTED	RESIDENCE AGE & TRADE	UNIT	RESULT OF BATTLE	PRISON	PRISON RELEASE
Carroll, James A. Private	Old Brunswick Town, North Carolina, 4/16/1862	Brunswick County, North Carolina, 44 Years Old	3rd Co. G, 36th Regiment North Carolina, 2nd N. C. Artillery	Captured, Defended Battery to the Left of Northeast Bastion	Elmira Prison, Elmira, New York	Died of Chronic Diarrhea, 5/16/1865
Carroll, Joel G. Private	Old Brunswick Town, Fort St. Philip, North Carolina, 4/16/1862	Brunswick County, North Carolina, 35 Years Old, Extra Duty as Hospital Attendant, July, 1864	3rd Co. G, 36th Regiment North Carolina, 2nd N. C. Artillery	Captured, Defended Battery to the Left of Northeast Bastion	Elmira Prison, Elmira, New York	Died of Pneumonia, 3/10/1865
Carroll, John Private	New Orleans, Louisiana, 5/3/1861	Providence, Rhode Island, Age Unknown	Co. B, Confederate States Marine Corp, Assigned to Guard duty Aboard CSS *Raleigh.*	Captured	Point Lookout Prison, Maryland	Oath of Allegiance 5/13/1865
Carroll, Joseph Corporal	Elizabeth-town, Bladen County, North Carolina, 5/6/1862	Prospect Hall, Bladen County, North Carolina, 21 Years Old Farmer	2nd Co. K, 40th Regiment, 3rd North Carolina Light Artillery	Captured	Elmira Prison, Elmira, New York	Died of Gangrene Of Feet, 3/9/1865
Carroll, Joseph A. Private	Bladen County, North Carolina, 5/6/1862	Unknown	3rd Co. G, 36th Regiment North Carolina, 2nd N. C. Artillery	Captured, Defended Battery to the Left of Northeast Bastion	Prison Unknown	Date Of Release Unknown, No Further Information
Carroll, Nathaniel Private	Fort Fisher, New Hanover County, North Carolina, 6/1/1863	Prospect Hall, Bladen County, North Carolina, 38 Years Old, Turpentine	2nd Co. K, 40th Regiment, 3rd North Carolina Light Artillery	Wounded & Captured	Elmira Prison, Elmira, New York	Exchanged On the James River 2/20/1865

NAME & RANK	ENLISTED	RESIDENCE AGE & TRADE	UNIT	RESULT OF BATTLE	PRISON	PRISON RELEASE
Carroll, Uriah Private	Brunswick County, North Carolina, 2/19/1862	Brunswick County, North Carolina, 35 Years Old Farmer	Co. K, 36th Regiment North Carolina, 2nd N. C. Artillery	Captured	Point Lookout Prison, Maryland	Oath of Allegiance 5/13/1865
Carroll, William O. Private	Fort St. Philip, Elizabeth-town, Bladen County, North Carolina, 5/6/1862	Prospect Hall, Bladen County, North Carolina, 31 Years Old Turpentine	2nd Co. K, 40th Regiment, 3rd North Carolina Light Artillery	Wounded in Leg & Knee & Captured	Prison Unknown	No Release on File
Carroll, William R. Private	Unknown, No Further Information	Mingo District, Sampson County, North Carolina, 20 Years Old Farm Laborer	Co. K, 36th Regiment North Carolina, 2nd N. C. Artillery	Captured	Point Lookout Prison, Maryland	Oath of Allegiance 5/13/1865
Carson, James Captain	Charleston, South Carolina 2/24/1862	Charleston, South Carolina, 29 Years Old	25th South Carolina Volunteers	Wounded in Head & Captured	Fort Delaware, DE	Oath of Allegiance 6/17/1865
Carter, Cenos Private	Duplin County, North Carolina, 11/11/1861	Duplin County, North Carolina, Age Unknown	Co. E, 36th Regiment North Carolina, 2nd N. C. Artillery	Killed In Action 1/15/1865		
Carter, George M. Private	New Hanover County, North Carolina, 4/28/1864	Gooding's District, Craven County, North Carolina, 18 Years Old	Co. E, 36th Regiment North Carolina, 2nd N. C. Artillery	Killed In Action 1/15/1865		
Carter, Henry C. Private	New Hanover County, North Carolina, 3/15/1863	Fayetteville, Cumberland County, North Carolina, 18 Years Old Farm Laborer	2nd Co. C, 36th Regiment North Carolina, 2nd N. C. Artillery	Captured, Defended River Road Gate	Elmira Prison, Elmira, New York	Oath of Allegiance 6/12/1865

NAME & RANK	ENLISTED	RESIDENCE AGE & TRADE	UNIT	RESULT OF BATTLE	PRISON	PRISON RELEASE
Carter, James Private	Sampson County, North Carolina, 9/21/1861	Clinton District, Sampson County, North Carolina, 18 Years Old Farm Laborer	2nd Co. A, 36th Regiment North Carolina, 2nd N. C. Artillery	Captured, Defended the Mound Battery	Point Lookout Prison, Maryland	Exchanged 2/13/1865
Carter, James Private	Lenoir County, North Carolina, 5/2/1862	Duplin County, North Carolina, 19 Years Old	Co. A, 40th Regiment, 3rd North Carolina Light Artillery	Captured	Point Lookout Prison, Maryland	Exchanged 2/14/1865, Died of continuous fever in Raleigh hospital, 3/8/1865
Carter, Joseph L. Private	Brunswick County, North Carolina, 11/21/1862	Whiteville, Columbus County, North Carolina, 20 Years Old	Co. E, 36th Regiment North Carolina, 2nd N. C. Artillery	Killed In Action 1/15/1865		
Carter, Tealens Private	Unknown, No Further Information	Unknown	Co. A, 36th Regiment North Carolina, 2nd N. C. Artillery	Killed In Action 1/15/1865		No Official Record Found, Name Appears On Report of Major C. E. Pearce, 2/17/1865
Cartwright, John W. Private	Brunswick County, North Carolina, 10/25/1863	Unknown, 18 Years Old	Co. E, 36th Regiment North Carolina, 2nd N. C. Artillery	Killed In Action 1/15/1865		
Carver, James B. Private	Cumberland County, North Carolina, 6/21/1861	Fayetteville, Cumberland County, North Carolina, 45 Years Old Farmer	Co. E, 36th Regiment North Carolina, 2nd N. C. Artillery	Captured	Elmira Prison, Elmira, New York	Oath of Allegiance 7/11/1865
Cary, Clarence Midshipmn	Place Unknown 8/5/1861	Unknown	Confederate States Navy	Wounded In Right Leg 12/25/1864	Not Captured	Served aboard *CSS Chickamauga* and *CSS Yadkin*

NAME & RANK	ENLISTED	RESIDENCE AGE & TRADE	UNIT	RESULT OF BATTLE	PRISON	PRISON RELEASE
Caryl, John Private	Unknown	Unknown	Co. B, Confederate States Marine Corp	Captured	Unknown	Unknown
Casey, Benjamin D. Private	Wayne County, North Carolina, 7/24/1863	Goldsboro, Wayne County, North Carolina, 17 Years Old	3rd Co. G, 40th Regiment, 3rd North Carolina Light Artillery	Captured, Defended Land Face	Elmira Prison, Elmira, New York	Died of Chronic Diarrhea, 2/28/1865
Casey, Benjamin F. Private	Wayne County, North Carolina, 4/14/1863	Indian Springs District, Wayne County, North Carolina, 18 Years Old	3rd Co. G, 40th Regiment, 3rd North Carolina Light Artillery	Captured, Defended Land Face	Elmira Prison, Elmira, New York	Oath of Allegiance 6/12/1865
Casey, Wright Private	Wayne County, North Carolina, 4/14/1863	Goldsboro, Wayne County, North Carolina, 21 Years Old	3rd Co. G, 40th Regiment, 3rd North Carolina Light Artillery	Captured, Defended Land Face	Elmira Prison, Elmira, New York	Exchanged 2/20/1865
Cashwell, Marshall Coporal	Cumberland County, North Carolina, 2/20/1862	Fayetteville, Cumberland County, North Carolina, 20 Years Old Farmer	2nd Co. C, 36th Regiment North Carolina, 2nd N. C. Artillery	Captured, Defended River Road Gate	Elmira Prison, Elmira, New York	Oath of Allegiance 6/12/1865
Caton, Mathew P. Private	Craven County, North Carolina, 1/23/1862	Bay River, North of Neuse River, Craven County, North Carolina, 19 Years Old Farm Hand	Co. D, 40th Regiment, 3rd North Carolina Light Artillery	Mortally Wounded, Fractured Skull & Captured		Died Of Wounds at Fort Fisher 1/21/1865

NAME & RANK	ENLISTED	RESIDENCE AGE & TRADE	UNIT	RESULT OF BATTLE	PRISON	PRISON RELEASE
Caul, Stephen Private	New Orleans, Louisiana, 6/14/1861	Unknown	Co. C, Confederate States Marine Corp, Assigned to Guard duty Aboard CSS *Raleigh* and CSS *Arctic.*	Captured	Point Lookout Prison, Maryland	Died Of Pneumonia, Point Lookout, Maryland . 3/8/1865, Grave 1245
Center, John A. Private	Camp Holmes, North Carolina, 10/13/1863	South Eastern District, Ashe County, North Carolina, 49 Years Old Farmer	2nd Co. D, 36th Regiment North Carolina, 2nd N. C. Artillery	Captured	Elmira Prison, Elmira, New York	Oath of Allegiance 7/3/1865
Chambers, James G. Private	Wilmington, New Hanover County, North Carolina, 10/4/1864	New Hanover County, North Carolina, Age Unknown	Co. K, 10th Reg. 1st North Carolina Artillery	Captured	Elmira Prison, Elmira, New York	Died of Chronic Diarrhea, Died On Route To Be Exchanged
Chapman, Robert P. Sergeant	Mecklenburg County, North Carolina, 4/22/1862	Charlotte, Mecklenburg County, North Carolina, 26 Years Old Stone Cutter	Co. D, 1st Battalion, North Carolina Heavy Artillery	Wounded In Face, 12/25/1864		Wounded In Face, 12/25/1864, Born in England
Chapman, Robert T. Captain	Unknown	Unknown	Confederate States Navy	Escaped		Evacated Battery Buchanan During the Evening of January 15th.
Chapman, Slade Private	Craven County, North Carolina, 4/13/1864	North of Neuse River, Craven County, North Carolina, 18 Years Old Farmer	Co. D, 40th Regiment, 3rd North Carolina Light Artillery	Captured	Point Lookout Prison, Maryland	Oath of Allegiance 6/26/1865

NAME & RANK	ENLISTED	RESIDENCE AGE & TRADE	UNIT	RESULT OF BATTLE	PRISON	PRISON RELEASE
Chappel, Morris C. Private	Fort Fisher, New Hanover County, North Carolina, 4/14/1864, Volunteer	Richmond County, North Carolina, 18 Years Old	Co. H, 36th Regiment North Carolina, 2nd N. C. Artillery	Wounded In Action 12/24/1864		
Chason, Joseph H. Private	Cumberland County, North Carolina, 2/20/1862	Fayetteville, Cumberland County, North Carolina, 20 Years Old Farmer	2nd Co. C, 36th Regiment North Carolina, 2nd N. C. Artillery	Captured, Defended River Road Gate	Point Lookout Prison, Maryland	Oath of Allegiance 6/26/1865
Chavans, Augustus Private	Brunswick County, North Carolina, 9/6/1864	Brunswick County, North Carolina, 15 Years Old	Co. D, 1st Battalion, North Carolina Heavy Artillery	Captured, Defended River Road Gate	Point Lookout Prison, Maryland	Exchanged 2/15/1865, Cox's Landing, James River, Virginia
Cheek, John D. Private	Chatham County, North Carolina, 3/26/1863	Alamance County, North Carolina, 37 Years Old	3rd Co. G, 40th Regiment, 3rd North Carolina Light Artillery	Captured, Defended Land Face	Elmira Prison, Elmira, New York	Oath of Allegiance 6/12/1865
Cherry, Charles C. Private	Brunswick County, North Carolina, 9/21/1863	Tarboro, Edgecombe County, North Carolina, 18 Years Old	Co. F, 36th Regiment North Carolina, 2nd N. C. Artillery	Wounded 12/25/1864		Wounded In Both Legs 12/25/1864, Right Leg Amputated
Cherry, George T. Private	Duplin County, North Carolina, 11/4/1863	Mount Olive, Duplin County, North Carolina, 23 Years Old, Farmer	3rd Co. G, 40th Regiment, 3rd North Carolina Light Artillery	Captured, Defended Land Face	Elmira Prison, Elmira, New York	Oath of Allegiance 6/12/1865
Cherry, Oliver H. Private	Martin County, North Carolina, 8/11/1862	Trauters Creek, Beaufort County, North Carolina, 24 Years Old	Co. D, 1st Battalion, North Carolina Heavy Artillery	Mortally Wounded & Captured, Defended River Road Gate	Treated At Mansfield Hospital, Morehead City, North Carolina	Died Of Wounds 3/4/1865

NAME & RANK	ENLISTED	RESIDENCE AGE & TRADE	UNIT	RESULT OF BATTLE	PRISON	PRISON RELEASE
Church, Robert R. Private	Morehead City, Carteret County, North Carolina, 7/5/1861	Carteret County, North Carolina, 45 Years Old Baker	Co. F, 10th Reg. 1st North Carolina Artillery	Mortally Wounded in Left Thigh & Captured		Died of Wounds at Fort Fisher 1/15/1865, Compound Fracture of Left Thigh
Clamps, W. C. Private	Unknown, No Further Information	Unknown	Co. E, 10th Reg. 1st North Carolina Artillery	Captured	Elmira Prison, Elmira, New York	Died of Chronic Diarrhea, 3/20/1865
Clark, Baty C. Private	Fort Fisher, New Hanover County, North Carolina, 3/11/1863	New Hanover County, North Carolina, 17 Years Old	2nd Co. I, 36th Regiment North Carolina, 2nd N. C. Artillery	Captured, Defended Shepperd's Battery	Elmira Prison, Elmira, New York	Died of Chronic Diarrhea, 3/8/1865
Clark, Daniel James Captain	Bladen County, North Carolina, 5/6/1862	White Creek, Bladen County, North Carolina, 29 Years Old Farmer	2nd Co. K, 40th Regiment, 3rd North Carolina Light Artillery	Wounded In Head & Captured	Fort Columbus Prison, New York	Exchanged 3/5/1865 Boulware's Wharf, James River, Virginia
Clark, David Thomas Private	Brunswick County, North Carolina, 2/2/1864	White Creek, Bladen County, North Carolina, 18 Years Old Farmer	Co. H, 36th Regiment North Carolina, 2nd N. C. Artillery	Wounded In Ankle		Wounded 12/24/1864
Clark, Duncan C. Private	Bladen County, North Carolina, 11/5/1861	Elizabethtown Bladen County, North Carolina, 30 Years Old Cooper	3rd Co. B, 36th Regiment North Carolina, 2nd N. C. Artillery	Captured	Fort Delaware Prison, Del.	Oath of Allegiance 6/19/1865

NAME & RANK	ENLISTED	RESIDENCE AGE & TRADE	UNIT	RESULT OF BATTLE	PRISON	PRISON RELEASE
Clark, Henry S. Private	Wilmington, New Hanover County, North Carolina, 1/1/1863	New Hanover County, North Carolina, Age Unknown	Co. K, 10th Reg. 1st North Carolina Artillery	Captured	Elmira Prison, Elmira, New York	Exchanged 2/13/1865
Clark, James C. Corporal	Bladen County, North Carolina, 3/11/1862	White Hall, Bladen County, North Carolina, 45 Years Old Farmer	Co. H, 36th Regiment North Carolina, 2nd N. C. Artillery	Wounded In Knee 12/25/1864 & Captured	Elmira Prison, Elmira, New York	Oath of Allegiance 7/11/1865
Clark, James D. Private	St Johns, North Carolina, 5/7/1862	Weldon, Halifax County, North Carolina, Age Unknown, Detailed On Garrison Boat, Fort Caswell	Co. C, 3rd Battalion, North Carolina Light Artillery	Captured	Elmira Prison, Elmira, New York	Oath of Allegiance 7/11/1865
Clark, John D. Private	Red Springs, Robeson County, North Carolina, 9/19/1861	Lumberton, Robeson County, N. C., 19 Years Old, Extra Duty As Blacksmith In Quartermaster Dept.	Co. E, 40th Regiment, 3rd North Carolina Light Artillery	Captured	Elmira Prison, Elmira, New York	Oath of Allegiance 7/11/1865
Clark, John J. Private	Bladen County, North Carolina, 3/11/1862	Bladen County, North Carolina, 18 Years Old Farmer	Co. H, 36th Regiment North Carolina, 2nd N. C. Artillery	Captured	Point Lookout Prison, Maryland	Exchanged 2/14/1865, Cox's Landing, James River, Virginia
Clark, John W. Private	Bladen County, North Carolina, 5/6/1862	Elizabethtown Bladen County, North Carolina, 23 Years Old Student	2nd Co. K, 40th Regiment, 3rd North Carolina Light Artillery	Captured	Elmira Prison, Elmira, New York	Oath of Allegiance 6/12/1865

NAME & RANK	ENLISTED	RESIDENCE AGE & TRADE	UNIT	RESULT OF BATTLE	PRISON	PRISON RELEASE
Clark, Robert C. Private	Marion District, South Carolina 1/26/1862	Charleston, South Carolina, 25 Years Old Laborer	Co. L, 21st South Carolina Volunteers	Killed In Action, 1/15/1865		Color Corp.
Clark, Stephen B. Sergeant	Elizabeth-town, Bladen County, North Carolina, 5/6/1862	Elizabethtown Bladen County, North Carolina, 26 Years Old Overseer	2nd Co. K, 40th Regiment, 3rd North Carolina Light Artillery	Gunshot Wound In Left Leg Below Knee & Captured	Point Lookout Prison General Hospital, Maryland	Oath of Allegiance 6/28/1865
Clark, William Savage Private	Fort Holmes, Brunswick County, North Carolina, 10/26/1864	White Hall, Bladen County, North Carolina, 17 Years Old	2nd Co. K, 40th Regiment, 3rd North Carolina Light Artillery	Captured	Elmira Prison, Elmira, New York	Oath of Allegiance 6/12/1865
Clayton, D. J. Private	Coles Island, South Carolina 4/11/1862	Poplar, Orangeburg District, South Carolina, 23 Years Old	Co. F, 25th South Carolina Volunteers	Captured	Elmira Prison, Elmira, New York	Exchanged On the James River, Virginia 3/2/1865, Recaptured in Richmond, 5/12/65, Oath 7/19/1865
Clayton, F. R. Private	James Island, South Carolina 3/7/1863	Unknown	Co. F, 25th South Carolina Volunteers	Captured	Elmira Prison, Elmira, New York	Died of Chronic Diarrhea 3/23/1865
Clayton, W. W. Private	Coles Island, South Carolina 4/11/1862	Unknown, 23 Years Old	Co. F, 25th South Carolina Volunteers	Captured	Elmira Prison, Elmira, New York	Exchanged 2/20/1865, Died Chronic Diarrhea 3/26/1865

NAME & RANK	ENLISTED	RESIDENCE AGE & TRADE	UNIT	RESULT OF BATTLE	PRISON	PRISON RELEASE
Clements, Charles S. Private	Smithville, Brunswick County, North Carolina, 2/19/1862, Volunteer	Shallotte, Brunswick County, North Carolina, 40 Years Old Laborer	Co. K, 36th Regiment North Carolina, 2nd N. C. Artillery	Wounded & Captured	Prison Unknown	No Release On File. May Have Died of Wounds
Clements, J. C. First Lieutenant	Darlington, South Carolina 1/1/1862	Darlington District, South Carolina, 22 Years Old	Co. B, 21st South Carolina Volunteers	Captured	Fort Columbus Prison, New York	Exchanged 2/25/1865
Clemmons, Edward M. Private	Fort Caswell, Brunswick County, North Carolina, 2/6/1863	Brunswick County, North Carolina, 37 Years Old, Extra Duty In Ordinance Dept., November 1863	3rd Co. G, 36th Regiment North Carolina, 2nd N. C. Artillery	Captured, Defended Battery to the Left of Northeast Bastion	Elmira Prison, Elmira, New York	Exchanged 3/2/1865 Boulware's Wharf, James River, Virginia
Clemmons, George M. Private	Fort Caswell, Brunswick County, North Carolina, 2/6/1863	Lockwood Folly District, Brunswick County, North Carolina, 35 Years Old Farmer	3rd Co. G, 36th Regiment North Carolina, 2nd N. C. Artillery	Captured, Defended Battery to the Left of Northeast Bastion	Elmira Prison, Elmira, New York	Died Of Pneumonia 4/24/1865
Clemmons, Thomas Private	Brunswick County, North Carolina, 2/6/1863	Wilmington, New Hanover County, North Carolina, 21 Years Old	3rd Co. G, 36th Regiment North Carolina, 2nd N. C. Artillery	Captured, Defended Battery to the Left of Northeast Bastion	Elmira Prison, Elmira, New York	Oath of Allegiance 7/11/1865

NAME & RANK	ENLISTED	RESIDENCE AGE & TRADE	UNIT	RESULT OF BATTLE	PRISON	PRISON RELEASE
Clemmons, Timothy E. Seaman	Place Unknown, 1/24/1862	Lockwood Folly District, Brunswick County, North Carolina, 24 Years Old Fisherman	Galloway Co. Confederate States Coast Guard	Captured	Prison Unknown	Date Of Release Unknown
Clemmons, William Seaman	Place Unknown, 5/13/1862	Lockwood Folly District, Brunswick County, North Carolina, 15 Years Old	Galloway Co. Confederate States Coast Guard	Captured	Prison Unknown	Date Of Release Unknown
Clewis, Samuel W. Private	Brunswick County, North Carolina, 11/2/1863	Columbus County, North Carolina, 17 Years Old	Co. K, 36th Regiment North Carolina, 2nd N. C. Artillery	Captured	Point Lookout Prison, Maryland	Oath of Allegiance 6/26/1865
Clines, Patrick Private	New Orleans, Louisiana, 4/27/1861	New Orleans, Louisiana, Age Unknown Seaman	Co. B, Confederate States Marine Corp, Assigned to Guard duty Aboard CSS *Arctic*.	Captured	Point Lookout Prison, Maryland	Oath of Allegiance 5/13/1865
Clifton, Watson T. Private	Bladen County, North Carolina, 11/20/1861	Elizabethtown Bladen County, North Carolina, 25 Years Old Wheelwright	3rd Co. B, 36th Regiment North Carolina, 2nd N. C. Artillery	Wounded & Captured	Fort Delaware Prison, Del.	Oath of Allegiance 6/19/1865
Coatin, Thomas Seaman	Date and Place Unknown	Unknown	Confederate States Navy	Wounded 12/25/1864, In Back From Exploding Gun		

NAME & RANK	ENLISTED	RESIDENCE AGE & TRADE	UNIT	RESULT OF BATTLE	PRISON	PRISON RELEASE
Cobb, Alexander M. Private	Robeson County, North Carolina, 4/28/1862	Lumberton, Robeson County, North Carolina, 28 Years Old	Co. C, 3rd Battalion, North Carolina Light Artillery	Wounded & Captured, Fracture of Forearm	Prison Unknown	No Release On File
Cobb, Calvin A. Private	Robeson County, North Carolina, 12/16/1862	Lumberton, Robeson County, North Carolina, 18 Years Old	Co. D, 1st Battalion, North Carolina Heavy Artillery	Captured, Defended River Road Gate	Elmira Prison, Elmira, New York	Died of Chronic Diarrhea, 3/26/1865
Cobb, Joseph Private	Edgecombe County, North Carolina, 3/24/1864	Tarboro, Edgecombe County, North Carolina, 17 Years Old	Co. D, 40th Regiment, 3rd North Carolina Light Artillery	Captured	Point Lookout Prison, Maryland	Oath of Allegiance 6/24/1865
Cobb, William R. Private	Edgecombe County, North Carolina, 7/11/1863	Tarboro, Edgecombe County, North Carolina, 17 Years Old Farmer	Co. D, 40th Regiment, 3rd North Carolina Light Artillery	Captured	Point Lookout Prison, Maryland	Exchanged 2/20/1865 Boulwares Wharf, James River, Virginia
Coble, Alexander Private	Wake County, North Carolina, 5/11/1863	Sandy Creek, Randolph County, North Carolina, 32 Years Old Farmer	Co. C, 3rd Battalion, North Carolina Light Artillery	Mortally Wounded & Captured	Point Lookout Prison, Maryland	Died of Wounds 2/16/1865
Cochran, Allen W. Private	Manning, South Carolina 8/22/1863	Manning, Clarenden District, South Carolina, 18 Years Old	Co. I, 25th South Carolina Volunteers	Captured	Elmira Prison, Elmira, New York	Died of Chronic Diarrhea 3/8/1865
Cochran, Elijah P. Private	Enfield, Halifax County, North Carolina, 10/9/1861	Enfield, Halifax County, North Carolina, 20 Years Old	Co. F, 36th Regiment North Carolina, 2nd N. C. Artillery	Captured	Elmira Prison, Elmira, New York	Died of Chronic Diarrhea, 3/1/1865

NAME & RANK	ENLISTED	RESIDENCE AGE & TRADE	UNIT	RESULT OF BATTLE	PRISON	PRISON RELEASE
Cochran, Robert J. Private	Enfield, Halifax County, North Carolina, 10/9/1861	Enfield, Halifax County, North Carolina, 34 Years Old, Extra Duty As Hospital Attendant, April 4, 1864	Co. F, 36th Regiment North Carolina, 2nd N. C. Artillery	Captured	Elmira Prison, Elmira, New York	Died of Pneumonia, 3/1/1865
Cohen, John B. Sergeant	Date and Place Unknown	Beaufort, South Carolina, 25 Years Old Clerk	Co. A, 21st South Carolina Volunteers	Killed In Action, 1/15/1865		
Coit, David G. Assistant Surgeon	Date Unknown, Enlisted 8th Regiment South Carolina	Unknown, Appointed to Fort Fisher January 1862	General Field and Staff, Confederate Army	Captured	Fort Columbus Prison, New York	Exchanged at City Point, Virginia 2/25/1865
Coker, John L. Private	Lenoir County, North Carolina, 4/4/1863	Kinston, Lenoir County, North Carolina, 18 Years Old	Co. K, 10th Reg. 1st North Carolina Artillery	Captured	Elmira Prison, Elmira, New York	Oath of Allegiance 5/15/1865
Coker, Thomas L. Private	Georgetown South Carolina 12/20/1861	Cheraw, Chesterfield County, South Carolina, 16 Years Old	Co. D, 21st South Carolina Volunteers	Captured	Elmira Prison, Elmira, New York	Exchanged On The James River 2/20/1865
Cole, Hosea Private	Craven County, North Carolina, 1/31/1862	Halifax County, North Carolina, 30 Years Old	Co. F, 36th Regiment North Carolina, 2nd N. C. Artillery	Captured	Point Lookout Prison, Maryland	Oath of Allegiance 6/10/1865, Resided Halifax County
Cole, William Bright Sergeant	Goldsboro, Wayne County, North Carolina, 7/14/1861	Bentonville, Johnston County, North Carolina, 20 Years Old Turpentine Maker	Co. F, 10th Reg. 1st North Carolina Artillery	Wounded In Right Hip & Captured	Elmira Prison, Elmira, New York	Oath of Allegiance 5/19/1865,

NAME & RANK	ENLISTED	RESIDENCE AGE & TRADE	UNIT	RESULT OF BATTLE	PRISON	PRISON RELEASE
Coleman, Asa Private	New Hanover County, North Carolina, 5/1/1862	Columbus County, North Carolina, 19 Years Old	2nd Co. D, 36th Regiment North Carolina, 2nd N. C. Artillery	Captured	Point Lookout Prison, Maryland	Oath of Allegiance 6/26/1865,
Coleman, Daniel J. Private	Columbus County, North Carolina, 2/22/1862	Fair Bluff, Columbus County, North Carolina, 19 Years Old	Co. E, 36th Regiment North Carolina, 2nd N. C. Artillery	Captured	Elmira Prison, Elmira, New York	Oath of Allegiance 7/3/1865
Coleman, Eli Corporal	New Hanover County, North Carolina, 5/1/1862	Columbus County, North Carolina, 28 Years Old	2nd Co. D, 36th Regiment North Carolina, 2nd N. C. Artillery	Captured	Point Lookout Prison, Maryland	Oath of Allegiance 6/26/1865
Coleman, Isham Q. Corporal	Columbus County, North Carolina, 2/22/1862	Columbus County, North Carolina, 22 Years Old	Co. E, 36th Regiment North Carolina, 2nd N. C. Artillery	Wounded 1/13/1865 & Captured	Point Lookout Prison, Maryland	Oath of Allegiance 6/26/1865, Captured at Hospital In Smithville, N. C., 1/18/1865
Coleman, Jackson M. Private	New Hanover County, North Carolina, 5/1/1862	Whiteville, Columbus County, North Carolina, 22 Years Old Farmer	2nd Co. D, 36th Regiment North Carolina, 2nd N. C. Artillery	Captured	Point Lookout Prison, Maryland	Oath of Allegiance 6/26/1865
Coleman, John Q. Private	Brunswick County, North Carolina, 5/3/1862	Brunswick County, North Carolina, 22 Years Old	Co. E, 36th Regiment North Carolina, 2nd N. C. Artillery	Wounded by Shell in Face, Nasal Bone Fractured & Captured	Elmira Prison, Elmira, New York	Died of Chronic Diarrhea, 4/21/1865
Coleman, Lott Caswell Private	New Hanover County, North Carolina, 5/1/1862	Whiteville, Columbus County, North Carolina, 28 Years Old Turpentine/ Farmer	Co. E, 36th Regiment North Carolina, 2nd N. C. Artillery	Shell Wound, Right Thigh & Captured	Point Lookout Prison, Maryland	Oath of Allegiance 6/3/1865

NAME & RANK	ENLISTED	RESIDENCE AGE & TRADE	UNIT	RESULT OF BATTLE	PRISON	PRISON RELEASE
Coleman, Moses E. Private	Brunswick County, North Carolina, 3/3/1864	Waccamaw District, Brunswick County, North Carolina, 17 Years Old	Co. K, 36th Regiment North Carolina, 2nd N. C. Artillery	Wounded & Captured	Point Lookout Prison, Maryland	Oath of Allegiance 6/26/1865
Coleman, S. J. Sergeant	Marion District, South Carolina 1/26/62	Marion District, South Carolina, 27 Years Old	Co. L, 21st South Carolina Volunteers	Gunshot Wound and Compound Fracture Of Left Elbow & Captured	Point Lookout Prison Hospital, Maryland	Oath of Allegiance 7/25/1865
Coleman, Travis Jr. Private	Columbus County, North Carolina, 3/7/1862	Caswell County, North Carolina, 21 Years Old	Co. E, 36th Regiment North Carolina, 2nd N. C. Artillery	Captured	Point Lookout Prison, Maryland	Oath of Allegiance 6/26/1865
Collins, John Private	Place Unknown, 4/6/1864	New York	Co. B, Confederate States Marine Corp, Assigned to Guard duty Aboard CSS *Raleigh*.	Captured	Point Lookout Prison, Maryland	Oath of Allegiance 5/13/1865
Collins, Richard H. Private	Marion District, South Carolina 2/3/1862	Marion County, South Carolina Farmer, Age Unknown	Co. L, 21st South Carolina Volunteers	Captured	Elmira Prison, Elmira, New York	Died of Typhoid Fever, 2/9/1865
Colly, Samuel Seaman	Date and Place Unknown	Unknown	Confederate States Navy	Wounded, Splinters In Back 12/25/1864 & Captured 1/15/1865	Prison Unknown	Date Of Release Unknown
Congleton, Joseph A. Corporal	Beaufort County, North Carolina, 9/23/1861	Washington, Beaufort County, North Carolina, 23 Years Old Coach Maker	Co. D, 13th Battalion, North Carolina Light Artillery	Captured, Defended River Road Gate	Point Lookout Prison, Maryland	Oath of Allegiance 6/24/1865, Promoted to Artificer

NAME & RANK	ENLISTED	RESIDENCE AGE & TRADE	UNIT	RESULT OF BATTLE	PRISON	PRISON RELEASE
Congleton, Owen Private	Wilmington, New Hanover County, North Carolina, 5/18/1864	Long Acre, Washington, Beaufort County, North Carolina, 17 Years Old Farmer	Co. H, 10th Reg. 1st North Carolina Artillery	Captured	Elmira Prison, Elmira, New York	Died of Typhoid Fever, 2/24/1865
Conner, Doctor R. Private	Whiteville, Columbus County, North Carolina, 2/9/1863	Columbus County, North Carolina, 23 Years Old	Co. E, 36th Regiment North Carolina, 2nd N. C. Artillery	Captured	Elmira Prison, Elmira, New York	Exchanged 2/20/1865
Conner, James B. Private	Union County, North Carolina, 8/27/1861	Cleveland County, North Carolina, 22 Years Old Farm Laborer	Co. E, 40th Regiment, 3rd North Carolina Light Artillery	Killed In Action, 1/15/1865		
Conner, Pinkney C. Private	Columbus County, North Carolina, 2/9/1863	Columbus County, North Carolina, 22 Years Old	Co. E, 36th Regiment North Carolina, 2nd N. C. Artillery	Captured	Elmira Prison, Elmira, New York	Oath of Allegiance 7/11/1865
Cook, Alexander Private	Myersville, South Carolina 5/3/1862	Beaufort District, Kingstree, South Carolina, 15 Years Old	Co. H, 25th South Carolina Volunteers	Captured	Elmira Prison, Elmira, New York	Oath of Allegiance 6/23/1865
Cook, D. H. Private	New Hanover County, North Carolina, 1863	Whiteville, Columbus County, North Carolina, 15 Years Old Farmer	Co. H, 36th Regiment North Carolina, 2nd N. C. Artillery	Captured	Prison Unknown	Date Of Release Unknown
Cook, Francis A. Private	Pocotaligo, South Carolina 8/5/1861	St. Peter's Parrish, Beaufort District, South Carolina, 17 Years Old Farm Laborer	Co. F, 11th South Carolina Volunteers	Captured	Point Lookout Prison, Maryland	Oath of Allegiance 6/26/1865

NAME & RANK	ENLISTED	RESIDENCE AGE & TRADE	UNIT	RESULT OF BATTLE	PRISON	PRISON RELEASE
Cook, Robert Private	Fort Fisher, New Hanover County, North Carolina, 6/1/1863	Northern Division, Sampson County, North Carolina, 36 Years Old Farmer	2nd Co. I, 36th Regiment North Carolina, 2nd N. C. Artillery	Gunshot Wound In wrist & Left Thigh & Captured, Defended Shepperd's Battery	Point Lookout Prison General Hospital, Maryland	Oath of Allegiance 6/26/1865
Cook, Stephen E. Private	Pocotaligo, South Carolina 8/5/1861	Unknown, 20 Years Old	Co. F, 11th South Carolina Volunteers	Captured	Point Lookout Prison, Maryland	Oath of Allegiance 6/26/1865
Cook, Thomas J. Private	Battery Island, South Carolina 4/12/1862	Kingston Parrish, Horry County, South Carolina, 24 Years Old	Co. C, 25th South Carolina Volunteers	Captured	Elmira Prison, Elmira, New York	Exchanged On the James River, Virginia 3/2/1865
Cook, William D. Private	Battery Island, South Carolina 4/12/1862	Kershaw County, South Carolina, 27 Years Old	Co. B, 25th South Carolina Volunteers	Captured	Elmira Prison, Elmira, New York	Died of Chronic Diarrhea 4/12/1865
Cook, William D. Lieutenant	Bennetts-ville, South Carolina 12/25/1861	Columbia, Richland County, North Carolina, 26 Years Old	Co. F, 21st South Carolina Volunteers	Mortally Wounded In Left Leg & Shoulder & Captured	Point Lookout Prison Hospital, Maryland	2/2/1865, Left Leg Amputated, Died Of Wounds
Cooper, Charles H. Private	Fort Fisher, North Carolina, 10/31/1862, Volunteer	Owensville, Sampson County, North Carolina, 29 Years Old Farmer	2nd Co. C, 36th Regiment North Carolina, 2nd N. C. Artillery	Captured, Defended River Road Gate	Elmira Prison, Elmira, New York	Died of Smallpox, 3/19/1865

NAME & RANK	ENLISTED	RESIDENCE AGE & TRADE	UNIT	RESULT OF BATTLE	PRISON	PRISON RELEASE
Cooper, Hiram B. Private	New Hanover County, North Carolina, 10/31/1862	Owensville, Sampson County, North Carolina, 34 Years Old Farmer	2nd Co. D, 36th Regiment North Carolina, 2nd N. C. Artillery	Captured	Elmira Prison, Elmira, New York	Died of Disease, Causes Unknown 8/11/1865
Cooper, J. J. Private	Fort Johnson, South Carolina 8/1/1863	Williamsburg District, South Carolina, 31 Years Old	Co K, 21st South Carolina Volunteers	Killed In Action, 1/15/1865		
Cooper, John S. Private	New Hanover County, North Carolina, 2/6/1863	Owensville, Sampson County, North Carolina, 39 Years Old Farmer	2nd Co. C, 36th Regiment North Carolina, 2nd N. C. Artillery	Killed In Action, 1/15/1865, Defended River Road Gate		Killed by a shell fired from the Mound Battery
Cooper, Wynget Private	Date and Place Unknown	Pittsboro, Chatham County, North Carolina, 31 Years Old Farmer	3rd Co. B, 36th Regiment North Carolina, 2nd N. C. Artillery	Killed In Action, 1/15/1865		
Copeland, William Private	Wayne County, North Carolina, 4/8/1864	Nahunta, Wayne County, North Carolina, 20 Years Old	Co. F, 10th Reg. 1st North Carolina Artillery	Mortal Shell Wound of Head & Captured	Treated At Mansfield Hospital Morehead City, N. C.	Died Of Wounds 2/5/1865
Corban, Charles Private	Whippy Swamp, South Carolina 7/15/1861	Pocotaligo, Beaufort County, South Carolina, 18 Years Old	Co. D, 11th South Carolina Volunteers	Captured	Elmira Prison, Elmira, New York	Oath of Allegiance 6/23/1865
Corbin, Edward Private	Whippy Swamp, South Carolina 7/15/1861	Prince William Parrish, Beaufort County, South Carolina, 28 Years Old	Co. D, 11th South Carolina Volunteers	Captured	Elmira Prison, Elmira, New York	Died of Smallpox, 3/23/1865

NAME & RANK	ENLISTED	RESIDENCE AGE & TRADE	UNIT	RESULT OF BATTLE	PRISON	PRISON RELEASE
Cordon, Sylverter Corporal	Washington, Beaufort County, North Carolina, 9/23/1861	South Creek, Beaufort County, North Carolina, 16 Years Old	Co. D, 13th Battalion, North Carolina Light Artillery	Captured, Defended River Road Gate	Elmira Prison, Elmira, New York	Died of Chronic Diarrhea, 3/8/1865
Cordon, William W. First Sergeant	Washington, Beaufort County, North Carolina, 4/22/1861,	Washington, Beaufort County, North Carolina, 21 Years Old Carpenter	Co. K, 10th Reg. 1st North Carolina Artillery	Captured	Elmira Prison, Elmira, New York	Oath of Allegiance 7/11/1865
Costin, Thomas Seaman	Date and Place Unknown	Unknown	Confederate States Navy	Wounded in Back By Bursting Cannon & Captured	Prison Unknown	Date Of Release Unknown
Cotchett, William Dana Lieutenant	Charleston, South Carolina 2/241862	Unknown, 21 Years Old	Co. A, 25th South Carolina Volunteers	Captured	Fort Columbus, New York Harbor	Exchanged 2/25/1865
Covington, Benjamin C. Private	Fort Fisher, New Hanover County, North Carolina, 7/21/1863, Volunteer	Rockingham District, Richmond County, North Carolina, 18 Years Old Farmer	2nd Co. I, 36th Regiment North Carolina, 2nd N. C. Artillery	Captured, Defended Shepperd's Battery	Elmira Prison, Elmira, New York	Oath of Allegiance 6/16/1865
Covington, Thomas B. Private	Fort Fisher, New Hanover County, North Carolina, 6/26/1863	Rockingham District, Richmond County, North Carolina, 18 Years Old Farmer	2nd Co. I, 36th Regiment North Carolina, 2nd N. C. Artillery	Captured, Defended Shepperd's Battery	Elmira Prison, Elmira, New York	Oath of Allegiance 6/16/1865
Cowan, H. F. Private	Date and Place Unknown	Unknown	Co. K, 36th Regiment North Carolina, 2nd N. C. Artillery	Captured	Prison Unknown	Date Of Release Unknown

NAME & RANK	ENLISTED	RESIDENCE AGE & TRADE	UNIT	RESULT OF BATTLE	PRISON	PRISON RELEASE
Cowan, James M. First Lieutenant	Brunswick County, North Carolina, 6/6/1861	Town Creek District, Brunswick County, North Carolina, 28 Years Old Farmer	2nd Co. D, 36th Regiment North Carolina, 2nd N. C. Artillery	Captured	Fort Columbus Prison, New York	Exchanged 3/5/1865 City Point, Virginia
Cowan, Thaddeus Private	New Hanover County, North Carolina, 3/29/1862	New Hanover County, North Carolina, 30 Years Old Farmer	Co. H, 36th Regiment North Carolina, 2nd N. C. Artillery	Captured in Smithville, North Carolina, Hospital 1/16/1865	Point Lookout Prison, Maryland	Oath of Allegiance 5/13/1865, Detailed Hospital in Smithville, North Carolina
Cowperth-wait, W. B. Private	Charleston, South Carolina 5/9/1862	Charleston, South Carolina, 25 Years Old	Co. A, 25th South Carolina Volunteers	Captured	Elmira Prison, Elmira, New York	Oath of Allegiance 6/19/1865
Cox, Bryant Private	New Hanover County, North Carolina, 10/28/1861	Kinston District, Lenoir County, N. C., 29 Years Old Cooper & Ship's Carpenter	2nd Co. D, 36th Regiment North Carolina, 2nd N. C. Artillery	Captured	Point Lookout Prison, Maryland	Oath of Allegiance 5/15/1865
Cox, Isaac B. Private	Fort Pender, Brunswick County, North Carolina, 11/24/1863, Volunteer	Brunswick County, North Carolina, 17 Years Old	Co. E, 36th Regiment North Carolina, 2nd N. C. Artillery	Captured	Elmira Prison, Elmira, New York	Died of Pneumonia, 3/2/1865
Cox, Samuel P. Private	Columbus County, North Carolina, Date Unknown	Columbus County, North Carolina, 17 Years Old	Co. F, 36th Regiment North Carolina, 2nd N. C. Artillery	Wounded 1/13/1865 & Captured Smithville, N. C., Hospital 1/16/1865	Point Lookout Prison, Maryland	Oath of Allegiance 6/26/1865
Cozzens, Richard W. Private	Washington, Beaufort County, North Carolina, 9/23/1861	North Creek, Beaufort County, North Carolina, 19 Years Old Farmer	Co. D, 13th Battalion, North Carolina Light Artillery	Captured, Defended River Road Gate	Elmira Prison, Elmira, New York	Died of Smallpox, 3/19/1865

NAME & RANK	ENLISTED	RESIDENCE AGE & TRADE	UNIT	RESULT OF BATTLE	PRISON	PRISON RELEASE
Cozzans, Thomas F. Private	Washington, Beaufort County, North Carolina, 9/23/1861	Beaufort County, North Carolina, 28 Years Old	Co. D, 13th Battalion, North Carolina Light Artillery	Captured, Defended River Road Gate	Elmira Prison, Elmira, New York	Died of Remittent Fever, 4/6/1865
Crawford, Mathias Private	Goldsboro, Wayne County, North Carolina, 9/25/1862, Conscript	Goldsboro, North Carolina, 25 Years Old	Co. F, 10th Reg. 1st North Carolina Artillery	Captured	Elmira Prison, Elmira, New York	Died of Pneumonia, 3/12/1865
Crawford, William E. Private	Coles Island, South Carolina 4/11/1862	Charleston, South Carolina, 26 Years Old Laborer	C. G, 25th South Carolina Volunteers	Captured	Elmira Prison, Elmira, New York	Died Of Pneumonia 3/7/1865
Crawley, Hider D. Private	Craven County, North Carolina, 2/18/1862	Brinkleyville, Halifax County, North Carolina, 18 Years Old Farmer	Co. F, 36th Regiment North Carolina, 2nd N. C. Artillery	Captured	Elmira Prison, Elmira, New York	Died of Pneumonia, 3/12/1865, On Route to Be Exchanged
Crawley, John W. Sergeant	New Berne, Craven County, North Carolina, 1/3/1862	Brinkleyville, Halifax County, North Carolina, 18 Years Old Farmer	Co. F, 36th Regiment North Carolina, 2nd N. C. Artillery	Captured	Prison Unknown	No Release On File
Creech, Doctor L. Private	Bennetts-ville, South Carolina 2/7/62	Marlboro District, South Carolina Laborer, 27 Years Old Teamster	Co. F, 21st South Carolina Volunteers	Captured	Elmira Prison, Elmira, New York	Died of Chronic Diarrhea, 6/3/1865
Cribb, A. J. Private	Georgetown South Carolina. 3/23/62	Georgetown, Prince George Parish, South Carolina, 21 Years Old	Co. A, 21st South Carolina Volunteers	Captured	Elmira Prison, Elmira, New York	Oath of Allegiance 7/7/1865
Cribb, William Private	Charleston, South Carolina. 4/12/64	Georgetown, South Carolina, 17 Years Old	Co. A, 21st South Carolina Volunteers	Captured 1/16/1865 Fort Caswell Hospital	Point Lookout Prison Hospital, Maryland	Oath of Allegiance 6/20/1865, Chronic Bronchitis

NAME & RANK	ENLISTED	RESIDENCE AGE & TRADE	UNIT	RESULT OF BATTLE	PRISON	PRISON RELEASE
Crickman, Solomon Private	New Berne, Craven County, North Carolina, 1/27/1862, Volunteer	Battleboro, Nash County, North Carolina, 19 Years Old Farmer	Co. F, 36th Regiment North Carolina, 2nd N. C. Artillery	Captured	Elmira Prison, Elmira, New York	Oath of Allegiance 7/11/1865
Crisp, Thomas W. Private	Edgecombe County, North Carolina, 8/1/1863	Tarboro, Edgecombe County, North Carolina, 40 Years Old	Co. D, 40th Regiment, 3rd North Carolina Light Artillery	Captured	Point Lookout Prison, Maryland	Oath of Allegiance 6/16/1865
Croom, Isaac Private	New Hanover County, North Carolina, 5/25/1863	New Hanover County, North Carolina, Age Unknown	Co. F, 10th Reg. 1st North Carolina Artillery	Captured	Elmira Prison, Elmira, New York	Oath of Allegiance 5/29/1865
Croom, John A. Private	Wilmington, New Hanover County, North Carolina, Volunteer, 4/18/1862	Wilmington, New Hanover County, North Carolina, 31 Years Old Fisherman	Co. D, 1st Battalion, North Carolina Heavy Artillery	Captured, Defended River Road Gate	Elmira Prison, Elmira, New York	Exchanged 3/2/1865 Boulware's Wharf, James River, Virginia
Cromartie, Junius Poynter Private	New Hanover County, North Carolina, 1/27/1864, Conscript	Elizabethtown Bladen County, North Carolina, 20 Years Old Student, Detailed as a Scout, 7/6/1864	Co. H, 36th Regiment North Carolina, 2nd N. C. Artillery	Captured Near Sugar Loaf, North Carolina, 1/14/1865	Fort Delaware Prison, Del.	Died of Chronic Diarrhea, 4/29/1865
Crosswell, A. L. Private	Date and Place Unknown	Unknown	C. K, 25th South Carolina Volunteers	Captured	Point Lookout Prison, Maryland	Oath of Allegiance 6/4/1865

NAME & RANK	ENLISTED	RESIDENCE AGE & TRADE	UNIT	RESULT OF BATTLE	PRISON	PRISON RELEASE
Crumpler, Micajah H. Private	New Hanover County, North Carolina, 7/23/1863, Volunteer	Clinton, Sampson County, North Carolina, 52 Years Old Farmer	3rd Co. G, 40th Regiment, 3rd North Carolina Light Artillery	Captured, Defended Land Face	Elmira Prison, New York	Died of Disease, On Route To Be Exchanged At James River, Virginia, 2/21/1865
Cudworth, Alfred Private	Charleston, South Carolina 2/24/1864	Charleston, South Carolina, 20 Years Old	C. A, 25th South Carolina Volunteers	Captured	Elmira Prison, New York	Oath of Allegiance 6/16/1865
Culbreth, Daniel M. Private	Sampson County, North Carolina, 9/13/1863, Volunteer	Owensville, Sampson County, North Carolina, 44 Years Old Farmer	3rd Co. B, 36th Regiment North Carolina, 2nd N. C. Artillery	Captured	Elmira Prison, New York	Died of Chronic Diarrhea, 2/21/1865
Culbreth, Noah Private	Bladen County, North Carolina, 5/8/1862	Elizabethtown Bladen County, North Carolina, 26 Years Old Farmer	Co. H, 36th Regiment North Carolina, 2nd N. C. Artillery	Captured in Smithville Hospital, N. C., 1/16/1865	Point Lookout Prison, Maryland	Oath of Allegiance 6/26/1865
Culbreth, William Private	Sampson County, North Carolina, 4/10/1863, Volunteer	Owensville, Sampson County, North Carolina, 18 Years Old Farmer	3rd Co. B, 36th Regiment North Carolina, 2nd N. C. Artillery	Captured	Elmira Prison, New York	Oath of Allegiance 7/26/1865
Cumbee, Benjamin Private	New Hanover County, North Carolina, 2/12/1862	New Hanover County, North Carolina, 18 Years Old	2nd Co. D, 36th Regiment North Carolina, 2nd N. C. Artillery	Captured	Elmira Prison, Elmira, New York	Died of Chronic Diarrhea, 3/18/1865
Cumbee, Solomon J. Private	Wilmington, New Hanover County, North Carolina, 2/12/1862, Volunteer	New Hanover County, North Carolina, 45 Years Old	2nd Co. D, 36th Regiment North Carolina, 2nd N. C. Artillery	Captured	Elmira Prison, Elmira, New York	Died of Smallpox, 4/12/1865

NAME & RANK	ENLISTED	RESIDENCE AGE & TRADE	UNIT	RESULT OF BATTLE	PRISON	PRISON RELEASE
Cummings, William W. Private	Date and Place Unknown	Kinston, Lenoir County, North Carolina, 33 Years Old Overseer	Co. D, 40th Regiment, 3rd North Carolina Light Artillery	Missing Believed Killed		No Official Record Found, Name Appears On List Of Killed Prepared by Major C. E. Pearce, 2/17/1865
Currie, Andrew Jackson Private	Robeson County, North Carolina, 6/1/1863	Lumberton, Robeson County, North Carolina, 18 Years Old Farmer	3rd Co. B, 36th Regiment North Carolina, 2nd N. C. Artillery	Captured	Point Lookout Prison, Maryland	Oath of Allegiance 6/3/1865
Currie, Nicholas D. Private	Bennetts-ville, South Carolina 2/2/1863	Marion District, South Carolina, 24 Years Old Overseer	Co. F, 21st South Carolina Volunteers	Captured	Elmira Prison, Elmira, New York	Died of Pneumonia 5/14/1865
Currie, Randal Franklin Private	Robeson County, North Carolina, 4/16/1864	Lumberton, Robeson County, North Carolina, 17 Years Old Farmer	Co. D, 1st Battalion, North Carolina Heavy Artillery	Captured, Defended River Road Gate	Point Lookout Prison, Maryland	Oath of Allegiance 6/26/1865
Currie, Robert Private	Robeson County, North Carolina, 4/18/1864	Lumberton, Robeson County, North Carolina, 17 Years Old Farmer	Co. D, 1st Battalion, North Carolina Heavy Artillery	Wounded & Captured, Defended River Road Gate	Fort Delaware Prison, Del.	Oath of Allegiance 6/19/1865
Curry, R. Private	Date and Place Unknown	Unknown	Co. C, 3rd Battalion, North Carolina Light Artillery	Wounded & Captured	Fort Monroe, Virginia	Sent to Fort Monroe, Va, 1/17/1865 On Steamer Champion, Date Of Release Unknown
Cutchen, William T. Private	Date and Place Unknown	Enfield, Halifax County, North Carolina, 33 Years Old Farmer	Co. F, 36th Regiment North Carolina, 2nd N. C. Artillery	Captured	Elmira Prison, Elmira, New York	Died of Pneumonia, 3/11/1865

NAME & RANK	ENLISTED	RESIDENCE AGE & TRADE	UNIT	RESULT OF BATTLE	PRISON	PRISON RELEASE
Dailey, Benjamin F. Private	Wayne County, North Carolina, 4/14/1863, Volunteer	Newhope District, Wayne County, North Carolina, 18 Years Old Farmer	3rd Co. G, 40th Regiment, 3rd North Carolina Light Artillery	Captured, Defended Land Face	Elmira Prison, Elmira, New York	Died Of Chronic Diarrhea 3/4/1865
Dale, James C. Private	Wilmington, New Hanover County, North Carolina, 10/21/1861, Volunteer	New Hanover County, North Carolina, 18 Years Old	2nd Co. D, 36th Regiment North Carolina, 2nd N. C. Artillery	Captured	Elmira Prison, Elmira, New York	Died Of Pneumonia 3/27/1865
Daley, H. Private	Date and Place Unknown	Unknown	Co. E, 40th Regiment, 3rd North Carolina Light Artillery	Wounded & Captured	Prison Unknown	Date Of Release Unknown
Daniel, David J. Private	Bladen County, North Carolina, 3/10/1862	West Brook, Bladen County, North Carolina, 18 Years Old Farmer	3rd Co. B, , 36th Regiment North Carolina, 2nd N. C. Artillery	Captured	Point Lookout Prison, Maryland	Oath of Allegiance 6/26/1865
Daniel, E. J. Private	Date and Place Unknown	Unknown	3rd Co. B, , 36th Regiment North Carolina, 2nd N. C. Artillery	Captured	Prison Unknown	Date Of Release Unknown
Daniel, Henry Private	Wayne County, North Carolina, 7/9/1861	Wayne County, North Carolina, 22 Years Old Painter	Co. F, 10th Reg. 1st North Carolina Artillery	Captured	Elmira Prison, Elmira, New York	Died from Acute Inflammation Of The Liver 4/18/1865
Daniel, William C. Second Lieutenant	Halifax County, North Carolina, 10/9/1861	Heathsville, Halifax County, N. C., 18 Years Old Student at Trinity College, N. C.	Co. F, 36th Regiment North Carolina, 2nd N. C. Artillery	Captured	Fort Columbus Prison, New York	Exchanged 3/5/1865 Boulware's Wharf, James River, Virginia

NAME & RANK	ENLISTED	RESIDENCE AGE & TRADE	UNIT	RESULT OF BATTLE	PRISON	PRISON RELEASE
Daniel, William E. Private	Fort Campbell, Brunswick County, North Carolina, 1/2/1864, Volunteer	West Brook, Bladen County, North Carolina, 17 Years Old	3rd Co. G, 36th Regiment North Carolina, 2nd N. C. Artillery	Captured, Defended Battery to the Left of Northeast Bastion	Elmira Prison, Elmira, New York	Died of Smallpox, 3/28/1865
Dantzlar, Allen P. Private	Coles Island, South Carolina 4/11/1862	Orangeburg, South Carolina, 17 Years Old	C. F, 25th South Carolina Volunteers	Captured	Elmira Prison, Elmira, New York	Exchanged 3/2/1865 Boulware's Wharf, James River, Virginia
Dantzlar, B. M. Private	Coles Island, South Carolina 4/11/1862	Orangeburg, South Carolina, 20 Years Old	C. F, 25th South Carolina Volunteers	Captured	Elmira Prison, Elmira, New York	Died Of Chronic Diarrhea 2/20/1865
Dantzler, David W. Private	Coles Island, South Carolina 4/11/1862	McCantsville, Orangeburg, South Carolina, 27 Years Old	Co. F, 25th South Carolina Volunteers	Captured	Elmira Prison, Elmira, New York	Died of Pneumonia, 4/1/1865
Dantzler, F. W. Private	Coles Island, South Carolina 4/11/1862	Orangeburg District, South Carolina, 16 Years Old	C. F, 25th South Carolina Volunteers	Captured	Elmira Prison, Elmira, New York	Oath of Allegiance 7/26/1865
Darden, George T. Private	Murfreesboro Hertford County, North Carolina, 6/12/1863	Hertford County, N. C., 24 Years Old Detailed To Carry Mail Between Fort Caswell and Smithville, June 1863	Co. C, 3rd Battalion, North Carolina Light Artillery	Captured	Elmira Prison, Elmira, New York	Exchanged 3/14/1865 Boulware's Wharf, James River, Virginia
Dardin, Calvin Private	Wayne County, North Carolina, 2/2/1863	Bull Head District, Greene County, North Carolina, 25 Years Old	Co. F, 10th Reg. 1st North Carolina Artillery	Captured	Elmira Prison, Elmira, New York	Oath of Allegiance 5/29/1865

NAME & RANK	ENLISTED	RESIDENCE AGE & TRADE	UNIT	RESULT OF BATTLE	PRISON	PRISON RELEASE
Darnell, D. J. Private	Date and Place Unknown	Warren County, North Carolina 55 Years Old Farmer	3rd Co. B, 36th Regiment North Carolina, 2nd N. C. Artillery	Captured	Point Lookout Prison, Maryland	Oath of Allegiance 6/26/1865
David, John Private	Gourdins Dept., South Carolina 12/29/1862	Williamsburg District, South Carolina. 33 Years Old	C. F, 25th South Carolina Volunteers	Captured	Elmira Prison, Elmira, New York	Exchanged 3/2/1865 Boulware's Wharf, James River, Virginia
Davidson, Thomas Private	Duplin County, North Carolina, 9/1/1864	Duplin County, North Carolina, Age Unknown	Co. D, 10th Reg. 1st North Carolina Artillery	Captured	Elmira Prison, Elmira, New York	Died Of Smallpox, 3/14/1865
Davis, Alexander Private	Brunswick County, North Carolina, 5/301863	Robeson County, North Carolina, 18 Years Old Farmer	Co. E, 40th Regiment, 3rd North Carolina Light Artillery	Captured	Point Lookout Prison, Maryland	Died Of Pneumonia 2/13/1865
Davis, Alexander Smith Private	Elizabeth-town, Bladen County, North Carolina, 5/5/1862	Cypress Creek, Bladen County, North Carolina, 33 Years Old Farmer	Co. H, 36th Regiment North Carolina, 2nd N. C. Artillery	Captured	Elmira Prison, Elmira, New York	Died Of Chronic Diarrhea 2/18/1865
Davis, Amos L. Private	Fort Fisher, New Hanover County, North Carolina, 4/16/1862	New Hanover County, North Carolina, 18 Years Old	2nd Co. I, 36th Regiment North Carolina, 2nd N. C. Artillery	Wounded & Captured, Defended Shepperd's Battery	Elmira Prison, Elmira, New York	Died of Smallpox, 3/28/1865
Davis, Archibald W. Private	Robeson County, North Carolina, 9/17/1861	Robeson County, North Carolina, 19 Years Old Farmer	Co. E, 40th Regiment, 3rd North Carolina Light Artillery	Captured	Point Lookout Prison, Maryland	Oath of Allegiance 6/26/1865

NAME & RANK	ENLISTED	RESIDENCE AGE & TRADE	UNIT	RESULT OF BATTLE	PRISON	PRISON RELEASE
Davis, David Private	Brunswick County, North Carolina, 7/28/1863	Smyrna, Carteret County, North Carolina, 35 Years Old Fisherman	2nd Co. D, 36th Regiment North Carolina, 2nd N. C. Artillery	Captured	Point Lookout Prison, Maryland	Oath of Allegiance 6/26/1865
Davis, E. W. Private	Date and Place Unknown	Stanly County, N. C., 50 Years Old Farmer	2nd Co. I, 36th Regiment North Carolina, 2nd N. C. Artillery	Captured, Defended Shepperd's Battery	Elmira Prison, Elmira, New York	Died Of Debility 5/26/1865
Davis, Edward W. Private	Fort St. Philip, Brunswick County, North Carolina, 7/7/1862, Volunteer	White Oak, Bladen County, N. C., 23 Years Old Detailed 1/5/1864 to build wharf at Fort Fisher	2nd Co. K, 40th Regiment, 3rd North Carolina Light Artillery	Captured	Elmira Prison, Elmira, New York	Exchanged 2/15/1865, Died of Consumption 5/17/1865, Richmond, Virginia, Hospital
Davis, Elias Private	Wilmington, New Hanover County, North Carolina, 6/1/1864	Wayne County, North Carolina, 19 Years Old	Co. C, 7th North Carolina, Battalion, Junior Reserves	Killed in Action, 12/25/1864		
Davis, Francis Seaman	Place Unknown 8/14/1861	Carteret County, North Carolina, 44 Years Old Seaman	Galloway Co. Confederate States Coast Guard	Captured	Prison Unknown	Date Of Release Unknown
Davis, Hiram Private	Elizabeth-town, Bladen County, North Carolina, 10/19/1861	Bladen County, North Carolina, 14 Years Old Farmer	2nd Co. I, 36th Regiment North Carolina, 2nd N. C. Artillery	Captured, Defended Shepperd's Battery	Elmira Prison, Elmira, New York	Died Of Disease 5/21/1865, Cause Unknown
Davis, John B. Private	Tarboro, Edgecombe County, North Carolina, 10/1/1862	Edgecombe County, North Carolina, 21 Years Old	Co. D, 13th Battalion, North Carolina Light Artillery	Captured, Defended River Road Gate	Point Lookout Prison, Maryland	Admitted to Hamond General Hospital 2/3/1865, Date Of Release Unknown

NAME & RANK	ENLISTED	RESIDENCE AGE & TRADE	UNIT	RESULT OF BATTLE	PRISON	PRISON RELEASE
Davis, John M. Private	Bladen County, North Carolina, 12/20/1861	White Creek, Bladen County, North Carolina, 19 Years Old	3rd Co. B, 36th Regiment North Carolina, 2nd N. C. Artillery	Captured	Point Lookout Prison, Maryland	Oath of Allegiance 6/4/1865, Drummer
Davis, John Richardson Private	Fort Fisher, New Hanover County, North Carolina, 3/16/1862	Elizabethtown Bladen County, North Carolina, 18 Years Old	2nd Co. I, 36th Regiment North Carolina, 2nd N. C. Artillery	Captured, Defended Shepperd's Battery	Elmira Prison, Elmira, New York	Oath of Allegiance 6/12/1865
Davis, John W. Sergeant	Carteret County, North Carolina, 10/10/1861, Volunteer	Beaufort, Carteret County, North Carolina, 24 Years Old Farmer	3rd Co. G, 40th Regiment , North Carolina, 3rd North Carolina Artillery	Captured, Defended Land Face	Elmira Prison, Elmira, New York	Oath of Allegiance 5/19/1865
Davis, Jordan D. Corporal	Fort St. Philip, Brunswick County, North Carolina, 5/14/1862, Volunteer	Lockwoods Folly District, Brunswick County, North Carolina, 33 Years Old Farmer	3rd Co. G, 36th Regiment North Carolina, 2nd N. C. Artillery	Wounded & Captured, Defended Battery to the Left of Northeast Bastion	Elmira Prison, Elmira, New York	Exchanged 3/2/1865 Boulware's Wharf, James River, Virginia
Davis, R. S. Private	Date and Place Unknown	Unknown	C. I, 25th South Carolina Volunteers	Wounded Severely & Captured	Fort Monroe, Virginia	Brought north on Steamer Champion 1/17/1865, No More Information
Davis, Richard J. Streety Private	Bladen County, North Carolina, Volunteer	Downingsville Bladen County, North Carolina, 21 Years Old	2nd Co. I, 36th Regiment North Carolina, 2nd N. C. Artillery	Mortal Shell Wound of Right Elbow & Captured, Defended Shepperd's Battery	Treated At Mansfield Hospital Morehead City, N. C.,	Died of Wounds 2/8/1865

NAME & RANK	ENLISTED	RESIDENCE AGE & TRADE	UNIT	RESULT OF BATTLE	PRISON	PRISON RELEASE
Davis, Simmons S. Seaman	Place Unknown 1/24/1861	Carteret County, North Carolina, Age Unknown Seaman	Galloway Co. Confederate States Coast Guard	Captured	Prison Unknown	Date Of Release Unknown
Davis, Thaddeus C. Sergeant	Carteret County, North Carolina, 10/16/1861, Volunteer	Morehead City, Carteret County, North Carolina, 19 Years Old	3rd Co. G, 40th Regiment, 3rd North Carolina Light Artillery	Captured, Defended Land Face	Elmira Prison, Elmira, New York	Oath of Allegiance 5/19/1865
Davis, Thomas Sergeant	Wilmington, New Hanover County, North Carolina, 1/1/1861, Volunteer	Prospect Hall, Bladen County, North Carolina, 23 Years Old Farmer	3rd Co. B, 36th Regiment North Carolina, 2nd N. C. Artillery	Captured	Elmira Prison, Elmira, New York	Exchanged 3/2/1865 Boulware's Wharf, James River, Virginia
Davis, Thomas Private	James Island, 3/13/1863	Kershaw County, South Carolina, 36 Years Old Farmer	Co. F, 25th South Carolina Volunteers	Mortally Wounded, Severely wounded In Left Leg & Captured	Point Lookout US Army General Hospital	Died Of Wounds 2/9/1865, Gunshot Wound In Left Thigh and Knee, Left Leg Amputated
Davis, William A. Private	Elizabeth-town, Bladen County, North Carolina, 10/19/1861, Volunteer	White Oak, Bladen County, North Carolina, 20 Years Old Farmer	2nd Co. I, 36th Regiment North Carolina, 2nd N. C. Artillery	Captured, Defended Shepperd's Battery	Elmira Prison, Elmira, New York	Exchanged 3/2/1865 Boulware's Wharf, James River, Virginia
Davis, William E. Seaman	Place Unknown 1/24/1861	Brunswick County, North Carolina, Age Unknown	Galloway Co. Confederate States Coast Guard	Captured	Prison Unknown	Date Of Release Unknown

NAME & RANK	ENLISTED	RESIDENCE AGE & TRADE	UNIT	RESULT OF BATTLE	PRISON	PRISON RELEASE
Davis, William H. Private	Fort Fisher, New Hanover County, North Carolina, 5/1/1862, Volunteer	New Hanover County, North Carolina, 18 Years Old	2nd Co. C, 36th Regiment North Carolina, 2nd N. C. Artillery	Captured, Defended River Road Gate	Elmira Prison, Elmira, New York	Died Of Pneumonia 4/27/1865
Daw, Jesse H. Private	Craven County, North Carolina, 9/21/1861	New Berne, Craven County, North Carolina, 21 Years Old Farmer	Co. D, 40th Regiment, 3rd North Carolina Light Artillery	Captured	Point Lookout Prison, Maryland	Oath of Allegiance 6/26/1865
Dawson, Burwell Private	Sampson County, North Carolina, 2/18/1863	Newton Grove, Sampson County, North Carolina, 18 Years Old Farm Laborer	2nd Co. A, 36th Regiment North Carolina, 2nd N. C. Artillery	Captured, Defended the Mound Battery	Point Lookout Prison, Maryland	Died Of Pneumonia, 3/17/1865
Deal, Linton W. Private	Wilmington, New Hanover County, North Carolina, 2/2/1863, Substitute for Jacob J. Edwards	Duplin County, North Carolina, 37 Years Old	Co. D, 1st Battalion, North Carolina Heavy Artillery	Captured, Defended River Road Gate	Elmira Prison, Elmira, New York	Exchanged 3/2/1865 Boulware's Wharf, James River, Virginia
Dean, Frank A. Private	Savannah, Georgia, 3/?/1863	Unknown, 22 Years Old	Co. B, Confederate States Marine Corp, Assigned to Guard duty Aboard CSS *Savannah.*	Wounded & Captured, Defended Sea Face	Elmira Prison, Elmira, New York	Wounded, Concussion Of Brain, Died Of Chronic Diarrhea 7/18/1865
Debese, D. G. Captain	Date and Place Unknown	Unknown	Co. B, Confederate States Marine Corp.	Captured	Unknown	No Information Found

NAME & RANK	ENLISTED	RESIDENCE AGE & TRADE	UNIT	RESULT OF BATTLE	PRISON	PRISON RELEASE
Dees, John A. W. Private	Richmond County, North Carolina, 4/29/1863, Volunteer	Pikesville, Wayne County, North Carolina, 19 Years Old Farmer	3rd Co. B, 36th Regiment North Carolina, 2nd N. C. Artillery	Captured	Elmira Prison, Elmira, New York	Died Of Chronic Diarrhea & Smallpox, 2/27/1865
DeLoach, James Private	6/2/1862, Coosawhatchie, South Carolina	Unknown, 36 Years Old	Co. F, 11th South Carolina Volunteers	Captured	Point Lookout, Maryland	Died of Chronic Diarrhea, 7/8/1865
Deloache, Nelson Private	Camp Hardee, Georgetown South Carolina 1/1/1862	Manning, Clarendon District, South Carolina, 37 Years Old Brick Mason	Co. I, 25th South Carolina Volunteers	Captured	Elmira Prison, Elmira, New York	Died Of Chronic Diarrhea 3/4/1865
Dempsey, Charles Private	Date and Place Unknown	Enfield, Halifax County, North Carolina, 18 Years Old Farmer Laborer	Co. F, 36th Regiment North Carolina, 2nd N. C. Artillery	Captured	Point Lookout Prison, Maryland	Exchanged 2/14/1865 Cox's Landing, James River, Virginia
Dempsey, Henry Private	Date and Place Unknown	Edenton, Chowan County, North Carolina, 46 Years Old	Co. F, 36th Regiment North Carolina, 2nd N. C. Artillery	Captured	Point Lookout Prison, Maryland	Exchanged 2/14/1865 Cox's Landing, James River, Virginia
Dempsey, Patrick C. Private	4/16/1864, Wilmington, New Hanover County, North Carolina	Teachey's Depot, North Carolina	2nd Co. I, 10th Regiment North Carolina, 1st N. C. Artillery	Wounded at the First Battle of Fort Fisher		Paroled at Greensboro, North Carolina, 5/1/1865
Denning, Nathan Private	3/10/1863, Johnston County, North Carolina	Newton Grove, Sampson County, North Carolina, 38 Years Old Farmer	3rd Co. B, 36th Regiment North Carolina, 2nd N. C. Artillery	Captured	Point Lookout Prison, Maryland	Oath of Allegiance 6/26/1865

NAME & RANK	ENLISTED	RESIDENCE AGE & TRADE	UNIT	RESULT OF BATTLE	PRISON	PRISON RELEASE
Derr, John C. Private	Fort Strong, New Hanover County, North Carolina, 2/2/1863, Volunteer	Teacher's Depot, Duplin County, North Carolina, 19 Years Old	Co. D, 1st Battalion, North Carolina Heavy Artillery	Captured, Defended River Road Gate	Elmira Prison, Elmira, New York	Oath of Allegiance 7/11/1865
DeVane, Robert Harvey Private	Fort Fisher, New Hanover County, North Carolina, 8/5/1863, Volunteer	Colvins Creek, New Hanover County, North Carolina, 18 Years Old	2nd Co. I, 36th Regiment North Carolina, 2nd N. C. Artillery	Captured, Defended the Mound Battery	Elmira Prison, Elmira, New York	Oath of Allegiance 6/12/1865
DeVoe, James H. Corporal	Charleston, South Carolina 4/16/1862	Unknown, 25 Years Old	Co. B, 25th South Carolina Volunteers	Captured	Elmira Prison, Elmira, New York	Exchanged 3/22/1865
Dewar, Henry B. Private	New Hanover County, North Carolina, 3/18/1863	Summerville, Harnett County, North Carolina, 36 Years Old Merchant	2nd Co. C, 36th Regiment North Carolina, 2nd N. C. Artillery	Captured, Defended River Road Gate	Point Lookout Prison, Maryland	Oath of Allegiance 6/26/1865
Dial, Jacob Private	Bennettsville, South Carolina 12/25/1861	Bennettsville, Marlboro District, South Carolina, 41 Years Old	Co. F, 21st South Carolina Volunteers	Captured	Elmira Prison, Elmira, New York	Died Of Pneumonia 3/10/1865
Dibble, M. W. Corporal	Residence Greenville, South Carolina	Greenville, South Carolina, Age Unknown	Co. B, 25th South Carolina Volunteers	Captured	Elmira Prison, Elmira, New York	Oath of Allegiance 6/15/1865
Dicken, George Private	Halifax County, North Carolina, 10/9/1861	Halifax County, North Carolina, 19 Years Old	Co. F, 36th Regiment North Carolina, 2nd N. C. Artillery	Captured	Point Lookout Prison, Maryland	Oath of Allegiance 6/12/1865

NAME & RANK	ENLISTED	RESIDENCE AGE & TRADE	UNIT	RESULT OF BATTLE	PRISON	PRISON RELEASE
Dicken, Hiram Private	Enfield, Halifax County, North Carolina, 10/9/1861, Volunteer	Heathsville, Halifax County, North Carolina. 35 Years Old Farmer	Co. F, 36th Regiment North Carolina, 2nd N. C. Artillery	Captured	Elmira Prison, Elmira, New York	Exchanged On the James River 3/14/1865
Dickens, Rowan Sergeant	Fort Caswell, Brunswick County, North Carolina, 8/71863, Volunteer	Halifax County, North Carolina, 18 Years Old	Co. F, 36th Regiment North Carolina, 2nd N. C. Artillery	Captured	Elmira Prison, Elmira, New York	Died Of Smallpox, 3/18/1865
Dickinson, James H. Sergeant	Charleston, South Carolina 2/24/1862	Greenville, South Carolina, 20 Years Old Farmer	Co. A, 25th South Carolina Volunteers	Captured	Elmira Prison, Elmira, New York	Exchanged 3/2/1865 Boulware's Wharf, James River, Virginia
Dicks, William W. Private	Bladen County, North Carolina, 3/15/1862, Volunteer	Elizabethtown Bladen County, North Carolina, 22 Years Old	2nd Co. I, 36th Regiment North Carolina, 2nd N. C. Artillery	Gunshot Wound Of Right Thigh & Captured, Defended the Mound Battery	Fort Delaware Prison, Del.	Died Of Colic 3/29/1865
Dickson, George W. Private	Secession-ville, South Carolina 7/25/1863	Columbia, Richland County, South Carolina, 30 Years Old Clerk	Co. I, 25th South Carolina Volunteers	Captured	Elmira Prison, Elmira, New York	Exchanged 3/14/1865
Dickson, James W. First Lieutenant	Bladen County, North Carolina, 5/6/1862	Town Creek, Bladen County, North Carolina, Years Old Clerk	2nd Co. K, 40th Regiment, 3rd North Carolina Light Artillery	Captured	Fort Columbus Prison, New York	Exchanged 3/5/1865, Boulware's Wharf, James River, Virginia
Dickson, M. R. Private	Date and Place Unknown	Unknown	Co. F, 36th Regiment North Carolina, 2nd N. C. Artillery	Killed in Action, 1/15/1865		

NAME & RANK	ENLISTED	RESIDENCE AGE & TRADE	UNIT	RESULT OF BATTLE	PRISON	PRISON RELEASE
Dill, Samuel L. Private	Wilmington, New Hanover County, North Carolina, 7/1/1863	Beaufort, Carteret County North Carolina, Age Unknown	Co. K, 10th Reg. 1st North Carolina Artillery	Captured	Elmira Prison, Elmira, New York	Exchanged 3/14/1865, Boulware's Wharf, James River, Virginia
Dillard, S. H. Private	Sampson County, North Carolina, 9/1/1864	Sampson County, North Carolina, Age Unknown Overseer	Co. D, 1st Battalion, North Carolina Heavy Artillery	Captured, Defended River Road Gate	Elmira Prison, Elmira, New York	Exchanged 2/20/1865, Died Of Typhoid Fever 3/8/1865, Hospital Richmond, Virginia
Dillon, John Private	Mobile, Alabama, 12/9/1863	New Orleans, Louisiana, 30 Years Old Laborer	Co. C, Confederate States Marine Corp, Assigned to Guard duty Aboard CSS *Tallahassee*.	Wounded in Hip & Captured	Prison Unknown	Date of Release Unknown
Dixon, James W. Private	Craven County, North Carolina, 9/21/1861, Volunteer	North of Neuse River, Craven County, North Carolina, 20 Years Old Farm Hand	Co. D, 40th Regiment, 3rd North Carolina Light Artillery	Shell Wound Left Elbow & Captured	Treated At Mansfield Hospital, Morehead City, N. C., Sent To Fort Delaware Prison, Del.	Died of Inflammation Of The Brain 4/1/1865
Dixon, William Private	Brunswick County, North Carolina, 9/13/1863	Craven County, North Carolina, 45 Years Old Farmer	3rd Co. G, 36th Regiment North Carolina, 2nd N. C. Artillery	Killed In Action 1/15/1865, Defended Battery to the Left of Northeast Bastion		

NAME & RANK	ENLISTED	RESIDENCE AGE & TRADE	UNIT	RESULT OF BATTLE	PRISON	PRISON RELEASE
Doares, James D. Private	Old Brunswick Town, North Carolina, 4/16/1862	Northwest District, Brunswick County, North Carolina, 16 Years Old Laborer	3rd Co. G, 36th Regiment North Carolina, 2nd N. C. Artillery	Captured, Defended Battery to the Left of Northeast Bastion	Elmira Prison, Elmira, New York	Oath of Allegiance 8/7/1865
Doak, Henry M. Second Lieutenant	Knoxville, Tenn., 6/11/1861, Transferred to Confederate Marine Corp. 11/12/1862	Washington County, Tennessee, Age Unknown	Co. B, Confederate States Marine Corp, Assigned to Guard duty Aboard CSS *Charleston,* CSS *Raleigh* and the CSS *Arctic.*	Wounded in Leg by shell Fragment, Partially Blinded & Captured	Treated at Fort Monroe, Transferred to Fort Delaware Prison, Del. , 2/11/1865	Exchanged 2/27/1865 at City Point, Virginia
Dobbs, Leonard W. Private	Savannah, Georgia, 3/6/1863	Unknown	Co. E, Confederate States Marine Corp, Assigned to Guard duty Aboard CSS *Savannah.*	Captured, Defended Sea Face	Point Lookout Prison, Maryland	Exchanged 2/10/1865
Dorden, Paul Private	Hertford County, North Carolina, 9/1/1864	Hertford County, North Carolina, Age Unknown	Co. C, 3rd Battalion, North Carolina Light Artillery	Captured	Elmira Prison, Elmira, New York	Died Of Pneumonia 4/2/1865
Dornin, T. L. Lieutenant	Date and Place Unknown	Unknown	Confederate States Navy, Served on *CSS Florida,* and the *CSS Rappahannock*	Wounded in Foot, 12/25/1864	Not Captured	
Dosher, Lafayette Seaman	Place Unknown 5/13/1862	Smithville, Brunswick County, North Carolina, 29 Years Old Raftsman	Galloway Co. Confederate States Coast Guard	Captured	Prison Unknown	Date Of Release Unknown

239

NAME & RANK	ENLISTED	RESIDENCE AGE & TRADE	UNIT	RESULT OF BATTLE	PRISON	PRISON RELEASE
Doughtie, Alpheus P. Private	Hertford County, North Carolina, 4/30/1862	Murfreesboro, Hertford County, North Carolina, 17 Years Old	Co. C, 3rd Battalion, North Carolina Light Artillery	Captured	Elmira Prison, Elmira, New York	Died Of Smallpox, 2/24/1865
Doughtry, Henry H. Private	Brunswick County, North Carolina, 1/31/1864,	Halls District, Sampson County, North Carolina, 23 Years Old Farm Laborer	Co. F, 36th Regiment North Carolina, 2nd N. C. Artillery	Captured	Point Lookout Prison, Maryland	Oath of Allegiance 6/3/1865
Douglas, Norman Private	Union County, North Carolina, 8/27/1861	Lumberton, Robeson County, North Carolina, 30 Years Old Farmer	Co. E, 40th Regiment, 3rd North Carolina Light Artillery	Mortal Gunshot Wound Right Elbow & Captured	Treated At Mansfield Hospital Morehead City, N. C.,	Died Of Wounds 2/10/1865
Douglass, Henry Private	Chesterfield, South Carolina 5/1/1863	Unknown	Co. D, 21st South Carolina Volunteers	Captured	Elmira Prison, Elmira, New York	Died Of Epilepsy 3/19/1865
Dove, Alexander J. Private	Bladen County, North Carolina, 5/8/1862	Elizabethtown Bladen County, North Carolina, 32 Years Old Turpentine	Co. H, 36th Regiment North Carolina, 2nd N. C. Artillery	Captured	Point Lookout Prison, Maryland	Oath of Allegiance 6/26/1865
Dove, James I. Private	Brunswick County, North Carolina, 3/7/1863, Volunteer	Elizabethtown Bladen County, North Carolina, 23 Years Old Farmer	Co. H, 36th Regiment North Carolina, 2nd N. C. Artillery	Severe Gunshot Wound, Left Hand & Face & Captured	Treated At Mansfield Hospital, Morehead City, N. C., Sent To David's Island Prison, New York Harbor	Oath of Allegiance 6/20/1865
Dove, John M. Private	Brunswick County, North Carolina, 3/7/1863	Elizabethtown Bladen County, North Carolina, 31 Years Old Turpentine	Co. H, 36th Regiment North Carolina, 2nd N. C. Artillery	Captured	Point Lookout Prison, Maryland	Oath of Allegiance 6/26/1865

NAME & RANK	ENLISTED	RESIDENCE AGE & TRADE	UNIT	RESULT OF BATTLE	PRISON	PRISON RELEASE
Dove, William J. Private	Brunswick County, North Carolina, 3/7/1863	Elizabethtown Bladen County, North Carolina, 24 Years Old Farmer	Co. H, 36th Regiment North Carolina, 2nd N. C. Artillery	Captured	Point Lookout Prison, Maryland	Oath of Allegiance 6/26/1865
Dowless, Elisha Private	Bladen County, North Carolina, 2/7/1862, Volunteer	Elizabethtown Bladen County, North Carolina, 33 Years Old Farmer	2nd Co. I, 36th Regiment North Carolina, 2nd N. C. Artillery	Wounded & Captured, Defended the Mound Battery	Point Lookout Prison, Maryland	Oath of Allegiance 6/26/1865
Dowless, Samuel A. Private	New Hanover County, North Carolina, 3/7/1862	Elizabethtown Bladen County, North Carolina, 35 Years Old Turpentine	2nd Co. I, 36th Regiment North Carolina, 2nd N. C. Artillery	Captured, Defended the Mound Battery	Point Lookout Prison, Maryland	Oath of Allegiance 6/26/1865
Downing, Hayes B. Private	Cumberland County, North Carolina, 10/10/1864	Fayetteville, Cumberland County, North Carolina, 15 Years Old	3rd Co. G, 36th Regiment North Carolina, 2nd N. C. Artillery	Captured, Defended Battery to the Left of Northeast Bastion	Elmira Prison, Elmira, New York	Oath of Allegiance 5/15/1865
Downing, John B. Private	Lock's Creek, Cumberland County, North Carolina, 1/24/1863, Volunteer	Fayetteville, Cumberland County, North Carolina, 28 Years Old Merchant	2nd Co. I, 36th Regiment North Carolina, 2nd N. C. Artillery	Captured, Defended the Mound Battery	Elmira Prison, Elmira, New York	Oath of Allegiance 6/17/1865
Downing, Neill Private	New Hanover County, North Carolina	Cumberland East District, Cumberland County, North Carolina, 16 Years Old	3rd Co. G, 36th Regiment North Carolina, 2nd N. C. Artillery	Wounded & Captured, Defended Battery to the Left of Northeast Bastion	Prison Unknown	No Release On File, May Have Died of Wounds at Fort Fisher

241

NAME & RANK	ENLISTED	RESIDENCE AGE & TRADE	UNIT	RESULT OF BATTLE	PRISON	PRISON RELEASE
Downing, Valentine Private	New Hanover County, North Carolina, 3/31/1864, Volunteer	Downingville, Bladen County, North Carolina, 18 Years Old	Co. H, 36th Regiment North Carolina, 2nd N. C. Artillery	Captured	Elmira Prison, Elmira, New York	Died Of Chronic Diarrhea 4/5/1865
Doyle, J. (Negro) Private	Date and Place Unknown	Unknown	Co. E, 40th Regiment, 3rd North Carolina Light Artillery	Captured	Point Lookout Prison, Maryland	Exchanged 3/16/1865, Boulware's Wharf, James River, Virginia
Dozier, J. Fred Private	Date and Place Unknown	Arringtons District, Nash County, North Carolina, 52 Years Old Farmer	Co. E, 36th Regiment North Carolina, 2nd N. C. Artillery	Captured	Elmira Prison, Elmira, New York	Died Of Chronic Diarrhea 3/9/1865
Draughan, George B. Private	Brunswick County, North Carolina, 3/8/1863	Mingo District, Sampson County, North Carolina, 25 Years Old Farmer	2nd Co. D, 36th Regiment North Carolina, 2nd N. C. Artillery	Captured	Point Lookout Prison, Maryland	Oath of Allegiance 5/13/1865
Drew, James Private	3/1/1861 in Co. A, 1st Georgia Infantry, Discharged to Enlist in CSMC, 4/5/1864	Unknown, 23 Years Old	Co. C, Confederate States Marine Corp, Assigned to Guard duty Aboard CSS *Tallahassee*.	Wounded & Captured	Elmira Prison, Elmira, New York	Died Of Pneumonia 2/27/1865
Drew, William W. First Lieutenant	Brunswick County, North Carolina, 2/19/1862, Volunteer	Town Creek District, Brunswick County, North Carolina, 21 Years Old Farmer	Co. K, 36th Regiment North Carolina, 2nd N. C. Artillery	Wounded & Captured	Fort Columbus Prison, New York	Exchanged 3/5/1865, Boulware's Wharf, James River, Va
DuBose, D. G. Captain	Georgetown South Carolina 5/1/1862	Sumter, South Carolina, 24 Years Old Clerk	Co. H, 21st South Carolina Volunteers	Captured	Fort Columbus Prison, New York	Exchanged 2/25/1865

NAME & RANK	ENLISTED	RESIDENCE AGE & TRADE	UNIT	RESULT OF BATTLE	PRISON	PRISON RELEASE
Dudley, Edward B. Captain	Transferred From Coast Guard, 3/3/1862	New Berne, Craven County, North Carolina, 42 Years Old Fisherman, Company Commander	2nd Co. D, 36th Regiment North Carolina, 2nd N. C. Artillery	Captured	Fort Columbus Prison, New York	Exchanged 3/5/1865, City Point, Va.
Dudley, John London Sergeant	Camp Wyatt, New Hanover County, North Carolina, 5/11/1864, Volunteer	Wilmington, New Hanover County, North Carolina, 18 Years Old	2nd Co. D, 36th Regiment North Carolina, 2nd N. C. Artillery	Wounded & Captured	Point Lookout Prison, Maryland	Oath of Allegiance 6/26/1865
Dudley, John R. Private	Fort Caswell, Brunswick County, North Carolina, 9/29/1863, Volunteer	Dismal District, Sampson County, North Carolina, 18 Years Old	2nd Co. A, 36th Regiment North Carolina, 2nd N. C. Artillery	Captured, Defended the Mound Battery	Elmira Prison, Elmira, New York	Oath of Allegiance 7/11/1865
Dudley, Sampson Private	Sampson County, North Carolina, 11/12/1861, Volunteer	Dismal District, Sampson County, North Carolina, 19 Years Old	2nd Co. A, 36th Regiment North Carolina, 2nd N. C. Artillery	Captured, Defended the Mound Battery	Elmira Prison, Elmira, New York	Died Of Bronchitis 5/26/1865
Duffy, Edward Seaman	Date and Place Unknown	Unknown	Confederate States Navy	Wounded In Shoulder 12/25/1864, & Captured 1/15/1865	Prison Unknown	Date Of Release Unknown
Duncan, John J. Private	Brunswick County, North Carolina, 12/15/1863, Volunteer	Enfield, Halifax County, North Carolina, 38 Years Old Farm Overseer	Co. F, 36th Regiment North Carolina, 2nd N. C. Artillery	Captured	Elmira Prison, Elmira, New York	Died Of Chronic Diarrhea 3/31/1865

NAME & RANK	ENLISTED	RESIDENCE AGE & TRADE	UNIT	RESULT OF BATTLE	PRISON	PRISON RELEASE
Duncan, William W. Private	Halifax County, North Carolina, 10/9/1861	Union County, North Carolina, 26 Years Old Farmer	Co. F, 36th Regiment North Carolina, 2nd N. C. Artillery	Killed In Action 1/15/1865		Wounded 12/24/1864, Hospitalized in Raleigh with Contusion 12/27/1864
Dunham, Thomas B. Private	Bladen County, North Carolina,	Bladen County, North Carolina, Age Unknown Farmer	Co. H, 36th Regiment North Carolina, 2nd N. C. Artillery	Captured	Point Lookout Prison, Maryland	Oath of Allegiance 6/26/1865
Dunn, Franklin Private	Edgecombe County, North Carolina, 4/1/1864, Volunteer	Edgecombe County, North Carolina, 26 Years Old	Co. D, 40th Regiment, 3rd North Carolina Light Artillery	Captured	Elmira Prison, Elmira, New York	Died Of Smallpox, 4/9/1865
Dunn, John Private	Mobile, Louisiana, 2/27/1863	Unknown	Co. E, Confederate States Marine Corp, Assigned to Guard duty Aboard CSS *Savannah* and CSS *Atlanta*.	Captured, Defended Sea Face	Fort Monroe, Virginia	Oath of Allegiance 7/6/1863
Dunning, William C. Sergeant	Hertford County, North Carolina, 2/26/1862	Windsor, Bertie County, North Carolina, 21 Years Old Farmer	Co. C, 3rd Battalion, North Carolina Light Artillery	Shell Wound Left Hand & Captured	Treated At Mansfield Hospital, Morehead City, N. C., Sent To Fort Delaware Prison, Del.	Oath of Allegiance 6/19/1865
Dupree, Joseph A. Private	Edgecombe County, North Carolina, 3/24/1864	Pitt County, North Carolina, 17 Years Old	Co. D, 40th Regiment, 3rd North Carolina Light Artillery	Captured	Point Lookout Prison, Maryland	Oath of Allegiance 6/11/1865

NAME & RANK	ENLISTED	RESIDENCE AGE & TRADE	UNIT	RESULT OF BATTLE	PRISON	PRISON RELEASE
Earls, Daniel Private	Cleveland County, North Carolina, 2/26/1863	New House, Cleveland County, North Carolina, 33 Years Old	Co. K, 10th Reg. 1st North Carolina Artillery	Captured	Elmira Prison, Elmira, New York	Died of Ulcer Around Neck, 4/1/1865
Easterling, Andrew Jackson Private	Bennetts-ville, South Carolina 5/12/1862	Bennettsville, District of Marlboro, South Carolina, 33 Years Old	Co. F, 21st South Carolina Volunteers	Captured	Elmira Prison, Elmira, New York	Died Of Intermittent Fever 3/19/1865
Easterling, William T. Private	Bennetts-ville, South Carolina 1/1/1864	Bennettsville, District of Marlboro, South Carolina, 19 Years Old	Co. F, 21st South Carolina Volunteers	Captured	Elmira Prison, Elmira, New York	Oath of Allegiance 7/11/1865
Earley, Moses C. Private	Hertford County, North Carolina, 9/12/1864	Bertie County, North Carolina, 17 Years Old	Co. C, 3rd Battalion, North Carolina Light Artillery	Captured	Elmira Prison, Elmira, New York	Died of Pneumonia & Typhoid Fever, 2/10/1865
Eason, James S. Private	Edgecombe County, North Carolina, 9/1/1863	Tarboro, Edgecombe County, North Carolina, 42 Years Old	Co. D, 40th Regiment, 3rd North Carolina Light Artillery	Captured	Point Lookout Prison, Maryland	Exchanged 2/20/1865 Boulware's Wharf, James River, Virginia
Eazeon, A. Private	Date and Place Unknown	Unknown	2nd Co. D, 36th Regiment North Carolina, 2nd N. C. Artillery	Captured	Prison Unknown	Date of Release Unknown
Edge, David S. Private	Brunswick County, North Carolina, 1/18/1863	Elizabethtown Bladen County, North Carolina, 37 Years Old	Co. H, 36th Regiment North Carolina, 2nd N. C. Artillery	Killed in Action, 1/15/1865		

NAME & RANK	ENLISTED	RESIDENCE AGE & TRADE	UNIT	RESULT OF BATTLE	PRISON	PRISON RELEASE
Edge, Hugh P. Private	Fort Fisher, New Hanover County, North Carolina 5/10/1863, Conscript	Elizabethtown Bladen County, North Carolina, 24 Years Old, Turpentine	2nd Co. I, 36th Regiment North Carolina, 2nd N. C. Artillery	Captured, Defended the Mound Battery	Elmira Prison, Elmira, New York	Exchanged 3/14/1865 Boulware's Wharf, James River, Virginia
Edge, Kelly Private	Elizabeth-town, Bladen County, North Carolina, 10/19/1861, Volunteer	White Oak, Bladen County, North Carolina, 40 Years Old Day Laborer	2nd Co. I, 36th Regiment North Carolina, 2nd N. C. Artillery	Captured, Defended the Mound Battery	Elmira Prison, Elmira, New York	Exchanged 2/20/1865 Boulware's Wharf, James River, Virginia
Edge, Robert D. Private	New Hanover County, North Carolina 3/16/1862, Volunteer	White Oak, Bladen County, North Carolina, 30 Years Old, Farmer Detailed as Carpenter at Fort Fisher	2nd Co. I, 36th Regiment North Carolina, 2nd N. C. Artillery	Captured	Elmira Prison, Elmira, New York	Died of Pneumonia, 3/17/1865
Edmondson, Josiah Private	Edgecombe County, North Carolina, 7/11/1863	Edgecombe County, North Carolina, 26 Years Old	Co. D, 40th Regiment, 3rd North Carolina Light Artillery	Captured	Point Lookout Prison, Maryland	Oath of Allegiance 6/11/1865
Edwards, David T. Private	Bladen County, North Carolina, 1/1/1864, Volunteer	Elizabethtown Bladen County, North Carolina, 18 Years Old Farmer	2nd Co. K, 40th Regiment, 3rd North Carolina Light Artillery	Mortal Gunshot Wound to Head, Fracture of left Temporal Bone & Captured	Fort Monroe Prison Hospital, Virginia	Died Of Wounds 1/23/1865

NAME & RANK	ENLISTED	RESIDENCE AGE & TRADE	UNIT	RESULT OF BATTLE	PRISON	PRISON RELEASE
Edwards, Edward F. Private	Elizabeth-town, Bladen County, North Carolina, 4/1/1862, Volunteer	Gravelly Hill, Bladen County, North Carolina, 16 Years Old Farmer, Turpentine	Co. H, 36th Regiment North Carolina, 2nd N. C. Artillery	Captured	Elmira Prison, Elmira, New York	Died of Smallpox, 3/11/1865
Edwards, George W. Private	Buncombe County, North Carolina, 4/26/1863	Reems Creek, Buncombe County, North Carolina, 23 Years Old Farmer	Co. C, 3rd Battalion, North Carolina Light Artillery	Gunshot Wound Of Right Foot & Captured	Point Lookout Prison, Maryland	Oath of Allegiance 6/26/1865
Edwards, Harman J. Private	New Hanover County, North Carolina, 6/3/1863	Bladen County, North Carolina, 18 Years Old	2nd Co. K, 40th Regiment, 3rd North Carolina Light Artillery	Captured	Point Lookout Prison, Maryland	Oath of Allegiance 6/28/1865
Edwards, Henry T. Private	Brunswick County, North Carolina, 8/20/1863	Edgecombe County, North Carolina, 18 Years Old	Co. F, 36th Regiment North Carolina, 2nd N. C. Artillery	Captured	Point Lookout Prison, Maryland	Died of Pneumonia, 2/7/1865
Edwards, Jasper Private	Date and Place Unknown	Bartow County, Georgia, Age Unknown Farmer	Co. B, Confederate States Marine Corp, Assigned to Guard duty Aboard CSS *Raleigh*.	Captured	Point Lookout Prison, Maryland	Date Of Release Unknown
Edwards, Jonas Private	Edgecombe County, North Carolina, 9/1/1863	Tarboro, Edgecombe County, North Carolina, 43 Years Old Farmer	Co. D, 40th Regiment, 3rd North Carolina Light Artillery	Captured	Point Lookout Prison, Maryland	Oath of Allegiance 5/13/1865

NAME & RANK	ENLISTED	RESIDENCE AGE & TRADE	UNIT	RESULT OF BATTLE	PRISON	PRISON RELEASE
Edwards, Ralsey Private	Elizabeth-town, Bladen County, North Carolina, 5/6/1862, Volunteer	Bladenboro, Bladen County, North Carolina, 19 Years Old Farmer	2nd Co. K, 40th Regiment, 3rd North Carolina Light Artillery	Captured	Elmira Prison, Elmira, New York	Oath of Allegiance 7/19/1865
Edwards, William L. Private	Edgecombe County, North Carolina, 4/10/1864	Dortches District, Edgecombe County, North Carolina, 60 Years Old Carpenter	Co. D, 40th Regiment, 3rd North Carolina Light Artillery	Wounded & Captured	Prison Unknown	May Have Died Of Wounds At Fort Fisher, N. C.
Edwards, William Private	Bladen County, North Carolina, 3/10/1863, Volunteer	White Creek, Bladen County, North Carolina, 29 Years Old Turpentine	3rd Co. B, 36th Regiment North Carolina, 2nd N. C. Artillery	Captured	Elmira Prison, Elmira, New York	Oath of Allegiance 7/11/1865
Eichhorn, John E. Private	Brunswick County, North Carolina, 2/19/1862	Brunswick County, North Carolina, 46 Years Old	Co. K, 36th Regiment North Carolina, 2nd N. C. Artillery	Captured	Point Lookout Prison, Maryland	Oath of Allegiance 6/4/1865
Eleanor, Charles G. Private	Craven County, North Carolina, 12/29/1861, Volunteer	Enfield, Halifax County, N. C., 33 Years Old Cabinet Maker, Extra Duty At Fort Caswell as Carpenter	Co. F, 36th Regiment North Carolina, 2nd N. C. Artillery	Wounded & Captured	Fort Delaware Prison, Del.	Oath of Allegiance 6/19/1865
Ellen, Cordia Norfleet F. Private	Fort Caswell, Brunswick County, North Carolina, 9/5/1863	Battleboro, Nash County, North Carolina, 43 Years Old Farmer	3rd Co. G, 36th Regiment North Carolina, 2nd N. C. Artillery	Wounded, Defended Battery to the Left of Northeast Bastion	Escaped	Died 5/12/1896 in Halifax District, Nash County, North Carolina

NAME & RANK	ENLISTED	RESIDENCE AGE & TRADE	UNIT	RESULT OF BATTLE	PRISON	PRISON RELEASE
Ellerbe, A. C. Private	Chesterfield, South Carolina 12/26/1861	Cheraw, Chesterfield, South Carolina, 34 Years Old Overseer	Co. G, 21st South Carolina Volunteers	Killed In Action, 1/15/1865		
Ellis, Charles T. Private	New Hanover County, North Carolina, 3/17/1864	New Hanover County, North Carolina, 44 Years Old Day Laborer	Co. K, 10th Reg. 1st North Carolina Artillery	Captured	Elmira Prison, Elmira, New York	Died of Chronic Diarrhea, 3/28/1865
Ellis, E. S. Private	Battery Island, South Carolina 4/12/1862	Unknown, 30 Years Old	Co. C, 25th South Carolina Volunteers	Captured	Elmira Prison, Elmira, New York	Died Of Chronic Diarrhea 5/17/1865
Ellis, William W. Private	Darlington, South Carolina 2/19/1863	Graniteville, Edgefield, South Carolina, 29 Years Old	Co. B, 21st South Carolina Volunteers	Captured	Elmira Prison, Elmira, New York	Died Of Chronic Diarrhea 3/6/1865
Elmore, N. S. Private	New Hanover County, North Carolina	New Hanover County, North Carolina, Age Unknown Farmer	Co. F, 36th Regiment North Carolina, 2nd N. C. Artillery	Captured	Point Lookout Prison, Maryland	Oath of Allegiance 5/13/1865
Emerson, David Private	Date and Place Unknown	Unknown, 42 Years Old	Co. D, 40th Regiment, 3rd North Carolina Light Artillery	Captured Smithville, North Carolina, 1/18/1865	Point Lookout Prison General Hospital, Maryland	Died of General Debility, 3/1/1865,
Englert, John W. Private	Charleston, South Carolina 3/25/1863	Charleston, South Carolina, 23 Years Old	Co. I, 25th South Carolina Volunteers	Captured	Elmira Prison, Elmira, New York	Oath of Allegiance 5/15/1865

NAME & RANK	ENLISTED	RESIDENCE AGE & TRADE	UNIT	RESULT OF BATTLE	PRISON	PRISON RELEASE
Enzor, Alva Corporal	Edgecombe County, North Carolina, 5/20/1863, Volunteer	Horry District, South Carolina	2nd Co. D, 36th Regiment, 2nd N. C. Artillery	Wounded & Captured	Point Lookout Prison, Maryland	Oath of Allegiance 6/26/1865
Epps, J. H. Sergeant	James Island, South Carolina 4/12/1862	Kingstree, South Carolina, 20 Years Old	Co. C, 25th South Carolina Volunteers	Captured	Elmira Prison, Elmira, New York	Oath of Allegiance 7/7/1865
Ervin, Lawrence Private	James Island, South Carolina 10/17/1863	Sumter, Clarendon District, South Carolina, 17 Years Old	Co. I, 25th South Carolina Volunteers	Captured	Elmira Prison, Elmira, New York	Oath of Allegiance 7/11/1865
Etheridge, James T. Private	Enfield, Halifax County, North Carolina, 10/9/1861, Volunteer	Tarboro, Edgecombe County, North Carolina, 20 Years Old Farmer	Co. F, 36th Regiment North Carolina, 2nd N. C. Artillery	Gunshot Wound of Right Fore Arm & Captured	Point Lookout Prison, Maryland	Oath of Allegiance 6/12/1865
Etheridge, Ransom Private	Brunswick County, North Carolina, 8/19/1863, Volunteer	Sprights District, Greene County, North Carolina, 42 Years Old Overseer	Co. F, 36th Regiment North Carolina, 2nd N. C. Artillery	Captured	Elmira Prison, Elmira, New York	Exchanged 2/20/1865, Died of Chronic Diarrhea, 4/6/1865, Jackson Hospital, Richmond, Virginia
Eure, William W. Sergeant	Halifax County, North Carolina, 10/9/1861, Volunteer	Enfield, Halifax County, North Carolina, 21 Years Old Mechanic	Co. F, 36th Regiment North Carolina, 2nd N. C. Artillery	Captured	Elmira Prison, Elmira, New York	Died of Chronic Diarrhea, 3/29/1865

NAME & RANK	ENLISTED	RESIDENCE AGE & TRADE	UNIT	RESULT OF BATTLE	PRISON	PRISON RELEASE
Evans, Angus J. Private	Fort Holmes, Brunswick County, North Carolina, 2/24/1864, Volunteer	Bladen County, North Carolina, 18 Years Old Laborer	2nd Co. K, 40th Regiment, 3rd North Carolina Light Artillery	Captured	Elmira Prison, Elmira, New York	Exchanged 3/14/1865 Boulware's Wharf, James River, Virginia
Evans, Archibald Private	Brunswick County, North Carolina, 11/20/1863, Volunteer	Brunswick County, North Carolina, 17 Years Old	Co. K, 36th Regiment North Carolina, 2nd N. C. Artillery	Wounded & Captured	Prison Unknown	May Have Died Of Wounds At Fort Fisher, N. C.
Evans, Daniel Private	Elizabeth-town, Bladen County, North Carolina, 10/19/1861	Bladen County, North Carolina, 21 Years Old, Detailed to catch deserters, 1862	2nd Co. I, 36th Regiment, 3rd North Carolina Light Artillery	Captured, Defended Shepperd's Battery	Elmira Prison, Elmira, New York	Died of Pneumonia, 2/9/1865
Evans, Henry C. First Lieutenant	New Hanover County, North Carolina, 4/26/1862	Edenton, Chowan County, North Carolina, 26 Years Old Farmer	Co. D, 1st Battalion, North Carolina Heavy Artillery	Captured, Defended River Road Gate	Fort Columbus Prison, New York	Exchanged 3/5/1865 Boulware's Wharf, James River, Virginia
Evans, J. H. Private	Charleston, South Carolina 5/16/1862	Marion District, South Carolina, 30 Years Old Farmer	Co. C, 25th South Carolina Volunteers	Captured	Elmira Prison, Elmira, New York	Scheduled For Exchange But Died Of Unknown Disease 7/21/1865
Evans, James Private	Fort Fisher, New Hanover County, North Carolina, 3/7/1862	New Hanover County, North Carolina, 24 Years Old	2nd Co. I, 36th Regiment North Carolina, 2nd N. C. Artillery	Captured, Defended Shepperd's Battery	Elmira Prison, Elmira, New York	Exchanged 3/2/1865 Boulware's Wharf, James River, Virginia,

NAME & RANK	ENLISTED	RESIDENCE AGE & TRADE	UNIT	RESULT OF BATTLE	PRISON	PRISON RELEASE
Evans, John O. Private	Fort Caswell, Brunswick County, North Carolina, 11/20/1863	Brunswick County, North Carolina, 17 Years Old	Co. K, 36th Regiment North Carolina, 2nd N. C. Artillery	Captured	Point Lookout Prison, Maryland	Oath of Allegiance 5/14/1865
Evans, John Private	Robeson County, North Carolina, 5/8/1862, Volunteer	Lumberton, Robeson County, North Carolina, 30 Years Old Farmer	Co. C, 40th Regiment, 3rd North Carolina Light Artillery	Captured	Elmira Prison, Elmira, New York	Oath of Allegiance 6/20/1865
Evans, N. C. Private	Date and Place Unknown	Unknown	Co. D, 1st Battalion, North Carolina Heavy Artillery	Wounded & Captured, Defended River Road Gate	Prison Unknown	Date Of Release Unknown
Evans, Nathan J. Private	Marion District, South Carolina 3/20/1864	Marion District, South Carolina, 19 Years Old Farmer	Co. L, 21st South Carolina Volunteers	Captured	Elmira Prison, Elmira, New York	Oath of Allegiance 7/11/1865
Evans, Richard A. Private	Wilmington, New Hanover County, North Carolina, 6/23/1863	Morrisville, Wake County, North Carolina, 26 Years Old Day Laborer	Co. D, 1st Battalion, North Carolina Heavy Artillery	Mortally Wounded, Gunshot Wound of Right Leg 1/15/1865 & Captured		Right Leg Amputated, Died of Wounds at Fort Fisher, Defended River Road Gate.
Evans, Robert Edward Private	New Hanover County, North Carolina, 5/10/1862	Colvin's Creek, New Hanover County, North Carolina, 29 Years Old Farmer	Co. D, 1st Battalion, North Carolina Heavy Artillery	Captured, Defended River Road Gate	Point Lookout Prison, Maryland	Oath of Allegiance 5/13/1865
Evans, R. M. Private	Coles Island, South Carolina 4/11/1862	Orangeburg, South Carolina, 27 Years Old Farmer	Co. F, 25th South Carolina Volunteers	Captured	Elmira Prison, Elmira, New York	Died of Pneumonia, 6/2/1865

NAME & RANK	ENLISTED	RESIDENCE AGE & TRADE	UNIT	RESULT OF BATTLE	PRISON	PRISON RELEASE
Everett, Nathan B. Private	Edgecombe County, North Carolina, 9/1/1863	Tarboro, Edgecombe County, North Carolina, 44 Years Old Farmer	Co. D, 40th Regiment, 3rd North Carolina Light Artillery	Captured	Point Lookout Prison, Maryland	Oath of Allegiance 6/12/1865
Everett, Neil Private	Cumberland County, North Carolina, Date Unknown	Fayetteville, Cumberland County, North Carolina, Age Unknown	2nd Co. C, 36th Regiment North Carolina, 2nd N. C. Artillery	Captured, Defended River Road Gate	Elmira Prison, Elmira, New York	Oath of Allegiance 6/12/1865
Everett, Riley Private	Bladen County, North Carolina, 2/24/1863	Bladen County, North Carolina, 32 Years Old	Co. E, 36th Regiment North Carolina, 2nd N. C. Artillery	Wounded Both Legs 12/25/1864		
Evers, David Private	Bladen County, North Carolina, 10/19/1861	Elizabethtown Bladen County, North Carolina, 22 Years Old Turpentine	2nd Co. I, 36th Regiment North Carolina, 2nd N. C. Artillery	Captured, Defended Shepperd's Battery	Point Lookout Prison, Maryland	Oath of Allegiance 6/26/1865
Evers, Dennis Private	Elizabeth-town, Bladen County, North Carolina, 10/23/1863, Volunteer	Elizabethtown Bladen County, North Carolina, 18 Years Old Farmer	2nd Co. K, 40th Regiment, 3rd North Carolina Light Artillery	Captured	Elmira Prison, Elmira, New York	Died of Smallpox, 3/29/1865
Evers, Ephraim Private	Fort Fisher, New Hanover County, North Carolina, 5/7/1863, Volunteer	Elizabethtown Bladen County, North Carolina, 23 Years Old Farmer	2nd Co. K, 40th Regiment, 3rd North Carolina Light Artillery	Captured	Elmira Prison, Elmira, New York	Died of Pneumonia, 3/14/1865
Evers, Joshua Private	Bladen County, North Carolina, 10/19/1862	Elizabethtown Bladen County, North Carolina, 20 Years Old Turpentine	2nd Co. I, 36th Regiment North Carolina, 2nd N. C. Artillery	Captured, Defended Shepperd's Battery	Point Lookout Prison, Maryland	Oath of Allegiance 6/26/1865

NAME & RANK	ENLISTED	RESIDENCE AGE & TRADE	UNIT	RESULT OF BATTLE	PRISON	PRISON RELEASE
Evers, William H. Private	New Hanover County, North Carolina, 10/27/1862, Volunteer	New Hanover County, North Carolina, 23 Years Old, Detailed 1/5/1864 to 8/31/1864 to build a wharf at Fort Fisher	2nd Co. K, 40th Regiment, 3rd North Carolina Light Artillery	Captured	Elmira Prison, Elmira, New York	Died of Smallpox, 3/27/1865
Evers, William J. Private	Bladen County, North Carolina, 5/6/1862	Elizabethtown Bladen County, North Carolina, 32 Years Old Cooper	2nd Co. K, 40th Regiment, 3rd North Carolina Light Artillery	Captured	Point Lookout Prison, Maryland	Oath of Allegiance 6/26/1865
Exum, Benjamin Private	Wayne County, North Carolina, 5/14/1863	Pikeville, Wayne County, North Carolina 18 Years Old Laborer	Co. F, 10th Reg. 1st North Carolina Artillery	Captured	Elmira Prison, Elmira, New York	Died of Smallpox, 3/10/1865
Ezzell, Lemuel J. Private	Duplin County, North Carolina, 9/15/1861	Magnolia, Southern Division, Duplin County, North Carolina, 43 Years Old	2nd Co. A, 36th Regiment North Carolina, 2nd N. C. Artillery	Captured, Defended the Mound Battery	Point Lookout Prison, Maryland	Oath of Allegiance 6/22/1865

NAME & RANK	ENLISTED	RESIDENCE AGE & TRADE	UNIT	RESULT OF BATTLE	PRISON	PRISON RELEASE
Faircloth, T. Private	Date and Place Unknown	Unknown	Co. E, 36th Regiment North Carolina, 2nd N. C. Artillery	Captured	Elmira Prison, Elmira, New York	Died of Rheumatism, 3/17/1865
Faircloth, Thomas G. Private	Brunswick County, North Carolina, 7/7/1862	Ellisville, Bladen County, North Carolina, 21 Years Old Farmer	2nd Co. K, 40th Regiment, 3rd North Carolina Artillery	Killed In Action, 1/15/1865		

NAME & RANK	ENLISTED	RESIDENCE AGE & TRADE	UNIT	RESULT OF BATTLE	PRISON	PRISON RELEASE
Faircloth, Thomas H. Private	Terribinth, 2/20/1862, Cumberland County, North Carolina	Ellisville, Bladen County, North Carolina, 20 Years Old Farmer	2nd Co. C, 36th Regiment North Carolina, 2nd N. C. Artillery	Captured, Defended River Road Gate	Elmira Prison, Elmira, New York	Died of Chronic Diarrhea, 3/14/1865
Faison, Edward L. First Lieutenant	Sampson County, North Carolina, 10/31/1861 Volunteer	Clinton, Sampson County, North Carolina, 30 Years Old Farmer	2nd Co. A, 36th Regiment North Carolina, 2nd N. C. Artillery	Captured, Defended the Mound Battery	Fort Columbus Prison, New York Harbor	Exchanged 3/5/1865 Boulware's Wharf, James River, Virginia,
Falk, James H. Corporal	Union County, North Carolina, 8/27/1861 Volunteer	Union County, North Carolina, 22 Years Old	Co. E, 40th Regiment, 3rd North Carolina Artillery	Captured	Point Lookout Prison, Maryland	Oath of Allegiance 6/27/1865
Farmer, James W. Private	Bertie County, North Carolina, 1/28/1862	Bertie County, N. C., Farmer, 26 Years Old, Detailed to cut wood for Fort Caswell, March-June 1864	Co. B, 3rd Battalion, North Carolina Light Artillery	Gunshot Wound of Right Foot & Captured	Point Lookout Prison, Maryland	Oath of Allegiance 6/26/1865
Farmer, John Private	Wayne County, North Carolina, 7/20/1863	Mount Olive, Wayne County, North Carolina, 42 Years Old Farmer	3rd Co. G, 40th Regiment, 3rd North Carolina Artillery	Captured, Defended Land Face	Point Lookout Prison, Maryland & Elmira, New York	Exchanged 3/20/1865, Recaptured At Hospital Richmond, Virginia, 4/3/1865, Oath of Allegiance 6/28/1865
Farrell, T. Private	Unknown	Unknown	Co. E, 36th Regiment North Carolina, 2nd N. C. Artillery	Captured	Prison Unknown	Date of Release Unknown

NAME & RANK	ENLISTED	RESIDENCE AGE & TRADE	UNIT	RESULT OF BATTLE	PRISON	PRISON RELEASE
Faucett, R. P. Private	New Hanover County, North Carolina, 4/18/1863	New Hanover County, North Carolina, 18 Years Old	2nd Co. C, 36th Regiment North Carolina, 2nd N. C. Artillery	Killed in Action, 1/15/1865, Defended River Road Gate		
Faulk, William H. Private	Fort St. Philip, Brunswick County, North Carolina, 4/9/1863, Substitute	Brunswick County, North Carolina, 15 Years Old	Co. E, 36th Regiment North Carolina, 2nd N. C. Artillery	Captured	Elmira Prison, Elmira, New York	Exchanged 3/2/1865 Boulware's Wharf, James River, Virginia
Fawcett, Robert B. Private	New Hanover County, North Carolina, 4/16/1864	Halifax County, North Carolina, 17 Years Old	Co. F, 36th Regiment North Carolina, 2nd N. C. Artillery	Captured	Point Lookout Prison, Maryland	Oath of Allegiance 6/27/1865
Felder, C. E. Private	Coles Island, South Carolina 4/11/1862	White Cain, Orangeburg, South Carolina, 19 Years Old	Co. F, 25th South Carolina Volunteers	Captured	Elmira Prison, Elmira, New York	Oath of Allegiance 7/11/1865
Felder, R.F.	Georgetown South Carolina 1/1/1862	Unknown, 25 Years Old	Co. I, 25th South Carolina Volunteers	Captured	Fort Columbus Prison, New York	Exchanged 2/23/1865
Ferebee, Willoughby D. First Sergeant	Craven County, North Carolina, 9/21/1861	Craven County, North Carolina, 31 Years Old	Co. D, 40th Regiment, 3rd North Carolina Artillery	Captured	Point Lookout Prison, Maryland	Oath of Allegiance 6/26/1865
Ferguson, Davis Private	Fort Holmes, Wake County, North Carolina, 5/11/1863	Wake County, North Carolina, Age Unknown	Co. C, 3rd Battalion, North Carolina Light Artillery	Captured	Elmira Prison, Elmira, New York	Died of Convulsions, 3/10/1865

NAME & RANK	ENLISTED	RESIDENCE AGE & TRADE	UNIT	RESULT OF BATTLE	PRISON	PRISON RELEASE
Ferrell, A. S. Private	New Hanover County, North Carolina, 11/25/1864	New Hanover County, North Carolina, Age Unknown	Co. D, 13th Battalion North Carolina Light Artillery	Captured, Defended River Road Gate	Elmira Prison, Elmira, New York	Exchanged 3/18/1865 Boulware's Wharf, James River, Virginia
Fersner, W. F. Ordinance Sergeant	Coles Island, South Carolina 4/11/1862	Orangeburg, South Carolina, Age Unknown	Field And Staff, 25th South Carolina Volunteers	Captured	Elmira Prison, Elmira, New York	Oath of Allegiance 7/7/1865
Fertic, John Private	Coles Island, South Carolina 4/11/1862	Orangeburg District, Louisville, South Carolina	Co. E, 25th South Carolina Volunteers	Captured	Elmira Prison, Elmira, New York	Oath of Allegiance 7/7/1865
Fields, Frederick B. Private	Lenoir County, North Carolina, 6/30/1862	Mosely Hall, Bear Creek District, Lenoir County, North Carolina, 23 Years Old Farmer	Co. D, 40th Regiment, 3rd North Carolina Artillery	Captured	Point Lookout Prison, Maryland	Oath of Allegiance 6/3/1865
Fields, Tobias Private	Fort Branch, Brunswick County, North Carolina, 7/24/1863, Volunteer	Moore County, North Carolina, 20 Years Old Farmer	3rd Co. G, 40th Regiment, 3rd North Carolina Artillery	Captured, Defended Land Face	Elmira Prison, Elmira, New York	Died of Pneumonia 3/4/1865
Fisher, John H. Private	Clinton, Sampson County, North Carolina, 7/19/1864	Owensville, Sampson County, North Carolina, 37 Years Old Farmer	2nd Co. D, 36th Regiment North Carolina, 2nd N. C. Artillery	Shell Wound In Head, Brain Concussion & Captured	Point Lookout Prison General Hospital, Maryland	Oath of Allegiance 6/4/1865,
Fisher, Marshall T. Private	Fort Fisher, New Hanover County, North Carolina, 3/15/1863, Volunteer	New Hanover County, North Carolina, 35 Years Old	2nd Co. C, 36th Regiment North Carolina, 2nd N. C. Artillery	Captured, Defended River Road Gate	Elmira Prison, Elmira, New York	Died of Chronic Diarrhea, 5/2/1865

NAME & RANK	ENLISTED	RESIDENCE AGE & TRADE	UNIT	RESULT OF BATTLE	PRISON	PRISON RELEASE
Fisher, William T. Private	Fort Fisher, New Hanover County, North Carolina, 3/15/1863, Volunteer	Fayetteville, Cumberland County, North Carolina, 39 Years Old	2nd Co. C, 36th Regiment North Carolina, 2nd N. C. Artillery	Captured, Defended River Road Gate	Elmira Prison, Elmira, New York	Oath of Allegiance 6/12/1865
Flanigan, Alfred Private	Fort Caswell, Brunswick County, North Carolina, 8/22/1863, Volunteer	Brunswick County, North Carolina, 29 Years Old	2nd Co. D, 36th Regiment North Carolina, 2nd N. C. Artillery	Captured	Elmira Prison, Elmira, New York	Exchanged 3/14/1865
Fleming, Joseph J. Private	Halifax County, North Carolina, 10/9/1861	Pitt County, North Carolina, Age Unknown	Co. F, 36th Regiment North Carolina, 2nd N. C. Artillery	Captured	Point Lookout Prison, Maryland	Oath of Allegiance 6/27/1865
Flemming, Samuel W. Private	James Island, South Carolina 8/20/1863	Columbia, Richland, South Carolina, 33 Years Old	Co I, 25th Regiment South Carolina Volunteers	Captured	Elmira Prison, Elmira, New York	Died of Pneumonia, 4/26/1865,
Flemming, W. D. Private	Georgetown South Carolina 1/1/1862	Kingstree, South Carolina, 19 Years Old	Co. I, 25th South Carolina Volunteers	Captured	Elmira Prison, Elmira, New York	Oath of Allegiance 7/11/1865
Flottwell, Richard Private	Charleston, South Carolina 3/19/1862	Mobile, Al, 27 Years Old	Co. E, 25th South Carolina Volunteers	Captured	Elmira Prison, Elmira, New York	Oath of Allegiance 5/29/1865
Flowers, Alfred C. Corporal	Brunswick County, North Carolina, 2/19/1862, Volunteer	Town Creek District, Brunswick County, North Carolina, 17 Years Old Farmer	Co. K, 36th Regiment North Carolina, 2nd N. C. Artillery	Wounded & Captured	Point Lookout Prison, Maryland	Oath of Allegiance 6/4/1865

NAME & RANK	ENLISTED	RESIDENCE AGE & TRADE	UNIT	RESULT OF BATTLE	PRISON	PRISON RELEASE
Flowers, Henry D. B. Private	Columbus County, North Carolina, 10/21/1861,	Whiteville, Columbus County, North Carolina, 16 Years Old Farmer	2nd Co. A, 36th Regiment North Carolina, 2nd N. C. Artillery	Captured, Defended the Mound Battery	Point Lookout Prison, Maryland	Oath of Allegiance 6/27/1865
Flowers, James Private	Fort St. Philip, Brunswick County, North Carolina, 5/5/1862, Volunteer	Brunswick County, North Carolina, 23 Years Old	3rd Co. G, 36th Regiment North Carolina, 2nd N. C. Artillery	Captured, Defended Battery to the Left of Northeast Bastion	Elmira Prison, Elmira, New York	Exchanged 2/20/1865
Flowers, Thomas Private	Darlington, South Carolina 9/10/1862	District of Sumter, South Carolina, 21 Years Old Printer	Co. G, 21st South Carolina Volunteers	Captured	Elmira Prison, Elmira, New York	Oath of Allegiance 7/11/1865
Floyd, William W. Private	Columbus County, North Carolina, 3/1/1862	Asheboro, Randolph County, North Carolina, 18 Years Old	Co. E, 36th Regiment North Carolina, 2nd N. C. Artillery	Killed In Action 1/15/1865		
Fogle, W. J. Private	Orangeburg South Carolina 4/19/1862	Orangeburg District, Bull Swamp, South Carolina, 42 Years Old Methodist Clergyman	Co. F, 25th South Carolina Volunteers	Captured	Elmira Prison, Elmira, New York	Died of Chronic Diarrhea, 3/16/1865
Foley, John Private	Brunswick County, North Carolina, 5/5/1862,	Horry District, South Carolina, 22 Years Old	2nd Co. A, 36th Regiment North Carolina, 2nd N. C. Artillery	Captured, Defended the Mound Battery	Point Lookout Prison, Maryland	Oath of Allegiance 6/27/1865
Foley, Ransom Private	Brunswick County, North Carolina, 4/24/1862,	Horry District, South Carolina, 19 Years Old	2nd Co. A, 36th Regiment North Carolina, 2nd N. C. Artillery	Captured, Defended the Mound Battery	Point Lookout Prison, Maryland	Oath of Allegiance 6/27/1865

NAME & RANK	ENLISTED	RESIDENCE AGE & TRADE	UNIT	RESULT OF BATTLE	PRISON	PRISON RELEASE
Folks, John A. Private	Columbus County, North Carolina, 10/21/1861, Volunteer	Whiteville, Columbus County, North Carolina 20 Years Old Farmer	2nd Co. A, 36th Regiment North Carolina, 2nd N. C. Artillery	Captured, Defended the Mound Battery	Elmira Prison, Elmira, New York	Died of Gangrene Of Feet, 3/14/1865
Foote, George A. Assistant Surgeon	Place Unknown 5/25/1861	Warrenton District, Warren County, North Carolina, 25 Years Old Medical Doctor	Confederate States Navy	Captured	Fort Columbus, New York Harbor	Exchanged 2/25/1865 Boulwares Wharf, James River, Va. Served aboard *CSS Albemarle* and *CSS Raleigh*
Footman, John M. First Sergeant	Battery Island, South Carolina 4/12/1862	Williamsburg, South Carolina, 31 Years Old	Co. C, 25th South Carolina Volunteers	Shell Wound of Right Knee & Captured	Treated At Fort Monroe, Va., Sent To Point Lookout, Maryland	Oath of Allegiance 6/5/1865
Forbes, Elbert Private	Edgecombe County, North Carolina, 5/24/1864	Tarboro, Edgecombe County, North Carolina, 18 Years Old	Co. D, 40th Regiment, 3rd North Carolina Artillery	Captured	Point Lookout Prison, Maryland	Oath of Allegiance 6/26/1865
Forbes, Samuel M. Private	Camp Holmes, North Carolina, 2/1/1863, Conscript	Hintonsville, Pasquotank County, North Carolina, 31 Years Old Farmer	3rd Co. G, 36th Regiment North Carolina, 2nd N. C. Artillery	Severely Wounded & Captured, Defended Battery to the Left of Northeast Bastion	Unknown	May Have Died Of Wounds At Fort Fisher, N. C.
Force, George H. Private	Charleston, South Carolina 3/18/1862	Greensboro, Georgia, 20 Years Old	Co. B, 25th South Carolina Volunteers	Captured	Elmira Prison, Elmira, New York	Oath of Allegiance 8/14/1865

NAME & RANK	ENLISTED	RESIDENCE AGE & TRADE	UNIT	RESULT OF BATTLE	PRISON	PRISON RELEASE
Ford, John H. Private	Fort Fisher, New Hanover County, North Carolina, 3/15/1864	Fayetteville, Cumberland County, North Carolina, 27 Years Old Turpentine	3rd Co. G, 36th Regiment North Carolina, 2nd N. C. Artillery	Captured, Defended Battery to the Left of Northeast Bastion	Elmira Prison, Elmira, New York	Exchanged 3/2/1865, Died of Typhoid Fever, Jackson Hospital, Richmond, Virginia, 5/2/1865
Ford, Thomas Captain	Camp Harllee, South Carolina 1/1/1862	Unknown	Co. A, 21st South Carolina Volunteers	Captured	Fort Columbus Prison, New York	Exchanged 2/25/1865
Forrest, John P. Private	Brunswick County, North Carolina, 7/28/1863	Albemarle, Stanly County, North Carolina, 38 Years Old Mechanic & Farmer	2nd Co. D, 36th Regiment North Carolina, 2nd N. C. Artillery	Captured	Point Lookout Prison, Maryland	Oath of Allegiance 6/26/1865
Foster, Perry A. Seaman	Date and Place Unknown	Unknown, Served Aboard *CSS Chickamauga* in 1864,	Confederate States Navy	Mortally Wounded In Mouth and Right Shoulder		Assigned to Defend Battery Buchanan in December, 1864
Foster, Thomas A. Private	Brunswick County, North Carolina, 7/12/1863	Heathsville, Halifax County, North Carolina, 40 Years Old Farmer	Co. F, 36th Regiment North Carolina, 2nd N. C. Artillery	Captured	Point Lookout Prison, Maryland	Exchanged 2/20/1865 Cox's Landing, James River, Virginia
Fountain, Joseph Henry Private	Halifax County, North Carolina, 10/9/1861	Edgecombe County, North Carolina, 20 Years Old	Co. F, 36th Regiment North Carolina, 2nd N. C. Artillery	Captured	Point Lookout Prison, Maryland	Oath of Allegiance 6/26/1865
Fowler, Joseph Private	Brunswick County, North Carolina, 5/20/1863	Brunswick County, North Carolina, 23 Years Old	2nd Co. D, 36th Regiment North Carolina, 2nd N. C. Artillery	Captured	Point Lookout Prison, Maryland	Oath of Allegiance 6/26/1865

NAME & RANK	ENLISTED	RESIDENCE AGE & TRADE	UNIT	RESULT OF BATTLE	PRISON	PRISON RELEASE
Fowler, Samuel L. Private	New Hanover County, North Carolina, 10/24/1863	Sampson County, North Carolina, Age Unknown	Co. E, 36th Regiment North Carolina, 2nd N. C. Artillery	Captured	Point Lookout Prison, Maryland	Oath of Allegiance 6/27/1865
Fowler, Stephen R. Private	Carteret County, North Carolina, 12/25/1864	Carteret County, North Carolina, Age Unknown Farmer	Co. D, 13th Battalion North Carolina Light Artillery	Captured, Defended River Road Gate	Point Lookout Prison, Maryland	Oath of Allegiance 5/15/1865
Fox, Isaiah Private	Chatham County, North Carolina, 3/26/1863, Volunteer	St. Lawrence, Chatham County, North Carolina, 34 Years Old	3rd Co. G, 40th Regiment, 3rd North Carolina Artillery	Captured, Defended Land Face	Elmira Prison, Elmira, New York	Died of Rheumatism, 4/4/1865
Fraim, John G. Second Lieutenant	Bertie County, North Carolina, 4/1/1862	Bertie County, North Carolina, Age Unknown	Co. C, 3rd Battalion, North Carolina Light Artillery	Captured	Fort Columbus Prison, New York Harbor	Exchanged 3/5/1865
Frazier, Linton H. Private	Beaufort County, North Carolina 9/23/1861	Beaufort County, North Carolina, 20 Years Old	Co. D, 13th Battalion North Carolina Light Artillery	Captured. Defended River Road Gate	Point Lookout Prison, Maryland	Oath of Allegiance 6/4/1865
Freeman, Chapman Private	Camp Harllee, South Carolina 1/1/1862	Cheraw, South Carolina, 15 Years Old	Co. D, 21st South Carolina Volunteers	Captured	Elmira Prison, Elmira, New York	Oath of Allegiance 7/11/1865
Freeman, George Private	Marion, South Carolina 4/20/1862	Marion, Gum Swamp, South Carolina, 16 Years Old Farmer	Co. I, 25th South Carolina Volunteers	Captured	Elmira Prison, Elmira, New York	Died of Pneumonia, 2/25/1865

NAME & RANK	ENLISTED	RESIDENCE AGE & TRADE	UNIT	RESULT OF BATTLE	PRISON	PRISON RELEASE
Freeman, William Private	Fort Branch, Brunswick County, North Carolina, 8/17/1863 Volunteer	Brunswick County, North Carolina, 43 Years Old	3rd Co. G, 40th Regiment, 3rd North Carolina Artillery	Captured, Defended Land Face	Elmira Prison, Elmira, New York	Died of Pneumonia, 2/9/1865
Fulford, Irvin Second Lieutenant	Beaufort County, North Carolina, 4/24/1862	Beaufort County, North Carolina, 22 Years Old	Co. K, 10th Reg. 1st North Carolina Artillery	Captured	Fort Columbus Prison, New York	Exchanged 3/5/1865 City Point, Virginia
Fuller, Thomas Private	Date and Place Unknown	Unknown	Co. B, Confederate States Marine Corp,	Captured	Point Lookout Prison, Maryland	Date of Release Unknown
Fullwood, William H. Seaman	Place Unknown 1/24/1862	Brunswick County, North Carolina, Age Unknown Seaman	Galloway Company, Confederate States Coast Guard	Captured	Unknown	Date Of Release Unknown
Fulmore, Zachariah T. Private	Robeson County, North Carolina, 5/5/1864	Lumberton, Robeson County, North Carolina, 17 Years Old Farmer	Co. D, 1st Battalion, North Carolina Heavy Artillery	Captured, Defended River Road Gate	Point Lookout Prison, Maryland	Oath of Allegiance 5/15/1865
Furr, John B. Private	Wilmington, New Hanover County, North Carolina, 3/24/1864	Wilmington, New Hanover County, North Carolina, Age Unknown	Co. K, 10th Reg. 1st North Carolina Artillery	Captured	Elmira Prison, Elmira, New York	Died of Smallpox, 3/3/1865
Furr, Martin Private	Camp Holmes, Wake County, North Carolina, 4/8/1863	Mount Pleasant, Cabarrus County, North Carolina, 20 Years Old Farmer	Co. C, 3rd Battalion, North Carolina Light Artillery	Captured	Elmira Prison, Elmira, New York	Died of Typhoid Fever, 2/22/1865

NAME & RANK	ENLISTED	RESIDENCE AGE & TRADE	UNIT	RESULT OF BATTLE	PRISON	PRISON RELEASE
Gafney, Dominick Private	New Orleans, Louisiana, 4/15/1861	Unknown, Age Unknown	Co. B, Confederate States Marine Corp, Assigned to Guard duty Aboard CSS *Richmond* and CSS *Arctic.*	Captured	Point Lookout Prison, Maryland	Oath of Allegiance 5/13/1865
Gainey, Thomas W. Private	Darlington, South Carolina 4/4/1863	Darlington District, South Carolina 4/4/1863, 24 Years Old Farmer	Co. G, 21st South Carolina Volunteers	Captured	Elmira Prison, Elmira, New York	Oath of Allegiance 7/11/1865
Gainor, William T. Private	Greenville, Pitt County, North Carolina, 5/14/1862	Washington, Beaufort County, North Carolina, Age Unknown	Co. K, 10th Reg. 1st North Carolina Artillery	Captured	Elmira Prison, Elmira, New York	Died of Chronic Diarrhea, 3/4/1865
Gaither, Kenneth Private	Edgecombe County, North Carolina, 9/1/1863, Conscripted	Tarboro, Edgecombe County, North Carolina, 41 Years Old Farmer	Co. D, 40th Regiment, 3rd North Carolina Artillery	Captured Fort Caswell Hospital North Carolina, 1/16/1865	Prison Unknown	Date Of Release Unknown
Galloway, Abram M. Private	Darlington, South Carolina 4/15/1861	Darlington District, South Carolina, 19 Years Old Farmer	Co. H, 21st South Carolina Volunteers	Captured	Elmira Prison, Elmira, New York	Oath of Allegiance 8/7/1865
Galloway, John Wesley Captain	Date and Place Unknown	Smithville, Brunswick County, North Carolina, 49 Years Old Light Ship Keeper	Galloway Co., Confederate States Coast Guard	Captured	Prison Unknown	Date Of Release Unknown
Galloway, L. Chappel Private	Darlington, South Carolina 5/20/1862	Darlington District, South Carolina, 24 Years Old Farmer	Co. B, 21st South Carolina Volunteers	Captured	Elmira Prison, Elmira, New York	Died of Chronic Diarrhea, 4/25/1865

NAME & RANK	ENLISTED	RESIDENCE AGE & TRADE	UNIT	RESULT OF BATTLE	PRISON	PRISON RELEASE
Galloway, Lorenzo Seaman	Place Unknown 8/24/1862	Brunswick County, North Carolina, Age Unknown Fisherman	Galloway Co., Confederate States Coast Guard	Captured	Prison Unknown	Date Of Release Unknown
Galloway, Pipkin Private	James Island, South Carolina 3/1/1864	Darlington District, South Carolina, 38 Years Old Farmer	Co. H, 21st South Carolina Volunteers	Captured	Elmira Prison, Elmira, New York	Died of Gangrene Of Feet 3/7/1865
Galloway, Samuel L. Seaman	Place Unknown 1/24/1862	Smithville, Brunswick County, North Carolina, 15 Years Old Fisherman	Galloway Co., Confederate States Coast Guard	Captured	Prison Unknown	Date Of Release Unknown
Gamble, Joseph M. Private	Gourdins Dept., South Carolina 12/29/1861	Sumter, South Carolina, 37 Years Old	Co. K, 25th South Carolina Volunteers	Captured	Elmira Prison, Elmira, New York	Oath of Allegiance 7/3/1865
Gamble, Thomas E. Private	Charleston, South Carolina 5/16/1862	New Zion, Clarendon County, South Carolina, 27 Years Old Farmer	Co. I, 25th South Carolina Volunteers	Captured	Elmira Prison, Elmira, New York	Died of Chronic Diarrhea, 4/7/1865,
Ganns, Wiley Private	Fort Caswell, North Carolina, 10/20/1863, Volunteer	Fair Bluff, Columbus County, North Carolina, 20 Years Old	2nd Co. D, 36th Regiment North Carolina, 2nd N. C. Artillery	Captured	Elmira Prison, Elmira, New York	Oath of Allegiance 7/7/1865
Ganus, Simeon Private	Brunswick County, North Carolina, 5/9/1864	Brunswick County, North Carolina, Age Unknown	Co. K, 36th Regiment North Carolina, 2nd N. C. Artillery	Captured	Point Lookout Prison, Maryland	Exchanged 2/20/1865 Boulware's Wharf, James River, Virginia

NAME & RANK	ENLISTED	RESIDENCE AGE & TRADE	UNIT	RESULT OF BATTLE	PRISON	PRISON RELEASE
Gardner, Benjamin W. Private	Smithville, Brunswick County, North Carolina, 5/15/1864	Stony Creek District, Goldsboro, Wayne County, North Carolina, 17 Years Old Farmer	Co. F, 10th Reg. 1st North Carolina Artillery	Captured	Elmira Prison, Elmira, New York	Died of Intermittent Fever, 3/5/1865
Gardner, Barney B. Private	Wilson County, North Carolina, 1/5/1864	Wilson District, Wilson County, North Carolina, 14 Years Old Farmer	Co. D, 40th Regiment, 3rd North Carolina Artillery	Captured	Point Lookout Prison, Maryland	Oath of Allegiance 6/27/1865
Gardner, M. Private	Date and Place Unknown	Unknown	Co. D, 40th Regiment, 3rd North Carolina Artillery	Captured	Point Lookout Prison, Maryland	Oath of Allegiance 6/27/1865
Gardner, Owen J. Private	Brunswick County, North Carolina, 12/18/1862	Elizabethtown Bladen County, North Carolina, 35 Years Old Farmer	Co. H, 36th Regiment North Carolina, 2nd N. C. Artillery	Captured in Smithville Hospital 1/18/1865	Point Lookout Prison, Maryland	Oath of Allegiance 5/13/1865
Gardner, Robinson Private	Bladen County, North Carolina, 10/19/1861, Volunteer	Fayetteville, Cumberland County, North Carolina, 16 Years Old	Co. E, 36th Regiment North Carolina, 2nd N. C. Artillery	Captured	Elmira Prison, Elmira, New York	Died of Smallpox, 3/2/1865
Garner, David F. Private	Shepards- ville, Carteret County, North Carolina, 7/20/1861, Volunteer	Shepardsville, Carteret County, North Carolina, 21 Years Old Farmer	Co. F, 10th Reg. 1st North Carolina Artillery	Captured	Elmira Prison, Elmira, New York	Died of Chronic Diarrhea, 5/8/1865

NAME & RANK	ENLISTED	RESIDENCE AGE & TRADE	UNIT	RESULT OF BATTLE	PRISON	PRISON RELEASE
Garner, William J. Private	Secession-ville, South Carolina 1/25/1864	Marion District, South Carolina, 29 Years Old	Co. K, 25th South Carolina Volunteers	Captured	Elmira Prison, Elmira, New York	Exchanged 7/3/1865, Died Of Unknown Disease 3/3/1865 In Howard's Grove Hospital, Richmond, Virginia
Garvey, Obediah B. Private	Brunswick County, North Carolina, 7/23/1863, Volunteer	Brunswick County, North Carolina, 18 Years Old	Co. K, 36th Regiment North Carolina, 2nd N. C. Artillery	Killed in Action 1/15/1865		
Gaskins, Major W. Private	Craven County, North Carolina, 1/24/1862	Swift Creek, North of Neuse River, Craven County, North Carolina, 19 Years Old Farmer	Co. D, 40th Regiment, 3rd North Carolina Artillery	Captured	Point Lookout Prison, Maryland	Oath of Allegiance 6/27/1865
Gasque, J. M. Private	Marion District, South Carolina 3/13/1862	Marion District, South Carolina, 18 Years Old	Co. L, 21st South Carolina Volunteers	Captured	Elmira Prison, Elmira, New York	Oath of Allegiance 7/11/1865
Gasque, Samuel O. Private	Marion District, South Carolina 5/14/1862	Marion District, South Carolina Farm, 21 Years Old Laborer	Co. L, 21st South Carolina Volunteers	Captured	Elmira Prison, Elmira, New York	Died of Chronic Diarrhea, 3/28/1865,
Gause, Lucian A. Seaman	Place Unknown 1/24/1862	Shallotte District, Brunswick County, N. C., 18 Years Old Farmer & Fisherman	Galloway Co., Confederate States Coast Guard	Captured	Prison Unknown	Date Of Release Unknown

NAME & RANK	ENLISTED	RESIDENCE AGE & TRADE	UNIT	RESULT OF BATTLE	PRISON	PRISON RELEASE
Gause, William Q. Private	Brunswick County, North Carolina, 2/26/1863, Volunteer	Whiteville, Columbus County, North Carolina, 18 Years Old	Co. H, 36th Regiment North Carolina, 2nd N. C. Artillery	Captured	Elmira Prison, Elmira, New York	Oath of Allegiance 7/7/1865
Gay, P. W. Private	Bennetts-ville, South Carolina 1/21/1864	Bennettsville, Marlboro District, South Carolina, 38 Years Old Farmer	Co. F, 21st South Carolina Volunteers	Captured	Elmira Prison, Elmira, New York	Died of Pneumonia 2/13/1865,
George, John R. Private	Brunswick County, North Carolina, 1/2/1864	Newton Grove, Johnston County, North Carolina, 17 Years Old Farmer	Co. K, 36th Regiment North Carolina, 2nd N. C. Artillery	Captured	Point Lookout Prison, Maryland	Oath of Allegiance 5/13/1865
Gerken, E. F. Henry Private	Charleston, South Carolina 2/22/1862	Charleston, South Carolina, 38 Years Old	Co. D, 25th South Carolina Volunteers	Captured	Elmira Prison, Elmira, New York	Oath of Allegiance 5/15/1865
Gibson, Albert Sergeant	Marion District, South Carolina 1/26/1862	Marion District, South Carolina, 23 Years Old	Co. L, 21st South Carolina Volunteers	Gunshot Wound Left Hip & Captured	Elmira Prison, Elmira, New York	Oath of Allegiance 7/11/1865
Gibson, Ebenezer B. Private	Richmond County, North Carolina, 8/17/1863, Volunteer	Richmond County, North Carolina, 18 Years Old	Co. E, 40th Regiment, 3rd North Carolina Artillery	Captured	Elmira Prison, Elmira, New York	Died of Chronic Diarrhea, 3/10/1865
Gibson, Oscar Private	Florence, South Carolina 6/15/1862	Marion District, South Carolina, 17 Years Old Farmer	Co. L, 21st South Carolina Volunteers	Severe Gunshot Wound Left Hip, Femur Fracture & Captured	Point Lookout USA Hosp., 7/24/1865, Transferred To Douglass USA Hosp. 8/17/1865	Discharged Douglass USA Hospital, Washington, DC, 8/24/1865

NAME & RANK	ENLISTED	RESIDENCE AGE & TRADE	UNIT	RESULT OF BATTLE	PRISON	PRISON RELEASE
Gibson, Raiford Private	Fort Holmes, Brunswick County, North Carolina, 12/24/1864	Williamson District, Richmond County, North Carolina, 16 Years Old Farmer	Co. E, 40th Regiment, 3rd North Carolina Artillery	Captured	Elmira Prison, Elmira, New York	Oath of Allegiance 6/12/1865
Gibson, Thomas P. Private	Shelby County, Louisiana, 2/21/1863	Unknown	Co. H, Confederate States Marine Corp, Assigned to Guard duty Aboard CSS *Tallahassee.*	Mortally Wounded in Leg & Captured	Not Sent to Prison	Amputation Of Left Leg, Died Of Wounds at Fort Fisher 1/17/1865
Gilchrist, Angus Private	Transferred From Co. B, 73rd Regiment, N. C. Troops, 9/1/1864	Montpelier, Vance County, North Carolina, 15 Years Old	Co. D, 1st Battalion, North Carolina Heavy Artillery	Captured, Defended River Road Gate	Point Lookout Prison, Maryland	Oath of Allegiance 6/27/1865
Gilcott, George H. Private	St. Johns, Hertford County, North Carolina, 7/1/1862	Plymouth, North Carolina, Age Unknown	Co. C, 3rd Battalion, North Carolina Light Artillery	Captured	Elmira Prison, Elmira, New York	Oath of Allegiance 6/12/1865
Gillespie, Elisha H. Private	Macon County, North Carolina, 3/23/1863	Franklin, Macon County, North Carolina, 37 Years Old Farmer	Co. D, 13th Battalion North Carolina Light Artillery	Killed in Action 1/15/1865, Defended River Road Gate		
Ginnett, Matthew Private	Goldsboro, Wayne County, North Carolina, 7/22/1861	Goldsboro, Wayne County, North Carolina, 19 Years Old Farmer	Co. F, 10th Reg. 1st North Carolina Artillery	Captured	Elmira Prison, Elmira, New York	Oath of Allegiance 7/11/1865

NAME & RANK	ENLISTED	RESIDENCE AGE & TRADE	UNIT	RESULT OF BATTLE	PRISON	PRISON RELEASE
Ginnett, Needham Private	Fort Holmes, New Hanover County, North Carolina, 1/10/1864	New Hanover County, North Carolina, Age Unknown	Co. F, 10th Reg. 1st North Carolina Artillery	Captured	Elmira Prison, Elmira, New York	Exchanged 2/20/1865
Gist, George W. Private	Battery Island, South Carolina 4/12/1862	Gridison, South Carolina, 32 Years Old	Co. C, 25th South Carolina Volunteers	Gunshot Wound Of Chest & Captured	Point Lookout Prison, Maryland	Oath of Allegiance 6/5/1865
Glennan, Mike G. Lieutenant	Date and Place Unknown	Unknown, Quartermaster Sergeant	Aide-De-Camp, 36th Regiment, 2nd North Carolina Artillery	Captured	Fort Columbus, New York Harbor	Paroled 2/25/1865 Boulware's Wharf, James River, Virginia
Glover, John B. Private	Charleston, South Carolina 2/24/1862	Augusta, Georgia, 25 Years Old	Co. B, 25th South Carolina Volunteers	Gunshot Wound Of Chest & Captured	Elmira Prison, Elmira, New York	Oath of Allegiance 7/26/1865
Godwin, Ichabod Private	Wilmington, New Hanover County, North Carolina, 3/1/1862, Volunteer	Fair Bluff, Columbus County, North Carolina, 17 Years Old	Co. E, 36th Regiment North Carolina, 2nd N. C. Artillery	Captured	Elmira Prison, Elmira, New York	Oath of Allegiance 7/11/1865
Godwin, Sebastian H. Private	New Hanover County, North Carolina, 7/28/1864	Sampson County, North Carolina, Age Unknown	2nd Co. A, 36th Regiment North Carolina, 2nd N. C. Artillery	Captured, Defended the Mound Battery	Point Lookout Prison, Maryland	Oath of Allegiance 6/27/1865
Golson, James D. Private	Coles Island, South Carolina 4/11/1862	St Mathews, Orangeburg County, South Carolina, 25 Years Old Farmer	Co. F, 25th South Carolina Volunteers	Mortally Wounded, Severe Gunshot Wound Of Face & Captured	Treated At Mansfield Hospital, Morehead City, North Carolina	Died Of Wounds 3/11/1865

NAME & RANK	ENLISTED	RESIDENCE AGE & TRADE	UNIT	RESULT OF BATTLE	PRISON	PRISON RELEASE
Gooden, David James Private	Elizabeth-town, Bladen County, North Carolina, 2/3/1862 Volunteer	Bladen County, North Carolina, 18 Years Old	2nd Co. I 36th Regiment North Carolina, 2nd N. C. Artillery	Captured	Elmira Prison, Elmira, New York	Exchanged 3/14/1865 Boulware's Wharf, James River, Virginia
Gooden, Neill Corporal	Bladen County, North Carolina, 10/19/1861	Elizabethtown Bladen County, North Carolina, 35 Years Old Farmer	2nd Co. I, 36th Regiment North Carolina, 2nd N. C. Artillery	Killed in Action 1/15/1865, Defended Shepperd's Battery		
Gooding, Eldred B. Sergeant	Whippy Swamp, South Carolina 7/15/1861	Prince William Parish, Beaufort District, South Carolina 17 Years Old Farmer	Co. E, 11th South Carolina Volunteers	Captured	Elmira Prison, Elmira, New York	Exchanged 3/2/1865 Boulware's Wharf, James River, Virginia
Goodman, Allison V. First Lieutenant	Brunswick County, North Carolina, 5/2/1862	Town Creek District, Brunswick County, North Carolina, 28 Years Old Farmer	3rd Co. G, 36th Regiment North Carolina, 2nd N. C. Artillery	Captured, Defended Battery to the Left of Northeast Bastion	Fort Columbus, New York Harbor	Exchanged 3/5/1865 Boulware's Wharf, James River, Virginia
Goodman, Henry E. Private	Lenoir County, North Carolina, 7/15/1863 Volunteer	Goldsboro, Wayne County, North Carolina, 41 Years Old	3rd Co. G, 40th Regiment, 3rd North Carolina Artillery	Captured, Defended Land Face	Elmira Prison, Elmira, New York	Oath of Allegiance 6/12/1865
Goodman, Henry H. Private	Old Brunswick Town, North Carolina, 4/16/1862, Volunteer	Town Creek District, Brunswick County, North Carolina, 32 Years Old Farmer	3rd Co. G, 36th Regiment North Carolina, 2nd N. C. Artillery	Captured, Defended Battery to the Left of Northeast Bastion	Elmira Prison, Elmira, New York	Died of Smallpox, 2/21/1865
Gordon, Edward S. Private	Wilson County, North Carolina, 2/27/1864	New Berne, Craven County, North Carolina, 17 Years Old	Co. D, 40th Regiment, 3rd North Carolina Artillery	Captured	Point Lookout Prison, Maryland	Exchanged 2/20/1865 Boulware's Wharf, James River, Virginia

NAME & RANK	ENLISTED	RESIDENCE AGE & TRADE	UNIT	RESULT OF BATTLE	PRISON	PRISON RELEASE
Gordon, George T. Lieutenant Colonel	Camp Gregg, Virginia, 12/14/1862	Unknown	Major General William H. C. Whiting's Staff	Not Captured		Carried a dispatch to Major General Braxton Bragg, 1/15/1865
Gore, Christopher C. Private	Brunswick County, North Carolina, 10/20/1863	Whiteville, Columbus County, North Carolina, 17 Years Old farmer	Co. K, 36th Regiment North Carolina, 2nd N. C. Artillery	Captured Near Fort Fisher	Point Lookout Prison, Maryland	Oath of Allegiance 5/13/1865
Gore, Cortenus Private	Brunswick County, North Carolina, 9/11/1863, Volunteer	Brunswick County, North Carolina, 18 Years Old Farmer	Co. K, 36th Regiment North Carolina, 2nd N. C. Artillery	Wounded 1/15/1865 & Captured 2/11/1865, Captured Near Fort Fisher	Point Lookout Prison, Maryland	Oath of Allegiance 5/13/1865
Gore, Jesse D. Private	Brunswick County, North Carolina, 8/6/1864	Shallotte, Brunswick County, North Carolina, 32 Years Old Laborer	Co. K, 36th Regiment North Carolina, 2nd N. C. Artillery	Captured	Point Lookout Prison, Maryland	Oath of Allegiance 5/13/1865
Gore, Joshua Private	Brunswick County, North Carolina, 10/16/1863, Volunteer	Whiteville, Columbus County, North Carolina, 18 Years Old Farmer	Co. K, 36th Regiment North Carolina, 2nd N. C. Artillery	Gunshot Wound Back, Left Scapula & Captured	Point Lookout Prison, Maryland	Oath of Allegiance 6/14/1865
Gowan, Henry F. Private	Columbus County, North Carolina, 3/26/1864	Wake County, North Carolina, Age Unknown	Co. K, 36th Regiment North Carolina, 2nd N. C. Artillery	Captured	Point Lookout Prison, Maryland	Oath of Allegiance 6/27/1865
Gowan, Peter Private	Charleston, South Carolina 2/24/1862	Charleston, South Carolina, 20 Years Old	Co. A, 25th South Carolina Volunteers	Captured	Elmira Prison, Elmira, New York	Oath of Allegiance 6/21/1865

NAME & RANK	ENLISTED	RESIDENCE AGE & TRADE	UNIT	RESULT OF BATTLE	PRISON	PRISON RELEASE
Gower, Henry S. Private	Camp Holmes, North Carolina, 10/13/1863	Wake County, North Carolina, Age Unknown	2nd Co. D, 36th Regiment North Carolina, 2nd N. C. Artillery	Captured	Elmira Prison, Elmira, New York	Died of Chronic Diarrhea, 5/14/1865
Grady, Charles C. Private	Duplin County, North Carolina, 5/18/1864	Mount Olive, Duplin County, North Carolina, 17 Years Old Farmer	Co. D, 40th Regiment, 3rd North Carolina Artillery	Captured	Point Lookout Prison, Maryland	Oath of Allegiance 6/21/1865
Grady, Lewis H. Private	Duplin County, North Carolina, 7/13/1863 Volunteer	Mount Olive, Duplin County, North Carolina, 22 Years Old Farmer	3rd Co. G, 40th Regiment, 3rd North Carolina Artillery	Captured, Defended Land Face	Elmira Prison, Elmira, New York	Exchanged 3/2/1865, Died of Pneumonia, 3/151865, General Hospital No. 9, Richmond, Virginia
Graham, Daniel W. Private	Robeson County, North Carolina, 1/1/1863	Lumberton, Robeson County, North Carolina, 40 Years Old	Co. D, 1st Battalion, North Carolina Heavy Artillery	Captured, Defended River Road Gate	Point Lookout Prison, Maryland	Oath of Allegiance 6/27/1865
Graham, James Private	Marion District, South Carolina 4/20/1862	Gum Swamp, Marion District, South Carolina, 18 Years Old Farmer	Co. D, 25th South Carolina Volunteers	Captured	Elmira Prison, Elmira, New York	Died of Remittent Fever, 2/4/1865,
Graham, Malcolm J. Sergeant	Cumberland County, North Carolina, 2/24/1862	Fayetteville, Cumberland County, North Carolina, 26 Years Old Painter	2nd Co. G, 36th Regiment North Carolina, 2nd N. C. Artillery	Captured	Point Lookout Prison, Maryland	Oath of Allegiance 6/23/1865
Grambling, Martin L. Private	Coles Island, South Carolina 4/11/1862	Orangeburg, South Carolina Farmer, 27 Years Old Teamster	Co. F, 25th South Carolina Volunteers	Captured	Elmira Prison, Elmira, New York	Oath of Allegiance 7/7/1865

NAME & RANK	ENLISTED	RESIDENCE AGE & TRADE	UNIT	RESULT OF BATTLE	PRISON	PRISON RELEASE
Grant, Solomon E. Private	Wilmington, New Hanover County, North Carolina, 4/16/1864	Wilmington, New Hanover County, North Carolina, 15 Years Old	Co. K, 10th Reg. 1st North Carolina Artillery	Captured	Elmira Prison, Elmira, New York	Died of Chronic Diarrhea, 3/6/1865
Grant, William R Private	Camp Harllee, South Carolina 1/1/1862	Marlboro District, South Carolina, 30 Years Old	Co. D, 21st South Carolina Volunteers	Captured	Elmira Prison, Elmira, New York	Exchanged 3/2/1865 Boulware's Wharf, James River, Virginia
Grantham, John Q. Private	Fort Holmes, Brunswick County, North Carolina, 12/11/1864	Brunswick County, North Carolina, Age Unknown	Co. E, 40th Regiment, 3rd North Carolina Artillery	Captured	Elmira Prison, Elmira, New York	Exchanged 3/18/1865, Died of Typhoid Fever 4/5/1865, Richmond, Virginia
Grantham, Josiah L. Private	Fort Caswell, Brunswick County, North Carolina, 8/19/1863 Volunteer	Brunswick County, North Carolina 44 Years Old	Co. E, 40th Regiment, 3rd North Carolina Artillery	Captured	Elmira Prison, Elmira, New York	Died of Chronic Diarrhea, 3/23/1865,
Grantham, Robert W. Private	Darlington, South Carolina 1/20/1862	Darlington District, South Carolina, 18 Years Old Farmer	Co. H, 21st South Carolina Volunteers	Captured	Elmira Prison, Elmira, New York	Died of Pneumonia 3/5/1865,
Graves, A. W. Private	Date and Place Unknown	Graham, Alamance County, North Carolina, 35 Years Old Farmer	Co. C, 3rd Battalion, North Carolina Light Artillery	Severe Gunshot Wound In Head & Captured		May Have Died Of Wounds At Fort Fisher, North Carolina
Graves, Joseph Lieutenant	Secession-ville, South Carolina 5/15/1862	Columbia, Richland County, South Carolina, 20 Years Old	Co. G, 25th South Carolina Volunteers	Captured	Fort Columbus, New York Harbor	Exchanged 2/25/1865

NAME & RANK	ENLISTED	RESIDENCE AGE & TRADE	UNIT	RESULT OF BATTLE	PRISON	PRISON RELEASE
Gray, James Alexander Private	Fort Fisher, New Hanover County, North Carolina, 7/16/1864	Wilmington, New Hanover County, North Carolina, 19 Years Old	2nd Co. C, 36th Regiment North Carolina, 2nd N. C. Artillery	Captured, Defended River Road Gate	Elmira Prison, Elmira, New York	Exchanged 3/2/1865 Boulware's Wharf, James River, Virginia
Grayson, J. M. Private	Battery Island, South Carolina 4/12/1862	Williamsburg District, South Carolina, 20 Years Old	Co. C, 25th South Carolina Volunteers	Gunshot Wound Left Thigh & Captured	Point Lookout Prison, Maryland	Oath of Allegiance 6/28/1865
Green, Edward B. Captain	Georgetown South Carolina 1/1/1862	Marion District, Mars Bluff, South Carolina, 32 Years Old Engineer	Co. K, 21st South Carolina Volunteers	Captured	Fort Columbus, New York Harbor	Exchanged 2/25/1865
Green, George Private	New Orleans, Louisiana, 4/30/1861	New Orleans, Louisiana, Age Unknown Laborer	Co. A, Confederate States Marine Corp, Assigned to Guard duty Aboard CSS *Arctic.*	Captured	Point Lookout Prison, Maryland	Oath of Allegiance 5/13/1865
Green, Samuel Private	Fort Pender, Brunswick County, North Carolina, 12/29/1863 Volunteer	Alamance County, North Carolina, 19 Years Old Farmer	Co. E, 36th Regiment North Carolina, 2nd N. C. Artillery	Captured	Elmira Prison, Elmira, New York	Oath of Allegiance 7/3/1865
Greer, William Robert Private	Charleston, South Carolina 1/4/1863	Charleston, South Carolina, 19 Years Old	Co. B, 25th South Carolina Volunteers	Captured	Elmira Prison, Elmira, New York	Oath of Allegiance 6/23/1865
Gregg, Alex M. Sergeant	Pee Dee, South Carolina 1/1/1862	Mars Bluff, Marion District, South Carolina, 19 Years Old	Co. K, 21st South Carolina Volunteers	Captured	Elmira Prison, Elmira, New York	Oath of Allegiance 6/23/1865

NAME & RANK	ENLISTED	RESIDENCE AGE & TRADE	UNIT	RESULT OF BATTLE	PRISON	PRISON RELEASE
Gregg, Thomas C. Private	Camp Manigault, South Carolina 5/2/1862	Mars Bluff, Marion District, South Carolina, 23 Years Old	Co. I, 21st South Carolina Volunteers	Captured	Elmira Prison, Elmira, New York	Oath of Allegiance 6/23/1865
Gregg, W. W. Private	Marion District, South Carolina 9/1/1863	Marion County, South Carolina, 19 Years Old	Co. I, 21st South Carolina Volunteers	Captured	Elmira Prison, Elmira, New York	Died Of Unknown Disease On Boat To Be Exchanged 3/3/1865
Gregory, Charles G. Assistant Surgeon	Raleigh, Wake County, North Carolina, 4/19/1861	Enfield, Halifax County, North Carolina, 25 Years Old Physician	36th Regiment North Carolina, 2nd N. C. Artillery	Captured	Point Lookout Prison, Maryland	Exchanged 2/14/1865 Cox's Landing, James River, Virginia
Gregory, Joseph H. First Sergeant	Craven County, North Carolina, 1/31/1862	Enfield, Halifax County, North Carolina, 28 Years Old Farmer	Co. F, 36th Regiment North Carolina, 2nd N. C. Artillery	Captured	Point Lookout Prison, Maryland	Oath of Allegiance 6/27/1865
Grice, E. G. Private	Bennetts-ville, South Carolina 9/24/1864	Bennettsville, Marlboro County, South Carolina, 35 Years Old Blacksmith	Co. F, 21st South Carolina Volunteers	Killed in Action 1/15/1865		
Grice, Giles W. Private	Sampson County, North Carolina, 10/23/1861, Volunteer	Warrensville, Sampson County, North Carolina, 32 Years Old Hireling	2nd Co. A, 36th Regiment North Carolina, 2nd N. C. Artillery	Captured, Defended the Mound Battery	Elmira Prison, Elmira, New York	Died of Chronic Diarrhea, 3/22/1865
Grier, Thomas C. Private	Georgetown South Carolina 1/1/1862	Prince George Parish, Georgetown, South Carolina, 34 Years Old Farmer	Co. A, 21st South Carolina Volunteers	Captured	Elmira Prison, Elmira, New York	Exchanged 3/2/1865 Boulware's Wharf, James River, Virginia

NAME & RANK	ENLISTED	RESIDENCE AGE & TRADE	UNIT	RESULT OF BATTLE	PRISON	PRISON RELEASE
Grier, William S. Private	Charleston, South Carolina 4/1/1864	Prince George Parish, Georgetown, South Carolina. 17 Years Old Farmer	Co. A, 21st South Carolina Volunteers	Captured	Elmira Prison, Elmira, New York	Died of Chronic Diarrhea, 3/12/1865,
Griffin, Absalom B. Private	Coles Island, South Carolina 4/11/1862	Unknown	Co. F, 25th South Carolina Volunteers	Captured	Elmira Prison, Elmira, New York	Died of Chronic Diarrhea, 5/6/1865,
Griffin, Henry J. F. Private	Coles Island, South Carolina 4/11/1862	Lance's Ferry, Orangeburg District, South Carolina, 36 Years Old Overseer	Co. F, 25th South Carolina Volunteers	Captured	Elmira Prison, Elmira, New York	Died of Chronic Diarrhea, 5/16/1865,
Griffin, Ignatius Q. Corporal	Columbus County, North Carolina, 3/1/1862	Columbus County, North Carolina, 21 Years Old	Co. E, 36th Regiment North Carolina, 2nd N. C. Artillery	Captured	Point Lookout Prison, Maryland	Oath of Allegiance 6/27/1865
Griffin, John Private	Coles Island, South Carolina 4/11/1862	Grady, South Carolina, 20 Years Old	Co. F, 25th South Carolina Volunteers	Shell Wound To Scalp & Captured	Point Lookout Prison, Maryland	Oath of Allegiance 6/27/1865
Griffin, N. J. Private	New Hanover County, North Carolina, 7/6/1864	Unknown	2nd Co. A, 36th Regiment North Carolina, 2nd N. C. Artillery	Captured, Defended the Mound Battery	Prison Unknown	Date Of Release Unknown
Griffin, S. D. Private	Coles Island, South Carolina 4/11/1862	Orangeburg, South Carolina, Age Unknown	Co. F, 25th South Carolina Volunteers	Captured	Elmira Prison, Elmira, New York	Oath of Allegiance 7/11/1865
Griffin, Silas Private	Brunswick County, North Carolina, 7/14/1862	Robeson County, North Carolina, 22 Years Old Farm Laborer	Co. E, 40th Regiment, 3rd North Carolina Artillery	Captured	Point Lookout Prison, Maryland	Oath of Allegiance 6/27/1865

NAME & RANK	ENLISTED	RESIDENCE AGE & TRADE	UNIT	RESULT OF BATTLE	PRISON	PRISON RELEASE
Griggs, Elisha Private	Fort Branch, Brunswick County, North Carolina, 7/25/1863 Volunteer	Charlotte, North Carolina, 18 Years Old	3rd Co. G, 40th Regiment, 3rd North Carolina Artillery	Captured, Defended Land Face	Elmira Prison, Elmira, New York	Oath of Allegiance 6/12/1865
Griggs, William W. Assistant Surgeon	Place Unknown 5/1/1863	Unknown	Confederate States Navy, Served Aboard Ironclad *CSS North Carolina,*	Captured	Fort Columbus, New York Harbor	Exchanged City Point, Va. 2/25/1865
Grimes, Edward F. Private	Bladen County, North Carolina, 8/28/1862	Bladen County, North Carolina, 21 Years Old	3rd Co. b, 36th Regiment, North Carolina 2nd N. C. Artillery	Captured	Point Lookout Prison, Maryland	Oath of Allegiance 6/27/1865
Grimsly, Charles M. Private	Bladen County, North Carolina, 12/26/1861	Elizabethtown Bladen County, North Carolina, 16 Years Old Farmer	3rd Co. B, 36th Regiment North Carolina, 2nd N. C. Artillery	Wounded in Knee 12/24/1864		
Gurgainus, James R. Private	Wilmington, New Hanover County, North Carolina, 10/20/1864	Tarboro, Edgecombe County, North Carolina, Age Unknown	Co. K, 10th Regiment, 3rd North Carolina Artillery	Captured	Elmira Prison, Elmira, New York	Oath of Allegiance 7/7/1865
Guy, William Private	Lillington, Harnett County, North Carolina, 4/30/1862 Volunteer	Morrisville, Wake County, North Carolina, 24 Years Old	2nd Co. C, 36th Regiment North Carolina, 2nd N. C. Artillery	Captured, Defended River Road Gate	Elmira Prison, Elmira, New York	Oath of Allegiance 6/12/1865
Guyton, Jacob Private	Fort Fisher, New Hanover County, North Carolina, 3/23/1862, Volunteer	Elizabethtown Bladen County, North Carolina, 23 Years Old Farmer	2nd Co. I, 36th Regiment North Carolina, 2nd N. C. Artillery	Wounded & Captured, Defended Shepperd's Battery	Prison Unknown	May Have Died Of Wounds At Fort Fisher, North Carolina

NAME & RANK	ENLISTED	RESIDENCE AGE & TRADE	UNIT	RESULT OF BATTLE	PRISON	PRISON RELEASE
Gwinn, W. B. Lieutenant	8/10/1863 Place Unknown	Unknown	Co. A, 2nd Engineers North Carolina Troops	Captured	Fort Columbus, New York Harbor	Paroled 2/25/1865 At City Point, Virginia
Gyles, F. A. Sergeant	Coles Island, South Carolina 3/22/1862	Unknown, 21 Years Old	Co. B, 25th South Carolina Volunteers	Captured	Elmira Prison, New York	Exchanged 3/14/1865

NAME & RANK	ENLISTED	RESIDENCE AGE & TRADE	UNIT	RESULT OF BATTLE	PRISON	PRISON RELEASE
Hagans, Amos Private	Edgecombe County, North Carolina, 9/1/1863	Sparta, Pitt County, North Carolina, 36 Years Old Farmer	Co. D, 40th Regiment, 3rd North Carolina Light Artillery	Captured	Point Lookout Prison, Maryland	Oath of Allegiance 6/27/1865
Haggard, John D. Private	St. Johns, Hertford County, North Carolina, 7/18/1864 Conscript	Garysburg, North Carolina, Age Unknown	Co. C, 3rd Battalion, North Carolina Light Artillery	Captured	Elmira Prison, Elmira, New York	Oath of Allegiance 5/29/1865
Haggerty, John Sergeant	New Orleans, Louisiana, 5/2/1861	New Orleans, Louisiana, Age Unknown	Co. A, Confederate States Marine Corp, Assigned to Guard duty Aboard CSS *North Carolina* and CSS *Arctic*	Captured	Point Lookout Prison, Maryland	Oath of Allegiance 5/13/1865
Haigh, William H. Private	New Hanover County, North Carolina, 8/27/1864	Fayetteville, Cumberland County, North Carolina, Age Unknown Lawyer	2nd Co. C, 36th Regiment North Carolina, 2nd N. C. Artillery	Captured, Defended River Road Gate	Point Lookout Prison, Maryland	Oath of Allegiance 6/9/1865

NAME & RANK	ENLISTED	RESIDENCE AGE & TRADE	UNIT	RESULT OF BATTLE	PRISON	PRISON RELEASE
Haigler, F. G. Private	Secession-ville, South Carolina 5/22/1862	Orangeburg District, South Carolina, 18 Years Old	Co. F, 25th South Carolina Volunteers	Captured	Elmira Prison, Elmira, New York	Oath of Allegiance 7/26/1865
Hales, Matthew Private	Bladen County, North Carolina, 11/21/1861, Volunteer	Blockersville, Cumberland County, N. C., 20 Years Old Assigned, Extra Duty On Revetment Turf, 1864	Co. H, 36th Regiment North Carolina, 2nd N. C. Artillery	Wounded in Shoulder 12/24/1864	Not Captured	Admitted to Wilmington Hospital 12/25/1864
Hales, Samuel Private	Blockers-ville, Cumberland County, North Carolina, 3/2/1862 Volunteer	Fayetteville, Cumberland County, North Carolina, 53 Years Old Farm Hand	2nd Co. D, 36th Regiment North Carolina, 2nd N. C. Artillery	Captured	Elmira Prison, Elmira, New York	Exchanged 3/2/1865 Boulware's Wharf, James River, Virginia
Haley, Harvey V. Corporal	Camp Hardee, Georgetown South Carolina 1/1/1862	Manning, Clarendon District, South Carolina, 33 Years Old	Co. I, 25th South Carolina Volunteers	Captured	Elmira Prison, Elmira, New York	Died Of Chronic Diarrhea 3/12/1865
Hall, Alexander A. Private	Hardeeville, South Carolina 3/6/1863	Unknown, 18 Years Old	Co. D, 11th South Carolina Volunteers	Captured	Elmira Prison, Elmira, New York	Died Of Rubeola 4/2/1865
Hall, Amos J. Private	Fort Fisher, New Hanover County, North Carolina, 12/20/1862 Volunteer	Fayetteville, Cumberland County, North Carolina, 31 Years Old	2nd Co. C, 36th Regiment North Carolina, 2nd N. C. Artillery	Captured, Defended River Road Gate	Elmira Prison, Elmira, New York	Exchanged 3/2/1865 Boulware's Wharf, James River, Virginia
Hall, C. F. Private	New Hanover County, North Carolina, 6/17/1864	New Hanover County, North Carolina, Age Unknown	2nd Co. A, 36th Regiment North Carolina, 2nd N. C. Artillery	Captured, Defended the Mound Battery	Point Lookout Prison, Maryland	Exchanged 2/18/1865 Boulware's Wharf, James River, Virginia

NAME & RANK	ENLISTED	RESIDENCE AGE & TRADE	UNIT	RESULT OF BATTLE	PRISON	PRISON RELEASE
Hall, Daniel	Sampson County, North Carolina, 2/26/1862	Owensville, Sampson County, North Carolina, 21 Years Old Laborer	2nd Co. C, 36th Regiment North Carolina, 2nd N. C. Artillery	Killed In Action 1/15/1865, Defended River Road Gate		
Hall, Daniel Private	Darlington, South Carolina 1/3/1862	Unknown, 25 Years Old	Co. G, 21st South Carolina Volunteers	Captured	Elmira Prison, Elmira, New York	Died of Pneumonia 2/25/1865
Hall, David T. Private	Ellisville, Bladen County, North Carolina, 3/4/1862 Volunteer	Ellisville, Bladen County, North Carolina, 28 Years Old	2nd Co. C, 36th Regiment North Carolina, 2nd N. C. Artillery	Captured, Defended River Road Gate	Elmira Prison, Elmira, New York	Oath of Allegiance 7/7/1865
Hall, Gaston W. Private	Fort Fisher, New Hanover County, North Carolina, 3/15/1864 Volunteer	Fayetteville, Cumberland County, North Carolina, 19 Years Old Detailed as Scout for Lt. Faison	Co. H, 36th Regiment North Carolina, 2nd N. C. Artillery	Captured	Elmira Prison, Elmira, New York	Died of Chronic Diarrhea, 3/1/1865
Hall, Henry Private	New Hanover County, North Carolina, 5/10/1864	Owensville, Sampson County, North Carolina, 19 Years Old Farm Laborer	2nd Co. A, 36th Regiment North Carolina, 2nd N. C. Artillery	Killed In Action 1/15/1865, Defended the Mound Battery		
Hall, James H. Private	Georgetown South Carolina 1/1/1862	New Prospect, Spartanburg, South Carolina, 23 Years Old	Co. K, 21st South Carolina Volunteers	Captured	Elmira Prison, Elmira, New York	Died of Chronic Diarrhea, 8/26/1865
Hall, Jesse Private	Fort Fisher, New Hanover County, North Carolina, 6/1/1863 Volunteer	Ellisville, Bladen County, North Carolina, 19 Years Old	2nd Co. I, 36th Regiment North Carolina, 2nd N. C. Artillery	Captured, Defended Shepperd's Battery	Elmira Prison, Elmira, New York	Died of Rubeola, 2/10/1865

NAME & RANK	ENLISTED	RESIDENCE AGE & TRADE	UNIT	RESULT OF BATTLE	PRISON	PRISON RELEASE
Hall, Lewis Private	St. Johns, Hertford County, North Carolina, 8/7/1864 Volunteer	Yadkinville, Yadkin County, North Carolina, 17 Years Old	Co. C, 3rd Battalion, North Carolina Light Artillery	Captured	Elmira Prison, Elmira, New York	Died of Chronic Diarrhea, 3/7/1865
Hall, Lewis D. Private	New Hanover County, North Carolina, 9/20/1863	New Hanover County, North Carolina, Age Unknown	2nd Co. A, 36th Regiment North Carolina, 2nd N. C. Artillery	Captured, Defended the Mound Battery	Elmira Prison, Elmira, New York	Died of Smallpox, 3/19/1865
Hall, Lorenzo Dow Private	Cumberland County, North Carolina, 9/8/1863 Volunteer	Fayetteville, Cumberland County, North Carolina, 45 Years Old	3rd Co. B, 36th Regiment North Carolina, 2nd N. C. Artillery	Captured	Elmira Prison, Elmira, New York	Oath of Allegiance 7/7/1865
Hall, Malcom Private	Fort Fisher, New Hanover County, North Carolina, 3/8/1863 Volunteer	Owensville, Sampson County, North Carolina, 45 Years Old Farmer	2nd Co. D, 36th Regiment North Carolina, 2nd N. C. Artillery	Captured	Elmira Prison, Elmira, New York	Oath of Allegiance 7/11/1865
Hall, Maurice Private	Fort Fisher, New Hanover County, North Carolina, 7/8/1862	Fayetteville, Cumberland County, North Carolina, Age Unknown	2nd Co. C, 36th Regiment North Carolina, 2nd N. C. Artillery	Captured, Defended River Road Gate	Elmira Prison, Elmira, New York	Oath of Allegiance 6/12/1865
Hall, Stephen W. Private	Harrison Creek, Cumberland County, North Carolina, 3/5/1862 Volunteer	Ellisville, Bladen County, North Carolina, 23 Years Old Farmer	2nd Co. C, 36th Regiment North Carolina, 2nd N. C. Artillery	Captured, Defended River Road Gate	Elmira Prison, Elmira, New York	Oath of Allegiance 6/12/1865

NAME & RANK	ENLISTED	RESIDENCE AGE & TRADE	UNIT	RESULT OF BATTLE	PRISON	PRISON RELEASE
Hall, Thomas H. Private	Fort Fisher, New Hanover County, North Carolina, 8/20/1864	New Hanover County, North Carolina, Age Unknown	2nd Co. I, 36th Regiment North Carolina, 2nd N. C. Artillery	Captured, Defended Shepperd's Battery	Elmira Prison, Elmira, New York	Died of Pneumonia, 2/16/1865
Hall, William D. Private	Clinton, Sampson County, North Carolina, 2/24/1863 Volunteer	Red Plains, Yadkin County, North Carolina, 24 Years Old Farm Laborer	2nd Co. C, 36th Regiment North Carolina, 2nd N. C. Artillery	Captured, Defended River Road Gate	Elmira Prison, Elmira, New York	Oath of Allegiance 7/7/1865
Hall, William J. Private	Fort Fisher, New Hanover County, North Carolina, 5/8/1862 Volunteer	Ellisville, Bladen County, North Carolina, 34 Years Old Turpentine	2nd Co. C, 36th Regiment North Carolina, 2nd N. C. Artillery	Captured, Defended River Road Gate	Elmira Prison, Elmira, New York	Oath of Allegiance 6/12/1865
Hamer, C. H. Private	Bennetts-ville, South Carolina 10/20/1863	Unknown, 38 Years Old	Co. F, 21st South Carolina Volunteers	Captured	Elmira Prison, Elmira, New York	Died of Pneumonia 2/6/1865
Hamer, James C. Private	Bennetts-ville, South Carolina 5/1/1864	Bennettsville, Marlboro District, South Carolina 36 Years Old Farmer	Co. F, 21st South Carolina Volunteers	Captured	Elmira Prison, Elmira, New York	Died of Chronic Diarrhea, 3/2/1865
Hamlet, Nathaniel M. Private	New Berne, Craven County, North Carolina, 1/1/1862	Weldon, Halifax County, North Carolina, Age Unknown Farmer	Co. F, 36th Regiment North Carolina, 2nd N. C. Artillery	Captured	Elmira Prison, Elmira, New York	Exchanged 3/2/1865 Boulware's Wharf, James River, Virginia
Hammonds Moses Private	Fort Caswell, Brunswick County, North Carolina, 5/3/1862 Volunteer	Asheboro, Randolph County, North Carolina, 27 Years Old Carpenter	Co. E, 36th Regiment North Carolina, 2nd N. C. Artillery	Captured	Elmira Prison, Elmira, New York	Oath of Allegiance 6/23/1865

NAME & RANK	ENLISTED	RESIDENCE AGE & TRADE	UNIT	RESULT OF BATTLE	PRISON	PRISON RELEASE
Hancock, Zumariah Private	Wilmington, New Hanover County, North Carolina, 7/18/1863	High Point, Guilford County, North Carolina, Age Unknown	Co. K, 10th Reg. 1st North Carolina Artillery	Captured	Elmira Prison, Elmira, New York	Oath of Allegiance 7/11/1865
Hanelsen, J. E. Private	Wilmington, New Hanover County, North Carolina	Wilmington, New Hanover County, North Carolina, 34 Years Old Merchant	Co. G, 36th Regiment North Carolina, 2nd N. C. Artillery	Missing Supposed To Be Killed, 1/15/1865		No Official Record, Name Appears On List Of Killed Prepared by Major C. E. Pearce, 2/17/1865
Hanie, Harvey Private	Fort Branch, Brunswick County, North Carolina, 8/19/1863	Wadesboro, Anson County, North Carolina, 33 Years Old	3rd Co. G, 40th Regiment, 3rd North Carolina Light Artillery	Gunshot Wound Right Side of Chest & Captured, Defended Land Face	Point Lookout Prison General Hospital, Maryland	Died Of Wounds 3/10/1865
Hardin, John D. Private	Sampson County, North Carolina,	Clinton, Sampson County, North Carolina, Age Unknown Day Laborer	2nd Co. A, 36th Regiment North Carolina, 2nd N. C. Artillery	Captured, Defended the Mound Battery	Point Lookout Prison, Maryland	Oath of Allegiance 6/27/1865
Hardison, Bates Private	Beaufort County, North Carolina, 2/15/1862	Washington, Beaufort County, North Carolina, 40 Years Old Laborer	Co. I, 40th Regiment, 3rd North Carolina Light Artillery	Wounded, Fracture Of Left Elbow & Captured	Point Lookout Prison, Maryland	Died of Encephalitis, 6/26/1865
Hardison, Elijah J. Private	Transferred From Co. B, 41st Regiment, North Carolina, 2/19/1864	Unknown, 33 Years Old	Co. D, 13th Battalion North Carolina Light Artillery	Severely Wounded & Captured, Defended River Road Gate	Prison Unknown	May Have Died Of Wounds At Fort Fisher, North Carolina
Hardison, William S. Private	Pitt County, North Carolina, 5/14/1862	Trauters Creek, Beaufort County, North Carolina, 28 Years Old Farmer	Co. K, 10th Reg. 1st North Carolina Artillery	Mortal Gunshot Wound of Right Shoulder and Neck & Captured	Treated At Mansfield Hospital Morehead City, North Carolina	Died Of Wounds 1/21/1865

NAME & RANK	ENLISTED	RESIDENCE AGE & TRADE	UNIT	RESULT OF BATTLE	PRISON	PRISON RELEASE
Hardy, John L. Private	Wilson County, North Carolina, 6/18/1863	Saratoga District, Wilson County, N. C., 28 Years Old Merchant	Co. D, 40th Regiment, 3rd North Carolina Light Artillery	Captured	Point Lookout Prison, Maryland	Oath of Allegiance 6/27/1865
Hardy, William C. Private	Fort Caswell, Brunswick County, North Carolina, 9/1/1863	Brinkleyville, Halifax County, North Carolina, 18 Years Old	Co. F, 36th Regiment North Carolina, 2nd N. C. Artillery	Killed In Action 1/15/1865		Gunshot Wound Left Thigh
Hare, Daniel Private	Lillington, Harnett County, North Carolina, 4/30/1862	Harnett County, North Carolina, 23 Years Old	2nd Co. C, 36th Regiment North Carolina, 2nd N. C. Artillery	Wounded Severely, Left Arm Amputated & Captured	Point Lookout Prison, Maryland	Oath of Allegiance 6/4/1865, Defended River Road Gate
Hare, James E. Private	New Hanover County, North Carolina, 2/22/1863	Kingsbury, Cumberland County, North Carolina, 37 Years Old	2nd Co. A, 36th Regiment North Carolina, 2nd N. C. Artillery	Killed In Action 1/15/1865, Defended the Mound Battery		
Hare, Reddin Private	New Hanover County, North Carolina, 2/22/1863	Sampson County, North Carolina, 35 Years Old Laborer	2nd Co. A, 36th Regiment North Carolina, 2nd N. C. Artillery	Captured, Defended the Mound Battery	Point Lookout Prison, Maryland	Oath of Allegiance 6/27/1865
Hare, Richard Private	Date and Place Unknown	Unknown	2nd Co. A, 36th Regiment North Carolina, 2nd N. C. Artillery	Wounded & Captured, Defended the Mound Battery	Prison Unknown	Date Of Release Unknown
Harman, Reddick H. Private	Camp Mangum, North Carolina, 5/27/1862	Murfreesboro, Hertford County, North Carolina, 21 Years Old Farmer	Co. C, 3rd Battalion, North Carolina Light Artillery	Gunshot Wound To Left Arm & Captured	Fort Delaware Prison, Del.	Oath of Allegiance 6/19/1865

NAME & RANK	ENLISTED	RESIDENCE AGE & TRADE	UNIT	RESULT OF BATTLE	PRISON	PRISON RELEASE
Harp, B. G. Private	Date and Place Unknown	Unknown	Co. F, 36th Regiment North Carolina, 2nd N. C. Artillery	Captured	Prison Unknown	Date Of Release Unknown
Harp, G. H. Private	Date and Place Unknown	Unknown	Co. F, 36th Regiment North Carolina, 2nd N. C. Artillery	Captured	Prison Unknown	Date Of Release Unknown
Harper, James A. Private	Craven County, North Carolina, 1/15/1862,	Heathsville, Halifax County, North Carolina, 21 Years Old	Co. F, 36th Regiment North Carolina, 2nd N. C. Artillery	Killed In Action 1/15/1865		
Harper, Riley A. Private	Craven County, North Carolina, 1/24/1862	New Berne, Craven County, North Carolina, 37 Years Old Farmer	Co. D, 40th Regiment, 3rd North Carolina Light Artillery	Captured	Point Lookout Prison, Maryland	Oath of Allegiance 6/27/1865
Harrell, Hugh W. Private	Robeson County, North Carolina, 2/22/1863,	Robeson County, North Carolina, 39 Years Old	Co. D, 1st Battalion, North Carolina Heavy Artillery	Captured, Defended River Road Gate	Point Lookout Prison, Maryland	Exchanged 2/15/1865, Boulware's Wharf, James River, Virginia
Harrell, Joel E. Private	Darlington, South Carolina 1/1/1862	Darlington District County, South Carolina, 18 Years Old	Co. B, 21st South Carolina Volunteers	Killed In Action 1/15/1865		
Harrell, John H. Private	Craven County, North Carolina, 4/15/1864	Tarboro, Edgecombe County, North Carolina, 18 Years Old	Co. D, 40th Regiment, 3rd Regiment, North Carolina Light Artillery	Captured	Point Lookout Prison, Maryland	Oath of Allegiance 6/27/1865

NAME & RANK	ENLISTED	RESIDENCE AGE & TRADE	UNIT	RESULT OF BATTLE	PRISON	PRISON RELEASE
Harrell, Levi Private	Edgecombe County, North Carolina, 10/10/1863	Edgecombe County, North Carolina, 17 Years Old	Co. D, 40th Regiment, 3rd Regiment, North Carolina Light Artillery	Captured	Point Lookout Prison, Maryland	Exchanged 2/20/1865, Boulware's Wharf, James River, Virginia
Harrelson, Brice Private	New Hanover County, North Carolina, 3/17/1864	Caswell County, North Carolina, Age Unknown	Co. K, 10th Reg. 1st North Carolina Artillery	Gunshot Wound & Fracture Of Left Elbow & Captured	Point Lookout Prison, Maryland	Oath of Allegiance 6/28/1865
Harrelson, Isham West Private	Old Brunswick Town, North Carolina, 4/16/1862	Lockwoods Folly District, Brunswick County, North Carolina, 25 Years Old Cooper	3rd Co. G, 36th Regiment North Carolina, 2nd N. C. Artillery	Captured, Defended Battery to the Left of Northeast Bastion	Elmira Prison, Elmira, New York	Exchanged 3/2/1865 Boulware's Wharf, James River, Virginia
Harrelson, John E. Private	Brunswick County, North Carolina, 10/2/1862, Volunteer	Graham, Alamance County, North Carolina, 25 Years Old Overseer	3rd Co. G, 36th Regiment North Carolina, 2nd N. C. Artillery	Killed In Action 1/15/1865, Defended Battery to the Left of Northeast Bastion		
Harris, Edward Private	Old Brunswick Town, North Carolina, 4/16/1862,	Town Creek District, Brunswick County, North Carolina, 40 Years Old Laborer	3rd Co. G, 36th Regiment North Carolina, 2nd N. C. Artillery	Wounded & Captured, Defended Battery to the Left of Northeast Bastion	Elmira Prison, Elmira, New York	Died of Pneumonia, 4/2/1865
Harris, Franklin H. Private	Darlington, South Carolina 1/20/1862	Charlotte, North Carolina, 18 Years Old Farmer	Co. H, 21st South Carolina Volunteers	Captured	Elmira Prison, Elmira, New York	Oath of Allegiance 7/11/1865
Harris, James T. Private	Brunswick County, North Carolina	Town Creek District, Brunswick County, North Carolina, Age Unknown Farmer	Co. F, 36th Regiment North Carolina, 2nd N. C. Artillery	Captured	Point Lookout Prison, Maryland	Oath of Allegiance 6/3/1865

NAME & RANK	ENLISTED	RESIDENCE AGE & TRADE	UNIT	RESULT OF BATTLE	PRISON	PRISON RELEASE
Harris, James W. Private	Lenoir County, North Carolina, 8/1/1861	Craven County, North Carolina, 25 Years Old Farmer	Co. D, 40th Regiment, 3rd Regiment, North Carolina Light Artillery	Captured	Point Lookout Prison, Maryland	Oath of Allegiance 5/13/1865
Harris, Patrick Corporal	Enlisted in CSMC 2/24/1864	Mobile, Alabama, Age Unknown Farmer	Co. B, Confederate States Marine Corp, Assigned to Guard duty Aboard CSS *Tallahassee.*	Captured	Point Lookout Prison, Maryland	Oath of Allegiance 5/13/1865
Harris, William H. Private	Lenoir County, North Carolina, 8/1/1861, Volunteer	Lenoir County, North Carolina, 24 Years Old	Co. D, 40th Regiment, 3rd Regiment, North Carolina Light Artillery	Captured	Point Lookout Prison, Maryland	Oath of Allegiance 6/27/1865
Harrison, William S. Private	Unknown 5/14/1864, Volunteer	Unknown	Co. D, 40th Regiment, 3rd Regiment, North Carolina Light Artillery	Mortally Wounded in right thigh & Captured	Treated At Mansfield Hospital Morehead City, North Carolina	Died Of Wounds 1/21/1865
Hart, Harris Private	Chatham County, North Carolina, 3/26/1863	Chatham County, North Carolina, Farm Laborer, 39 Years Old Wood Cutter	3rd Co. G, 40th Regiment, 3rd Regiment, North Carolina Light Artillery	Captured, Defended Land Face	Elmira Prison, Elmira, New York	Exchanged Boulware's Wharf, James River, Virginia, 3/19/1865
Hart, Hugh Private	Chatham County, North Carolina, 3/26/1863, Volunteer	Pittsboro, Chatham County, North Carolina, 37 Years Old Farmer	3rd Co. G, 40th Regiment, 3rd Regiment, North Carolina Light Artillery	Gunshot Wound Left Thigh & Captured, Defended Land Face	Treated At Fort Monroe, Va, Sent To Fort Delaware Prison, Del.	Oath of Allegiance 6/19/1865

NAME & RANK	ENLISTED	RESIDENCE AGE & TRADE	UNIT	RESULT OF BATTLE	PRISON	PRISON RELEASE
Hart, William Private	New Hanover County, North Carolina, 8/15/1863	Tarboro, Edgecombe County, North Carolina, 41 Years Old Merchant	2nd Co. C, 36th Regiment North Carolina, 2nd N. C. Artillery	Captured, Defended River Road Gate	Prison Unknown	Date Of Release Unknown
Harvey, Robert Private	New Berne, Craven County,, North Carolina, 10/19/1861 Volunteer	Elizabethtown Bladen County, North Carolina, 16 Years Old	2nd Co. I, 36th Regiment North Carolina, 2nd N. C. Artillery	Killed In Action 1/15/1865, Defended Shepperd's Battery		Shot And Killed On Top Of Parapet At Third Gun Chamber
Harvey, Robert James Sergeant	New Berne, Craven County, North Carolina, 1/23/1862 Volunteer	New Berne, Craven County, North Carolina, 49 Years Old Turpentine Distillery	Co. F, 36th Regiment North Carolina, 2nd N. C. Artillery	Captured	Elmira Prison, Elmira, New York	Exchanged 3/14/1865
Harvy, Joel Private	New Hanover County, North Carolina, 8/1/1864	Elizabethtown Bladen County, North Carolina, 16 Years Old	Co. H, 36th Regiment North Carolina, 2nd N. C. Artillery	Captured	Point Lookout Prison, Maryland	Died of Pneumonia, 2/12/1865
Hasing, Daniel Private	Date and Place Unknown	Unknown	Co. F, 36th Regiment North Carolina, 2nd N. C. Artillery	Captured	Prison Unknown	Date Of Release Unknown
Haskins, William Private	Wayne County, North Carolina, 10/11/1864	Wayne County, North Carolina, Age Unknown	Co. D, 40th Regiment, 3rd Regiment, North Carolina Light Artillery	Captured	Elmira Prison, Elmira, New York	Died of Chronic Diarrhea, 3/21/1865
Hassell, William First Lieutenant	Craven County, North Carolina, 10/16/1861	Craven County, North Carolina, 26 Years Old	3rd Co. G, 40th Regiment, 3rd Regiment, North Carolina Light Artillery	Captured, Defended Land Face	Fort Columbus, New York Harbor,	Exchanged 3/5/1865

NAME & RANK	ENLISTED	RESIDENCE AGE & TRADE	UNIT	RESULT OF BATTLE	PRISON	PRISON RELEASE
Haste, Calvin A. Private	St. Johns, Hertford County, North Carolina, 7/8/1862	Hertford County, North Carolina, 30 Years Old Farmer	Co. C, 3rd Battalion North Carolina Artillery	Captured	Elmira Prison, Elmira, New York	Died of Peritonitis, 2/14/1865
Hatcher, William H. Private	Chesterfield, South Carolina 12/31/1863	Bennettsville, Marlboro District, South Carolina, 14 Years Old	Co. D, 21st South Carolina Volunteers	Captured	Elmira Prison, Elmira, New York	Died Of Pneumonia 6/29/1865
Havens, Alfred Private	Mobile, Alabama, 8/10/1861,	Mobile, Alabama, Age Unknown Waterman	Co. C, Confederate States Marine Corp, Assigned to Guard duty Aboard CSS *Jamestown* and CSS *Tallahassee.*	Captured	Point Lookout Prison, Maryland	Oath of Allegiance 5/13/1865
Hawes, McKinnon Private	Brunswick, County, North Carolina, 1/31/1864	Brunswick, County, North Carolina, 17 Years Old	Co. D, 13th Battalion North Carolina Light Artillery	Captured, Defended River Road Gate	Point Lookout Prison, Maryland	Exchanged Cox's Landing, James River, Virginia, 2/14/1865
Hawkins, Major B. Private	Enfield, Halifax County, North Carolina, 10/9/1861 Volunteer	Halifax County, North Carolina, 19 Years Old	Co. F, 36th Regiment North Carolina, 2nd N. C. Artillery	Captured	Elmira Prison, Elmira, New York	Died of Pneumonia, 2/13/1865
Hawley, Francis O. Private	Cumberland County, North Carolina, 3/21/1864, Volunteer	Fayetteville, Cumberland County, North Carolina, 18 Years Old	2nd Co. C, 36th Regiment North Carolina, 2nd N. C. Artillery	Severe Gunshot Wound To Face And Nose & Captured	Treated At Mansfield Hospital, Morehead City, N. C., Sent To Fort Delaware, Del.	Oath of Allegiance 6/19/1865, Defended River Road Gate
Hays, Charles F. Private	Marion District, South Carolina 4/20/1862	Unknown	Co. D, 25th South Carolina Volunteers	Captured	Elmira Prison, Elmira, New York	Died of Pneumonia, 3/20/1865

NAME & RANK	ENLISTED	RESIDENCE AGE & TRADE	UNIT	RESULT OF BATTLE	PRISON	PRISON RELEASE
Hays, James N. Private	James Island, South Carolina 6/6/1863	Oak Grove, Marion District, South Carolina, 33 Years Old Farmer	Co. D, 25th South Carolina Volunteers	Captured	Elmira Prison, Elmira, New York	Oath of Allegiance 6/23/1865
Hayes, Francis S. Private	Columbus County, North Carolina, 2/19/1862	Columbus County, North Carolina, 29 Years Old	Co. E, 36th Regiment North Carolina, 2nd N. C. Artillery	Captured	Point Lookout Prison, Maryland	Oath of Allegiance 6/28/1865
Hayes, Loyd Private	Columbus County, North Carolina, 2/19/1862, Volunteer	Columbus County, North Carolina, 33 Years Old	Co. E, 36th Regiment North Carolina, 2nd N. C. Artillery	Wounded	Prison Unknown	Release Unknown
Haynes, Francis L. Private	Robeson County, North Carolina, 12/26/1863	Lumberton, Robeson County, North Carolina, 39 Years Old	2nd Co. D, 36th Regiment North Carolina, 2nd N. C. Artillery	Captured	Point Lookout Prison, Maryland	Oath of Allegiance 6/28/1865
Hazzell, P. G. Lieutenant	Date and Place Unknown	Age Unknown Clerk for General Whiting	Aide-De-Camp 1st Co. A, 36th Regiment North Carolina, 2nd N. C. Artillery	Wounded & Captured	Fort Columbus, New York Harbor,	Exchanged 3/5/1865, Boulware's Wharf, James River, Virginia
Heady, Charles Private	Wilmington, New Hanover County, North Carolina, 10/23/1861 Volunteer	Wilmington, New Hanover County, North Carolina, 30 Years Old	2nd Co. D, 36th Regiment North Carolina, 2nd N. C. Artillery	Captured	Elmira Prison, Elmira, New York	Died of Rheumatism, 5/27/1865
Heape, Benjamin A. Private	Coosawhatchie, South Carolina 7/10/1862	Sand Hill, Beaufort District, South Carolina, 24 Years Old Farmer	Co. F, 11th South Carolina Volunteers	Captured	Point Lookout Prison, Maryland	Oath of Allegiance 6/28/1865

NAME & RANK	ENLISTED	RESIDENCE AGE & TRADE	UNIT	RESULT OF BATTLE	PRISON	PRISON RELEASE
Heckle, Andrew J. Private	James Island, South Carolina 9/1/1862	Unknown	Co F, 25th Regiment South Carolina Volunteers	Captured	Elmira Prison, Elmira, New York	Died of Typhoid Fever, 2/9/1865
Hedgepath, John S. Private	Date and Place Unknown	Tarboro, Edgecombe County, North Carolina, 17 Years Old	Co. F, 36th Regiment North Carolina, 2nd N. C. Artillery	Captured	Elmira Prison, Elmira, New York	Died of Pneumonia, 2/10/1865.
Herring, Benjamin Private	Brunswick, County, North Carolina, 9/25/1864 Volunteer	Lumberton, Robeson County, North Carolina, 38 Years Old Farmer	3rd Co. G, 40th Regiment, 3rd Regiment, North Carolina Light Artillery	Captured, Defended Land Face	Elmira Prison, Elmira, New York	Died of Chronic Diarrhea, 5/22/1865
Herring, Benjamin F. Corporal	Red Banks, Robeson County, North Carolina, 10/14/1861 Volunteer	Colvin's Creek, New Hanover County, North Carolina, 15 Years Old	3rd Co. G, 40th Regiment, 3rd Regiment, North Carolina Light Artillery	Captured, Defended Land Face	Elmira Prison, Elmira, New York	Oath of Allegiance 5/17/1865
Herring, Daniel Negro	Date and Place Unknown	Cook, Age Unknown	Co. F, 36th Regiment North Carolina, 2nd N. C. Artillery	Captured	Point Lookout Prison, Maryland	Oath of Allegiance 6/19/1865
Herring, James Private	Wayne County, North Carolina, 2/12/1862 Volunteer	Sleepy Creek, Indian Springs District, Wayne County, North Carolina 16 Years Old	3rd Co. G, 40th Regiment, 3rd Regiment, North Carolina Light Artillery	Captured, Defended Land Face	Elmira Prison, Elmira, New York	Died of Chronic Diarrhea, 4/21/1865,
Herrington, John C. Private	Washington, Beaufort County, North Carolina, 9/23/1861	Grove, Chatham County, North Carolina, 20 Years Old	Co. D, 13th Battalion North Carolina Light Artillery	Killed In Action 1/15/1865, Defended River Road Gate		

NAME & RANK	ENLISTED	RESIDENCE AGE & TRADE	UNIT	RESULT OF BATTLE	PRISON	PRISON RELEASE
Hester, David D. Private	Elizabeth-town, Bladen County, North Carolina, 1/1/1864, Volunteer	Elizabethtown Bladen County, North Carolina 18 Years Old Farmer	2nd Co. K, 40th Regiment, 3rd Regiment, North Carolina Light Artillery	Captured	Elmira Prison, Elmira, New York	Died of Pneumonia-Typhoid, 2/6/1865
Hester, Jasper Private	Fort Holmes, Brunswick, County, North Carolina, 6/8/1864	Elizabethtown Bladen County, North Carolina, 18 Years Old	2nd Co. K, 40th Regiment, 3rd Regiment, North Carolina Light Artillery	Captured	Elmira Prison, Elmira, New York	Died of Typhoid Fever, 2/28/1865
Hester, William B. Private	Elizabeth-town, Bladen County, North Carolina, 1/1/1864 Volunteer	Elizabethtown Bladen County, North Carolina, 18 Years Old Farmer	2nd Co. K, 40th Regiment, 3rd Regiment, North Carolina Light Artillery	Captured	Elmira Prison, Elmira, New York	Exchanged 3/2/1865 Boulware's Wharf, James River, Virginia
Hester, William J. Private	Elizabeth-town, North Carolina, 5/6/1862, Mustered in at Fort St. Philip, Volunteer	Elizabethtown Bladen County, North Carolina, 22 Years Old Farmer	2nd Co. K, 40th Regiment, 3rd Regiment, North Carolina Light Artillery	Captured	Elmira Prison, Elmira, New York	Died of Pneumonia, 3/29/1865
Hewett, Benjamin E. Sergeant	Brunswick, County, North Carolina, 5/10/1862, Volunteer	Lockwood Folly District, Brunswick, County, North Carolina, 25 Years Old Farmer	Co. K, 36th Regiment North Carolina, 2nd N. C. Artillery	Wounded 1/14/1865		Nothing Further
Hewett, B. Thomas Private	Brunswick, County, North Carolina, 2/19/62	Brunswick, County, North Carolina, 33 Years Old	Co. K, 36th Regiment North Carolina, 2nd N. C. Artillery	Captured	Point Lookout Prison, Maryland	Oath of Allegiance 6/5/1865,

NAME & RANK	ENLISTED	RESIDENCE AGE & TRADE	UNIT	RESULT OF BATTLE	PRISON	PRISON RELEASE
Hewett, Ethelebread Seaman	Place Unknown 1/24/1862	Lockwood Folly District, Brunswick, County, N. C., 22 Years Old Detached to Signal Service 1/10/1863 Fisherman	Galloway Co. C.S. Coast Guard	Captured	Prison Unknown	Release Unknown
Hewett, George W. Seaman	Place Unknown 8/19/1861	Brunswick County, North Carolina, 19 Years Old Fisherman	Galloway Co. C.S. Coast Guard	Captured	Prison Unknown	Release Unknown
Hewett, Henry M. Private	Brunswick, County, North Carolina, 2/19/62, Volunteer	Shallotte,, Brunswick, County, North Carolina, 22 Years Old Farmer	Co. K, 36th Regiment North Carolina, 2nd N. C. Artillery	Wounded & Captured	Point Lookout Prison, Maryland	Oath of Allegiance 6/28/1865,
Hewett, Isaac P. Seaman	Date and Place Unknown	Brunswick, County, N. C., Age Unknown Detached as Boatman, Seaman	Galloway Co. C.S. Coast Guard	Captured	Prison Unknown	Release Unknown
Hewett, James H. Private	Brunswick, County, North Carolina, 2/18/62	Lockwood Folly District, Brunswick, County, North Carolina, 20 Years Old	Co. K, 36th Regiment North Carolina, 2nd N. C. Artillery	Captured	Point Lookout Prison, Maryland	Died of Consumption, 2/27/1865,
Hewett, John L. Seaman	Place Unknown 8/14/1861	Brunswick, County, North Carolina, 33 Years Old Fisherman	Galloway Co. C.S. Coast Guard	Captured	Prison Unknown	Release Unknown
Hewett, Joseph Seaman	Place Unknown 1/24/1862	Brunswick, County, North Carolina, 28 Years Old Fisherman & Farmer	Galloway Co. C.S. Coast Guard	Captured	Prison Unknown	Release Unknown

NAME & RANK	ENLISTED	RESIDENCE AGE & TRADE	UNIT	RESULT OF BATTLE	PRISON	PRISON RELEASE
Hewett, Rhesa E. Seaman	Place Unknown 8/14/1861	Brunswick, County, North Carolina, 20 Years Old Fisherman	Galloway Co. C.S. Coast Guard	Captured	Prison Unknown	Release Unknown
Hewett, Simeon Private	Brunswick, County, North Carolina, 12/31/62, Volunteer	Lockwood Folly District, Brunswick, County, North Carolina, 18 Years Old Farmer	Co. K, 36th Regiment North Carolina, 2nd N. C. Artillery	Wounded & Captured	Point Lookout Prison, Maryland	Oath of Allegiance 6/28/1865,
Hewett, Stephen L. Seaman	Place Unknown 1/24/1862	Lockwood Folly District, Brunswick, County, North Carolina, 27 Years Old Mariner, Fisherman	Galloway Co. C.S. Coast Guard	Captured	Prison Unknown	Release Unknown
Hewett, Stewart Seaman	Place Unknown 1/24/1862	Lockwood Folly District, Brunswick, County, North Carolina, 26 Years Old Fisherman	Galloway Co. C.S. Coast Guard	Captured	Prison Unknown	Release Unknown
Hewitt, Dority W. Private	Fort Campbell, Brunswick, County, North Carolina, 10/26/63	Brunswick, County, North Carolina, 17 Years Old Extra duty at Quarter Master Dept.	3rd Co. G, 36th Regiment North Carolina, 2nd N. C. Artillery	Captured, Defended Battery to the Left of Northeast Bastion	Elmira Prison, Elmira, New York	Died of Pneumonia, 3/26/1865
Hewitt, Ephram Private	Brunswick, County, North Carolina, 5/4/64	Lockwood Folly District, Brunswick, County, North Carolina, 19 Years Old Farmer	3rd Co. G, 36th Regiment North Carolina, 2nd N. C. Artillery	Captured, Defended Battery to the Left of Northeast Bastion	Elmira Prison, Elmira, New York	Exchanged 3/2/1865 Boulware's Wharf, James River, Virginia
Hewitt, G. Private	Date and Place Unknown	Unknown	3rd Co. G, 36th Regiment North Carolina, 2nd N. C. Artillery	Captured, Defended Battery to the Left of Northeast Bastion	Fort Monroe, Virginia	Release Unknown, Sent to Fort Monroe, Virginia 1/17/1865

NAME & RANK	ENLISTED	RESIDENCE AGE & TRADE	UNIT	RESULT OF BATTLE	PRISON	PRISON RELEASE
Hewitt, Isaiah Private	Fort Caswell, Brunswick, County, North Carolina, 9/4/63, Volunteer	Piney Greene, Onslow County, North Carolina, 33 Years Old Farm Laborer	3rd Co. G, 36th Regiment North Carolina, 2nd N. C. Artillery	Captured, Defended Battery to the Left of Northeast Bastion	Elmira Prison, Elmira, New York	Exchanged 2/20/1865
Hewitt, J. R. Private	Date and Place Unknown	Unknown	3rd Co. B, 36th Regiment North Carolina, 2nd N. C. Artillery	Captured	Elmira Prison, Elmira, New York	Oath of Allegiance 7/13/1865
Hewitt, Watson Private	Brunswick, County, North Carolina, 9/29/62, Volunteer	Brunswick, County, North Carolina, 34 Years Old	3rd Co. G, 36th Regiment North Carolina, 2nd N. C. Artillery	Gunshot Wound Right Thigh & Captured, Defended Battery to the Left of Northeast Bastion	Treated At Mansfield Hospital, Morehead City, N. C., Sent To Fort Delaware, Del.	Oath of Allegiance 6/7/1865,
Hickey, John Private	New Orleans, Louisiana, 6/11/1861	New Orleans, Louisiana, Age Unknown Laborer	Co. C, Confederate States Marine Corp, Assigned to Guard duty Aboard CSS *Virginia* and CSS *Arctic*.	Captured	Point Lookout Prison, Maryland	Oath of Allegiance 5/13/1865
Hickman, Henry Private	Smithville, Brunswick, County, North Carolina, 2/19/1862	Shallotte, Brunswick, County, North Carolina, 24 Years Old Farmer	Co. K, 36th Regiment North Carolina, 2nd N. C. Artillery	Gunshot Wound In Right Arm & Captured	Point Lookout Prison Hospital, Maryland	Died From Pyemia After Right Arm Was Amputated, 2/7/1865
Hickman, Stewart Corporal	Old Brunswick, North Carolina, 4/16/1962,	Shallotte, Brunswick, County, North Carolina, 24 Years Old Laborer	3rd Co. G, 36th Regiment North Carolina, 2nd N. C. Artillery	Captured, Defended Battery to the Left of Northeast Bastion	Elmira Prison, Elmira, New York	Oath of Allegiance taken at Elmira US Hospital 8/7/1865

NAME & RANK	ENLISTED	RESIDENCE AGE & TRADE	UNIT	RESULT OF BATTLE	PRISON	PRISON RELEASE
Hickman, Thomas Lieutenant	Brunswick, County, North Carolina, 2/19/62	Shallotte, Brunswick, County, North Carolina, 29 Years Old Farmer	Co. K, 36th Regiment North Carolina, 2nd N. C. Artillery	Captured	Fort Columbus, New York Harbor,	Exchanged 3/5/1865, Boulware's Wharf, James River, Virginia
Hickman, William B. Private	Date and Place Unknown	Whiteville, Columbus County, North Carolina, 17 Years Old Farmer	Co. E, 36th Regiment North Carolina, 2nd N. C. Artillery	Captured	Elmira Prison, Elmira, New York	Died of Chronic Diarrhea, 2/28/1865
Hicks, Calvin B. Private	Place Unknown 3/21/64	Pickesville District, Wayne County, North Carolina, 29 Years Old Sheriff	Co. K, 40th Regiment, 3rd Regiment, North Carolina Light Artillery	Captured	Point Lookout Prison, Maryland	Oath of Allegiance 6/27/1865,
Hicks, Elias F. Private	Wilmington, New Hanover County, North Carolina, 4/16/1864	Piney Grove, Sampson County, North Carolina, 18 Years Old Farmer	Co. K, 10th Regiment, 1st Regiment North Carolina Artillery	Killed In Action 1/15/1865		
Hicks, George T. Private	Fort Johnston, Brunswick, County, North Carolina, 6/25/63 Volunteer	North Western District, Wake County, North Carolina, 18 Years Old	3rd Co. G, 40th Regiment North Carolina, 2nd N. C. Artillery	Captured, Defended Land Face	Elmira Prison, Elmira, New York	Died of Pneumonia, 3/31/1865
Hicks, James M. Assistant Surgeon	Orange County, North Carolina, 8/31/1863	Orange County, North Carolina, 19 Years Old	Confederate States Navy	Captured	Fort Columbus, New York Harbor,	Paroled at City Point, Virginia, February 25, 1865
Higgins, A. G. Private	Date and Place Unknown	Unknown	Co. D, 40th Regiment, 3rd Regiment, North Carolina Light Artillery	Captured	Prison Unknown	Release Unknown

NAME & RANK	ENLISTED	RESIDENCE AGE & TRADE	UNIT	RESULT OF BATTLE	PRISON	PRISON RELEASE
Higgins, John F. Seaman	Date and Place Unknown	Born at St. Mary's in Maryland, Age Unknown	Confederate States Navy, Served Aboard *CSS Virginia*, and Fought against *USS Moniter*	Severely Wounded, Right Leg Shot Off	None, Treated in Wilmington	Leg Amputated at upper third of Thigh 12/25/1864
Hilborn, Zadock Private	New Hanover County, North Carolina, 3/3/1862, Volunteer	Whiteville, Columbus County, North Carolina, 45 Years Old Laborer	Co. E, 36th Regiment North Carolina, 2nd N. C. Artillery	Gunshot Wound Right Arm & Captured	Treated At Mansfield Hospital, Morehead City, N. C., Sent To Fort Delaware, Del.	Oath of Allegiance 6/19/1865,
Hildreth, Thomas Private	Fort Branch, Brunswick, County, North Carolina, 8/20/1863, Volunteer	Anson County, North Carolina, 43 Years Old	3rd Co. G, 40th Regiment, 3rd Regiment, North Carolina Light Artillery	Captured, Defended Land Face	Elmira Prison, Elmira, New York	Died of Pneumonia, 3/2/1865
Hill, Daniel J. Private	Brunswick, County, North Carolina, 1/10/64	Brunswick, County, North Carolina, Age Unknown	Co. E, 40th Regiment, 3rd Regiment, North Carolina Light Artillery	Captured	Point Lookout Prison, Maryland	Died of Pneumonia, 2/9/1865
Hill, Elias Private	Darlington, South Carolina 5/12/1862	York County, South Carolina, 43 Years Old Teamster	Co. B, 21st South Carolina Volunteers	Captured	Elmira Prison, Elmira, New York	Died Of Chronic Diarrhea 5/2/1865
Hill, Ezekiel M. Private	Smithville, Brunswick, County, North Carolina, 2/19/1862	Asheboro, Randolph County, North Carolina, 35 Years Old Farm Laborer	Co. K, 36th Regiment North Carolina, 2nd N. C. Artillery	Killed In Action 1/15/1865		
Hill, James Major	6/26/1861, Florida	Unknown	General Whiting's Staff	Captured	Fort Columbus, New York Harbor	3/5/1865 Paroled at Zarina

NAME & RANK	ENLISTED	RESIDENCE AGE & TRADE	UNIT	RESULT OF BATTLE	PRISON	PRISON RELEASE
Hill, Webb H. Private	Enfield, Halifax County, North Carolina, 10/9/1861, Volunteer	Goldsboro, Wayne County, North Carolina, 21 Years Old Detailed as blacksmith	Co. F, 36th Regiment North Carolina, 2nd N. C. Artillery	Captured	Elmira Prison, Elmira, New York	Oath of Allegiance 5/29/1865,
Hillsworth, T. Private	Date and Place Unknown	Unknown	3rd Co. G, 40th Regiment, 3rd Regiment, North Carolina Light Artillery	Captured, Defended Land Face	Prison Unknown	Release Unknown
Hines, Hugh Private	New Hanover County, North Carolina, 10/23/1861, Volunteer	New Hanover County, North Carolina, 26 Years Old	2nd Co. D, 36th Regiment North Carolina, 2nd N. C. Artillery	Wounded & Captured	Prison Unknown	Release Unknown, May Have Died of Wounds at Fort Fisher
Hines, Lewis II. Private	Craven County, North Carolina, 1/29/1862	Nash County, North Carolina, 23 Years Old	Co. F, 36th Regiment North Carolina, 2nd N. C. Artillery	Wounded & Captured	Point Lookout Prison, Maryland	Oath of Allegiance 6/27/1865,
Hinson, Eli Private	Fort Pender, Brunswick, County, North Carolina, 12/8/1863	Whiteville, Columbus County, North Carolina, 17 Years Old Farmer	Co. E, 36th Regiment North Carolina, 2nd N. C. Artillery	Captured	Elmira Prison, Elmira, New York	Oath of Allegiance 7/19/1865,
Hinson, Elias H. Corporal	Wilmington, New Hanover County, North Carolina, 3/4/1862, Volunteer	Whiteville, Columbus County, North Carolina, 21 Years Old Farmer	Co. E, 36th Regiment North Carolina, 2nd N. C. Artillery	Captured	Elmira Prison, Elmira, New York	Died of Pneumonia, 3/13/1865

NAME & RANK	ENLISTED	RESIDENCE AGE & TRADE	UNIT	RESULT OF BATTLE	PRISON	PRISON RELEASE
Hinson, Jimpsey Private	New Hanover County, North Carolina, 4/28/1864	New Hanover County, North Carolina, Age Unknown	Co. E, 36th Regiment North Carolina, 2nd N. C. Artillery	Captured	Elmira Prison, Elmira, New York	Died of Chronic Diarrhea, 3/7/1865
Hinson, John Private	Camp Harllee, South Carolina 1/1/1862	Bennettsville, Marlboro District, South Carolina, 19 Years Old Clerk	Co. A, 21st South Carolina Volunteers	Captured	Elmira Prison, Elmira, New York	Died of Pneumonia, 5/18/1865
Hinson, Joshua P. Private	Fort Anderson, Brunswick, County, North Carolina, 7/29/1863, Volunteer	Brunswick, County, North Carolina, 18 Years Old	Co. E, 36th Regiment North Carolina, 2nd N. C. Artillery	Captured	Elmira Prison, Elmira, New York	Died of Chronic Diarrhea, 4/7/1865
Hinson, Richard D. Private	Goldsboro, Wayne County, North Carolina, 4/28/1864	Goldsboro, Wayne County, North Carolina, 64 Years Old Farmer	Co. F, 10th Reg. 1st North Carolina Artillery	Captured	Elmira Prison, Elmira, New York	Oath of Allegiance 5/29/1865
Hinson, William H. Private	Bladen County, North Carolina, 3/26/1863, Volunteer	Graham, Alamance County, North Carolina, 36 Years Old	3rd Co. G, 40th Regiment North Carolina, 3rd North Carolina Artillery	Captured, Defended Land Face	Elmira Prison, Elmira, New York	Oath of Allegiance 6/12/1865
Hinton, Bernard A. Private	Bladen County, North Carolina, 10/19/1861, Volunteer	White Oak, Bladen County, North Carolina, 21 Years Old Farmer	2nd Co. I, 36th Regiment North Carolina, 2nd N. C. Artillery	Captured, Defended Shepperd's Battery	Elmira Prison, Elmira, New York	Exchanged 3/2/1865 Boulware's Wharf, James River, Virginia
Hinton, William Private	Bladen County, North Carolina, 10/19/1861	Rolesville, Wake County, North Carolina, 20 Years Old Farmer	2nd Co. I, 36th Regiment North Carolina, 2nd N. C. Artillery	Killed In Action 1/15/1865, Defended Shepperd's Battery		

NAME & RANK	ENLISTED	RESIDENCE AGE & TRADE	UNIT	RESULT OF BATTLE	PRISON	PRISON RELEASE
Hirschler, Isaac Private	Wilmington, New Hanover County, North Carolina, 7/7/1862, Volunteer	Wilmington, New Hanover County, North Carolina, 22 Years Old	Co. D, 1st Battalion, North Carolina Heavy Artillery	Captured, Defended River Road Gate	Elmira Prison, Elmira, New York	Oath of Allegiance 5/13/1865
Hobbs, George A. Corporal	Williamston Martin County, North Carolina, 3/31/1862	Hamilton, Martin County, North Carolina, Age Unknown	Co. K, 10th Reg. 1st North Carolina Artillery	Captured	Elmira Prison, Elmira, New York	Died of Phthisis, 3/21/1865
Hobbs, William W. Private	Brunswick, County, North Carolina, 12/31/1863	Sampson County, North Carolina, 17 Years Old Student	2nd Co. A, 36th Regiment North Carolina, 2nd N. C. Artillery	Captured, Defended the Mound Battery	Point Lookout Prison, Maryland	Oath of Allegiance 6/13/1865
Hockaday, Bennett Private	Fayetteville, Cumberland County, North Carolina, 2/26/1862, Volunteer	Rockfish, Hoke County, North Carolina, 26 Years Old, Detached service at Battery Gatlin	2nd Co. A, 36th Regiment North Carolina, 2nd N. C. Artillery	Captured, Defended the Mound Battery	Elmira Prison, Elmira, New York	Died of Smallpox, 3/5/1865,
Hodge, John P. Private	Whippy Swamp, South Carolina 7/15/1861	Gillisonville, St. Peter's Parrish, Beaufort District, South Carolina, 18 Years Old Farmer	Co. D, 11th South Carolina Volunteers	Captured	Elmira Prison, Elmira, New York	Oath of Allegiance 8/7/1865
Hodge, James B. Private	Camp Harlee, Georgetown South Carolina 1/1/1862	Brewington, Clarendon District, South Carolina, 23 Years Old Farmer	Co. I, 25th South Carolina Volunteers	Captured	Elmira Prison, Elmira, New York	Died Of Chronic Diarrhea 4/10/1865

NAME & RANK	ENLISTED	RESIDENCE AGE & TRADE	UNIT	RESULT OF BATTLE	PRISON	PRISON RELEASE
Hodge, Jordan Private	Union County, North Carolina, 8/27/1861	Robeson County, North Carolina, 22 Years Old Farmer	Co. E, 40th Regiment, 3rd Regiment, North Carolina Light Artillery	Captured	Point Lookout Prison, Maryland	Oath of Allegiance 5/13/1865,
Hodge, Lewis Private	Whippy Swamp, South Carolina 7/15/1861	Gillisonville, St. Peters Parrish Beaufort District, South Carolina, 22 Years Old Farmer	Co. D, 11th South Carolina Volunteers	Captured	Elmira Prison, Elmira, New York	Oath of Allegiance 7/13/1865
Hodge, Samuel D. Private	Camp Harlee, Georgetown South Carolina 1/1/1862	Clarendon District, South Carolina, 21 Years Old Farmer	Co. I, 25th South Carolina Volunteers	Captured	Elmira Prison, Elmira, New York	Died of Died Of Chronic Diarrhea 2/11/1865
Hodges, Elihue S. Private	Camp Hardee, Georgetown South Carolina 1/1/1862	Sumter District, South Carolina, 18 Years Old Farmer	Co. I, 25th South Carolina Volunteers	Captured	Elmira Prison, Elmira, New York	Exchanged 2/20/1865, Died Of Unknown Disease at Wayside Hospital No. 9, Richmond, Virginia, 3/4/1865
Hodges, James A. Private	Bladen County, North Carolina, 4/30/1862	Bladen County, North Carolina, 23 Years Old	Co. H, 36th Regiment North Carolina, 2nd N. C. Artillery	Captured	Point Lookout Prison, Maryland	Oath of Allegiance 6/28/1865
Hodges, John A. Private	New Hanover County, North Carolina, 4/30/1862	Bladen County, North Carolina, 23 Years Old Farmer	Co. H, 36th Regiment North Carolina, 2nd N. C. Artillery	Captured	Point Lookout Prison, Maryland	Exchanged Cox's Landing, James River, Virginia, 2/14/1865

NAME & RANK	ENLISTED	RESIDENCE AGE & TRADE	UNIT	RESULT OF BATTLE	PRISON	PRISON RELEASE
Hodges, John H. Private	Robeson County, North Carolina, 9/1/1863, Volunteer	Pleasant Exchange, Lumberton, North Carolina, Robeson County, North Carolina, 44 Years Old Farmer	3rd Co. B, 36th Regiment North Carolina, 2nd N. C. Artillery	Captured	Elmira Prison, Elmira, New York	Exchanged Boulware's Wharf, James River, Virginia, 3/14/1865, Died of Chronic Diarrhea, 3/27/1865, Way Hospital #2, Greensboro, N. C.
Hodges, John H. Private	Robeson County, North Carolina, Date Unknown	Lumberton, Robeson County, North Carolina, 26 Years Old Laborer	Co. K, 36th Regiment North Carolina, 2nd N. C. Artillery	Captured	Point Lookout Prison, Maryland	Oath of Allegiance 6/28/1865,
Hodges, William H. Sergeant	Georgetown South Carolina 1/1/1862	Manning, Clarendon District, South Carolina, 21 Years Old Farmer	Co. K, 21st South Carolina Volunteers	Captured	Elmira Prison, Elmira, New York	Died Of Chronic Diarrhea 3/7/1865
Hogan, Joseph C. Private	New Orleans, Louisiana, 4/13/1861	Chapel Hill, Orange County, North Carolina, 27 Years Old Farmer	Co. A, Confederate States Marine Corp, Assigned to Guard duty Aboard CSS *Savannah,* and CSS *Raleigh*	Captured, Defended Sea Face	Point Lookout Prison, Maryland	Oath of Allegiance 5/13/1865
Holden, Benjamin F. Private	Fort Caswell, Brunswick, County, North Carolina, 9/23/1862	Franklinton District, Franklin County, North Carolina, 17 Years Old Farmer	3rd Co. G, 36th Regiment North Carolina, 2nd N. C. Artillery	Killed In Action 1/15/1865, Defended Battery to the Left of Northeast Bastion		

NAME & RANK	ENLISTED	RESIDENCE AGE & TRADE	UNIT	RESULT OF BATTLE	PRISON	PRISON RELEASE
Holden, Lewis W. Seaman	Place Unknown 5/13/1862	Lockwood Folly District, Brunswick, County, North Carolina, 22 Years Old Farmer	Galloway Co. C.S. Coast Guard	Captured	Prison Unknown	Release Unknown
Holden, Nathan E. Private	Brunswick, County, North Carolina, 9/25/1862	Brunswick, County, North Carolina, 20 Years Old	3rd Co. G, 36th Regiment North Carolina, 2nd N. C. Artillery	Captured, Defended Battery to the Left of Northeast Bastion	Elmira Prison, Elmira, New York	Died of Chronic Diarrhea, 2/28/1865
Holden, Richard A. Private	Fort Fisher, New Hanover County, North Carolina, 2/28/1864, Volunteer	Brunswick County, North Carolina, 17 Years Old	3rd Co. G, 36th Regiment North Carolina, 2nd N. C. Artillery	Wounded & Captured, Defended Battery to the Left of Northeast Bastion	Elmira Prison, Elmira, New York	Oath of Allegiance 7/3/1865
Holden, Richard W. Private	Fort Caswell, Brunswick, County, North Carolina, 8/24/1863	Brunswick, County, North Carolina, 42 Years Old	3rd Co. G, 36th Regiment North Carolina, 2nd N. C. Artillery	Gunshot Wound, Right Breast & Captured, Defended Battery to the Left of Northeast Bastion	Treated At Mansfield Hospital, Morehead City, N. C., Sent To Fort Delaware Prison, Del.	Taken North To Morehead City on Steamer USS Champion 1/17/1865, Oath of Allegiance 6/19/1865
Holden, Richard W., Jr. Private	Fort Campbell, Brunswick, County, North Carolina, 10/9/1863, Volunteer	Brunswick, County, North Carolina, 18 Years Old	3rd Co. G, 36th Regiment North Carolina, 2nd N. C. Artillery	Wounded & Captured,	Elmira Prison, Elmira, New York	Exchanged 2/20/1865, Died of Chronic Diarrhea, 3/12/1865, Howard Grove Hospital, Richmond, Virginia
Holland, Matthew Private	Clinton, Sampson County, North Carolina, 2/9/1863, Volunteer	Clinton, Sampson County, North Carolina, 36 Years Old Farmer	2nd Co. C, 36th Regiment North Carolina, 2nd N. C. Artillery	Captured, Defended River Road Gate	Elmira Prison, Elmira, New York	Died of Chronic Diarrhea, 4/7/1865

NAME & RANK	ENLISTED	RESIDENCE AGE & TRADE	UNIT	RESULT OF BATTLE	PRISON	PRISON RELEASE
Hollowman Alfred B. Private	Lillington, Harnett County, North Carolina, 4/30/1862	Harnett County, North Carolina, 25 Years Old	2nd Co. C, 36th Regiment North Carolina, 2nd N. C. Artillery	Captured, Defended River Road Gate	Point Lookout Prison, Maryland	Oath of Allegiance 6/27/1865
Holmes, William E. Corporal	Charleston, South Carolina, 5/9/1862	Spartanburg, South Carolina, 27 Years Old	Co. A, 25th South Carolina Volunteers	Captured	Elmira Prison, Elmira, New York	Oath of Allegiance 6/19/1865
Holstein, Joseph A. Private	James Island, South Carolina 4/21/1863	Ridge, Edgefield District, South Carolina, 17 Years Old Farmer	Co. G, 21st South Carolina Volunteers	Captured	Elmira Prison, Elmira, New York	Died of Chronic Diarrhea, 3/7/1865
Holt, Thomas Lewis Private	Alamance County, North Carolina, Date Unknown	Alamance County, North Carolina, Age Unknown	3rd Co. B, 36th Regiment North Carolina, 2nd N. C. Artillery	Captured	Point Lookout Prison, Maryland	Oath of Allegiance 6/13/1865
Honett, S. R. Private	Date and Place Unknown	Unknown	Co. K, 36th Regiment North Carolina, 2nd N. C. Artillery	Captured	Prison Unknown	Release Unknown
Honeycutt, Hillery H. Private	Wilmington, New Hanover County, North Carolina, 7/23/1863, Volunteer	Sampson County, North Carolina, 42 Years Old	3rd Co. G, 40th Regiment, 3rd Regiment, North Carolina Light Artillery	Captured, Defended Land Face	Elmira Prison, Elmira, New York	Exchanged 3/2/1865 Boulware's Wharf, James River, Virginia
Hood, Ezekiel Lieutenant	Goldsboro, Wayne County, North Carolina, 7/22/1861, Volunteer	Falling Creek, Cross Roads District, Wayne County, North Carolina, 19 Years Old Farmer	Co. F, 10th Reg. 1st North Carolina Artillery	Severely Wounded & Captured	Fort Columbus, New York Harbor,	Exchanged 2/25/1865, City Point, Virginia

NAME & RANK	ENLISTED	RESIDENCE AGE & TRADE	UNIT	RESULT OF BATTLE	PRISON	PRISON RELEASE
Hook, Samuel P. Private	Coles Island, South Carolina 4/11/1862	Saluda Town, Columbia, Lexington County, South Carolina, 21 Years Old	Co. D, 25th South Carolina Volunteers	Captured	Elmira Prison, Elmira, New York	Died of Pneumonia, 3/8/1865
Hooker, Henry H. First Lieutenant	Craven County, North Carolina, 10/28/1861, Volunteer	Swift Creek, North of Neuse River, Craven County, North Carolina, 32 Years Old Farmer	Co. D, 40th Regiment, 3rd Regiment, North Carolina Light Artillery	Captured	Fort Columbus, New York Harbor,	Exchanged Boulware's Wharf, James River, Virginia, 3/5/1865
Horn, Arthur Private	Bladen County, North Carolina, 5/15/1863	Ellisville, Bladen County, North Carolina, 36 Years Old Farmer	2nd Co. C, 36th Regiment North Carolina, 2nd N. C. Artillery	Killed In Action 1/15/1865, Defended River Road Gate		
Horn, Little Berry Private	Wilmington, New Hanover County, North Carolina, 3/5/1862, Volunteer	Columbus County, North Carolina, 33 Years Old	Co. E, 36th Regiment North Carolina, 2nd N. C. Artillery	Captured	Elmira Prison, Elmira, New York	Exchanged 2/20/1865
Horn, W. W. Private	Gourdins Dept., South Carolina 5/11/1862	Kingston, South Carolina, 38 Years Old	Co. K, 25th South Carolina Volunteers	Captured	Elmira Prison, Elmira, New York	Oath of Allegiance 7/11/1865
Horne, Daniel W. Private	Fort Fisher, New Hanover County, North Carolina, 5/7/1862, Volunteer	New Hanover County, North Carolina, 31 Years Old	2nd Co. C, 36th Regiment North Carolina, 2nd N. C. Artillery	Captured, Defended River Road Gate	Elmira Prison, Elmira, New York	Died of Smallpox, 3/26/1865

306

NAME & RANK	ENLISTED	RESIDENCE AGE & TRADE	UNIT	RESULT OF BATTLE	PRISON	PRISON RELEASE
Horne, George T. Private	New Hanover County, North Carolina, 5/7/1862, Volunteer	Downingsville Bladen County, North Carolina, 21 Years Old Turpentine	2nd Co. C, 36th Regiment North Carolina, 2nd N. C. Artillery	Severe Gunshot Wound Right Ankle & Captured	Fort Delaware Prison, Del.	Oath of Allegiance 6/19/1865, Defended River Road Gate
Horne, William J. Private	Fort Fisher, New Hanover County, North Carolina, 7/26/1863, Volunteer	Downingsville Bladen County, North Carolina, 18 Years Old Farmer	2nd Co. C, 36th Regiment North Carolina, 2nd N. C. Artillery	Captured, Defended River Road Gate	Elmira Prison, Elmira, New York	Died of Chronic Diarrhea, 3/7/1865
Horton, George P. Private	Fort Holmes, North Carolina, 6/29/1864	Oak Spring, Flint Hill District, Rutherford County, North Carolina, 24 Years Old Farmer	3rd Co. G, 40th Regiment, 3rd Regiment, North Carolina Light Artillery	Captured, Defended Land Face	Elmira Prison, Elmira, New York	Oath of Allegiance 6/12/1865
House, George A. Private	Pee Dee, South Carolina 4/28/1862	Darlington District, South Carolina, 32 Years Old	Co. K, 21st South Carolina Volunteers	Killed In Action 1/15/1865		
House, John H. Private	Brunswick, County, North Carolina, 9/15/1863, Volunteer	Halifax County, North Carolina, 18 Years Old	Co. F, 36th Regiment North Carolina, 2nd N. C. Artillery	Captured	Elmira Prison, Elmira, New York	Oath of Allegiance 7/7/1865
Howard, Lorenzo Private	New Hanover County, North Carolina, 9/29/1863	Magnolia, Duplin County, North Carolina, 18 Years Old Farmer	Co. D, 1st Battalion, North Carolina Heavy Artillery	Captured, Defended River Road Gate	Point Lookout Prison, Maryland	Exchanged Boulware's Wharf, James River, Virginia, 2/21/1865
Howard, William Private	Duplin County, North Carolina, 9/1/1864	Magnolia, Duplin County, North Carolina, 18 Years Old Farmer	Co. D, 1st Battalion, North Carolina Heavy Artillery	Captured, Defended River Road Gate	Elmira Prison, Elmira, New York	Died of Chronic Diarrhea, 5/1/1865,

NAME & RANK	ENLISTED	RESIDENCE AGE & TRADE	UNIT	RESULT OF BATTLE	PRISON	PRISON RELEASE
Howell, Curtis D. Private	Goldsboro, Wayne County, North Carolina, 9/20/1862	Goldsboro, Stony Creek District, Wayne County, North Carolina, 18 Years Old Farmer	Co. F, 10th Reg. 1st North Carolina Artillery	Captured	Elmira Prison, Elmira, New York	Oath of Allegiance 5/29/1865
Howell, Levi D. Private	Goldsboro, Wayne County, North Carolina 3/8/1864	Goldsboro, Fork District, Wayne County, North Carolina, 43 Years Old	Co. F, 10th Reg. 1st North Carolina Artillery	Captured	Elmira Prison, Elmira, New York	Died of Chronic Diarrhea, 5/22/1865,
Howell, Richard Mills Private	Beaufort, Carteret County, North Carolina 6/28/1861	Goldsboro, Fork District, Wayne County, North Carolina, 22 Years Old Farm Laborer	Co. F, 10th Reg. 1st North Carolina Artillery	Wounded & Captured	Elmira Prison, Elmira, New York	Exchanged 2/20/1865
Howell, Ralph Private	Wilmington, New Hanover County, North Carolina, 3/3/1862	Fayetteville, Cumberland County, North Carolina, 22 Years Old	2nd Co. D, 36th Regiment North Carolina, 2nd N. C. Artillery	Captured	Elmira Prison, Elmira, New York	Oath of Allegiance 7/7/1865
Howenton, Alexander Private	Enfield, Halifax County, North Carolina, 10/9/1861	Tarboro, Edgecombe County, North Carolina, 25 Years Old Farmer	Co. F, 36th Regiment North Carolina, 2nd N. C. Artillery	Gunshot Wound Left Arm & Captured	Point Lookout Prison Hospital, Maryland	Oath of Allegiance 6/3/1865
Howinson, William Private	Date and Place Unknown	Unknown	Co. D, 40th Regiment, 3rd Regiment, North Carolina Light Artillery	Gunshot Wound Right Thigh & Captured	Prison Unknown	Date Of Release Unknown

NAME & RANK	ENLISTED	RESIDENCE AGE & TRADE	UNIT	RESULT OF BATTLE	PRISON	PRISON RELEASE
Hubbard, John B. Private	Date and Place Unknown	Martin's Creek, Pickens District, South Carolina, 16 Years Old	Co. H, 25th South Carolina Volunteers	Captured	Elmira Prison, Elmira, New York	Oath of Allegiance 7/19/1865
Hucks, Henry K. Captain	Whippy Swamp, South Carolina 7/15/1861	Prince William Parish, Pocotaligo, South Carolina, 25 Years Old Engineer	Co. D, 11th South Carolina Volunteers	Captured	Fort Columbus, New York Harbor,	Exchanged 2/25/1865
Hudgins, William G. First Lieutenant	Confederate States Navy, 5/26/1863	Mathews County, Virginia, Age Unknown	Confederate States Navy, Assigned Duty on CSS *Savannah*.	Wounded in Mouth by Shell Fragment & Captured, Defended Sea Face	Fort Monroe, Va.	Exchanged 4/26/1865
Hudson, Benajah Private	Sampson County, North Carolina, 9/5/1863	Newton Grove, Sampson County, North Carolina, 41 Years Old Farmer	2nd Co. A, 36th Regiment North Carolina, 2nd N. C. Artillery	Captured, Defended the Mound Battery	Point Lookout Prison, Maryland	Died of Chronic Diarrhea, 5/22/1865
Hudson, Holly Private	Brunswick County, North Carolina, 11/13/1863, Volunteer	Newton Grove, Sampson County, North Carolina, 18 Years Old Farmer	2nd Co. A, 36th Regiment North Carolina, 2nd N. C. Artillery	Wounded & Captured, Defended the Mound Battery	Point Lookout Prison, Maryland	Oath of Allegiance 6/13/1865
Hudson, Seth H. Private	Cabarrus County, North Carolina, 4/8/1863	Concord, Cabarrus County, North Carolina, 39 Years Old Farmer	Co. C, 3rd Battalion, North Carolina Light Artillery	Captured Hospital at Fort Caswell, North Carolina	Point Lookout Prison, Maryland	Oath of Allegiance 5/13/1865
Hudson, Thomas Private	Fort Johnson, South Carolina 9/8/1863	Darlington District, South Carolina, 27 Years Old Farmer	Co. K, 21st South Carolina Volunteers	Captured	Elmira Prison, Elmira, New York	Oath of Allegiance 6/30/1865

NAME & RANK	ENLISTED	RESIDENCE AGE & TRADE	UNIT	RESULT OF BATTLE	PRISON	PRISON RELEASE
Huff, George B. Private	Date and Place Unknown	Unknown	Co. E, Confederate States Marine Corp, Assigned to Guard Duty Aboard CSS *Savannah* and CSS *Georgia.*	Captured, Defended Sea Face	Point Lookout Prison, Maryland	Oath of Allegiance 5/12/1865
Huffman, Andrew Private	Coles Island, South Carolina 4/11/1862	St. Matthews, Orangeburg District, South Carolina, 24 Years Old	Co. F, 25th South Carolina Volunteers	Captured	Elmira Prison, Elmira, New York	Died of Chronic Diarrhea, 4/6/1865
Huffman, D. J. Private	Coles Island, South Carolina 4/11/1862	Louisville, South Carolina, 38 Years Old	Co. F, 25th South Carolina Volunteers	Captured	Elmira Prison, Elmira, New York	Oath of Allegiance 7/11/1865
Huffman, Milton Private	Camp Wyatt, New Hanover County, North Carolina, 4/14/1864	New Hanover County, North Carolina, 18 Years Old	2nd Co. D, 36th Regiment North Carolina, 2nd N. C. Artillery	Captured	Elmira Prison, Elmira, New York, Recaptured and Sent to Point Lookout, Maryland 5/2/1865	Exchanged 3/14/1865, Captured in Jackson Hospital, Richmond, Va, 4/3/1865, Released 6/28/1865
Huggins, Christopher Private	Marion District, South Carolina 2/21/1862	Mullins Depot, South Carolina, 24 Years Old	Co. K, 21st South Carolina Volunteers	Captured	Elmira Prison, Elmira, New York	Oath of Allegiance 6/23/1865
Huggins, William Private	Marion District, South Carolina 5/21/1862	Richland County, South Carolina, 23 Years Old	Co. L, 21st South Carolina Volunteers	Killed In Action 1/15/1865		

NAME & RANK	ENLISTED	RESIDENCE AGE & TRADE	UNIT	RESULT OF BATTLE	PRISON	PRISON RELEASE
Hunnings, Robert L. Private	Craven County, North Carolina, 9/21/1861	Newbern, Craven County, North Carolina, 19 Years Old Shoemaker	Co. D, 40th Regiment, 3rd Regiment, North Carolina Light Artillery	Captured	Point Lookout Prison, Maryland	Oath of Allegiance 5/13/1865
Hunnings, William W. Private	Craven County, North Carolina, 9/28/1861	Newbern, Craven County, North Carolina, 21 Years Old Farm Hand	Co. D, 40th Regiment, 3rd Regiment, North Carolina Light Artillery	Mortal Gunshot Wound of the Anus, exiting the Right Groin & Captured	Point Lookout Prison, Maryland	Died of Wounds 2/14/1865
Hunter, Exum Lewis First Lieutenant	Halifax County, North Carolina, 2/1/1862	Enfield, Halifax County, North Carolina, 25 Years Old, Company Commander	Co. F, 36th Regiment North Carolina, 2nd N. C. Artillery	Captured	Fort Columbus, New York Harbor	Exchanged Boulware's Wharf, James River, Virginia, 3/5/1865
Hunter, James T. B. Private	Enfield, Halifax County, North Carolina, 10/9/1861 Volunteer	Enfield, Halifax County, North Carolina, 20 Years Old Clerk	Co. F, 36th Regiment North Carolina, 2nd N. C. Artillery	Killed In Action 1/15/1865		
Hunter, William W. Private	Lenoir County, North Carolina, 10/16/1861	Kinston, Lenoir County, North Carolina, 19 Years Old	3rd Co. G, 40th Regiment, 3rd Regiment, North Carolina Artillery	Captured, Defended Land Face	Elmira Prison, New York	Oath of Allegiance 6/12/1865
Huntley, Elijah D. Corporal	Fort Branch, Brunswick, County, North Carolina, 7/20/1863	Wadesboro, Anson County, North Carolina, 30 Years Old Farmer	3rd Co. G, 40th Regiment, 3rd Regiment, North Carolina Artillery	Captured, Defended Land Face	Elmira Prison, New York	Exchanged Boulware's Wharf, James River, Virginia, 3/14/1865

NAME & RANK	ENLISTED	RESIDENCE AGE & TRADE	UNIT	RESULT OF BATTLE	PRISON	PRISON RELEASE
Hussey, John B. Private	Brunswick, County, North Carolina, 9/9/1863, Volunteer	Kenansville, Duplin County, North Carolina, 19 Years Old Student	2nd Co. C, 36th Regiment, North Carolina, 2nd N. C. Artillery	Gunshot Wound, Left Arm and Left Hip & Captured	Treated At Mansfield Hospital, Morehead City, N. C., Sent To Ft. Delaware Prison, Del.	Oath of Allegiance 6/19/1865, Defended River Road Gate
Hutchinson B. Private	Date and Place Unknown	Unknown	2nd Co. A, 36th Regiment, North Carolina, 2nd N. C. Artillery	Captured, Defended the Mound Battery	Prison Unknown	Date Of Release Unknown
Hutchinson H. Private	Date and Place Unknown	Unknown	2nd Co. A, 36th Regiment, North Carolina, 2nd N. C. Artillery	Captured, Defended the Mound Battery	Prison Unknown	Date Of Release Unknown
Hux, Benjamin G. Private	Fort Caswell, Brunswick, County, North Carolina, 6/18/1863	Western District, Halifax County, North Carolina, 17 Years Old Farmer	Co. F, 36th Regiment, North Carolina, 2nd N. C. Artillery	Captured	Elmira Prison, New York	Oath of Allegiance 7/26/1865
Hux, Francis M. Private	Fort Caswell, Brunswick, County, North Carolina, 10/10/1863	Enfield, Halifax County, North Carolina, 18 Years Old Farmer	Co. F, 36th Regiment, North Carolina, 2nd N. C. Artillery	Wounded, Left Ear Taken Off By Shell Causing Deafness, Captured	Point Lookout Prison Hospital, Maryland	Oath of Allegiance 7/28/1865
Hux, Gardner H. Private	Halifax County, North Carolina, 10/25/1864	Western District, Halifax County, North Carolina, 15 Years Old Farmer	Co. F, 36th Regiment, North Carolina, 2nd N. C. Artillery	Captured	Elmira Prison, New York	Oath of Allegiance 6/23/1865

NAME & RANK	ENLISTED	RESIDENCE AGE & TRADE	UNIT	RESULT OF BATTLE	PRISON	PRISON RELEASE
Inabet, Andrew J. Private	Coles Island, South Carolina 4/11/1862	St. Matthews, Orangeburg, South Carolina, 41 Years Old	Co. G, 25th South Carolina Volunteers	Captured	Elmira Prison, Elmira, New York	Oath of Allegiance 6/23/1865
Inabet, Charles G. Private	Coles Island, South Carolina 4/11/1862	Orangeburg, South Carolina, Age Unknown	Co. G, 25th South Carolina Volunteers	Captured	Elmira Prison, Elmira, New York	Oath of Allegiance 7/7/1865
Ingram, William G. Private	Northampton County, North Carolina, 2/3/1862, Volunteer	Gaston, Northampton County, North Carolina, 19 Years Old Farmer	Co. C, 3rd Battalion North Carolina Light Artillery	Gunshot Wound Left side of Hip & Captured	Point Lookout, Maryland	Oath of Allegiance 6/14/1865
Inman, Alexander Private	Brunswick County, North Carolina, 10/5/1863	Lumberton, Robison County, North Carolina, 40 Years Old Farmer	Co. E, 40th Regiment N. C., 3rd N. C. Artillery	Captured	Point Lookout, Maryland	Died of Pneumonia, 3/9/1865
Ipock, Albert Sergeant	Craven County, North Carolina, 1/23/1862	Craven County, North Carolina, 27 Years Old	Co. D, 40th Regiment N. C., 3rd N. C. Artillery	Captured	Point Lookout, Maryland	Died of Disease of Heart, 2/18/1865
Irby, William Private	Fort Caswell, Brunswick County, North Carolina, 2/2/1863	Enfield, Halifax County, North Carolina, 18 Years Old	Co. F, 36th Regiment North Carolina, 2nd N. C. Artillery	Captured	Elmira Prison, Elmira, New York	Oath of Allegiance 6/12/1865, Enlisted As a Substitute
Ireland, Wesley F. Private	Alamance County, North Carolina, 2/15/1864	Alamance County, North Carolina, 18 Years Old	3rd Co. B, 36th Regiment North Carolina, 2nd N. C. Artillery	Captured	Point Lookout, Maryland	Oath of Allegiance 6/3/1865

NAME & RANK	ENLISTED	RESIDENCE AGE & TRADE	UNIT	RESULT OF BATTLE	PRISON	PRISON RELEASE
Irick, Elliott H. Private	Secession-ville, South Carolina 5/1/1862	St. Matthews, Orangeburg, South Carolina, 32 Years Old Farmer	Co. G, 25th South Carolina Volunteers	Captured	Elmira Prison, Elmira, New York	Exchanged 2/20/1865
Irick, Laban A. Private	Coles Island, South Carolina 4/15/1862	Orangeburg, South Carolina, Age Unknown	Co. G, 25th South Carolina Volunteers	Captured	Elmira Prison, Elmira, New York	Oath of Allegiance 7/11/1865
Ivey, John A. Private	Fort Fisher, New Hanover County, North Carolina, 12/21/1861	New Hanover County, North Carolina, 46 Years Old, Dispatch Bearer in Fort Fisher Telegraph Office	2nd Co. I, 36th Regiment North Carolina, 2nd N. C. Artillery	Captured, Defended Shepperd's Battery	Elmira Prison, Elmira, New York	Exchanged 3/2/1865 Boulware's Wharf, James River, Virginia
Ivey, Richard Private	Bladen County, North Carolina, 3/26/1862	Bladen County, North Carolina, 18 Years Old Farmer	Co. H, 36th Regiment North Carolina, 2nd N. C. Artillery	Captured	Point Lookout, Maryland	Oath of Allegiance 6/5/1865
Ivey, W. Private	Date and Place Unknown	Unknown	Co. H, 36th Regiment North Carolina, 2nd N. C. Artillery	Captured	Point Lookout, Maryland	Oath of Allegiance 6/5/1865
Izlar, Adolphus M. Private	Coles Island, South Carolina 4/11/1862	Unknown	Co. G, 25th South Carolina Volunteers	Captured	Elmira Prison, Elmira, New York	Exchanged 3/14/1865
Izlar, Benjamin P. First Sergeant	Coles Island, South Carolina 4/11/1862	Orangeburg, South Carolina, 25 Years Old Teacher	Co. G, 25th South Carolina Volunteers	Captured	Elmira Prison, Elmira, New York	Oath of Allegiance 6/14/1865

NAME & RANK	ENLISTED	RESIDENCE AGE & TRADE	UNIT	RESULT OF BATTLE	PRISON	PRISON RELEASE
Izlar, James F. Captain	Coles Island, South Carolina 4/11/1862	Unknown	Co. G, 25th South Carolina Volunteers	Captured	Fort Columbus, New York Harbor	Exchanged 2/25/1865

NAME & RANK	ENLISTED	RESIDENCE AGE & TRADE	UNIT	RESULT OF BATTLE	PRISON	PRISON RELEASE
Jackson, Alfred W. Private	Fort Fisher, New Hanover County, North Carolina, 10/25/1863	Fayetteville, Cumberland County, North Carolina, 37 Years Old Farmer	Co. E, 36th Regiment North Carolina, 2nd N. C. Artillery	Captured	Elmira Prison, New York	Exchanged 3/2/1865 Died of Chronic Diarrhea 3/24/1865 at Way Hospital #1, Weldon, N. C.
Jackson, Allen M. Private	Fort Fisher, New Hanover County, North Carolina, 5/6/1863	Fayetteville, Cumberland County, North Carolina, 42 Years Old Farmer	Co. E, 36th Regiment North Carolina, 2nd N. C. Artillery	Captured	Elmira Prison, New York	Oath of Allegiance 7/3/1865
Jackson, Blackman Private	Sampson County, North Carolina, 2/18/1863	Dismal District, Sampson County, North Carolina, 34 Years Old, Farm Laborer	2nd Co. A, 36th Regiment North Carolina, 2nd N. C. Artillery	Captured, Defended the Mound Battery	Elmira Prison, New York	Exchanged 3/21/1865, Boulware's Wharf, James River, Virginia
Jackson, George W. Private	Bladen County, North Carolina, 8/20/1864	Bladen County, North Carolina, 32 Years Old Turpentine	2nd Co. I, 36th Regiment North Carolina, 2nd N. C. Artillery	Captured, Defended Shepperd's Battery	Point Lookout Prison, Maryland	Oath of Allegiance 6/28/1865
Jackson, James Private Bugler	Sampson County, North Carolina, 2/18/1863	Sampson County, North Carolina, Farmer, 38 Years Old Mason	Co. D, 13th Battalion, North Carolina Light Artillery	Mortal Gunshot Wound Left Knee and Thigh, & Captured, Defended River Road Gate	Point Lookout Prison Hospital, Maryland	Died of Wounds 2/5/1865

NAME & RANK	ENLISTED	RESIDENCE AGE & TRADE	UNIT	RESULT OF BATTLE	PRISON	PRISON RELEASE
Jackson, John N. Private	Sampson County, North Carolina, 2/18/1863	Northern Division, Sampson County, North Carolina, 36 Years Old Laborer	2nd Co. A, 36th Regiment North Carolina, 2nd N. C. Artillery	Captured, Defended the Mound Battery	Point Lookout Prison, Maryland	Oath of Allegiance 6/3/1865
Jackson, Nathan H. Private	Sampson County, North Carolina, 2/18/1863	Mingo District, Sampson County, North Carolina, 38 Years Old Farmer	2nd Co. A, 36th Regiment North Carolina, 2nd N. C. Artillery	Captured, Defended the Mound Battery	Elmira Prison, New York	Died of Pneumonia, 2/11/1865
Jackson, Newette Private	Union County, North Carolina, 8/27/1861	Unknown, 20 Years Old	Co. E, 40th Regiment North Carolina Artillery	Severe Gunshot Wound Right Thigh & Captured	Point Lookout Prison General Hospital, Maryland	Oath of Allegiance 6/5/1865
Jackson, Olin Private	Sampson County, North Carolina, 7/22/1862	Northern Mingo District, Sampson County, North Carolina, 18 Years Old Farmer	2nd Co. A, 36th Regiment North Carolina, 2nd N. C. Artillery	Captured, Defended the Mound Battery	Point Lookout Prison, Maryland	Oath of Allegiance 6/28/1865
Jackson, Olline C. Private	Brunswick County, North Carolina 1/3/1864	Northern District, Sampson County, North Carolina, 18 Years Old Farmer	2nd Co. A, 36th Regiment North Carolina, 2nd N. C. Artillery	Captured, Defended the Mound Battery	Point Lookout Prison, Maryland	Oath of Allegiance 6/28/1865
Jackson, Wiley Private	Brunswick County, North Carolina, 1/4/1864	Fayetteville, Cumberland County, North Carolina, 18 Years Old	2nd Co. A, 36th Regiment North Carolina, 2nd N. C. Artillery	Captured, Defended the Mound Battery	Point Lookout Prison, Maryland	Oath of Allegiance 6/14/1865
Jackson, William A. Private	Sampson County, North Carolina, 2/18/1863	Sampson County, North Carolina, 34 Years Old Farmer	2nd Co. A, 36th Regiment North Carolina, 2nd N. C. Artillery	Captured, Defended the Mound Battery	Point Lookout Prison, Maryland	Oath of Allegiance 6/28/1865

NAME & RANK	ENLISTED	RESIDENCE AGE & TRADE	UNIT	RESULT OF BATTLE	PRISON	PRISON RELEASE
Jacobs, Snowden Private	Bennetts-ville, South Carolina 12/25/1861	Bennettsville, Marlboro District, South Carolina, 24 Years Old	Co. F, 21st South Carolina Volunteers	Captured	Elmira Prison, Elmira, New York	Oath of Allegiance 7/7/1865
James, H. V. Private	James Island, South Carolina 6/23/1863	Madisonville, Florida, Age Unknown	Co. H, 25th South Carolina Volunteers	Captured	Elmira Prison, Elmira, New York	Oath of Allegiance 7/19/1865
Jeffords, Joseph B. Private	Pee Dee, South Carolina 2/20/1862	Timmonsville, Darlington District, South Carolina, 26 Years Old Carpenter	Co. K, 21st South Carolina Volunteers	Captured	Elmira Prison, Elmira, New York	Oath of Allegiance 7/3/1865
Jeller, F. A. Private	Date and Place Unknown	Unknown	3rd Co. G, 36th Regiment North Carolina, 2nd N. C. Artillery	Captured	Prison Unknown	Release Unknown
Jenerett, Isaac Private	Brunswick County, North Carolina, 1/4/1864	Brunswick County, North Carolina, 33 Years Old	Co. K, 36th Regiment North Carolina, 2nd N. C. Artillery	Captured	Point Lookout Prison, Maryland	Oath of Allegiance 6/27/1865
Jenkins, Charles T. Private	Hertford County, North Carolina, 6/1/1863	Hertford County, North Carolina, Age Unknown	Co. I, 3rd Battalion North Carolina Artillery	Gunshot Wound of Right Wrist & Captured	Point Lookout Prison, Maryland	Amputation Right Forearm, Oath of Allegiance 6/3/1865
Jenkins, James E. Private	Hertford County, North Carolina, 8/23/1864	Murfreesboro, Hertford County, North Carolina, 48 Years Old Day Laborer	Co. I, 3rd Battalion North Carolina Artillery	Killed in Action, 1/15/1865		

NAME & RANK	ENLISTED	RESIDENCE AGE & TRADE	UNIT	RESULT OF BATTLE	PRISON	PRISON RELEASE
Jenkins, M. G. Private	Warren County, North Carolina, Date Unknown	Warrenton, Warren County, North Carolina, 35 Years Old	Co. F, 36th Regiment North Carolina, 2nd N. C. Artillery	Captured	Point Lookout Prison, Maryland	Oath of Allegiance 6/28/1865
Jenkins, Samuel Private	Fort Branch, Brunswick County, North Carolina, 8/19/1863	Ragland District, Granville County, North Carolina, 41 Years Old Farmer	3rd Co. G, 40th Regiment North Carolina Artillery	Captured, Defended Land Face	Elmira Prison, Elmira, New York	Oath of Allegiance 6/23/1865
Jernigan, Elijah W. Private	New Hanover County, North Carolina, 3/5/1862	Columbus County, North Carolina, 23 Years Old	2nd Co. D, 36th Regiment North Carolina, 2nd N. C. Artillery	Captured	Point Lookout Prison, Maryland	Oath of Allegiance 6/28/1865
Jernigan, Isaac Private	New Hanover County, North Carolina, 3/5/1862	Columbus County, North Carolina, 20 Years Old	2nd Co. D, 36th Regiment North Carolina, 2nd N. C. Artillery	Captured	Point Lookout Prison, Maryland	Oath of Allegiance 6/28/1865
Jernigan, Levi S. Private	New Hanover County, North Carolina, 3/5/1862	Columbus County, North Carolina, 23 Years Old	2nd Co. D, 36th Regiment North Carolina, 2nd N. C. Artillery	Captured	Point Lookout Prison, Maryland	Oath of Allegiance 6/28/1865
Jessup, James H. Private	New Hanover County, North Carolina, 8/1/1864	Elizabethtown Bladen County, North Carolina, 16 Years Old Farmer	Co. H, 36th Regiment North Carolina, 2nd N. C. Artillery	Wounded & Captured, 1/15/1865	Prison Unknown	Release Unknown

NAME & RANK	ENLISTED	RESIDENCE AGE & TRADE	UNIT	RESULT OF BATTLE	PRISON	PRISON RELEASE
Jessup, Jasper N. Corporal	Brunswick County, North Carolina, 7/7/1862, Volunteer	White Oak, Bladen County, North Carolina, 33 Years Old Farmer	2nd Co. K, 40th Regiment North Carolina Artillery	Mortal Gunshot Wound Of Face and Scalp & Captured	Treated At Mansfield Hospital Morehead City, North Carolina	Died of Wounds 3/21/1865
Jessup, Thomas H. Private	Bladen County, North Carolina, 10/19/1861	Elizabethtown Bladen County, North Carolina, 17 Years Old Farmer	2nd Co. I, 36th Regiment North Carolina, 2nd N. C. Artillery	Captured, Defended Shepperd's Battery	Point Lookout Prison, Maryland	Oath of Allegiance 6/28/1865
Jewitt, J. Private	Date and Place Unknown	Unknown	Co. K, 36th Regiment North Carolina, 2nd N. C. Artillery	Captured	Prison Unknown	Release Unknown
Johnson, Amos Private	Robeson County, North Carolina, 1/25/1862	Fayetteville, Cumberland County, North Carolina, 28 Years Old Cooper	3rd Co. B, 36th Regiment North Carolina, 2nd N. C. Artillery	Captured	Elmira Prison, Elmira, New York	Died of Chronic Diarrhea 4/16/1865
Johnson, Amos Neil Private	New Hanover County, North Carolina, 1/21/1864	Lisbon District, Sampson County, North Carolina, 44 Years Old Farmer	2nd Co. K, 40th Regiment North Carolina Artillery	Captured	Point Lookout Prison, Maryland	Oath of Allegiance 6/28/1865
Johnson, Daniel T. Private	Brunswick County, North Carolina, 4/30/1862	Northwest District, Brunswick County, North Carolina, 37 Years Old Laborer	3rd Co. G, 36th Regiment North Carolina, 2nd N. C. Artillery	Mortally Wounded In Both Arms & Captured, Defended Battery to the Left of Northeast Bastion	Point Lookout Prison, Maryland	Wounded Both arms, Right Arm Amputated, Died Of Wounds 2/28/1865

NAME & RANK	ENLISTED	RESIDENCE AGE & TRADE	UNIT	RESULT OF BATTLE	PRISON	PRISON RELEASE
Johnson, James Private	Fort Fisher, New Hanover County, North Carolina, 5/16/1863	Unknown. 18 Years Old	2nd Co. C, 36th Regiment North Carolina, 2nd N. C. Artillery	Captured, Defended River Road Gate	Elmira Prison, Elmira, New York	Exchanged 2/20/1865
Johnson, James F. Private	Craven County, North Carolina, 5/16/1863	Goldsboro, Wayne County, North Carolina, 27 Years Old Farmer	Co. D, 40th Regiment North Carolina Artillery	Killed in Action, 1/15/1865		
Johnson, James H. Private	Carteret County, North Carolina, 7/21/1861	Wayne County, North Carolina, 25 Years Old Farmer	Co. F, 10th Regiment North Carolina Artillery	Wounded Right Arm, 12/24/1864	None	
Johnson, James Henry Sergeant	Goldsboro, Wayne County, North Carolina, 7/21/1861	Goldsboro, Wayne, County, North Carolina, 23 Years Old Farmer	Co. F, 10th Regiment North Carolina Artillery	Captured	Elmira Prison, Elmira, New York	Oath of Allegiance 7/13/1865
Johnson, John B. Private	Marion City Hall, South Carolina 4/20/1864	Marion County, South Carolina, 17 Years Old	Co. D, 25th South Carolina Volunteers	Mortally Wounded, Gunshot Wound In Rectum and Abdomen & Captured	Point Lookout Prison, Maryland	Died Of Wounds 4/8/1865
Johnson, John Private	Goldsboro, Wayne County, North Carolina, 7/9/1861	Goldsboro, Wayne County, North Carolina, 45 Years Old	Co. F, 10th Regiment North Carolina Artillery	Captured	Elmira Prison, Elmira, New York	Oath of Allegiance 7/11/1865
Johnson, John A. Private	Fort Fisher, New Hanover County, North Carolina, 1/6/1863,	Summerville, Harnett County, North Carolina, 18 Years Old Farmer	2nd Co. C, 36th Regiment North Carolina, 2nd N. C. Artillery	Captured, Defended River Road Gate	Elmira Prison, Elmira, New York	Died from Dysentery, 2/23/1865

NAME & RANK	ENLISTED	RESIDENCE AGE & TRADE	UNIT	RESULT OF BATTLE	PRISON	PRISON RELEASE
Johnson, John F. Private	Marrion City Hall, South Carolina 4/20/1862	Unknown, 16 Years Old	Co. D, 25th South Carolina Volunteers	Captured	Elmira Prison, Elmira, New York	Exchanged On The James River 2/20/1865
Johnson, John J. Private	Camp Harlee, Georgetown South Carolina 1/1/1862	Unknown, 38 Years Old	Co. D, 25th South Carolina Volunteers	Captured	Elmira Prison, Elmira, New York	Died from Remittant Fever, 2/16/1865
Johnson, Larry Private	Wayne County, North Carolina, 7/8/1861	Goldsboro, Wayne County, North Carolina, 23 Years Old Farmer	Co. F, 10th Regiment North Carolina Artillery	Captured	Elmira Prison, Elmira, New York	Died from Pneumonia, 2/26/1865
Johnson, Levi E. Sergeant	Carteret County, North Carolina, 7/21/1861	Beaufort, Carteret County, North Carolina, 21 Years Old Engineer	Co. F, 10th Regiment North Carolina Artillery	Gunshot Wound, Scalp & Captured	Fort Delaware, Del.	Oath of Allegiance 6/7/1865
Johnson, Matthew C. Private	Craven County, North Carolina, 1/13/1862	Halifax County, North Carolina, 18 Years Old	Co. F, 36th Regiment North Carolina, 2nd N. C. Artillery	Captured	Point Lookout Prison, Maryland	Oath of Allegiance 6/28/1865
Johnson, M. P. Private	James Island, South Carolina 8/1/1863	Unknown	Co I, 25th Regiment South Carolina Volunteers	Captured	Elmira Prison, Elmira, New York	Died of Smallpox, 3/23/1865
Johnson, Nathan Thomas Private	Brunswick County, North Carolina, 8/28/1863	Wayne County, North Carolina, Age Unknown	Co. F, 10th Regiment North Carolina Artillery	Captured	Elmira Prison, Elmira, New York	Oath of Allegiance 7/11/1865
Johnson, Nicholson F. Private	Bladen County, North Carolina, 10/23/1863	Cypress Creek, Bladen County, North Carolina, 17 Years Old Farmer	2nd Co. K, 40th Regiment North Carolina Artillery	Captured	Point Lookout Prison, Maryland	Oath of Allegiance 5/13/1865

NAME & RANK	ENLISTED	RESIDENCE AGE & TRADE	UNIT	RESULT OF BATTLE	PRISON	PRISON RELEASE
Johnson, Richard M. Private	Cumberland County, North Carolina, 1/3/1865	Hunting Creek, Wilkes County, North Carolina, 18 Years Old Farmer	2nd Co. C, 36th Regiment North Carolina, 2nd N. C. Artillery	Captured, Defended River Road Gate	Elmira Prison, Elmira, New York	Died from Pneumonia, 2/20/1865
Johnson, Richard M. Private	New Hanover County, North Carolina, 8/15/1863	Fayetteville, Cumberland County, North Carolina, 27 Years Old Laborer	2nd Co. K, 40th Regiment North Carolina Artillery	Captured	Point Lookout Prison, Maryland	Oath of Allegiance 6/4/1865
Johnson, Robert A. Private	Richmond County, North Carolina, 4/16/1864	Montpelier, Laurel Hill District, Richmond County, North Carolina, 18 Years Old Farmer	Co. D, 1st Battalion North Carolina Heavy Artillery	Gunshot Wound Right Thigh & Groin & Captured, Defended River Road Gate	Point Lookout Prison General Hospital, Maryland	Oath of Allegiance 6/14/1865
Johnson, William F. Private	Wilmington, New Hanover County, North Carolina, 10/28/1861, Volunteer	Wilmington, New Hanover County, North Carolina, 27 Years Old	Co. E, 36th Regiment North Carolina, 2nd N. C. Artillery	Captured	Elmira Prison, Elmira, New York	Exchanged 3/2/1865, Died from Chronic Diarrhea Moore Hospital, Richmond Virginia, 3/9/1865
Johnson, William H. Private	Fort Fisher, New Hanover County, North Carolina, 2/19/1863	Forsyth County, North Carolina, 19 Years Old Mechanic	Co. H., 36th Regiment North Carolina, 2nd N. C. Artillery	Not Captured		Detailed as a Scout by General Whiting, Admitted Greensboro Hospital with Fever 1/19/1865
Johnston, Beazar B. Private	Lenoir County, North Carolina, 6/23/1862	Lenoir County, North Carolina, Age Unknown	Co. D, 13th Battalion, North Carolina Light Artillery	Captured, Defended River Road Gate	Point Lookout Prison, Maryland	Exchanged at Cox's Landing, James River, Virginia, 2/15/1865

NAME & RANK	ENLISTED	RESIDENCE AGE & TRADE	UNIT	RESULT OF BATTLE	PRISON	PRISON RELEASE
Johnston, John M. Private	Bladen County, North Carolina, 8/14/1862	Elizabethtown Bladen County, North Carolina, 18 Years Old Farmer	Co. H, 36th Regiment North Carolina, 2nd N. C. Artillery	Wounded in Left Arm and Head & Captured	Point Lookout Prison, Maryland	Oath of Allegiance 6/28/1865
Jolly, W. F. Seaman	Date and Place Unknown	Unknown	Confederate States Navy	Wounded, Burned when gun burst 12/25/1864	None	
Jones, Amos Private	Bladen County, North Carolina, 3/31/1864	Bladen County, North Carolina, 18 Years Old, Assigned Lt. Faison's Scouts	Co. H, 36th Regiment North Carolina, 2nd N. C. Artillery	Killed in Action, 12/25/1865		Shot and Killed near Shepperd's Battery
Jones, Alexander McC First Lieutenant	Beaufort County, North Carolina, 3/7/1862	Washington, Beaufort County, North Carolina, 32 Years Old Teacher	Co. I, 40th Regiment North Carolina Artillery	Captured	Fort Columbus, New York Harbor	Exchanged 3/5/1865, Boulware's Wharf, James River, Virginia
Jones, Bartemus P. Ordinance Sergeant	Beaufort County, North Carolina, 9/30/1861	North Creek, Beaufort County, North Carolina, 33 Years Old Laborer	Co. B, 40th Regiment North Carolina Artillery	Wounded in Face, 12/25/1864, & Captured 1/15/1865	Elmira Prison, Elmira, New York	Died of Smallpox, 4/1/1865
Jones, D. H. Sergeant	Charleston, South Carolina 7/2/1862	Charleston, South Carolina, 20 Years Old	Co A, 25th Regiment South Carolina Volunteers	Captured	Elmira Prison, Elmira, New York	Oath of Allegiance 6/19/1865
Jones, Daniel S. Private	New Hanover County, North Carolina, 6/17/1863	South Division, Guilford County, North Carolina, 16 Years Old	Co. K, 10th Regiment, North Carolina Artillery	Captured	Elmira Prison, Elmira, New York	Oath of Allegiance 6/23/1865

NAME & RANK	ENLISTED	RESIDENCE AGE & TRADE	UNIT	RESULT OF BATTLE	PRISON	PRISON RELEASE
Jones, David Britton Private	Washington County, North Carolina, 8/21/1864	Rocky Mount, Edgecombe County, North Carolina, Age Unknown	Co. D, 40th Regiment North Carolina Artillery	Captured	Elmira Prison, Elmira, New York	Oath of Allegiance 7/7/1865
Jones, Franklin Private	Wayne County, Transferred From N. C. Local Defense Troops 8/17/1864	Goldsboro, Wayne County, North Carolina, Age Unknown	Co. D, 40th Regiment North Carolina Artillery	Captured	Elmira Prison, Elmira, New York	Oath of Allegiance 5/29/1865
Jones, James A. Private	Marion District, South Carolina 1/23/1864	Floydsville, Marion District, South Carolina, 46 Years Old	Co. L, 21st South Carolina Volunteers	Captured	Elmira Prison, Elmira, New York	Died of Chronic Diarrhea, 2/26/1865
Jones, Jacob Private	Date and Place Unknown	Unknown	2nd Co. A, 36th Regiment North Carolina, 2nd N. C. Artillery	Captured, Defended the Mound Battery	Prison Unknown	Release Unknown
Jones, James Private	Wayne County, North Carolina, 3/23/1864	Goldsboro, Wayne County, North Carolina, 17 Years Old Carriage Trimmer	Co. D, 40th Regiment North Carolina Artillery	Captured	Point Lookout Prison, Maryland	Oath of Allegiance 5/29/1865
Jones, James E. Private	Edgecombe County, North Carolina, 3/23/1864	Tarboro, Edgecombe County, North Carolina, 18 Years Old Farmer	Co. D, 40th Regiment North Carolina Artillery	Captured	Elmira Prison, Elmira, New York	Oath of Allegiance 6/21/1865
Jones, John E. Private	Nash County, North Carolina, 6/2/1864	Moore County, North Carolina, 24 Years Old	Co. D, 40th Regiment North Carolina Artillery	Captured	Point Lookout Prison, Maryland	Exchanged 2/15/1865, Boulware's Wharf, James River, Virginia

NAME & RANK	ENLISTED	RESIDENCE AGE & TRADE	UNIT	RESULT OF BATTLE	PRISON	PRISON RELEASE
Jones, John Pembroke Corporal	Mobile, Alabama, 9/18/1861	Mobile, Alabama, 24 Years Old	Co. B, Confederate States Marine Corp, Assigned to Guard Duty Aboard CSS *Edith*	Captured	Point Lookout Prison, Maryland	Oath of Allegiance 6/14/1865
Jones, Joseph S. Private	Butler, Alabama, 3/18/1863,	Unknown	Co. A, Confederate States Marine Corp, Assigned to Guard Duty Aboard CSS *Tallahassee.*	Captured	Point Lookout Prison, Maryland	Oath of Allegiance 6/6/1865
Jones, Levy W. Private	New Hanover County, North Carolina, 5/9/1863	White Oak, Bladen County, North Carolina, 19 Years Old	2nd Co. I, 36th Regiment North Carolina, 2nd N. C. Artillery	Killed in Action, 1/15/1865, Defended Shepperd's Battery		
Jones, Marvin Private	Whiteville, North Carolina, 4/27/1863, Conscript	Whiteville, Columbus County, North Carolina, 26 Years Old	Co. E, 36th Regiment North Carolina, 2nd N. C. Artillery	Wounded, January 1865	Not Captured	
Jones, P. D. Private	Date and Place Unknown	Unknown	Co. D, 40th Regiment North Carolina Artillery	Captured	Elmira Prison, Elmira, New York	Oath of Allegiance 7/7/1865
Jones, Robert Daniel Private	Craven County, North Carolina, 1/24/1862, Volunteer	New Berne, Craven County, North Carolina, 18 Years Old	Co. D, 40th Regiment North Carolina Artillery	Captured	Point Lookout Prison, Maryland	Oath of Allegiance 6/28/1865
Jones, Thomas Private	Craven County, North Carolina, 9/28/1861	New Berne, North of Neuse River, Craven County, North Carolina, 29 Years Old Farmer	Co. D, 40th Regiment North Carolina Artillery	Captured	Prison Unknown	Release Unknown

NAME & RANK	ENLISTED	RESIDENCE AGE & TRADE	UNIT	RESULT OF BATTLE	PRISON	PRISON RELEASE
Jones, Thomas J. Private	Brunswick County, North Carolina, 7/17/1863	West Brook, Bladen County, North Carolina, 33 Years Old Farmer	2nd Co. D, 36th Regiment North Carolina, 2nd N. C. Artillery	Captured	Point Lookout Prison, Maryland	Exchanged at Cox's Landing, James River, Virginia, 2/15/1865
Jones, William H. Private	Wayne County, North Carolina, 8/8/1863	New Berne, Craven County, North Carolina, 33 Years Old Farmer	Co. D, 40th Regiment North Carolina Artillery	Captured	Point Lookout Prison, Maryland	Exchanged at Cox's Landing, James River, Virginia, 2/21/1865
Jordan, Kenion Private	Carteret County, North Carolina, 7/29/1861	Wayne County, North Carolina, 23 Years Old Farmer	Co. F, 10th Regiment North Carolina Artillery	Captured	Elmira Prison, Elmira, New York	Died of Chronic Diarrhea 3/10/1865
Jordan, Rivers C. Private	Bladen County, North Carolina, 5/3/1862	Elizabethtown Bladen County, North Carolina, 21 Years Old Farmer	Co. H, 36th Regiment North Carolina, 2nd N. C. Artillery	Captured	Point Lookout Prison, Maryland	Oath of Allegiance 6/28/1865
Jordan, Wilson Private	Newland, Avery County, North Carolina, 3/26/1862	Morrisville, Wake County, North Carolina, 58 Years Old Farmer	Co. C, 3rd Battalion North Carolina Artillery	Captured	Elmira Prison, Elmira, New York	Exchanged 3/14/1865, Boulware's Wharf, James River, Virginia
Joyce, John Corporal	New Orleans, Louisiana, 4/30/1861	New Orleans, Louisiana, Age Unknown Sailor	Co. A, Confederate States Marine Corp, Assigned to Guard Duty Aboard CSS *Savannah* and CSS *North Carolina.*	Captured, Defended Sea Face	Point Lookout Prison, Maryland	Oath of Allegiance 5/13/1865

NAME & RANK	ENLISTED	RESIDENCE AGE & TRADE	UNIT	RESULT OF BATTLE	PRISON	PRISON RELEASE
Joyce, Patrick Private	Mobile, Alabama, 9/2/1861	Unknown	Co C, Confederate States Marine Corp, Assigned to Guard Duty Aboard CSS *Jamestown* and CSS *Arctic.*	Captured	Prison Unknown	Oath of Allegiance 5/12/1865
Joyner, Edward Noah Private	New Hanover County, North Carolina, 10/18/1864	Marlboro, Pitt County, North Carolina, 16 Years Old Student	Co. D, 13th Battalion, North Carolina Light Artillery	Gunshot Wound of Forehead & Scalp, Left Side & Captured, Defended River Road Gate	Point Lookout Prison Hospital, Maryland	Oath of Allegiance 7/25/1865
Joyner, James H. Private	Fort St. Philip, Brunswick County, North Carolina, 5/16/1862, Volunteer	Pitt County, North Carolina, 34 Years Old, Extra Duty As Carpenter At Fort Caswell, N. C.	3rd Co. G, 36th Regiment North Carolina, 2nd N. C. Artillery	Wounded & Captured, Defended Battery to the Left of Northeast Bastion	Elmira Prison, Elmira, New York	Exchanged 2/20/1865, Died of Unknown Disease at Richmond Hospital 3/20/1865
Joyner, Samuel Sergeant	Columbus County, North Carolina, 3/1/1862	Whiteville, Columbus County, North Carolina, 43 Years Old Merchant	Co. E, 36th Regiment North Carolina, 2nd N. C. Artillery	Captured	Elmira Prison, Elmira, New York	Died of Gangrene of Feet, 2/28/1865
Judge, John J. Sergeant	Halifax County, North Carolina, 10/9/1861, Volunteer	Halifax County, North Carolina, 20 Years Old	Co. F, 36th Regiment North Carolina, 2nd N. C. Artillery	Captured	Elmira Prison, Elmira, New York	Exchanged 3/19/1865, Boulware's Wharf, James River, Virginia
Judkins, William G. Sergeant	Beaufort County, North Carolina, 9/23/1861	Washington, Beaufort County, North Carolina, 32 Years Old	Co. D, 13th Battalion North Carolina Artillery	Captured, Defended River Road Gate	Point Lookout Prison, Maryland	Oath of Allegiance 6/28/1865

NAME & RANK	ENLISTED	RESIDENCE AGE & TRADE	UNIT	RESULT OF BATTLE	PRISON	PRISON RELEASE
Junes, S. N. Private	Battery Island, South Carolina 4/12/1862	Gourdine Station, South Carolina, 17 Years Old	Co C, 25th Regiment South Carolina Volunteers	Captured	Elmira Prison, Elmira, New York	Oath of Allegiance 7/13/1865
Justice, Benjamin H. Musician	Date Unknown, Conscripted 4/4/1863	New Hanover County, North Carolina, 25 Years Old Sail Maker	3rd Co. G, 36th Regiment North Carolina, 2nd N. C. Artillery	Captured, Defended Battery to the Left of Northeast Bastion	Elmira Prison, Elmira, New York	Oath of Allegiance 5/15/1865

NAME & RANK	ENLISTED	RESIDENCE AGE & TRADE	UNIT	RESULT OF BATTLE	PRISON	PRISON RELEASE
Keel, Nathan Seaman	Pitt County, North Carolina, 8/19/1861	Pitt County, North Carolina, 30 Years Old Seaman	Galloway Co, Confederate States Coast Guard	Captured	Prison Unknown	Release Unknown
Keife, Frank Sergeant	Mobile, Alabama, 11/24/1862	Louisville, Kentucky, Age Unknown Tailor	Co. B, Confederate States Marine Corp, Assigned to Guard Duty Aboard CSS *Raleigh.*	Captured	Point Lookout Prison, Maryland	Oath of Allegiance 5/13/1865
Keith, Duncan Private	Wilmington, New Hanover County, North Carolina, 4/24/1863	Fayetteville, Cumberland County, North Carolina, Age Unknown	Co. F, 10th Regiment North Carolina, 1st North Carolina Artillery	Captured	Elmira Prison, Elmira, New York	Oath of Allegiance 6/12/1865
Kelley, James Private	Date and Place Unknown	Kershaw County, South Carolina, 39 Years Old Overseer	Co. B, 25th South Carolina Volunteers	Captured	Elmira Prison, Elmira, New York	Died Of Disease 2/6/1865

NAME & RANK	ENLISTED	RESIDENCE AGE & TRADE	UNIT	RESULT OF BATTLE	PRISON	PRISON RELEASE
Kelley, John Private	Anderson, South Carolina 5/1/1862	Greenville County, South Carolina, 37 Years Old Farmer	Co. H, 25th South Carolina Volunteers	Captured	Elmira Prison, Elmira, New York	Died Of Smallpox, 2/28/1865
Kelley, John M. Private	Charleston, South Carolina 5/28/1862	Charleston, South Carolina, 24 Years Old	Co. H, 25th South Carolina Volunteers	Captured	Elmira Prison, Elmira, New York	Died of Pneumonia, 2/13/1865,
Kelley, Simon Private	Darlington, South Carolina 3/15/1864	Bishopville, Sumter County, South Carolina, 18 Years Old	Co. G, 21st South Carolina Volunteers	Captured	Elmira Prison, Elmira, New York	Died Of Pneumonia 2/16/1865
Kelly, Colin M. Sergeant	Bladen County, North Carolina, 9/10/1861, Volunteer	Elizabethtown Bladen County, North Carolina, 24 Years Old Teacher	3rd Co. B, 36th Regiment, North Carolina, 2nd N. C. Artillery	Wounded In Face, 12/24/1864, & Captured 1/15/1865	Point Lookout Prison, Maryland	Oath of Allegiance 5/15/1865, Wounded in Action 12/24/1864
Kelly, Daniel C. Corporal	Bladen County, North Carolina, 1/28/1862, Volunteer	Elizabethtown Bladen County, North Carolina, 21 Years Old Farmer	3rd Co. B, 36th Regiment, North Carolina, 2nd N. C. Artillery	Wounded & Captured	Point Lookout Prison, Maryland	Oath of Allegiance 5/15/1865
Kelly, Henry Private	Date and Place Unknown	Darlington District, South Carolina, 16 Years Old	Co. G, 21st South Carolina Volunteers	Captured	Elmira Prison, Elmira, New York	Oath of Allegiance 6/14/1865
Kelly, James A. Private	Darlington, South Carolina 1/1/1862	Darlington District, South Carolina, 18 Years Old	Co. B, 21st South Carolina Volunteers	Captured	Elmira Prison, Elmira, New York	Died Of Pneumonia 2/6/1865

NAME & RANK	ENLISTED	RESIDENCE AGE & TRADE	UNIT	RESULT OF BATTLE	PRISON	PRISON RELEASE
Kelly, John Neill First Lieutenant	Bladen County, North Carolina, 9/10/1861	Elizabethtown Bladen County, North Carolina, 25 Years Old Turpentine	3rd Co. B, 36th Regiment, North Carolina, 2nd N. C. Artillery	Captured	Fort Columbus, New York Harbor	Exchanged Boulware's Wharf, James River, Virginia, 3/5/1865
Kelly, Thomas Private	Darlington, South Carolina 5/1/1862	Darlington District, South Carolina, 38 Years Old Farmer	Co. G, 21st South Carolina Volunteers	Captured	Elmira Prison, Elmira, New York	Oath of Allegiance 7/3/1865
Kelly, William A. Private	Bladen County, North Carolina, 3/26/1862	Elizabethown, Bladen County, North Carolina, 17 Years Old Laborer	3rd Co. B, 36th Regiment, North Carolina, 2nd N. C. Artillery	Captured	Point Lookout Prison, Maryland	Oath of Allegiance 6/3/1865
Kemp, William J. Sergeant	Bladen County, North Carolina, 8/4/1862, Volunteer	White Creek, Bladen County, North Carolina, 26 Years Old Farmer	Co. H, 36th Regiment, North Carolina, 2nd N. C. Artillery	Severely Wounded & Captured	Prison Unknown	Release Unknown, May have died at Fort Fisher, N. C.
Kennedy, James D. Private	Camp Lamb, New Hanover County, North Carolina, 7/9/1863, Volunteer	Mount Olive, North Division, Duplin County, North Carolina, 18 Years Old	Co. D, 1st Battalion North Carolina Heavy Artillery	Gunshot Wound Right Ankle & Captured, Defended River Road Gate or Middle Sallyport	Point Lookout Prison General Hospital, Maryland	Oath of Allegiance 6/26/1865
Kennedy, Levi B. Private	Wake County, North Carolina, 4/15/1864	Kinston District, Lenoir County, North Carolina, 20 Years Old Farmer	Co. K, 10th Regiment North Carolina, 1st N. C. Artillery	Captured	Elmira Prison, Elmira, New York	Died of Chronic Diarrhea 4/13/1865
Kennedy, William J. Private	Fort Fisher, New Hanover County, North Carolina, 3/15/1863	Fayetteville, Cumberland County, North Carolina, 39 Years Old	2nd Co. C, 36th Regiment, North Carolina, 2nd N. C. Artillery	Captured, Defended River Road Gate	Elmira Prison, Elmira, New York	Oath of Allegiance 6/12/1865

NAME & RANK	ENLISTED	RESIDENCE AGE & TRADE	UNIT	RESULT OF BATTLE	PRISON	PRISON RELEASE
Kerr, Charles Stevens Private	Wake County, North Carolina, 12/29/1863	New Hanover County, North Carolina, 18 Years Old Farmer	2nd Co. C, 36th Regiment, North Carolina, 2nd N. C. Artillery	Escaped Capture At Fort Fisher		Paroled 4/25/1865, Defended River Road Gate
King, Athedon D. Private	Craven County, North Carolina, 1/20/1862	Eastern Division, Halifax County, North Carolina, 22 Years Old Farmer	Co. F, 36th Regiment, North Carolina, 2nd N. C. Artillery	Captured	Point Lookout Prison, Maryland	Oath of Allegiance 6/28/1865
King, Barnabus S. Private	New Hanover County, North Carolina, 3/30/1863	Johnston County, North Carolina, 46 Years Old	Co. F, 10th Regiment North Carolina, 1st N. C. Artillery	Captured	Elmira Prison, Elmira, New York	Died of Chronic Diarrhea 2/4/1865
King, George Private	Elizabeth-town, Bladen County, North Carolina, 5/6/1862	Bladenboro, Bladen County, North Carolina, 18 Years Old Farmer	2nd Co. K, 40th Regiment North Carolina, 3rd N. C. Artillery	Captured	Elmira Prison, Elmira, New York	Oath of Allegiance 6/21/1865
King, I. P. Z. Sergeant	Darlington, South Carolina 3/15/1863	Charlotte, North Carolina, Age Unknown	Co. B, 21st South Carolina Volunteers	Captured	Elmira Prison, Elmira, New York	Oath of Allegiance 7/11/1865
King, James Private	Bladen County, North Carolina, 8/2/1862	West Brook, Bladen County, North Carolina, 31 Years Old	3rd Co. G, 36th Regiment, North Carolina, 2nd N. C. Artillery	Captured, Defended Battery to the Left of Northeast Bastion	Elmira Prison, Elmira, New York	Died of Smallpox, 3/2/1865
King, John C. Private	Brunswick County, North Carolina, 9/9/1863	Fayetteville, Cumberland County, North Carolina, 39 Years Old Overseer	Co. F, 36th Regiment, North Carolina, 2nd N. C. Artillery	Captured	Point Lookout Prison, Maryland	Oath of Allegiance 6/28/1865

NAME & RANK	ENLISTED	RESIDENCE AGE & TRADE	UNIT	RESULT OF BATTLE	PRISON	PRISON RELEASE
King, John W. Private	Halifax County, North Carolina, 10/9/1861	Raleigh, Wake County, North Carolina, 26 Years Old Stone Mason	Co. F, 36th Regiment, North Carolina, 2nd N. C. Artillery	Captured	Point Lookout Prison, Maryland	Exchanged 2/15/1865 Cox's Landing, James River, Virginia
King, T. P. Private	Darlington, South Carolina 2/20/1862	Charlotte, North Carolina, 18 Years Old	Co. B, 21st South Carolina Volunteers	Captured	Elmira Prison, Elmira, New York	Oath of Allegiance 7/11/1865
King, W. Private	Date and Place Unknown	Unknown	Co. E, 25th South Carolina Volunteers	Captured	Elmira Prison, Elmira, New York	Died Of Disease 6/3/1865
King, Wesley Private	James Island, South Carolina 12/9/1863	Darlington District, South Carolina, 35 Years Old	Co. H, 21st South Carolina Volunteers	Captured	Elmira Prison, Elmira, New York	Died Of Chronic Diarrhea 6/23/1865
Kingman, John W. Private	Charleston, South Carolina 2/18/1862	Charleston, South Carolina, 30 Years Old Clerk	Co A, 25th Regiment South Carolina Volunteers	Captured	Elmira Prison, Elmira, New York	Exchanged 3/14/1865
Kinlaw, Anderson W. Private	Fort Holmes, Brunswick County, North Carolina, 11/20/1864	Brunswick County, North Carolina, Age Unknown Farmer	2nd Co. K, 40th Regiment North Carolina, 3rd N. C. Artillery	Captured	Elmira Prison, Elmira, New York	Exchanged On the James River, Virginia, 2/20/1865
Kinlaw, Benjamin Corporal	Elizabeth-town, Bladen County, North Carolina, Volunteer	Prospect Hall, Bladen County North Carolina, 27 Years Old Farmer & Turpentine Distiller	2nd Co. K, 40th Regiment North Carolina, 3rd N. C. Artillery	Captured	Elmira Prison, Elmira, New York	Died of Chronic Diarrhea 4/16/1865

NAME & RANK	ENLISTED	RESIDENCE AGE & TRADE	UNIT	RESULT OF BATTLE	PRISON	PRISON RELEASE
Kinlaw, James T. Private	Fort Fisher, New Hanover County, North Carolina, 6/1/1863 Conscript	Bladen County, North Carolina, 18 Years Old	2nd Co. K, 40th Regiment North Carolina, 3rd N. C. Artillery	Shell Wound Left Side & Captured	Point Lookout General Hospital, Maryland	Oath of Allegiance 6/28/1865
Kinlaw, Neil Private	Robeson County, North Carolina, 5/6/1862, Volunteer	Lumberton, Robeson County, North Carolina, 38 Years Old Farmer	2nd Co. K, 40th Regiment North Carolina, 3rd N. C. Artillery	Captured	Elmira Prison, Elmira, New York	Died of Chronic Diarrhea 2/20/1865
Kinzel, John Francis Private	Transferred in From Co. B, 31st Regiment North Carolina Troops, 1/1/1864, Volunteer	Unknown, 35 Years Old	2nd Co. D, 36th Regiment, North Carolina, 2nd N. C. Artillery	Captured	Point Lookout Prison, Maryland	Oath of Allegiance 6/12/1865
Kirby, Dixon Private	Camp Homes, Brunswick County, North Carolina, 3/29/1864	Wake County, North Carolina, Age Unknown	Co. K, 10th Regiment North Carolina, 1st N. C. Artillery	Captured	Elmira Prison, Elmira, New York	Died of Smallpox, 4/13/1865
Kirby, Ezekiel H. Private	James Island, South Carolina 4/13/1863	Williamsburg District, South Carolina, 27 Years Old	Co D, 25th Regiment South Carolina Volunteers	Gunshot Wound To Shoulder & Captured	Point Lookout Prison, Maryland	Oath of Allegiance 5/14/1865
Kirby, Robert Seaman	Place Unknown, 1/24/1862	Brunswick County, North Carolina, Age Unknown Fisherman	Galloway Co, Confederate States Coast Guard	Captured	Prison Unknown	Release Unknown

NAME & RANK	ENLISTED	RESIDENCE AGE & TRADE	UNIT	RESULT OF BATTLE	PRISON	PRISON RELEASE
Kirkland, John F. Private	Calhoun County, Alabama, 2/18/1863	Unknown, 37 Years Old	Co. B, Confederate States Marine Corp, Assigned to Guard duty Aboard CSS *Savannah*.	Captured, Defended Sea Face	Point Lookout Prison, Maryland	Oath of Allegiance 6/6/1865
Kitchen, J. H. Private	Date and Place Unknown	Unknown	Co. F, 36th Regiment, North Carolina, 2nd N. C. Artillery	Captured	Prison Unknown	Release Unknown
Knight, John Private	Hertford County, North Carolina, 8/3/1864	Gates County, North Carolina, 26 Years Old	Co. C, 3rd Battalion North Carolina Light Artillery	Captured	Elmira Prison, Elmira, New York	Died of Typhoid Fever 4/13/1865
Knight, Patrick Private	New Orleans, Louisiana, 4/27/1861	New Orleans, Louisiana, Age Unknown Laborer	Co. A, Confederate States Marine Corp, Assigned to Guard Duty aboard CSS *Savannah*, CSS *Atlanta* and CSS *Arctic*.	Captured, Defended Sea Face	Point Lookout Prison, Maryland	Oath of Allegiance 5/13/1865
Kornegay, C. Private	Date and Place Unknown	Unknown	3rd Co. G, 40th Regiment North Carolina, 3rd N. C. Artillery	Gunshot Wound of Right Thigh & Captured, Defended Land Face	Point Lookout Prison, Maryland	Oath of Allegiance 6/22/1865
Kornegay, Dixon W. Corporal	Wayne County, North Carolina, 10/16/1861	Sleepy Creek, Indian Springs District, Wayne County, North Carolina, 16 Years Old Farmer	3rd Co. G, 40th Regiment North Carolina, 3rd N. C. Artillery	Captured, Defended Land Face	Elmira Prison, Elmira, New York	Exchanged 2/20/1865, Died Chronic Diarrhea 4/27/1865

NAME & RANK	ENLISTED	RESIDENCE AGE & TRADE	UNIT	RESULT OF BATTLE	PRISON	PRISON RELEASE
Kornegay, Joseph E. Private	Fort Holmes, Duplin County, North Carolina, 11/7/1861	Mount Olive, Duplin County, North Carolina, 16 Years Old Farmer	3rd Co. G, 40th Regiment North Carolina, 3rd N. C. Artillery	Captured, Defended Land Face	Elmira Prison, Elmira, New York	Exchanged 3/2/1865 Boulware's Wharf, James River, Virginia
Kornegay, Leonidas Private	Fort Holmes, Brunswick County, North Carolina, 4/13/1864	Sleepy Creek, Wayne County, North Carolina, 18 Years Old Farmer	3rd Co. G, 40th Regiment North Carolina, 3rd N. C. Artillery	Gunshot Wound Left Thigh & Captured. Defended Land Face	Point Lookout General Hospital, Maryland	Oath of Allegiance 6/22/1865
Kornegay, Marshall Private	Brunswick County, North Carolina, 1/26/1864	Mount Olive, Duplin County, North Carolina, 20 Years Old Student	2nd Co. A, 36th Regiment, North Carolina, 2nd N. C. Artillery	Captured, Defended the Mound Battery	Point Lookout Prison, Maryland	Died of pneumonia 3/28/1865
Kornegay, Wesley Corporal	Duplin County, North Carolina, 10/16/1861	Duplin County, North Carolina, 17 Years Old	3rd Co. G, 40th Regiment North Carolina, 3rd N. C. Artillery	Captured, Defended Land Face	Elmira Prison, Elmira, New York	Died of Chronic Diarrhea 4/27/1865

NAME & RANK	ENLISTED	RESIDENCE AGE & TRADE	UNIT	RESULT OF BATTLE	PRISON	PRISON RELEASE
Lamb, James Private	New Hanover County, North Carolina, 1/10/1864	Colvin Creek, New Hanover County, North Carolina, 44 Years Old Farm Laborer	Co. F, 10th Regiment North Carolina, 1st N. C. Artillery	Captured	Elmira Prison, New York	Died of Chronic Diarrhea 2/19/1865
Lamb, William Colonel	Norfolk, Virginia, 4/18/1861	Norfolk, Virginia, 25 Years Old Publisher & Editor, Argus News	36th Regiment North Carolina, 2nd N. C. Artillery	Gunshot Wound, Hip & Captured	Fort Monroe, Virginia	Paroled 5/1/1865

NAME & RANK	ENLISTED	RESIDENCE AGE & TRADE	UNIT	RESULT OF BATTLE	PRISON	PRISON RELEASE
Lamberson, Eli Private	Bladen County, North Carolina, 3/20/1862	White Creek, Bladen County, North Carolina, 21 Years Old Turpentine	Co. H, 36th Regiment North Carolina, 2nd N. C. Artillery	Captured	Elmira Prison, New York	Died of Chronic Diarrhea 3/7/1865
Lancaster, Edward R. Seaman	Place Unknown, 8/14/1861	Craven County, North Carolina, 21 Years Old Fisherman	Galloway Co., Confederate States Coast Guard	Captured	Prison Unknown	Release Unknown
Lancaster, L. L. Private	Date and Place Unknown	Unknown, 29 Years Old	Co. K, 36th Regiment North Carolina, 2nd N. C. Artillery	Captured	Point Lookout, Maryland	Died of Typhoid-Pneumonia, 6/5/1865
Lancaster, William A. Seaman	Place Unknown, 1/24/1862	Pitt County, North Carolina, Age Unknown Fisherman	Galloway Co., Confederate States Coast Guard	Captured	Prison Unknown	Release Unknown
Lane, James S. Captain	Craven County, North Carolina, 9/21/1861	Craven County, North Carolina, 34 Years Old	Co. D, 40th Regiment North Carolina, 3rd N. C. Artillery	Wounded 1/15/1865	Escaped Fort Fisher	Treated at Hospital #3, Greensboro, North Carolina
Lane, Robert J. Private	Enfield, Halifax County, North Carolina, 10/9/1861	Edgecomb County, North Carolina, 19 Years Old	Co. F, 36th Regiment North Carolina, 2nd N. C. Artillery	Gunshot Wound Back of Neck & Captured	Point Lookout, Maryland	Oath of Allegiance 7/25/1865
Lanneau, W. S. Private	Charleston, South Carolina 5/9/1863	Unknown, 24 Years Old	Co A, 25th Regiment South Carolina Volunteers	Captured	Elmira Prison, Elmira, New York	Oath of Allegiance 6/14/1865
Lardingood W. A. Private	Date and Place Unknown	Unknown	2nd Co. A, 36th Regiment North Carolina, 2nd N. C. Artillery	Captured, Defended the Mound Battery	Prison Unknown	Paroled, Release Date Unknown

NAME & RANK	ENLISTED	RESIDENCE AGE & TRADE	UNIT	RESULT OF BATTLE	PRISON	PRISON RELEASE
Lassiter, James Henry Private	Winton, Hertford County, North Carolina, 2/13/1862	Murfreesboro, Herford County, North Carolina, 24 Years Old Farmer	Co. C, 3rd Battalion, North Carolina Light Artillery	Captured	Elmira Prison, Elmira, New York	Oath of Allegiance 6/12/1865
Lassiter, John W. Private	Winton, Hertford County, North Carolina, 1/28/1862,	Murfreesboro, Herford County, North Carolina, 19 Years Old Day Laborer	Co. C, 3rd Battalion North Carolina Light Artillery	Captured	Elmira Prison, New York	Oath of Allegiance 6/12/1865
Lassiter, Leroy Private	Winton, Hertford County, North Carolina, 1/28/1862	Murfreesboro, Herford County, North Carolina, 34 Years Old Farmer	Co. C, 3rd Battalion North Carolina Light Artillery	Captured	Elmira Prison, New York	Oath of Allegiance 6/12/1865
Lassiter, Richard Private	St. Johns, Hertford County, North Carolina, 4/15/1862	Green Plaines, Northampton County, North Carolina, 19 Years Old	Co. C, 3rd Battalion North Carolina Light Artillery	Captured	Elmira Prison, New York	Oath of Allegiance 5/17/1865
Latham, Charles H. First Lieutenant	Beaufort County, North Carolina, 10/9/1861	Washington, Beaufort County, North Carolina, 31 Years Old	Co. D, 13th Battalion North Carolina Light Artillery	Captured, Defended River Road Gate	Fort Columbus, New York Harbor	Exchanged 3/5/1865 at Boulware's Wharf, James River, Virginia
Latham, J. Private	Date and Place Unknown	Unknown	2nd Co. A, 36th Regiment North Carolina, 2nd N. C. Artillery	Captured, Defended the Mound Battery	Prison Unknown	Paroled, Release Date Unknown
Latham, James W. T. Sergeant	Beaufort County, North Carolina, 9/23/1861	Beaufort County, North Carolina, 22 Years Old	2nd Co. G, 36th Regiment North Carolina, 2nd N. C. Artillery	Killed In Action 1/15/1865		

NAME & RANK	ENLISTED	RESIDENCE AGE & TRADE	UNIT	RESULT OF BATTLE	PRISON	PRISON RELEASE
Latham, W. W. Private	New Hanover County, North Carolina, 5/1/1863	Carteret County, North Carolina, Age Unknown	Co. D, 13th Battalion North Carolina Light Artillery	Captured, Defended River Road Gate	Fort Delaware, Del.	Oath of Allegiance 5/15/1865
Lawhon, James Private	Duplin County, North Carolina, 11/6/1861	Mount Olive, Duplin County, North Carolina, 39 Years Old	2nd Co. A, 36th Regiment North Carolina, 2nd N. C. Artillery	Captured, Defended the Mound Battery	Elmira Prison, New York	Died of Chronic Diarrhea 4/10/1865
Lawley, William H. Private	Wilmington, North Carolina	Unknown	Co. B, Confederate States Marine Corp, Assigned to Guard duty Aboard Aboard CSS *Raleigh.*	Captured	Point Lookout, Maryland	Oath of Allegiance 5/13/1865
Lawrence, James M. Private	Craven County, North Carolina, 1/1/1862	Tarboro, Edgecombe County, North Carolina, 26 Years Old Farmer	Co. F, 36th Regiment North Carolina, 2nd N. C. Artillery	Captured	Elmira Prison, New York	Died of Pneumonia 4/23/1865
Lawson, James T. Private	Darlington, South Carolina 1/20/1863	Cedar Bluff, Union County, South Carolina, 22 Years Old Laborer	Co. H, 21st South Carolina Volunteers	Killed In Action 1/15/1865		
Lawson, William Private	Date and Place Unknown	Unknown	Co. K, 10th Regiment North Carolina, 1st N. C. Artillery	Captured	Elmira Prison, New York	Died of Chronic Diarrhea 2/20/1865
Lawson, William R. S. Sergeant	Georgetown South Carolina 1/25/1862	Charlotte, Anson County, North Carolina, 25 Years Old	Co. H, 21st South Carolina Volunteers	Captured	Elmira Prison, Elmira, New York	Oath of Allegiance 7/11/1865

NAME & RANK	ENLISTED	RESIDENCE AGE & TRADE	UNIT	RESULT OF BATTLE	PRISON	PRISON RELEASE
Leach, Hugh Private	Randolph County, North Carolina, 3/16/1863	Trinity College, Randolph County, North Carolina, 31 Years Old	Co. K, 10th Regiment North Carolina, 1st N. C. Artillery	Captured	Elmira Prison, New York	Died of Chronic Diarrhea 3/30/1865
Leady, Charles C. Private	Date and Place Unknown	Unknown	Co. D, 40th Regiment North Carolina, 3rd N. C. Artillery	Captured	Prison Unknown	Release Unknown
Leary, Lemuel Private	Enfield, Halifax County, North Carolina, 10/9/1861	Halifax County, North Carolina, 18 Years Old	Co. F, 36th Regiment North Carolina, 2nd N. C. Artillery	Captured	Elmira Prison, New York	Exchanged 3/2/1865 Boulware's Wharf, James River, Virginia
Ledondew, Thomas D. Private	Date and Place Unknown	Unknown	Co. D, 40th Regiment North Carolina, 3rd N. C. Artillery	Captured	Prison Unknown	Release Unknown
Lee, Nelson H. Private	Craven County, North Carolina, 1/24/1862, Volunteer	Swift Creek, North of Neuse River, Craven County, North Carolina, 22 Years Old Farm Laborer	Co. D, 40th Regiment North Carolina, 3rd N. C. Artillery	Captured	Point Lookout, Maryland	Died of Pneumonia 1/30/1865
Lee, W. J. Private	Pee Dee, South Carolina 4/27/1862	Timmonsville, South Carolina, 42 Years Old	Co. K, 21st South Carolina Volunteers	Captured	Elmira Prison, Elmira, New York	Oath of Allegiance 7/11/1865
Legett, Andrew J. Private	Bennetts-ville, South Carolina 4/4/1862	Marion County, South Carolina, 25 Years Old Farm Laborer	Co. F, 21st South Carolina Volunteers	Captured	Elmira Prison, Elmira, New York	Oath of Allegiance 6/14/1865
Leggett, Jesse Private	Brunswick County, North Carolina, 8/19/1863	Brunswick County, North Carolina, 18 Years Old	Co. E, 40th Regiment North Carolina, 3rd N. C. Artillery	Captured	Point Lookout, Maryland	Oath of Allegiance 6/9/1865

NAME & RANK	ENLISTED	RESIDENCE AGE & TRADE	UNIT	RESULT OF BATTLE	PRISON	PRISON RELEASE
Legrand, Hosmar Private	Fort Fisher, New Hanover County, North Carolina, 9/1/1863	Mangum, Richmond County, North Carolina, 18 Years Old Farmer	2nd Co. I, 36th Regiment North Carolina, 2nd N. C. Artillery	Captured, Defended Shepperd's Battery	Elmira Prison, New York	Died on route to be Exchanged at James River of Chronic Diarrhea-Typhoid Fever 3/8/1865
Legrand, Julius E. Private	New Hanover County, North Carolina, 3/8/1864	Mangum, Richmond County, North Carolina, 17 Years Old Farmer	2nd Co. I, 36th Regiment North Carolina, 2nd N. C. Artillery	Captured, Defended Shepperd's Battery	Elmira Prison, New York	Exchanged 3/2/1865, Died of Chronic Diarrhea-Typhoid Fever 3/10/1865
Legrand, Nash First Lieutenant	New Hanover County, North Carolina, 12/27/1861	Anson County, North Carolina, 24 Years Old	2nd Co. I, 36th Regiment North Carolina, 2nd N. C. Artillery	Captured, Defended Shepperd's Battery	Fort Columbus, New York Harbor	Exchanged 3/5/1865 Boulware's Wharf, James River, Virginia,
Lehue, Benjamin W. Private	Fort St. Philip, Brunswick County, North Carolina, 5/14/1862	Brunswick County, North Carolina, 28 Years Old	3rd Co. G, 36th Regiment North Carolina, 2nd N. C. Artillery	Captured, Defended Battery to the Left of Northeast Bastion	Elmira Prison, New York	Exchanged 3/2/1865 Boulware's Wharf, James River, Virginia
Leman, Leaman B. Private	Ridgeville, South Carolina 8/20/1861	Unknown, 20 Years Old	Co. G, 11th South Carolina Volunteers	Captured	Point Lookout, Maryland	Died of Chronic Diarrhea-Typhoid Fever, 3/10/1865
Lemon, Alexander Private	Elizabeth-town, Bladen County, North Carolina, 5/7/1862	Elizabethtown Bladen County, North Carolina, 27 Years Old Cooper	Co. H, 36th Regiment North Carolina, 2nd N. C. Artillery	Captured	Elmira Prison, New York	Oath of Allegiance 6/12/1865
Lemon, Neil J. Sergeant	Bladen County, North Carolina, 3/7/1862	Elizabethtown Bladen County, North Carolina, 27 Years Old Turpentine	Co. H, 36th Regiment North Carolina, 2nd N. C. Artillery	Gunshot Wound Left Arm & Captured	Point Lookout, Maryland	Oath of Allegiance 6/29/1865

NAME & RANK	ENLISTED	RESIDENCE AGE & TRADE	UNIT	RESULT OF BATTLE	PRISON	PRISON RELEASE
Lemons, John A. Private	Union County, North Carolina, 3/23/1863	Iredell County, North Carolina, 31 Years Old Farmer	Co. K, 10th Regiment North Carolina, 1st N. C. Artillery	Captured	Elmira Prison, New York	Died of Pneumonia 5/20/1865
Lennon, Joseph E. Private	Bladen County, North Carolina, 8/28/1862	Bladen County, North Carolina, 20 Years Old	3rd Co. B, 36th Regiment North Carolina, 2nd N. C. Artillery	Captured	Point Lookout, Maryland	Oath of Allegiance 6/29/1865
Leonard, Asa Corporal	Fort St. Philip, Brunswick County, North Carolina, 5/16/1862	Shallotte District, Brunswick County, North Carolina, 32 Years Old Farmer	3rd Co. G, 36th Regiment North Carolina, 2nd N. C. Artillery	Captured, Defended Battery to the Left of Northeast Bastion	Elmira Prison, New York	Oath of Allegiance 7/7/1865
Leonard, Benjamin W. Private	Brunswick County, North Carolina, 1/2/1864	Shallotte District, Brunswick County, North Carolina, 18 Years Old Farmer	Co. K, 36th Regiment North Carolina, 2nd N. C. Artillery	Wounded & Captured	Point Lookout, Maryland	Oath of Allegiance 5/13/1865
Leonard, C. C. Private	Date and Place Unknown	Unknown	Co. K, 36th Regiment North Carolina, 2nd N. C. Artillery	Wounded & Captured	Prison Unknown	Release Unknown
Lesesne, James Private	Fort Holmes, Bladen County, North Carolina, 5/25/1864	Elizabethtown Bladen County, North Carolina, 17 Years Old	2nd Co. K, 40th Regiment North Carolina, 3rd N. C. Artillery	Captured	Elmira Prison, New York	Oath of Allegiance 6/12/1865
Lesesue, Paul Private	Fort Fisher, North Carolina, 12/4/1862 Volunteer	Elizabethtown Bladen County, North Carolina, 17 Years Old Student	2nd Co. K, 40th Regiment North Carolina, 3rd N. C. Artillery	Captured	Elmira Prison, New York	Exchanged 3/14/1865 Boulware's Wharf, James River, Virginia

NAME & RANK	ENLISTED	RESIDENCE AGE & TRADE	UNIT	RESULT OF BATTLE	PRISON	PRISON RELEASE
Lessene, Charles First Lieutenant	Williamsburg South Carolina 12/29/1862	Kingstree, Williamsburg, South Carolina, 23 Years Old Clerk	Co K, 25th Regiment South Carolina Volunteers	Wounded In Right Hip By Shell Fragment & Captured	Fort Delaware, Del.	Oath of Allegiance 6/17/1865
Lewis, Alexander Private	Fort St. Philip, Brunswick County, North Carolina, 4/16/1862	Lumberton, Robeson County, North Carolina, 23 Years Old	3rd Co. G, 36th Regiment North Carolina, 2nd N. C. Artillery	Captured, Defended Battery to the Left of Northeast Bastion	Elmira Prison, New York	Exchanged 2/20/1865, Died in Hospital in Raleigh of Pneumonia 3/20/1865
Lewis, Andrew W. Private	Halifax County, North Carolina, 10/9/1861	Enfield, Halifax County, North Carolina, 18 Years Old Farm Laborer	Co. F, 36th Regiment North Carolina, 2nd N. C. Artillery	Wounded in Shoulder 12/24/1864 & Captured	Point Lookout, Maryland	Oath of Allegiance 6/28/1865,
Lewis, C. M. Private	Date and Place Unknown	Unknown	Co. K, 36th Regiment North Carolina, 2nd N. C. Artillery	Wounded	Prison Unknown	Release Unknown
Lewis, Dallas F. Private	Fort Caswell, Brunswick County, North Carolina, 5/30/1863	Lumberton, Robeson County, North Carolina, 18 Years Old Farm Laborer	Co. E, 40th Regiment North Carolina, 3rd N. C. Artillery	Captured	Point Lookout, Maryland	Oath of Allegiance 6/28/1865
Lewis, Gains Private	Fort Branch, Brunswick County, North Carolina, 7/23/1863	Wayne County, North Carolina, 28 Years Old	3rd Co. G, 40th Regiment North Carolina, 3rd N. C. Artillery	Captured, Defended Land Face	Elmira Prison, New York	Exchanged 2/20/1865
Lewis, Thomas W. Private	Fort Caswell, Brunswick County, N. C., 3/6/1862	Unknown, 28 Years Old	Co. K, 36th Regiment North Carolina, 2nd N. C. Artillery	Gunshot Wound Right Side of Back & Captured	Point Lookout Prison Hospital, Maryland	Died of Gunshot wound 5/5/1865

NAME & RANK	ENLISTED	RESIDENCE AGE & TRADE	UNIT	RESULT OF BATTLE	PRISON	PRISON RELEASE
Lewis, William E. Private	Wayne County, North Carolina, 10/6/1863	Goldsboro, Wayne County, North Carolina, 17 Years Old	Co. F, 10th Regiment North Carolina, 1st N. C. Artillery	Captured	Elmira Prison, New York	Oath of Allegiance 5/29/1865
Liddon, David S. Private	Fort Okracoke, Beaufort County, North Carolina, 4/22/1861	Washington, Beaufort County, North Carolina, 21 Years Old	Co. K, 10th Regiment North Carolina, 1st N. C. Artillery	Captured	Elmira Prison, New York	Oath of Allegiance 5/14/1865
Lide, Robert T. Private	Chesterfield, South Carolina 2/24/1863	Cheraw, Chesterfield, South Carolina, 26 Years Old	Co. D, 21st South Carolina Volunteers	Captured	Elmira Prison, Elmira, New York	Oath of Allegiance 7/7/1865
Lifrage, Theodore M. Sergeant	Williamsburg South Carolina 12/29/1861	Murray's Ferry, Williamsburg, South Carolina, 29 Years Old	Co K, 25th Regiment South Carolina Volunteers	Captured	Elmira Prison, Elmira, New York	Died of Chronic Diarrhea, 4/3/1865
Lilly, William B. Private	Beaufort County, North Carolina, 10/5/1861	Tarboro, Edgecombe County, North Carolina, 18 Years Old	Co. K, 10th Regiment North Carolina, 1st N. C. Artillery	Captured	Elmira Prison, New York	Oath of Allegiance 7/19/1865
Lime, William Private	Date and Place Unknown	Unknown	2nd Co. I, 36th Regiment North Carolina, 2nd N. C. Artillery	Captured, Defended Shepperd's Battery	Elmira Prison, New York	Died of Unknown Disease 3/31/1865
Lines, Samuel Private	Date and Place Unknown	Salisbury, Rowan County, North Carolina, 37 Years Old Carpenter	3rd Co. G, 36th Regiment North Carolina, 2nd N. C. Artillery	Wounded & Captured, Defended Battery to the Left of Northeast Bastion	Prison Unknown	Release Unknown, May Have Died at Fort Fisher

NAME & RANK	ENLISTED	RESIDENCE AGE & TRADE	UNIT	RESULT OF BATTLE	PRISON	PRISON RELEASE
Little, Alexander H. Private	Fort Okracoke, Beaufort County, North Carolina, 7/24/1861	Long Acre, Beaufort County, North Carolina, 18 Years Old	Co. K, 10th Regiment North Carolina, 1st N. C. Artillery	Wounded Severe & Captured	Prison Unknown	Release Unknown, May have Died of Wounds at Fort Fisher
Little, Bennett Private	Fort Caswell, Brunswick County, North Carolina, 12/6/1863, Volunteer	Unknown, 45 Years Old	Co. K, 36th Regiment North Carolina, 2nd N. C. Artillery	Wounded & Captured	Prison Unknown	Release Unknown
Little, Henry D. Private	Edgecombe County, North Carolina, 9/1/1863	Tarboro, Edgecombe County, North Carolina, 43 Years Old Farmer	Co. D, 40th Regiment North Carolina, 3rd N. C. Artillery	Captured	Point Lookout, Maryland	Oath of Allegiance 6/28/1865
Little, Leonidas Private	Edgecombe County, North Carolina, 7/7/1863	Tarboro, Edgecombe County, North Carolina, 25 Years Old	Co. D, 40th Regiment North Carolina, 3rd N. C. Artillery	Captured	Point Lookout, Maryland	Oath of Allegiance 6/28/1865
Little, Robert Augustus Private	Beaufort County, North Carolina, 1/22/1862	Tranter's Creek, Beaufort County, North Carolina, 31 Years Old	Co. D, 13th Battalion North Carolina Light Artillery	Captured, Defended River Road Gate	Elmira Prison, New York	Died of Chronic Diarrhea 3/20/1865
Lock, Thomas J. Private	Fort Caswell, Brunswick County, North Carolina, 1/14/1864	Halifax County, North Carolina, 18 Years Old	Co. F, 36th Regiment North Carolina, 2nd N. C. Artillery	Gunshot Wound & Fracture of Right Forearm & Captured	Point Lookout Hospital, Maryland	Oath of Allegiance 6/3/1865

NAME & RANK	ENLISTED	RESIDENCE AGE & TRADE	UNIT	RESULT OF BATTLE	PRISON	PRISON RELEASE
Lock, William Private	Brunswick County, North Carolina, 8/11/1863	Unknown, 18 Years Old	Co. E, 40th Regiment North Carolina, 2nd N. C. Artillery	Wounded & Captured	Prison Unknown	Release Unknown
Lockay, L. Private	Date and Place Unknown	Fayetteville, Cumberland County, North Carolina, 36 Years Old Wagoner	Co. F, 36th Regiment North Carolina, 2nd N. C. Artillery	Captured	Prison Unknown	Release Unknown
Lockemy, Resin Private	Fort Caswell, Brunswick County, North Carolina, 7/6/1863	Brunswick County, North Carolina, 28 Years Old	2nd Co. D, 36th Regiment North Carolina, 2nd N. C. Artillery	Captured	Elmira Prison, New York	Died of Pneumonia 3/13/1865
Lockerman John Mason Private	Fayetteville, Cumberland County, North Carolina, 7/6/1863	Sampson County, North Carolina, 33 Years Old Carpenter	2nd Co. C, 36th Regiment North Carolina, 2nd N. C. Artillery	Gunshot Wound above Elbow & Captured	Point Lookout Prison Hospital, Maryland	Amputation of Right Arm, Oath of Allegiance 6/26/1865, Defended River Road Gate
Lockrema, Daniel Private	Date and Place Unknown	Northern Division, Sampson County, North Carolina, 30 Years Old Cooper	2nd Co. D, 36th Regiment North Carolina, 2nd N. C. Artillery	Captured	Elmira Prison, New York	Died of Typhoid Fever 4/29/1865
Lofton, Isaac N. Private	Fort Holmes, Brunswick County, North Carolina, 4/20/1864	Jerecho, Indian Springs District, Wayne County, North Carolina, 18 Years Old	3rd Co. G, 40th Regiment North Carolina, 3rd N. C. Artillery	Captured, Defended Land Face	Elmira Prison, New York	Died of Chronic Diarrhea 3/30/1865
Logan, Calhoun Captain	Battery Island, South Carolina 4/12/1862	Williamsburg District, South Carolina, 25 Years Old	Co. B, 25th South Carolina Volunteers	Captured	Fort Columbus, New York Harbor	Exchanged 2/25/1865

NAME & RANK	ENLISTED	RESIDENCE AGE & TRADE	UNIT	RESULT OF BATTLE	PRISON	PRISON RELEASE
Logan, John J.\n\nCaptain	Camp Harlee, Georgetown South Carolina 1/1/1862	Clarendon District, South Carolina, 28 Years Old Printer	Co. H, 25th South Carolina Volunteers	Gunshot Wound Left Shoulder & Captured	Fort Delaware, DE	Oath of Allegiance 6/17/1865
Lone, S. Q.\n\nPrivate	Date and Place Unknown	Unknown	Co. K, 36th Regiment North Carolina, 2nd N. C. Artillery	Missing believed Killed		No Official Record Found, Name Appears On Report of Major C. E. Pearce, 2/17/1865
Long, Alexander\n\nPrivate	Elizabeth-town, Bladen County, North Carolina, 10/19/1861	Elizabethtown Bladen County, North Carolina, 20 Years Old Day Laborer	2nd Co. I, 36th Regiment North Carolina, 2nd N. C. Artillery	Captured, Defended Shepperd's Battery	Elmira Prison, New York	Oath of Allegiance 7/11/1865
Long, George M.\n\nPrivate	Wilmington, New Hanover County, N. C., 6/1/1864	Columbus County, North Carolina, Age Unknown Farmer	Co. B, 7th Battalion Junior Reserves	Wounded Left Shoulder 12/25/1864	Not Captured	
Long, J. M.\n\nPrivate	Transferred from S.C. Waccamaw Light Artillery 8/6/1864	Unknown	Co. K, 36th Regiment North Carolina, 2nd N. C. Artillery	Captured	Point Lookout, Maryland	Oath of Allegiance 5/13/1865
Long, J. Q.\n\nPrivate	Transferred from S.C. Waccamaw Light Artillery	Unknown	Co. K, 36th Regiment North Carolina, 2nd N. C. Artillery	Captured	Prison Unknown	Release Unknown
Long, J. W.\n\nPrivate	Date and Place Unknown	Unknown	Co. K, 36th Regiment North Carolina, 2nd N. C. Artillery	Wounded & Captured	Prison Unknown	Release Unknown

NAME & RANK	ENLISTED	RESIDENCE AGE & TRADE	UNIT	RESULT OF BATTLE	PRISON	PRISON RELEASE
Long, John Private	Brunswick County, North Carolina, 7/9/1864	Shallotte District, Brunswick County, North Carolina, 17 Years Old Farmer	Co. K, 36th Regiment North Carolina, 2nd N. C. Artillery	Captured	Point Lookout, Maryland	Oath of Allegiance 6/13/1865
Long, Joseph N. Corporal	Brunswick County, North Carolina, 2/19/1862	Shallotte District, Brunswick County, North Carolina, 27 Years Old	Co. K, 36th Regiment North Carolina, 2nd N. C. Artillery	Captured	Point Lookout, Maryland	Oath of Allegiance 6/29/1865
Long, Lillington D. Private	Elizabeth-town, Bladen County, North Carolina, 2/3/1862	Downingsville, North Carolina, 26 Years Old Turpentine	2nd Co. I, 36th Regiment North Carolina, 2nd N. C. Artillery	Captured, Defended Shepperd's Battery	Elmira Prison, New York	Exchanged 2/20/1865 Died Disease at Howard Grove Hospital, Richmomnd, Virginia, 4/2/1865
Long, M. C. Private	Transferred from S.C. Waccamaw Light Artillery	Anson County, North Carolina, Age Unknown Farmer	Co. K, 36th Regiment North Carolina, 2nd N. C. Artillery	Killed In Action 1/15/1865		
Long, William C. Private	Brunswick County, North Carolina, 4/22/1862	Shallotte District, Brunswick County, North Carolina, 19 Years Old Farmer	Co. K, 36th Regiment North Carolina, 2nd N. C. Artillery	Wounded & Captured while a patient in Smithville Hospital	Point Lookout, Maryland	Oath of Allegiance 6/26/1865
Love, Robert A. Private	Red Springs, Robeson County, North Carolina, 9/15/1861	Unknown, 24 Years Old	Co. E, 40th Regiment North Carolina, 3rd N. C. Artillery	Captured	Elmira Prison, New York	Exchanged 3/2/1865 Boulware's Wharf, James River, Virginia

NAME & RANK	ENLISTED	RESIDENCE AGE & TRADE	UNIT	RESULT OF BATTLE	PRISON	PRISON RELEASE
Love, Thomas J. Sergeant	Red Springs, Robeson County, North Carolina, 9/19/1861	Wilmington, New Hanover County, North Carolina, 24 Years Old Railroad Agent	Co. E, 40th Regiment North Carolina, 3rd N. C. Artillery	Captured	Elmira Prison, New York	Exchanged 3/2/1865 Died in Raleigh General Hospital #8 of Chronic Diarrhea 3/15/1865
Love, William T. Private	Date and Place Unknown	Manchester, Cumberland County, North Carolina, 43 Years Old	Co. C, 3rd Battalion North Carolina Light Artillery	Missing Believed Killed		
Lovett, H. Private	Randolph County, North Carolina, 3/28/1863	Greensboro, Guilford County, North Carolina, 24 Years Old Laborer	Co. D, 13th Battalion North Carolina Light Artillery	Mortally Wounded December 1864		
Lowder, H. S. Private	Camp Harlee, Georgetown South Carolina 5/16/1862	Manning, Clarendon District, South Carolina, 31 Years Old Farmer	Co. I, 25th South Carolina Volunteers	Captured	Elmira Prison, New York	Exchanged 3/14/1865
Lowder, James D. Private	Charleston, South Carolina 5/28/1862	Manning, Clarendon District, South Carolina, 29 Years Old Farmer	Co. I, 25th South Carolina Volunteers	Gunshot Wound To Chin & Captured	Elmira Prison, New York	Oath of Allegiance 7/3/1865
Lowe, William T. Private	Wilmington, New Hanover County, North Carolina, 4/31863	Murfreesboro, Hertford County, North Carolina, 15 Years Old	Co. C, 3rd Battalion North Carolina Light Artillery	Concussion From Explosion & Captured	Point Lookout, Maryland	Oath of Allegiance 5/13/1865
Lucas, Henry Private	Clinton, Sampson County, North Carolina, 2/91863	Owensville, Sampson County, North Carolina, 36 Years Old Farmer	2nd Co. D, 36th Regiment North Carolina, 2nd N. C. Artillery	Captured	Elmira Prison, New York	Exchanged 3/14/1865 at Boulware's Wharf, James River, Virginia

NAME & RANK	ENLISTED	RESIDENCE AGE & TRADE	UNIT	RESULT OF BATTLE	PRISON	PRISON RELEASE
Lucas, John T. Private	Transferred From Provost Guard, 3/20/1864, Goldsboro, Wayne County, N. C.	Black Creek District, Wilson County, North Carolina, 19 Years Old	Co. F, 10th Regiment North Carolina, 1st N. C. Artillery	Captured	Elmira Prison, New York	Died of Chronic Diarrhea 4/15/1865
Ludlum, Benjamin Private	Brunswick County, North Carolina, 2/19/1862	Waccamaw District, Brunswick County, North Carolina, 39 Years Old Farmer	Co. K, 36th Regiment North Carolina, 2nd N. C. Artillery	Captured	Point Lookout, Maryland	Died of pneumonia 3/16/1865
Ludlum, John Private	Brunswick County, North Carolina, 2/19/1862	Waccamaw District, Brunswick County, North Carolina, 37 Years Old Farmer	Co. K, 36th Regiment North Carolina, 2nd N. C. Artillery	Captured	Point Lookout, Maryland	Oath of Allegiance 6/29/1865
Lupton, John D. Private	Craven County, North Carolina, 3/1/1863, Substitute for William Tunnell	North of Neuse River, Craven County, North Carolina, 18 Years Old Farmer	Co. D, 40th Regiment North Carolina, 3rd N. C. Artillery	Captured	Point Lookout, Maryland	Died of Acute Diarrhea 6/29/1865
Lynch, Elias Private	Williamsburg South Carolina 12/10/1862	Murray's Ferry, Williamsburg, South Carolina, 31 Years Old	Co. H, 25th South Carolina Volunteers	Gunshot Wound, Chin & Captured	Point Lookout, Maryland	Oath of Allegiance 6/29/1865
Lyons, Thomas J. Private	Date and Place Unknown	Unknown	Co. E, Confederate States Marine Corp. Assigned to Guard aboard CSS *Savannah.*	Captured, Defended Sea Face	Point Lookout, Maryland	Oath of Allegiance 6/28/1865

NAME & RANK	ENLISTED	RESIDENCE AGE & TRADE	MILTARY UNIT	RESULT OF BATTLE	PRISON	PRISON RELEASE
Mace, Joseph C. Private	Marion District, 4/13/1863	Unknown	Co. K, 21st South Carolina Volunteers	Killed in Action 1/15/1865		
Mallison, David B. Private	Wilmington, New Hanover County, North Carolina, 1/1/1863	Washington, Beaufort County, North Carolina, 17 Years Old Apprentice	Co. K, 10th Regiment North Carolina, 1st N. C. Artillery	Captured	Elmira Prison, New York	Oath of Allegiance 5/19/1865
Malloy, Edward Private	Robeson County, North Carolina, 5/9/1862	Lumberton, Robeson County, North Carolina, 29 Years Old Farmer, Born in Scotland	Co. D, 1st Battalion North Carolina Heavy Artillery	Captured, Defended River Road Gate or Middle Sallyport	Elmira Prison, New York	Died of Chronic Diarrhea 4/19/1865
Maness, Lewis W. Private	Wilmington, New Hanover County, North Carolina, 3/14/1863	Unknown, 27 Years Old	Co. K, 10th Regiment North Carolina, 1st N. C. Artillery	Mortally Wounded, Gunshot Wound of Left Side and Lung & Captured	Point Lookout Prison General Hospital, Maryland	Died of wounds 2/15/1865
Markes, Joseph N. Private	Brunswick County, North Carolina, 8/19/1863	Edgecombe County, North Carolina, 44 Years Old	Co. F, 36th Regiment North Carolina, 2nd N. C. Artillery	Mortal Gunshot to Back of Head & Captured	Point Lookout Prison, General Hospital, Maryland	Died of Wounds, 4/5/1865
Marlain, William T. Private	Robeson County, North Carolina, 1/6/1865	Wadesboro, Anson County, North Carolina, 17 Years Old	Co. D, 1st Battalion North Carolina Heavy Artillery	Captured, Defended River Road Gate or Middle Sallyport	Elmira Prison, New York	Oath of Allegiance 5/17/1865
Marler, Jesse Private	Goldsboro, Wayne County, North Carolina, 9/20/1863	Goldsboro, Wayne County, North Carolina, Age Unknown	Co. K, 10th Regiment North Carolina, 1st N. C. Artillery	Captured	Elmira Prison, New York	Oath of Allegiance 6/23/1865

NAME & RANK	ENLISTED	RESIDENCE AGE & TRADE	MILTARY UNIT	RESULT OF BATTLE	PRISON	PRISON RELEASE
Marsh, David C. Private	Charleston, South Carolina 2/24/1862	Charleston, South Carolina, 29 Years Old Proprietor of Dry Dock	Co. A, 25th South Carolina Volunteers	Gunshot Wound To Left Knee & Captured	Point Lookout, Maryland	Oath of Allegiance 6/29/1865
Marsh, Neill Private	Cumberland County, North Carolina, 9/20/1863	Fayetteville, Cumberland County, North Carolina, 40 Years Old Farmer	3rd Co. B, 36th Regiment North Carolina, 2nd N. C. Artillery	Captured	Elmira Prison, New York	Exchanged 3/2/1865 Died of Typhoid/Pneumonia in Raleigh Hospital 3/20/1865
Marshall, Andrew M. Private	Fort Branch, Brunswick County, North Carolina, 8/17/1863	Orange County, North Carolina, 44 Years Old	3rd Co. G, 40th Regiment North Carolina, 3rd N. C. Artillery	Captured, Defended Land Face	Elmira Prison, New York	Oath of Allegiance 6/12/1865
Martin, Allen Corporal	Savannah, Georgia, 7/?/1863	Unknown, 21 Years Old	Co. E, Confederate States Marine Corp, Assigned to Guard Duty Aboard CSS *Georgia*.	Wounded in Right Knee & Captured	Point Lookout, Maryland	Oath of Allegiance 6/4/1865
Martin, James F. Private	Fort Branch, Brunswick County, North Carolina, 7/24/1863	Mt Giliad District, Montgomery County, North Carolina, 24 Years Old Farmer	3rd Co. G, 40th Regiment North Carolina, 3rd N. C. Artillery	Gunshot Wound Right Thigh & Captured, Defended Land Face	Point Lookout Prison General Hospital, Maryland	Oath of Allegiance 6/3/1865
Martin, John Private	Charleston, South Carolina 4/15/1862	Charleston, South Carolina, 39 Years Old	Co. E, 25th South Carolina Volunteers	Wounded & Captured	Elmira Prison, New York	Oath of Allegiance 5/17/1865
Martin, John W. Private	Beaufort County, North Carolina, 10/23/1861	New Castle, Wilkes County, North Carolina, 22 Years Old Farmer	Co. D, 13th Battalion North Carolina Light Artillery	Killed in Action 1/15/1865, Defended River Road Gate		

NAME & RANK	ENLISTED	RESIDENCE AGE & TRADE	MILTARY UNIT	RESULT OF BATTLE	PRISON	PRISON RELEASE
Matheson, James S. Private	Fort Branch, Brunswick County, North Carolina, 7/22/1863	Montgomery County, North Carolina, 18 Years Old	3rd Co. G, 40th Regiment North Carolina, 3rd N. C. Artillery	Wounded in Back & Captured, Defended Land Face	Point Lookout Prison, Maryland	Oath of Allegiance 7/30/1865,
Mathews, Archibald B. Private	Brunswick County, North Carolina, 5/15/1863	Lumberton, Robeson County, North Carolina, 18 Years Old Farmer	Co. E, 40th Regiment North Carolina, 3rd N. C. Artillery	Captured	Elmira Prison, New York	Died of Pneumonia 2/10/1865
Mathews, Charles M. Private	Gourdins Dept., South Carolina 4/15/1862	Unknown, 16 Years Old	Co. K, 25th South Carolina Volunteers	Captured	Elmira Prison, New York	Oath of Allegiance 7/13/1865
Mathews, J. M. Private	Battery Island, South Carolina 4/12/1862	Williamsburg District, South Carolina, 22 Years Old Farmer	Co. B, 25th South Carolina Volunteers	Captured	Elmira Prison, New York	Oath of Allegiance 7/11/1865
Mathews, W. J. Private	Meyersville, South Carolina 5/3/1862	Murray's Ferry, Williamsburg District, South Carolina, 24 Years Old Clerk	Co H, 25th Regiment South Carolina Volunteers	Captured	Elmira Prison, New York	Died of Smallpox, 4/7/1865
Matthews, Allen Private	Harnett County, North Carolina, 2/26/1862	Unknown, 18 Years Old	2nd Co. C, 36th Regiment North Carolina, 2nd N. C. Artillery	Captured, Defended River Road Gate	Prison Unknown	Date of Release Unknown
Matthews, Daniel Private	Blockers-ville, Cumberland County, North Carolina, 2/26/1862, Volunteer	Guilford County, North Carolina, 21 Years Old Farm Laborer, Born in Cumberland County	2nd Co. C, 36th Regiment North Carolina, 2nd N. C. Artillery	Severely Wound in Right Arm & Left Hand & Captured, Defended River Road Gate	Hammond General Hospital, Point Lookout Prison, Maryland	Oath of Allegiance 6/26/1865, Right forearm Arm Amputated and Three Fingers of the Left Hand

NAME & RANK	ENLISTED	RESIDENCE AGE & TRADE	MILTARY UNIT	RESULT OF BATTLE	PRISON	PRISON RELEASE
Matthews, Edwin J. Private	Cumberland County, North Carolina, 2/26/1862	Cumberland County, North Carolina, 18 Years Old	2nd Co. C, 36th Regiment North Carolina, 2nd N. C. Artillery	Captured, Defended River Road Gate	Elmira Prison, New York	Died of Pneumonia 3/17/1865
Matthews, Gideon P. Private	Fort Caswell, Brunswick County, North Carolina, 9/1/1863, Volunteer	Brinkleyville, Halifax County, North Carolina, 18 Years Old Farm Laborer	Co. F, 36th Regiment North Carolina, 2nd N. C. Artillery	Mortally Wounded, Compound Fracture of Right Thigh, & Captured		Died of Wounds at Fort Fisher 1/18/1865
Mathews, Hudson Sergeant	Harnett County, North Carolina, 2/20/1862	Summerville, Harnett County, North Carolina, 39 Years Old	2nd Co. C, 36th Regiment North Carolina, 2nd N. C. Artillery	Captured, Defended River Road Gate	Point Lookout Prison, Maryland	Oath of Allegiance 6/29/1865
Matthews, Jacob M. Private	Cumberland County, North Carolina, 2/26/1862	Summerville, Harnett County, North Carolina, 22 Years Old Farm Laborer	2nd Co. C, 36th Regiment North Carolina, 2nd N. C. Artillery	Captured, Defended River Road Gate	Elmira Prison, New York	Died of Smallpox 4/19/1865
Matthews, James Thomas Private	Sampson County, North Carolina, 7/28/1863	Sampson County, North Carolina, 20 Years Old Farmer	2nd Co. C, 36th Regiment North Carolina, 2nd N. C. Artillery	Captured, Defended River Road Gate	Point Lookout Prison, Maryland	Oath of Allegiance 6/29/1865
Matthews, John Allen Musician	Lillington, Harnett County, North Carolina, 2/20/1862, Volunteer	Raleigh, Wake County, North Carolina, 28 Years Old	2nd Co. C, 36th Regiment North Carolina, 2nd N. C. Artillery	Captured, Defended River Road Gate	Elmira Prison, New York	Oath of Allegiance 6/12/1865

NAME & RANK	ENLISTED	RESIDENCE AGE & TRADE	MILTARY UNIT	RESULT OF BATTLE	PRISON	PRISON RELEASE
Matthews, John R. Private	Fort Caswell, Brunswick County, North Carolina, 3/8/1863, Volunteer	Sampson County, North Carolina, 24 Years Old Farmer	2nd Co. D, 36th Regiment North Carolina, 2nd N. C. Artillery	Wounded & Captured	Elmira Prison, New York	Exchanged 3/2/1865 Boulware's Wharf, James River, Virginia
Matthews, Neill A. Private	Fort Fisher, New Hanover County, North Carolina, 12/12/1862	Raleigh, Wake County, North Carolina, 18 Years Old	2nd Co. C, 36th Regiment North Carolina, 2nd N. C. Artillery	Captured, Defended River Road Gate	Elmira Prison, New York	Oath of Allegiance 6/12/1865
Matthews, Reuben Private	Cumberland County, North Carolina, 5/12/1862	Summerville, Harnett County, North Carolina, 24 Years Old	2nd Co. C, 36th Regiment North Carolina, 2nd N. C. Artillery	Captured, Defended River Road Gate	Point Lookout Prison, Maryland	Oath of Allegiance 6/29/1865
Matthews, William H. Private	Lillington, Harnett County, North Carolina, 2/26/1862	Harnett County, North Carolina, 26 Years Old	2nd Co. C, 36th Regiment North Carolina, 2nd N. C. Artillery	Captured, Defended River Road Gate	Elmira Prison, New York	Died of Smallpox 3/27/1865
Matthis, Neill Private	Harnett County, North Carolina, 11/15/1863	Raleigh, Wake County, North Carolina, 37 Years Old	3rd Co. B, 36th Regiment North Carolina, 2nd N. C. Artillery	Captured	Elmira Prison, New York	Oath of Allegiance 7/7/1865
Maultsby, Gilford R. Private	Columbus County, North Carolina, 1/20/1864, Volunteer	Whiteville, Columbus County, North Carolina, 18 Years Old Farmer	3rd Co. B, 36th Regiment North Carolina, 2nd N. C. Artillery	Unknown	Prison Unknown	Date of Release Unknown, Archives Reports Gilford R. Maulsby Was in the Base Hospital With the Mumps 1/25/1865

NAME & RANK	ENLISTED	RESIDENCE AGE & TRADE	MILTARY UNIT	RESULT OF BATTLE	PRISON	PRISON RELEASE
Maultsby, Henry C. Private	Bladen County, North Carolina, 1/11/1864	Westbrook, Bladen County, North Carolina, 18 Years Old	3rd Co. B, 36th Regiment North Carolina, 2nd N. C. Artillery	Wounded in Shoulder, 12/24/1864		Sent to Hospital in Raleigh, N. C.
Maxwell, Whitford Private	Camp Wyatt, New Hanover County, North Carolina, 6/16/1864	New Hanover County, North Carolina, 35 Years Old Farmer	2nd Co. D, 36th Regiment North Carolina, 2nd N. C. Artillery	Captured	Elmira Prison, New York	Died of Chronic Diarrhea 3/11/1865
Maxwell, William S. Private	Camp Wyatt, New Hanover County, North Carolina, 3/15/1864	New Hanover County, North Carolina, 35 Years Old	2nd Co. D, 36th Regiment North Carolina, 2nd N. C. Artillery	Captured	Elmira Prison, New York	Exchanged 3/14/1865
May, Hugh M. Private	Brunswick County, N. C., 8/5/1863, Volunteer	Silesville, Anson County, North Carolina, 37 Years Old Farmer	2nd Co. D, 36th Regiment North Carolina, 2nd N. C. Artillery	Killed in Action 1/15/1865		
May, James Private	Darlington, South Carolina 5/16/1863	Pendleton, Anderson County, 30 Years Old Carpenter	Co. G, 21st South Carolina Volunteers	Killed in Action 1/15/1865		
May, Patrick F. Private	Charleston, South Carolina 2/22/1862	Unknown, 18 Years Old	Co. E, 25th South Carolina Volunteers	Captured	Elmira Prison, New York	Oath of Allegiance 5/17/1865
Mayo, Benjamin F. Corporal	Carteret County, North Carolina, 8/5/1863	Carteret District, Carteret County, North Carolina, 20 Years Old Clerk	Co. D, 13th Battalion North Carolina Light Artillery	Captured, Defended River Road Gate	Point Lookout Prison, Maryland	Oath of Allegiance 5/15/1865

NAME & RANK	ENLISTED	RESIDENCE AGE & TRADE	MILTARY UNIT	RESULT OF BATTLE	PRISON	PRISON RELEASE
McArthur, Neil T. Corporal	Cumberland County, North Carolina, 2/20/1862	Robeson County, North Carolina, 19 Years Old	2nd Co. C, 36th Regiment North Carolina, 2nd N. C. Artillery	Captured, Defended River Road Gate	Point Lookout Prison, Maryland	Oath of Allegiance 6/29/1865
McBryde, Malcolm H. Captain	Union County, North Carolina, 8/27/1861	Stewartville District, Richmond County, North Carolina, 25 Years Old School Teacher	Co. E, 40th Regiment North Carolina, 3rd N. C. Artillery	Captured	Fort Columbus, New York Harbor	Exchanged 3/5/1865 at Boulware's Wharf, James River, Virginia
McCalister, J. E. Private	Williamsburg South Carolina 5/13/1862	Murray's Ferry, Williamsburg District, South Carolina, 18 Years Old Farmer	Co. H, 25th South Carolina Volunteers	Captured	Elmira Prison, New York	Died of Smallpox 4/20/1865
McCall, Barnabus Private	Marion District, South Carolina 5/12/1862	Selkirk, Marion District, South Carolina, 20 Years Old Farm Laborer	Co. K, 21st South Carolina Volunteers	Captured	Elmira Prison, Elmira, New York	Oath of Allegiance 7/7/1865
McCallum, Daniel S. Sergeant	Robeson County, North Carolina, 9/29/1861, Volunteer	Lumberton, Robeson County, North Carolina, 36 Years Old	Co. E, 40th Regiment North Carolina, 3rd N. C. Artillery	Killed in Action 1/15/1865		
McCallum, Doddridge Private	Union County, North Carolina, 8/27/1861	Lumberton, Robeson County, North Carolina, 28 Years Old Farm Laborer	Co. E, 40th Regiment North Carolina, 3rd N. C. Artillery	Captured	Point Lookout Prison, Maryland	Oath of Allegiance 6/29/1865
McCallum, Neill Private	Union County, North Carolina, 8/27/1861	Robeson County, North Carolina, 26 Years Old Schoolteacher	Co. E, 40th Regiment North Carolina, 3rd N. C. Artillery	Captured	Point Lookout Prison, Maryland	Oath of Allegiance 6/29/1865

NAME & RANK	ENLISTED	RESIDENCE AGE & TRADE	MILTARY UNIT	RESULT OF BATTLE	PRISON	PRISON RELEASE
McCallum, William H. Private	Brunswick County, North Carolina, 1/23/1863	Robeson County, North Carolina, 18 Years Old	Co. E, 40th Regiment North Carolina, 3rd N. C. Artillery	Captured	Point Lookout Prison, Maryland	Oath of Allegiance 6/29/1865
McCabe, Patrick Private	Mobile, Alabama, 8/28/1862	Nashville, Tennessee, Age Unknown Carpenter	Co. E, Confederate States Marine Corp, Served Aboard the *CSS Atlanta* and the *CSS Georgia*.	Captured	Point Lookout Prison, Maryland	Oath of Allegiance 5/14/1865
McCartney James Private	New Hanover County, North Carolina, 9/2/1861	Unknown	2nd Co. I, 10th Regiment North Carolina, 1st N. C. Artillery	Captured	Fort Monroe, Virginia	Oath of Allegiance 2/4/1865
McCaskill, Francis M. Private	Montgomery County, North Carolina, 4/29/1863	Bruton's District, High Point, Guilford County, North Carolina, 18 Years Old	3rd Co. B, 36th Regiment North Carolina, 2nd N. C. Artillery	Captured	Elmira Prison, New York	Oath of Allegiance 7/11/1865
McCaskill, John C. Private	Fort Branch, North Carolina, 7/30/1863	Rock Spring District, Montgomery County, North Carolina, 40 Years Old	3rd Co. G, 40th Regiment North Carolina, 3rd N. C. Artillery	Captured, Defended Land Face	Elmira Prison, New York	Died of Rheumatism 3/18/1865
McCaskill, Nelson Private	Brunswick County, North Carolina, 7/22/1863, Volunteer	Rock Spring District, Montgomery County, North Carolina, 20 Years Old	3rd Co. G, 40th Regiment North Carolina, 3rd N. C. Artillery	Shell Wound, Right Side of Face & Captured, Defended Land Face	Fort Delaware, Del.	Oath of Allegiance 6/19/1865

NAME & RANK	ENLISTED	RESIDENCE AGE & TRADE	MILTARY UNIT	RESULT OF BATTLE	PRISON	PRISON RELEASE
McCauley, John Private	Fort Caswell, Brunswick County, North Carolina, 12/19/1862	Brunswick County, North Carolina, Age Unknown	2nd Co. D, 36th Regiment North Carolina, 2nd N. C. Artillery	Captured	Elmira Prison, New York	Exchanged 3/2/1865 Boulware's Wharf, James River, Virginia
McClary, D. S. Private	James Island, South Carolina 4/5/1864	Kingstree, Murray's Ferry, Williamsburg District, South Carolina, 16 Years Old Farmer	Co. C, 25th South Carolina Volunteers	Captured	Elmira Prison, New York	Oath of Allegiance 7/11/1865
McClendon Joel Private	Fort Branch, Brunswick County, North Carolina, 7/24/1863	Montgomery County, North Carolina, 30 Years Old	3rd Co. G, 40th Regiment North Carolina, 3rd N. C. Artillery	Captured, Defended Land Face	Elmira Prison, New York	Died of Remittent Fever 2/18/1865
McCorkle, J. F. Private	Marion District, South Carolina 4/20/1862	Marion District, South Carolina, Age Unknown	Co. D, 25th South Carolina Volunteers	Captured	Elmira Prison, New York	Oath of Allegiance 7/7/1865
McCormic, Dugal Private	Robeson County, North Carolina, 5/14/1862	Robeson County, North Carolina, 28 Years Old Farmer	Co. D, 1st Battalion North Carolina Heavy Artillery	Captured, Defended River Road Gate or Middle Sallyport	Point Lookout Prison, Maryland	Oath of Allegiance 6/29/1865
McCormic, James L. Captain	Robeson County, North Carolina, 5/14/1862, Volunteer	Robeson County, North Carolina, 30 Years Old Merchant	Co. D, 1st Battalion North Carolina Heavy Artillery	Killed in Action 1/15/1865, Defended River Road Gate		

NAME & RANK	ENLISTED	RESIDENCE AGE & TRADE	MILTARY UNIT	RESULT OF BATTLE	PRISON	PRISON RELEASE
McCormick, Duncan Private	Red Springs, Robeson County, North Carolina, 9/17/1861	Lumberton, Robeson County, North Carolina, Farm Laborer, 19 Years Old Carpenter	Co. E, 40th Regiment North Carolina, 3rd N. C. Artillery	Captured	Elmira Prison, New York	Died of Unknown Causes 7/21/1865
McCormick, James D. Private	Robeson County, North Carolina	Lumberton, Robeson County, North Carolina, 19 Years Old Farmer	Co. E, 40th Regiment North Carolina, 3rd N. C. Artillery	Captured	Prison Unknown	Date of Release Unknown
McCormick, James A. Private	Union County, North Carolina, 8/27/1861	Lumberton, Robeson County, North Carolina, 18 Years Old Farmer	Co. E, 40th Regiment North Carolina, 3rd N. C. Artillery	Captured	Point Lookout Prison, Maryland	Oath of Allegiance 6/29/1865
McCotter, Benjamin Franklin Sr. Corporal	Craven County, North Carolina, 10/23/1861	Craven County, North Carolina, 19 Years Old	Co. D, 40th Regiment North Carolina, 3rd N. C. Artillery	Captured	Point Lookout Prison, Maryland	Oath of Allegiance 6/29/1865
McCurdy, Samuel Sergeant	Mobile, Alabama, 12/22/1862	Unknown	Co. E, Confederate States Marine Corp, Assigned to Guard Duty Aboard CSS *Savannah.*	Captured, Defended Sea Face	Point Lookout Prison, Maryland	Oath of Allegiance 6/29/1865
McDade, John Private	New Orleans, Louisiana, 4/19/1861	New Orleans, Louisiana, Age Unknown Laborer	Co. B, Confederate States Marine Corp, Assigned to Guard Duty aboard CSS *North Carolina* and CSS *Arctic.*	Wounded & Captured	Point Lookout Prison, Maryland	Oath of Allegiance 5/14/1865

NAME & RANK	ENLISTED	RESIDENCE AGE & TRADE	MILTARY UNIT	RESULT OF BATTLE	PRISON	PRISON RELEASE
McDaniel, Joe R. Sergeant	Marion District, South Carolina 1/8/1862	Allen's Bridge, Marion District, South Carolina, 23 Years Old Farmer	Co. I, 21st South Carolina Volunteers	Captured	Elmira Prison, Elmira, New York	Died of Pneumonia, 6/11/1865
McDaniel, Love Private	New Hanover County, North Carolina, 12/14/1862	Ellisville, Bladen County, North Carolina, 18 Years Old Farmer	2nd Co. C, 36th Regiment North Carolina, 2nd N. C. Artillery	Captured, Defended River Road Gate	Point Lookout Prison, Maryland	Oath of Allegiance 6/29/1865
McDaniel, William L. Private	Fort Branch, New Hanover County, North Carolina, 8/1/1863	New Berne, Craven County, North Carolina, 44 Years Old	3rd Co. G, 40th Regiment North Carolina, 3rd N. C. Artillery	Captured, Defended Land Face	Elmira Prison, New York	Oath of Allegiance 6/12/1865
McDonald, John M. Private	Raleigh, Wake County, North Carolina, 7/16/1862	Lumberton, Robeson County, North Carolina, 17 Years Old Farmer	Co. E, 40th Regiment North Carolina, 3rd N. C. Artillery	Captured	Point Lookout Prison, Maryland	Oath of Allegiance 6/29/1865
McDuffie, Daniel K. Private	Fort St. Philip, Brunswick County, North Carolina, 7/16/1862	Brunswick County, North Carolina, 21 Years Old	2nd Co. K, 40th Regiment North Carolina, 3rd N. C. Artillery	Captured	Elmira Prison, New York	Exchanged 3/2/1865 Boulware's Wharf, James River, Virginia
McDuffie, Henry F. Private	Fort St. Philip, Brunswick County, North Carolina, 7/16/1862	Wilmington, New Hanover County, North Carolina, 18 Years Old Mail Carrier	2nd Co. K, 40th Regiment North Carolina, 3rd N. C. Artillery	Captured	Elmira Prison, New York	Died of Unknown Disease on Boat to be Exchanged, 2/20/1865

NAME & RANK	ENLISTED	RESIDENCE AGE & TRADE	MILTARY UNIT	RESULT OF BATTLE	PRISON	PRISON RELEASE
McEachin, Daniel Private	New Hanover County, North Carolina, 2/25/1863	Lumberton, Robeson County, North Carolina, 20 Years Old Farmer	Co. D, 1st Battalion North Carolina Heavy Artillery	Captured, Defended River Road Gate or Middle Sallyport	Point Lookout Prison, Maryland	Oath of Allegiance 6/29/1865
McEwen, Archibald Daniel Corporal	Elizabeth-town, Bladen County, North Carolina, 5/6/1862	Elizabethtown Bladen County, North Carolina, 23 Years Old Farmer	2nd Co. K, 40th Regiment North Carolina, 3rd N. C. Artillery	Captured	Elmira Prison, New York	Oath of Allegiance 6/12/1865, Died of Chronic Diarrhea June 19th at Manchester, Va.
McFeeley, James G. Private	Charleston, South Carolina 5/5/1862	Unknown	Co. H, 25th South Carolina Volunteers	Captured	Elmira Prison, New York	Oath of Allegiance 5/7/1865
McGee, Stephen Private	Bladen County, North Carolina, 10/19/1861	Bladen County, North Carolina, 17 Years Old	2nd Co. I, 36th Regiment North Carolina, 2nd N. C. Artillery	Captured, Defended Shepperd's Battery	Point Lookout Prison, Maryland	Oath of Allegiance 5/14/1865
McGhee, William H. Private	Elizabeth-town, Bladen County, North Carolina, 10/19/1861	Bladen County, North Carolina, 19 Years Old	2nd Co. I, 36th Regiment North Carolina, 2nd N. C. Artillery	Captured, Defended Shepperd's Battery	Elmira Prison, New York	Exchanged 3/14/1865 at Boulware's Wharf, James River, Virginia,
McGinnis, Patrick Private	New Orleans, Louisiana, 6/4/1861	New Orleans, Louisiana, Age Unknown	Co. C, Confederate States Marine Corp, Assigned to Guard Duty aboard CSS *Virginia* and CSS *Arctic*.	Wounded & Captured	Point Lookout Prison, Maryland	Oath of Allegiance 5/14/1865

NAME & RANK	ENLISTED	RESIDENCE AGE & TRADE	MILTARY UNIT	RESULT OF BATTLE	PRISON	PRISON RELEASE
McGirt, John Archibald Private	Brunswick County, North Carolina, 5/17/1862	Lumberton, Robeson County, North Carolina, 21 Years Old Farmer	Co. E, 40th Regiment North Carolina, 3rd N. C. Artillery	Captured	Point Lookout Prison, Maryland	Oath of Allegiance 6/29/1865
McGirt, Joseph T. Sergeant	Union County, North Carolina, 8/30/1861	Robeson County, North Carolina, 30 Years Old Carpenter	Co. E, 40th Regiment North Carolina, 3rd N. C. Artillery	Captured	Point Lookout Prison, Maryland	Oath of Allegiance 6/29/1865
McGoogan James A. Private	Robeson County, North Carolina, 9/1/1864	Robeson County, North Carolina, Age Unknown Farmer	Co. D, 1st Battalion North Carolina Heavy Artillery	Shell Wound, Left Shoulder & Captured, Defended River Road Gate	Fort Monroe, Va, Sent to Point Lookout Prison, Maryland	Oath of Allegiance 6/21/1865
McGoogan Nathaniel Private	Robeson County, North Carolina, 5/6/1862, Volunteer	Lumberton, Robeson County, North Carolina, 18 Years Old Farmer	Co. D, 1st Battalion North Carolina Heavy Artillery	Killed in Action 1/15/1865, Defended River Road Gate		
McGoogan James A. Private	Robeson County, North Carolina, 9/1/1864	Robeson County, North Carolina, Age Unknown Farmer	Co. C, 3rd Battalion North Carolina Light Artillery	Wounded & Captured	Point Lookout Prison, Maryland	Oath of Allegiance 6/21/1865
McGregor, Benjamin F. Private	Fort Caswell, Brunswick County, North Carolina, 1/23/1863	Williamson District, Richmond County, North Carolina, 18 Years Old	Co. E, 40th Regiment North Carolina, 3rd N. C. Artillery	Captured	Elmira Prison, New York	Oath of Allegiance 6/12/1865
McGuire, Edward Private	Mobile, Alabama, 2/18/1861, Discharged and enlisted in CSMC 2/23/1864	Unknown, Laborer	Co. A, Confederate States Marine Corp, Assigned to Guard Duty Aboard CSS *Morgan* and CSS *Edith*	Captured	Point Lookout Prison, Maryland	Oath of Allegiance 5/14/1865

NAME & RANK	ENLISTED	RESIDENCE AGE & TRADE	MILTARY UNIT	RESULT OF BATTLE	PRISON	PRISON RELEASE
McIntosh, Daniel Private	Camp Holmes, North Carolina, 4/12/1864	Moore County, North Carolina, 18 Years Old Farmer	Co. K, 10th Regiment North Carolina, 1st N. C. Artillery	Captured	Elmira Prison, New York	Died of Chronic Diarrhea 4/2/1865
McIntosh, Peter Private	Richmond County, North Carolina, 4/12/1864	Laurel Hill District, Richmond County, North Carolina, 17 Years Old Merchant	Co. D, 1st Battalion North Carolina Heavy Artillery	Captured, Defended River Road Gate or Middle Sallyport	Point Lookout Prison, Maryland	Oath of Allegiance 6/29/1865
McIntyre, Duncan Musician	Wilmington, New Hanover County, North Carolina, 2/6/1863	Cumberland County, North Carolina, 38 Years Old Farmer	Co. F, 10th Regiment North Carolina, 1st N. C. Artillery	Captured	Elmira Prison, New York	Oath of Allegiance 5/15/1865
McIntyre, John T. Sergeant	Bennetts-ville, South Carolina 5/12/1862	Bennettsville, Marlboro District, South Carolina, 17 Years Old	Co. F, 21st South Carolina Volunteers	Captured	Elmira Prison, Elmira, New York	Died of Chronic Diarrhea, 3/5/1865
McIver, Calvin D. Sergeant	Robeson County, North Carolina, 9/17/1861 Volunteer	Robeson County, North Carolina, 19 Years Old Farmer	Co. E, 40th Regiment North Carolina, 3rd N. C. Artillery	Captured	Point Lookout Prison, Maryland	Oath of Allegiance 5/15/1865
McIver, David A. Private	Coles Island, South Carolina 4/11/1862	Unknown	Co. F, 25th South Carolina Volunteers	Captured	Elmira Prison, New York	Exchanged 3/2/1865 Boulware's Wharf, James River, Virginia
McIver, David R. W. Captain	Chesterfield, South Carolina 6/1/1863	Cheraw, South Carolina, 31 Years Old	Co. K, 21st South Carolina Volunteers	Gunshot Wound & Fracture of Left Arm & Captured	Point Lookout Prison General Hospital, Maryland	Oath of Allegiance 6/16/1865, Amputated Lower third of Left Arm

NAME & RANK	ENLISTED	RESIDENCE AGE & TRADE	MILTARY UNIT	RESULT OF BATTLE	PRISON	PRISON RELEASE
McKay, Artemus Private	Robeson County, North Carolina, 8/5/1863	Lumberton, Robeson County, North Carolina, 19 Years Old	3rd Co. B, 36th Regiment North Carolina, 2nd N. C. Artillery	Captured	Point Lookout Prison, Maryland	Oath of Allegiance 6/4/1865
McKay, John L. Private	Fort Fisher, New Hanover County, North Carolina, 7/22/1863	Elizabethtown Bladen County, North Carolina, 18 Years Old Farmer	2nd Co. K, 40th Regiment North Carolina, 3rd N. C. Artillery	Captured	Elmira Prison, New York	Exchanged 3/14/1865 Boulware's Wharf, James River, Virginia
McKay, William Private	Richmond County, North Carolina, 8/17/1863	Laurel Hill, Scotland, North Carolina, 42 Years Old Farmer	Co. E, 40th Regiment North Carolina, 3rd N. C. Artillery	Killed in Action 1/15/1865		
McKee, Archibald Private	Bladen County, North Carolina,	Elizabethtown Bladen County, North Carolina, 16 Years Old Farmer	Co. H, 36th Regiment North Carolina, 2nd N. C. Artillery	Captured	Point Lookout Prison, Maryland	Oath of Allegiance 6/29/1865
McKee, Daniel B. Private	Bladen County, North Carolina, 4/1/1862	Elizabethtown Bladen County, North Carolina, 16 Years Old Farmer	Co. H, 36th Regiment North Carolina, 2nd N. C. Artillery	Captured	Point Lookout Prison, Maryland	Oath of Allegiance 6/26/1865
McKeener, A. Adjutant	Date and Place Unknown	Unknown	25th South Carolina Volunteers	Wounded & Captured	Prison Unknown	Date of Release Unknown
McKiethan Daniel B. Private	Brunswick County, North Carolina, 8/10/1863	Brunswick County, North Carolina, 44 Years Old	Co. K, 36th Regiment North Carolina, 2nd N. C. Artillery	Captured	Point Lookout Prison, Maryland	Exchanged 2/21/1865 at Boulware's Wharf, James River, Virginia

NAME & RANK	ENLISTED	RESIDENCE AGE & TRADE	MILTARY UNIT	RESULT OF BATTLE	PRISON	PRISON RELEASE
McKenzie, Hugh A. Private	Red Spring, Robeson County, North Carolina, 9/6/1861, Volunteer	Lumberton, Robeson County, North Carolina, 22 Years Old Farmer	Co. E, 40th Regiment North Carolina, 3rd N. C. Artillery	Wounded & Captured	Prison Unknown	Date of Release Unknown
McKinnie, Robert Private	Camp Holmes, North Carolina, 9/22/1863	Wayne County, North Carolina, 44 Years Old	3rd Co. G, 40th Regiment North Carolina, 3rd N. C. Artillery	Captured, Defended Land Face	Elmira Prison, New York	Exchanged 2/20/1865
McKinnon, Daniel P. Private	Camp Holmes, North Carolina, 10/29/1864	Robeson County, North Carolina, Age Unknown Farmer	Co. E, 40th Regiment North Carolina, 3rd N. C. Artillery	Captured	Point Lookout Prison, Maryland	Oath of Allegiance 5/15/1865
McKinnon, John M. Lieutenant	Union County, North Carolina, 8/27/1861	Robeson County, North Carolina, 23 Years Old	Co. E, 40th Regiment North Carolina, 3rd N. C. Artillery	Captured	Fort Columbus, New York Harbor	Exchanged 3/5/1865 at Boulware's Wharf, James River, Virginia
McKinnon, Kenneth B. Private	Robeson County, North Carolina, 5/15/1863	Robeson County, North Carolina, 18 Years Old	Co. D, 1st Battalion North Carolina Heavy Artillery	Mortal Gunshot Wound of Right Arm, fractured Humerous & Captured	Point Lookout Prison, Maryland	Died of Wounds 3/26/1865, Defended River Road Gate.
McKinnon, McKay Private	Brunswick County, North Carolina, 5/20/1863	Laurel Hill District, Richmond County, North Carolina, 18 Years Old Farmer	Co. E, 40th Regiment North Carolina, 3rd N. C. Artillery	Captured	Point Lookout Prison, Maryland	Oath of Allegiance 6/29/1865
McKinnon, Murdoch M. Private	Brunswick County, North Carolina, 6/4/1863	Richmond County, North Carolina, 18 Years Old	Co. E, 40th Regiment North Carolina, 3rd N. C. Artillery	Captured	Point Lookout Prison, Maryland	Oath of Allegiance 6/12/1865

NAME & RANK	ENLISTED	RESIDENCE AGE & TRADE	MILTARY UNIT	RESULT OF BATTLE	PRISON	PRISON RELEASE
McKnight, William M. Corporal	Battery Island, South Carolina 4/12/1862	Unknown 28 Years Old	Co. C, 25th South Carolina Volunteers	Captured	Elmira Prison, New York	Exchanged 2/20/1865
McLain, Joshua B. Private	Fort St. Philips, Brunswick County, North Carolina, 7/2/1863	Brunswick County, North Carolina, 17 Years Old	Co. E, 36th Regiment North Carolina, 2nd N. C. Artillery	Wounded In Right Thigh & Captured	Elmira Prison, New York	Died of Unknown Disease 5/10/1865
McLauchlin, John Private	Brunswick County, North Carolina, 4/16/1863	Lumberton, Robeson County, North Carolina, 37 Years Old Painter	Co. H, 36th Regiment North Carolina, 2nd N. C. Artillery	Wounded Left Thigh 12/25/1864 & Captured 1/15/1865	Point Lookout Prison, Maryland	Oath of Allegiance 6/29/1865
McLaughlin, Joseph Private	New Orleans, Louisiana, 4/17/1861	Mobile, Alabama, Age Unknown Laborer	Co. B, Confederate States Marine Corp, Assigned to Guard Duty Aboard CSS *North Carolina*	Captured	Point Lookout Prison, Maryland	Oath of Allegiance 5/14/1865
McLaurin, John Private	Fort Branch, Brunswick County, North Carolina, 8/18/1863	Marvin, Anson County, North Carolina, 41 Years Old Farmer	3rd Co. G, 40th Regiment North Carolina, 3rd N. C. Artillery	Captured, Defended Land Face	Elmira Prison, New York	Died of Eyrsipelas 2/13/1865
McLawlin, E. Private	Date and Place Unknown	Salisbury, Rowan County, North Carolina, Age Unknown Clerk	3rd Co. B, 36th Regiment North Carolina, 2nd N. C. Artillery	Captured	Prison Unknown	Date of Release Unknown
McLean, Albert A. Private	New Hanover County, North Carolina, 5/9/1862	Lumberton, Robeson County, North Carolina, 18 Years Old Farm Laborer	Co. D, 1st Battalion North Carolina Heavy Artillery	Captured, Defended River Road Gate or Middle Sallyport	Point Lookout Prison, Maryland	Died of Chronic Diarrhea 5/1/1865

NAME & RANK	ENLISTED	RESIDENCE AGE & TRADE	MILTARY UNIT	RESULT OF BATTLE	PRISON	PRISON RELEASE
McLean, Angus Private	Richmond County, North Carolina, 5/11/1862	Wolf Pitt District, Richmond County, North Carolina, 23 Years Old Farmer	Co. H, 36th Regiment North Carolina, 2nd N. C. Artillery	Captured	Point Lookout Prison, Maryland	Oath of Allegiance 6/29/1865
McLean, Artemus Private	Union County, North Carolina, 8/27/1861	Robeson County, North Carolina, 20 Years Old Farmer	Co. D, 1st Battalion North Carolina Heavy Artillery	Captured, Defended River Road Gate or Middle Sallyport	Point Lookout Prison, Maryland	Oath of Allegiance 6/24/1865
McLean, Benjamin Franklin Private	Robeson County, North Carolina, 12/15/1863	Lumberton, Robeson County, North Carolina, 15 Years Old	Co. D, 1st Battalion North Carolina Heavy Artillery	Captured, Defended River Road Gate or Middle Sallyport	Point Lookout Prison, Maryland	Oath of Allegiance 6/6/1865
McLean, Lauchlin J. Private	Cumberland County, North Carolina, 12/15/1863	Cumberland County, North Carolina, Age Unknown	3rd Co. B, 36th Regiment North Carolina, 2nd N. C. Artillery	Captured	Point Lookout Prison, Maryland	Oath of Allegiance 6/29/1865
McLean, Murdock Private	Robeson County, North Carolina, 5/14/1864	Lumberton, Robeson County, North Carolina, 18 Years Old Farm Laborer	Co. D, 1st Battalion North Carolina Heavy Artillery	Captured, Defended River Road Gate or Middle Sallyport	Point Lookout Prison, Maryland	Oath of Allegiance 6/12/1865, Report on file at National Archives that Mudock Died at Point Lookout of Unknown Causes
McLean, Neill T. Private	Brunswick County, North Carolina, 3/18/1862	Lumberton, Robeson County, North Carolina, 19 Years Old Farmer	Co. E, 40th Regiment North Carolina, 3rd N. C. Artillery	Captured	Point Lookout Prison, Maryland	Oath of Allegiance 6/29/1865

NAME & RANK	ENLISTED	RESIDENCE AGE & TRADE	MILTARY UNIT	RESULT OF BATTLE	PRISON	PRISON RELEASE
McLeish, John W. Sergeant	Charleston, South Carolina 2/22/1862	Charleston, South Carolina, 26 Years Old	Co. E, 25th South Carolina Volunteers	Captured	Elmira Prison, New York	Oath of Allegiance 5/29/1865
McLellan, Enos T. Private	Camp Harllee, Marion District, South Carolina 5/1/1862	Britton's Neck, Marion District, South Carolina, 17 Years Old	Co. I, 21st South Carolina Volunteers	Captured	Elmira Prison, Elmira, New York	Died of Chronic Diarrhea 3/2/1865
McLendon, Duncan Private	Robeson County, North Carolina, 5/14/1862	Lumberton, Robeson County, North Carolina, 21 Years Old Day Laborer	Co. D, 1st Battalion North Carolina Heavy Artillery	Captured, Defended River Road Gate or Middle Sallyport	Point Lookout Prison, Maryland	Oath of Allegiance 6/29/1865
McLeod, Daniel Private	Harnett County, North Carolina, 4/30/1862	Harnett County, North Carolina, 33 Years Old Farmer	2nd Co. C, 36th Regiment North Carolina, 2nd N. C. Artillery	Captured, Defended River Road Gate	Elmira Prison, New York	Oath of Allegiance 6/12/1865
McLeod, Evander J. Private	Bladen County, North Carolina, 5/5/1862	Bladen County, North Carolina, 21 Years Old Farmer	Co. H, 36th Regiment North Carolina, 2nd N. C. Artillery	Captured	Point Lookout Prison, Maryland	Oath of Allegiance 6/3/1865
McLeod, John H. Private	Elizabeth-town, Bladen County, North Carolina, 5/6/1862	Elizabethtown Bladen County, North Carolina, 21 Years Old Turpentine	2nd Co. K, 40th Regiment North Carolina, 3rd N. C. Artillery	Shell Wound of Left Calf & Thigh & Captured	Point Lookout Prison General Hospital, Maryland	Oath of Allegiance 6/4/1865
McLeod, Malcom Corporal	Bladen County, North Carolina, 10/19/1861, Volunteer	Elizabethtown Bladen County, North Carolina, 32 Years Old Turpentine	2nd Co. I, 36th Regiment North Carolina, 2nd N. C. Artillery	Wounded & Captured, Defended Shepperd's Battery	Fort Delaware, Del.	Oath of Allegiance 6/19/1865

NAME & RANK	ENLISTED	RESIDENCE AGE & TRADE	MILTARY UNIT	RESULT OF BATTLE	PRISON	PRISON RELEASE
McLeod, Malcolm G. Sergeant	Bladen County, North Carolina, 5/5/1862	Elizabethtown Bladen County, North Carolina, 25 Years Old Farmer	Co. H, 36th Regiment North Carolina, 2nd N. C. Artillery	Wounded Right Thigh & Captured	Fort Delaware, Delaware	Oath of Allegiance 6/19/1865
McLvane, J. H. Private	Darlington, South Carolina 1/1/1862	Florence, South Carolina, 22 Years Old	Co. B, 21st South Carolina Volunteers	Captured	Elmira Prison, New York	Oath of Allegiance 7/7/1865
McMasters, Wesley W. Private	Asheboro, Randolph County, North Carolina, 3/25/1863	Reed Creek, Eastern Division, Randolph County, North Carolina, 29 Years Old Carpenter	3rd Co. G, 40th Regiment North Carolina, 3rd N. C. Artillery	Captured, Defended Land Face	Elmira Prison, New York	Exchanged 3/2/1865, Died of Remittent Fever 3/18/1865 At Jackson Hospital, Richmond, Virginia
McMillan, Archibald Sergeant	Wilmington, New Hanover County, North Carolina, 11/4/1861, Volunteer	Bladen County, North Carolina, 45 Years Old Laborer	2nd Co. I, 36th Regiment North Carolina, 2nd N. C. Artillery	Severe Gunshot Wound Right Knee & Captured, Defended Shepperd's Battery	Treated At Mansfield Hospital Morehead City, N. C., Sent To Fort Delaware, Del.	Oath of Allegiance 6/19/1865
McMillan, Archibald M. Private	Robeson County, North Carolina, 4/26/1862	Robeson County, North Carolina, 30 Years Old	Co. D, 1st Battalion North Carolina Heavy Artillery	Captured, Defended River Road Gate or Middle Sallyport	Point Lookout Prison, Maryland	Oath of Allegiance 6/29/1865
McMillan, Daniel Private	Fort Caswell, Brunswick County, North Carolina, 8/12/1864	Fayetteville, Cumberland County, North Carolina, 16 Years Old Farmer	Co. C, 3rd Battalion North Carolina Light Artillery	Captured	Elmira Prison, New York	Oath of Allegiance 6/12/1865, Also reported as having "died on the route" to be exchanged 2/20/1865

NAME & RANK	ENLISTED	RESIDENCE AGE & TRADE	MILTARY UNIT	RESULT OF BATTLE	PRISON	PRISON RELEASE
McMillan, Francis McNish Private	Cumberland County, North Carolina, 8/12/1864	Cumberland County, North Carolina, 19 Years Old Farmer	Co. H, 36th Regiment North Carolina, 2nd N. C. Artillery	Wounded & Captured	Point Lookout Prison, Maryland	Oath of Allegiance 6/29/1865
McMillan, Thomas M. Private	Robeson County, North Carolina, 9/1/1864	Robeson County, North Carolina, Age Unknown	Co. D, 1st Battalion North Carolina Heavy Artillery	Captured, Defended River Road Gate or Middle Sallyport	Prison Unknown	Paroled But Date of Release Unknown
McMillan, William James Private	Robeson County, North Carolina, 9/1/1864	Lumberton, Robeson County, North Carolina, 21 Years Old	Co. D, 1st Battalion North Carolina Heavy Artillery	Captured, Defended River Road Gate or Middle Sallyport	Point Lookout Prison, Maryland	Died of Unknown Causes 6/7/1865
McMillan, William N. D. Private	Robeson County, North Carolina, 11/1/1863	Robeson County, North Carolina, 33 Years Old	Co. D, 1st Battalion North Carolina Heavy Artillery	Shell Wound Below Knee & Captured	Point Lookout Prison General Hospital, Maryland	Oath of Allegiance 6/4/1865, Defended River Road Gate or Middle Sallyport
McMillen, M. T. Private	Date and Place Unknown	Unknown	Co. D, 13th Battalion North Carolina Light Artillery	Captured, Defended River Road Gate	Fort Fisher, North Carolina	Died of Pneumonia 1/27/1865
McNair, Archibald James First Lieutenant	Union County, North Carolina, 8/27/1861	Robeson County, North Carolina, 21 Years Old Student	Co. E, 40th Regiment North Carolina, 3rd N. C. Artillery	Captured	Fort Columbus, New York Harbor	Exchanged 3/5/1865 at Boulware's Wharf, James River, Virginia
McNair, Daniel P. Private	Robeson County, North Carolina, 8/8/1863	Robeson County, North Carolina, 38 Years Old Farmer	3rd Co. B, 36th Regiment North Carolina, 2nd N. C. Artillery	Wounded & Captured, Wounded in Hand 12/24/1864	Elmira Prison, New York	Died of Chronic Diarrhea 3/10/1865

NAME & RANK	ENLISTED	RESIDENCE AGE & TRADE	MILTARY UNIT	RESULT OF BATTLE	PRISON	PRISON RELEASE
McNair, Jonathan E. Private	Union County, North Carolina, 8/27/1861	Robeson County, North Carolina, 23 Years Old Farm Laborer	Co. E, 40th Regiment North Carolina, 3rd N. C. Artillery	Captured	Point Lookout Prison, Maryland	Oath of Allegiance 6/9/1865
McNair, Luther S.	Brunswick County, North Carolina, 12/2/1863	Robeson County, North Carolina, 18 Years Old Farm Laborer	Co. E, 40th Regiment North Carolina, 3rd N. C. Artillery	Captured	Point Lookout Prison, Maryland	Oath of Allegiance 6/9/1865
McNair, Samuel P. Private	Fort Caswell, Brunswick County, North Carolina, 9/22/1863, Volunteer	Stewartsville District, Springfield, Richmond County, North Carolina, 16 Years Old	Co. E, 40th Regiment North Carolina, 3rd N. C. Artillery	Captured	Prison Unknown	Date of Release Unknown
McNeill, Angus D. Private	Robeson County, North Carolina, 9/1/1864	Lumberton, Robeson County, North Carolina, 23 Years Old Farmer	Co. D, 1st Battalion North Carolina Heavy Artillery	Gunshot Wound Right Foot & Captured	Fort Monroe, Newport News, Virginia	Oath of Allegiance 6/30/1865, Defended River Road Gate or Middle Sallyport
McNeill, Albert Sellers Private	Robeson County, North Carolina, 4/16/1864	Lumberton, Robeson County, North Carolina, 17 Years Old Farmer	Co. D, 1st Battalion North Carolina Heavy Artillery	Killed in Action 1/15/1865, Defended River Road Gate		
McNeill, Archibald A. Private	Richmond County, North Carolina, 5/15/1862	Richmond County, North Carolina, 26 Years Old	Co. D, 1st Battalion North Carolina Heavy Artillery	Captured, Defended River Road Gate or Middle Sallyport	Point Lookout Prison, Maryland	Oath of Allegiance 6/29/1865

NAME & RANK	ENLISTED	RESIDENCE AGE & TRADE	MILTARY UNIT	RESULT OF BATTLE	PRISON	PRISON RELEASE
McNeill, Daniel Private	Cumberland County, North Carolina, 11/21/1863	Fayetteville, Cumberland East, Cumberland County, North Carolina, 18 Years Old	3rd Co. B, 36th Regiment North Carolina, 2nd N. C. Artillery, Detailed as scout under Lt. Faison	Captured,	Elmira Prison, New York	Died of Chronic Diarrhea 3/10/1865, Evidence Suggests that McNeill died of suffocation aboard the transport *North Point* while sailing to Point Lookout, Md.
McNeill, David T. Private	Brunswick County, North Carolina, 6/7/1863	Lumberton, Robeson County, North Carolina, 37 Years Old	Co. E, 40th Regiment North Carolina, 3rd N. C. Artillery	Captured	Point Lookout Prison, Maryland	Oath of Allegiance 6/29/1865
McNeill, Franklin Purcell Private	Robeson County, North Carolina, 4/22/1863	Lumberton, Robeson County, North Carolina, 18 Years Old Farmer	Co. D, 1st Battalion North Carolina Heavy Artillery	Captured, Defended River Road Gate or Middle Sallyport	Elmira Prison, New York	Oath of Allegiance 6/26/1865
McNeill, Lauchlin Private	Richmond County, North Carolina, 4/22/1863	Laurel Hill District, Richmond County, North Carolina, 29 Years Old	Co. D, 1st Battalion North Carolina Heavy Artillery	Captured, Defended River Road Gate or Middle Sallyport	Point Lookout Prison, Maryland	Oath of Allegiance 6/29/1865
McNeill, Malcom Private	Brunswick County, North Carolina, 3/27/1863, Volunteer	Lumberton, Robeson County, North Carolina, 18 Years Old	Co. E, 40th Regiment North Carolina, 3rd N. C. Artillery	Mortally Wounded 1/15/1865		
McNeill, Malcom D. Private	Robeson County, North Carolina, 4/22/1863	Lumberton, Robeson County, North Carolina, 16 Years Old Farmer	Co. D, 1st Battalion North Carolina Heavy Artillery	Wounded Left Hip & Captured, Defended River Road Gate	Point Lookout Prison, Maryland	Oath of Allegiance 6/4/1865
McNeill, Thomas A. Sergeant	Robeson County, North Carolina, 7/7/1862	Lumberton, Robeson County, North Carolina, 20 Years Old Farmer	Co. D, 1st Battalion North Carolina Heavy Artillery	Captured, Defended River Road Gate or Middle Sallyport	Point Lookout Prison, Maryland	Oath of Allegiance 6/29/1865

NAME & RANK	ENLISTED	RESIDENCE AGE & TRADE	MILTARY UNIT	RESULT OF BATTLE	PRISON	PRISON RELEASE
McNorton, Daniel Private	Wilmington, New Hanover County, North Carolina, 12/20/1861	White Creek, Bladen County, North Carolina, 20 Years Old Turpentine Distiller	3rd Co. B, 36th Regiment North Carolina, 2nd N. C. Artillery	Mortally Wounded in both Legs & Captured, Contusion Left Hip 12/24/1864		Amputated Both Legs, Died Of Wounds at Fort Fisher 1/16/1865
McPhaul, Laughlin D. Private	Robeson County, North Carolina, 4/22/1863	Lumberton, Robeson County, North Carolina, 22 Years Old Farmer	Co. D, 1st Battalion North Carolina Heavy Artillery	Killed in Action 1/15/1865, Defended River Road Gate		
McPherson, William D. Private	Richmond County, North Carolina, 8/17/1863	Robeson County, North Carolina, 18 Years Old	Co. E, 40th Regiment North Carolina, 3rd N. C. Artillery	Captured	Point Lookout Prison, Maryland	Oath of Allegiance 6/29/1865
McQueen, Daniel M. Private	Date and Place Unknown	Lumberton, Robeson County, North Carolina, 16 Years Old	Co. E, 40th Regiment North Carolina, 3rd N. C. Artillery	Captured	Elmira Prison, New York	Died of Chronic Diarrhea 2/22/1865
McQueen, Henry C. Corporal	Robeson County, North Carolina, 4/22/1863	Lumberton, Robeson County, North Carolina, 17 Years Old Farmer	Co. D, 1st Battalion North Carolina Heavy Artillery	Gunshot Wound Left Thigh & Captured, Defended River Road Gate	Point Lookout Prison, Maryland	Oath of Allegiance 6/4/1865
McRacken, William W. Lieutenant	Brunswick County, North Carolina, 5/5/1862	Brunswick County, North Carolina, 25 Years Old	3rd Co. G, 36th Regiment North Carolina, 2nd N. C. Artillery	Captured, Defended Battery to the Left of Northeast Bastion	Fort Columbus, New York Harbor	Exchanged 3/5/1865 at Boulware's Wharf, James River, Virginia
McRae, Alexander C. Private	Cumberland County, North Carolina, 1/14/1864	Fayetteville, Cumberland County, North Carolina, 18 Years Old Farmer	3rd Co. B, 36th Regiment North Carolina, 2nd N. C. Artillery	Captured	Point Lookout Prison, Maryland	Oath of Allegiance 6/6/1865

NAME & RANK	ENLISTED	RESIDENCE AGE & TRADE	MILTARY UNIT	RESULT OF BATTLE	PRISON	PRISON RELEASE
Meadows, Turner W. Private	Carteret County, North Carolina, 10/16/1861	Carteret District, Carteret County, North Carolina, 21 Years Old Farm Laborer	3rd Co. G, 40th Regiment North Carolina, 3rd N. C. Artillery	Shell Wound, Right Forearm & Captured, Defended Land Face	Treated At Mansfield Hospital, Morehead City, N. C., Sent To Fort Delaware, Del.	Oath of Allegiance 5/10/1865
Mears, Elihu Private	Elizabeth-town, Bladen County, North Carolina, 10/19/1861	Elizabethtown Bladen County, North Carolina, 19 Years Old	2nd Co. I, 36th Regiment North Carolina, 2nd N. C. Artillery	Captured, Defended Shepperd's Battery	Elmira Prison, New York	Oath of Allegiance 6/12/1865
Meeks, Brantley Private	Wilmington, New Hanover County, North Carolina, 2/27/1863	New Hanover County, North Carolina, 26 Years Old	Co. D, 1st Battalion North Carolina Heavy Artillery	Captured, Defended River Road Gate or Middle Sallyport	Elmira Prison, New York	Exchanged 3/14/1865, Died of Scurvy in Jackson Hospital, Richmond, Virginia 4/2/1865
Megginnis, Patrick Private	Unknown	Unknown	Co. C, Confederate States Marine Corp	Captured	Point Lookout Prison, Md.	Unknown
Mellichampe, James M. Private	Charleston, South Carolina 2/24/1862	Charleston, South Carolina, 25 Years Old Clerk	Co A, 25th Regiment South Carolina Volunteers	Captured	Elmira Prison, Elmira New York	Died of Pneumonia 2/12/1865
Melvin, Daniel M. Private	Wilmington, New Hanover County, North Carolina, 1/1/1861	Downingsville Bladen County, North Carolina, 19 Years Old Turpentine	2nd Co. I, 36th Regiment North Carolina, 2nd N. C. Artillery	Captured, Defended Shepperd's Battery	Elmira Prison, New York	Died of Pneumonia 3/18/1865

NAME & RANK	ENLISTED	RESIDENCE AGE & TRADE	MILTARY UNIT	RESULT OF BATTLE	PRISON	PRISON RELEASE
Melvin, John S. Seaman	Date and Place Unknown	Unknown	Galloway Co., Confederate States Coast Guard	Captured	Prison Unknown	Date of Release Unknown
Melvin, John T. Captain	Fort Fisher, New Hanover County, North Carolina, 11/16/1861	Elizabethtown Bladen County, North Carolina, 34 Years Old Constable, Company Commander	2nd Co. I, 36th Regiment North Carolina, 2nd N. C. Artillery	Captured, Defended Shepperd's Battery	Fort Columbus, New York Harbor	Exchanged 3/5/1865 at Boulware's Wharf, James River, Virginia,
Melvin, Joseph M. Seaman	Date and Place Unknown	Unknown	Galloway Co., Confederate States Coast Guard	Captured	Prison Unknown	Date of Release Unknown
Melvin, Marshall H. Private	Fort Fisher, New Hanover County, North Carolina, 3/7/1862	Cumberland East, Harrison's Creek, North Carolina, 17 Years Old Farmer	2nd Co. I, 36th Regiment North Carolina, 2nd N. C. Artillery	Captured, Defended Shepperd's Battery	Elmira Prison, New York	Oath of Allegiance 7/11/1865
Melvin, A. W. Private	Fayetteville, Cumberland County, North Carolina, 2/26/1862	Fayetteville, Cumberland, North Carolina, 26 Years Old Farmer	2nd Co. C, 36th Regiment North Carolina, 2nd N. C. Artillery	Captured, Defended River Road Gate	Elmira Prison, New York	Died of Smallpox 3/18/1865
Melvin, William Private	Alamance County, North Carolina, 3/14/1863	Alamance County, North Carolina, Age Unknown	Co. K, 10th Regiment North Carolina, 1st N. C. Artillery	Captured	Elmira Prison, New York	Oath of Allegiance 6/12/1865
Melvin, William Snowden Private	Bladen County, North Carolina, 5/13/1862	Ellisville, Bladen County, North Carolina, 51 Years Old Farmer	Co. H, 36th Regiment North Carolina, 2nd N. C. Artillery	Captured	Elmira Prison, New York	Died of Unknown Causes 3/18/1865

NAME & RANK	ENLISTED	RESIDENCE AGE & TRADE	MILTARY UNIT	RESULT OF BATTLE	PRISON	PRISON RELEASE
Mercer, Absalum Private	Fort Caswell, Brunswick County, North Carolina, 5/5/1864	Mount Olive, Duplin County, North Carolina, 18 Years Old Farmer	2nd Co. A, 36th Regiment North Carolina, 2nd N. C. Artillery	Captured, Defended the Mound Battery	Elmira Prison, New York	Died On Route to Be Exchanged, 2/20/1865
Mercer, Calvin W. Private	Fort Caswell, Brunswick County, North Carolina, 5/14/1862	Mount Olive, Duplin County, North Carolina, 24 Years Old Farmer	2nd Co. A, 36th Regiment North Carolina, 2nd N. C. Artillery	Captured, Defended The Mound Battery	Elmira Prison, New York	Exchanged 3/2/1865, Died of Unknown Causes in Richmond Hospital 3/29/1865
Mercer, Chancy G. Private	Fort Caswell, Brunswick County, North Carolina, 1/9/1864	Mount Olive, Duplin County, North Carolina, 20 Years Old Farmer	2nd Co. A, 36th Regiment North Carolina, 2nd N. C. Artillery	Captured Defended The Mound Battery	Elmira Prison, New York	Died From "Gangrene of Feet" 3/11/1865
Mercer, Christopher C. Private	Brunswick County, North Carolina, 2/19/1863	Lumberton, Robeson County, North Carolina, 37 Years Old Farmer	Co. E, 40th Regiment North Carolina, 3rd N. C. Artillery	Captured	Point Lookout Prison, Maryland	Died of Pneumonia 2/7/1865
Mercer, Lott Private	Duplin County, North Carolina, 11/6/1861	Mount Olive, Duplin County, North Carolina, 44 Years Old	2nd Co. A, 36th Regiment North Carolina, 2nd N. C. Artillery	Captured, Defended the Mound Battery	Elmira Prison, New York	Exchanged 2/20/1865
Mercer, Noah J. Private	Fort Caswell, Brunswick County, North Carolina, 5/14/1862	Mount Olive, Duplin County, North Carolina, 27 Years Old Farmer	2nd Co. A, 36th Regiment North Carolina, 2nd N. C. Artillery	Captured, Defended the Mound Battery	Elmira Prison, New York	Died of Typhoid Fever 3/17/1865
Mercer, Robert R. Private	Edgecombe County, North Carolina, 9/9/1864	Unknown, 38 Years Old	Co. D, 40th Regiment North Carolina, 3rd N. C. Artillery	Captured	Point Lookout Prison, Maryland	Died of Pneumonia 3/11/1865

NAME & RANK	ENLISTED	RESIDENCE AGE & TRADE	MILTARY UNIT	RESULT OF BATTLE	PRISON	PRISON RELEASE
Meritt, Richard D. Private	Fort St. Philip, Brunswick County, North Carolina, 4/21/1863	Elizabethtown Bladen County, North Carolina, 35 Years Old, Turpentine	Co. E, 36th Regiment North Carolina, 2nd N. C. Artillery	Captured	Elmira Prison, New York	Exchanged 3/14/1865 at Boulware's Wharf, James River, Virginia
Merrett, Andrew J. Private	New Hanover County, North Carolina, 4/16/1864	Enfield, Halifax County, North Carolina, 17 Years Old	Co. F, 36th Regiment North Carolina, 2nd N. C. Artillery	Captured	Point Lookout Prison, Maryland	Oath of Allegiance 6/29/1865
Merritt, Benjamin R. Private	Craven County, North Carolina, 4/16/1864	Enfield, Halifax County, North Carolina, 21 Years Old	Co. F, 36th Regiment North Carolina, 2nd N. C. Artillery	Wounded Left Arm Above Elbow 12/24/1864		Amputation of Left Arm
Merritt, James R. Private	Halifax County, North Carolina, 10/9/1861	Enfield, Halifax County, North Carolina, 18 Years Old Farmer	Co. F, 36th Regiment North Carolina, 2nd N. C. Artillery	Wounded 12/24/1864		
Merritt, John A. Private	Enfield, Halifax County, North Carolina, 10/9/1861	Enfield, Halifax County, North Carolina, 20 Years Old Farmer	Co. F, 36th Regiment North Carolina, 2nd N. C. Artillery	Captured	Elmira Prison, New York	Oath of Allegiance 6/12/1865
Merritt, Joseph Private	Bladen County, North Carolina, 10/19/1861	Windsor, Bertie County, North Carolina, 30 Years Old Farmer	2nd Co. I, 36th Regiment North Carolina, 2nd N. C. Artillery	Captured, Defended Shepperd's Battery	Point Lookout Prison, Maryland	Oath of Allegiance 6/29/1865
Merritt, Marshall Private	Bladen County, North Carolina, 10/19/1861	Bladen County, North Carolina, 20 Years Old	2nd Co. I, 36th Regiment North Carolina, 2nd N. C. Artillery	Wounded in Right Arm & Captured, Defended Shepperd's Battery	DeCamp U.S. Army Hospital, David's Island, New York Harbor	Oath of Allegiance 6/20/1865

NAME & RANK	ENLISTED	RESIDENCE AGE & TRADE	MILTARY UNIT	RESULT OF BATTLE	PRISON	PRISON RELEASE
Merritt, Patrick Private	Sampson County, North Carolina, 12/19/1862	Mount Olive, Duplin County, North Carolina, 38 Years Old Hotel Keeper	2nd Co. A, 36th Regiment North Carolina, 2nd N. C. Artillery	Missing in Action 1/15/1865, Defended the Mound Battery		Survived War
Miller, Alexander Private	Beaufort County, North Carolina, 2/15/1862	Unknown	2nd Co. A, 36th Regiment North Carolina, 2nd N. C. Artillery	Captured, Defended the Mound Battery	Elmira Prison, New York	Exchanged 2/20/1865
Miller, Archibald B. Private	Robeson County, North Carolina, 10/14/1861	Lumberton, Robeson County, North Carolina, 18 Years Old	Co. E, 40th Regiment North Carolina, 3rd N. C. Artillery	Captured	Point Lookout Prison, Maryland	Oath of Allegiance 6/21/1865
Miller, Chancy W. Private	Fort Caswell, Brunswick County, North Carolina, 2/6/1864	Brunswick County, North Carolina, 17 Years Old	2nd Co. A, 36th Regiment North Carolina, 2nd N. C. Artillery	Captured, Defended the Mound Battery	Elmira Prison, New York	Exchanged On the James River 2/20/1865
Miller, Clayton Private	Charleston, South Carolina 12/5/1863	Parish of Prince George, George Town, South Carolina, 15 Years Old	Co. A, 21st South Carolina Volunteers	Captured	Elmira Prison, New York	Exchanged On the James River 2/20/1865
Miller, Daniel Private	Charleston, South Carolina 12/5/1863	3rd Ward, Charleston, South Carolina, 21 Years Old Tinner	Co. A, 21st South Carolina Volunteers	Captured	Elmira Prison, New York	Exchanged 2/20/1865
Miller, John Private	Wilmington, New Hanover County, North Carolina, 7/3/1861	Hanover County, North Carolina, 23 Years Old	Co. F, 36th Regiment North Carolina, 2nd N. C. Artillery	Mortally Wounded In Right Temple & Captured		Died Of Wounds at Fort Fisher 1/21/1865

NAME & RANK	ENLISTED	RESIDENCE AGE & TRADE	MILTARY UNIT	RESULT OF BATTLE	PRISON	PRISON RELEASE
Millican, Francis O. Sergeant	Wilmington, New Hanover County, North Carolina, 3/5/1862	Whiteville, Columbus County, North Carolina, 26 Years Old	Co. E, 36th Regiment North Carolina, 2nd N. C. Artillery	Captured	Elmira Prison, New York	Died of Chronic Diarrhea 3/16/1865
Milliken, Lorenzo F. Private	Fort Caswell, Brunswick County, North Carolina, 2/19/1862, Volunteer	Waccamaw District, Brunswick County, North Carolina, 17 Years Old	Co. K, 36th Regiment North Carolina, 2nd N. C. Artillery	Mortally Wounded (Fractured Skull) & Captured		Died of Wounds at Fort Fisher 1/15/1865
Milliken, Moses Private	Brunswick County, North Carolina, 2/17/1863	Brunswick County, North Carolina, Age Unknown Farmer	Co. K, 36th Regiment North Carolina, 2nd N. C. Artillery	Captured	Point Lookout Prison, Maryland	Oath of Allegiance 5/14/1865
Milliken, Nathan Private	Brunswick County, North Carolina, 7/15/1862, Volunteer	Unknown, 33 Years Old	Co. K, 36th Regiment North Carolina, 2nd N. C. Artillery	Wounded & Captured	Prison Unknown	May Have Died of Wounds at Fort Fisher
Milliken, Robert R. First Sergeant	Brunswick County, North Carolina, 2/19/1862, Volunteer	Waccamaw District, Brunswick County, North Carolina, 35 Years Old Farmer	Co. K, 36th Regiment North Carolina, 2nd N. C. Artillery	Wounded & Captured	Prison Unknown	May Have Died of Wounds at Fort Fisher

NAME & RANK	ENLISTED	RESIDENCE AGE & TRADE	MILTARY UNIT	RESULT OF BATTLE	PRISON	PRISON RELEASE
Mills, John H. Private	Old Brunswick, North Carolina, 4/16/1862, Mustered in Fort St. Philip	Town Creek District, Brunswick County, North Carolina, 41 Years Old Shoemaker	3rd Co. G, 36th Regiment North Carolina, 2nd N. C. Artillery	Captured, Defended Battery to the Left of Northeast Bastion	Elmira Prison, New York	Exchanged 3/2/1865 Boulware's Wharf, James River, Virginia
Miltear, Robert Private	Enfield, Halifax County, North Carolina, 10/9/1861	Halifax County, North Carolina, 30 Years Old	Co. F, 36th Regiment North Carolina, 2nd N. C. Artillery	Captured	Prison Unknown	Date of Release Unknown
Miner, Dougal Private	Date and Place Unknown	Unknown	3rd Co. G, 40th Regiment North Carolina, 3rd N. C. Artillery	Captured, Defended Land Face	Prison Unknown	Date of Release Unknown
Miner, G. L. Private	Date and Place Unknown	Unknown	Co. F, 25th South Carolina Volunteers	Captured	Prison Unknown	Date of Release Unknown
Mims, Alfred J. First Lieutenant	Charleston, South Carolina 2/22/1862	Unknown, 23 Years Old	Co. E, 25th South Carolina Volunteers	Captured	Fort Delaware, Delaware	Oath of Allegiance 5/15/1865
Mims, Josiah P. Lieutenant	Hilton Head, South Carolina 7/26/1861	Unknown, 21 Years Old	Co. H, 11th South Carolina Volunteers	Captured	Fort Columbus, New York Harbor	Exchanged 2/25/1865
Mints, Henry Private	Brunswick County, North Carolina, 4/16/1862, Volunteer	Brunswick County, North Carolina, 23 Years Old	3rd Co. G, 36th Regiment North Carolina, 2nd N. C. Artillery	Wounded & Captured, Defended Battery to the Left of Northeast Bastion	Prison Unknown	May Have Died of Wounds at Fort Fisher

NAME & RANK	ENLISTED	RESIDENCE AGE & TRADE	MILTARY UNIT	RESULT OF BATTLE	PRISON	PRISON RELEASE
Mints, John F. Private	Fort Fisher, New Hanover County, North Carolina, 4/17/1864	Brunswick County, North Carolina, 17 Years Old	3rd Co. G, 36th Regiment North Carolina, 2nd N. C. Artillery	Gunshot Wound Left Shoulder & Captured Defended Battery to the Left of Northeast Bastion	Point Lookout General Hospital, Maryland	Oath of Allegiance 6/3/1865
Mints, Stephen Private	Old Brunswick, North Carolina, 4/16/1862, Mustered in Fort St. Philip	Brunswick County, North Carolina, 48 Years Old	3rd Co. G, 36th Regiment North Carolina, 2nd N. C. Artillery	Captured, Defended Battery to the Left of Northeast Bastion	Elmira Prison, New York	Exchanged 2/20/1865, Died of Unknown Disease in Howard Grove Hospital, Richmond, Virginia, 3/20/1865
Mints, William Private	Old Brunswick, North Carolina, 4/16/1862, Mustered in Fort St. Philip	Brunswick County, North Carolina, 21 Years Old	3rd Co. G, 36th Regiment North Carolina, 2nd N. C. Artillery	Captured, Defended Battery to the Left of Northeast Bastion	Elmira Prison, New York	Died of Typhoid Fever 4/10/1865
Mitchum, John S. Private	Battery Island, South Carolina 4/12/1862	Kingston, South Carolina, 21 Years Old	Co. K, 25th South Carolina Volunteers	Captured	Elmira Prison, New York	Oath of Allegiance 7/11/1865
Mitchum, S. S. Sergeant	Battery Island, South Carolina 4/12/1862	Unknown, 45 Years Old	Co. C, 25th South Carolina Volunteers	Captured	Elmira Prison, New York	Exchanged On James River, Virginia, 2/20/1865
Mitchum, W. E. Private	Gourdins Dept, South Carolina 5/1/1864	Kingstree, South Carolina, 20 Years Old	Co. K, 25th South Carolina Volunteers	Captured	Elmira Prison, New York	Oath of Allegiance 7/7/1865

NAME & RANK	ENLISTED	RESIDENCE AGE & TRADE	MILTARY UNIT	RESULT OF BATTLE	PRISON	PRISON RELEASE
Mixon, A. W. Private	Camp Harllee, Georgetown South Carolina 1/1/1862	Unknown, 41 Years Old	Co. I, 25th South Carolina Volunteers	Captured	Elmira Prison, New York	Died Of Disease 2/14/1865, Chronic Diarrhea
Mixon, W. P. Sergeant	Darlington, South Carolina 1/20/1862	Darlington District, South Carolina, 20 Years Old Farmer	Co. H, 21st South Carolina Volunteers	Captured	Elmira Prison, New York	Exchanged On James River 2/20/1865
Molloy, Lawrence E. Private	James Island, South Carolina 5/4/1862	Charleston, South Carolina, Age Unknown	Co. B, 25th South Carolina Volunteers	Captured	Elmira Prison, New York	Oath of Allegiance 7/7/1865
Monroe, Thomas Private	Fort Caswell, Brunswick County, North Carolina, 6/4/1863	Western Division, Argyle, Cumberland County, North Carolina, 33 Years Old	Co. E, 40th Regiment North Carolina, 3rd N. C. Artillery	Captured	Point Lookout Prison, Maryland	Died of Chronic Dysentery 1/30/1865
Monroe, Thomas L. Private	New Hanover County, North Carolina, 3/15/1862, Volunteer	New Hanover County, North Carolina, 23 Years Old Laborer	Co. H, 36th Regiment North Carolina, 2nd N. C. Artillery	Wounded & Captured	Point Lookout Prison, Maryland	Oath of Allegiance 5/14/1865, Born in Scotland
Montgomery, Edward P. Private	Battery Island, South Carolina 4/12/1862	Kingstree, South Carolina, 20 Years Old	Co. C, 25th South Carolina Volunteers	Captured	Elmira Prison, New York	Oath of Allegiance In USA General Hospital 8/7/1865
Montgomery, Isaac Sergeant	Georgetown South Carolina 1/1/1862	Kingstree, South Carolina, 25 Years Old	Co. C, 25th South Carolina Volunteers	Captured	Elmira Prison, New York	Oath of Allegiance 7/26/1865

NAME & RANK	ENLISTED	RESIDENCE AGE & TRADE	MILTARY UNIT	RESULT OF BATTLE	PRISON	PRISON RELEASE
Montgomery, J. A. Private	Battery Island, South Carolina 4/12/1862	Kingstree, South Carolina, 22 Years Old	Co. C, 25th South Carolina Volunteers	Captured	Elmira Prison, New York	Oath of Allegiance 7/26/1865
Montgomery, James A. Private	New Hanover County, North Carolina, 10/20/1863	New Hanover County, North Carolina, 18 Years Old	3rd Co. B, 36th Regiment North Carolina, 2nd N. C. Artillery	Captured	Point Lookout Prison, Maryland	Oath of Allegiance 5/15/1865
Montgomery, S. E. Private	Georgetown South Carolina 4/17/1862	Unknown, 29 Years Old Overseer at Holms House	Co. B, 25th South Carolina Volunteers	Captured	Elmira Prison, New York	Exchanged On James River 3/14/1865
Moody, Nathanial R. Private	Chatham County, North Carolina, 10/20/1863, Volunteer	Chatham County, North Carolina, 36 Years Old	3rd Co. G, 40th Regiment North Carolina, 3rd N. C. Artillery	Wounded in Back & Captured, Defended Land Face	Point Lookout Prison, Maryland	Oath of Allegiance 6/29/1865
Mooney, John C. Corporal	Fort Johnson, Smithville, Brunswick County, North Carolina, 2/19/1862, Volunteer	Waccamaw District, Brunswick County, North Carolina, 20 Years Old Laborer	Co. K, 36th Regiment North Carolina, 2nd N. C. Artillery	Wounded & Captured	Point Lookout Prison, Maryland	Exchanged 2/21/1865 at Boulware's Wharf, James River, Virginia
Moore, Andrew Private	Fort Fisher, New Hanover County, North Carolina, 3/13/1862	Fayetteville, Cumberland County, North Carolina, 22 Years Old	2nd Co. I, 36th Regiment North Carolina, 2nd N. C. Artillery	Captured, Defended Shepperd's Battery	Elmira Prison, New York	Oath of Allegiance 6/12/1865
Moore, Benjamin Franklin Private	Darlington, South Carolina 5/19/1863	Bennettsville, Marlboro District, South Carolina, 16 Years Old	Co. B, 21st South Carolina Volunteers	Captured	Elmira Prison, New York	Died Of Chronic Diarrhea 4/10/1865

NAME & RANK	ENLISTED	RESIDENCE AGE & TRADE	MILTARY UNIT	RESULT OF BATTLE	PRISON	PRISON RELEASE
Moore, Enoch Private	Fort Caswell, Brunswick County, North Carolina, 12/8/1863	Pitt County, North Carolina, 18 Years Old	Co. F, 36th Regiment North Carolina, 2nd N. C. Artillery	Captured	Elmira Prison, New York	Exchanged 2/20/1865
Moore, George W. First Sergeant	Pocotaligo, South Carolina 8/5/1861	Beaufort District, South Carolina, 20 Years Old	Co. F, 11th South Carolina Volunteers	Captured	Point Lookout Prison, Maryland	Oath of Allegiance 6/29/1865
Moore, J. F. Private	Darlington, South Carolina 1/1/1862	Columbia, South Carolina, 19 Years Old Carpenter	Co. B, 21st South Carolina Volunteers	Captured	Elmira Prison, New York	Oath of Allegiance 8/7/1865
Moore, James R. First Sergeant	Bennetts- ville, South Carolina 12/25/1861	Charleston District, South Carolina, 28 Years Old Sailor	Co. F, 21st South Carolina Volunteers	Captured	Elmira Prison, New York	Died Of Unknown Disease 7/18/1865
Moore, James R. Private	Brunswick County, North Carolina, 7/24/1863	Anson County, North Carolina, 40 Years Old	3rd Co. G, 40th Regiment North Carolina, 3rd N. C. Artillery	Captured, Defended Land Face	Elmira Prison, New York	Exchanged 2/21/1865
Moore, John J. Corporal	Brunswick County, North Carolina, 7/11/1863	Edgecombe County, North Carolina, 40 Years Old	Co. D, 40th Regiment North Carolina, 3rd N. C. Artillery	Captured	Point Lookout Prison, Maryland	Oath of Allegiance 6/29/1865
Moore, William C. Private	Enlistment Place and Date Unknown	Abbeville, South Carolina, 26 Years Old Merchant	Co. K, 21st South Carolina Volunteers	Wounded & Captured	Fort Monroe, Virginia	Sent North on Steamer USS Champion

NAME & RANK	ENLISTED	RESIDENCE AGE & TRADE	MILTARY UNIT	RESULT OF BATTLE	PRISON	PRISON RELEASE
Moore, William A. Private	Brunswick County, North Carolina, 12/31/1862	Brunswick County, North Carolina, 16 Years Old	Co. K, 36th Regiment North Carolina, 2nd N. C. Artillery	Captured	Point Lookout Prison, Maryland	Oath of Allegiance 6/29/1865
Moore, William H. Private	Brunswick County, North Carolina, 7/27/1863	Anson County, North Carolina, 18 Years Old	3rd Co. G, 40th Regiment North Carolina, 3rd N. C. Artillery	Captured, Defended Land Face	Elmira Prison, New York	Died of Remittent Fever 2/28/1865
Moore, William P. Private	Date and Place Unknown	Oglethorpe County, Georgia, 26 Years Old	Co. E, Confederate States Marine Corp, Assigned to Guard Duty Aboard CSS *Savannah.*	Wounded in Leg, Shock & Captured, Defended Sea Face	Point Lookout Prison, Maryland	Oath of Allegiance 6/26/1865
Moore, Wilson E. Private	New Hanover County, North Carolina, 4/13/1863	New Hanover County, North Carolina, Age Unknown	Co. K, 10th Regiment North Carolina, 1st N. C. Artillery	Gunshot Wound Left Side Of Face & Captured	Fort Delaware, Del.	Oath of Allegiance 6/12/1865
Morgan, Benjamin F. Private	Brunswick County, North Carolina, 10/1/1863	Caswell County, North Carolina, 35 Years Old	2nd Co. D, 36th Regiment North Carolina, 2nd N. C. Artillery	Captured	Point Lookout Prison, Maryland	Oath of Allegiance 6/29/1865
Morgan, John W. Private	Brunswick County, North Carolina, 3/1/1864	Unknown, 18 Years Old	Co. D, 13th Battalion North Carolina Light Artillery	Gunshot Wound Right Thigh & Captured, Defended River Road Gate	Point Lookout Prison, Maryland	7/24/1865, Oath of Allegiance 8/29/1865

NAME & RANK	ENLISTED	RESIDENCE AGE & TRADE	MILTARY UNIT	RESULT OF BATTLE	PRISON	PRISON RELEASE
Morris, Anderson Private	New Hanover County, North Carolina, 3/30/1863	Orange County, North Carolina, Age Unknown	Co. D, 13th Battalion North Carolina Light Artillery	Severe Gunshot Wound Left Arm & Captured, Defended River Road Gate	Treated at Mansfield Hospital, Morehead City, N. C., Sent to Fort Delaware, Del.	Oath of Allegiance 6/19/1865
Morris, Garry Private	Halifax County, North Carolina, 10/9/1861	Edgecombe County, North Carolina, 22 Years Old	Co. F, 36th Regiment North Carolina, 2nd N. C. Artillery	Captured	Point Lookout Prison, Maryland	Oath of Allegiance 6/4/1865
Morris, Robert G. Private	Halifax County, North Carolina, 10/9/1861	Halifax County, North Carolina, 18 Years Old	Co. F, 36th Regiment North Carolina, 2nd N. C. Artillery	Captured	Point Lookout Prison, Maryland	Oath of Allegiance 6/29/1865
Morris, William T. Private	Craven County, North Carolina, 10/1/1861	Craven County, North Carolina, 39 Years Old	Co. D, 40th Regiment North Carolina, 3rd N. C. Artillery	Captured	Point Lookout Prison, Maryland	Oath of Allegiance 6/29/1865
Morrison, John H. Private	Robeson County, North Carolina, 7/28/1863, Volunteer	Amhurst County, Virginia, 18 Years Old Extra Duty Cutting Wood	Co. E, 40th Regiment North Carolina, 3rd N. C. Artillery	Shell Wound Lower Right Leg & Captured	Treated at Fort Monroe Hospital, Va, Sent to Point Lookout Prison, Maryland	Oath of Allegiance 6/15/1865
Morse, Allen M. Seaman	5/1/1862 Substitute For Endorous Holden	Unknown	Galloway Co., Confederate States Coast Guard	Captured	Prison Unknown	Date of Release Unknown
Morrisy, Thomas K. Private	Duplin County, North Carolina, 9/15/1861	Warsaw, Duplin County, North Carolina, 42 Years Old Laborer	2nd Co. A, 36th Regiment North Carolina, 2nd N. C. Artillery	Captured, Defended The Mound Battery	Point Lookout Prison, Maryland	Exchanged 2/21/1865 at Boulware's Wharf, James River, Virginia

NAME & RANK	ENLISTED	RESIDENCE AGE & TRADE	MILTARY UNIT	RESULT OF BATTLE	PRISON	PRISON RELEASE
Morton, Benjamin Private	Onslow County, North Carolina, 1/25/1862, Volunteer	Onslow County, North Carolina, 34 Years Old	3rd Co. B, 36th Regiment North Carolina, 2nd N. C. Artillery	Gunshot Wound Fore Finger of Right Hand & Captured	Treated at Fort Monroe Hospital, Va, Sent to Fort Delaware, Delaware	Oath of Allegiance 6/19/1865
Morton, Hardy Owen Private	Bladen County, North Carolina, 1/28/1862	Flemington, North Carolina, 26 Years Old	3rd Co. B, 36th Regiment North Carolina, 2nd N. C. Artillery	Wounded in Left Knee & Captured	Elmira Prison, New York	Oath of Allegiance 7/3/1865
Morton, Jones Private	Carteret County, North Carolina, 10/16/1861, Volunteer	Carteret County, North Carolina, 17 Years Old Extra Duty as Teamster	3rd Co. G, 40th Regiment North Carolina, 3rd N. C. Artillery	Gunshot Wound Right Hip & Captured, Defended Land Face	Treated at Fort Monroe Hospital, Va, Sent To Point Lookout Prison, Maryland	Oath of Allegiance 6/29/1865
Morton, Julius H. Private	Alamance County, North Carolina, 1/25/1862	Graham, Alamance County, North Carolina, 17 Years Old	3rd Co. B, 36th Regiment North Carolina, 2nd N. C. Artillery	Captured	Point Lookout Prison, Maryland	Oath of Allegiance 6/3/1865
Morton, William F. Private	Brunswick County, North Carolina, 10/16/1861	Montgomery County, North Carolina, 43 Years Old	3rd Co. G, 40th Regiment North Carolina, 3rd N. C. Artillery	Mortally Wounded & Captured, Defended Land Face		Died Of Wounds at Fort Fisher 1/18/1865
Mott, Daniel W. Private	New Hanover County, North Carolina, 3/30/1863	New Hanover County, North Carolina, Age Unknown	Co. D, 13th Battalion North Carolina Light Artillery	Severe Shell Wound of Left Ankle Joint & Captured at Hospital in Smithville, North Carolina	Point Lookout Prison, Maryland	Oath of Allegiance 7/7/1865, Lower Left Leg Amputated, Defended River Road Gate

NAME & RANK	ENLISTED	RESIDENCE AGE & TRADE	MILTARY UNIT	RESULT OF BATTLE	PRISON	PRISON RELEASE
Muirhead, R. J. Assistant Surgeon	Date and Place Unknown	Unknown	3rd Military District Department of North Carolina	Captured	Fort Columbus, New York Harbor	Exchanged City Point, Va. 2/25/1865
Muldoon, Arthur Private	New Orleans, Louisiana, 4/27/1861	New Orleans, Louisiana, Age Unknown	Co. A, Confederate States Marine Corp, Assigned to Guard Duty Aboard CSS *Raleigh*	Captured	Fort Monroe, Virginia	Oath of Allegiance 2/4/1865
Mulford, Charles B. Private	Brunswick County, North Carolina, 9/2/1863	Gravelly Hill, Bladen County, North Carolina, 44 Years Old Turpentine	Co. H, 36th Regiment North Carolina, 2nd N. C. Artillery	Captured	Point Lookout Prison, Maryland	Exchanged 2/21/1865 at Boulware's Wharf, James River, Virginia
Mundine, John G. Private	Talladega, Alabama, 3/16/1863	Shelby County, Alabama, Age Unknown	Co. B, Confederate States Marine Corp, Assigned to Guard Duty Aboard CSS *Arctic.*	Captured	Point Lookout Prison, Maryland	Exchanged 2/10/1865
Munn, Daniel Captain	Bladen County, North Carolina, 9/10/1861	Prospect Hill, Bladen County, North Carolina, 30 Years Old Farmer, Company Commander 3rd Co. B, 36th Regiment N. C.	3rd Co. B, 36th Regiment North Carolina, 2nd N. C. Artillery	Captured	Fort Columbus, New York Harbor	Exchanged 3/5/1865 at Boulware's Wharf, James River, Virginia
Munn, John B. Private	Brunswick County, North Carolina, 8/13/1863	Montgomery County, North Carolina, 18 Years Old	3rd Co. G, 40th Regiment North Carolina, 3rd N. C. Artillery	Captured, Defended Land Face	Elmira Prison, New York	Died of Phthisis Pulmonalis 2/26/1865

NAME & RANK	ENLISTED	RESIDENCE AGE & TRADE	MILTARY UNIT	RESULT OF BATTLE	PRISON	PRISON RELEASE
Murdoch, James Campbell Second Lieutenant	Place Unknown, 4/8/1863	California, Age Unknown	Co. C, Confederate States Marine Corp, Assigned to Guard Duty Aboard CSS *Richmond.*	Captured	Fort Columbus, New York Harbor	Exchanged 2/25/1865 at Boulware's Wharf, James River, Va
Murph, Daniel Washington Private	Lincoln County, North Carolina, 3/12/1863	Shields Ford, Catawba County, North Carolina, 34 Years Old Farm Hand	Co. K, 10th Regiment North Carolina, 1st N. C. Artillery	Killed in Action 12/25/1864		
Murphy, B. F. Private	Date and Place Unknown	Unknown	Co. G, 25th South Carolina Volunteers	Captured	Elmira Prison, New York	Died of Smallpox, 3/24/1865
Murphy, David F. Private	Orangeburg, South Carolina 4/30/1862	Orangeburg District, South Carolina, 27 Years Old Farm Laborer	Co. G, 25th South Carolina Volunteers	Captured	Elmira Prison, New York	Died of Chronic Diarrhea, 2/28/1865
Murphy, James W. Private	Brunswick County, North Carolina, 6/25/1863	Brunswick County, North Carolina, 26 Years Old	3rd Co. G, 40th Regiment North Carolina, 3rd N. C. Artillery	Captured, Defended Land Face	Elmira Prison, New York	Exchanged 2/20/1865, Died of Unknown Disease At Richmond Hospital 3/16/1865
Murphy, Matthew J. Private	New Hanover County, North Carolina, 4/18/1864	Taylor's Bridge, Sampson County, North Carolina, 18 Years Old	2nd Co. A, 36th Regiment North Carolina, 2nd N. C. Artillery	Killed in Action 1/15/1865 Defended the Mound Battery		
Murphy, Miles Private	Wake County, North Carolina, 3/29/1864	Unknown	Co. K, 10th Regiment North Carolina, 1st N. C. Artillery	Captured, Face Burned By Gunpowder 12/25/1864	Elmira Prison, Maryland	Exchanged 3/2/1865 Boulware's Wharf, James River, Virginia

NAME & RANK	ENLISTED	RESIDENCE AGE & TRADE	MILTARY UNIT	RESULT OF BATTLE	PRISON	PRISON RELEASE
Murphy, Robert J. Captain	Transferred From Co. A, 61st Regiment North Carolina Troops 10/31/1861	Sampson County, North Carolina, 29 Years Old, Company Commander 2nd Co. A, 36th Regiment N. C.	2nd Co. A, 36th Regiment North Carolina, 2nd N. C. Artillery	Captured, Defended the Mound Battery	Fort Columbus, New York Harbor	Exchanged 3/5/1865 at Boulware's Wharf, James River, Virginia
Murphy, Thomas Private	Mobile, Alabama, 8/26/1861	New Orleans, Louisiana, Age Unknown Laborer	Co. C, Confederate States Marine Corp, Assigned to Guard Duty Aboard CSS *Patrick Henry* and CSS *Arctic*.	Wounded & Captured	Point Lookout Prison, Maryland	Oath of Allegiance 5/14/1865
Murphy, William F. Private	Randolph County, North Carolina, 3/23/1863	Taylor's Bridge, Sampson County, North Carolina, Age Unknown	Co. K, 10th Regiment North Carolina, 1st N. C. Artillery	Wounded in Thigh and Penis & Captured	Point Lookout Prison, Maryland	Oath of Allegiance 6/3/1865
Murrell, George W. Private	Camp Holmes, Wake County, North Carolina, 9/5/1863	Wilmington, New Hanover County, North Carolina, 32 Years Old	3rd Co. B, 36th Regiment North Carolina, 2nd N. C. Artillery	Captured	Elmira Prison, New York	Oath of Allegiance 7/11/1865
Muse, James Private	Craven County, North Carolina, 6/25/1861	Craven County, North Carolina, 26 Years Old Farmer	Co. D, 40th Regiment North Carolina, 3rd N. C. Artillery	Captured	Point Lookout Prison, Maryland	Oath of Allegiance 6/29/1865
Myers, Fred Private	James Island, South Carolina 10/19/63	Branchville, Orangeburg, South Carolina, 43 Years Old	Co. G, 25th South Carolina Volunteers	Captured	Elmira Prison, Elmira, New York	Oath of Allegiance 6/23/1865

NAME & RANK	ENLISTED	RESIDENCE AGE & TRADE	MILTARY UNIT	RESULT OF BATTLE	PRISON	PRISON RELEASE
Myers, Luther Private	Coles Island, South Carolina 4/11/62	Midway, Orangeburg District, South Carolina, 31 Years Old Farmer	Co. G, 25th South Carolina Volunteers	Captured	Elmira Prison, Elmira, New York	Oath of Allegiance 7/7/1865

NAME & RANK	ENLISTED	RESIDENCE AGE & TRADE	UNIT	RESULT OF BATTLE	PRISON	PRISON RELEASE
Nance, Daniel Private	Brunswick County, North Carolina, 2/19/1862	Shallotte, Brunswick County, North Carolina, 37 Years Old Farmer	Co. K, 36th Regiment North Carolina, 2nd North Carolina Artillery	Killed in Action 1/15/1865		
Nance, Edward J. Private	Robeson County, North Carolina, 9/13/1863	Robeson County, North Carolina, 19 Years Old	3rd Co. B, 36th Regiment North Carolina, 2nd North Carolina Artillery	Wounded Severely, Gunshot Wound Of Left Foot & Captured	Hammond General Hospital, Point Lookout Prison, Maryland	Oath of Allegiance 6/29/1865
Nance, Everett Private	Cero Gordo, Brunswick County, North Carolina, 11/17/1862	Fair Bluff, Columbus County, North Carolina, 28 Years Old	Co. E, 36th Regiment North Carolina, 2nd North Carolina Artillery	Captured	Elmira Prison, Elmira, New York	Oath of Allegiance 7/3/1865
Neal, George M. Private	Enfield, Halifax County, North Carolina, 10/9/1861	Edgecombe County, North Carolina, 18 Years Old	Co. F, 36th Regiment North Carolina, 2nd North Carolina Artillery	Captured	Elmira Prison, Elmira, New York	Exchanged 2/20/1865
New, F. B. Private	Date and Place Unknown	Unknown, 18 Years Old	Co. C, 3rd Battalion North Carolina Light Artillery	Captured	Fort Monroe, Virginia	Release Date Unknown

NAME & RANK	ENLISTED	RESIDENCE AGE & TRADE	UNIT	RESULT OF BATTLE	PRISON	PRISON RELEASE
New, Henry Z. Private	New Hanover County, North Carolina, 7/23/1863, Volunteer	Wilmington, New Hanover County, North Carolina, 37 Years Old Day Laborer	Co. D, 1st Battalion North Carolina Heavy Artillery	Mortally Wounded & Captured, Defended River Road Gate		Died Of Wounds at Fort Fisher 1/16/1865
Newman, Archibald W. Private	Fort Caswell, Brunswick County, North Carolina, 7/15/1862	Sampson County, North Carolina, 31 Years Old Farmer	2nd Co. A, 36th Regiment North Carolina, 2nd North Carolina Artillery	Captured, Defended the Mound Battery	Elmira Prison, Elmira, New York	Oath of Allegiance 8/7/1865
Newman, Jesse Private	Columbus County, North Carolina, 7/15/1862	Whiteville, Columbus County, North Carolina, 27 Years Old Cooper	Co. E, 36th Regiment North Carolina, 2nd North Carolina Artillery	Killed In Action 1/15/1865		
Newton, D. D. Corporal	Bennetts-ville, South Carolina 11/18/1862	Cheraw, South Carolina, 19 Years Old	Co. F, 21st South Carolina Volunteers	Captured	Elmira Prison, New York	Oath of Allegiance 7/11/1865
Nichols, Hazard Private	Fayetteville, North Carolina, Cumberland County, 2/20/1862	Gray's Creek, Cumberland County, North Carolina, 22 Years Old	2nd Co. C, 36th Regiment North Carolina, 2nd North Carolina Artillery	Captured, Defended River Road Gate	Elmira Prison, Elmira, New York	Died of Chronic Diarrhea 3/20/1865
Nichols, William A. Private	Hertford County, North Carolina, 7/15/1862	Weldon, Halifax County, North Carolina, 25 Years Old Farmer	Co. C, 3rd Battalion North Carolina Light Artillery	Captured	Elmira Prison, Elmira, New York	Oath of Allegiance 7/11/1865

NAME & RANK	ENLISTED	RESIDENCE AGE & TRADE	UNIT	RESULT OF BATTLE	PRISON	PRISON RELEASE
Nicholson, Richard J. Private	Date and Place Unknown	Unknown, 18 Years Old	Co. E, Confederate States Marine Corp, Assigned to Guard Duty Aboard CSS *Savannah.*	Captured, Defended Sea Face	Point Lookout Prison, Maryland	Died Of Pneumonia 2/8/1865
Niven, Dougal Private	Brunswick County, North Carolina, 7/27/1863	Mecklenburg County, North Carolina, 36 Years Old	3rd Co. G, 40th Regiment North Carolina, 3rd Regiment N. C. Artillery	Captured, Defended Land Face	Elmira Prison, Elmira, New York	Oath of Allegiance 6/12/1865
Nobles, J. N. Private	Date and Place Unknown	Unknown	Co. E, 36th Regiment North Carolina, 2nd North Carolina Artillery	Captured	Point Lookout Prison, Maryland	Exchanged 2/15/1865, Cox's Landing, James River, Virginia
Nobles, John Private	Cero Gordo, Columbus County, North Carolina, 3/3/1862	Fair Bluff, Columbus County, North Carolina, 18 Years Old	Co. E, 36th Regiment North Carolina, 2nd North Carolina Artillery	Captured	Elmira Prison, Elmira, New York	Oath of Allegiance 7/7/1865
Nobles, Jackson Musician	Columbus County, North Carolina, 2/19/1862, Volunteer	Lumberton, Robeson County, North Carolina, 17 Years Old	Co. E, 36th Regiment North Carolina, 2nd North Carolina Artillery	Wounded 1/14/1865	Prison Unknown	
Noles, Alfred Private	Cero Gordo, Columbus County, North Carolina, 3/4/1862	Columbus County, North Carolina, 22 Years Old	Co. E, 36th Regiment North Carolina, 2nd North Carolina Artillery	Captured	Elmira Prison, Elmira, New York	Died of Chronic Diarrhea 5/21/1865

NAME & RANK	ENLISTED	RESIDENCE AGE & TRADE	UNIT	RESULT OF BATTLE	PRISON	PRISON RELEASE
Norman, James S. Coporal	Washington, Beaufort County, N. C., North Carolina 4/16/1862	Washington, Beaufort County, North Carolina, 26 Years Old Sail Maker	Co, K, 10th Regiment North Carolina, 1st N.C Artillery	Captured	Elmira Prison, Elmira, New York	Oath of Allegiance 7/11/1865
Norris, Ed J. Lieutenant	Charleston, South Carolina 4/20/62	Charleston, South Carolina, 17 Years Old Clerk	Co. E, 25th South Carolina Volunteers	Captured	Fort Columbus, New York Harbor	Transferred to Fort Delaware, Del., 4/26/1865, Oath of Allegiance 5/15/1865
Norris, Samuel F. Private	Brunswick County, North Carolina, 10/13/1863	Columbus County, North Carolina, 18 Years Old	2nd Co. D, 36th Regiment North Carolina, 3rd Regiment N. C. Artillery	Captured	Point Lookout Prison, Maryland	Oath of Allegiance 6/29/1865
Northcutt, Henry L. Private	Marion District, South Carolina 2/29/1864	Mullins, South Carolina, Age Unknown	Co. I, 21st South Carolina Volunteers	Captured	Elmira Prison, New York	Oath of Allegiance 7/11/1865
Northcutt, John Corporal	Darlington, South Carolina 11/1/1863	Darlington District, South Carolina, 42 Years Old Farmer	Co. B, 21st South Carolina Volunteers	Captured	Elmira Prison, New York	Exchanged 3/2/1865 Boulware's Wharf, James River, Virginia
Northcutt, S. T. Private	Darlington, South Carolina 1/25/1862	Darlington District, South Carolina, 20 Years Old	Co. B, 21st South Carolina Volunteers	Captured	Elmira Prison, New York	Oath of Allegiance 7/19/1865
Nugent, James Private	Mobile, Alabama, 4/4/1864	Philadelphia, Pennsylvania, 18 Years Old	Co. B, Confederate States Marine Corp, Assigned to Guard Duty Aboard CSS *Tallahassee*.	Captured	Point Lookout Prison, Maryland	Oath of Allegiance 5/14/1865

NAME & RANK	ENLISTED	RESIDENCE AGE & TRADE	UNIT	RESULT OF BATTLE	PRISON	PRISON RELEASE
Nunn, Benjamin F. Sergeant	Lenoir County, North Carolina, 10/16/1861	Lenoir County, North Carolina, 18 Years Old	3rd Co. G, 40th Regiment North Carolina, 3rd Regiment N. C. Artillery	Captured, Defended Land Face	Elmira Prison, Elmira, New York	Exchanged 2/20/1865

NAME & RANK	ENLISTED	RESIDENCE AGE & TRADE	UNIT	RESULT OF BATTLE	PRISON	PRISON RELEASE
Oats, J. P. Private	Darlington, South Carolina 1/1/1862	Darlington District, South Carolina, 19 Years Old	Co. B, 21st South Carolina Volunteers	Captured	Elmira Prison, Elmira, New York	Oath of Allegiance 7/7/1865
Oats, John C. Private	New Hanover County, North Carolina, Date Unknown	Town Creek District, Brunswick County, North Carolina, 16 Years Old	3rd Co. G, 36th Regiment North Carolina, 2nd N. C. Artillery	Wounded Severe & Captured, Defended Battery to the Left of Northeast Bastion	Elmira Prison, Elmira, New York	Oath of Allegiance 6/23/1865
Odom, Arnold Private	Fort Fisher, New Hanover County, North Carolina, 11/28/1862	New Hanover County, North Carolina, 24 Years Old	2nd Co. I, 36th Regiment North Carolina, 2nd N. C. Artillery	Captured, Defended Shepperd's Battery	Elmira Prison, Elmira, New York	Exchanged 3/14/1865 Boulware's Wharf, James River, Virginia,
Odom, William B. Sergeant	Bennetts-ville, South Carolina 12/25/1861	Charlotte, North Carolina, 21 Years Old	Co. I, 21st South Carolina Volunteers	Captured	Elmira Prison, Elmira, New York	Oath of Allegiance 7/26/1865
O'Keife, Robert Private	Date and Place Unknown	Unknown, 28 Years Old	Co. A, Confederate States Marine Corp	Wounded, Gunshot wound & Fracture Right arm & Captured	Point Lookout Prison, Maryland	Oath of Allegiance 11/3/1865

NAME & RANK	ENLISTED	RESIDENCE AGE & TRADE	UNIT	RESULT OF BATTLE	PRISON	PRISON RELEASE
Oliver, John P. Private	Robeson County, North Carolina, 9/24/1861	Robeson County, North Carolina, 19 Years Old Farmer	Co. E, 40th Regiment North Carolina, 3rd N. C. Artillery	Captured	Point Lookout Prison, Maryland	Oath of Allegiance 5/15/1865
Oliver, John Q. Private	Brunswick County, North Carolina, 10/5/1863	Lumberton, Robeson County, North Carolina, 42 Years Old Farmer	Co. E, 40th Regiment North Carolina, 3rd N. C. Artillery	Killed In Action 1/15/1865		
Oliver, Joseph R. Private	Fort Caswell, Brunswick County, North Carolina, 4/22/1862	Robeson County, North Carolina, 18 Years Old Farmer	Co. E, 40th Regiment North Carolina, 3rd N. C. Artillery	Captured	Point Lookout Prison, Maryland	Oath of Allegiance 5/15/1865
Oliver, Sidney S. Private	Morris Island, South Carolina 2/27/1863	Darlington District, South Carolina, 19 Years Old	Co. K, 21st South Carolina Volunteers	Killed In Action 1/15/1865		
Ott, Elmore W. Private	Secession-ville, South Carolina 3/10/1864	Poplar, Orangeburg District, South Carolina, 13 Years Old Farmer	Co. G, 25th South Carolina Volunteers	Captured	Elmira Prison, Elmira, New York	Died of Pneumonia, 3/5/1865
Ott, John Private	Date and Place Unknown	Charleston, South Carolina, Age Unknown	Co. G, 25th South Carolina Volunteers	Captured	Elmira Prison, Elmira, New York	Died of Disease While Going Home
Ott, Samuel Private	Secession-ville, South Carolina 5/9/62	St. Matthews, Orangeburg District, South Carolina, 23 Years Old Farmer	Co. E, 25th South Carolina Volunteers	Captured	Elmira Prison, Elmira, New York	Oath of Allegiance 7/14/1865
Ott, William E. Private	Date and Place Unknown	Unknown, 18 Years Old	Co C, 25th Regiment South Carolina Volunteers	Captured	Elmira Prison, Elmira, New York	Died of Unknown Disease, 3/5/1865

NAME & RANK	ENLISTED	RESIDENCE AGE & TRADE	UNIT	RESULT OF BATTLE	PRISON	PRISON RELEASE
Ottaway, Robert M. Private	Fort Fisher, North Carolina, 2/25/1864	Brunswick County, North Carolina, 17 Years Old	3rd Co. G, 36th Regiment North Carolina, 2nd N. C. Artillery	Captured, Defended Battery to the Left of Northeast Bastion	Elmira Prison, Elmira, New York	Died of Smallpox, 5/5/1865
Outlaw, Jackson K. Private	Brunswick County, North Carolina, 4/26/1864	Mount Olive, Duplin County, North Carolina, 17 Years Old	3rd Co. G, 40th Regiment North Carolina, 3rd N. C. Artillery	Captured, Defended Land Face	Elmira Prison, Elmira, New York	Exchanged 2/20/1865
Outlaw, John Lewis Private	Winton, Hertford County, North Carolina, 2/5/1862	Bertie County, North Carolina, 26 Years Old Farmer	Co. C, 3rd Battalion North Carolina Light Artillery	Captured	Elmira Prison, Elmira, New York	Died of Pneumonia, 3/28/1865
Owen, James Lieutenant	New Hanover County, North Carolina, 11/19/1862	Unknown	2nd Co. C, 36th Regiment North Carolina, 2nd N. C. Artillery	Captured, Defended River Road Gate	Fort Columbus, New York Harbor	Exchanged City Point, Virginia, 3/5/1865
Owen, John W. Private	Fort Caswell, Brunswick County, North Carolina, 12/31/1863	Sampson County, North Carolina, 17 Years Old Student	2nd Co. C, 36th Regiment North Carolina, 2nd N. C. Artillery	Captured, Defended River Road Gate	Point Lookout Prison, Maryland	Oath of Allegiance 6/29/1865
Owen, Michael Private	Elizabeth-town, Bladen County, North Carolina, 10/19/1861	Bladen County, North Carolina, 19 Years Old	2nd Co. I, 36th Regiment North Carolina, 2nd N. C. Artillery	Captured, Defended Shepperd's Battery	Elmira Prison, Elmira, New York	Died of Chronic Diarrhea 4/19/1865

NAME & RANK	ENLISTED	RESIDENCE AGE & TRADE	UNIT	RESULT OF BATTLE	PRISON	PRISON RELEASE
Owen, Owen W. Private	Fort Caswell, Brunswick County, North Carolina, 12/31/1863	Sampson County, North Carolina, 17 Years Old	2nd Co. A, 36th Regiment North Carolina, 2nd N. C. Artillery	Captured, Defended The Mound Battery	Point Lookout Prison, Maryland	Oath of Allegiance 6/29/1865
Owen, Thomas S. Private	Fort Fisher, New Hanover County, North Carolina, 3/7/1862	Fayetteville, Cumberland County, North Carolina, 25 Years Old	2nd Co. I, 36th Regiment North Carolina, 2nd N. C. Artillery	Captured, Defended Shepperd's Battery	Elmira Prison, Elmira, New York	Oath of Allegiance 6/21/1865
Owens, Samuel Private	Charleston, South Carolina Morris Island, 2/20/1863	Charleston, South Carolina, Age Unknown	Co A, 21st Regiment South Carolina Volunteers	Captured	Elmira Prison, Elmira, New York	Died of "Lung Fever" 2/21/1865
Owens, William Private	Georgetown South Carolina 1/5/1862	Prince George Parish, Georgetown, South Carolina, 18 Years Old	Co. C, 21st South Carolina Volunteers	Captured	Elmira Prison, Elmira, New York.	Died of Chronic Diarrhea 4/26/1865
Owens, William C. Sergeant	Charleston, South Carolina Charleston, 2/24/1862	Prince George Parish, Georgetown, South Carolina, 19 Years Old	Co K, 25th Regiment South Carolina Volunteers	Captured	Elmira Prison, Elmira, New York	Died of Catarrh, 3/21/1865

NAME & RANK	ENLISTED	RESIDENCE AGE & TRADE	UNIT	RESULT OF BATTLE	PRISON	PRISON RELEASE
Paddison, John R. Private	Rowan County, North Carolina, 5/16/1864	McDowell County, North Carolina, Age Unknown, Telegraph operator at Fort Fisher	Co. D, 13th Battalion North Carolina Light Artillery	Captured at Battery Buchanan sending a message	Point Lookout Prison, Maryland	Oath of Allegiance 6/16/1865

NAME & RANK	ENLISTED	RESIDENCE AGE & TRADE	UNIT	RESULT OF BATTLE	PRISON	PRISON RELEASE
Padget, Edward J. Private	New Hanover County, North Carolina, 3/3/1862	New Hanover County, North Carolina, 24 Years Old	2nd Co. D, 36th Regiment North Carolina, 2nd N. C. Artillery	Captured	Point Lookout Prison, Maryland	Oath of Allegiance 6/17/1865
Padget, Lewis H. Private	New Hanover County, North Carolina, 1/4/1864	Unknown	Co. D, 13th Battalion North Carolina Light Artillery	Wounded & Captured, Defended River Road Gate	Point Lookout Prison, Maryland	Oath of Allegiance 5/12/1865
Page, Archibald K. Private	Sampson County, North Carolina, 11/4/1861	Sampson County, North Carolina, 19 Years Old Farm Laborer	2nd Co. A, 36th Regiment North Carolina, 2nd N. C. Artillery	Captured, Defended the Mound Battery	Point Lookout Prison, Maryland	Oath of Allegiance 6/17/1865
Page, Bennett Private	Fort Caswell, Brunswick County, North Carolina, 2/24/1863	Charlotte, North Carolina, 37 Years Old	3rd Co. G, 36th Regiment North Carolina, 2nd N. C. Artillery	Captured, Defended Battery to the Left of Northeast Bastion	Elmira Prison, Elmira, New York	Died of "Rheumatic Pericarditis" 3/7/1865
Page, John S. Private	Sampson County, North Carolina, 11/4/1861	Sampson County, North Carolina, 24 Years Old Farmer & Laborer	2nd Co. A, 36th Regiment North Carolina, 2nd N. C. Artillery	Captured, Defended the Mound Battery	Point Lookout Prison, Maryland	Oath of Allegiance 6/17/1865
Page, Marion Dempsey Private	Edgecombe County, North Carolina, 3/24/1864	Tarboro, Edgecombe County, North Carolina, 17 Years Old Farmer	Co. D, 40th Regiment North Carolina, 3rd N. C. Artillery	Wounded in Side & Captured	Point Lookout Prison, Maryland	Oath of Allegiance 6/3/1865
Page, William R. Sergeant	Sampson County, North Carolina, 11/4/1861	Hawley's Store, Sampson County, North Carolina, 24 Years Old Farmer & Laborer	2nd Co. A, 36th Regiment North Carolina, 2nd N. C. Artillery	Killed In Action 1/15/1865, Defended the Mound Battery		

NAME & RANK	ENLISTED	RESIDENCE AGE & TRADE	UNIT	RESULT OF BATTLE	PRISON	PRISON RELEASE
Page, Zachariah Private	Caswell County, North Carolina, 8/30/1864	Caswell County, North Carolina, Age Unknown	Co. D, 40th Regiment North Carolina, 3rd N. C. Artillery	Captured	Point Lookout Prison, Maryland	Oath of Allegiance 6/17/1865
Parker, Abner P. Private	Mount Tabor, Forsyth County, North Carolina, 7/15/1863	Boykin Station, Virginia, Age Unknown	Co. C, 3rd Battalion North Carolina Light Artillery	Captured	Elmira Prison, Elmira, New York	Oath of Allegiance 6/12/1865
Parker, Alva Private	Union County, North Carolina, 8/27/1864, Volunteer	Robeson County, North Carolina, 22 Years Old	Co. E, 40th Regiment North Carolina, 3rd N. C. Artillery	Gunshot Wound Right Arm & Captured	Treated At Fort Monroe Hospital, Va, Sent to Fort Delaware, Del.	Oath of Allegiance 6/18/1865
Parker, Badgegood B. Private	Chesterfield, South Carolina 1/8/1862	Unknown, 32 Years Old	Co. E, 21st South Carolina Volunteers	Captured	Elmira Prison, Elmira, New York	Died of Chronic Diarrhea 7/12/1865
Parker, Charles D. Private	Date and Place Unknown	Unknown	Co. H, 36th Regiment North Carolina, 2nd N. C. Artillery	Captured	Point Lookout Prison, Maryland	Exchanged 2/15/1865 at Cox's River Landing, Virginia
Parker, George D. First Lieutenant	Date and Place Unknown	Age Unknown, Detached service at Battery Gatlin	Field & Staff, 36th Regiment North Carolina, 2nd N. C. Artillery	Captured	Fort Columbus, New York Harbor	Exchanged 3/5/1865 at Boulware's Wharf, James River, Virginia
Parker, George F. Private	Kinston, Lenoir County, North Carolina, 9/20/1863	Everittsville, Cross Roads District, Wayne County, North Carolina, 30 Years Old Farmer	Co. F, 10th Regiment North Carolina, 1st N. C. Artillery	Captured	Elmira Prison, Elmira, New York	Oath of Allegiance 7/11/1865

NAME & RANK	ENLISTED	RESIDENCE AGE & TRADE	UNIT	RESULT OF BATTLE	PRISON	PRISON RELEASE
Parker, George R. Private	Fort Caswell, Brunswick County, North Carolina, 7/15/1862	Brunswick County, North Carolina, 36 Years Old	2nd Co. A, 36th Regiment North Carolina, 2nd N. C. Artillery	Captured, Defended the Mound Battery	Elmira Prison, Elmira, New York	Died of Chronic Diarrhea 6/18/1865
Parker, Jackson Private	Macon County, North Carolina, 3/11/1863	Macon County, North Carolina, Age Unknown	Co. D, 13th Battalion North Carolina Light Artillery	Captured, Defended River Road Gate	Elmira Prison, New York, Point Lookout Prison, Maryland	Exchanged From Elmira 3/2/1865, Captured Again At Richmond Hospital, 4/3/1865, Oath of Allegiance 7/19/1865
Parker, John Private	New Hanover County, North Carolina, 12/15/1864	Pitt County, North Carolina, 19 Years Old Laborer	Co. D, 13th Battalion North Carolina Light Artillery	Captured, Defended River Road Gate	Elmira Prison, Elmira, New York	Exchanged 2/20/1865
Parker, John W. Private	Sampson County, North Carolina, 218/1863	Sampson County, North Carolina, 26 Years Old Farmer	2nd Co. A, 36th Regiment North Carolina, 2nd N. C. Artillery	Captured, Defended the Mound Battery	Point Lookout Prison, Maryland	Oath of Allegiance 6/17/1865
Parnell, Joshua	Morris Island, South Carolina 6/12/1863	Darlington District, South Carolina, 18 Years Old Farmer	Co. H, 21st South Carolina Volunteers	Captured	Elmira Prison, Elmira, New York	Oath of Allegiance 6/14/1865
Parnell, Thomas N. Private	Darlington, South Carolina 1/1/1862	Darlington District, South Carolina, 22 Years Old Farmer	Co. B, 21st South Carolina Volunteers	Captured	Elmira Prison, Elmira, New York	Exchanged 3/14/1865

NAME & RANK	ENLISTED	RESIDENCE AGE & TRADE	UNIT	RESULT OF BATTLE	PRISON	PRISON RELEASE
Parrott, Joseph M. Sergeant	Darlington, South Carolina 5/12/1862	Darlington District, South Carolina, 39 Years Old Farmer	Co. B, 21st South Carolina Volunteers	Captured	Elmira Prison, Elmira, New York	Died Of Unknown Disease 7/17/1865
Parsons, Andrew J. Private	Battery Island, South Carolina 2/24/1862	Murray's Ferry, Williamsburg District, South Carolina, 28 Years Old Farmer	Co C, 25th Regiment South Carolina Volunteers	Captured	Point Lookout Prison, Maryland	Exchanged 4/12/1865
Parten, Elisha Private	Fort Caswell, Brunswick County, North Carolina, 6/25/1863	Heathsville, Halifax County, North Carolina, 18 Years Old Farm Laborer	Co. F, 36th Regiment North Carolina, 2nd N. C. Artillery	Mortally Wounded, Gunshot Wound To Left Thigh, Fractured Femur & Captured	Point Lookout Prison General Hospital, Maryland	Died Of Wounds 2/8/1865
Parterson, J. K. Private	Date and Place Unknown	Unknown	Co. D, 13th Battalion North Carolina Light Artillery	Captured, Defended River Road Gate	Prison Unknown	Release Date Unknown
Partin, John Private	Wake County, North Carolina, 8/18/1863	Wake County, North Carolina, 44 Years Old	3rd Co. B, 36th Regiment North Carolina, 2nd N. C. Artillery	Captured	Elmira Prison, Elmira, New York	Died of Chronic Diarrhea 3/10/1865
Partin, John C. Private	New Hanover County, North Carolina, 6/10/1863	Harnett County, North Carolina, 18 Years Old	2nd Co. C, 36th Regiment North Carolina, 2nd N. C. Artillery	Captured, Defended River Road Gate	Point Lookout Prison, Maryland	Oath of Allegiance 6/17/1865
Pate, Alfred D. Private	Bennetts- ville, South Carolina 5/12/1862	Bennettsville, Marlboro, South Carolina, 32 Years Old Farm Laborer	Co. F, 21st South Carolina Volunteers	Killed In Action 1/15/1865		

NAME & RANK	ENLISTED	RESIDENCE AGE & TRADE	UNIT	RESULT OF BATTLE	PRISON	PRISON RELEASE
Pate, Asa Private	Fort Holmes, North Carolina, 2/5/1864	Wayne County, North Carolina, Age Unknown	Co. F, 10th Regiment North Carolina, 1st N. C. Artillery	Captured	Elmira Prison, Elmira, New York	Died of Pneumonia 4/2/1865
Pate, Daniel Private	Bladen County, North Carolina, 5/6/1862	Wayne County, North Carolina, 24 Years Old Farmer	2nd Co. K, 40th Regiment North Carolina, 3rd N. C. Artillery	Captured	Elmira Prison, Elmira, New York	Died of Chronic Diarrhea 5/9/1865
Pate, Daniel Private	Goldsboro, Wayne County, North Carolina, 12/8/1862	Goldsboro, Creek District, Wayne County, North Carolina, 19 Years Old	Co. F, 10th Regiment North Carolina, 1st N. C. Artillery	Captured	Elmira Prison, Elmira, New York	Oath of Allegiance 7/3/1865
Pate, Edwin A. Private	Columbus County, North Carolina, 5/15/1862	Whiteville, Columbus County, North Carolina, 54 Years Old Farmer	1st Battalion, North Carolina Heavy Artillery.	Captured	Elmira Prison, Elmira, New York	Oath of Allegiance 7/3/1865
Pate, Gabriel G. First Sergeant	Brunswick County, North Carolina, 5/16/1862	Wayne County, North Carolina, 30 Years Old	Co. E, 36th Regiment North Carolina, 2nd N. C. Artillery	Captured	Point Lookout Prison, Maryland	Oath of Allegiance 6/17/1865
Pate, Jackson Private	Beaufort, Carteret County, North Carolina, 7/6/1861	Goldsboro, Wayne County, North Carolina, 24 Years Old Farmer	Co. F, 10th Regiment North Carolina, 1st N. C. Artillery	Captured	Elmira Prison, Elmira, New York	Oath of Allegiance 5/29/1865
Pate, John C. Private	Brunswick County, North Carolina, 3/20/1864	Brunswick County, North Carolina, 18 Years Old	2nd Co. K, 40th Regiment North Carolina, 3rd N. C. Artillery	Captured	Elmira Prison, Elmira, New York	Died of Remittent Fever 3/26/1865

NAME & RANK	ENLISTED	RESIDENCE AGE & TRADE	UNIT	RESULT OF BATTLE	PRISON	PRISON RELEASE
Pate, John Lewis Private	Beaufort, Carteret County, North Carolina, 3/20/1864	Goldsboro, Wayne County, North Carolina, 19 Years Old Farmer	Co. F, 10th Regiment North Carolina, 1st N. C. Artillery	Captured	Elmira Prison, Elmira, New York	Oath of Allegiance 7/26/1865
Pate, Richard W. Private	Beaufort, Carteret County, North Carolina, 7/2/1861	Goldsboro, Wayne County, North Carolina, 20 Years Old Farmer	Co. F, 10th Regiment North Carolina, 1st N. C. Artillery	Captured	Elmira Prison, Elmira, New York	Oath of Allegiance 7/7/1865
Pate, Stephen Private	Brunswick County, North Carolina, 9/23/1863	Bladen County, North Carolina, 27 Years Old Farmer	2nd Co. K, 40th Regiment North Carolina, 3rd N. C. Artillery	Captured	Elmira Prison, Elmira, New York	Exchanged 3/2/1865 Boulware's Wharf, James River, Virginia
Patterson, Daniel Captain	Bladen County, North Carolina, 5/16/1862	Bladen County, North Carolina, Age Unknown, Company Commander	Co. H, 36th Regiment North Carolina, 2nd N. C. Artillery	Captured	Fort Columbus, New York Harbor	Exchanged 3/5/1865 at Boulware's Wharf, James River, Virginia
Paul, George H. Private	Craven County, North Carolina, 6/18/1862	Craven County, North Carolina, 18 Years Old	Co. D, 40th Regiment North Carolina, 3rd N. C. Artillery	Captured	Point Lookout Prison, Maryland	Oath of Allegiance 6/30/1865
Paul, John P. Private	Union County, North Carolina, 8/27/1861	Unknown, 18 Years Old	Co. E, 40th Regiment North Carolina, 3rd N. C. Artillery	Captured	Point Lookout Prison, Maryland	Oath of Allegiance 6/4/1865
Paul, Peter Private	Brunswick County, North Carolina, 12/28/1863	Lumberton, Robeson County, North Carolina, 18 Years Old	2nd Co. K, 40th Regiment North Carolina, 3rd N. C. Artillery	Captured	Elmira Prison, Elmira, New York	Oath of Allegiance 6/4/1865

NAME & RANK	ENLISTED	RESIDENCE AGE & TRADE	UNIT	RESULT OF BATTLE	PRISON	PRISON RELEASE
Pearson, J. W. Private	Orangeburg, South Carolina 12/20/1862	Orangeburg, South Carolina, Age Unknown	Co H, 25th Regiment South Carolina Volunteers	Captured	Elmira Prison, Elmira, New York	Oath of Allegiance 7/11/1865
Peel, James Private	Brunswick County, North Carolina, 10/31/1864	Brunswick County, North Carolina, Age Unknown	3rd Co. G, 40th Regiment North Carolina, 3rd N. C. Artillery	Captured, Defended Land Face	Elmira Prison, Elmira, New York	Died of "Dropsy From Hepatic Disease" 4/4/1865
Peelle, Joseph J. Private	Northampton County, North Carolina, 5/14/1863	Bertie County, North Carolina, Age Unknown	Co. C, 3rd Battalion North Carolina Light Artillery	Gunshot Wound Of Upper Left Leg, Fracture of Tibia & Knee, & Captured	Point Lookout Prison, Maryland	Oath of Allegiance 6/12/1865, Left Leg Amputated
Peeples, Abraham Private	Beaufort District, Date Unknown	Sand Hill, Beaufort County, South Carolina, 37 Years Old Farmer	Co. F, 11th South Carolina Volunteers	Killed In Action 1/15/1865		
Peltier, L. L. Private	Chesterfield, South Carolina 2/1/1863	Cheraw, Chesterfield, South Carolina, 34 Years Old Cooper	Co. D, 21st South Carolina Volunteers	Captured	Elmira Prison, Elmira, New York	Oath of Allegiance 7/7/1865
Pendergrass, John M. First Lieutenant	Georgetown South Carolina 3/18/1862	Charleston, South Carolina, 30 Years Old Laborer	Co G, 25th Regiment South Carolina Volunteers	Captured	Fort Columbus, New York Harbor	Exchanged 2/25/1865
Penfield, Charles S. Private	Bladen County, North Carolina, 4/1/1862	Moore County, North Carolina, 24 Years Old Farmer	Co. H, 36th Regiment North Carolina, 2nd N. C. Artillery	Captured	Point Lookout Prison, Maryland	Oath of Allegiance 5/13/1865

405

NAME & RANK	ENLISTED	RESIDENCE AGE & TRADE	UNIT	RESULT OF BATTLE	PRISON	PRISON RELEASE
Penfield, James W. Private	Bladen County, North Carolina, 4/1/1862	Robeson County, North Carolina, 26 Years Old Farmer	Co. H, 36th Regiment North Carolina, 2nd N. C. Artillery	Captured	Point Lookout Prison, Maryland	Oath of Allegiance 6/17/1865
Penfield, Thomas N. Private	Bladen County, North Carolina, 8/2/1863, Volunteer	Unknown, 18 Years Old	Co. H, 36th Regiment North Carolina, 2nd N. C. Artillery	Wounded & Captured	Point Lookout Prison, Maryland	Oath of Allegiance 5/13/1865
Penny, James S. Private	Columbus County, North Carolina, 2/25/1864	Columbus County, North Carolina, 18 Years Old	Co. D, 1st Battalion North Carolina Heavy Artillery	Captured, Defended River Road Gate or Middle Sallyport	Point Lookout Prison, Maryland	Died of Pneumonia 2/25/1865
Perdue, Charles Private	Lenoir County, North Carolina, 10/16/1861	Lenoir County, North Carolina, 30 Years Old	3rd Co. G, 40th Regiment North Carolina, 3rd N. C. Artillery	Captured, Defended Land Face	Elmira Prison, Elmira, New York	Died of "Continued Fever" 3/22/1865
Perdue, Charles Private	Chesterfield, South Carolina 5/1/1862	Unknown, 17 Years Old	Co. E, 21st South Carolina Volunteers	Captured	Elmira Prison, Elmira, New York	Died of Pneumonia 6/21/1865
Perdue, William Private	Brunswick County, North Carolina, 4/22/1863	Lenoir County, North Carolina, 49 Years Old	3rd Co. G, 40th Regiment North Carolina, 3rd N. C. Artillery	Captured, Defended Land Face	Elmira Prison, Elmira, New York	Exchanged 3/2/1865, Died of "Chronic Diarrhea and Febris Typhoides" 3/21/1865 at Raleigh Hospital
Perry, A. C. Private	Date and Place Unknown	Unknown	3rd Co. B, 36th Regiment North Carolina, 2nd N. C. Artillery	Captured	Prison Unknown	Release Date Unknown

NAME & RANK	ENLISTED	RESIDENCE AGE & TRADE	UNIT	RESULT OF BATTLE	PRISON	PRISON RELEASE
Perry, Alfred W. Corporal	Martin County, North Carolina, 8/11/1862	Beaufort County, North Carolina, 37 Years Old	Co. D, 13th Battalion North Carolina Light Artillery	Mortally Wounded in Right Arm & Captured, Defended River Road Gate		Died 3/22/1865 In Mansfield Hospital, Morehead City, North Carolina, After Amputation of Right Arm
Perry, Daniel Roland First Lieutenant	Bladen County, North Carolina, 11/5/1861	White Creek, Bladen County, North Carolina, 27 Years Old Turpentine Distiller	3rd Co. G, 36th Regiment North Carolina, 2nd N. C. Artillery	Killed In Action 1/15/1865		Killed while charging the Federals with Colonel Lamb in the interior of the fort
Perry, Elijah M. Private	Bladen County, North Carolina, 11/10/1861	White Creek, Bladen County, North Carolina, 20 Years Old Farmer	3rd Co. B, 36th Regiment North Carolina, 2nd N. C. Artillery	Captured	Prison Unknown	Release Date Unknown
Perry, John C. Private	Brunswick County, North Carolina, 3/20/1864	Bladen County, North Carolina, 18 Years Old Farmer	3rd Co. B, 36th Regiment North Carolina, 2nd N. C. Artillery	Captured	Elmira Prison, Elmira, New York	Died of Smallpox, 3/20/1865
Perry, Levi H. Corporal	Bladen County, North Carolina, 12/26/1861	White Creek, Bladen County, North Carolina, 23 Years Old Farmer	3rd Co. B, 36th Regiment North Carolina, 2nd N. C. Artillery	Wounded in Back From Shell Fragment 12/25/1864, Captured 1/15/1865	Prison Unknown	Release Date Unknown,
Perry, Lewis H. Private	Wilmington, New Hanover County, North Carolina, 10/20/1864	Tarboro, Edgecombe County, North Carolina, Age Unknown	Co. K, 10th Regiment North Carolina, 1st N. C. Artillery	Captured	Elmira Prison, Elmira, New York	Oath of Allegiance 7/19/1865

NAME & RANK	ENLISTED	RESIDENCE AGE & TRADE	UNIT	RESULT OF BATTLE	PRISON	PRISON RELEASE
Perry, Orren Private	Chatham County, North Carolina, 10/20/1864	Chatham County, North Carolina, 37 Years Old	3rd Co. G, 40th Regiment North Carolina, 3rd N. C. Artillery	Captured, Defended Land Face	Elmira Prison, Elmira, New York	Died of Chronic Diarrhea 4/2/1865
Perry, Wiley N. Private	Bladen County, North Carolina, 1/28/1862	Bladen County, North Carolina, 19 Years Old	3rd Co. B, 36th Regiment North Carolina, 2nd N. C. Artillery	Captured	Elmira Prison, Elmira, New York	Exchanged 3/2/1865, Died in Moore Hospital, Richmond, Va, of Typhoid Fever 3/15/1865
Perry, William Private	Bladen County, North Carolina, 5/15/1862	St. Laurence, Chatham County, North Carolina, 27 Years Old Farmer	Co. K, 40th Regiment North Carolina, 3rd N. C. Artillery	Killed In Action 1/15/1865		
Peterson, Columbus A. Private	New Hanover County, North Carolina, 5/9/1862	Bladen County, North Carolina, 18 Years Old	Co. D, 1st Battalion North Carolina Heavy Artillery	Captured, Defended River Road Gate or Middle Sallyport	Point Lookout Prison, Maryland	Oath of Allegiance 6/30/1865, National Archives also reports Peterson died at Point Lookout Prison
Peterson, Gaston Private	Sampson County, North Carolina, 12/19/1862	Sampson County, North Carolina, 37 Years Old	2nd Co. A, 36th Regiment North Carolina, 2nd N. C. Artillery	Captured, Defended the Mound Battery	Point Lookout Prison, Maryland	Oath of Allegiance 6/17/1865
Peterson, James M. Private	Date and Place Unknown	Unknown	2nd Co. A, 36th Regiment North Carolina, 2nd N. C. Artillery	Captured, Defended the Mound Battery	Point Lookout Prison, Maryland	Died Of Pneumonia 3/6/1865

NAME & RANK	ENLISTED	RESIDENCE AGE & TRADE	UNIT	RESULT OF BATTLE	PRISON	PRISON RELEASE
Peterson, Monroe Private	New Hanover County, North Carolina, 8/19/1863	Bladen County, North Carolina, 35 Years Old	2nd Co. K, 40th Regiment North Carolina, 3rd N. C. Artillery	Captured	Point Lookout Prison, Maryland	Exchanged 3/16/1865 at Boulware's Wharf, James River, Virginia
Peterson, Thomas A. Private	Elizabeth-town, Bladen County, North Carolina, 4/8/1862	French's Creek, Bladen County, North Carolina, 21 Years Old Farmer & Turpentine Distiller	Co. H, 36th Regiment North Carolina, 2nd N. C. Artillery	Severe Gunshot Wound To Right Shoulder & Captured	Point Lookout General Hospital, Maryland	No Release Date, May Have Died Of Wounds
Phelps, Samuel P. Seaman	Place Not Listed, 1/24/1862	Lockwood Folly District, Brunswick County, N. C., 19 Years Old Laborer, Fisherman	Galloway Co., Confederate States Coast Guard	Captured	Prison Unknown	Release Date Unknown
Phelps, Timothy Seaman	Place Not Listed, 1/24/1862	Lockwood Folly District, Brunswick County, N. C., 22 Years Old Laborer, Fisherman	Galloway Co., Confederate States Coast Guard	Captured	Prison Unknown	Release Date Unknown
Phelps, William P. Seaman	Place Not Listed, 1/24/1862	Lockwood Folly District, Brunswick County, N. C., 19 Years Old Laborer & Fisherman	Galloway Co., Confederate States Coast Guard	Captured	Prison Unknown	Release Date Unknown
Phelps, William Thomas Private	Windsor, Bertie County, North Carolina, 1/23/1862	Plymouth, North Carolina, 21 Years Old Farmer	Co. C, 3rd Battalion North Carolina Light Artillery	Wounded In Leg & back & Captured	Elmira, New York	Oath of Allegiance 6/12/1865

NAME & RANK	ENLISTED	RESIDENCE AGE & TRADE	UNIT	RESULT OF BATTLE	PRISON	PRISON RELEASE
Philips, Charles Private	Union County, North Carolina, 11/29/1861	Unknown	Co. C, 3rd Battalion North Carolina Light Artillery	Captured	Fort Monroe, Virginia	Release Date Unknown
Phillips, Bryant Private	Chatham County, North Carolina, 11/29/1861	Chatham County, North Carolina, 18 Years Old	3rd Co. G, 40th Regiment North Carolina, 3rd N. C. Artillery	Captured, Defended Land Face	Elmira Prison, Elmira, New York	Died of Chronic Diarrhea 4/8/1865
Phillips, Cornelius Private	Robeson County, North Carolina, 11/29/1861	Robeson County, North Carolina, Age Unknown	Co. D, 1st Battalion North Carolina Heavy Artillery	Gunshot Wound Left thigh & Captured, Defended River Road Gate	Hamilton, Virginia, then sent to Fort Delaware, Del.	Oath of Allegiance 6/19/1865
Phillips, Eli Private	Georgetown South Carolina 1/1/1864	Marion District, South Carolina, 34 Years Old Farmer	Co. A, 21st South Carolina Volunteers	Captured	Elmira Prison, Elmira, New York	Died of Chronic Diarrhea 2/20/1865
Phillips, John Private	Camp Harllee, Georgetown South Carolina 1/1/1862	Prince George Parish, Georgetown, South Carolina, 32 Years Old	Co. A, 21st South Carolina Volunteers	Captured	Elmira Prison, Elmira, New York	Died of Chronic Diarrhea 2/6/1865
Phillips, Nelson Private	Georgetown South Carolina 11/29/1862	Marion County, South Carolina, 44 Years Old Farmer	Co. A, 21st South Carolina Volunteers	Killed In Action 1/15/1865		
Phillips, Richard T. Private	Edgecombe County, North Carolina, 7/11/1863	Edgecombe County, North Carolina, 43 Years Old	Co. D, 40th Regiment North Carolina, 3rd N. C. Artillery	Captured	Point Lookout Prison, Maryland	Oath of Allegiance 6/16/1865

NAME & RANK	ENLISTED	RESIDENCE AGE & TRADE	UNIT	RESULT OF BATTLE	PRISON	PRISON RELEASE
Phipps, Richard Private	Columbus County, North Carolina, 10/25/1861	Columbus County, North Carolina, 22 Years Old	2nd Co. A, 36th Regiment North Carolina, 2nd N. C. Artillery	Captured, Defended the Mound Battery	Elmira Prison, Elmira, New York	Oath of Allegiance 7/13/1865
Pickett, George W. Private	New Hanover County, North Carolina, 8/30/1863	New Hanover County, North Carolina, 18 Years Old	Co. K, 36th Regiment North Carolina, 2nd N. C. Artillery	Captured	Point Lookout Prison, Maryland	Oath of Allegiance 6/16/1865
Pierce, James M. Corporal	Bladen County, North Carolina, 3/26/1862, Volunteer	Bladen County, North Carolina, 18 Years Old	3rd Co. B, 36th Regiment North Carolina, 2nd N. C. Artillery	Wounded & Captured	Point Lookout Prison, Maryland	Oath of Allegiance 6/17/1865
Pierce, Richard Private	Date and Place Unknown	Unknown, 33 Years Old	Co. F, Confederate States Marine Corp	Gunshot Wound Upper Thigh, Captured	Point Lookout Prison, Maryland	Oath of Allegiance 6/6/1865
Pitman, Benjamin F. Private	Bladen County, North Carolina, 11/25/1861	Bladen County, North Carolina, 19 Years Old	3rd Co. B, 36th Regiment North Carolina, 2nd N. C. Artillery	Captured	Point Lookout Prison, Maryland	Oath of Allegiance 6/17/1865
Pittman, Henry Private	Brunswick County, North Carolina, 9/1/1863	Halifax County, North Carolina, 44 Years Old	Co. F, 36th Regiment North Carolina, 2nd N. C. Artillery	Captured	Point Lookout Prison, Maryland	Died of Gangrene 3/11/1865
Pittman, James M. Private	Mobile, Alabama, 4/30/1864	Troup County, Georgia, 28 Years Old	Co. B, Confederate States Marine Corp, Assigned to Guard Duty Aboard CSS *Tallahassee* and CSS *Arctic.*	Captured	Point Lookout Prison, Maryland	Oath of Allegiance 6/17/1865

411

NAME & RANK	ENLISTED	RESIDENCE AGE & TRADE	UNIT	RESULT OF BATTLE	PRISON	PRISON RELEASE
Player, Robert H. Private	Darlington, South Carolina 3/22/1863	Darlington District, South Carolina, 19 Years Old	Co. G, 21st South Carolina Volunteers	Killed In Action 1/15/1865		
Plowden, John Covert Private	Georgetown South Carolina 3/18/1862	Manning, Clarendon District, South Carolina, 36 Years Old Farmer	Co I, 25th South Carolina Volunteers	Captured	Elmira Prison, Elmira, New York	Died of Chronic Diarrhea 5/3/1865
Polk, Joel C. Private	Petersburg, Virginia, 5/20/1864	Darlington District, South Carolina, 19 Years Old Farmer	Co. D, 21st South Carolina Volunteers	Captured	Elmira Prison, Elmira, New York	Oath of Allegiance 7/7/1865
Pope, Asmond Private	Brunswick County, North Carolina, 9/1/1863	Sampson County, North Carolina, 22 Years Old	2nd Co. A, 36th Regiment North Carolina, 2nd N. C. Artillery	Captured, Defended the Mound Battery	Point Lookout Prison, Maryland	Oath of Allegiance 6/30/1865
Pope, Benjamin E. Private	Brunswick County, North Carolina, 11/5/1863	Halifax County, North Carolina, 18 Years Old	Co. F, 36th Regiment North Carolina, 2nd N. C. Artillery	Gunshot Wound Right Thigh, Fractured Femur & Captured	Point Lookout Prison, Maryland	Oath of Allegiance 6/26/1865
Pope, Furney Private	Sampson County, North Carolina, 2/18/1863	Sampson County, North Carolina, 38 Years Old Farmer	2nd Co. A, 36th Regiment North Carolina, 2nd N. C. Artillery	Captured, Defended the Mound Battery	Point Lookout Prison, Maryland	Oath of Allegiance 6/17/1865
Pope, Hinton Private	Brunswick County, North Carolina, 11/4/1861, Volunteer	Clinton, Sampson County, North Carolina, 23 Years Old Laborer, Fort Caswell, North Carolina	2nd Co. A, 36th Regiment North Carolina, 2nd N. C. Artillery	Killed In Action 1/15/1865, Defended the Mound Battery		

NAME & RANK	ENLISTED	RESIDENCE AGE & TRADE	UNIT	RESULT OF BATTLE	PRISON	PRISON RELEASE
Pope, Stephen Private	Brunswick County, North Carolina, 9/23/1863	Duplin County, North Carolina, 41 Years Old	3rd, Co. G, 40th Regiment North Carolina, 2nd N. C. Artillery	Captured, Defended Land Face	Elmira Prison, Elmira, New York	Oath of Allegiance 6/12/1865
Pope, William Streety Private	Elizabeth-town, Bladen County, North Carolina, 10/19/1861	Fayetteville, Cumberland County, North Carolina, 28 Years Old	2nd Co. I, 36th Regiment North Carolina, 2nd N. C. Artillery	Captured, Defended Shepperd's Battery	Elmira Prison, Elmira, New York	Oath of Allegiance 6/12/1865
Porter, Joseph W. Private	Halifax County, North Carolina, 10/9/1861	Halifax County, North Carolina, Age Unknown	Co. F, 36th Regiment North Carolina, 2nd N. C. Artillery	Captured	Point Lookout Prison, Maryland	Died of Pneumonia 2/12/1865
Potter, F. H. Private	Brunswick County, North Carolina, 8/20/1864	Unknown, 18 Years Old	Co. K, 36th Regiment North Carolina, 2nd N. C. Artillery	Captured	Point Lookout Prison, Maryland	Exchanged 2/21/1865 at Boulware's Wharf, James River, Virginia
Potter, John M. Private	Brunswick County, North Carolina, 2/19/1862, Volunteer	Brunswick County, North Carolina, 29 Years Old	Co. K, 36th Regiment North Carolina, 2nd N. C. Artillery	Shell Wound, Left Lumbar Region & Captured	Fort Delaware, Maryland	Oath of Allegiance 6/19/1865
Potter, Rufus H. Private	Bladen County, North Carolina, 12/4/1861	Bladen County, North Carolina, 17 Years Old	3rd Co. B, 36th Regiment North Carolina, 2nd N. C. Artillery	Captured	Elmira Prison, Elmira, New York	Died of Chronic Diarrhea 4/9/1865
Potter, S. Private	Date and Place Unknown	Unknown	3rd Co. G, 36th Regiment North Carolina, 2nd N. C. Artillery	Wounded & Captured	Prison Unknown	Release Date Unknown

NAME & RANK	ENLISTED	RESIDENCE AGE & TRADE	UNIT	RESULT OF BATTLE	PRISON	PRISON RELEASE
Pouns, Jacob A. Sergeant	Old Brunswick, North Carolina, 4/23/1862, Mustered in at Fort St. Philip, N. C.	Brunswick County, North Carolina, 22 Years Old	3rd Co. G, 36th Regiment North Carolina, 2nd N. C. Artillery	Captured, Defended Battery to the Left of Northeast Bastion	Elmira Prison, Elmira, New York	Died of Pneumonia 2/13/1865
Pouns, Samuel J. Private	Fort Fisher, New Hanover County, North Carolina, 4/19/1864	New Hanover County, North Carolina, 17 Years Old	3rd Co. G, 36th Regiment North Carolina, 2nd N. C. Artillery	Captured, Defended Battery to the Left of Northeast Bastion	Elmira Prison, Elmira, New York	Died on Route to be Exchanged, Cause Unknown 2/20/1865
Powe, Ellerbe Private	Camp Harllee, South Carolina 1/1/1862	Cheraw, South Carolina, 40 Years Old	Co. D, 21st South Carolina Volunteers	Captured	Elmira Prison, Elmira, New York	Oath of Allegiance 7/7/1865
Powe, James F. Private	Camp Marrigault, Chesterfield, South Carolina 4/3/1862	Cheraw, Chesterfield, South Carolina, 36 Years Old Farmer	Co. D, 21st South Carolina Volunteers	Captured	Elmira Prison, Elmira, New York	Died of Pneumonia 5/5/1865
Powe, Joseph Corporal	Chesterfield, South Carolina 4/30/1862	Cheraw, Chesterfield, South Carolina, 48 Years Old Overseer	Co. D, 21st South Carolina Volunteers	Captured	Elmira Prison, Elmira, New York	Died of Pneumonia 3/8/1865
Powell, Alexander F. Hospital Steward	Brunswick County, North Carolina, 8/19/1863	Columbus County, North Carolina, 20 Years Old	Co. E, 36th Regiment North Carolina, 2nd N. C. Artillery	Captured	Fort Columbus, New York Harbor	Exchanged 3/5/1865 at Boulware's Wharf, James River, Virginia
Powell, Charles Private	Myersville, South Carolina 5/13/1862	Cheraw, Chesterfield, South Carolina, 15 Years Old	Co. H, 25th South Carolina Volunteers	Captured	Elmira Prison, Elmira, New York	Exchanged 3/2/1865, Admitted To Charlotte Hospital with Variola 3/15/1865

NAME & RANK	ENLISTED	RESIDENCE AGE & TRADE	UNIT	RESULT OF BATTLE	PRISON	PRISON RELEASE
Powell, David Private	Myersville, South Carolina 5/13/1862	Unknown	Co. H, 25th South Carolina Volunteers	Captured	Elmira Prison, Elmira, New York	Exchanged On the James River 2/20/1865,
Powell, E. Private	Myersville, South Carolina 5/7/1862	Unknown	Co. H, 25th South Carolina Volunteers	Captured	Elmira Prison, Elmira, New York	Died of Inflammation of the Liver, 6/23/1865
Powell, Henry D. Private	Craven County, North Carolina, 10/15/1861	Craven County, North Carolina, 18 Years Old Farmer	Co. D, 40th Regiment North Carolina, 3rd N. C. Artillery	Captured	Point Lookout Prison, Maryland	Oath of Allegiance 5/14/1865
Powell, Isaac Private	Bladen County, North Carolina, 9/16/1863	Bladen County, North Carolina, 42 Years Old	2nd Co. I, 36th Regiment North Carolina, 2nd N. C. Artillery	Captured, Defended Shepperd's Battery	Point Lookout Prison, Maryland	Oath of Allegiance 6/16/1865
Powell, Jackson M. Private	Brunswick County, North Carolina, 5/20/1863	Horry District, South Carolina, Age Unknown	2nd Co. D, 36th Regiment North Carolina, 2nd N. C. Artillery	Captured	Point Lookout Prison, Maryland	Oath of Allegiance 6/16/1865
Powell, James W. Sergeant Major	Columbus County, North Carolina, 3/12/1862	Whiteville, Columbus County, North Carolina, 18 Years Old Farmer	Field & Staff, 36th Regiment North Carolina, 2nd N. C. Artillery	Captured	Fort Columbus, New York Harbor	Exchanged 3/5/1865 at Boulware's Wharf, James River, Virginia
Powell, John R. First Lieutenant	Bertie County, North Carolina, 4/15/1862	Bertie County, North Carolina, Age Unknown	Co. C, 3rd Battalion North Carolina Light Artillery	Captured	Fort Columbus, New York Harbor	Exchanged 3/5/1865 at Boulware's Wharf, James River, Virginia

NAME & RANK	ENLISTED	RESIDENCE AGE & TRADE	UNIT	RESULT OF BATTLE	PRISON	PRISON RELEASE
Powell, John W. Private	Brunswick County, North Carolina, 5/8/1862	Lumberton, Robeson County, North Carolina, 33 Years Old Farmer	Co. E, 40th Regiment North Carolina, 3rd N. C. Artillery	Captured	Point Lookout Prison, Maryland	Oath of Allegiance 6/5/1865
Powell, Oliver Hazzard Captain	Columbus County, North Carolina, 3/7/1862	Columbus County, North Carolina, 35 Years Old Farmer, Company Commander	Co. E, 36th Regiment North Carolina, 2nd N. C. Artillery	Captured	Fort Columbus, New York Harbor	Exchanged 3/5/1865 at Boulware's Wharf, James River, Virginia
Powell, Warren T. Private	Robeson County, North Carolina, 9/24/1861	Robeson County, North Carolina, 20 Years Old	Co. E, 40th Regiment North Carolina, 3rd N. C. Artillery	Captured	Elmira Prison, Elmira, New York	Exchanged 3/2/1865, Died of Chronic Diarrhea in Richmond Hospital 4/24/1865
Powers, Alfred Private	Bladen County, North Carolina, 5/6/1862	Whiteville, Columbus County, North Carolina, 21 Years Old Farmer	2nd Co. K, 40th Regiment North Carolina, 3rd N. C. Artillery	Killed In Action 1/15/1865		
Powers, David G. Private	Bladen County, North Carolina, 5/6/1862	Whiteville, Columbus County, North Carolina, 23 Years Old Farmer	2nd Co. K, 40th Regiment North Carolina, 3rd N. C. Artillery	Wounded Left Leg & Captured	Point Lookout Prison, Maryland	Left Leg Amputated, Died of "Pyaemia from Gunshot Wound" 2/12/1865
Pratt, Thomas St. George Lieutenant	Enlisted in CSMC, 10/8/1862	Born Maryland, 1841, Age Unknown Law Student	Co. E, Confederate States Marine Corp, Assigned to Guard Duty Aboard CSS *Savannah*.	Wounded by minnie ball in foot & Captured, Defended Sea Face	Treated at Camp Hamilton, Va., Transferred to Fort Monroe, Va.	Oath of Allegiance 5/25/1865

NAME & RANK	ENLISTED	RESIDENCE AGE & TRADE	UNIT	RESULT OF BATTLE	PRISON	PRISON RELEASE
Pressley, H. M. Private	James Island, South Carolina 4/9/1863	Murray's Ferry, Williamsburg District, South Carolina, 17 Years Old Farmer	Co. C, 25th South Carolina Volunteers	Captured	Elmira Prison, Elmira, New York	Exchanged 3/2/1865 Boulware's Wharf, James River, Virginia
Price, J. W. Private	Date and Place Unknown	Unknown	Co. F, 36th Regiment North Carolina, 2nd N. C. Artillery	Captured	Point Lookout Prison, Maryland	Oath of Allegiance 6/16/1865
Price, Robert T. Private	Wayne County, North Carolina, 8/19/1863	Wayne County, North Carolina, 18 Years Old	3rd Co. G, 40th Regiment North Carolina, 3rd N. C. Artillery	Captured, Defended Land Face	Elmira Prison, Elmira, New York	Died of Pneumonia 2/13/1865
Prickett, Joseph H. Private	Coles Island, South Carolina 4/12/1862	St. Matthew, South Carolina, Age Unknown	Co. H, 25th South Carolina Volunteers	Captured	Elmira Prison, Elmira, New York	Died of Chronic Diarrhea 6/15/1865
Pridgen, Edwin S. Private	Brunswick County, North Carolina, 7/23/1863	Lenoir County, North Carolina, 17 Years Old Student	3rd Co. G, 40th Regiment North Carolina, 3rd N. C. Artillery	Captured, Defended Land Face	Elmira Prison, Elmira, New York	Oath of Allegiance 6/12/1865
Pridgen, Matthew Washington First Lieutenant	Bladen County, North Carolina, 3/20/1862	Gravelly Hill, Bladen County, North Carolina, 29 Years Old	Co. H, 36th Regiment North Carolina, 2nd N. C. Artillery	Concussion from exploding shell 12/25/1864, & Captured 1/15/1865	Fort Columbus, New York Harbor	Exchanged 3/5/1865 at Boulware's Wharf, James River, Virginia
Pridgen, Melvin Private	New Hanover County, North Carolina, 3/3/1862	Wilmington, New Hanover County, North Carolina, 20 Years Old	2nd Co. D, 36th Regiment North Carolina, 2nd N. C. Artillery	Captured	Elmira Prison, Elmira, New York	Died of Chronic Diarrhea 4/15/1865

NAME & RANK	ENLISTED	RESIDENCE AGE & TRADE	UNIT	RESULT OF BATTLE	PRISON	PRISON RELEASE
Pridgen, Peter Private	New Hanover County, North Carolina, 3/13/1862	Wilmington, New Hanover County, North Carolina, 60 Years Old Farmer	2nd Co. D, 36th Regiment North Carolina, 2nd N. C. Artillery	Killed In Action 1/15/1865		
Pridgen, Thomas J. Sergeant	Fort Caswell, North Carolina, 2/16/1863	Canetuck, Pender County, North Carolina, 28 Years Old	2nd Co. D, 36th Regiment North Carolina, 2nd N. C. Artillery	Captured	Elmira Prison, Elmira, New York	Oath of Allegiance 6/16/1865
Pridgen, William Lafayette Private	Wilmington, New Hanover County, North Carolina, 5/15/1862	Canetuck, Pender County, North Carolina, 20 Years Old	2nd Co. D, 36th Regiment North Carolina, 2nd N. C. Artillery	Captured	Elmira Prison, Elmira, New York	Oath of Allegiance 6/16/1865
Priest, John A. Private	Wilmington, New Hanover County, North Carolina, 11/12/1861	White Hall, Bladen County, North Carolina, 18 Years Old	3rd Co. B, 36th Regiment North Carolina, 2nd N. C. Artillery	Captured	Elmira Prison, Elmira, New York	Oath of Allegiance 7/7/1865
Priest, John Hector Private	Bladen County, North Carolina, 11/18/1862	Bladen County, North Carolina, 18 Years Old	3rd Co. B, 36th Regiment North Carolina, 2nd N. C. Artillery	Captured	Point Lookout Prison, Maryland	Oath of Allegiance 6/17/1865
Prince, John E. Lieutenant	Charleston, South Carolina 2/22/1862	Charleston, South Carolina, 20 Years Old Printer's Apprentice	Co. E, 25th South Carolina Volunteers	Captured	Fort Delaware, Del.	Oath of Allegiance 5/15/1865
Provansana Mario Seaman	Date and Place Unknown	Unknown	Confederate States Navy, Served Aboard *CSS Chattahoochee*	Wounded Left Breast		

NAME & RANK	ENLISTED	RESIDENCE AGE & TRADE	UNIT	RESULT OF BATTLE	PRISON	PRISON RELEASE
Provost, Clarence Private	Charleston, South Carolina 2/24/1862	Anderson, South Carolina, 28 Years Old Merchant	Co. A, 25th South Carolina Volunteers	Captured	Elmira Prison, Elmira, New York	Oath of Allegiance 6/19/1865
Pugh, William Washington Private	Wilmington, New Hanover County, North Carolina, 4/22/1861	Beaufort County, North Carolina, 19 Years Old	Co. F, 10th Regiment North Carolina, 1st N. C. Artillery	Captured	Elmira Prison, Elmira, New York	Exchanged 2/20/1865
Purcell, Duncan Private	Fort Fisher, New Hanover County, North Carolina, 3/12/1862	New Hanover County, North Carolina, 35 Years Old	2nd Co. C, 36th Regiment North Carolina, 2nd N. C. Artillery	Captured, Defended River Road Gate	Elmira Prison, Elmira, New York	Died of Chronic Diarrhea 4/10/1865
Purnell, Calvin Private	Robeson County, North Carolina, 9/24/1861	Robeson County, North Carolina, 30 Years Old	Co. E, 40th Regiment North Carolina, 3rd N. C. Artillery	Captured	Elmira Prison, Elmira, New York	Died of Chronic Diarrhea 3/15/1865
Purvis, Henry Private	Georgetown South Carolina 1/1/1862	Darlington District, South Carolina, 25 Years Old Farmer	Co. K, 21st South Carolina Volunteers	Captured	Elmira Prison, Elmira, New York	Died of Chronic Diarrhea 2/12/1865

NAME & RANK	ENLISTED	RESIDENCE AGE & TRADE	UNIT	RESULT OF BATTLE	PRISON	PRISON RELEASE
Quick, Angus P. Private	Bennetts-ville, South Carolina 12/25/1861	Unknown, 32 Years Old	Co. F, 21st South Carolina Volunteers	Captured	Elmira Prison, Elmira, New York	Exchanged 3/2/1865 Boulware's Wharf, James River, Virginia

NAME & RANK	ENLISTED	RESIDENCE AGE & TRADE	UNIT	RESULT OF BATTLE	PRISON	PRISON RELEASE
Quick, John B. Private	Bennetts-ville, South Carolina 12/25/1861	Bennettsville, South Carolina Marlboro County, South Carolina, 33 Years Old Laborer	Co. F, 21st South Carolina Volunteers	Mortally Wounded, Severe Gunshot Wound & Fracture of Left Wrist & Captured	Point Lookout Prison Hospital, Maryland	Died Of Wounds 3/9/1865
Quinn, Franklin W. Private	Duplin County, North Carolina, 7/11/1863	Duplin County, North Carolina, 27 Years Old	3rd Co. G, 40th Regiment North Carolina, 3rd N. C. Artillery	Gunshot Wound of Left Thigh & Captured, Defended Land Face	Point Lookout Prison General Hospital, Maryland	Oath of Allegiance 6/17/1865
Quinn, John T. Private	Wilmington, New Hanover County, North Carolina, 4/26/1862	Magnolia, Duplin County, North Carolina, 23 Years Old	Co. D, 1st Battalion North Carolina Heavy Artillery	Captured, Defended River Road Gate or Middle Sallyport	Elmira Prison, Elmira, New York	Exchanged 3/2/1865, Admitted To Hospital in Richmond 3/8/1865 with Debility
Quinn, Sylonus Private	Date and Place Unknown	Duplin County, North Carolina, 47 Years Old Cooper	Co. D, 40th Regiment North Carolina, 3rd N. C. Artillery	Captured	Elmira Prison, Elmira, New York	Exchanged 3/2/1865 Boulware's Wharf, James River, Virginia
Quinn, William F. Private	New Orleans, Louisiana, 5/8/1861	Unknown, 30 Years Old	Co. B, Confederate States Marine Corp, Assigned to Guard Duty Aboard CSS *Savannah*, CSS *Raleigh* and CSS *North Carolina.*	Mortally Wounded In Left Leg, Amputation of Left Foot & Captured, Defended Sea Face	Fort Monroe, Virginia	Left Leg Amputated, Died of Wounds 1/24/1865

NAME & RANK	ENLISTED	RESIDENCE & TRADE	UNIT	RESULT OF BATTLE	PRISON	PRISON RELEASE
Rabon, George W. Private	Old Brunswick Town, North Carolina, 4/16/1862	Wilmington, New Hanover County, North Carolina, 33 Years Old	3rd Co. G, 36th Regiment North Carolina, 2nd N. C. Artillery	Captured, Defended Battery to the Left of Northeast Bastion	Elmira Prison, New York	Oath of Allegiance 7/19/1865
Rabon, William P. Private	Fort Caswell, North Carolina, 9/11/1863	Wilmington, New Hanover County, North Carolina, 18 Years Old	3rd Co. G, 36th Regiment North Carolina, 2nd N. C. Artillery	Captured, Defended Battery to the Left of Northeast Bastion	Elmira Prison, New York	Oath of Allegiance 7/3/1865
Rackley, James E. Private	Brunswick County, North Carolina, 2/19/1862	Cypress Creek, Bladen County, North Carolina, 18 Years Old	Co. K, 36th Regiment North Carolina, 2nd N. C. Artillery	Killed In Action 1/15/1865		
Rackley, William G. Private	Brunswick County, North Carolina, 2/19/1862, Volunteer	Unknown, 14 Years Old	Co. K, 36th Regiment North Carolina, 2nd N. C. Artillery	Wounded & Captured	Prison Unknown	Release Date Unknown, May have Died of Wounds at Fort Fisher, Enlisted As A Musician
Randolph, William H. Private	Halifax County, North Carolina, 10/9/1861	Halifax County, North Carolina, 18 Years Old	Co. F, 36th Regiment North Carolina, 2nd N. C. Artillery	Gunshot Wound Of Right Arm & Captured	Point Lookout Prison, Maryland	Oath of Allegiance 6/19/1865
Rascoe, Alexander H. Private	Bennetts-ville, South Carolina 12/25/1861	Bennettsville, Marlboro District, South Carolina, 23 Years Old Farmer	Co. F, 21st South Carolina Volunteers	Captured	Elmira Prison, Elmira, New York	Exchanged 3/14/1865
Ratley, Hinant Private	Fort Fisher, New Hanover County, North Carolina, 3/19/1863	New Hanover County, North Carolina, 50 Years Old	2nd Co. K, 40th Regiment North Carolina, 3rd N. C. Artillery	Captured	Elmira Prison, New York	Died of Chronic Diarrhea 2/10/1865

NAME & RANK	ENLISTED	RESIDENCE & TRADE	UNIT	RESULT OF BATTLE	PRISON	PRISON RELEASE
Rawls, Hosey Private	St. Johns, Hertford County, North Carolina, 7/27/1864	Murfreesboro, Hertford County, North Carolina, 26 Years Old	Co. C, 3rd Battalion North Carolina Artillery	Captured	Elmira Prison, New York	Died of Debility 5/27/1865
Rawles, John Private	Date and Place Unknown	Vicinity of Rocky Well, Lexington, South Carolina, 17 Years Old	Co. K, 21st South Carolina Volunteers	Captured	Elmira Prison, Elmira, New York	Exchanged 3/14/1865
Rawles, James Private	Georgetown South Carolina 12/20/1861	Georgetown, Prince George Parish, South Carolina, 30 Years Old Farmer	Co. A, 21st South Carolina Volunteers	Captured	Elmira Prison, Elmira, New York	Died of Chronic Diarrhea 4/5/1865
Rawls, Joseph A. Private	St. Johns, Hertford County, North Carolina, 8/3/1864	Plymouth, North Carolina, Age Unknown	Co. C, 3rd Battalion North Carolina Artillery	Captured	Elmira Prison, New York	Exchanged 3/21/1865 At Boulware's Wharf, James River, Virginia, Died of Debility In Jackson Hospital 3/23/1865, Richmond, Virginia
Rawls, Joseph J. Private	Greenville, Pitt County, North Carolina, 5/14/1862	Tarboro, Edgecombe County, North Carolina, Age Unknown	Co. K, 10th Regiment North Carolina, 1st N. C. Artillery	Shot In Arm & Breast, Face Burned by Powder 12/25/1864, Captured 1/15/1865	Elmira Prison, New York	Oath of Allegiance 7/26/1865
Rawls, William R. Private	St. Johns, Hertford County, North Carolina, 7/28/1864	Murfreesboro, Hertford County, North Carolina, 32 Years Old	Co. C, 3rd Battalion North Carolina Artillery	Captured	Elmira Prison, New York	Exchanged 3/14/1865 At Boulware's Wharf, James River, Virginia

NAME & RANK	ENLISTED	RESIDENCE & TRADE	UNIT	RESULT OF BATTLE	PRISON	PRISON RELEASE
Rayfield, Edward J. Private	Beaufort County, North Carolina, 5/8/1862	Beaufort County, North Carolina, Age Unknown	Co. K, 10th Regiment North Carolina, 1st N. C. Artillery	Shell Wound In Back & Captured	Treated At Fort Monroe, Va, Sent To Fort Delaware, Del.	Oath of Allegiance 6/7/1865
Raymond, Ebenezer Private	Brunswick County, North Carolina, 2/19/1862	Unknown, 20 Years Old	Co. K, 36th Regiment North Carolina, 2nd N. C. Artillery	Captured	Point Lookout Prison, Maryland	Exchanged 2/21/1865 At Boulware's Wharf, James River, Virginia
Reaves, Jerry P. Private	New Hanover County, North Carolina, 5/8/1863	New Hanover County, North Carolina, 40 Years Old Detailed in Gatlin Battery, North of Fort Fisher	2nd Co. I, 36th Regiment North Carolina, 2nd N. C. Artillery	Captured, Defended Shepperd's Battery	Elmira Prison, New York	Exchanged 2/20/1865
Reaves, John Edward Private	Whiteville, Columbus County, North Carolina, 4/27/1863, Conscript	Bladen County, North Carolina, 34 Years Old	Co. E, 36th Regiment North Carolina, 2nd N. C. Artillery	Captured	Point Lookout Prison, Maryland	Oath of Allegiance 6/19/1865
Reaves, John W. Private	Fort Caswell, Brunswick County, North Carolina, 10/7/1863	Brunswick County, North Carolina, 33 Years Old	2nd Co. D, 36th Regiment North Carolina, 2nd N. C. Artillery	Captured	Elmira Prison, New York	Died of Bronchitis 3/26/1865
Reaves, Samuel F. Private	Old Brunswick, Brunswick County, North Carolina, 4/16/1862	Whiteville, Columbus County, North Carolina, 35 Years Old	3rd Co. G, 36th Regiment North Carolina, 2nd N. C. Artillery	Captured, Defended Battery to the Left of Northeast Bastion	Elmira Prison, New York	Died of Smallpox, 4/13/1865

NAME & RANK	ENLISTED	RESIDENCE & TRADE	UNIT	RESULT OF BATTLE	PRISON	PRISON RELEASE
Reaves, Samuel W. Private	Fort Anderson, North Carolina, 4/27/1863	Columbus County, North Carolina	Co. E, 36th Regiment North Carolina, 2nd N. C. Artillery	Captured	Elmira Prison, New York	Exchanged 3/2/1865 Boulware's Wharf, James River, Virginia
Reed, James Private	Charleston, South Carolina 4/2/1862	Orangeburg District, South Carolina, 35 Years Old Farmer	Co. H, 25th South Carolina Volunteers	Captured	Elmira Prison, New York	Died of Smallpox, 3/13/1865
Reeves, Robert H. Ordinance Sergeant	Marion District, South Carolina 9/29/1864	Tumbling Shoals, Laurens County, South Carolina, 22 Years Old	Field & Staff, 21st South Carolina Volunteers	Killed In Action 1/15/1865		
Regan, Addison Private	Fort Fisher, New Hanover County, North Carolina, 6/28/1863, Volunteer	Robeson County, North Carolina, 17 Years Old	2nd Co. I, 36th Regiment North Carolina, 2nd N. C. Artillery	Captured, Defended Shepperd's Battery	Elmira Prison, New York	Exchanged 3/21/1865 At Boulware's Wharf, James River, Virginia
Regan, Neill Private	Fort Fisher, New Hanover County, North Carolina, 3/4/1864, Volunteer	New Hanover County, North Carolina, 17 Years Old Detailed as mounted scout, Fort Fisher	2nd Co. I, 36th Regiment North Carolina, 2nd N. C. Artillery	Captured, Defended Shepperd's Battery	Elmira Prison, New York	Died of Pneumonia 5/23/1865
Register, Ira Private	Darlington, South Carolina 3/14/1862	Darlington County, South Carolina, 32 Years Old Farmer	Co. B, 21st South Carolina Volunteers	Killed while Defending River Road gate, 1/15/1865		
Register, Miles C. Private	Bladen County, North Carolina, 10/19/1861	Bladen County, North Carolina, 20 Years Old	2nd Co. I, 36th Regiment North Carolina, 2nd N. C. Artillery	Captured, Defended Shepperd's Battery	Point Lookout Prison, Maryland	Oath of Allegiance 6/17/1865

NAME & RANK	ENLISTED	RESIDENCE & TRADE	UNIT	RESULT OF BATTLE	PRISON	PRISON RELEASE
Register, Nathan Private	Bladen County, North Carolina, 2/19/1862, Volunteer	Brunswick County, North Carolina, 45 Years Old	Co. K, 36th Regiment North Carolina, 2nd N. C. Artillery	Wounded, Concussion From Shell & Captured	Treated at Mansfield Hospital, Morehead City, N. C., Sent To Fort Delaware, Del.	Oath of Allegiance 6/19/1865
Register, Owen Private	Bladen County, North Carolina, 10/19/1861	Bladen County, North Carolina, 22 Years Old	2nd Co. I, 36th Regiment North Carolina, 2nd N. C. Artillery	Captured, Defended Shepperd's Battery	Point Lookout Prison, Maryland	Oath of Allegiance 6/19/1865
Reid, Louis H. Sergeant Major	Washington, Beaufort County, North Carolina, 9/23/1861	Wilson, Wilson County, North Carolina 21 Years Old	Co. D, 13th Battalion North Carolina Light Artillery	Captured, Defended River Road Gate	Elmira Prison, New York	Oath of Allegiance 6/14/1865
Reilly, James Major	New Hanover County, North Carolina, 5/31/1861	New Hanover County, North Carolina, 30 Years Old	Field & Staff, 10th Regiment North Carolina, 1st N. C. Artillery	Captured	Fort Delaware, Del.	Oath of Allegiance 5/15/1865
Renneker, John H. Private	James Island, South Carolina 3/21/1863	Charleston, South Carolina, Age Unknown	Co. B, 25th South Carolina Volunteers	Captured	Elmira Prison, New York	Oath of Allegiance 6/23/1865
Renneker, F. W. Private	Charleston, South Carolina 2/24/1862	Unknown, 21 Years Old	Co. B, 25th South Carolina Volunteers	Captured	Elmira Prison, New York	Exchanged 3/14/1865
Rentfrow, James Private	Smithville, Brunswick County, North Carolina, 7/11/1863	Brunswick County, North Carolina, Age Unknown	Co. F, 10th Regiment North Carolina, 1st N. C. Artillery	Captured	Elmira Prison, New York	Died of Pneumonia 3/4/1865

NAME & RANK	ENLISTED	RESIDENCE & TRADE	UNIT	RESULT OF BATTLE	PRISON	PRISON RELEASE
Reynolds, James M. Private	Fort Caswell, Brunswick County, North Carolina, 5/4/1863, Volunteer	Brunswick County, North Carolina, 37 Years Old	3rd Co. G, 36th Regiment North Carolina, 2nd N. C. Artillery	Captured, Defended Battery to the Left of Northeast Bastion	Elmira Prison, New York	Exchanged 2/20/1865
Reynolds, James W. Private	Sampson County, North Carolina, Date Unknown	Sampson County, North Carolina, 33 Years Old Farm Laborer	3rd Co. G, 36th Regiment North Carolina, 2nd N. C. Artillery	Captured, Defended Battery to the Left of Northeast Bastion	Elmira Prison, New York	Died of Pneumonia 4/9/1865
Reynolds, William Private	Sampson County, North Carolina, 2/18/1863, Volunteer	Sampson County, North Carolina, 37 Years Old	2nd Co. A, 36th Regiment North Carolina, 2nd N. C. Artillery	Captured, Defended the Mound Battery	Elmira Prison, New York	Died of Pneumonia 3/5/1865
Reynolds, William H. Private	Brunswick County, North Carolina, 2/19/1862	Town Creek, Brunswick County, North Carolina, 39 Years Old	Co. K, 36th Regiment North Carolina, 2nd N. C. Artillery	Captured	Elmira Prison, New York	Exchanged 2/20/1865
Rhames, Nathaniel E. Private	Charleston, South Carolina 4/17/1864	Unknown	Co. A, 21st South Carolina Volunteers	Captured	Elmira Prison, New York	Died of Chronic Diarrhea 6/10/1865
Rhea, Jesse Private	Craven County, North Carolina, 2/2/1862	Halifax County, North Carolina, 28 Years Old	Co. F, 36th Regiment North Carolina, 2nd N. C. Artillery	Captured	Point Lookout Prison, Maryland	Oath of Allegiance 6/17/1865
Rhodes, A. J. Private	Darlington, South Carolina 10/23/1863	Darlington District, South Carolina, Age Unknown	Co. B, 21st South Carolina Volunteers	Captured	Elmira Prison, Elmira, New York	Oath of Allegiance 7/7/1865

NAME & RANK	ENLISTED	RESIDENCE & TRADE	UNIT	RESULT OF BATTLE	PRISON	PRISON RELEASE
Rhodes, John D. Private	Fort Caswell, North Carolina, 3/26/1862	Fair Bluff, Columbus County, North Carolina, 18 Years Old	Co. E, 36th Regiment North Carolina, 2nd N. C. Artillery	Captured	Elmira Prison, New York	Oath of Allegiance 7/7/1865
Rice, James Private	Craven County, North Carolina, 1/24/1862	Craven County, North Carolina, 25 Years Old	Co. D, 40th Regiment North Carolina, 3rd N. C. Artillery	Captured	Point Lookout Prison, Maryland	Oath of Allegiance 6/19/1865
Rice, Noah Private	Craven County, North Carolina, 9/21/1861	Craven County, North Carolina, 21 Years Old	Co. D, 40th Regiment North Carolina, 3rd N. C. Artillery	Captured	Point Lookout Prison, Maryland	Oath of Allegiance 6/19/1865
Rich, Zachariah Private	Harnett County, North Carolina, 2/20/1862	Harnett County, North Carolina, 29 Years Old	2nd Co. C, 36th Regiment North Carolina, 2nd N. C. Artillery	Captured, Defended River Road Gate	Point Lookout Prison, Maryland	Oath of Allegiance 6/17/1865
Richards, Myer Sergeant	Marion, South Carolina 4/20/1862	Marion, South Carolina, 24 Years Old Merchant	Co. D, 25th South Carolina Volunteers	Captured	Elmira Prison, New York	Oath of Allegiance 5/13/1865
Richardson, P. G. Private	Camp Harllee, South Carolina 2/14/1862	Kingstree, South Carolina, Age Unknown	Co. I, 21st South Carolina Volunteers	Captured	Elmira Prison, Elmira, New York	Oath of Allegiance 7/11/1865
Richburg, Benjamin D. Private	James Island, South Carolina 2/23/1863	Bradford Springs, Sumter District, South Carolina, 29 Years Old Overseer	Co. I, 25th South Carolina Volunteers	Captured	Elmira Prison, New York	Died of Pneumonia 4/24/1865

NAME & RANK	ENLISTED	RESIDENCE & TRADE	UNIT	RESULT OF BATTLE	PRISON	PRISON RELEASE
Richburgh, J. E. Private	Camp Harllee, Georgetown South Carolina 1/1/1862	Kingstree, South Carolina, 18 Years Old	Co. I, 25th South Carolina Volunteers	Captured	Elmira Prison, New York	Oath of Allegiance 6/23/1865
Ridgeway, Joseph M. Private	James Island, South Carolina 11/15/1861	Unknown	Co. I, 25th South Carolina Volunteers	Captured	Elmira Prison, New York	Died of Pneumonia 4/6/1865
Ridgeway, Joseph N. Private	Camp Harllee, Georgetown South Carolina 2/23/1863	Manning, Clarendon District, South Carolina, 33 Years Old Miller	Co. I, 25th South Carolina Volunteers	Captured	Elmira Prison, New York	Died of Unknown Disease 4/24/1865
Ridgeway, Reuben F. Sergeant	James Island, South Carolina 10/24/1862	Manning, Clarendon District, South Carolina, 30 Years Old Farmer	Co. I, 25th South Carolina Volunteers	Captured	Elmira Prison, New York	Exchanged On the James River 2/20/1865
Riley, Daniel Private	Fort Fisher, New Hanover County, North Carolina, 3/15/1863, Volunteer	Fayetteville,, Cumberland County, North Carolina, 32 Years Old Farmer	2nd Co. D, 36th Regiment North Carolina, 2nd N. C. Artillery	Captured	Elmira Prison, New York	Died of Pneumonia 2/16/1865
Riley, John Private	Wilmington, New Hanover County, North Carolina, 3/18/1862	Unknown, 32 Years Old	2nd Co. C, 36th Regiment North Carolina, 2nd N. C. Artillery	Shell Wound Left Side of Head & Captured	Point Lookout Prison General Hospital, Maryland	Oath of Allegiance 5/14/1865, Defended River Road Gate

NAME & RANK	ENLISTED	RESIDENCE & TRADE	UNIT	RESULT OF BATTLE	PRISON	PRISON RELEASE
Riley, William Private	Cumberland County, North Carolina, 3/18/1862	Ellisville, Bladen County, North Carolina, 35 Years Old Farmer	Co. H, 36th Regiment North Carolina, 2nd N. C. Artillery	Captured	Point Lookout Prison, Maryland	Oath of Allegiance 5/14/1865
Rin, J. Private	Date and Place Unknown	Unknown	3rd Co. G, 36th Regiment North Carolina, 2nd N. C. Artillery	Wounded & Captured	Prison Unknown	Date Of Release Unknown
Rinaldi, Eugene W. Private	Fort Holmes, Brunswick County, North Carolina, 8/21/1864	Elizabethtown Bladen County, North Carolina, 17 Years Old	2nd Co. K, 40th Regiment North Carolina, 3rd N. C. Artillery	Captured	Elmira Prison, New York	Died of Chronic Diarrhea 4/26/1865
Rivers, Frank Lieutenant	Chesterfield, South Carolina 5/18/1862	Unknown	Co. E, 21st South Carolina Volunteers	Captured	Fort Columbus, New York Harbor	Exchanged 2/25/1865
Rivers, Jacob M. Private	Whippy Swamp, South Carolina 7/15/1861	Prince William Parish, Beaufort District, South Carolina, 25 Years Old Farmer	Co. D, 11th South Carolina Volunteers	Captured	Elmira Prison, Elmira, New York	Exchanged 3/2/1865 Boulware's Wharf, James River, Virginia
Rives, William C. Private	Secession-ville, South Carolina 5/11/1862	Orangeburg, South Carolina, 20 Years Old	Co. G, 25th South Carolina Volunteers	Captured	Elmira Prison, New York	Oath of Allegiance 6/16/1865
Roach, David L. 1st Sergeant	Place Unknown, 8/14/1861	Craven County, North Carolina, 31 Years Old Fisherman	Galloway Co., Confederate States Coast Guard	Captured	Prison Unknown	Date Of Release Unknown

NAME & RANK	ENLISTED	RESIDENCE & TRADE	UNIT	RESULT OF BATTLE	PRISON	PRISON RELEASE
Robbins, John C. Private	Brunswick County, North Carolina, 4/16/1862, Volunteer,	Brunswick County, North Carolina, 22 Years Old	3rd Co. G, 36th Regiment North Carolina, 2nd N. C. Artillery	Wounded & Captured 1/15/1865, Defended Battery to the Left of Northeast Bastion	Prison Unknown	Date Of Release Unknown, May Have Died of Wounds at Fort Fisher
Robbins, William W. Private	Fort Caswell, Brunswick County, North Carolina, 8/29/1863, Volunteer	Brunswick County, North Carolina, 36 Years Old	3rd Co. G, 36th Regiment North Carolina, 2nd N. C. Artillery	Wounded & Captured, Defended Battery to the Left of Northeast Bastion	Elmira Prison, New York	Died of Smallpox, 3/22/1865
Roberson, Dexter Seaman	Place Unknown, 9/20/1863	Unknown	Galloway Co., Confederate States Coast Guard	Captured	Prison Unknown	Date Of Release Unknown
Roberson, Harrison Private	Transferred From Company F, 17th Regiment 4/27/1864, North Carolina Troops	Martin County, North Carolina, 21 Years Old	Co. K, 10th Regiment North Carolina, 1st N. C. Artillery	Captured	Elmira Prison, New York	Died of Pneumonia 3/7/1865
Robert, Henry Clay Private	Brunswick County, North Carolina, 5/8/1862	Lumberton, Robeson County, North Carolina, 18 Years Old Farmer	Co. E, 40th Regiment North Carolina, 3rd N. C. Artillery	Captured	Point Lookout Prison, Maryland	Oath of Allegiance 5/15/1865
Roberts, J. DeBerniere Second Lieutenant	Columbia, South Carolina, 7/15/1861, Co. G, Hampton's Legion, Transferred to CSMC 6/9/1864	Craven County, North Carolina, 20 Years Old	Co. C, Confederate States Marine Corp	Captured	Fort Columbus, New York Harbor	Exchanged Boulwares Wharf, Va. 3/5/1865

NAME & RANK	ENLISTED	RESIDENCE & TRADE	UNIT	RESULT OF BATTLE	PRISON	PRISON RELEASE
Roberts, John Troy Private	Fort Fisher, New Hanover County, North Carolina, 6/21/1864	Spout Spring Depot, North Carolina, 17 Years Old Student	Co. H, 36th Regiment North Carolina, 2nd N. C. Artillery	Captured	Elmira Prison, New York	Oath of Allegiance 7/11/1865
Roberts, Stephen Gaskill Private	New Hanover County, North Carolina, 4/30/1863	Portsmouth, Carteret County, North Carolina, 18 Years Old Mariner	Co. D, 13th Battalion North Carolina Light Artillery	Captured, Defended River Road Gate	Point Lookout Prison, Maryland	Oath of Allegiance 5/25/1865
Roberts, Wilson A. Private	Coosawhatchie, South Carolina 1/1/1863	Gillisonville, Beaufort District, South Carolina, 38 Years Old Blacksmith & Wheel Wright	Co. F, 11th South Carolina Volunteers	Captured	Point Lookout Prison, Maryland	Died Consumption 6/3/1865
Roberts, William Private	Robeson County, North Carolina, 9/17/1861	Lumberton, Robeson County, North Carolina, 24 Years Old Farm Laborer	Co. E, 40th Regiment North Carolina, 3rd N. C. Artillery	Killed In Action 1/15/1865		
Robeson, Albert Private	Fort Pender, Brunswick County, North Carolina, 9/2/1863	White Hall, Bladen County, North Carolina, 18 Years Old	Co. H, 36th Regiment North Carolina, 2nd N. C. Artillery	Captured	Fort McHenry, Maryland	Oath of Allegiance 5/18/1865, Died Of Chronic Diarrhea 5/27/1865
Robeson, Malcolm Private	Bladen County, North Carolina, 5/5/1862	Bladen County, North Carolina, 31 Years Old Farmer	Co. H, 36th Regiment North Carolina, 2nd N. C. Artillery	Captured	Point Lookout Prison, Maryland	Exchanged 3/16/1865 At Boulware's Wharf, James River, Virginia

NAME & RANK	ENLISTED	RESIDENCE & TRADE	UNIT	RESULT OF BATTLE	PRISON	PRISON RELEASE
Robeson, Matthew P. Private	Elizabeth-town, Bladen County, North Carolina, 3/15/1862, Volunteer	Duplin County, North Carolina, 42 Years Old Farmer	Co. H, 36th Regiment North Carolina, 2nd N. C. Artillery	Captured	Elmira Prison, New York	Died of Smallpox, 2/22/1865
Robinson, F. Private	Date and Place Unknown	Unknown	2nd Co. I, 36th Regiment North Carolina, 2nd N. C. Artillery	Captured	Prison Unknown	Date Of Release Unknown,
Robinson, Henry L. Seaman	Place Unknown, 1/24/1862	Lockwood Folly, Brunswick County, North Carolina, 22 Years Old Fisherman	Galloway Co., Confederate States Coast Guard	Captured	Prison Unknown	Date Of Release Unknown
Robinson, Jesse Private	Goldsboro, Wayne County, North Carolina, 7/3/1863	Greene County, North Carolina, 36 Years Old Farmer	Co. F, 10th Regiment North Carolina, 1st N. C. Artillery	Captured	Elmira Prison, New York	Died of Rubeola (measles) 2/19/1865
Robinson, John Frieze Private	Sampson County, North Carolina, 12/`19/1862	Sampson County, North Carolina, 35 Years Old Farmer	2nd Co. A, 36th Regiment North Carolina, 2nd N. C. Artillery	Captured, Defended the Mound Battery	Point Lookout Prison, Maryland	Oath of Allegiance 6/3/1865
Robinson, John P. Private	Fort St. Philip, Brunswick County, North Carolina, 5/14/1862, Volunteer	Brunswick County, North Carolina, 28 Years Old	3rd Co. G, 36th Regiment North Carolina, 2nd N. C. Artillery	Captured, Defended Battery to the Left of Northeast Bastion	Elmira Prison, New York	Oath of Allegiance 7/3/1865

NAME & RANK	ENLISTED	RESIDENCE & TRADE	UNIT	RESULT OF BATTLE	PRISON	PRISON RELEASE
Robinson, Julius C. Private	Fort Fisher, New Hanover County, North Carolina, 3/1/1864, Volunteer	New Hanover County, North Carolina, 18 Years Old	2nd Co. I, 36th Regiment North Carolina, 2nd N. C. Artillery	Captured, Defended Shepperd's Battery	Elmira Prison, New York	Died of Chronic Diarrhea 2/15/1865
Robinson, Michael Private	Date and Place Unknown	Unknown	Co. H, 36th Regiment North Carolina, 2nd N. C. Artillery	Captured	Prison Unknown	Date Of Release Unknown
Robinson, Napoleon A. Private	Fort Branch, Brunswick County, North Carolina, 7/9/1863	Charlotte, North Carolina, 17 Years Old	3rd Co. G, 40th Regiment North Carolina, 3rd N. C. Artillery	Captured, Defended Land Face	Elmira Prison, New York	Oath of Allegiance 6/12/1865
Robinson, Samuel F. Sergeant	Date and Place Unknown	Lockwood Folly, Brunswick County, North Carolina, 24 Years Old Fisherman	Galloway Co., Confederate States Coast Guard	Captured	Prison Unknown	Date Of Release Unknown
Robinson, Sion Private	Transferred From Co. D, 38th North Carolina Troops 10/22/1861	Sampson County, North Carolina, 21 Years Old Farmer	2nd Co. I, 36th Regiment North Carolina, 2nd N. C. Artillery	Captured, Defended Shepperd's Battery	Point Lookout Prison, Maryland	Oath of Allegiance 6/19/1865
Robinson, Thomas R. Seaman	Place Unknown 1/24/1862	Lockwood Folly, Brunswick County, North Carolina, 17 Years Old Fisherman	Galloway Co., Confederate States Coast Guard	Captured	Prison Unknown	Date Of Release Unknown
Robinson, Thomas M. Corporal	Sampson County, North Carolina, 12/`19/1862	Taylor's Bridge, Sampson County, North Carolina, 33 Years Old Cooper	2nd Co. A, 36th Regiment North Carolina, 2nd N. C. Artillery	Killed In Action 1/15/1865, Defended the Mound Battery		

NAME & RANK	ENLISTED	RESIDENCE & TRADE	UNIT	RESULT OF BATTLE	PRISON	PRISON RELEASE
Robison, A. Private	Date and Place Unknown	Unknown	Co. H, 36th Regiment North Carolina, 2nd N. C. Artillery	Captured	Elmira Prison, New York	Exchanged 3/21/1865 At Boulware's Wharf, James River, Virginia
Robinson, William Private	Goldsboro, Wayne County, North Carolina, 8/23/1862	Goldsboro, Wayne County, North Carolina, 20 Years Old	Co. F, 10th Regiment North Carolina, 1st N. C. Artillery	Captured	Elmira Prison, New York	Died of Pneumonia 3/7/1865
Robison, T. Seaman	Date and Place Unknown	Unknown	Confederate States Navy	Wounded Severely In Head 12/25/1864		
Rodgers, Henry Private	Halifax County, North Carolina, 10/9/1861	Halifax County, North Carolina, 28 Years Old	Co. F, 36th Regiment North Carolina, 2nd N. C. Artillery	Captured	Point Lookout Prison, Maryland	Oath of Allegiance 6/19/1865
Rogers, Thomas G. Private	Camp Harllee, Georgetown South Carolina 1/8/1862	Marion District, South Carolina, 27 Years Old Silver Smith	Co. I, 21st South Carolina Volunteers	Captured	Elmira Prison, Elmira, New York	Died of Chronic Diarrhea, 2/16/1865
Rodgers, William J. J. Private	Enfield, Halifax County, North Carolina, 10/9/1861, Volunteer	Wayne County, North Carolina, 23 Years Old	Co. F, 36th Regiment North Carolina, 2nd N. C. Artillery	Captured	Elmira Prison, New York	Died of Typhoid Fever 2/27/1865
Rogers, Warren Private	Wilson County, North Carolina, 11/4/1863	Unknown, 18 Years Old	Co. D, 40th Regiment North Carolina, 3rd N. C. Artillery	Captured	Point Lookout Prison, Maryland	Oath of Allegiance 6/3/1865

NAME & RANK	ENLISTED	RESIDENCE & TRADE	UNIT	RESULT OF BATTLE	PRISON	PRISON RELEASE
Rook, E. C. Private	Coles Island, South Carolina 4/11/1862	Unknown	Co. F, 25th South Carolina Volunteers	Captured	Elmira Prison, New York	Exchanged 3/2/1865 Boulware's Wharf, James River, Virginia
Ross, James A. Private	Cross Roads, Cumberland County, North Carolina, 2/23/1862, Volunteer	Unknown, 19 Years Old	2nd Co. C, 36th Regiment North Carolina, 2nd N. C. Artillery	Wounded & Captured, Defended River Road Gate	Prison Unknown	Date Of Release Unknown, May Have Died Of Wounds at Fort Fisher
Ross, John A. Private	Rockfish, Hoke County, North Carolina, 2/26/1862, Volunteer	Duplin County, North Carolina, 21 Years Old	2nd Co. C, 36th Regiment North Carolina, 2nd N. C. Artillery	Wounded In Face By Shell, Carrying Away The Eyeball and Part of the Bones of the Nose, Captured	Hammond Hospital, Point Lookout Prison, Maryland	Oath of Allegiance 6/3/1865, Defended River Road Gate
Ross, Thomas Private	Date and Place Unknown	Unknown	Co. H, 36th Regiment North Carolina, 2nd N. C. Artillery	Captured	Point Lookout Prison, Maryland	Died of Remittent Fever 2/11/1865
Rouse, Noah Private	Fort Fisher, New Hanover County, North Carolina, 2/9/1863	Whiteville, Columbus County, North Carolina, 21 Years Old	2nd Co. K, 40th Regiment North Carolina, 3rd N. C. Artillery	Captured	Elmira Prison, New York	Oath of Allegiance 6/12/1865
Rowan, John J. Private	Bladen County, North Carolina, 2/14/1863	Bladen County, North Carolina, 35 Years Old	3rd Co. B, 36th Regiment North Carolina, 2nd N. C. Artillery	Severely Wounded In Both Legs By Exploding Shell, Wounded Left Thigh & Captured	Hammond Hospital, Point Lookout Prison, Maryland	Oath of Allegiance 6/26/1865

NAME & RANK	ENLISTED	RESIDENCE & TRADE	UNIT	RESULT OF BATTLE	PRISON	PRISON RELEASE
Rowan, W. P. Private	Date and Place Unknown	Unknown	3rd Co. G, 36th Regiment North Carolina, 2nd N. C. Artillery	Captured, Defended Battery to the Left of Northeast Bastion	Prison Unknown	Date Of Release Unknown
Rowland, Benjamin W. Private	Fort Caswell, Brunswick County, North Carolina, 8/2/1863	Henderson, Vance County, North Carolina, 18 Years Old	Co. F, 36th Regiment North Carolina, 2nd N. C. Artillery	Captured	Elmira Prison, New York	Oath of Allegiance 6/12/1865
Royal, Molton Private	Fort Fisher, New Hanover County, North Carolina, 10/31/1862, Volunteer	Unknown, 22 Years Old	2nd Co. C, 36th Regiment North Carolina, 2nd N. C. Artillery	Captured, Defended River Road Gate	Elmira Prison, New York	Exchanged 3/2/1865 Boulware's Wharf, James River, Virginia
Royal, Ollin Private	Sampson County, North Carolina, 2/18/1863	Warsaw, Duplin County, North Carolina, 35 Years Old	2nd Co. A, 36th Regiment North Carolina, 2nd N. C. Artillery	Captured, Defended the Mound Battery	Elmira Prison, New York	Oath of Allegiance 6/12/1865
Rozier, Reuben Private	Fort Fisher, New Hanover County, North Carolina, 8/1/1863	Lumberton, Robeson County, North Carolina, 43 Years Old	2nd Co. K, 40th Regiment North Carolina, 3rd N. C. Artillery	Captured	Elmira Prison, New York	Oath of Allegiance 6/12/1865
Ruark, Robert M. Seaman	Place Unknown 5/13/1862	Smithville, Brunswick County, North Carolina, 20 Years Old Raftsman	Galloway Co., Confederate States Coast Guard	Captured	Prison Unknown	Date Of Release Unknown

NAME & RANK	ENLISTED	RESIDENCE & TRADE	UNIT	RESULT OF BATTLE	PRISON	PRISON RELEASE
Ruffin, Andrew Private	Halifax County, North Carolina, 10/9/1861	Wilson, Wilson County, North Carolina, 18 Years Old	Co. F, 36th Regiment North Carolina, 2nd N. C. Artillery	Killed In Action 1/15/1865		
Rush, E. R. Lieutenant	Battery Island, South Carolina 4/12/1862	Unknown, 23 Years Old	Co, A, 25th South Carolina Volunteers	Captured	Fort Columbus, N.Y. Harbor	Exchanged 2/25/1865
Rush, Robert T. Private	Fort Branch, Brunswick County, North Carolina, 7/20/1863, Volunteer	Montgomery County, North Carolina, 18 Years Old	3rd Co. G, 40th Regiment North Carolina, 3rd N. C. Artillery	Captured, Defended Land Face	Elmira Prison, New York	Exchanged 3/2/1865 Boulware's Wharf, James River, Virginia
Rushing, James B. Private	Marion District, South Carolina 4/20/1862	Marion County, South Carolina, 17 Years Old	Co. D, 25th South Carolina Volunteers	Captured	Elmira Prison, New York	Exchanged On the James River 2/20/1865
Russ, Edward Private	New Hanover County, North Carolina, 12/3/1862	Elizabethtown Bladen County, North Carolina, 37 Years Old	Co. E, 36th Regiment North Carolina, 2nd N. C. Artillery	Captured Smithville, North Carolina	Point Lookout Prison, Maryland	Died of Chronic Rheumatism 2/11/1865
Russ, Thomas James Private	Bladen County, North Carolina, 8/1/1863	Bladen County, North Carolina, 27 Years Old Farmer	2nd Co. K, 40th Regiment North Carolina, 3rd N. C. Artillery	Captured	Point Lookout Prison, Maryland	Oath of Allegiance 6/17/1865
Russ, William H. Private	Fort Campbell, Brunswick County, North Carolina, 1/16/1864	Wilmington, New Hanover County, North Carolina, 17 Years Old	3rd Co G, 36th Regiment North Carolina, 2nd N. C. Artillery	Captured	Elmira Prison, New York	Oath of Allegiance 7/7/1865

NAME & RANK	ENLISTED	RESIDENCE & TRADE	UNIT	RESULT OF BATTLE	PRISON	PRISON RELEASE
Russ, William Henry Sergeant	Bladen County, North Carolina, 9/24/1861	Bladen County, North Carolina, 30 Years Old	2nd Co A, 36th Regiment North Carolina, 2nd N. C. Artillery	Captured	Point Lookout Prison, Maryland	Oath of Allegiance 6/17/1865
Russell, John Private	Fort Branch, Brunswick County, North Carolina, 7/28/1863, Volunteer	Anson County, North Carolina, 42 Years Old	3rd Co. G, 40th Regiment North Carolina, 3rd N. C. Artillery	Captured, Defended Land Face	Elmira Prison, New York	Died of Pneumonia 3/4/1865
Russell, Calvin L. Private	Place Unknown, 8/?/1863	Unknown	Co. E, Confederate States Marine Corp	Captured	Point Lookout Prison, Maryland	Died of Pneumonia 4/16/1865
Rutherford, George Private	Date and Place Unknown	Augusta, Georgia, Age Unknown	Co. E, Confederate States Marine Corp, Assigned to Guard Duty Aboard CSS *Savannah.*	Captured, Defended Sea Face	Point Lookout Prison, Maryland	Oath of Allegiance 6/17/1865
Ryan, James T. Private	Fort Caswell, Brunswick County, North Carolina, 7/1/1863	Enfield, Halifax County, North Carolina, 18 Years Old	Co. F, 36th Regiment North Carolina, 2nd N. C. Artillery	Captured	Elmira Prison, New York	Oath of Allegiance 7/7/1865
Ryland, Robert Private	Fort Caswell, Columbus County, North Carolina, 4/10/1862	Unknown, 27 Years Old	Co. E, 36th Regiment North Carolina, 2nd N. C. Artillery	Mortally Wounded In Left Lung & Captured	Point Lookout Prison, Maryland	Died Of "Pyaemia From Gunshot Wound" 2/10/1865

NAME & RANK	ENLISTED	RESIDENCE AGE & TRADE	UNIT	RESULT OF BATTLE	PRISON	PRISON RELEASE
Sadler, William E. Private	Craven County, North Carolina, 9/21/1861	Craven County, North Carolina, 31 Years Old Farmer	Co. D, 40th Regiment North Carolina, 3rd N. C. Artillery	Captured	Point Lookout Prison, Maryland	Oath of Allegiance 5/14/1865
Salmon, David D. Private	Brunswick County, North Carolina, 11/20/1863	Robeson County, North Carolina, 18 Years Old Farmer	Co. E, 40th Regiment North Carolina, 3rd N. C. Artillery	Captured	Point Lookout Prison, Maryland	Oath of Allegiance 5/15/1865
Salmon, Sidney Private	Chatham County, North Carolina, 3/26/1863, Volunteer	Goldstone, Chatham County, North Carolina, 18 Years Old Farmer, Wood Cutter	3rd Co. G, 40th Regiment North Carolina, 3rd N. C. Artillery	Captured, Defended Land Face	Elmira Prison, New York	Exchanged 3/2/1865 at James River, Virginia, Died of unknown Disease 3/2/1865
Salters, William H. Lieutenant	James Island, South Carolina 7/1/1862	Kingstree, Williamsburg District, South Carolina, 21 Years Old	Co. K, 25th South Carolina Volunteers	Captured	Fort Columbus, N.Y. Harbor	Exchanged 2/25/1865
Sampson, Ely Private	Date and Place Unknown	Unknown	Co. H, 36th Regiment North Carolina, 2nd N. C. Artillery	Captured	Prison Unknown	Release Date Unknown
Sanders, Benjamin H. Private	Coles Island, South Carolina 4/11/1862	Midway, Barnwell County, South Carolina, 14 Years Old	Co. G, 25th South Carolina Volunteers	Captured	Elmira Prison, New York	Oath of Allegiance 7/7/1865
Sanders, Joseph T. Sergeant	Charleston, South Carolina 4/1/1862	Charleston, South Carolina, 19 Years Old Clerk	Co. E, 25th South Carolina Volunteers	Captured	Elmira Prison, New York	Exchanged 2/20/1865

NAME & RANK	ENLISTED	RESIDENCE AGE & TRADE	UNIT	RESULT OF BATTLE	PRISON	PRISON RELEASE
Sanders, Samuel D.	Camp Harllee, South Carolina 1/1/1862	Cheraw, Chesterfield County, South Carolina, 40 Years Old School Teacher	Co. D, 21st South Carolina Volunteers	Captured	Fort Columbus, New York Harbor	Exchanged 2/25/1865
Sanford, Jesse Private	Columbia, South Carolina 8/13/1864	Blackville, Orangeburg District, South Carolina, 34 Years Old Mechanic	Co. G, 25th South Carolina Volunteers	Captured	Elmira Prison, New York	Died of Chronic Diarrhea 3/20/1865
Sasser, William Private	Goldsboro, Wayne County, North Carolina, 12/25/1861	Unknown	Co F, 10th Regiment North Carolina, 1st N. C. Artillery	Captured	Point Lookout Prison, Maryland	Oath of Allegiance 5/14/1865
Satterfield, G. W. R. Private	Brunswick County, North Carolina, 3/1/1864	Person County, North Carolina, Age Unknown	Co. D, 13th Battalion North Carolina Light Artillery	Captured in Hospital in Smithville 1/16/1865, Defended River Road Gate	Point Lookout Prison, Maryland	Oath of Allegiance 6/26/1865
Saterthwaite Benjamin F. Corporal	Beaufort County, North Carolina, 9/23/1861	Unknown, 30 Years Old	Co. D, 13th Battalion North Carolina Light Artillery	Captured Defended River Road Gate	Prison Unknown	Release Date Unknown
Saunders, James E. Corporal	Hertford County, North Carolina, 5/1/1862	Hertford County, North Carolina, Age Unknown	Co. C, 3rd Battalion North Carolina Light Artillery	Gunshot Wound Left Forearm & Fractured Jaw & Captured	Treated At Mansfield Hospital, Morehead City, N. C., Sent To Fort Delaware Prison, Del.	Oath of Allegiance 6/19/1865
Saunders, James R. Private	Fort Caswell, Brunswick County, North Carolina, 7/15/1863	Halifax County, North Carolina, 18 Years Old	Co. F, 36th Regiment North Carolina, 2nd N. C. Artillery	Captured	Elmira Prison, New York	Exchanged 3/14/1865 at Boulware's Wharf, James River, Virginia

NAME & RANK	ENLISTED	RESIDENCE AGE & TRADE	UNIT	RESULT OF BATTLE	PRISON	PRISON RELEASE
Saunders, William Major	District of Darlington, South Carolina, 11/11/1862	District of Darlington, South Carolina, 27 Years Old Planter	Chief of Artillery to General Louis Hebert	Not Captured, Wounded		Evacuated Battery Buchanan With Captain Robert Chapman
Savage, Richard Private	Brunswick County, North Carolina, 10/7/1863	New Hanover County, North Carolina, 35 Years Old	2nd Co. D, 36th Regiment North Carolina, 2nd N. C. Artillery	Captured	Point Lookout Prison, Maryland	Oath of Allegiance 5/14/1865
Schirer, John Private	James Island, South Carolina 7/20/1862	Providence, Rhode Island, Age Unknown	Co. B, 25th South Carolina Volunteers	Captured	Elmira Prison, New York	Oath of Allegiance 6/16/1865
Schuler, George L. V. S. Private	Cole's Island, South Carolina 4/11/1862	McCantsville, Orangeburg, South Carolina, 25 Years Old Carpenter	Co. F, 25th South Carolina Volunteers	Captured	Elmira Prison, New York	Exchanged 3/2/1865 Boulware's Wharf, James River, Virginia
Schuler, Fred P.H. Private	Cole's Island, South Carolina 4/11/1862	Orangeburg District, South Carolina, 15 Years Old	Co. F, 25th South Carolina Volunteers	Captured	Elmira Prison, New York	Exchanged 3/2/1865, Died at Jackson Hospital Of Chronic Diarrhea 4/3/1865
Schulte, J. H. Private	Charleston, South Carolina 4/4/1862	Charleston, South Carolina, 29 Years Old Lumber Dealer	Co. B, 25th South Carolina Volunteers	Captured	Elmira Prison, New York	Oath of Allegiance 7/7/1865
Scott, J. E. Private	James Island, South Carolina 5/16/1863	Murray's Ferry, Williamsburg District, South Carolina, 18 Years Old	Co. C, 25th South Carolina Volunteers	Captured	Elmira Prison, New York	Oath of Allegiance 6/30/1865

NAME & RANK	ENLISTED	RESIDENCE AGE & TRADE	UNIT	RESULT OF BATTLE	PRISON	PRISON RELEASE
Scott, John L. Private	James Island, South Carolina 8/29/1863	Lynchburg, Sumter District, South Carolina, 34 Years Old Contractor	Co. G, 25th South Carolina Volunteers	Captured	Elmira Prison, New York	Oath of Allegiance 7/11/1865
Seagraves, James M. Private	Camp Hill, North Carolina, 8/8/1862	Age Unknown, Brick Mason	Co. C, 3rd Battalion North Carolina Light Artillery	Captured	Elmira Prison, New York	Exchanged 3/14/1865 at Boulware's Wharf, James River, Virginia
Sealey, Neverson Private	Robeson County, North Carolina, 4/11/1864, Volunteer	Robeson County, North Carolina, 17 Years Old	Co. D, 1st Battalion North Carolina Heavy Artillery	Wounded Left Side & Captured, Defended River Road Gate	Point Lookout Prison, Maryland	Oath of Allegiance 6/30/1865
Secrest, Lafayette A. Private	Wilmington, New Hanover County, North Carolina, 5/11/1864	Monroe, Union County, North Carolina, 18 Years Old	Co K, 10th Regiment North Carolina, 1st N. C. Artillery	Captured	Elmira Prison, New York	Died of "Spasm Of Glottis" 4/13/1865
Sellars, David Private	Fort Caswell, North Carolina, 10/20/1863, Volunteer	New Hanover County, North Carolina, 35 Years Old	2nd Co. D, 36th Regiment North Carolina, 2nd N. C. Artillery	Captured	Elmira Prison, New York	Died of Smallpox, 3/20/1865
Sellars, Duncan C. Private	Bladen County, North Carolina, 1/28/1862	Rosendale, North Carolina, 26 Years Old	3rd Co. B, 36th Regiment North Carolina, 2nd N. C. Artillery	Captured	Elmira Prison, New York	Oath of Allegiance 7/3/1865
Sellars, George Private	Wilmington, New Hanover County, North Carolina, 10/28/1861, Volunteer	Wilmington, New Hanover County, North Carolina, 19 Years Old	2nd Co. D, 36th Regiment North Carolina, 2nd N. C. Artillery	Captured	Elmira Prison, New York	Oath of Allegiance 5/27/1865, Died of Chronic Diarrhea 5/27/1865

NAME & RANK	ENLISTED	RESIDENCE AGE & TRADE	UNIT	RESULT OF BATTLE	PRISON	PRISON RELEASE
Sellars, John Private	Wilmington, New Hanover County, North Carolina, 3/3/1862, Volunteer	New Hanover County, North Carolina, 38 Years Old	2nd Co. D, 36th Regiment North Carolina, 2nd N. C. Artillery	Wounded & Captured	Elmira Prison, New York	Died of Smallpox, 3/1/1865
Sellars, William Private	New Hanover County, North Carolina, 3/3/1862	New Hanover County, North Carolina, 28 Years Old	2nd Co. D, 36th Regiment North Carolina, 2nd N. C. Artillery	Captured	Elmira Prison, New York	Died of "Congestion Of Lungs" 2/10/1865
Sellers, Elisha Private	Brunswick County, North Carolina, 2/6/1863	Wilmington, New Hanover, County, North Carolina, 43 Years Old Ship's Carpenter	3rd Co. G, 36th Regiment North Carolina, 2nd N. C. Artillery	Killed In Action 1/15/1865, Defended Battery to the Left of Northeast Bastion		
Sellers, James B. Private	Fort Fisher, New Hanover County, North Carolina, 5/23/1864	Town Creek District, Brunswick County, North Carolina, 17 Years Old	3rd Co. G, 36th Regiment North Carolina, 2nd N. C. Artillery	Captured, Defended Battery to the Left of Northeast Bastion	Elmira Prison, New York	Oath of Allegiance 7/7/1865
Sellers, John First Sergeant	Fort St. Philip, Brunswick County, North Carolina, 5/14/1862, Volunteer	Brunswick County, North Carolina, 34 Years Old Detailed to string Telegraph lines to Fort Caswell, N. C.	3rd Co. G, 36th Regiment North Carolina, 2nd N. C. Artillery	Captured, Defended Battery to the Left of Northeast Bastion	Elmira Prison, New York	Died of Chronic Diarrhea 3/29/1865
Sellers, John M. Private	Old Brunswick Town, North Carolina, 4/16/1862, Volunteer	Brunswick County, North Carolina, 41 Years Old	3rd Co. G, 36th Regiment North Carolina, 2nd N. C. Artillery	Captured, Defended Battery to the Left of Northeast Bastion	Elmira Prison, New York	Died of Smallpox, 3/20/1865

NAME & RANK	ENLISTED	RESIDENCE AGE & TRADE	UNIT	RESULT OF BATTLE	PRISON	PRISON RELEASE
Sellers, John W. Musician	Fort Caswell, Brunswick County, North Carolina, 2/24/1863, Volunteer	Brunswick County, North Carolina, 37 Years Old	3rd Co. G, 36th Regiment North Carolina, 2nd N. C. Artillery	Captured, Defended Battery to the Left of Northeast Bastion	Elmira Prison, New York	Died of Smallpox, 5/14/1865
Sellers, Lorenzo Private	Fort Caswell, Brunswick County, North Carolina, 9/25/1862, Volunteer	Lockwood Folly, Brunswick County, North Carolina, 21 Years Old Worked extra duty as a nurse in the hospital	3rd Co. G, 36th Regiment North Carolina, 2nd N. C. Artillery	Captured, Defended Battery to the Left of Northeast Bastion	Elmira Prison, New York	Exchanged 3/21/1865 at Boulware's Wharf, James River, Virginia
Sellers, Robert A. Private	Fort Johnson, Brunswick County, North Carolina, 3/16/1863, Volunteer	Smithville, North Carolina, 17 Years Old	3rd Co. G, 40th Regiment North Carolina, 3rd N. C. Artillery	Captured, Defended Land Face	Elmira Prison, New York	Oath of Allegiance 6/12/1865
Sellers, Thomas A. Private	Fort Caswell, Brunswick County, North Carolina, 2/8/1863, Volunteer	Brunswick County, North Carolina, 38 Years Old	3rd Co. G, 36th Regiment North Carolina, 2nd N. C. Artillery	Captured, Defended Battery to the Left of Northeast Bastion	Elmira Prison, New York	Exchanged 2/20/1865 at Boulware's Wharf, James River, Virginia
Sellers, William H. Private	Cero Gordo, North Carolina, 3/5/1862, Volunteer	Whiteville, Columbus County, North Carolina, 25 Years Old	Co. E, 36th Regiment North Carolina, 2nd N. C. Artillery	Wounded & Captured	Elmira Prison, New York	Oath of Allegiance 7/3/1865
Sellers, William R. Private	Brunswick County, North Carolina, 8/24/1863, Volunteer	Brunswick County, North Carolina, 30 Years Old	3rd Co. G, 36th Regiment North Carolina, 2nd N. C. Artillery	Wounded & Captured, Defended Battery to the Left of Northeast Bastion	Elmira Prison, New York	Died of Congestion Of Lungs (Pneumonia), 2/10/1865

NAME & RANK	ENLISTED	RESIDENCE AGE & TRADE	UNIT	RESULT OF BATTLE	PRISON	PRISON RELEASE
Senter, John A. Private	Camp Holmes, North Carolina, 10/13/1863	Raleigh, Wake County, North Carolina, Age Unknown	2nd Co. D, 36th Regiment North Carolina, 2nd N. C. Artillery	Captured	Elmira Prison, New York	Oath of Allegiance 7/3/1865
Sessoms, Alexander Corporal	Sampson County, North Carolina, 8/20/1863	Owensville, Sampson County, North Carolina, 20 Years Old	3rd Co. B, 36th Regiment North Carolina, 2nd N. C. Artillery	Severely Wounded In Right Foot & Captured	Point Lookout Prison, Maryland	Oath of Allegiance 6/29/1865, Right Foot Amputated
Sessoms, Alexander Sergeant	Fayetteville, Cumberland County, North Carolina, 2/16/1862	Unknown, 28 Years Old	2nd Co. C, 36th Regiment North Carolina, 2nd N. C. Artillery	Shell Wound to Left Thigh & Captured	General Hospital At Fort Monroe, Camp Hamilton, Virginia	Oath of Allegiance 5/29/1865, Defended River Road Gate
Sessoms, James Gilbert Private	Sampson County, North Carolina, 11/1/1862, Volunteer	Sampson County, North Carolina, 26 Years Old Extra Duty As Teamster, Day Laborer	2nd Co. C, 36th Regiment North Carolina, 2nd N. C. Artillery	Severely Wounded & Captured	Point Lookout Prison, Maryland	Oath of Allegiance 6/20/1865, Defended River Road Gate
Sessoms, Neill Private	Blockersville, North Carolina, 2/26/1862, Volunteer	Fayetteville, Cumberland County, North Carolina, 26 Years Old	2nd Co. C, 36th Regiment North Carolina, 2nd N. C. Artillery	Captured, Defended River Road Gate	Elmira Prison, New York	Oath of Allegiance 6/12/1865
Sessoms, Thomas S. Private	Wilmington, New Hanover County, North Carolina, 11/4/1861, Volunteer	Harrison's Creek Landing, North Carolina, 21 Years Old	2nd Co. I, 36th Regiment North Carolina, 2nd N. C. Artillery	Captured, Defended Shepperd's Battery	Elmira Prison, New York	Oath of Allegiance 6/12/1865

NAME & RANK	ENLISTED	RESIDENCE AGE & TRADE	UNIT	RESULT OF BATTLE	PRISON	PRISON RELEASE
Sessoms, William J. Private	Cumberland County, North Carolina, 2/26/1862	Prospect Hall, Bladen County, North Carolina, 32 Years Old Turpentine Distiller	2nd Co. C, 36th Regiment North Carolina, 2nd N. C. Artillery	Wounded Severely In Right Knee and Foot & Captured	Hammond General Hospital, Point Lookout Prison, Maryland	Died of Wounds 4/23/1865, Defended River Road Gate
Shadding, Henry J. Private	Fort Pender, Brunswick County, North Carolina, 12/7/1863, Volunteer	Brunswick County, North Carolina, 18 Years Old	Co. H, 36th Regiment North Carolina, 2nd N. C. Artillery	Captured	Elmira Prison, New York	Died of Chronic Diarrhea 3/31/1865
Shaffer, R. R. Private	Charleston, South Carolina 2/24/1862	Charleston, South Carolina, 33 Years Old	Co. B, 25th South Carolina Volunteers	Captured	Elmira Prison, New York	Oath of Allegiance 7/11/1865
Shavender, Aaron G. Private	Beaufort County, North Carolina, 9/23/1861	Beaufort County, North Carolina, 18 Years Old	Co. D, 13th Battalion North Carolina Light Artillery	Captured, Defended River Road Gate	Point Lookout Prison, Maryland	Oath of Allegiance 5/13/1865
Shaw, A. M. Private	May Have Transferred From Co. K, 18th North Carolina	Unknown	2nd Co. K, 40th Regiment North Carolina, 3rd N. C. Artillery	Captured	Prison Unknown	Release Date Unknown
Shaw, Angus First Sergeant	Richmond County, North Carolina, 5/15/1861, Volunteer	Richmond County, North Carolina, 25 Years Old	Co. D, 1st Battalion North Carolina Heavy Artillery	Severely Wounded & Captured, Defended River Road Gate	Point Lookout Prison, Maryland	Oath of Allegiance 6/19/1865

NAME & RANK	ENLISTED	RESIDENCE AGE & TRADE	UNIT	RESULT OF BATTLE	PRISON	PRISON RELEASE
Shaw, Bennett Private	Elizabeth-town, Bladen County, North Carolina, 5/6/1862, Volunteer	Brown Marsh, Bladen County, North Carolina, 22 Years Old Farmer	2nd Co. K, 40th Regiment North Carolina, 3rd N. C. Artillery	Captured	Elmira Prison, New York	Oath of Allegiance 6/12/1865
Shaw, Colin Private	Brunswick County, North Carolina, 7/18/1862, Volunteer	Unknown, 29 Years Old Extra Duty As Teamster	2nd Co. K, 40th Regiment North Carolina, 3rd N. C. Artillery	Severely Wounded & Captured	Prison Unknown	Release Date Unknown, Possibly Died Of Wounds At Fort Fisher, North Carolina
Shaw, Daniel F. Private	Elizabeth-town, Bladen County, North Carolina, 5/6/1862, Volunteer	Brown Marsh, Bladen County, North Carolina, 33 Years Old Farmer	2nd Co. K, 40th Regiment North Carolina, 3rd N. C. Artillery	Captured	Elmira Prison, New York	Oath of Allegiance 6/12/1865
Shaw, Daniel J. Sergeant	Bladen County, North Carolina, 4/1/1862	Moore County, North Carolina, 51 Years Old Farmer	Co. H, 36th Regiment North Carolina, 2nd N. C. Artillery	Captured	Point Lookout Prison, Maryland	Exchanged At Cox's Landing, James River, Virginia, 2/15/1865
Shaw, Daniel M. Private	Fort Caswell, Brunswick County, North Carolina, 9/19/1863, Volunteer	Brunswick County, North Carolina, 41 Years Old	Co. E, 40th Regiment North Carolina, 3rd N. C. Artillery	Captured	Elmira Prison, New York	Exchanged 3/2/1865 Boulware's Wharf, James River, Virginia
Shaw, Duncan Private	Elizabeth-town, Bladen County, North Carolina, 5/6/1862, Volunteer	Brown Marsh, Bladen County, North Carolina, 18 Years Old Farmer	2nd Co. K, 40th Regiment North Carolina, 3rd N. C. Artillery	Captured	Elmira Prison, New York	Oath of Allegiance 6/12/1865

NAME & RANK	ENLISTED	RESIDENCE AGE & TRADE	UNIT	RESULT OF BATTLE	PRISON	PRISON RELEASE
Shaw, H. D. Private	Battery Island, South Carolina 4/12/1862	Kingstree, Murray's Ferry, Williamsburg District, South Carolina, 17 Years Old	Co. C, 25th South Carolina Volunteers	Captured	Elmira Prison, New York	Oath of Allegiance 7/11/1865
Shaw, Jack S. Private	Richmond County, North Carolina, 9/1/1864	Whiteville, Columbus County, North Carolina, 17 Years Old	Co. D, 1st Battalion North Carolina Heavy Artillery	Killed In Action 1/15/1865, Defended River Road Gate		
Shaw, John Private	Wilmington, New Hanover County, North Carolina, 12/28/1861, Volunteer	Fayetteville, Cumberland County, North Carolina, 40 Years Old	Co. E, 36th Regiment North Carolina, 2nd N. C. Artillery	Captured	Elmira Prison, New York	Oath of Allegiance 7/3/1865
Shaw, John A. Private	Cumberland County, North Carolina, 11/10/1862	Unknown, 18 Years Old	2nd Co. C, 36th Regiment North Carolina, 2nd N. C. Artillery	Captured, Defended River Road Gate	Point Lookout Prison, Maryland	Died of Measles 4/13/1865
Shaw, John W. Private	Elizabeth-town, Bladen County, North Carolina, 5/6/1862, Volunteer	Elizabethtown Bladen County, North Carolina, 18 Years Old	2nd Co. K, 40th Regiment North Carolina, 3rd N. C. Artillery	Captured	Elmira Prison, New York	Oath of Allegiance 6/12/1865
Shaw, Laughlin Private	Date and Place Unknown	Unknown	3rd Co. B, 36th Regiment North Carolina, 2nd N. C. Artillery	Wounded & Captured	Prison Unknown	Release Date Unknown
Shaw, Malcom Private	Date and Place Unknown	Whiteville, Columbus County, North Carolina, 16 Years Old	Co. K, 36th Regiment North Carolina, 2nd N. C. Artillery	Captured	Elmira Prison, New York	Oath of Allegiance 7/7/1865

NAME & RANK	ENLISTED	RESIDENCE AGE & TRADE	UNIT	RESULT OF BATTLE	PRISON	PRISON RELEASE
Shaw, Mitchell Private	Fort Holmes, Brunswick County, North Carolina, 10/26/1864	Brunswick County, North Carolina, 41 Years Old	2nd Co. K, 40th Regiment North Carolina, 3rd N. C. Artillery	Captured	Elmira Prison, New York	Exchanged 3/2/1865 Boulware's Wharf, James River, Virginia
Shaw, Neill Private	Cumberland County, North Carolina, 1/20/1864	Summersville, Harnett County, North Carolina, 18 Years Old	3rd Co. B, 36th Regiment North Carolina, 2nd N. C. Artillery	Mortally Wounded & Captured		Died Of Wounds at Fort Fisher 1/15/1865
Shaw, Solomon Musician	Fort St. Philip, Brunswick County, North Carolina, 2/7/1863, Volunteer	Whiteville, Columbus County, North Carolina, 36 Years Old	Co. E, 36th Regiment North Carolina, 2nd N. C. Artillery	Captured	Elmira Prison, New York	Exchanged 3/14/1865 at Boulware's Wharf, James River, Virginia
Shaw, William Jr. Captain	Beaufort County, North Carolina, 4/22/1861	Beaufort County, North Carolina, 33 Years Old	Co K, 10th Regiment North Carolina, 1st N. C. Artillery	Captured	Fort Columbus, New York Harbor	Exchanged 3/5/1865 at City Point, Virginia
Sheahan, William S. Private	St John, Hertford County, North Carolina, 5/2/1862	Hertford County, North Carolina, Age Unknown	Co. C, 3rd Battalion North Carolina Light Artillery	Captured	Elmira Prison, New York	Oath of Allegiance 8/7/1865
Shearin, Lucius A. Private	Halifax County, North Carolina, 1/20/1862	Brinkleyville, Halifax County, North Carolina, 30 Years Old Farm Laborer	Co. F, 36th Regiment North Carolina, 2nd N. C. Artillery	Killed In Action 1/15/1865		

NAME & RANK	ENLISTED	RESIDENCE AGE & TRADE	UNIT	RESULT OF BATTLE	PRISON	PRISON RELEASE
Sheehan, John Private	2/12/1861, Co. D, 1st Alabama Artillery, Transferred to CSMC 6/8/1864	Born in Ireland in 1823, 38 Years Old	Co. B, Confederate States Marine Corp, Assigned to Guard Duty Aboard CSS *Savannah* and CSS *Georgia*.	Captured, Defended Sea Face	Point Lookout Prison, Maryland	Oath of Allegiance 6/6/1865
Shelly, D. D. Private	Date and Place Unknown	Unknown	3rd Co. G, 36th Regiment North Carolina, 2nd N. C. Artillery	Captured	Prison Unknown	Release Date Unknown
Shepard, Joseph C. Assistant Surgeon	6/5/1862, Camp Davis, New Hanover County, North Carolina	Scotts Hill, Pender County, North Carolina, Age Unknown	Confederate States Army, 3rd Military District, Department of North Carolina	Captured	Governor's Island, N.Y. Harbor	Exchanged Six Weeks After Capture
Shephard, John J. Private	Wilmington, New Hanover County, North Carolina, 2/13/1862	Wilmington, New Hanover County, North Carolina, 49 Years Old	2nd Co. D, 36th Regiment North Carolina, 2nd N. C. Artillery	Captured	Elmira Prison, New York	Exchanged 3/21/1865 at Boulware's Wharf, James River, Virginia
Shepherd, Ethemore Private	Cerogordo, North Carolina, 3/1/1862	Fair Bluff, Columbus County, North Carolina, 18 Years Old	Co. E, 36th Regiment North Carolina, 2nd N. C. Artillery	Captured	Elmira Prison, New York	Oath of Allegiance 7/26/1865
Shepperd, George E. Private	Transferred From Co. A, 41st North Carolina Troops 4/1863	Unknown, 18 Years Old	Co. D, 13th Battalion North Carolina Light Artillery	Wounded & Captured, Defended River Road Gate	Prison Unknown	Release Date Unknown, May Have Died of Wounds at Fort Fisher

NAME & RANK	ENLISTED	RESIDENCE AGE & TRADE	UNIT	RESULT OF BATTLE	PRISON	PRISON RELEASE
Shields, C. W. Private	Date and Place Unknown	Unknown	Co. F, 36th Regiment North Carolina, 2nd N. C. Artillery	Captured	Point Lookout Prison, Maryland	Died of Chronic Diarrhea 3/7/1865
Shields, William T. Private	Craven County, North Carolina, 1/30/1862, Volunteer	Halifax County, North Carolina, 21 Years Old	Co. F, 36th Regiment North Carolina, 2nd N. C. Artillery	Captured	Prison Unknown	Release Date Unknown
Shipman, William Private	Bladen County, North Carolina, 7/8/1862	Elizabethtown Bladen County, North Carolina, 24 Years Old	3rd Co. B, 36th Regiment North Carolina, 2nd N. C. Artillery	Captured	Elmira Prison, New York	Oath of Allegiance 7/7/1865
Shirer, Henry W. Private	Cole's Island, South Carolina 4/11/1862	Charleston, South Carolina, 23 Years Old	Co. F, 25th South Carolina Volunteers	Captured	Elmira Prison, New York	Died of Variola 6/30/1865
Shirley, John Private	Fort Ellis, Craven County, North Carolina, 12/25/1861, Volunteer	Gibbs Woods District, Currituck County, North Carolina, 25 Years Old	Co. F, 36th Regiment North Carolina, 2nd N. C. Artillery	Captured	Elmira Prison, New York	Exchanged 2/20/1865
Shoemaker Ira Thomas Sergeant	Coles Island, South Carolina 4/11/62	Grahams P.O., South Carolina, Age Unknown	Co. G, 25th South Carolina Volunteers	Captured	Elmira Prison, New York	Oath of Allegiance 6/14/1865
Shoulars, George J. Sergeant	Bertie County, North Carolina, 4/15/1862	Bertie County, North Carolina, Age Unknown	Co. C, 3rd Battalion North Carolina Light Artillery	Wounded, Fracture of wrist, severe, 12/25/1864		

NAME & RANK	ENLISTED	RESIDENCE AGE & TRADE	UNIT	RESULT OF BATTLE	PRISON	PRISON RELEASE
Shotwell, F. A. Private	Smithville, Brunswick County, North Carolina, 5/18/1864	Unknown, 18 Years Old	Co F, 10th Regiment North Carolina, 1st N. C. Artillery	Gunshot Wound of Left Side, Fracturing 12th Rib & Captured	Point Lookout Prison, Hammond General Hospital Maryland	Oath of Allegiance 6/3/1865
Sikes, Amos Private	Fort Fisher, New Hanover County, North Carolina, 9/28/1863, Conscript	New Hanover County, North Carolina, 42 Years Old	2nd Co. I, 36th Regiment North Carolina, 2nd N. C. Artillery	Captured, Defended Shepperd's Battery	Elmira Prison, New York	Died of Typhoid Fever 5/6/1865
Sikes, Lucian Private	Fort Fisher, New Hanover County, North Carolina, 5/12/1862, Conscript	New Hanover County, North Carolina, 28 Years Old	2nd Co. I, 36th Regiment North Carolina, 2nd N. C. Artillery	Captured, Defended Shepperd's Battery	Elmira Prison, New York	Exchanged at James River, Va, 3/14/1865, Died of Debility In Jackson Hospital, Richmond, Va, 4/7/1865,,
Sikes, Stephen Thomas Private	Bladen County, North Carolina, 10/19/1861	Bladen County, North Carolina, 16 Years Old	Co. H, 36th Regiment North Carolina, 2nd N. C. Artillery	Captured	Point Lookout Prison, Maryland	Exchanged At Cox's Landing, James River, Virginia, 2/15/1865
Sillivent, Hardy Private	Goldsboro, Wayne County, North Carolina, 8/27/1862	Goldsboro, Wayne County, North Carolina, Age Unknown	Co F, 10th Regiment North Carolina, 1st N. C. Artillery	Captured	Elmira Prison, New York	Died of Typhoid Fever 4/20/1865
Simmons, Asberry Private	Fort St. Philip, Brunswick County, North Carolina, 5/13/1862, Volunteer	Smithville, North Carolina, 33 Years Old	3rd Co. G, 36th Regiment North Carolina, 2nd N. C. Artillery	Captured, Defended Battery to the Left of Northeast Bastion	Elmira Prison, New York	Oath of Allegiance 6/23/1865

NAME & RANK	ENLISTED	RESIDENCE AGE & TRADE	UNIT	RESULT OF BATTLE	PRISON	PRISON RELEASE
Simmons, Benjamin Private	Brunswick County, North Carolina, 7/22/1863	Brunswick County, North Carolina, 45 Years Old	Co. K, 36th Regiment North Carolina, 2nd N. C. Artillery	Captured	Point Lookout Prison, Maryland	Oath of Allegiance 6/20/1865
Simmons, Henry L. Private	Brunswick County, North Carolina, 2/19/1862	Brunswick County, North Carolina, 31 Years Old	Co. K, 36th Regiment North Carolina, 2nd N. C. Artillery	Captured	Point Lookout Prison, Maryland	Oath of Allegiance 6/20/1865
Simmons, John W. Private	Fort Fisher, New Hanover County, North Carolina, 6/11/1864, Conscript	Sampson County, North Carolina, 36 Years Old Farmer	2nd Co. I, 36th Regiment North Carolina, 2nd N. C. Artillery	Captured, Defended Shepperd's Battery	Elmira Prison, New York	Exchanged 3/14/1865 at Boulware's Wharf, James River, Virginia,
Simmons, Joseph Private	Brunswick County, North Carolina, 2/19/1862	Brunswick County, North Carolina, 19 Years Old	Co. K, 36th Regiment North Carolina, 2nd N. C. Artillery	Captured	Point Lookout Prison, Maryland	Oath of Allegiance 6/20/1865
Simmons, Samuel Private	Fort Fisher, New Hanover County, North Carolina, 7/13/1864	Sampson County, North Carolina, 34 Years Old Farmer	3rd Co. G, 36th Regiment North Carolina, 2nd N. C. Artillery	Captured, Defended Battery to the Left of Northeast Bastion	Elmira Prison, New York	Exchanged 3/2/1865 Boulware's Wharf, James River, Virginia
Simms, John H. Private	Fort Fisher, New Hanover County, North Carolina, 3/15/1863, Volunteer	New Hanover County, North Carolina, 18 Years Old	2nd Co. C, 36th Regiment North Carolina, 2nd N. C. Artillery	Captured, Defended River Road Gate	Elmira Prison, New York	Died of Chronic Diarrhea-Pneumonia 2/24/1865
Simons, W. Lucas Private	Charleston, South Carolina 5/1/1862	Unknown, 19 Years Old	Co. B, 25th South Carolina Volunteers	Captured	Elmira Prison, New York	Exchanged On The James River 3/10/1865

NAME & RANK	ENLISTED	RESIDENCE AGE & TRADE	UNIT	RESULT OF BATTLE	PRISON	PRISON RELEASE
Simpson, F. Private	Date and Place Unknown	Unknown	3rd Co. B, 36th Regiment North Carolina, 2nd N. C. Artillery	Captured	Point Lookout Prison, Maryland	Oath of Allegiance 6/3/1865
Simpson, James R. Private	Alamance County, North Carolina, 3/15/1863	Unknown, 18 Years Old	3rd Co. B, 36th Regiment North Carolina, 2nd N. C. Artillery	Captured	Point Lookout Prison, Maryland	Oath of Allegiance 6/3/1865
Sinclair, James J. Private	Fort Holmes, Brunswick County, North Carolina, 3/24/1864, Volunteer	Brunswick County, North Carolina, 18 Years Old	2nd Co. K, 40th Regiment North Carolina, 3rd N. C. Artillery	Captured	Elmira Prison, New York	Exchanged 3/2/1865 Boulware's Wharf, James River, Virginia
Singletary, Calvin Private	Elizabeth-town, Bladen County, North Carolina, 5/6/1862, Volunteer	Bladen County, North Carolina, 33 Years Old Farmer	2nd Co. K, 40th Regiment North Carolina, 3rd N. C. Artillery	Captured	Elmira Prison, New York	Died of Pneumonia 2/24/1865
Singletary, Dennis Lennon Private	Elizabeth-town, Bladen County, North Carolina, 5/6/1862, Volunteer	Bladen County, North Carolina, 34 Years Old Farmer, Detailed to build a wharf at Fort Fisher, 1/5/1864	2nd Co. K, 40th Regiment North Carolina, 3rd N. C. Artillery	Captured	Elmira Prison, New York	Exchanged 3/2/1865 Boulware's Wharf, James River, Virginia
Singletary, George S. Private	Elizabeth-town, Bladen County, North Carolina, 5/6/1862, Volunteer	Lumberton, Robeson County, North Carolina, 23 Years Old Farmer	2nd Co. K, 40th Regiment North Carolina, 3rd N. C. Artillery	Captured	Elmira Prison, New York	Oath of Allegiance 6/12/1865

NAME & RANK	ENLISTED	RESIDENCE AGE & TRADE	UNIT	RESULT OF BATTLE	PRISON	PRISON RELEASE
Singletary, Jonathan L. Private	Elizabethtown, Bladen County, North Carolina, 5/6/1862, Volunteer	Elizabethtown Bladen County, North Carolina, 20 Years Old Farmer	2nd Co. K, 40th Regiment North Carolina, 3rd N. C. Artillery	Captured	Elmira Prison, New York	Oath of Allegiance 6/12/1865
Singletary, Joshua K. Private	Bladen County, North Carolina, 8/28/1862, Volunteer	Bladen County, North Carolina, 20 Years Old	3rd Co. B, 36th Regiment North Carolina, 2nd N. C. Artillery	Captured	Elmira Prison, New York	Exchanged 3/2/1865 Boulware's Wharf, James River, Virginia
Singletary, Matthew Young Private	Bladen County, North Carolina, 12/20/1861, Volunteer	Pleasant Exchange, North Carolina, 25 Years Old	3rd Co. B, 36th Regiment North Carolina, 2nd N. C. Artillery	Captured	Elmira Prison, New York	Exchanged on the James River, Va, 2/20/1865, Extra Duty as Hospital Nurse at post
Singletary, Wright Private	Wilmington, New Hanover County, North Carolina, 1/1/1862, Volunteer	Elizabethtown Bladen County, North Carolina, 30 Years Old	3rd Co. B, 36th Regiment North Carolina, 2nd N. C. Artillery	Captured	Elmira Prison, New York	Oath of Allegiance 7/7/1865
Singleton, Asa Y. Private	Martin County, North Carolina, 8/11/1862	Martin County, North Carolina, Formerly of Braxton County, Virginia, 39 Years Old	Co. D, 13th Battalion North Carolina Light Artillery	Killed In Action 1/15/1865, Defended River Road Gate		
Singleton, Spiers Surgeon	Appointed Surgeon 11/16/1861	Unknown	Field & Staff, 36th Regiment North Carolina, 2nd N. C. Artillery	Captured	Fort Columbus, New York Harbor	Exchanged 3/5/1865 at Boulware's Wharf, James River, Virginia

NAME & RANK	ENLISTED	RESIDENCE AGE & TRADE	UNIT	RESULT OF BATTLE	PRISON	PRISON RELEASE
Sizemore, Wiiliam J. Private	Chatham County, North Carolina, 3/26/1863, Volunteer	Halifax County, North Carolina, 37 Years Old	3rd Co. G, 40th Regiment North Carolina, 3rd N. C. Artillery	Captured, Defended Land Face	Elmira Prison, New York	Died of Pneumonia 3/21/1865
Skinner, Franklin Private	James Island, South Carolina 9/1/1863	Age Unknown Carpenter	Co. H, 21st South Carolina Volunteers	Captured	Elmira Prison, New York	Died of Chronic Diarrhea 4/9/1865
Skipper, Thomas Private	Date and Place Unknown	Bennettsville, Marlboro County, South Carolina, 20 Years Old	Co. G, 21st South Carolina Volunteers	Killed In Action 1/15/1865		
Skipper, William M. Private	Old Brunswick Town, North Carolina, 4/23/1862, Volunteer	Brunswick County, North Carolina, 15 Years Old	3rd Co. G, 36th Regiment North Carolina, 2nd N. C. Artillery	Wounded & Captured, Defended Battery to the Left of Northeast Bastion	Elmira Prison, New York	Exchanged 3/2/1865 Boulware's Wharf, James River, Virginia
Sledge, Herbert A. Private	Brunswick County, North Carolina, 8/4/1862, Volunteer	Brinkleyville, Western District, Halifax County, North Carolina, 18 Years Old Farmer	Co. F, 36th Regiment North Carolina, 2nd N. C. Artillery	Captured, Wounded	Point Lookout Prison, Maryland	Oath of Allegiance 6/20/1865
Sledge, Isham C. Private	Brunswick County, North Carolina, 12/4/1862, Volunteer	Nash County, North Carolina, 18 Years Old	Co. F, 36th Regiment North Carolina, 2nd N. C. Artillery	Captured	Point Lookout Prison, Maryland	Oath of Allegiance 6/20/1865
Smith, Alexander Private	New Hanover County, North Carolina, 5/8/1862	Bladen County, North Carolina, 28 Years Old Farmer	Co. H, 36th Regiment North Carolina, 2nd N. C. Artillery	Captured	Point Lookout Prison, Maryland	Oath of Allegiance 6/19/1865

NAME & RANK	ENLISTED	RESIDENCE AGE & TRADE	UNIT	RESULT OF BATTLE	PRISON	PRISON RELEASE
Smith, Amos Private	Bladen County, North Carolina, 10/19/1861	Bladen County, North Carolina, 27 Years Old	2nd Co. I, 36th Regiment North Carolina, 2nd N. C. Artillery	Captured, Defended Shepperd's Battery	Point Lookout Prison, Maryland	Oath of Allegiance 6/19/1865
Smith, Amos W. Private	New Hanover County, North Carolina, 3/7/1862, Volunteer	Unknown, 45 Years Old	2nd Co. I, 36th Regiment North Carolina, 2nd N. C. Artillery	Gunshot Wound Right Arm & Captured, Defended Shepperd's Battery	Treated at Mansfield Hospital, Morehead City, N. C., Sent To Fort Delaware, Del.	Died of Typhoid Fever 3/13/1865
Smith, Archibald Private	Fort Fisher, New Hanover County, North Carolina, 10/16/1863, Conscripted	Elizabethtown Bladen County, N. C., 45 Years Old Detailed to Cut Timber in Bladen County, N. C., July 1864	2nd Co. I, 36th Regiment North Carolina, 2nd N. C. Artillery	Captured, Defended Shepperd's Battery	Elmira Prison, New York	Oath of Allegiance 6/12/1865
Smith, Azor J. Private	Brunswick County, North Carolina, 8/20/1864	Horry County, North Carolina, Age Unknown Farmer	Co. K, 36th Regiment North Carolina, 2nd N. C. Artillery	Captured	Point Lookout Prison, Maryland	Oath of Allegiance 5/14/1865
Smith, Benjamin F. Private	New Hanover County, North Carolina, 4/5/1864	Warrensville, Sampson County, North Carolina, 19 Years Old	Co. H, 36th Regiment North Carolina, 2nd N. C. Artillery	Killed In Action 1/15/1865		
Smith, Bunyon M. Private	Elizabethtown, Bladen County, North Carolina, 10/19/1861, Volunteer	Fayetteville, Cumberland County, North Carolina, 18 Years Old	2nd Co. I, 36th Regiment North Carolina, 2nd N. C. Artillery	Captured, Defended Shepperd's Battery	Elmira Prison, New York	Oath of Allegiance 6/12/1865

NAME & RANK	ENLISTED	RESIDENCE AGE & TRADE	UNIT	RESULT OF BATTLE	PRISON	PRISON RELEASE
Smith, Chesley Private	Sampson County, North Carolina, 10/18/1861, Volunteer	Bladen County, North Carolina, 38 Years Old	2nd Co. A, 36th Regiment North Carolina, 2nd N. C. Artillery	Captured, Defended the Mound Battery	Elmira Prison, New York	Died of Chronic Diarrhea 6/23/1865
Smith, Cogdell Private	Sampson County, North Carolina, 4/16/1863	Sampson County, North Carolina, 18 Years Old	2nd Co. A, 36th Regiment North Carolina, 2nd N. C. Artillery	Captured, Defended the Mound Battery	Point Lookout Prison, Maryland	Oath of Allegiance 6/20/1865
Smith, Daniel Private	Elizabeth-town, Bladen County, North Carolina, 7/8/1862, Volunteer	Bladen County, North Carolina, 27 Years Old Detailed as a Carpenter Building Batteries, Oct. 1862	2nd Co. I, 36th Regiment North Carolina, 2nd N. C. Artillery	Captured, Defended Shepperd's Battery	Elmira Prison, New York	Died of Smallpox, 3/29/1865
Smith, David Private	Brunswick County, North Carolina, 12/14/1863	Unknown, 18 Years Old	Co. H, 36th Regiment North Carolina, 2nd N. C. Artillery	Captured	Point Lookout Prison, Maryland	Died of Chronic Diarrhea 6/23/1865
Smith, E. B. Private	Marion District, South Carolina 4/26/1864	Marion District, South Carolina, 26 Years Old	Co. D, 21st South Carolina Volunteers	Captured	Elmira Prison, Elmira, New York	Died On Route To Be Exchanged 3/2/1865,
Smith, Edom Private	Fort Fisher, New Hanover County, North Carolina, 6/11/1863, Volunteer	New Hanover County, North Carolina, 20 Years Old Detailed as a Carpenter	2nd Co. I, 36th Regiment North Carolina, 2nd N. C. Artillery	Captured, Defended Shepperd's Battery	Elmira Prison, New York	Died of Pneumonia 2/18/1865
Smith, F. C. Private	Resided Duplin County, North Carolina	Warsaw, Duplin County, North Carolina, Age Unknown	2nd Co. A, 36th Regiment North Carolina, 2nd N. C. Artillery	Captured, Defended the Mound Battery	Elmira Prison, New York	Oath of Allegiance 7/11/1865

NAME & RANK	ENLISTED	RESIDENCE AGE & TRADE	UNIT	RESULT OF BATTLE	PRISON	PRISON RELEASE
Smith, H. Private	Date and Place Unknown	Unknown	2nd Co. I, 36th Regiment North Carolina, 2nd N. C. Artillery	Captured, Defended Shepperd's Battery	Prison Unknown	Release Date Unknown,
Smith, Henry Clay Private	Pitt County, North Carolina, 8/17/1864	Maysville, Jones County, North Carolina, 21 Years Old	Co. D, 40th Regiment North Carolina, 3rd N. C. Artillery	Captured	Elmira Prison, New York	Exchanged 3/14/1865 at Boulware's Wharf, James River, Virginia
Smith, J. T. Private	Date and Place Unknown	Unknown	2nd Co. I, 36th Regiment North Carolina, 2nd N. C. Artillery	Captured, Defended Shepperd's Battery	Prison Unknown	Release Date Unknown,
Smith, James Sergeant	Date and Place Unknown	Brunswick County, North Carolina, 20 Years Old Laborer	Galloway Co., Confederate States Coast Guard	Captured	Prison Unknown	Release Date Unknown
Smith, James A. Private	Robeson County, North Carolina, 4/16/1864	Robeson County, North Carolina, 17 Years Old	Co. D, 1st Battalion North Carolina Heavy Artillery	Gunshot wound of mouth & Captured, Defended River Road Gate	Point Lookout Prison, Maryland	Oath of Allegiance 6/3/1865
Smith, James H. Private	Sampson County, North Carolina, 2/18/1863	Buck Swamp, Wayne County, North Carolina, 20 Years Old	2nd Co. A, 36th Regiment North Carolina, 2nd N. C. Artillery	Killed In Action 1/15/1865, Defended the Mound Battery		
Smith, John B. Private	Chatham County, North Carolina, 3/26/1863, Volunteer	Chatham County, North Carolina, 37 Years Old Detailed as Wood Cutter, Smithville, N. C., November 1863	3rd Co. G, 40th Regiment North Carolina, 3rd N. C. Artillery	Captured, Defended Land Face	Elmira Prison, New York	Died of Pneumonia 2/8/1865

NAME & RANK	ENLISTED	RESIDENCE AGE & TRADE	UNIT	RESULT OF BATTLE	PRISON	PRISON RELEASE
Smith, John B. Private	Fort Fisher, New Hanover County, North Carolina, 10/26/1863, Conscript	New Hanover County, North Carolina, 45 Years Old Detailed as a Carpenter, August, 1864	2nd Co. I, 36th Regiment North Carolina, 2nd N. C. Artillery	Captured, Defended Shepperd's Battery	Elmira Prison, New York	Died of Pneumonia 4/10/1865
Smith, John C. Private	Robeson County, North Carolina, 2/23/1863	Robeson County, North Carolina, 25 Years Old	Co. D, 1st Battalion North Carolina Heavy Artillery	Captured, Defended River Road Gate or Middle Sallyport	Point Lookout Prison, Maryland	Oath of Allegiance 6/3/1865
Smith, John G. Private	Fort Fisher, New Hanover County, North Carolina, 5/29/1863	Robeson County, North Carolina, 34 Years Old	2nd Co. K, 40th Regiment North Carolina, 3rd N. C. Artillery	Shell Wound of Left Foot & Ankle & Captured	Point Lookout Prison General Hospital, Maryland	Oath of Allegiance 6/26/1865
Smith, John O. D. Private	Wilmington, New Hanover County, North Carolina, 10/19/1861, Volunteer	Bladen County, North Carolina, 19 Years Old	2nd Co. I, 36th Regiment North Carolina, 2nd N. C. Artillery	Captured, Defended Shepperd's Battery	Elmira Prison, New York	Exchanged 3/2/1865, Died of Chronic Diarrhea At Richmond Hospital 3/16/1865
Smith, John W. Private	Orangeburg, South Carolina 3/30/1862	Vance's Ferry, Orangeburg District, South Carolina, 29 Years Old	Co. F, 25th South Carolina Volunteers	Captured	Elmira Prison, New York	Oath of Allegiance 7/11/1865
Smith, Josephus C. Private	New Hanover County, North Carolina, 6/11/1863	Unknown, 18 Years Old	2nd Co. I, 36th Regiment North Carolina, 2nd N. C. Artillery	Captured, Defended Shepperd's Battery	Elmira Prison, New York	Died of Chronic Diarrhea 3/22/1865

NAME & RANK	ENLISTED	RESIDENCE AGE & TRADE	UNIT	RESULT OF BATTLE	PRISON	PRISON RELEASE
Smith, K. F. Private	Date and Place Unknown	Unknown	Co. D, 1st Battalion North Carolina Heavy Artillery	Captured, Defended River Road Gate or Middle Sallyport	Prison Unknown	Release Date Unknown
Smith, Larkin G. Private	Bradly's Store, Cumberland County, North Carolina, 2/26/1862	Unknown, 28 Years Old Carpenter	2nd Co. C, 36th Regiment North Carolina, 2nd N. C. Artillery	Severe Gundshot Wound Left Arm & Captured, Defended River Road Gate	Hammond General Hospital, Point Lookout Prison, Maryland	Left Forearm Arm Amputated, Died of Pyemia 2/15/1865
Smith, Murdock H. Private	Bladen County, North Carolina, 5/1/1862	Bladen County, North Carolina, 28 Years Old Farmer	Co. H, 36th Regiment North Carolina, 2nd N. C. Artillery	Captured	Point Lookout Prison, Maryland	Oath of Allegiance 6/19/1865
Smith, Nathan Private	Fort Fisher, New Hanover County, North Carolina, 5/5/1864	New Hanover County, North Carolina, 26 Years Old	2nd Co. A, 36th Regiment North Carolina, 2nd N. C. Artillery	Captured, Defended the Mound Battery	Elmira Prison, New York	Died of Pneumonia 2/24/1865
Smith, Peter W. Private	Fort Fisher, North Carolina, 4/5/1864, Volunteer	New Hanover County, North Carolina, 17 Years Old	Co. H, 36th Regiment North Carolina, 2nd N. C. Artillery	Captured	Elmira Prison, New York	Died of Chronic Diarrhea 3/13/1865
Smith, Philip D. Private	Darlington, South Carolina 1/20/1862	Darlington District, South Carolina, 23 Years Old Farmer	Co. H, 21st South Carolina Volunteers	Captured	Elmira Prison, Elmira, New York	Oath of Allegiance 7/11/1865

NAME & RANK	ENLISTED	RESIDENCE AGE & TRADE	UNIT	RESULT OF BATTLE	PRISON	PRISON RELEASE
Smith, Philip Sergeant	New Orleans, Louisiana, 5/29/1861	St. Louis, Missouri, Age Unknown	Co. C, Confederate States Marine Corp, Assigned to Guard Duty Aboard CSS *Patrick Henry* and CSS *Arctic.*	Captured	Point Lookout Prison, Maryland	Oath of Allegiance 2/4/1865
Smith, Randal H. Private	Lillington, Harnett County, North Carolina, 4/30/1862, Volunteer	Harnett County, North Carolina, 26 Years Old	2nd Co. C, 36th Regiment North Carolina, 2nd N. C. Artillery	Captured, Defended River Road Gate	Elmira Prison, New York	Exchanged 3/14/1865
Smith, Richard F. Private	New Hanover County, North Carolina, 5/9/1862	Bladen County, North Carolina, 24 Years Old Farmer	Co. H, 36th Regiment North Carolina, 2nd N. C. Artillery	Captured	Point Lookout Prison, Maryland	Oath of Allegiance 6/19/1865
Smith, Richard W. Private	Bladen County, North Carolina, 3/5/1862, Volunteer	Bladen County, North Carolina, 27 Years Old Farmer	Co. H, 36th Regiment North Carolina, 2nd N. C. Artillery	Shell Wound Left Shoulder & Captured	Treated At Fort Monroe Hospital, Va, Sent To Fort Delaware Prison, Del.	Oath of Allegiance 6/19/1865
Smith, Robert Private	Elizabeth-town, Bladen County, North Carolina, 4/5/1862, Volunteer	Cypress Creek, Bladen County, North Carolina, 31 Years Old Farmer	Co. H, 36th Regiment North Carolina, 2nd N. C. Artillery	Captured	Elmira Prison, New York	Exchanged 2/20/1865, Died On Route To Be Exchanged.
Smith, Robert J. Private	James Island, South Carolina 3/24/1864	Bradford Springs, Sumter District, South Carolina, 17 Years Old Farmer	Co. F, 25th South Carolina Volunteers	Captured	Elmira Prison, New York	Died of Chronic Diarrhea 2/24/1865

NAME & RANK	ENLISTED	RESIDENCE AGE & TRADE	UNIT	RESULT OF BATTLE	PRISON	PRISON RELEASE
Smith, Simeon Private	Fort Caswell, Brunswick County, North Carolina, 3/6/1863, Volunteer	Laurinburg, Scotland County, North Carolina, 25 Years Old	Co. E, 40th Regiment North Carolina, 3rd N. C. Artillery	Captured	Elmira Prison, New York	Oath of Allegiance 6/12/1865
Smith, Stephen Allen Private	Wilmington, New Hanover County, North Carolina, 3/3/1862, Volunteer	New Hanover County, North Carolina, 19 Years Old	2nd Co. D, 36th Regiment North Carolina, 2nd N. C. Artillery	Wounded & Captured	Elmira Prison, New York	Died of Smallpox, 3/1/1865
Smith, Stephen Blount Private	Wayne County, North Carolina, 10/16/1861, Volunteer	Wayne County, North Carolina, Detailed as Carpenter	Co. G, 40th Regiment North Carolina, 3rd N. C. Artillery	Escaped		
Smith, Thomas Gibson Private	Fort Caswell, Brunswick County, North Carolina, 3/6/1863, Volunteer	Laurinburg, Scotland County, North Carolina, 20 Years Old	Co. E, 40th Regiment North Carolina, 3rd N. C. Artillery	Captured	Elmira Prison, New York	Oath of Allegiance 6/12/1865
Smith, Thomas M. Private	Fort Fisher, North Carolina, 10/26/1863, Conscripted	Elizabethtown Bladen County, North Carolina, 45 Years Old	Co. K, 36th Regiment North Carolina, 2nd N. C. Artillery	Captured	Elmira Prison, New York	Oath of Allegiance 6/30/1865
Smith, Thomas S. Private	New Hanover County, North Carolina, 4/5/1864	Unknown, 17 Years Old	Co. H, 36th Regiment North Carolina, 2nd N. C. Artillery	Captured In Smithville Hospital, N. C., 1/16/1865	Point Lookout Prison, Maryland	Oath of Allegiance 6/4/1865
Smith, Valentine Private	Brunswick County, North Carolina, 3/4/1864	Brunswick County, North Carolina, 17 Years Old	Co. K, 36th Regiment North Carolina, 2nd N. C. Artillery	Captured In Smithville Hospital, N. C., 1/16/1865	Point Lookout Prison, Maryland	Oath of Allegiance 6/20/1865

NAME & RANK	ENLISTED	RESIDENCE AGE & TRADE	UNIT	RESULT OF BATTLE	PRISON	PRISON RELEASE
Smith, William A. Private	Date and Place Unknown	Spartanburg County, South Carolina, 18 Years Old, Worked On Gun Boat, 1862	Co. I, 25th South Carolina Volunteers	Wounded & Captured	Fort Monroe, Virginia	Date Of Release Unknown
Smith, William E. Private	Fort Fisher, New Hanover County, North Carolina, 2/12/1864, Volunteer	Halifax County, North Carolina, 18 Years Old	2nd Co. C, 36th Regiment North Carolina, 2nd N. C. Artillery	Captured, Defended River Road Gate	Elmira Prison, New York	Oath of Allegiance 7/7/1865
Smith, William H. Private	Brunswick County, North Carolina, 12/4/1862	Halifax County, North Carolina, 18 Years Old	Co. F, 36th Regiment North Carolina, 2nd N. C. Artillery	Captured	Elmira Prison, New York	Oath of Allegiance 7/7/1865
Smithwick, William Hyman Sergeant	Windsor, Bertie County, North Carolina, 1/23/1862,	Plymouth, North Carolina, 21 Years Old Farmer	Co. C, 3rd Battalion North Carolina Light Artillery	Captured	Elmira Prison, New York	Oath of Allegiance 6/12/1865
Smoke, Andrew E. Private	Orangeburg, South Carolina 4/24/1864	Bull Swamp, Orangeburg District, South Carolina, 23 Years Old Farmer	Co. H, 25th South Carolina Volunteers	Captured	Elmira Prison, New York	Died of Chronic Diarrhea 2/21/1865
Smothers, Simeon Private	Chesterfield, South Carolina 12/26/1861	Unknown, 24 Years Old	Co. G, 21st South Carolina Volunteers	Captured	Elmira Prison, Elmira, New York	Exchanged On The James River, Virginia, 2/20/1865
Smothers, Wiley Private	Chesterfield County, South Carolina 2/9/1864	Cheraw, Chesterfield County, South Carolina, 40 Years Old Farmer	Co. G, 21st South Carolina Volunteers	Killed In Action 1/15/1865		

NAME & RANK	ENLISTED	RESIDENCE AGE & TRADE	UNIT	RESULT OF BATTLE	PRISON	PRISON RELEASE
Smothers, William Private	Chesterfield, South Carolina 4/5/1864	Cheraw, Chesterfield County, South Carolina, 18 Years Old	Co. G, 21st South Carolina Volunteers	Killed In Action 1/15/1865		
Snead, Jonathan Bonaparte Private	Old Brunswick Town, North Carolina, 4/30/1862, Volunteer	Wilmington, New Hanover County, N. C., 30 Years Old Detailed Sept. 1863 as guard for the Wilmington & Manchester Railroad	3rd Co. G, 36th Regiment North Carolina, 2nd N. C. Artillery	Captured, Defended Battery to the Left of Northeast Bastion	Elmira Prison, New York	Oath of Allegiance 5/29/1865
Snipes, John Private	Goldsboro, Wayne County, North Carolina, 7/6/1861	Goldsboro, Wayne County, North Carolina, 24 Years Old Mason	Co F, 10th Regiment North Carolina, 1st N. C. Artillery	Captured	Elmira Prison, New York	Died of Pneumonia 2/20/1865
Snipes, Sion Private	Elizabeth-town, Bladen County, North Carolina, 2/3/1862, Volunteer	Elizabethtown Bladen County, North Carolina, 25 Years Old Turpentine	Co. E, 36th Regiment North Carolina, 2nd N. C. Artillery	Captured	Elmira Prison, New York	Oath of Allegiance 8/7/1865
Somerset, J. Calvin Private	Brunswick County, North Carolina, 2/19/1862	Unknown, 36 Years Old	Co. K, 36th Regiment North Carolina, 2nd N. C. Artillery	Captured	Point Lookout Prison, Maryland	Exchanged 2/21/1865 at Boulware's Wharf, James River, Virginia
Sommerset, Marvin K. Corporal	Brunswick County, North Carolina, 4/4/1864, Volunteer	Whiteville, Columbus County, North Carolina, 17 Years Old	Co. K, 36th Regiment North Carolina, 2nd N. C. Artillery	Killed In Action 1/15/1865		

NAME & RANK	ENLISTED	RESIDENCE AGE & TRADE	UNIT	RESULT OF BATTLE	PRISON	PRISON RELEASE
Son, J. D. Private	Enfield, South Carolina 5/19/1864	Vicinity of Hollow Creek, Lexington, South Carolina, 36 Years Old Farmer	Co. H, 25th South Carolina Volunteers	Shell Wound On Right Side of Chin and Clavicle & Captured	Point Lookout, Hammond General Hospital, Maryland	Oath of Allegiance 6/6/1865
Soots, Adam Private	Camp Holmes, North Carolina, 5/9/1863	Wake County, North Carolina, Age Unknown	Co. C, 3rd Battalion North Carolina Light Artillery	Captured	Elmira Prison, New York	Died of Chronic Diarrhea 3/1/1865
Souls, William C. Private	Georgetown South Carolina 1/20/1862	Columbus County, North Carolina, Age Unknown Farmer	3rd Co. G, 36th Regiment North Carolina, 2nd N. C. Artillery	Wounded & Captured, Defended Battery to the Left of Northeast Bastion	Point Lookout, Maryland	Oath of Allegiance 5/14/1865
Southerland, Duncan D. Private	Brunswick County, North Carolina, 7/28/1863	Richmond County, North Carolina, 18 Years Old	Co. E, 40th Regiment North Carolina, 3rd N. C. Artillery	Captured	Point Lookout Prison, Maryland	Oath of Allegiance 6/28/1865
Southerland, Thomas J. Captain	New Hanover County, North Carolina, 7/3/1861	Tarboro, Edgecombe County, North Carolina, Age Unknown	2nd Co I, 10th Regiment North Carolina, 1st N. C. Artillery	Shell Wound Left Side Of Head, 1/14/1865, Escaped	Treated In Wilmington Military Hospital #4	Paroled At Greensboro 5/1/1865
Sowles, Joshua First Lieutenant	Columbus County, North Carolina, 10/23/1861	Columbus County, North Carolina, 29 Years Old	2nd Co. A, 36th Regiment, North Carolina, 2nd N. C. Artillery	Captured, Defended the Mound Battery, Led half of Company A to defend land face	Fort Columbus Prison, New York Harbor	Exchanged 3/5/1865 Boulware's Wharf, James River, Virginia

NAME & RANK	ENLISTED	RESIDENCE AGE & TRADE	UNIT	RESULT OF BATTLE	PRISON	PRISON RELEASE
Spell, David Private	Fort Fisher, New Hanover County, North Carolina, 4/10/1863, Volunteer	New Hanover County, North Carolina, 18 Years Old	2nd Co. C, 36th Regiment North Carolina, 2nd N. C. Artillery	Captured, Defended River Road Gate	Elmira Prison, New York	Died of Chronic Diarrhea 3/24/1865
Spell, Hardy Private	Fort Fisher, New Hanover County, North Carolina, 10/18/1862, Volunteer	New Hanover County, North Carolina, 18 Years Old	2nd Co. C, 36th Regiment North Carolina, 2nd N. C. Artillery	Captured, Defended River Road Gate	Elmira Prison, New York	Died of Chronic Diarrhea 2/13/1865
Spell, Lewis B. Private	New Hanover County, North Carolina, 10/31/1862, Volunteer	Sampson County, North Carolina, 19 Years Old Laborer	2nd Co. C, 36th Regiment North Carolina, 2nd N. C. Artillery	Gunshot Wound Left Shoulder & Captured, Defended River Road Gate	Treated At Fort Monroe Hospital, Va, Sent To Fort Delaware Prison, Del.	Oath of Allegiance 6/19/1865
Spell, Love A. Private	Sampson County, North Carolina, 8/31/1864	Sampson County, North Carolina, 17 Years Old Farm Laborer	2nd Co. A, 36th Regiment North Carolina, 2nd N. C. Artillery	Captured, Defended the Mound Battery	Point Lookout Prison, Maryland	Oath of Allegiance 6/20/1865
Spence, John A. Private	Fort Fisher, New Hanover County, North Carolina, 3/15/1863, Volunteer	New Hanover County, North Carolina, 18 Years Old Laborer	2nd Co. D, 36th Regiment North Carolina, 2nd N. C. Artillery	Captured	Elmira Prison, New York	Died of "Congestion Of Lungs" 2/10/1865

467

NAME & RANK	ENLISTED	RESIDENCE AGE & TRADE	UNIT	RESULT OF BATTLE	PRISON	PRISON RELEASE
Spencer, Charles Seaman	Place Unknown 10/1/1861	Unknown, 30 Years Old Boatman	Galloway Co., Confederate States Coast Guard	Captured	Prison Unknown	Release Date Unknown
Spencer, William Seaman	Place Unknown 1/24/1862	Smithville, Brunswick County, North Carolina, 19 Years Old Apprentice	Galloway Co., Confederate States Coast Guard	Captured	Prison Unknown	Release Date Unknown
Spigner, Edward Private	Cole's Island, South Carolina 5/19/1864	Orangeburg District, South Carolina, 29 Years Old Overseer	Co. F, 25th South Carolina Volunteers	Captured	Elmira Prison, New York	Oath of Allegiance 7/7/1865
Spivey, William J. Private	Fort Fisher, New Hanover County, North Carolina, 4/28/1864	Whiteville, Columbus County, North Carolina, 17 Years Old Laborer	Co. E, 36th Regiment North Carolina, 2nd N. C. Artillery	Captured	Elmira Prison, New York	Oath of Allegiance 7/7/1865
Springs, William Vincent Private	Charleston, South Carolina 4/7/1864	Mars Bluff, Marion County, South Carolina, 18 Years Old Laborer	Co. A, 21st South Carolina Volunteers	Captured	Elmira Prison, New York	Died of Chronic Diarrhea 2/19/1865
Squires, John F. Private	Craven County, North Carolina, 6/25/1861	Craven County, North Carolina, 23 Years Old Farmer	Co. D, 40th Regiment North Carolina, 3rd N. C. Artillery	Captured	Point Lookout Prison, Maryland	Oath of Allegiance 5/14/1865
Squires, John H. Musician	Bladen County, North Carolina 3/7/1862, Volunteer	Bladen County, North Carolina, 23 Years Old	3rd Co. B, 36th Regiment North Carolina, 2nd N. C. Artillery	Captured	Elmira Prison, New York	Exchanged 3/2/1865 Boulware's Wharf, James River, Virginia

NAME & RANK	ENLISTED	RESIDENCE AGE & TRADE	UNIT	RESULT OF BATTLE	PRISON	PRISON RELEASE
Stallings, Slade R. Private	Washington, Beaufort County, North Carolina, 4/22/1861	Greeneville, North Carolina, 26 Years Old	Co K, 10th Regiment North Carolina, 1st N. C. Artillery	Captured	Elmira Prison, New York	Died of Pneumonia 3/10/1865
Stanaland, Stephen B. Private	Fort Caswell, Brunswick County, North Carolina, 6/21/1863, Volunteer	Columbus County, North Carolina, 17 Years Old	Co. E, 40th Regiment North Carolina, 3rd N. C. Artillery	Captured	Elmira Prison, New York	Oath of Allegiance 7/26/1865
Stancell, John Private	Columbus County, North Carolina, 2/22/1862	Columbus County, North Carolina, 35 Years Old	Co. E, 36th Regiment North Carolina, 2nd N. C. Artillery	Captured	Fort Columbus, N.Y. Harbor	Exchanged 3/5/1865 at Boulware's Wharf, James River, Virginia
Standin, William H. Private	New Hanover County, North Carolina, 8/7/1863	Edenton, Chowan County, North Carolina, 50 Years Old	Co. D, 13th Battalion North Carolina Light Artillery	Captured, Defended River Road Gate	Elmira Prison, New York	Oath of Allegiance 6/27/1865
Stanley, James H. Private	Fort Caswell, Brunswick County, North Carolina, 3/10/1862	New Hanover County, North Carolina, Age Unknown	Co. K, 36th Regiment North Carolina, 2nd N. C. Artillery	Wounded & Captured	Point Lookout Prison, Maryland	Exchanged 2/21/1865 at Boulware's Wharf, James River, Virginia, Died Of Chronic Diarrhea On Way Home 3/8/1865
Stanley, John M. Private	Brunswick County, North Carolina, 8/9/1864	Brunswick County, North Carolina, Age Unknown	Co. K, 36th Regiment North Carolina, 2nd N. C. Artillery	Wounded, Shell Concussion & Captured	Treated At Mansfield Hospital, Morehead City, N. C., Sent To Fort Delaware Prison, Del.	Oath of Allegiance 6/19/1865

NAME & RANK	ENLISTED	RESIDENCE AGE & TRADE	UNIT	RESULT OF BATTLE	PRISON	PRISON RELEASE
Stanely, Solomon K. Seaman	Place Unknown 1/24/1862	Brunswick County, North Carolina, Age Unknown Detached as Raftsman, Fisherman	Galloway Co., Confederate States Coast Guard	Captured	Prison Unknown	Release Date Unknown
Stanley, R. Seaman	Date and Place Unknown	Unknown	Galloway Co., Confederate States Coast Guard	Captured	Prison Unknown	Release Date Unknown
Stanly, William F. First Lieutenant	Lenoir County, North Carolina, 1/10/1862, Volunteer	Lenoir County, North Carolina, 18 Years Old	3rd Co. G, 40th Regiment North Carolina, 3rd N. C. Artillery	Captured, Defended Land Face	Fort Columbus, N.Y. Harbor	Exchanged 3/5/1865 at Boulware's Wharf, James River, Virginia
Starling, Simeon Private	Cumberland County, North Carolina, Date Unknown	Cumberland County, North Carolina, Age Unknown	2nd Co. A, 36th Regiment North Carolina, 2nd N. C. Artillery	Captured, Defended the Mound Battery	Point Lookout Prison, Maryland	Oath of Allegiance 6/20/1865
Starling, Thomas E. Private	Fort Fisher, New Hanover County, North Carolina, 5/1/1863, Volunteer	Fayetteville, Cumberland County, North Carolina, 38 Years Old	2nd Co. D, 36th Regiment North Carolina, 2nd N. C. Artillery	Captured	Elmira Prison, New York Prison, Maryland	Oath of Allegiance 7/19/1865
Stean, Allen Private	Bennettsville South Carolina 9/13/1864	Bennettsville, Marlboro District, South Carolina, 18 Years Old Farm Laborer	Co. F, 21st South Carolina Volunteers	Captured	Elmira Prison, New York	Died of Pneumonia 2/17/1865
Stephens, James Private	Chesterfield, South Carolina 12/25/1861	Cheraw, Chesterfield County, South Carolina 27 Years Old Laborer	Co. F, 21st South Carolina Volunteers	Captured	Elmira Prison, Elmira, New York	Died of Pneumonia 2/23/1865

NAME & RANK	ENLISTED	RESIDENCE AGE & TRADE	UNIT	RESULT OF BATTLE	PRISON	PRISON RELEASE
Stephens, Joel F. Private	Robeson County, North Carolina, 5/3/1862, Volunteer	Robeson County, North Carolina, 20 Years Old	Co. D, 1st Battalion North Carolina Heavy Artillery	Wounded & Captured, Defended River Road Gate	Point Lookout Prison, Maryland	Oath of Allegiance 6/20/1865
Stephenson Newitt Private	Fort Fisher, New Hanover County, North Carolina, 3/15/1863, Volunteer	Unknown, 36 Years Old	2nd Co. C, 36th Regiment North Carolina, 2nd N. C. Artillery	Severely Wounded & Captured, Fracture Of Knee, Defended River Road Gate	Prison Unknown	No Official Release, Possibly Died Of Wounds At Fort Fisher, North Carolina
Stevenson, James Chapman Private	4/18/1864, Fort Fisher, N. C.	New Hanover County, N. C., Assigned to Signal Corps	Co. A, 36th Regiment North Carolina, 2nd N. C. Artillery	Escaped, Captured At Bentonville, N. C., 3/19/1865	Point Lookout Prison, Md.	Oath of Allegiance 6/20/1865, Evacuated fort on 1/15/1865
Stevenson, James Martin Major	New Hanover County, North Carolina, 4/16/1861	New Hanover County, North Carolina, Age Unknown	Field & Staff, 36th Regiment North Carolina, 2nd N. C. Artillery	Captured	Fort Columbus, N.Y. Harbor	Died of Pneumonia 2/18/1865
Stevenson, William M. Private	Asheboro, Randolph County, North Carolina, 3/25/1863, Volunteer	Greensboro, Guilford County, North Carolina, 31 Years Old	3rd Co. G, 40th Regiment North Carolina, 3rd N. C. Artillery	Captured, Defended Land Face	Elmira Prison, New York	Oath of Allegiance 5/29/1865
Stewart, Archibald S. Private	Union County, North Carolina, 8/27/1861	Robeson County, North Carolina, 23 Years Old	Co. E, 40th Regiment North Carolina, 3rd N. C. Artillery	Wounded 1/15/1865		Hospitalized In Greensboro, North Carolina, 1/19/1865

NAME & RANK	ENLISTED	RESIDENCE AGE & TRADE	UNIT	RESULT OF BATTLE	PRISON	PRISON RELEASE
Stewart, Auguis Private	Camp Wyatt, New Hanover County, North Carolina, 4/1/1864, Volunteer	New Hanover County, North Carolina, 40 Years Old	2nd Co. D, 36th Regiment North Carolina, 2nd N. C. Artillery	Captured	Elmira Prison, New York	Died of Pneumonia 3/14/1865
Stewart, Charles A. Musician	Sampson County, North Carolina, 11/4/1861, Volunteer	Sampson County, North Carolina, 26 Years Old	2nd Co. A, 36th Regiment North Carolina, 2nd N. C. Artillery	Captured, Defended The Mound Battery	Elmira Prison, New York	Died of Smallpox, 3/14/1865
Stewart, Duncan J. Musician	Fort Caswell, Brunswick County, North Carolina, 10/20/1863	Fayetteville, Cumberland County, North Carolina, 25 Years Old	2nd Co. D, 36th Regiment North Carolina, 2nd N. C. Artillery	Captured	Elmira Prison, New York	Oath of Allegiance 7/7/1865
Stewart, John Private	Brunswick County, North Carolina, 10/20/1863, Volunteer	Brunswick County, North Carolina, 35 Years Old	2nd Co. D, 36th Regiment North Carolina, 2nd N. C. Artillery	Captured	Elmira Prison, New York	Died of Chronic Diarrhea 4/9/1865
Stewart, Samuel C. Private	Darlington, South Carolina 1/1/1862	Darlington District, South Carolina, 17 Years Old	Co. B, 21st South Carolina Volunteers	Captured	Elmira Prison, New York	Died of Chronic Diarrhea 4/9/1865
Stinson, Henry M. Private	Chatham County, North Carolina, 7/21/1862, Volunteer	Chatham County, North Carolina, 18 Years Old Employed in Signal Corp. at Fort Holmes and Wilmington,	2nd Co. I, 36th Regiment North Carolina, 2nd N. C. Artillery,	Captured, Defended Shepperd's Battery	Elmira Prison, New York	Died of "Jaundice" 5/17/1865

NAME & RANK	ENLISTED	RESIDENCE AGE & TRADE	UNIT	RESULT OF BATTLE	PRISON	PRISON RELEASE
Stokes, William D. Private	Edgecombe County, North Carolina, 5/8/1864	Wilson County, North Carolina, Age Unknown	Co. D, 40th Regiment North Carolina, 3rd N. C. Artillery	Captured	Point Lookout Prison, Maryland	Oath of Allegiance 6/19/1865
Storm, David Private	Bladen County, North Carolina, 3/14/1863	Elizabethtown Bladen County, North Carolina, 35 Years Old Turpentine Distiller	Co. H, 36th Regiment North Carolina, 2nd N. C. Artillery	Killed In Action 1/15/1865		
Stoy, Walter P. Private	Charleston, South Carolina 3/14/1862	Augusta, Georgia, 19 Years Old	Co. E, 25th South Carolina Volunteers	Captured	Elmira Prison, New York	Oath of Allegiance 8/7/1865
Streets, William E. Private	New Hanover County, North Carolina, 7/27/1864	New Hanover County, North Carolina, 16 Years Old	Co. D, 1st Battalion North Carolina Heavy Artillery	Killed 1/15/1865, Defended River Road Gate		
Strickland, Alexander Private	Cerrogordo, Columbus County, North Carolina, 3/12/1862, Volunteer	Columbus County, North Carolina, 18 Years Old	Co. E, 36th Regiment North Carolina, 2nd N. C. Artillery	Captured	Elmira Prison, New York	Died of Typhoid-Pneumonia 2/18/1865
Strickland, Alston Private	Whiteville, Columbus County, North Carolina, 2/9/1862	Columbus County, North Carolina, 18 Years Old	Co. E, 36th Regiment North Carolina, 2nd N. C. Artillery	Gunshot Wound Left Leg, below knee & Captured	Point Lookout Prison, Maryland	Oath of Allegiance 7/25/1865
Strickland, Alva Private	Wilmington, New Hanover County, North Carolina, 5/1/1862, Volunteer	New Hanover County, North Carolina, 18 Years Old	2nd Co. D, 36th Regiment North Carolina, 2nd N. C. Artillery	Captured	Elmira Prison, New York	Died of Typhoid Fever 4/23/1865

NAME & RANK	ENLISTED	RESIDENCE AGE & TRADE	UNIT	RESULT OF BATTLE	PRISON	PRISON RELEASE
Strickland, Calvin Private	Brunswick County, North Carolina, 10/10/1863, Volunteer	Columbus County, North Carolina, 40 Years Old	2nd Co. D, 36th Regiment North Carolina, 2nd N. C. Artillery	Captured	Point Lookout Prison, Maryland	Oath of Allegiance 6/20/1865
Strickland, David Private	Cerro Gordo, North Carolina, 3/1/1862	Fair Bluff, Columbus County, North Carolina, 20 Years Old	Co. E, 36th Regiment North Carolina, 2nd N. C. Artillery	Captured	Elmira Prison, New York	Oath of Allegiance 7/7/1865
Strickland, Emanuel Private	Enlisted 4/29/1863, Place Unknown	Unknown, 27 Years Old	Co. E, 36th Regiment North Carolina, 2nd N. C. Artillery	Captured	Prison Unknown	Release Date Unknown
Strickland, Henry, Jr. Private	Columbus County, North Carolina, 3/1/1862	Unknown, 20 Years Old Detailed as Boatman	Co. E, 36th Regiment North Carolina, 2nd N. C. Artillery	Wounded In Right Leg, Severe Compound Fracture 12/25/1864		
Strickland, Jacob Private	Cerogordo, Columbus County, North Carolina, 3/11/1862	Columbus County, North Carolina, 18 Years Old Detailed at Fort Pender as a Teamster, 1863	Co. E, 36th Regiment North Carolina, 2nd N. C. Artillery	Captured	Elmira Prison, New York	Died of Chronic Diarrhea 5/16/1865
Strickland, Madison A. Private	Johnston County, North Carolina, 3/1/1862, Volunteer	Division East of Neuse River, Johnston County, North Carolina, 19 Years Old	Co. D, 40th Regiment North Carolina, 3rd N. C. Artillery	Captured	Point Lookout Prison, Maryland	Exchanged At Cox's Landing, James River, Virginia, 2/15/1865

NAME & RANK	ENLISTED	RESIDENCE AGE & TRADE	UNIT	RESULT OF BATTLE	PRISON	PRISON RELEASE
Strickland, Martin Private	Sampson County, North Carolina, 2/18/1863, Volunteer	Sampson County, North Carolina, 36 Years Old	2nd Co. A, 36th Regiment North Carolina, 2nd N. C. Artillery	Captured, Defended the Mound Battery	Elmira Prison, New York	Died of Chronic Diarrhea 4/8/1865
Strickland, Matthew M. Private	Sampson County, North Carolina, 2/18/1863	Sampson County, North Carolina, 38 Years Old	2nd Co. A, 36th Regiment North Carolina, 2nd N. C. Artillery	Captured, Defended the Mound Battery	Point Lookout Prison, Maryland	Oath of Allegiance 6/20/1865
Strickland, Nathaniel Private	Wilmington, New Hanover County, North Carolina, 3/1/1864, Conscripted	Wilmington, New Hanover County, North Carolina, 45 Years Old	Co. E, 36th Regiment North Carolina, 2nd N. C. Artillery	Captured	Elmira Prison, New York	Died of Pneumonia 3/12/1865
Strickland, Rueben S. Private	Cumberland County, North Carolina, 2/26/1862	Cumberland County, North Carolina, 25 Years Old	2nd Co. C, 36th Regiment North Carolina, 2nd N. C. Artillery	Captured, Defended River Road Gate	Point Lookout Prison, Maryland	Oath of Allegiance 6/20/1865
Strickland, Thomas B. Private	Sampson County, North Carolina, 2/18/1863	Sampson County, North Carolina, 21 Years Old	2nd Co. A, 36th Regiment North Carolina, 2nd N. C. Artillery	Captured, Defended the Mound Battery	Point Lookout Prison, Maryland	Oath of Allegiance 6/20/1865

NAME & RANK	ENLISTED	RESIDENCE AGE & TRADE	UNIT	RESULT OF BATTLE	PRISON	PRISON RELEASE
Strickland, Timothy J. First Sergeant	Duplin County, North Carolina, 9/15/1861	Duplin County, North Carolina, 18 Years Old	2nd Co. A, 36th Regiment North Carolina, 2nd N. C. Artillery	Shell Wound In Back & Captured, Defended the Mound Battery	Treated At Mansfield Hospital, Morehead City, N. C., Sent To Fort Delaware Prison, Del.	Oath of Allegiance 6/19/1865
Strickland, William G. Private	Date Of Enlistment Unknown	Columbus County, North Carolina, Age Unknown	Co. E, 36th Regiment North Carolina, 2nd N. C. Artillery	Captured	Point Lookout Prison, Maryland	Oath of Allegiance 6/20/1865
Strickland, William H. Private	Whiteville, Columbus County, North Carolina, 2/9/1863, Conscripted	Whiteville, Columbus County, North Carolina, 36 Years Old	Co. E, 36th Regiment North Carolina, 2nd N. C. Artillery	Captured	Elmira Prison, New York	Exchanged 3/14/1865 at Boulware's Wharf, James River, Virginia, Died From Unknown Disease At Richmond Hospital, 3/31/1865
Strock, Emery B. Private	Coles Island, South Carolina 4/13/1864	Vicinity of Vance's Ferry, Orangeburg District, South Carolina 17 Years Old Farmer	Co. E, 25th South Carolina Volunteers	Captured	Elmira Prison, New York	Exchanged 2/20/1865, Died 3/16/1865 of Rubeola, Jackson Hospital, Richmond, Virginia
Stroman, Charles Private	Cole's Island, South Carolina 4/11/1862	St. Matthews, Orangeburg District, South Carolina 24 Years Old Farmer	Co. F, 25th South Carolina Volunteers	Captured	Elmira Prison, New York	Died of Variola 5/10/1865

NAME & RANK	ENLISTED	RESIDENCE AGE & TRADE	UNIT	RESULT OF BATTLE	PRISON	PRISON RELEASE
Strong, W. C. Captain	Date and Place Unknown	Unknown	Aide To General Whiting	Wounded 12/25/1864, Contusion Of Left Hip		
Stubbs, D. D. Private	Bennetts-ville, South Carolina 12/25/1861	Charlotte, North Carolina, 18 Years Old	Co. F, 21st South Carolina Volunteers	Captured	Elmira Prison, New York	Oath of Allegiance 7/11/1865
Stubbs, Samuel F. Private	Bennetts-ville, South Carolina 4/16/1863	Bennettsville, Marlboro District, South Carolina, 22 Years Old Student	Co. F, 21st South Carolina Volunteers	Captured	Elmira Prison, New York	Died of Typhoid Fever-Pneumonia 2/11/1865
Stubbs, James A. Private	Bladen County, North Carolina, 3/6/1862	Bladen County, North Carolina, 35 Years Old Farmer	Co. H, 36th Regiment North Carolina, 2nd N. C. Artillery	Captured	Point Lookout Prison, Maryland	Oath of Allegiance 6/20/1865
Stubbs, Jonathan A. Corporal	Wilmington, New Hanover County, North Carolina, 3/4/1862, Volunteer	Unknown, 17 Years Old	2nd Co. D, 36th Regiment North Carolina, 2nd N. C. Artillery	Wounded & Captured	Prison Unknown	Release Date Unknown, May Have Died of Wounds at Fort Fisher
Suggs, James McKay Private	Fort Anderson, Brunswick County, North Carolina, 12/18/1862, Volunteer	Brunswick County, North Carolina, 38 Years Old	Co. H, 36th Regiment North Carolina, 2nd N. C. Artillery	Captured	Elmira Prison, New York	Died of Smallpox, 4/19/1865
Suggs, William P. Private	Brunswick County, North Carolina, 2/19/1862	Brunswick County, North Carolina, 26 Years Old	Co. K, 36th Regiment North Carolina, 2nd N. C. Artillery	Captured	Point Lookout Prison, Maryland	Oath of Allegiance 6/30/1865

NAME & RANK	ENLISTED	RESIDENCE AGE & TRADE	UNIT	RESULT OF BATTLE	PRISON	PRISON RELEASE
Suit, William J. Private	Fort Branch Brunswick County, North Carolina, 8/17/1863, Volunteer	Durham, North Carolina, 40 Years Old Detailed as Nurse in Hospital	3rd Co. G, 40th Regiment North Carolina, 3rd N. C. Artillery	Captured, Defended Land Face	Elmira Prison, New York	Exchanged on the James River 2/20/1865
Sullivan, Benjamin Private	Beaufort County, North Carolina, 9/23/1861	Unknown, 26 Years Old	Co. D, 13th Battalion North Carolina Light Artillery	Wounded & Captured, Defended River Road Gate	Prison Unknown	Release Date Unknown, May Have Died of Wounds at Fort Fisher
Sullivan, John Private	New Orleans, Louisiana, 6/1/1861	New Orleans, Louisiana, Age Unknown Laborer	Co. C, Confederate States Marine Corp, Assigned to Guard Duty Aboard CSS *North Carolina* and CSS *Arctic.*	Captured	Point Lookout Prison, Maryland	Oath of Allegiance 5/14/1865
Sullivan, John S. Private	Mobile, Alabama, 9/26/1862	Unknown	Co. E, Confederate States Marine Corp, Assigned to Guard Duty Aboard CSS *Savannah.*	Captured, Defended Sea Face	Point Lookout Prison, Maryland	Oath of Allegiance 5/14/1865
Sullivan, Richard T. Private	Fort Fisher, New Hanover County, North Carolina, 7/14/1863, Volunteer	New Hanover County, North Carolina, 18 Years Old	2nd Co. I, 36th Regiment North Carolina, 2nd N. C. Artillery	Captured, Defended Shepperd's Battery	Elmira Prison, New York	Died of Pneumonia 2/28/1865

NAME & RANK	ENLISTED	RESIDENCE AGE & TRADE	UNIT	RESULT OF BATTLE	PRISON	PRISON RELEASE
Sumerlin, Wiley N. Private	Wilmington, New Hanover County, North Carolina, 3/20/1864	Goldsboro, Wayne County, North Carolina, 40 Years Old Appointed Artificer in Smithville, 6/1/1864, Carpenter	Co F, 10th Regiment North Carolina, 1st N. C. Artillery	Captured	Elmira Prison, New York	Died of Chronic Diarrhea 3/20/1865
Sutton, Bryan Private	Wilmington, New Hanover County, North Carolina, 1/3/1863	Sampson County, North Carolina, 29 Years Old Farmer	Co F, 10th Regiment North Carolina, 1st N. C. Artillery	Captured	Elmira Prison, New York	Died of Pneumonia 3/6/1865
Sutton, John C. Private	Transferred From CS Navy 8/5/1863	Unknown, 18 Years Old	3rd Co. G, 36th Regiment North Carolina, 2nd N. C. Artillery	Captured, Defended Battery to the Left of Northeast Bastion	Elmira Prison, New York	Died of Pneumonia 4/16/1865
Sutton, John C. Private	Brunswick County, North Carolina, 6/4/1864	Unknown	2nd Co. K, 40th Regiment North Carolina, 3rd N. C. Artillery	Captured	Point Lookout Prison, Maryland	Exchanged At Cox's Landing, James River, Virginia, 2/15/1865
Sutton, John M. Captain	Wake County, North Carolina, 2/22/1862	Bertie County, North Carolina, 19 Years Old	Co. C, 3rd Battalion North Carolina Light Artillery	Captured	Fort Columbus, N.Y. Harbor	Exchanged at City Point, Virginia, 3/5/1865
Sutton, Joseph Private	Sampson County, North Carolina, 10/5/1861	Duplin County, North Carolina, 20 Years Old Farmer	2nd Co. A, 36th Regiment North Carolina, 2nd N. C. Artillery	Captured, Defended the Mound Battery	Point Lookout Prison, Maryland	Oath of Allegiance 5/14/1865

NAME & RANK	ENLISTED	RESIDENCE AGE & TRADE	UNIT	RESULT OF BATTLE	PRISON	PRISON RELEASE
Sutton, Stephen Wesley Private	Smithville, Brunswick County, North Carolina, 8/6/1863	Sampson County, North Carolina, Age Unknown	Co F, 10th Regiment North Carolina, 1st N. C. Artillery	Gunshot Wound Scalp & Captured	Treated At Fort Monroe, Virginia, Sent To Point Lookout Prison, Maryland	Exchanged 2/20/1865 at Boulware's Wharf, James River, Virginia
Sutton, Thomas J. Private	Date and Place Unknown	Unknown	Co. H, 36th Regiment North Carolina, 2nd N. C. Artillery	Captured	Point Lookout Prison, Maryland	Died Of Rubeola 2/10/1865
Sutton, W. C. Private	Date and Place Unknown	Hertford, Perquimans County, North Carolina, 35 Years Old Merchant	Co. H, 36th Regiment North Carolina, 2nd N. C. Artillery	Mortally Wounded & Captured	Fort Monroe Prison Hospital, Virginia	Died Of Wounds 1/26/1865, Compound Fracture Of Left Hip
Sutton, William E. Private	Fort Pender, Brunswick County, North Carolina, 7/15/1863	Unknown, 18 Years Old	Co. H, 36th Regiment North Carolina, 2nd N. C. Artillery	Gunshot Wound Near Spine & Right Thigh, Captured	Point Lookout General Hospital, Maryland	Oath of Allegiance 6/6/1865
Sutton, William J. Private	Brunswick County, North Carolina, 7/31/1863. Volunteer	Alfordsville, North Carolina, 18 Years Old	Co. F, 40th Regiment North Carolina, 3rd N. C. Artillery	Severely Wounded & Captured	Prison Unknown	Release Date Unknown, May Have Died Of Wounds At Fort Fisher, N. C.
Sutton, William T. Private	Sampson County, North Carolina, 12/19/1862	Sampson County, North Carolina, 37 Years Old	2nd Co. A, 36th Regiment North Carolina, 2nd N. C. Artillery	Captured, Defended the Mound Battery	Point Lookout Prison, Maryland	Oath of Allegiance 6/20/1865

NAME & RANK	ENLISTED	RESIDENCE AGE & TRADE	UNIT	RESULT OF BATTLE	PRISON	PRISON RELEASE
Swain, George T. Private	Brunswick County, North Carolina, 3/19/1863, Substitute	Brunswick County, North Carolina, 17 Years Old	3rd Co. G, 36th Regiment North Carolina, 2nd N. C. Artillery	Wounded & Captured, Defended Battery to the Left of Northeast Bastion	Prison Unknown	Release Date Unknown, May Have Died Of Wounds At Fort Fisher, North Carolina,
Swain, Thomas W. Private	Brunswick County, North Carolina, 12/19/1862, Volunteer	Smithville, Brunswick County, North Carolina, 33 Years Old	3rd Co. G, 36th Regiment North Carolina, 2nd N. C. Artillery	Severely Wounded & Captured, Defended Battery to the Left of Northeast Bastion	Prison Unknown	Release Date Unknown, May Have Died Of Wounds At Fort Fisher, North Carolina,
Swain, William Lieutenant	Brunswick County, North Carolina, 5/5/1862	Brunswick County, North Carolina, 36 Years Old, Company Commander	3rd Co. G, 36th Regiment North Carolina, 2nd N. C. Artillery	Captured, Defended Battery to the Left of Northeast Bastion	Fort Delaware Prison, Del.	Oath of Allegiance 5/15/1865
Swindell, Thomas D. Corporal	Craven County, North Carolina, 9/28/1861	Craven County, North Carolina, 25 Years Old Farmer	Co. D, 40th Regiment North Carolina, 3rd N. C. Artillery	Captured	Point Lookout Prison, Maryland	Oath of Allegiance 5/14/1865
Sykes, Edmund Private	Fort Fisher, North Carolina, 5/1/1862	New Hanover County, North Carolina, 28 Years Old	2nd Co. C, 36th Regiment North Carolina, 2nd N. C. Artillery	Captured, Defended River Road Gate	Elmira Prison, New York	Died of Chronic Diarrhea 3/3/1865
Syphret, Obedia J. Private	Orangeburg, South Carolina 4/15/1862	Orangeburg, South Carolina, Age Unknown	Co. G, 25th South Carolina Volunteers	Captured	Elmira Prison, New York	Oath of Allegiance 6/23/1865

NAME & RANK	ENLISTED	RESIDENCE AGE & TRADE	UNIT	RESULT OF BATTLE	PRISON	PRISON RELEASE

NAME & RANK	ENLISTED	RESIDENCE AGE & TRADE	UNIT	RESULT OF BATTLE	PRISON	PRISON RELEASE
Tallivast, Alex Private	Darlington, South Carolina 9/1/1863	Unknown	Co. B, 21st South Carolina Volunteers	Captured	Elmira Prison, New York	Died of Chronic Diarrhea 4/4/1865
Talton, A. J. Private	Chesterfield, South Carolina 1/8/1862	Cheraw, Chesterfield District, South Carolina, 20 Years Old	Co. E, 21st South Carolina Volunteers	Captured	Elmira Prison, New York	Oath of Allegiance 7/7/1865
Tarby, Henry F. Private	New Hanover County, North Carolina, 3/21/1862	Born in Lancaster County, Pa., 27 Years Old Gunsmith	Co. H, 36th Regiment North Carolina, 2nd N. C. Artillery	Captured	Point Lookout, Maryland	Oath of Allegiance 5/13/1865
Tatom, Alexander J. Private	Fort Anderson, North Carolina, 12/12/1862, Volunteer	Brunswick, County, North Carolina, 30 Years Old	Co. H, 36th Regiment North Carolina, 2nd N. C. Artillery	Captured	Elmira Prison, New York	Died of Smallpox, 3/13/1865
Taylor, A. J. Private	Date and Place Unknown	Richardson's District, Craven County, North Carolina, 30 Years Old	2nd Co. K, 40th Regiment North Carolina, 3rd N. C. Artillery	Captured	Elmira Prison, New York	Died of Chronic Diarrhea 2/16/1865
Taylor, Isaac J. Private	Fort Caswell, North Carolina,, 2/20/1862, Volunteer	Brunswick, County, North Carolina, 28 Years Old	2nd Co. A, 36th Regiment North Carolina, 2nd N. C. Artillery	Captured, Defended The Mound Battery	Elmira Prison, New York	Died of Chronic Diarrhea 3/11/1865
Taylor, James W. Private	Edgefield, South Carolina 5/1/1864	Graniteville, Edgefield, South Carolina, 25 Years Old	Co. H, 25th South Carolina Volunteers	Wounded Severely & Captured	Fort Monroe, Virginia	Transported North on Steamer USS Champion 1/17/1865, Release Unknown

NAME & RANK	ENLISTED	RESIDENCE AGE & TRADE	UNIT	RESULT OF BATTLE	PRISON	PRISON RELEASE
Taylor, John Private	Brunswick, County, North Carolina, 8/20/1863, Volunteer	Unknown, 38 Years Old Extra Duty As Laborer at Fort Caswell, North Carolina	Co. K, 36th Regiment North Carolina, 2nd N. C. Artillery	Severe Gunshot Wound Left Shoulder, & Captured	Mansfield Hospital, Morehead City, N. C., Sent To Fort Delaware Prison, Del.	Oath of Allegiance 6/8/1865
Taylor, John W. Private	Brunswick, County, North Carolina, 8/2/1862	Brunswick, County, North Carolina, 30 Years Old	3rd Co. G, 36th Regiment North Carolina, 2nd N. C. Artillery	Gunshot Wound Right Breast & Captured, Defended Battery to the Left of Northeast Bastion	Treated At Mansfield Hospital, Morehead City, N. C., Sent To Fort Delaware, Del.	Oath of Allegiance 6/19/1865
Taylor, Joseph S. Private	New Hanover County, North Carolina, 5/29/1863, Volunteer	Unknown, 41 Years Old Overseer	2nd Co. K, 40th Regiment North Carolina, 3rd N. C. Artillery	Captured	Camp Hamilton, Virginia, Then Sent To New York 1/28/1865	Release Unknown
Taylor, Middleton E. Private	Coles Island, South Carolina 4/11/1862	Orangeburg District, South Carolina, 27 Years Old Overseer, Ambulance Driver	Co. F, 25th South Carolina Volunteers	Captured	Elmira Prison, New York	Exchanged On the James River 2/20/1865,
Taylor, P. H. Private	Coles Island, South Carolina 4/11/1862	Georgia Station, Orangeburg District, South Carolina, 26 Years Old Farmer	Co. F, 25th South Carolina Volunteers	Captured	Elmira Prison, New York	Oath of Allegiance 7/7/1865
Teabout, Thomas Private	New Hanover County, North Carolina, 11/4/1862	Cumberland County, North Carolina, 28 Years Old	2nd Co. I, 36th Regiment North Carolina, 2nd N. C. Artillery	Captured, Defended Shepperd's Battery	Fort Delaware, Del.	Oath of Allegiance 6/19/1865

NAME & RANK	ENLISTED	RESIDENCE AGE & TRADE	UNIT	RESULT OF BATTLE	PRISON	PRISON RELEASE
Teabout, Thomas Private	Date and Place Unknown	Unknown	Co. G, 25th South Carolina Volunteers	Wounded Severely & Captured	Fort Monroe, Virginia	Release Unknown
Teal, G. W. Private	Chesterfield, South Carolina 1/25/1864	Unknown	Co. D, 21st South Carolina Volunteers	Captured	Elmira Prison, New York	Died of Pneumonia 4/8/1865
Terry, George W. Corporal	Williamsburg South Carolina 2/6/1862	Kingstree, South Carolina, 21 Years Old	Co. F, 25th South Carolina Volunteers	Captured	Elmira Prison, New York	Oath of Allegiance 7/11/1865
Tew, Thomas L. Private	New Hanover County, North Carolina, 3/15/1863	Columbus County, North Carolina, 20 Years Old Employed At Stage Coach Station	2nd Co. A, 36th Regiment North Carolina, 2nd N. C. Artillery	Captured, Defended the Mound Battery	Point Lookout, Maryland	Oath of Allegiance 6/21/1865
Thaggard, Amos Jerome Private	Elizabeth-town, Bladen County, North Carolina, 5/6/1862	Bladen County, North Carolina, 30 Years Old Farmer	2nd Co. K, 40th Regiment North Carolina, 3rd N. C. Artillery	Captured	Elmira Prison, New York	Exchanged 3/2/1865 Boulware's Wharf, James River, Virginia
Thaggard, J. C. Private	Cumberland County, North Carolina	Fayetteville, Cumberland County, North Carolina, 18 Years Old	3rd Co. B, 36th Regiment North Carolina, 2nd N. C. Artillery	Killed In Action 1/15/1865		

NAME & RANK	ENLISTED	RESIDENCE AGE & TRADE	UNIT	RESULT OF BATTLE	PRISON	PRISON RELEASE
Thaggard, James B. Private	Fort Fisher, New Hanover County, North Carolina, 3/15/1863, Volunteer	Fayetteville, Cumberland County, North Carolina, 35 Years Old	2nd Co. C, 36th Regiment North Carolina, 2nd N. C. Artillery	Captured, Defended River Road Gate	Elmira Prison, New York	Oath of Allegiance 6/12/1865, Died of Chronic Diarrhea in Hospital At City Point, Virginia, 6/27/1865
Thally, David J. Private	Old Brunswick, North Carolina, 4/16/1862, Mustered in at Fort St. Philip, Volunteer	Duplin County, North Carolina, 21 Years Old	3rd Co. G, 36th Regiment North Carolina, 2nd N. C. Artillery	Captured, Defended Battery to the Left of Northeast Bastion	Elmira Prison, New York	Exchanged 2/20/1865, Died of Bronchitis 4/9/1865 at CSA General Hospital, Charlotte, North Carolina
Thames, Alexander Private	Cumberland County, North Carolina, 2/26/1862	Fayetteville, Cumberland County, North Carolina, 20 Years Old Farm Hand	2nd Co. C, 36th Regiment North Carolina, 2nd N. C. Artillery	Killed In Action 1/15/1865		Defended River Road Gate
Thigpen, Franklin L. Private	Edgecombe County, North Carolina, 3/26/1864	Tarboro, Edgecombe County, North Carolina, 17 Years Old	Co. D, 40th Regiment North Carolina, 3rd N. C. Artillery	Captured	Point Lookout, Maryland	Exchanged At Boulware's Wharf, James River, Virginia, 2/21/1865
Thomas, J. H. Private	Chesterfield, South Carolina 1/24/1864	Cheraw, Chesterfield County, South Carolina, 17 Years Old Farmer	Co. D, 21st South Carolina Volunteers	Captured	Elmira Prison, New York	Oath of Allegiance 7/7/1865
Thomas, John D. Private	Brunswick County, North Carolina, 10/21/1863	Unknown	Co. K, 36th Regiment North Carolina, 2nd N. C. Artillery	Wounded & Captured	Prison Unknown	Release Unknown, May Have Died of Wounds at Fort Fisher

NAME & RANK	ENLISTED	RESIDENCE AGE & TRADE	UNIT	RESULT OF BATTLE	PRISON	PRISON RELEASE
Thomas, Richard G. Private	Elizabeth-town, Bladen County, North Carolina, 10/21/1863	Bladen County, North Carolina, 45 Years Old Farmer	Co. H, 36th Regiment North Carolina, 2nd N. C. Artillery	Captured	Point Lookout, Maryland, Military Prison Newport News, Virginia	Exchanged At Cox's Landing, James River, Virginia, 2/15/1865, Recaptured at Richmond Hospital 4/3/1865, Died in Prison of Chronic Diarrhea 6/24/1865
Thomas, William A. Private	Bladen County, North Carolina, 3/20/1862	Bladen County, North Carolina, 16 Years Old Farmer	Co. H, 36th Regiment North Carolina, 2nd N. C. Artillery	Captured	Prison Unknown	Release Unknown
Thompson, Willis Andrew Private	Fort Fisher, New Hanover County, North Carolina, 6/4/1863	Warsaw, Duplin County, North Carolina, Age Unknown	2nd Co. C, 36th Regiment North Carolina, 2nd N. C. Artillery	Captured, Defended River Road Gate	Elmira Prison, New York	Oath of Allegiance 6/12/1865
Thompson, David V. Private	Coles Island, South Carolina 4/11/1862	Orangeburg District, South Carolina, 16 Years Old Farm Laborer	Co. F, 25th South Carolina Volunteers	Captured	Elmira Prison, New York	Oath of Allegiance 7/11/1865
Thompson, Edward D. Private	Date & Place Unknown	Lumberton, Robeson County, North Carolina, Age Unknown	Co. F, 40th Regiment North Carolina, 3rd N. C. Artillery	Captured	Elmira Prison, New York	Oath of Allegiance 7/11/1865
Thompson, George R. Private	Fort St. Philip, Brunswick County, North Carolina, 5/15/1862	Bladen County, North Carolina, 29 Years Old Farmer	2nd Co. K, 40th Regiment North Carolina, 3rd N. C. Artillery	Gunshot Wound of Right Hand & Captured	Point Lookout General Hospital, Maryland	Oath of Allegiance 6/6/1865, Two Fingers of Right Hand Amputated

NAME & RANK	ENLISTED	RESIDENCE AGE & TRADE	UNIT	RESULT OF BATTLE	PRISON	PRISON RELEASE
Thompson, James D. Private	Union County, North Carolina, 8/30/1861, Volunteer	Lumberton, Robeson County, North Carolina, 23 Years Old	Co. F, 40th Regiment North Carolina, 3rd N. C. Artillery	Captured	Elmira Prison, New York	Oath of Allegiance 7/11/1865
Thompson, John W.	Charlotte, Virginia, 3/18/1863, Conscript	Unknown, 22 Years Old	3rd Co. G, 36th Regiment North Carolina, 2nd N. C. Artillery	Wounded & Captured, Defended Battery to the Left of Northeast Bastion	Prison Unknown	Release Unknown, May Have Died of Wounds at Fort Fisher
Thompson, Wesley Private	Richmond County, North Carolina, 8/17/1863, Volunteer	Lumberton, Robeson County, North Carolina, 18 Years Old	Co. F, 40th Regiment North Carolina, 3rd N. C. Artillery	Captured	Elmira Prison, New York	Oath of Allegiance 7/11/1865
Thompson, William Berry Private	New Hanover County, North Carolina, 5/15/1862	Robeson County, North Carolina, Age Unknown	Co. D, 1st Battalion North Carolina Heavy Artillery	Captured, Defended River Road Gate or Middle Sallyport	Point Lookout, Maryland	Oath of Allegiance 6/20/1865
Thompson, William F. Private	Date and Place Unknown	Georgetown, Prince George Parish, South Carolina, 34 Years Old Farmer	Co. B, 21st South Carolina Volunteers	Captured	Elmira Prison, New York	Died of Chronic Diarrhea 2/17/1865
Thorn, George P. Private	Date and Place Unknown	Unknown	2nd Co. C, 36th Regiment North Carolina, 2nd N. C. Artillery	Captured, Defended River Road Gate	Fort Delaware, Del.	Release Unknown
Thorp, James Corporal	Old Brunswick Town, North Carolina, 4/16/1862, Volunteer	Brunswick County, North Carolina, 21 Years Old	3rd Co. G, 36th Regiment North Carolina, 2nd N. C. Artillery	Wounded & Captured, Defended Battery to the Left of Northeast Bastion	Elmira Prison, New York	Oath of Allegiance 7/7/1865

NAME & RANK	ENLISTED	RESIDENCE AGE & TRADE	UNIT	RESULT OF BATTLE	PRISON	PRISON RELEASE
Thrower, Benjamin Private	Enfield, Halifax County, North Carolina, 10/9/1861	Halifax County, North Carolina, 26 Years Old	Co. F, 36th Regiment North Carolina, 2nd N. C. Artillery	Mortally Wounded (Fractured Skull) & Captured		Died Of Wounds at Fort Fisher (Fractured Skull) 1/19/1865
Tillery, Elephlet Private	Craven County, North Carolina, 1/20/1862	Halifax County, North Carolina, 18 Years Old	Co. F, 36th Regiment North Carolina, 2nd N. C. Artillery	Captured	Point Lookout, Maryland	Oath of Allegiance 6/21/1865
Tillman, John R. Private	Fort Fisher, New Hanover County, North Carolina, 10/28/1863, Conscript	Charlotte, North Carolina, 25 Years Old	2nd Co. I, 36th Regiment North Carolina, 2nd N. C. Artillery	Captured, Defended Shepperd's Battery	Elmira Prison, New York	Oath of Allegiance 6/12/1865
Tindall, Calvin Private	Fort Fisher, North Carolina, 10/31/1862, Volunteer	New Hanover County, North Carolina, 19 Years Old	2nd Co. C, 36th Regiment North Carolina, 2nd N. C. Artillery	Captured, Defended River Road Gate	Elmira Prison, New York	Died of Chronic Diarrhea 3/4/1865
Tindall, Owen S. Private	Sampson County, North Carolina, Date Unknown	Sampson County, North Carolina, Age Unknown	2nd Co. A, 36th Regiment North Carolina, 2nd N. C. Artillery	Captured, Defended the Mound Battery	Point Lookout, Maryland	Oath of Allegiance 6/20/1865
Tingle, John W. Private	Craven County, North Carolina, 1/24/1862	North of Neuse River, Craven County, North Carolina, 36 Years Old Farmer	Co. D, 40th Regiment North Carolina, 3rd N. C. Artillery	Captured	Point Lookout, Maryland	Exchanged 2/20/1865
Tisdale, W. W. Private	Battery Island, South Carolina 4/12/1862	Kingston, South Carolina, 19 Years Old	Co. B, 25th South Carolina Volunteers	Captured	Elmira Prison, New York	Oath of Allegiance 6/30/1865

NAME & RANK	ENLISTED	RESIDENCE AGE & TRADE	UNIT	RESULT OF BATTLE	PRISON	PRISON RELEASE
Tisdell, Kelly Private	Johnston County, North Carolina, 10/5/1863	Wilson County, North Carolina, 17 Years Old	Co. D, 40th Regiment North Carolina, 3rd N. C. Artillery	Captured	Point Lookout, Maryland	Exchanged At Cox's Landing, James River, Virginia, 2/15/1865
Tobias, John S. Private	Charleston, South Carolina 2/1/1864	Brewington, Clarendon District, South Carolina, 18 Years Old Farmer	Co. I, 25th South Carolina Volunteers	Captured	Elmira Prison, New York	Died of Pneumonia 2/23/1865
Tolar, Needham S. Private	Cumberland County, North Carolina, 11/19/1863	Cumberland County, North Carolina, 18 Years Old	1st Co. C, 36th Regiment North Carolina, 2nd N. C. Artillery	Wounded, Contusion Of Left Arm & Hip 12/25/1864		
Tolar, Robert M. Private	Bladen County, North Carolina 11/6/1864, Volunteer	Fayetteville, Cumberland County, North Carolina, 34 Years Old, Extra Duty Setting Range Lights	3rd Co. B, 36th Regiment North Carolina, 2nd N. C. Artillery	Captured	Elmira Prison, New York	Oath of Allegiance 7/7/1865
Tumage, Luke Private	Date and Place Unknown	Cheraw, Chesterfield County, South Carolina, 26 Years Old Laborer	Co. F, 21st South Carolina Volunteers	Captured	Elmira Prison, New York	Oath of Allegiance 7/3/1865
Tune, Thomas Private	Enfield, Halifax County, North Carolina, 10/9/1861, Volunteer	Halifax County, North Carolina, 28 Years Old	Co. F, 36th Regiment North Carolina, 2nd N. C. Artillery	Captured	Elmira Prison, New York	Died of Pneumonia 4/1/1865
Tune, William Private	New Berne, Craven County, North Carolina, 1/30/1862, Volunteer	Halifax County, North Carolina, 27 Years Old	Co. F, 36th Regiment North Carolina, 2nd N. C. Artillery	Captured	Elmira Prison, New York	Died of Smallpox, 3/31/1865

NAME & RANK	ENLISTED	RESIDENCE AGE & TRADE	UNIT	RESULT OF BATTLE	PRISON	PRISON RELEASE
Turner, John Private	Wilmington, New Hanover County, North Carolina, 5/8/1862, Volunteer	Bladen County, North Carolina, 32 Years Old Farmer	Co. H, 36th Regiment North Carolina, 2nd N. C. Artillery	Captured	Elmira Prison, New York	Died of Pneumonia 3/8/1865
Turrentine, M. H. Sergeant	Brunswick County, North Carolina, 1/29/1863	Brunswick County, North Carolina, 19 Years Old	2nd Co. D, 36th Regiment North Carolina, 2nd N. C. Artillery	Killed In Action 1/15/1865		
Turrentine, William G. Private	Brunswick County, North Carolina, 7/17/1863	Orange County, North Carolina, 18 Years Old	2nd Co. D, 36th Regiment North Carolina, 2nd N. C. Artillery	Captured	Point Lookout, Maryland	Oath of Allegiance 6/21/1865
Tyler, James Private	Fort Caswell, Brunswick County, North Carolina, 1/25/1862, Volunteer	Fair Bluff, Columbus County, North Carolina, 31 Years Old	2nd Co. A, 36th Regiment North Carolina, 2nd N. C. Artillery,	Captured, Defended the Mound Battery	Elmira Prison, New York	Oath of Allegiance 7/11/1865
Tyler, Lucius A. Private	St. John's, Hertford County, North Carolina, 4/1/1862	Hertford County, North Carolina, Age Unknown	Co. D, 3rd Battalion North Carolina Light Artillery	Captured	Elmira Prison, New York	Oath of Allegiance 6/21/1865
Tyson, Gideon A. Private	Wilmington, New Hanover County, North Carolina, 4/30/1862, Volunteer	Greenville, North Carolina, 22 Years Old Cooper, Extra Duty at Fort Holmes as Overseer, January 1864	Co. H, 36th Regiment North Carolina, 2nd N. C. Artillery	Captured	Elmira Prison, New York	Oath of Allegiance 7/7/1865

NAME & RANK	ENLISTED	RESIDENCE AGE & TRADE	UNIT	RESULT OF BATTLE	PRISON	PRISON RELEASE
Tyson, Moses Private	Columbus County, North Carolina, 3/7/1862	Columbus County, North Carolina, 30 Years Old	Co. E, 36th Regiment North Carolina, 2nd N. C. Artillery	Gunshot Wound Right Arm & Captured	Point Lookout, Maryland	Oath of Allegiance 5/15/1865

NAME & RANK	ENLISTED	RESIDENCE AGE & TRADE	UNIT	RESULT OF BATTLE	PRISON	PRISON RELEASE
Ulmer, George L. Private	Coles Island, South Carolina 4/11/1862	Poplar, Orangeburg District, South Carolina, 20 Years Old Farm Laborer	Co. F, 25th South Carolina Volunteers	Captured	Elmira Prison, New York	Oath of Allegiance 7/11/1865
Upchurch, Benjamin Private	Harnett County, North Carolina, 2/26/1862	Harnett County, North Carolina, 34 Years Old	2nd Co. C, 36th North Carolina, 2nd N. C. Artillery	Captured, Defended River Road Gate	Point Lookout Prison, Maryland	Oath of Allegiance 6/21/1865
Utley, Jasper T. Musician	Orange County, North Carolina, 6/23/1864	Hillsboro, Orange County, North Carolina, 34 Years Old	Co. D, 1st Battalion North Carolina Heavy Artillery	Captured, Defended River Road Gate or Middle Sallyport	Elmira Prison, New York	Oath of Allegiance 6/23/1865, Appointed Drummer 7/1864
Utley, Moses C. Private	Wake County, North Carolina, 2/24/1863	Wake County, North Carolina, 32 Years Old	2nd Co. D, 36th North Carolina, 2nd N. C. Artillery	Captured	Point Lookout Prison, Maryland	Oath of Allegiance 6/26/1865

NAME & RANK	ENLISTED	RESIDENCE AGE & TRADE	UNIT	RESULT OF BATTLE	PRISON	PRISON RELEASE
Van Benthuysen Alfred C. Captain	New Orleans, Louisiana, 3/30/1861	New Orleans, Louisiana, 24 Years Old	Confederate States Marine Corp, Commanding Officer of the CSMC Guard at Wilmington, N. C.	Wounded Severely in head by shell Fragment & Captured	Fort Columbus, New York Harbor	Exchanged 2/25/1865

NAME & RANK	ENLISTED	RESIDENCE AGE & TRADE	UNIT	RESULT OF BATTLE	PRISON	PRISON RELEASE
Veal, Joseph T. Private	Enlisted In November Of 1864	Windsor, Bertie County, North Carolina, 17 Years Old	Co. D, 3rd Battalion North Carolina, 3rd N. C. Light Artillery	Captured	Elmira Prison, New York	Supposedly Exchanged 2/20/1865, No Record of Exchanged taking Place
Vickers, John C. Private	Date and Place Unknown	Clarke County, Georgia, Age Unknown	Co. E, Confederate States Marine Corp, Served Aboard CS Ironclad *Savannah*	Captured	Point Lookout Prison, Maryland	Oath of Allegiance 6/30/1865
Vincent, D. J. Private	Date and Place Unknown	Unknown	Co. F, 36th Regiment North Carolina, 2nd N. C. Artillery	Wounded in Face & Captured	Unknown	Release Unknown, May Have Died of Wounds at Fort Fisher
Vines, Henry Private	Old Brunswick Town, North Carolina, 4/30/1862 Volunteer	Brunswick County, North Carolina, 18 Years Old Extra Duty in Engineering Dept. October 1863	3rd Co. G, 36th North Carolina, 2nd N. C. Artillery	Captured, Defended Battery to the Left of Northeast Bastion	Elmira Prison, New York	Oath of Allegiance 7/26/1865, Had both legs amputated to the knees because of Frostbite.
Vinson, Daniel J. Private	Goldsboro, Wayne County, North Carolina, 6/8/1863	Goldsboro, Stoney Creek District, Wayne County, North Carolina, 18 Years Old Farm Laborer	Co. F, 10th Regiment North Carolina, 1st N. C. Artillery	Wounded In Face & Captured	Elmira Prison, New York	Died Of Chronic Diarrhea 3/16/1865
Vinson, Nathan Private	New Hanover County, North Carolina, 9/24/1864	Goldsboro, Stoney Creek District, Wayne County, North Carolina, 19 Years Old Farm Laborer	Co. F, 10th Regiment North Carolina, 1st N. C. Artillery	Wounded 12/25/1864		

NAME & RANK	ENLISTED	RESIDENCE AGE & TRADE	UNIT	RESULT OF BATTLE	PRISON	PRISON RELEASE
Vinson, Samuel Private	Bladen County, North Carolina, 2/26/1862, Volunteer	Bladen County, North Carolina, 34 Years Old Farmer Extra Duty Ordinance Dept.	2nd Co. C, 36th North Carolina, 2nd N. C. Artillery	Captured, Defended River Road Gate	Point Lookout Prison, Maryland	Oath of Allegiance 5/13/1865
Vinson, Uriah T. Private	Goldsboro, Wayne County, North Carolina, 9/12/1862	Goldsboro, Stoney Creek District, Wayne County, North Carolina, 19 Years Old Detailed to Fort Anderson	Co. F, 10th Regiment North Carolina, 1st N. C. Artillery	Wounded In Face & Captured	Elmira Prison, New York	Died Of Pneumonia 3/19/1865
Vocelle, Augustus Private	Charleston, South Carolina 2/22/1862	Charleston, South Carolina, 37 Years Old	Co. F, 25th South Carolina Volunteers	Captured	Elmira Prison, New York	Died Of Pneumonia 3/21/1865

NAME & RANK	ENLISTED	RESIDENCE AGE & TRADE	UNIT	RESULT OF BATTLE	PRISON	PRISON RELEASE
Waddell, Richard Private	New Hanover County, North Carolina, 5/1/1862, Volunteer	Columbus County, North Carolina, 30 Years Old	2nd Co. D, 36th Regiment North Carolina, 2nd N. C. Artillery	Gunshot Wound, Neck & Captured	Treated At Mansfield Hospital, Morehead City, N. C., Sent To Fort Delaware, De.	Oath of Allegiance 6/19/1865
Walden, Aurebus Private	Enlisted CSMC At Mobile, Alabama, 4/9/1864	Alabama, 26 Years Old Carpenter	Confederate States Marine Corp, Assigned to Guard Duty Aboard CSS *Chickamauga*	Wounded Severely in Hip, 12/25/1864 Not Captured	Not Sent to Prison	
Walker, David J. Private	Brunswick County, North Carolina, 9/7/1863, Volunteer	Brunswick County, North Carolina, 18 Years Old	3rd Co. G, 36th Regiment North Carolina, 2nd N. C. Artillery	Captured, Defended Battery to the Left of Northeast Bastion	Elmira Prison, New York	Died Of Chronic Diarrhea 3/21/1865

NAME & RANK	ENLISTED	RESIDENCE AGE & TRADE	UNIT	RESULT OF BATTLE	PRISON	PRISON RELEASE
Wall, Mial Private	Fort Branch, Brunswick County, North Carolina, 8/17/1863, Volunteer	Charlotte, North Carolina, 41 Years Old, Extra Duty as Keeper of the Lights	3rd Co. G, 40th Regiment North Carolina, 3rd N. C. Artillery	Captured, Defended Land Face	Elmira Prison, New York	Oath of Allegiance 6/12/1865
Wallace, Henry W. Private	Fort St. Philip, North Carolina, 5/15/1862, Volunteer	Brunswick County, North Carolina, 48 Years Old	3rd Co. G, 36th Regiment North Carolina, 2nd N. C. Artillery	Captured, Defended Battery to the Left of Northeast Bastion	Elmira Prison, New York	Died Of Pneumonia 2/18/1865
Waller, James W. Private	Edgecombe County, North Carolina, 9/2/1863	Tarboro, Edgecombe County, North Carolina, 45 Years Old Farmer	Co. D, 40th Regiment North Carolina, 3rd N. C. Artillery	Captured	Point Lookout, Maryland	Died Of Pneumonia 2/24/1865
Walling, J. A. Private	Coles Island, South Carolina 4/11/1862	Columbia, South Carolina, Age Unknown	Co. F, 25th South Carolina Volunteers	Captured	Elmira Prison, New York	Oath of Allegiance 7/7/1865
Walsh, Edward D. Captain	Carteret County, North Carolina, 5/16/1861	Carteret County, North Carolina, 21 Years Old Lawyer	Co. F, 10th Regiment North Carolina, 1st N. C. Artillery	Captured	Fort Columbus, New York Harbor	Exchanged 2/25/1865 At City Point, Virginia
Walsh, Maurice Private	Mobile, Alabama, 8/25/1862	Unknown	Co. E, Confederate States Marine Corp, Assigned to Guard Duty Aboard CSS *Atlanta,* and CSS *Georgia.*	Captured	Point Lookout, Maryland	Oath of Allegiance 6/6/1865

NAME & RANK	ENLISTED	RESIDENCE AGE & TRADE	UNIT	RESULT OF BATTLE	PRISON	PRISON RELEASE
Walton, Thomas W. Private	Fort St. Philips, Brunswick County, North Carolina, 4/16/1862	Brunswick County, North Carolina, 25 Years Old	3rd Co. G, 36th Regiment North Carolina, 2nd N. C. Artillery	Gunshot Wound In Left Calf & Captured, Defended Battery to the Left of Northeast Bastion	Point Lookout Prison General Hospital, Maryland	Oath of Allegiance 6/21/1865
Ward, Arren Private	Transferred From Waccamaw Light Artillery	Unknown	Co. K, 36th Regiment North Carolina, 2nd N. C. Artillery	Captured	Point Lookout, Maryland	Oath of Allegiance 6/21/1865
Ward, James M. Private	Fort St. Philip, North Carolina, 5/16/1862, Substitute	Brunswick County, North Carolina, 17 Years Old	3rd Co. G, 36th Regiment North Carolina, 2nd N. C. Artillery	Captured, Defended Battery to the Left of Northeast Bastion	Elmira Prison, New York	Died Of Chronic Diarrhea 3/17/1865
Ward, Joel Reaves Sergeant	Old Brunswick, North Carolina, 4/16/1862, Volunteer	Brunswick County, North Carolina, 18 Years Old Extra Duty Engineering Dept. July 1864	3rd Co. G, 36th Regiment North Carolina, 2nd N. C. Artillery	Captured, Defended Battery to the Left of Northeast Bastion	Elmira Prison, New York	Exchanged 3/14/1865 Boulware's Wharf, James River, Virginia
Ward, Joseph W. Private	Fort Ellis, North Carolina, 11/1/1861, Volunteer	Halifax County, North Carolina 39 Years Old	Co. F, 36th Regiment North Carolina, 2nd N. C. Artillery	Captured	Elmira Prison, New York	Exchanged 2/20/1865 Boulware's Wharf, James River, Virginia
Ward, Solomon R. Private	Old Brunswick Town, North Carolina, 4/16/1862, Volunteer	Brunswick County, North Carolina, 19 Years Old, Extra Duty at Fort Caswell & Smithville Engineering Dept. working on Revetment Turf	3rd Co. G, 36th Regiment North Carolina, 2nd N. C. Artillery	Captured, Defended Battery to the Left of Northeast Bastion	Elmira Prison, New York	Exchanged on the James River 3/14/1865, Admitted to USA Hospital Bermuda Hundred 3/21/1865 with Smallpox

NAME & RANK	ENLISTED	RESIDENCE AGE & TRADE	UNIT	RESULT OF BATTLE	PRISON	PRISON RELEASE
Ward, William J. Jr. Private	Brunswick County, North Carolina, 10/25/1863	Unknown, 17 Years Old	Co. E, 36th Regiment North Carolina, 2nd N. C. Artillery	Wounded Both Legs 12/25/1864		Died After Amputation Of Right Leg
Ware, John H. Private	New Hanover County, North Carolina, 6/1/1864	Yanceyville, Caswell County, North Carolina, 24 Years Old, Extra Duty for Engineering Dept. as Foreman of Carpenters	Co. D, 13th Battalion North Carolina Light Artillery	Captured, Defended River Road Gate	Elmira Prison, New York	Exchanged 3/2/1865 Boulware's Wharf, James River, Virginia
Warner, Francis Private	Beaufort County, North Carolina, 11/4/1861	Beaufort, Carteret County, North Carolina, 19 Years Old	Co. D, 13th Battalion, N. C. Light Artillery	Mortally Wounded, Gunshot Left Arm and Side & Captured	Treated At Mansfield Hospital, Morehead City, North Carolina	Died Of Wounds 1/28/1865, Defended River Road Gate
Warren, John A. Private	Edgecombe County, North Carolina, 3/26/1864	Tarboro, Edgecombe County, North Carolina, 17 Years Old Farmer	Co. D, 40th Regiment North Carolina, 3rd N. C. Artillery	Captured	Point Lookout, Maryland	Died Of Pneumonia 2/26/1865
Warren, William H. Private	Beaufort County, North Carolina, 9/30/1861, Volunteer	Beaufort County, North Carolina, 41 Years Old, Detailed to Engineering Dept as Carpenter	Co. C, 40th Regiment North Carolina, 3rd N. C. Artillery	Captured	Elmira Prison, New York	Exchanged 3/2/1865 Boulware's Wharf, James River, Virginia
Warrick, William Private	Goldsboro, Wayne County, North Carolina, 10/28/1862	Falling Creek, Cross Roads District, Wayne County, North Carolina, 29 Years Old	Co. F, 10th Regiment North Carolina, 1st N. C. Artillery	Captured	Elmira Prison, New York	Died of Smallpox, 2/26/1865

NAME & RANK	ENLISTED	RESIDENCE AGE & TRADE	UNIT	RESULT OF BATTLE	PRISON	PRISON RELEASE
Waters, James C. Private	Washington, Beaufort County, North Carolina, 4/24/1861,	Unknown	Co. K, 10th Regiment North Carolina, 1st N. C. Artillery	Captured	Elmira Prison, New York	Exchanged 2/20/1865
Watson, Charles Private	Mobile, Alabama, 7/7/1862, Enlisted Again at Decatur, Georgia, 6/30/1863	Cincinnati, Ohio, 24 Years Old Tinner	Co. B, Confederate States Marine Corp, Assigned to Guard Duty Aboard CSS *Dalman,* and CSS *Tallahassee.*	Captured	Point Lookout, Maryland	Oath of Allegiance 5/14/1865
Watson, Charles McS Corporal	Union County, North Carolina, 8/27/1861	Robeson County, North Carolina, 19 Years Old	Co. F, 40th Regiment North Carolina, 3rd N. C. Artillery	Captured	Point Lookout, Maryland	Oath of Allegiance 6/9/1865
Watson, Daniel Private	Union County, North Carolina, 8/30/1861	Unknown, 22 Years Old	Co. F, 40th Regiment North Carolina, 3rd N. C. Artillery	Captured	Point Lookout, Maryland	Exchanged 3/2/1865 Boulware's Wharf, James River, Virginia
Watson, John Private	New Berne, Craven County, North Carolina, 1/27/1862, Volunteer	Edgecombe County, North Carolina, 38 Years Old Extra Duty as Laborer and Boatman at Fort Caswell, North Carolina	Co. F, 36th Regiment North Carolina, 2nd N. C. Artillery	Captured	Elmira Prison, New York	Oath of Allegiance 7/26/1865
Watson, John H. Private	Elizabeth-town, Bladen County, North Carolina, 10/19/1861, Volunteer	Bladen County, North Carolina, 19 Years Old	Co. E, 36th Regiment North Carolina, 2nd N. C. Artillery	Captured	Elmira Prison, New York	Oath of Allegiance 8/7/1865

NAME & RANK	ENLISTED	RESIDENCE AGE & TRADE	UNIT	RESULT OF BATTLE	PRISON	PRISON RELEASE
Watson, J. W. Private	Date and Place Unknown	Unknown	3rd Co. G, 36th Regiment North Carolina, 2nd N. C. Artillery	Captured, Defended Battery to the Left of Northeast Bastion	Prison Unknown	Date Of Release Unknown
Watson, Michael R. Private	Union County, North Carolina, 9/24/1861	Lumberton, Robeson County, North Carolina, 21 Years Old School Master	Co. F, 40th Regiment North Carolina, 3rd N. C. Artillery	Captured	Point Lookout, Maryland	Oath of Allegiance 6/6/1865
Watson, Nathaniel S. Private	Red Springs, Robeson County, North Carolina, 9/5/1861, Volunteer	Robeson County, North Carolina, 18 Years Old	Co. F, 40th Regiment North Carolina, 3rd N. C. Artillery	Captured	Elmira Prison, New York	Died Of Pneumonia 3/18/1865
Watson, Robert Seaman	Transferred to C. S. Navy from Co. K, 7th Florida Infantry, 3/?/1864	Unknown,	Confederate States Navy, Assigned to the CSS Savannah	Not Captured, Defended Sea Face		Evacuated Battery Buchanan with Captain Robert Chapman
Watts, Luke Private	Brunswick County, North Carolina, 11/14/1861	Columbus County, North Carolina, 17 Years Old Student	2nd Co. A, 36th Regiment North Carolina, 2nd N. C. Artillery	Captured, Defended The Mound Battery	Point Lookout, Maryland	Oath of Allegiance 6/21/1865
Way, W. B. Private	Coles Island, South Carolina 4/11/1862	McCantsville, Orangeburg District, South Carolina, 20 Years Old	Co. F, 25th South Carolina Volunteers	Captured	Elmira Prison, New York	Oath of Allegiance 7/26/1865

NAME & RANK	ENLISTED	RESIDENCE AGE & TRADE	UNIT	RESULT OF BATTLE	PRISON	PRISON RELEASE
Weaver, John Private	New Berne, Craven County, North Carolina, 1/1/1862	Chapel Hill, Orange County, North Carolina, 32 Years Old	Co. F, 36th Regiment North Carolina, 2nd N. C. Artillery	Wounded Severely In Left Side	Point Lookout Prison General Hospital, Maryland	Release Unknown, May Have Died of Wounds
Weeks, Bennett Private	Camp Lamb, New Hanover County, North Carolina, 7/23/1863	Sampson County, North Carolina, 41 Years Old Farmer	Co. D, 1st Battalion North Carolina Heavy Artillery	Wounded & Captured, Defended River Road Gate	Prison Unknown	May Have Died Of Wounds At Fort Fisher
Weeks, James Private	Bladen County, North Carolina, 10/19/1861	Bladen County, North Carolina, 25 Years Old	2nd Co. I, 36th Regiment North Carolina, 2nd N. C. Artillery	Captured, Defended Shepperd's Battery	Point Lookout, Maryland	Oath of Allegiance 6/21/1865
Weeks, S. T. Private	Date and Place Unknown	Unknown	Co. D, 1st Battalion North Carolina Heavy Artillery	Captured, Defended River Road Gate or Middle Sallyport	Prison Unknown	Paroled, Date Of Release Unknown
Welch, John Private	Chatham County, North Carolina, 3/26/1863, Volunteer	Chatham County, North Carolina, 19 Years Old, Extra Duty in Smithville, North Carolina as Woodcutter for Garrison	3rd Co. G, 40th Regiment North Carolina, 3rd N. C. Artillery	Captured, Defended Land Face	Elmira Prison, New York	Died Of Pneumonia 3/22/1865
Wells, Alfred M. Private	Date and Place Unknown	Unknown	3rd Co. G, 36th Regiment North Carolina, 2nd N. C. Artillery	Captured, Defended Battery to the Left of Northeast Bastion	Elmira Prison, New York	Exchanged on James River, Va, 2/20/1865, Died Of Smallpox 3/5/1865, US Army Hospital, Bermuda Hundred, Virginia

NAME & RANK	ENLISTED	RESIDENCE AGE & TRADE	UNIT	RESULT OF BATTLE	PRISON	PRISON RELEASE
Wells, David Private	Wilson, Wilson County, North Carolina, 8/18/1863, Volunteer	Edgecombe County, North Carolina, 41 Years Old	Co. D, 40th Regiment North Carolina, 3rd N. C. Artillery	Captured	Elmira Prison, New York	Exchanged 3/14/1865 Boulware's Wharf, James River, Virginia
Wells, E. M. Sergeant	Chesterfield, South Carolina 1/29/1864	Cheraw, Chesterfield, South Carolina, 34 Years Old Merchant	Co. G, 21st South Carolina Volunteers	Severe Gunshot Wound to Left Side Of Chest & Captured	Point Lookout, Maryland . Hammond General Hospital	Oath of Allegiance 6/3/1865
Wells, Jacob Private	Fort Caswell, North Carolina, 8/23/1863	Brunswick County, North Carolina, Age Unknown	2nd Co. D, 36th Regiment North Carolina, 2nd N. C. Artillery	Captured	Elmira Prison, New York	Died Of Pneumonia 2/15/1865
Wescoat, George W. Private	Fort Holmes, North Carolina, 9/5/1863, Conscript	Wake County, North Carolina, 40 Years Old	3rd Co. G, 36th Regiment North Carolina, 2nd N. C. Artillery	Captured, Defended Battery to the Left of Northeast Bastion	Elmira Prison, New York	Exchanged 3/2/1865 Boulware's Wharf, James River, Virginia
Wescoat, St. Julian D. Private	Charleston, South Carolina 5/13/1862	Edisto Island, St John's Colton, South Carolina, 18 Years Old, Planter	Co. F, 25th South Carolina Volunteers	Captured	Elmira Prison, New York	Exchanged on the James River 2/20/1865
Wescott, Jeremiah Private	Brunswick County, North Carolina, 8/17/1863	Brunswick County, North Carolina, 44 Years Old	Co. K, 36th Regiment North Carolina, 2nd N. C. Artillery	Captured	Point Lookout, Maryland	Oath of Allegiance 6/21/1865
Wescott, Benjamin Seaman	1/24/1862 Place Unknown	Smithville, Brunswick County, North Carolina, 18 Years Old Fisherman	Galloway Co., Confederate States Coast Guard	Captured	Prison Unknown	Date Of Release Unknown

NAME & RANK	ENLISTED	RESIDENCE AGE & TRADE	UNIT	RESULT OF BATTLE	PRISON	PRISON RELEASE
Wescott, John T. Private	Brunswick County, North Carolina, 7/15/1863, Volunteer	Brunswick County, North Carolina, 19 Years Old	Co. K, 36th Regiment North Carolina, 2nd N. C. Artillery	Gunshot Wound Left Hip & Captured	Fort Columbus, New York Harbor	Exchanged 3/5/1865 Boulware's Wharf, James River, Virginia
Wescott, William J. Seaman	1/24/1862 Place Unknown	Smithville, Brunswick County, North Carolina, 18 Years Old Fisherman	Galloway Co., Confederate States Coast Guard	Captured	Prison Unknown	Date Of Release Unknown
West, Arthur M. Private	Elizabeth-town, Bladen County, North Carolina, 10/19/1861, Volunteer	Fayetteville, Cumberland County, North Carolina, 18 Years Old, Assistant in Ordinance Department at Fort Fisher	2nd Co. I, 36th Regiment North Carolina, 2nd N. C. Artillery	Captured, Defended Shepperd's Battery	Elmira Prison, New York	Oath of Allegiance 6/12/1865
West, Daniel James Private	Duplin County, North Carolina, 5/4/1864	Kenansville, Duplin County, North Carolina, 17 Years Old	Co. D, 1st Battalion North Carolina Heavy Artillery	Mortally Wounded & Captured, Defended River Road Gate		Died Of Wounds at Fort Fisher 1/15/1865
West, George W. Private	Fort Fisher, New Hanover County, North Carolina, 8/1/1864	Fayetteville, Cumberland County, North Carolina, 16 Years Old	Co. H, 36th Regiment North Carolina, 2nd N. C. Artillery	Captured	Elmira Prison, New York	Oath of Allegiance 6/12/1865
West, Henry J. Private	Cumberland County, North Carolina, 11/1/1863	Unknown, 35 Years Old	Co. E, 36th Regiment North Carolina, 2nd N. C. Artillery	Captured	Point Lookout, Maryland	Exchanged 2/15/1865 Cox's Landing, James River, Virginia

NAME & RANK	ENLISTED	RESIDENCE AGE & TRADE	UNIT	RESULT OF BATTLE	PRISON	PRISON RELEASE
West, James W. Private	New Hanover County, North Carolina, 7/5/1863, Conscript	Unknown, 35 Years Old	Co. E, 36th Regiment North Carolina, 2nd N. C. Artillery	Captured	Point Lookout, Maryland	Date Of Release Unknown, May Have Died in Prison, J. W. West is listed in Point Lookout Cemetery
West, John Wright Private	New Hanover County, North Carolina, 10/4/1862	Kenansville, Duplin County, North Carolina, 18 Years Old Student	Co. D, 1st Battalion North Carolina Heavy Artillery	Captured, Defended River Road Gate or Middle Sallyport	Point Lookout, Maryland	Oath of Allegiance 6/22/1865
West, Ransom Private	Sampson County, North Carolina, 2/18/1863	Newton Grove, Sampson County, North Carolina, 18 Years Old Farm Laborer	2nd Co. A, 36th Regiment North Carolina, 2nd N. C. Artillery	Captured, Defended the Mound Battery	Point Lookout, Maryland	Oath of Allegiance 6/21/1865
West, Wiley Private	Sampson County, North Carolina, 2/18/1863	Sampson County, North Carolina, 40 Years Old	2nd Co. A, 36th Regiment North Carolina, 2nd N. C. Artillery	Captured, Defended the Mound Battery	Point Lookout, Maryland	Oath of Allegiance 6/21/1865
West, William J. Private	Elizabeth-town, Bladen County, North Carolina, 10/19/1861, Volunteer	Bladen County, North Carolina, 21 Years Old	2nd Co. I, 36th Regiment North Carolina, 2nd N. C. Artillery	Captured, Defended Shepperd's Battery	Elmira Prison, New York	Died Of Acute Dysentery 4/9/1865
Westcott, A. Lieutenant	Date and Place Unknown	Unknown	Co. K, 36th Regiment North Carolina, 2nd N. C. Artillery	Captured	Fort Columbus, New York Harbor	Date Of Release Unknown

NAME & RANK	ENLISTED	RESIDENCE AGE & TRADE	UNIT	RESULT OF BATTLE	PRISON	PRISON RELEASE
Westcott, W. S. Private	Date and Place Unknown	Unknown	Co. K, 36th Regiment North Carolina, 2nd N. C. Artillery	Captured	Point Lookout, Maryland	Exchanged 2/15/1865 Cox's Landing, James River, Virginia
Wester, William J. Private	Cumberland County, North Carolina, 2/26/1862, Substitute	Harnett County, North Carolina, 32 Years Old	2nd Co. C, 36th Regiment North Carolina, 2nd N. C. Artillery	Captured, Defended River Road Gate	Point Lookout, Maryland	Oath of Allegiance 6/21/1865
Wheeler, Amos J. Private	Fayetteville, Cumberland County, North Carolina, 2/26/1862	Cumberland County, North Carolina, 22 Years Old	2nd Co. D, 36th Regiment North Carolina, 2nd N. C. Artillery	Wounded Left Ankle & Captured	Point Lookout Prison General Hospital, Maryland	Oath of Allegiance 6/4/1865
Wheeler, Owen Private	Fayetteville, Cumberland County, North Carolina, 2/26/1862, Volunteer	Cumberland County, North Carolina, 40 Years Old	2nd Co. D, 36th Regiment North Carolina, 2nd N. C. Artillery	Captured	Elmira Prison, New York	Died Of Pneumonia 5/3/1865
Whitaker, John B. Private	Fort Caswell, Brunswick County, North Carolina, 9/1/1863, Volunteer	Halifax County, North Carolina, 42 Years Old	Co. F, 36th Regiment North Carolina, 2nd N. C. Artillery	Captured	Point Lookout, Maryland	Exchanged 2/18/1865 Boulware's Wharf, James River, Virginia
White, Eli M. Private	Date and Place Unknown	Waccamaw District, Brunswick County, North Carolina, 23 Years Old Farm Laborer	2nd Co. K, 40th Regiment North Carolina, 3rd N. C. Artillery	Captured	Elmira Prison, New York	Died Of Pneumonia 4/23/1865
White, Hugh B. Lieutenant	Chesterfield, South Carolina 1/9/1862	Darlington District, South Carolina, 30 Years Old Clerk	Co. B, 21st South Carolina Volunteers	Captured	Fort Columbus, New York Harbor	Exchanged 2/25/1865

NAME & RANK	ENLISTED	RESIDENCE AGE & TRADE	UNIT	RESULT OF BATTLE	PRISON	PRISON RELEASE
White, Hardy Private	Date and Place Unknown	Scotland's Neck, Halifax County, North Carolina, 17 Years Old	3rd Co. G, 36th Regiment North Carolina, 2nd N. C. Artillery	Captured, Defended Battery to the Left of Northeast Bastion	Elmira Prison, New York	Exchanged 3/14/1865 Boulware's Wharf, James River, Virginia
White, J. B. Private	Camp Harllee, Georgetown South Carolina 1/1/1862	Sumter, South Carolina, 42 Years Old	Co. I, 25th South Carolina Volunteers	Captured	Elmira Prison, New York	Oath of Allegiance 6/23/1865
White, J. B. Private	Chesterfield, South Carolina 1/1/1862	Cheraw, Chesterfield, South Carolina, 18 Years Old	Co. D, 21st South Carolina Volunteers	Captured	Elmira Prison, New York	Exchanged 3/2/1865 Boulware's Wharf, James River, Virginia
White, James R. Private	Bertie County, North Carolina, 3/13/1862	Bertie County, North Carolina, 23 Years Old	Co. D, 3rd Battalion North Carolina Light Artillery	Gunshot Wound Lower Right Leg, & Captured	Point Lookout, Maryland	Oath of Allegiance 6/26/1865, Amputation Of Lower Right Leg
White, Jerry M. Private	Georgetown South Carolina 1/1/1862	Darlington District, South Carolina, 18 Years Old	Co. K, 21st South Carolina Volunteers	Captured	Elmira Prison, New York	Exchanged 3/2/1865 Boulware's Wharf, James River, Virginia
White, William R. Private	Camp Harllee, Georgetown South Carolina 1/1/1862	Darlington District, South Carolina, 42 Years Old	Co. I, 25th South Carolina Volunteers	Captured	Elmira Prison, New York	Oath of Allegiance 6/27/1865
Whitehead, Eli M. Private	New Berne, Craven County, North Carolina, 1/1/1862, Volunteer	Craven County, North Carolina, 22 Years Old	Co. F, 36th Regiment North Carolina, 2nd N. C. Artillery	Captured	Elmira Prison, New York	Died Of Chronic Diarrhea 4/10/1865

NAME & RANK	ENLISTED	RESIDENCE AGE & TRADE	UNIT	RESULT OF BATTLE	PRISON	PRISON RELEASE
Whitehurst, Moses E. Private	Craven County, North Carolina, 3/26/1864	Craven County, North Carolina, 17 Years Old	Co. D, 40th Regiment North Carolina, 3rd N. C. Artillery	Captured	Point Lookout, Maryland	Oath of Allegiance 6/21/1865
Whiting, William H. Major General	Captain of Engineers in Federal Army, Enlisted 3/16/1861, Charleston, South Carolina	Born in Mississippi, 1825, 36 Years Old	Field & Staff Confederate States Army	Severe Gunshot Wound of Right Thigh & Captured	Fort Columbus, Governor's Island, New York Harbor	Died Of Diarrhea 3/10/1865
Whitley, Thomas L. Private	Wilmington, New Hanover County, North Carolina, 10/20/1864	Martin County, North Carolina, 28 Years Old	Co. K, 10th Regiment North Carolina, 1st N. C. Artillery	Wounded Severely In Right Arm & Captured	US Army Mansfield Hospital, Morehead City, North Carolina, Fort Delaware, Del.	Oath of Allegiance 6/7/1865, Right Arm Amputated
Whitley, William P. Private	Wayne County, North Carolina, 4/13/1864	Rowan County, North Carolina, Age Unknown	Co. D, 40th Regiment North Carolina, 3rd N. C. Artillery	Captured	Point Lookout, Maryland	Oath of Allegiance 6/21/1865
Whitlock, William Private	Brunswick County, North Carolina, 8/25/1863	Moore County, North Carolina, 41 Years Old Wagoner	3rd Co. G, 40th Regiment North Carolina, 3rd N. C. Artillery	Wounded Severely & Captured, Defended Land Face	Confined At DeCamp US Army Hospital, David's Island, New York Harbor	Oath of Allegiance 6/20/1865
Whittaker, W. H. Private	New Hanover County, North Carolina, 11/20/1864	Unknown	Co. F, 36th Regiment North Carolina, 2nd N. C. Artillery	Captured	Point Lookout, Maryland	Exchanged 2/21/1865 Boulware's Wharf, James River, Virginia

NAME & RANK	ENLISTED	RESIDENCE AGE & TRADE	UNIT	RESULT OF BATTLE	PRISON	PRISON RELEASE
Whitted, James McKay Private	Elizabeth-town, Bladen County, North Carolina, 4/26/1861	Unknown, 18 Years Old	Co. H, 36th Regiment North Carolina, 2nd N. C. Artillery	Gunshot Wound Upper Left Thigh & Captured	Point Lookout General Hospital, Maryland	Oath of Allegiance 7/7/1865
Wicker, Eli M. Private	Chatham County, North Carolina, 2/21/1862	Pittsboro, Chatham County, North Carolina, 29 Years Old Farm Laborer	2nd Co. C, 36th Regiment North Carolina, 2nd N. C. Artillery	Captured, Defended River Road Gate	Point Lookout, Maryland	Oath of Allegiance 6/22/1865
Wiggs, Henry L. Private	Goldsboro, Wayne County, North Carolina, 7/24/1861,	Goldsboro, Wayne County, North Carolina, 16 Years Old Farmer	Co. F, 10th Regiment North Carolina, 1st N. C. Artillery	Captured	Elmira Prison, New York	Oath of Allegiance 7/11/1865
Wilbon, John D. Private	New Hanover County, North Carolina, 3/8/1862, Volunteer	Hillsboro, Orange County, North Carolina, 39 Years Old Saddler	2nd Co. D, 36th Regiment North Carolina, 2nd N. C. Artillery	Captured	Point Lookout, Maryland	Exchanged 2/15/1865 Cox's Landing, James River, Virginia
Wilder, Benjamin K. Private	Gourdin's Dept., South Carolina 5/1/1862	Vicinity of Murray's Ferry, Williamsburg District, South Carolina, 39 Years Old	Co. K, 25th South Carolina Volunteers	Captured	Elmira Prison, New York	Died Of Pneumonia 3/16/1865
Wilder, L. E. Private	James Island, South Carolina 3/10/1863	Vicinity of Murray's Ferry, Williamsburg District, South Carolina 32 Years Old Farm Laborer	Co. K, 25th South Carolina Volunteers	Captured	Elmira Prison, New York	Died Of Intermittent Fever 4/2/1865

NAME & RANK	ENLISTED	RESIDENCE AGE & TRADE	UNIT	RESULT OF BATTLE	PRISON	PRISON RELEASE
Wiles, William Private	Coles Island, South Carolina 4/11/1862	Poplar, Orangeburg District, South Carolina 26 Years Old Overseer	Co. F, 25th South Carolina Volunteers	Captured	Elmira Prison, New York	Died Of Acute Diarrhea 5/11/1865
Wilkes, Andrew J. Private	Cumberland County, North Carolina, 2/20/1862	Cumberland County, North Carolina, 27 Years Old	2nd Co. C, 36th Regiment North Carolina, 2nd N. C. Artillery	Captured, Defended River Road Gate	Point Lookout, Maryland	Oath of Allegiance 6/21/1865
Wilkes, Henry Private	Richmond County, North Carolina, 9/1/1864	Williamson District, Richmond County, North Carolina, 16 Years Old	Co. D, 1st Battalion North Carolina Heavy Artillery	Killed In Action 1/15/1865, Defended River Road Gate		
Wilkes, Thomas J. Private	Cumberland County, North Carolina, 2/20/1862	Cumberland County, North Carolina, 27 Years Old	2nd Co. C, 36th Regiment North Carolina, 2nd N. C. Artillery	Captured, Defended River Road Gate	Point Lookout, Maryland	Oath of Allegiance 6/21/1865
Wilkinson, George D. Private	Union County, North Carolina, 8/30/1861	Brier Creek, Wilkes County, North Carolina, 26 Years Old	Co. E, 40th Regiment North Carolina, 3rd N. C. Artillery	Killed In Action 1/15/1865		
Wilkinson, James Private	Marion District, South Carolina 4/20/1862	Fair Bluff, Robeson, North Carolina, 42 Years Old, Company Cook	Co. D, 25th South Carolina Volunteers	Captured	Elmira Prison, New York	Oath of Allegiance 7/7/1865
Willets, Benjamin B. Private	Fort St. Philip, Brunswick County, North Carolina, 7/20/1862, Volunteer	Wilmington, New Hanover County, North Carolina, 18 Years Old	3rd Co. G, 36th Regiment North Carolina, 2nd N. C. Artillery	Captured, Defended Battery to the Left of Northeast Bastion	Elmira Prison, New York	Oath of Allegiance 7/11/1865

NAME & RANK	ENLISTED	RESIDENCE AGE & TRADE	UNIT	RESULT OF BATTLE	PRISON	PRISON RELEASE
Willets, George F. Sergeant	Brunswick County, North Carolina, 4/16/1862	Town Creek, Brunswick County, North Carolina, 20 Years Old	3rd Co. G, 36th Regiment North Carolina, 2nd N. C. Artillery	Killed In Action 1/15/1865, Defended Battery to the Left of Northeast Bastion		
Willets, Jacob L. Private	Old Brunswick Town, North Carolina, 4/16/1862, Volunteer	Brunswick County, North Carolina, 22 Years Old	3rd Co. G, 36th Regiment North Carolina, 2nd N. C. Artillery	Wounded & Captured, Defended Battery to the Left of Northeast Bastion	Elmira Prison, New York	Died Of Chronic Diarrhea 4/14/1865
Willets, John J. Private	Old Brunswick Town, North Carolina, 4/16/1862, Volunteer	Brunswick County, N. C., 21 Years Old Extra Duty Engineer Work, Smithville and Fort Caswell	3rd Co. G, 36th Regiment North Carolina, 2nd N. C. Artillery	Wounded & Captured, Defended Battery to the Left of Northeast Bastion	Elmira Prison, New York	Died Of Pneumonia 5/7/1865
Willets, William J. Private	Old Brunswick Town, North Carolina, 4/16/1862, Volunteer	Brunswick County, North Carolina, 26 Years Old	3rd Co. G, 36th Regiment North Carolina, 2nd N. C. Artillery	Wounded & Captured, Defended Battery to the Left of Northeast Bastion	Elmira Prison, New York	Died Of Pneumonia 3/4/1865
Williams, Alexander Private	Chesterfield, South Carolina 1/25/1862	Cheraw, Chesterfield, South Carolina, 37 Years Old Farmer	Co. D, 21th South Carolina Volunteers	Captured	Elmira Prison, New York	Died Of Acute Diarrhea 4/20/1865
Williams, Amos Private	Wilmington, New Hanover County, North Carolina, 3/7/1862, Volunteer	Whiteville, Columbus County, North Carolina, 38 Years Old Detailed as Mounted Scout	Co. E, 36th Regiment North Carolina, 2nd N. C. Artillery	Captured	Elmira Prison, New York	Died On Route To Be Exchanged 2/20/1865

NAME & RANK	ENLISTED	RESIDENCE AGE & TRADE	UNIT	RESULT OF BATTLE	PRISON	PRISON RELEASE
Williams, Andrew T. Private	Bladen County, North Carolina, 2/16/1863, Volunteer	Bladenboro, Bladen County, North Carolina, 22 Years Old	3rd Co. B, 36th Regiment North Carolina, 2nd N. C. Artillery	Captured	Elmira Prison, New York	Oath of Allegiance 7/11/1865
Williams, Charles Private	Wake County, North Carolina	Eagle Rock, Wake County, North Carolina, 20 Years Old	2nd Co. D, 36th Regiment North Carolina, 2nd N. C. Artillery	Killed In Action 1/15/1865		
Williams, Charles J. First Lieutenant	Cumberland County, North Carolina, 2/15/1862, Volunteer	Cumberland County, North Carolina, 25 Years Old	2nd Co. C, 36th Regiment North Carolina, 2nd N. C. Artillery	Gunshot Wound Of Right Shoulder & Captured, Defended River Road Gate	Treated At Fort Monroe, Va, Sent To Fort Delaware, Del.	Oath of Allegiance 6/17/1865
Williams, Charles O. Private	Union County, North Carolina, 8/27/1861, Volunteer	Robeson County, North Carolina, 30 Years Old	Co. E, 40th Regiment North Carolina, 3rd N. C. Artillery	Captured	Elmira Prison, New York	Exchanged 3/2/1865 Boulware's Wharf, James River, Virginia
Williams, Edward McQ Private	Place Of Enlistment Unknown 11/4/1864	Unknown	Co. E, 40th Regiment North Carolina, 3rd N. C. Artillery	Wounded & Captured	Point Lookout, Maryland	Oath of Allegiance 6/3/1865
Williams, Finnigan Private	Robeson County, North Carolina, 9/6/1861, Volunteer	Robeson County, North Carolina, 32 Years Old	Co. E, 40th Regiment North Carolina, 3rd N. C. Artillery	Gunshot Wound Left Arm & Captured	Treated At Fort Monroe, Va, Fort Delaware, Del.	Oath of Allegiance 6/19/1865

NAME & RANK	ENLISTED	RESIDENCE AGE & TRADE	UNIT	RESULT OF BATTLE	PRISON	PRISON RELEASE
Williams, Isaac W. Private	Fort Caswell, Brunswick County, North Carolina, 3/5/1863, Volunteer	Brunswick County, North Carolina, 22 Years Old Detailed as Cart Driver Engineer Dept.	Co. E, 40th Regiment North Carolina, 3rd N. C. Artillery	Captured	Elmira Prison, New York	Exchanged 2/20/1865, Died Of Chronic Diarrhea 3/12/1865 Richmond Hospital, Virginia
Williams, J. H. Private	Date and Place Unknown	Bladen County, North Carolina, 20 Years Old Detailed as a Carpenter on Smith Island, North Carolina	Co. F, 40th Regiment North Carolina, 3rd N. C. Artillery	Captured	Elmira Prison, New York	Died Of Chronic Diarrhea 4/3/1865
Williams, James A. Private	Union County, North Carolina, 8/27/1861	Robeson County, North Carolina, Age Unknown	Co. E, 40th Regiment North Carolina, 3rd N. C. Artillery	Captured	Point Lookout, Maryland.	Oath of Allegiance 6/21/1865
Williams, Joel Private	Clinton, Sampson County, North Carolina, 2/9/1863, Volunteer	Owensville, Sampson County, North Carolina, 34 Years Old Farmer	2nd Co. D, 36th Regiment North Carolina, 2nd N. C. Artillery	Captured	Elmira Prison, New York	Died Of Pneumonia 3/4/1865
Williams, John Private	New Orleans, Louisiana, 4/29/1861	New Orleans, Louisiana, Age Unknown	Co. A, Confederate States Marine Corp, Assigned to Guard Duty Aboard CSS *Savannah,* CSS *North Carolina* and CSS *Arctic.*	Captured, Defended Sea Face	Fort Monroe, Virginia	Oath of Allegiance 2/4/1865
Williams, John Private	Bennetts-ville, South Carolina 4/4/1862	Cheraw, Chesterfield, South Carolina, 32 Years Old Farmer	Co. I, 21st South Carolina Volunteers	Captured	Elmira Prison, New York	Oath of Allegiance 7/11/1865

NAME & RANK	ENLISTED	RESIDENCE AGE & TRADE	UNIT	RESULT OF BATTLE	PRISON	PRISON RELEASE
Williams, John W. Private	Fort Holmes, North Carolina, 5/18/1864	Brunswick County, North Carolina, Age Unknown	2nd Co. K, 40th Regiment North Carolina, 3rd N. C. Artillery	Captured	Elmira Prison, New York	Died Of Typhoid Fever 3/24/1865
Williams, Richard Private	Clinton, Sampson County, North Carolina, 2/9/1863, Volunteer	Sampson County, North Carolina, 36 Years Old Farmer	2nd Co. C, 36th Regiment North Carolina, 2nd N. C. Artillery	Captured, Defended River Road Gate	Elmira Prison, New York	Exchanged On the James River, Virginia 3/2/1865, Died shortly after returning home.
Williams, Starkey H. Sergeant	Duplin County, North Carolina, 11/7/1861	Duplin County, North Carolina, 19 Years Old	3rd Co. G, 40th Regiment North Carolina, 3rd N. C. Artillery	Severe Gunshot Wound Of Upper Jaw & Captured, Defended Land Face	Prison Unknown	No Release On File, May Have Died Of Wounds At Fort Fisher
Williams, T. W. Private	Brunswick County, North Carolina, Date Unknown	Brunswick County, North Carolina, Age Unknown	Co. K, 36th Regiment North Carolina, 2nd N. C. Artillery	Captured	Point Lookout, Maryland	Oath of Allegiance 6/21/1865
Williams, William Calon Private	Union County, North Carolina, 8/27/1861	Robeson County, North Carolina, 18 Years Old, Laborer	Co. E, 40th Regiment North Carolina, 3rd N. C. Artillery	Wounded By Shell Fragment In Head & Captured	Point Lookout, Maryland	Oath of Allegiance 6/21/1865
Williams, William D. Private	Robeson County, North Carolina, 6/10/1862, Volunteer	Lumberton, Robeson County, North Carolina, 18 Years Old	Co. E, 40th Regiment North Carolina, 3rd N. C. Artillery	Captured	Elmira Prison, New York	Oath of Allegiance 7/11/1865

NAME & RANK	ENLISTED	RESIDENCE AGE & TRADE	UNIT	RESULT OF BATTLE	PRISON	PRISON RELEASE
Williams, William W. Private	New Hanover County, North Carolina, 4/24/1862, Volunteer	South Carolina, 31 Years Old	Co. D, 1st Battalion North Carolina Heavy Artillery	Mortally Wounded & Captured, Defended River Road Gate	Treated At Mansfield Hospital, Morehead City, North Carolina	Died Of Wounds 6/15/1865
Williamson Alvin D. Private	Brunswick County, North Carolina, 2/26/1863	Columbus County, North Carolina, 22 Years Old	Co. E, 36th Regiment North Carolina, 2nd N. C. Artillery	Captured	Point Lookout, Maryland	Oath of Allegiance 5/14/1865
Williamson Dallas M. Private	Wilmington, New Hanover County, North Carolina, 3/3/1862, Volunteer	Fair Bluff, Columbus County, North Carolina, 18 Years Old	Co. E, 36th Regiment North Carolina, 2nd N. C. Artillery	Captured	Elmira Prison, New York	Oath of Allegiance 7/11/1865
Williamson Daniel S. Private	Fort Caswell, Brunswick County, North Carolina, 5/8/1862, Volunteer	Brunswick County, North Carolina, 30 Years Old	Co. E, 36th Regiment North Carolina, 2nd N. C. Artillery	Captured	Elmira Prison, New York	Died Of Chronic Diarrhea 3/14/1865
Williamson David F. Sergeant	Columbus County, North Carolina, 3/7/1862, Volunteer	Cerro Gordo, Columbus County, North Carolina, 25 Years Old	Co. E, 36th Regiment North Carolina, 2nd N. C. Artillery	Wounded Severely Fractured Jaw & Captured	Prison Unknown	Date Of Release Unknown, May Have Died of Wounds at Fort Fisher
Williamson David N. Private	Date and Place Unknown	Williston, Orangeburg, South Carolina, 24 Years Old Farm Laborer	Co. F, 21st South Carolina Volunteers	Wounded Left Shoulder & Captured	Prison Unknown	Date Of Release Unknown

NAME & RANK	ENLISTED	RESIDENCE AGE & TRADE	UNIT	RESULT OF BATTLE	PRISON	PRISON RELEASE
Williamson Hezekiah D. First Lieutenant	Columbus County, North Carolina, 2/19/1862	Columbus County, North Carolina, 21 Years Old	Co. E, 36th Regiment North Carolina, 2nd N. C. Artillery	Captured	Fort Columbus Prison, New York Harbor	Exchanged 3/5/1865 Boulware's Wharf, James River, Virginia
Williamson Hosea W. Private	Wilmington, New Hanover County, North Carolina, 3/1/1862, Volunteer	Fair Bluff, Columbus County, North Carolina, 20 Years Old	Co. E, 36th Regiment North Carolina, 2nd N. C. Artillery	Captured	Elmira Prison, New York	Oath of Allegiance 7/11/1865
Williamson James Private	Whiteville, Columbus County, North Carolina, 8/20/1863, Volunteer	Columbus County, North Carolina, 42 Years Old	Co. E, 36th Regiment North Carolina, 2nd N. C. Artillery	Captured	Elmira Prison, New York	Died Of Pneumonia 4/11/1865
Williamson James Wilds Sergeant	Darlington, South Carolina 3/18/1862	Charleston, South Carolina, 27 Years Old Carpenter	Co. B, 21th South Carolina Volunteers	Captured	Elmira Prison, New York	Died Of Pneumonia 3/15/1865
Williamson John R. Private	Cerro Gordo, Columbus County, North Carolina, 3/1/1862, Volunteer	Columbus County, North Carolina, 19 Years Old	Co. E, 36th Regiment North Carolina, 2nd N. C. Artillery	Captured	Elmira Prison, New York	Died Of "Congestion Of Lungs" 2/15/1865
Williamson Joseph W. Private	Fort Caswell, North Carolina, 7/16/1862, Volunteer	Columbus County, North Carolina, 34 Years Old	Co. E, 36th Regiment North Carolina, 2nd N. C. Artillery	Captured	Elmira Prison, New York	Died Of Chronic Diarrhea 6/21/1865

NAME & RANK	ENLISTED	RESIDENCE AGE & TRADE	UNIT	RESULT OF BATTLE	PRISON	PRISON RELEASE
Williamson Josiah Private	Brunswick County, North Carolina, 5/30/1863	Horry County, South Carolina, 25 Years Old	2nd Co. D, 36th Regiment North Carolina, 2nd N. C. Artillery	Captured	Point Lookout, Maryland	Oath of Allegiance 6/21/1865
Williamson Robert L. First Sergeant	Marion District, South Carolina 1/26/1862	Marion District, South Carolina, 25 Years Old, Book Keeper	Co. L, 21st South Carolina Volunteers	Killed In Action 1/15/1865		
Williamson William First Sergeant	Lexington County, South Carolina	Oakville, Lexington County, South Carolina, 28 Years Old Farm Hand	Co. L, 21st South Carolina Volunteers	Killed In Action 1/15/1865		
Williamson Samuel W. Private	Marion District, South Carolina 3/31/1862	Darlington County, South Carolina, 32 Years Old Huntsman	Co. L, 21st South Carolina Volunteers	Killed In Action 1/15/1865		
Williford, Willie H. First Lieutenant	Halifax County, North Carolina, 10/9/1861	Edgecombe County, North Carolina, 19 Years Old Farmer	Co. F, 36th Regiment North Carolina, 2nd N. C. Artillery	Killed In Action 1/15/1865		Died From Gunshot Wound During General Whiting's Charge
Willis, Cass Private	Fort Fisher, New Hanover County, North Carolina, 4/24/1863, Substitute	Fayetteville, Cumberland County, North Carolina, 16 Years Old	2nd Co. I, 36th Regiment North Carolina, 2nd N. C. Artillery	Wounded & Captured, Defended Shepperd's Battery	Elmira Prison, New York	Oath of Allegiance 6/12/1865
Willis, Charles T. Private	New Hanover County, North Carolina, 7/1/1862	Washington, Beaufort County North Carolina, 16 Years Old	Co. K, 10th Regiment North Carolina, 1st N. C. Artillery	Captured	Elmira Prison, New York	Oath of Allegiance 6/16/1865

NAME & RANK	ENLISTED	RESIDENCE AGE & TRADE	UNIT	RESULT OF BATTLE	PRISON	PRISON RELEASE
Willis, Francis M. Corporal	Bladen County, North Carolina, 11/24/1861	Bladen County, North Carolina, 17 Years Old	3rd Co. B, 36th Regiment North Carolina, 2nd N. C. Artillery	Captured	Point Lookout, Maryland	Oath of Allegiance 6/21/1865
Willis, John S. Sergeant	Elizabeth-town, Bladen County, North Carolina, 1/6/1861, Volunteer	Fayetteville, Cumberland County, North Carolina, Years Old	2nd Co. I, 36th Regiment North Carolina, 2nd N. C. Artillery	Captured, Defended Shepperd's Battery	Elmira Prison, New York	Oath of Allegiance 6/12/1865,
Willis, William Assistant Surgeon	Date and Place Unknown	Unknown	Confederate States Navy	Captured	Prison Unknown	Date Of Release Unknown
Willis, William First Lieutenant	Bladen County, North Carolina, 3/20/1862	Bladen County, North Carolina, Age Unknown	Co. H, 36th Regiment North Carolina, 2nd N. C. Artillery	Captured	Point Lookout, Maryland	Exchanged 2/15/1865 Cox's Landing, James River, Virginia
Willis, William N. Private	Fort Fisher, New Hanover County, North Carolina, 8/29/1863, Volunteer	Fayetteville, Cumberland County, North Carolina, 17 Years Old Detailed to Tend Range Lights	2nd Co. I, 36th Regiment North Carolina, 2nd N. C. Artillery	Wounded & Captured, Defended Shepperd's Battery	Elmira Prison, New York	Oath of Allegiance 6/12/1865
Wilson, Burrell Private	Date and Place Unknown	Vicinity of Hawley's Store, Sampson County, North Carolina, 20 Years Old Farmer	2nd Co. A, 36th Regiment North Carolina, 2nd N. C. Artillery	Wounded & Captured, Defended the Mound Battery	Elmira Prison, New York	Exchanged 3/2/1865 Boulware's Wharf, James River, Virginia

NAME & RANK	ENLISTED	RESIDENCE AGE & TRADE	UNIT	RESULT OF BATTLE	PRISON	PRISON RELEASE
Wilson, Byron Private	Date and Place Unknown	Unknown	2nd Co. A, 36th Regiment North Carolina, 2nd N. C. Artillery	Captured, Defended the Mound Battery	Prison Unknown	Date Of Release Unknown
Wilson, George Fennell Corporal	New Hanover County, North Carolina, 7/9/1863	Taylor's Bridge District, Sampson County, North Carolina, 18 Years Old	Co. D, 1st Battalion North Carolina Heavy Artillery	Killed In Action 1/15/1865, Defended River Road Gate		
Wilson, George W. Private	James Island, 12/31/1863	Limestone Springs, Spartanburg, South Carolina, 22 Years Old Blacksmith	Co. K, 21st South Carolina Volunteers	Killed In Action 1/15/1865		
Wilson, Harvey Lieutenant	Georgetown South Carolina 1/25/1862	Unknown, 35 Years Old Farmer	Co. K, 21st South Carolina Volunteers	Captured	Fort Columbus, New York Harbor	Exchanged 2/25/1865
Wilson, J. Private	Date and Place Unknown	Unknown	3rd Co. G, 40th Regiment North Carolina, 3rd N. C. Artillery	Captured, Defended Land Face	Prison Unknown	Date Of Release Unknown
Wilson, James D. Private	Elizabeth-town, Bladen County, North Carolina, 5/6/1862	Bladen County, North Carolina, 19 Years Old Farmer	2nd Co. K, 40th Regiment North Carolina, 3rd N. C. Artillery	Shell Wound Left Arm & Captured	Point Lookout General Hospital, Maryland	Oath of Allegiance 6/28/1865
Wilson, James O. Private	Bladen County, North Carolina, 11/5/1861, Volunteer	Unknown, 18 Years Old	3rd Co. B, 36th Regiment North Carolina, 2nd N. C. Artillery	Wounded & Captured	Prison Unknown	Date Of Release Unknown, May Have Died of Wounds at Fort Fisher

516

NAME & RANK	ENLISTED	RESIDENCE AGE & TRADE	UNIT	RESULT OF BATTLE	PRISON	PRISON RELEASE
Wilson, John H. Private	Sampson County, North Carolina, 2/18/1863, Volunteer	Sampson County, North Carolina, 20 Years Old	2nd Co. A, 36th Regiment North Carolina, 2nd N. C. Artillery	Captured, Defended the Mound Battery	Elmira Prison, New York	Exchanged 3/2/1865 Boulware's Wharf, James River, Virginia
Wilson, Lucian W. Private	Fort Caswell, Brunswick County, North Carolina, 1/6/1864, Volunteer	Brunswick County, North Carolina, 18 Years Old	2nd Co. D, 36th Regiment North Carolina, 2nd N. C. Artillery	Captured	Elmira Prison, New York	Died Of Chronic Diarrhea 4/3/1865
Wilson, Thomas Seaman	Date and Place Unknown	Unknown	Confederate States Navy	Wounded In Face 12/25/1864		
Windham, John Private	Williamsburg Gourdin's Dept., South Carolina 4/20/1862	Vicinity of Murray's Ferry, Williamsburg District, 18 Years Old Farm Laborer	Co. K, 25th South Carolina Volunteers	Captured	Elmira Prison, New York	Exchanged On the James River 2/20/1865
Windham, William J. Private	Georgetown South Carolina 12/28/1861	Darlington District, South Carolina, 32 Years Old Farmer	Co. K, 21st South Carolina Volunteers	Gunshot Wound To Face, Carrying Away Eye, exiting nose & Captured	Point Lookout, Maryland, Hammond General Hospital	Oath of Allegiance 5/13/1865

NAME & RANK	ENLISTED	RESIDENCE AGE & TRADE	UNIT	RESULT OF BATTLE	PRISON	PRISON RELEASE
Winslett, William F. Private	Choctaw County, Alabama, 3/1/1863	Unknown	Co. C, Confederate States Marine Corp, Assigned to Guard Duty Aboard CSS *Arctic*.	Captured	Point Lookout, Maryland	Oath of Allegiance 6/211865
Wise, V. F. Private	James Island, South Carolina 3/5/1863	Unknown	Co. F, 25th South Carolina Volunteers	Captured	Elmira Prison, New York	Exchanged On the James River 2/20/1865
Wise, Wiley W. Lieutenant	Coles Island, South Carolina 4/11/1862	Unknown	Co. F, 25th South Carolina Volunteers	Captured	Fort Columbus, New York Harbor	Exchanged On the James River 2/25/1865
Wolf, D. W. Private	Date and Place Unknown	Unknown	Co. G, 25th South Carolina Volunteers	Captured	Elmira Prison, New York	Died Of Chronic Diarrhea 3/1/1865
Wolfe, Jacob A. Corporal	Orangeburg, South Carolina 4/24/1864	Orangeburg District, South Carolina, 46 Years Old Farmer	Co. H, 25th South Carolina Volunteers	Captured	Elmira Prison, New York	Oath of Allegiance 7/7/1865
Wolfe, Peter Private	Date and Place Unknown	Unknown	25th South Carolina Volunteers	Killed In Action 1/15/1865		
Wood, David R. Private	Date and Place Unknown	Unknown	Co. D, 13th Battalion North Carolina Light Artillery	Captured, Defended River Road Gate	Prison Unknown	Date Of Release Unknown
Wood, George W. Corporal	South Mills, North Carolina, 4/24/1862, Volunteer	Unknown	Co. D, 13th Battalion North Carolina Light Artillery	Captured, Defended River Road Gate	Point Lookout, Maryland	Oath of Allegiance 6/21/1865

NAME & RANK	ENLISTED	RESIDENCE AGE & TRADE	UNIT	RESULT OF BATTLE	PRISON	PRISON RELEASE
Wood, Joseph D. Private	Craven County, North Carolina, 1/25/1862	Halifax County, North Carolina, 24 Years Old	Co. F, 36th Regiment North Carolina, 2nd N. C. Artillery	Captured	Point Lookout, Maryland	Oath of Allegiance 6/21/1865
Woodard, John A. Private	Fort Fisher, New Hanover County, North Carolina, 4/5/1864, Volunteer	New Hanover County, North Carolina, 19 Years Old	Co. H, 36th Regiment North Carolina, 2nd N. C. Artillery	Captured	Elmira Prison, New York	Died Of Pneumonia 2/7/1865
Woodbury, William D. First Lieutenant	Marion District, South Carolina 3/13/1862	Marion District, South Carolina, 21 Years Old	Co. L, 21st South Carolina Volunteers	Captured	Fort Columbus, New York Harbor	Exchanged 2/25/1865
Woodside, Samuel H. Private	Date and Place Unknown	Smithville, Brunswick County, North Carolina, 31 Years Old, Detached to Signal Service, Boatman	Galloway Co., Confederate States Coast Guard	Captured	Prison Unknown	Date Of Release Unknown
Wooten, Amos Private	Edgecombe County, North Carolina, 4/10/1864	Edgecombe County, North Carolina, Age Unknown	Co. D, 40th Regiment North Carolina, 3rd N. C. Artillery	Captured	Point Lookout, Maryland	Oath of Allegiance 6/14/1865
Wooten, Stephen W. Private	Edgecombe County, North Carolina, 9/1/1863	Edgecombe County, North Carolina, 44 Years Old	Co. D, 40th Regiment North Carolina, 3rd N. C. Artillery	Captured	Point Lookout, Maryland	Oath of Allegiance 6/21/1865
Word, John T. Private	Campbell County, Georgia, 2/19/1862	Milledgeville, Baldwin County, Georgia, Age Unknown	Co. E., 27th Georgia Infantry	Gunshot Wound left hand, Hip and Abdomen 1/15/1865		Wounded On Hoke's Line North Of Fort Fisher

NAME & RANK	ENLISTED	RESIDENCE AGE & TRADE	UNIT	RESULT OF BATTLE	PRISON	PRISON RELEASE
Worley, Alfred M. Private	Columbus County, North Carolina, 5/15/1862, Volunteer	Unknown 22 Years Old	Co. E, 36th Regiment North Carolina, 2nd N. C. Artillery	Captured	Point Lookout, Maryland	Date Of Release Unknown
Worley, Return S. Private	New Hanover County, North Carolina, 3/13/1862	Columbus County, North Carolina, 41 Years Old	2nd Co. D, 36th Regiment North Carolina, 2nd N. C. Artillery	Captured	Point Lookout, Maryland	Oath of Allegiance 6/3/1865`
Worrell, Ervin Private	Wilmington, New Hanover County, North Carolina, 2/15/1863	Goldsboro, Wayne County, North Carolina, 41 Years Old Barrel Maker	Co. F, 10th Regiment North Carolina, 1st N. C. Artillery	Captured	Elmira Prison, New York	Died Of Pneumonia 2/9/1865
Worrell, Isaiah Josiah Private	Wayne County, North Carolina, 4/26/1861	Wayne County, North Carolina, 34 Years Old Farmer	Co. F, 10th Regiment North Carolina, 1st N. C. Artillery	Captured	Point Lookout, Maryland	Oath of Allegiance 5/14/1865
Worrell, John Private	Goldsboro, Wayne County, North Carolina, 10/15/1862	Nahunta District, Wayne County, North Carolina, 26 Years Old Farmer	Co. F, 10th Regiment North Carolina, 1st N. C. Artillery	Captured	Elmira Prison, New York	Died Of Pneumonia 3/11/1865
Worrell, Robert W. Private	Wayne County, North Carolina, 7/26/1861	Nahunta District, Wayne County, North Carolina, 24 Years Old Farmer	Co. F, 10th Regiment North Carolina, 1st N. C. Artillery	Mortally Wounded & Captured		Died Of Wounds at Fort Fisher 1/15/1865
Worsham, Joseph R. Private	Camp Glover, Ridgeville, South Carolina 6/10/1861	Brewington, Clarendon County, South Carolina, 21 Years Old	Co. I, 25th South Carolina Volunteers	Captured	Elmira Prison, New York	Died Of Pneumonia 2/24/1865

NAME & RANK	ENLISTED	RESIDENCE AGE & TRADE	UNIT	RESULT OF BATTLE	PRISON	PRISON RELEASE
Wright, James D. Private	Brunswick County, North Carolina, 1/18/1864, Volunteer	Halifax County, North Carolina, 18 Years Old	Co. F, 36th Regiment North Carolina, 2nd N. C. Artillery	Captured	Elmira Prison, New York	Exchanged 2/20/1865, Died Of Smallpox, Jackson Hospital, Richmond, Virginia, 5/28/1865
Wright, James L. Private	Camp Holmes, North Carolina, 4/10/1864	Montgomery County, North Carolina, 34 Years Old	Co. K, 10th Regiment North Carolina, 1st N. C. Artillery	Captured	Elmira Prison, New York	Died of Smallpox, 4/18/1865
Wright, James T. Private	Wake County, North Carolina, 5/17/1863	Beans District, Montgomery County, North Carolina, 19 Years Old	Co. D, 3rd Battalion North Carolina Light Artillery	Killed In Action 1/15/1865		Missing at Fort Fisher, Report Killed
Wright, James T. Private	Brunswick County, North Carolina, 10/26/1864	Unknown	2nd Co. K, 40th Regiment North Carolina, 3rd N. C. Artillery	Captured	Point Lookout, Maryland	Exchanged 2/21/1865 Boulware's Wharf, James River, Virginia
Wright, John C. Private	New Hanover County, North Carolina, 3/3/1863	Unknown, 36 Years Old	2nd Co. K, 40th Regiment North Carolina, 3rd N. C. Artillery	Captured	Point Lookout, Maryland	Exchanged 2/21/1865 Boulware's Wharf, James River, Virginia
Wright, John T. Private	Craven County, North Carolina, 1/31/1862, Volunteer	Halifax County, North Carolina, 25 Years Old Detailed As Raftsman at Smithville, Fort Caswell	Co. F, 36th Regiment North Carolina, 2nd N. C. Artillery	Captured	Prison Unknown	Date Of Release Unknown
Wyndham, P. M. Private	Louisa City Hall, Virginia, 4/8/1862	Sumter, South Carolina, Age Unknown	Co. I, 25th South Carolina Volunteers	Captured	Elmira Prison, New York	Oath of Allegiance 7/11/1865

NAME & RANK	ENLISTED	RESIDENCE AGE & TRADE	UNIT	RESULT OF BATTLE	PRISON	PRISON RELEASE
Wynne, Thomas Private	Mobile, Alabama, 8/15/1862	Cincinnati, Ohio, Age Unknown	Co. E, Confederate States Marine Corp, Assigned to Guard Duty Aboard CSS *Atlanta* and CSS *Georgia.*	Captured	Elmira Prison, New York	Oath of Allegiance 5/29/1865

NAME & RANK	ENLISTED	RESIDENCE AGE & TRADE	UNIT	RESULT OF BATTLE	PRISON	PRISON RELEASE
Yarboro, Moses Private	Georgetown South Carolina 1/25/1862	Society Hill, South Carolina, 23 Years Old	Co. D, 21st South Carolina Volunteers	Captured	Elmira Prison, New York	Oath of Allegiance 7/26/1865
Yarborough, Thomas L. Private	Darlington, South Carolina 5/19/1862	Darlington District, South Carolina, 30 Years Old Farmer	Co. B, 21st South Carolina Volunteers	Captured	Elmira Prison, New York	Died Of Pneumonia 4/28/1865
Yelverton, John Private	Wayne County, North Carolina, 9/8/1863	Wayne County, North Carolina, 42 Years Old	Co. D, 40th Regiment North Carolina, 3rd N. C. Artillery	Captured	Point Lookout Prison, Maryland	Oath of Allegiance 6/22/1865
Yelverton, Robert Sauls Sergeant	Wilson County, North Carolina, 6/18/1863	Wilson County, North Carolina, 38 Years Old	Co. D, 40th Regiment North Carolina, 3rd N. C. Artillery	Captured	Point Lookout Prison, Maryland	Oath of Allegiance 6/22/1865
Young, James H. Private	Battery Island, South Carolina 4/12/1862	Unknown, 18 Years Old	Co. C, 25th South Carolina Volunteers	Captured	Elmira Prison, New York	Exchanged 3/2/1865 Boulware's Wharf, James River, Virginia

NAME & RANK	ENLISTED	RESIDENCE AGE & TRADE	UNIT	RESULT OF BATTLE	PRISON	PRISON RELEASE
Zednue, Henry Private	New Hanover County, North Carolina, 9/1/1864	New Hanover County, Alamance County, North Carolina, 41 Years Old	Co. D, 1st Battalion North Carolina Heavy Artillery	Mortal Gunshot Wound of Left Lung & Captured	Treated At Mansfield Hospital, Morehead City, North Carolina	Died Of Wounds 1/26/1865 Defended River Road Gate
Zimmerman, T. D. Lieutenant	Darlington, South Carolina 10/1/1862	Unknown, 23 Years Old	Co. B, 21st South Carolina Volunteers	Gunshot Wound Left Hand Losing Several Fingers & Captured	Fort Columbus, New York Harbor	Exchanged 2/25/1865

Chapter 12

Fort Fisher Statistics

Confederate Soldiers Present 1/15/1865	Captured	Wounded	Killed	Mortally Wounded	Men Sent To Elmira Prison, Elmira, New York	Men Who Died of Disease At Elmira Prison, Elmira, New York	Men Who Died of Wounds At Elmira, N. Y.
2,442	1,957	397	129	86	1,124	518	0

Men Sent To Point Lookout Prison, Maryland	Men Who Died of Disease At Point Lookout Prison, Maryland	Men Who Died of Wounds At Point Lookout Prison, Maryland	Men Sent To Fort Columbus Prison, New York Harbor	Men Who Died of Disease At Fort Columbus Prison, New York Harbor	Men Who Died of Wounds At Fort Columbus Prison, New York Harbor
643	56	15	97	2	0

Men Sent To Fort Delaware Prison, Del.	Men Who Died of Disease At Fort Delaware Prison, Del.	Men Who Died of Wounds At Fort Delaware Prison, Del.	Men Who Died of Wounds At Fort Fisher, North Carolina	Men Who Died of Wounds At Mansfield Hospital, Morehead City, North Carolina	Men Who Died of Wounds At North Carolina Hospitals
62	4	0	18	12	1

CASUALTIES BY UNIT

1st North Carolina Heavy Artillery Battalion					
Men	Captured	Wounded	Mortally Wounded	Killed	Killed or Wounded
59	49	14	5	10	48%

3rd Battalion North Carolina Light Artillery					
Men	Captured	Wounded	Mortally Wounded	Killed	Killed or Wounded
63	59	16	2	4	33%

10th Regiment, North Carolina Artillery

Men	Captured	Wounded	Mortally Wounded	Killed	Killed or Wounded
130	122	29	5	2	29 %

13th Battery, North Carolina Artillery

Men	Captured	Wounded	Mortally Wounded	Killed	Killed or Wounded
55	51	13	5	4	40%

36th Regiment, North Carolina, 2nd Artillery

Men	Captured	Wounded	Mortally Wounded	Killed	Killed or Wounded
1,095	1,030	205	41	65	28%

40th Regiment, North Carolina, 3rd Artillery

Men	Captured	Wounded	Mortally Wounded	Killed	Killed or Wounded
423	411	50	14	12	18%

11th Regiment South Carolina Volunteers

Men	Captured	Wounded	Mortally Wounded	Killed	Killed or Wounded
22	21	0	0	1	4.5%

21st Regiment South Carolina Volunteers

Men	Captured	Wounded	Mortally Wounded	Killed	Killed or Wounded
186	160	16	3	26	24%

25th Regiment South Carolina Volunteers					
Men	Captured	Wounded	Mortally Wounded	Killed	Killed or Wounded
258	257	25	3	1	11%

Confederate States Coast Guard					
Men	Captured	Wounded	Mortally Wounded	Killed	Killed or Wounded
50	50	0	0	0	0%

Confederate States Navy					
Men	Captured	Wounded	Mortally Wounded	Killed	Killed or Wounded
60	13	12	0	0	20%

Confederate States Marine Corp					
Men	Captured	Wounded	Mortally Wounded	Killed	Killed or Wounded
75	74	17	3	1	28%

DEATHS BY DISEASE IN PRISON

Diarrhea	Pneumonia	Smallpox	Typhoid Fever	Remittent Fever
224	149	63	32	12

Gangrene	Other Diseases	Total
8	127	615

Many times the figures for soldiers present and the men killed and captured do not agree. This is because some of the soldiers fled Battery Buchanan before they were captured.

Orders of Battle

Second Battle of Fort Fisher, January 13-15, 1865

Confederate States Army, Department of North Carolina, Third Military District, Major General Braxton Bragg, commander

FORT FISHER

Major General William Henry Chase Whiting,
observer and adviser

Colonel William Lamb,
36th Regiment North Carolina Troops, 2nd North Carolina Artillery, commander

1st Battalion North Carolina Heavy Artillery, Company D,
Captain James L. McCormic

3rd Battalion North Carolina Heavy Artillery, Company C, (Sutton's Battery)
Captain John M. Sutton

10th North Carolina Troops, 1st North Carolina Artillery,
Major James Reilly, commander
Company F, Captain Edward D. Walsh
Company K, (Shaw's Battery), Captain William Shaw, Jr.

13th Battalion North Carolina Artillery, Company D,
Captain Zachariah T. Adams

36th Regiment North Carolina Troops, 2nd North Carolina Artillery,
Colonel William Lamb, commander
2nd Company A, (Murphy's Battery) Captain Robert Murphy
2nd Company C, (Braddy's Battery), Captain Kinchen Braddy
2nd Company D, (Anderson's Artillery), Captain Edward Dudley
Company E, (Powell's Artillery), Captain Oliver Powell
Company F, (Hunter's Company), Captain Exum Lewis Hunter
3rd Company G, (Russell's Battery), Lieutenant William Swain
Company H, (Clarendon Guards), Captain Daniel Patterson
2nd Company I, (Bladen Artillery), Captain John T. Melvin
Company K, (Brunswick Artillery), Captain William Brooks

40th Regiment North Carolina Troops, 3rd North Carolina Artillery,
Company D, (Bay River Artillery), Captain James Lane
Company E, (Scotch Greys), Captain Malcomb H. McBrydie
3rd Company G, Captain George Buchan
2nd Company K, (Bladen Artillery Guards), Captain Daniel James Clark

Detachment of Confederate States Navy
Lieutenant Robert T. Chapman

Detachment of Confederate States Marines
Captain Alfred C. Benthuysen

Johnson Hagood's Brigade
11th South Carolina Infantry (detachment),
21st South Carolina Infantry (detachment), Captain D. G. DuBose
25th South Carolina Infantry (detachment), Captain James Carson

SUGAR LOAF

Hoke's Division, Major General Robert F. Hoke

Clingman's Brigade, Colonel Hector McKethan
8th North Carolina Infantry, Lt. Colonel Rufus A. Barrier
31st North Carolina Infantry, Lt. Colonel Charles Knight
51st North Carolina Infantry, Captain James W. Lippitt
61st North Carolina Infantry, Colonel William S. Devane

Colquitt's Brigade, Brig. General Alfred H. Colquitt
6th Georgia Infantry, Colonel John T. Lofton
19th Georgia Infantry, Colonel James H. Neal
23rd Georgia Infantry, Colonel Marcus R. Ballenger
27th Georgia Infantry, Captain Elisha D. Graham
28th Georgia Infantry, Captain John A. Johnson

Hagood's Brigade, Colonel Robert F. Graham
7th Battalion South Carolina Infantry, Lt. Colonel James H. Rion
11th South Carolina Infantry, Colonel F Hay Gantt
21st South Carolina Infantry,
25th South Carolina Infantry,
27th South Carolina Infantry,

Kirkland's Brigade, Brig. General William W. Kirkland
17th North Carolina Infantry, Lt. Colonel Thomas H. Sharp
42nd North Carolina Infantry, Colonel John E. Brown
66th North Carolina Infantry, Colonel John H. Nethercutt
2nd South Carolina Cavalry, Colonel Thomas J. Lipscomb

3rd Battalion North Carolina Light Artillery
Company A, (Northampton Artillery), Captain Andrew J. Ellis

10th Regiment North Carolina Troops, 1st North Carolina Artillery
2nd Company I, (Southerland's Battery), Captain Thomas Southerland

Staunton Hill Artillery (Paris' Battery) Captain Andrew B. Paris

FEDERAL FORCES

United States Army, Department of Virginia and North Carolina, Terry's Provisional Corps, Bvt. Major General Alfred H. Terry, commander

XXIV Army Corps

First Division

Second Brigade

Colonel Joseph C. Abbott,Commander
6th Connecticut Infantry, Colonel Alfred P. Rockwell
7th Connecticut Infantry, Captain John Thompson
Captain William S. Marble
3rd New Hampshire Infantry, Captain William H. Trickey
7th New Hampshire Infantry, Lt. Colonel Augustus W. Rollins

16th New York Heavy Artillery (detachment)
Companies A, B, C, F, G, K, Major Frederick W. Prince

Second Division

Brig. General Adelbert Ames, commander

First Brigade

Colonel N. Martin Curtis, commander
Major Ezra L. Walrath

3rd New York Infantry, Captain James H. Reeve
Lt. Edwin A. Behan
112th New York Infantry, Colonel John F. Smith
117th New York Infantry, Lt. Colonel Francis X. Meyer
142nd New York Infantry, Lt. Colonel Albert M. Barney

Second Brigade

Colonel Galusha Pennypacker, commander
Major Oliver P. Harding

47th New York Infantry, Captain Joseph M. McDonald
48th New York Infantry, Lt. Colonel William B. Coan,
Major Nere A. Elfwing
76th Pennsylvania Infantry, Colonel John S. Littell,
Major Charles Knerr
97th Pennsylvania Infantry, Lt. John Wainwright
203rd Pennsylvania Infantry, Colonel John W. Moore
Lt. Colonel Jonas W. Lyman
Major Oliver P. Harding
Captain Heber B. Essington

Third Brigade

Colonel Louis Bell, commander
Colonel Alonzo Alden

13th Indiana Infantry, Lt. Colonel Samuel M. Zent
4th New Hampshire Infantry, Captain John H. Roberts
115th New York Infantry, Lt. Colonel Nathan J. Johnson
169th New York Infantry, Colonel Alonzo Alden
Lt. Colonel James A. Colvin

Artillery Brigade, Captain Richard H. Lee
16th New York Independent Battery Light Artillery (detachment)

XXV Army Corps

Third Division

Brig. General Charles J. Paine, commander

Second Brigade

Colonel John W. Ames, commander

4th U.S. Colored Troops, Lt. Colonel George Rogers
6th U.S. Colored Troops, Major Augustus S. Boernstein
30th U.S. Colored Troops, Lt. Colonel Hiram A. Oakman
39th U.S. Colored Troops, Colonel Ozora P. Stearns

Third Brigade

Colonel Elias Wright, commander

1st U.S. Colored Troops, Lt. Colonel Giles H. Rich
5th U.S. Colored Troops, Major William R. Brazie
10th U.S. Colored Troops, Lt. Colonel Edward H. Powell
27th U.S. Colored Troops, Bvt Brig. General Albert M. Blackman
37th U.S. Colored Troops, Colonel Nathan Goff, Jr.

Artillery Brigade

1st Connecticut Heavy Artillery
Companies B, G, L, Captain William G. Pride
3rd U.S. Regular Army, Battery E, Lt. John Myrick
Artillery Bvt. Brig. General Henry L. Abbot
New York Light, 16th Battery, Captain Richard H. Lee

Engineers
15th New York
Companies A, I, Lt. K. Samuel O'Keefe

United States Navy, North Atlantic Blockading Squadron, Cape Fear Task Force,
Rear Admiral David D. Porter, commanding fleet

Line No. 1

VESSEL	GUNS	COMMANDING OFFICER
Brooklyn	26	Captain James Alden
Canonicus (monitor)	2	Lt. Cmdr. George Belknap
Huron	5	Lt. Cmdr. Thomas O. Selfridge
Kansas	8	Lt. Cmdr. Pendleton Watmough
Mahopac (monitor)	2	Lt. Cmdr. A.W. Weaver
Maumee	8	Lt. Cmdr. Ralph Chandler
Mohican	9	Cmdr. Daniel Ammen
Monadnock (monitor)	4	Cmdr. Enoch G. Parrott
New Ironsides (ironclad)	20	Cmdr. William Radford
Nyack	4	Lt. Cmdr. L.H. Newman
Pawtuxet	10	Cmdr. James H. Spotts
Pequot	8	Lt. Cmdr. Daniel Braine
Pontoosuc	12	Lt. Cmdr. William G. Temple
Saugus (monitor)	2	Cmdr. Edmund R. Colhoun
Seneca	5	Lt. Cmdr. Montgomery Sicard
Tacony	12	Lt. Cmdr. William T. Truxtun
Unadilla	6	Lt. Cmdr. Frank M. Ramsey
Yantic	5	Lt. Cmdr. Thomas C. Harris

Line No. 2

VESSEL	GUNS	COMMANDING OFFICER
Colorado	50	Commodore Henry K. Thatcher
Juanita	14	Captain William R. Taylor
Mackinaw	10	Cmdr. John C. Beaumont
Minnesota	46	Commodore Joseph Lanman
Powhatan	24	Commodore James F. Schenck
Shenandoah	6	Captain Daniel B. Ridgely
Susquehanna	18	Commodore Sylvanus W. Godon
Ticonderoga	14	Captain Charles Steedman
Tuscarora	10	Cmdr. James M. Frailey
Vanderbilt	16	Captain Charles W. Pickering
Vicksburg	7	Lt. Cmdr. Baker
Wabash	44	Captain Melancton Smith

Line No. 3

VESSEL	GUNS	COMMANDING OFFICER
Alabama	10	Acting Vol. Lt. Amos Langthorne
Chippewa	6	Lt. Cmdr. E.E. Potter
Fort Jackson	11	Captain Benjamin F. Sands
Iosco	10	Cmdr. John Guest

Keystone State	16	Cmdr. H. Rolando
Maratanza	6	Lt. Cmdr. George Young
Montgomery	6	Acting Vol. Lt. Thomas C. Dunn
Monticello	6	Lt. Cmdr. William B. Cushing
Osceola	10	Cmdr. J.M.B. Clitz
Quaker City	7	Cmdr. William F. Spicer
R.R. Cuyler	12	Cmdr. Charles H.B. Caldwell
Rhode Island	12	Cmdr. Stephen D. Trenchard
Santiago de Cuba	11	Captain Oliver S. Glisson
Sassacus	12	Lt. Cmdr. John L. Davis

Reserves

VESSEL	GUNS	COMMANDING OFFICER
A.D. Vance	5	Lt. Cmdr. John H. Upshur
Aries	7	Acting Vol. Lt. Francis S. Wells
Britannia	6	Acting Vol. Lt. William Sheldon
Cherokee	6	Acting Vol. Lt. William Dennison
Emma	8	Acting Vol. Lt. James Williams
Eolus	4	Acting Mstr. Edward S. Keyser
Fort Donelson	1	Acting Mstr. George W. Frost
Gettysburg	7	Lt. R. H. Lamson
Gov Buckingham	6	Acting Vol. Lt. J. MacDiarmid
Howquah	9	Acting Vol. Lt. Balch
Launch No. 6	1	Gunner Hubert Peters
Lillian	2	Acting Vol. Lt. T.A. Harris
Little Ada	2	Acting Mstr. Samuel P. Crafts
Malvern	12	Lt. Cmdr. Benjamin H. Porter
Moccasin	3	Acting Ensign Brown
Nansemond	3	Acting Mstr. James H. Porter
Nereus	11	Cmdr. J.C. Howell
Republic	1	Acting Mstr. John W. Bennett
Tristram Shandy	4	Acting Vol. Lt. Edward F. Green
Wilderness	4	Acting Mstr. Henry Arey

U.S. Army Transports

Atlantic, Blackstone, California, Champion, Charles Leary, Commodore DuPont, DeMolay, Euterpe, General Lyon, Governor Chase, Idaho, L.C. Livingston, McCellan, Montauk, North Point, Prometheus, Russia, Thames, Thomas, R. Scott, Tonawanda, Varuna, Weybosett

Civil War Medical Terminology

Disease	Meaning
Abcpsia	Blindness
Abscessus	A swollen, inflamed area of the body where pus gathers
Acute	Severe
Aegrotantem	Illness, sickness
Ague	Recurring fever and chills of malaria
Ambustio	A burn or scald
Anasaica	Generalized edema or generalized dropsy
Anchylosis	A stiffening of the joints
Aphonia	A lost of voice due to organic or psychological causes
Apoplexy	Stroke
Ascites	Accumulation of serous fluid in the abdominal cavity
Billious Fever	Any fever that exhibited the symptom of nausea or vomiting in addition to an increase in internal body temperature and strong diarrhea.
Bad Blood	Syphilis
Bilious fever	Fever caused by liver disorder
Black Death	Bubonic plague
Bloody Flux	Dysentery
Bright's Disease	Kidney disease
Catarrh	Inflammation of mucous membrane most commonly in the throat and nose, accompanied by an increased secretion mucous, sometimes accompanied by fever, or, rarely cerebral hemorrhage
Cephalalgia	Headache
Chilblain	Swelling of the extremities caused by exposure to cold
Chin Cough	Whooping Cough
Chorea	Disease characterized by convulsions and contortions
Chronic	Continuing for a long period of time
Colica	Acute abdominal pains, caused by abnormal condition of the bowel
Congestiva	Excessive accumulation of blood in parts of the body
Congestion of the Brain	This disease consists of an accumulation of blood in the cerebral tissue. It is caused by any impediment to the return of blood from the brain, such as a tumor of the neck, smallpox, heart disease or an injury such as a fall were the victim has a contusion of his head.
Congestion of the Lungs	Pneumonia

Disease	Meaning
Congestive Fever	Malaria
Conjunctivitis	Inflammation of the eye or eyelid
Consecutiva	Unrelated illness following another
Consumption	Tuberculosis
Continua	Without interruption
Contusion	A bruise or injury where the skin is not broken
Cramp Colic	Appendicitis
Crop Sickness	Overextended stomach
Croup	Laryngitis, diphtheria, or strep throat
Debilitas	Weakness or feebleness
Debility	Weakness or feebleness
Delirium Tremens	Hallucinations & seizures due to alcohol withdrawal
Diphtheria	Contagious disease of the throat
Dropsy of the Brain	Encephalitis, disease with acute onset of fever, headache, confusion, and sometimes seizures
Dropsy	Edema, an abnormal accumulation of fluid in the tissue spaces, cavities, or joint capsules of the body, causing swelling of the area.
Dropsy Hepatic	Edema, an abnormal accumulation of fluid in the liver.
Dysentery	Inflammation of intestinal membrane
Dyspepsia	Acid indigestion
Encephalitis	Swelling of the brain
Enteritis	Inflammation of the bowels
Erysipelas	An acute infectious disease of the mucous membranes characterized by the inflammation of the skin, accompanied by a fever.
Febris	Fever
Flux	Discharge of fluid from the body
Galloping Consumption	Pulmonary Tuberculosis
Glandular Fever	Mononucleosis, a sore throat where the patient's tonsils become swollen and develop a whitish-yellow covering. The lymph nodes in the neck are frequently swollen and painful.
Green Sickness	Anemia, disease of the blood characterized by weakness, or fatigue, general malaise, and sometimes poor concentration.
Gripe	Influenza
Hemophthis	Spitting of blood
Hemorrhia	Heavy Bleeding
Herpes	An inflammatory virus disease of the skin or mucous membranes

Disease	Meaning
Incipt Hydrothorax	An abnormal amount of watery fluid in the pleural cavity
Inflammation of Lungs	Pneumonia
Intermittent	Stopping and Starting, usually referring to Intermittent Fever
Intermittent Fever	A fever that comes and goes.
Jail Fever	Typhus is a bacterial disease spread by lice or fleas. It is characterized abdominal pain, headache, red rash and high fever.
Jaundice	Yellowing of the skin due to liver dysfunction (hyperbilirubinemia)
Lock Jaw	Tetanus, prolonged muscle spasms that affect the jaw, chest, neck, back and abdominal muscles. Mortality rates reported vary from 48% to 73%.
Lumbago	A back ache
Lung Fever	Pneumonia
Lung Sickness	Tuberculosis
Mania	Insanity
Miasma	Poisonous vapors thought to infect the air
Morbi Cutis	A skin disease
Morsal	Gangrene
Mortis	Death
Myelitis	Inflammation of the spine
Myocarditits	Inflammation of the heart muscles
Necrosis	Mortification of bones or tissue, usually skin
Nephritis	Inflammation of the kidneys
Nostalgia	Disease marked by homesickness, melancholia and loss of appetite
Ophthalmia	Relating to the eyes
Otalgia	Earache
Palsy	Paralysis or loss of muscle control
Paronychia	A painful, pus-producing inflammation at the end of a toe or finger
Parotitis	Mumps
Paroxysm	Convulsion
Phlegmon	Inflammation, especially of the connective tissues, leading to ulceration or abscess
Phthisis Pulmonalis	Consumption of the lungs; strictly applied to the tuberculosis variety.
Pleurisy	Inflammation of the lung
Pleuritis	Pleurisy, inflammation of the lining of the pleural cavity surrounding the lungs. Characterized by a sharp, stabbing pain in the chest that gets worse with deep breathing, coughing, sneezing, or laughing.
Podagra	Gout
Pott's Disease	Tuberculosis of the spinal vertebrae

Disease	Meaning
Pox	Syphilis
Pulmonalis	Relating to the heart
Putrid Fever	Typhus, so called from the decomposing and offensive state of the discharges and diseased textures of the body.
Pyemia	Widespread abscesses caused by pus-forming organisms in the blood.
Qyotidiana	A fever occurring or returning daily
Remittent	A fever that drops, but does not altogether disappear
Rickets	Disease of the skeletal system
Rheumatic Pericarditis	Inflammation and swelling of the pericardium (fibrous sac surrounding the heart) that occurs as a complication in people with rheumatism.
Rheumatism	Condition characterized by inflammation or pain in muscles, joints
Rubeola	Measles
Scarlet Fever	Disease characterized by a red rash and sore
Scorbutus	Scurvy
Screws	Rheumatism
Scrofula	Tuberculosis of the neck lymph nodes or lymphatic glands
Ship's Fever	Typhus
Softening of the Brain	Sudden impairment of neurological function, especially that resulting from a cerebral hemorrhage; a stroke.
Spotted Fever	Typhus, cerebrospinal meningitis fever
St. Vitus Dance	Nervous twitches, chorea
Sub-Laxatio	An incomplete dislocation
Typhus	Disease transmitted especially by body lice and is marked by high fever, stupor alternating with delirium, intense headache, and a dark red rash
Variola	Smallpox
Venesection	Bleeding
Viper's Dance	St. Vitus' Dance, An abnormal involuntary movement disorder.
Vulnus Incisum	Relating to a wound caused by a cut
Vulnus Punctum	Relating to a wound caused by a puncture
Vulnus Sclopeticum	Relating to a wound caused by a gunshot wound
Vulnus	Relating to a wound
Whitlow	A painful, pus-producing inflammation at the end of a toe or finger
Winter Fever	Pneumonia
Yellow Jack	Yellow Fever

Notes

Chapter 1 Lincoln Takes Office

1. Lincoln, President Abraham, *First Inaugural Address*, March 4, 1861
2. Fonvielle Jr., Dr. Chris E., *The Wilmington Campaign: Last Rays of Departing Hope*, pages. 6-7; Gragg, Rod, *Confederate Goliath: The Battle of Fort Fisher*, page 8
3. Lamb, William, *Colonel Lamb's Story of Fort Fisher*, pages 2-5; *Histories of Several Regiments and Battalions from North Carolina in the Great War 1861-65*, by Walter Clark, Volume V, pages 218-220
4. *The Atlas to Accompany the Official Records of the Union and Confederate Armies*, Plate 75, numbers 1-3, Plate 76, numbers 2, 4, Washington, D.C.: U.S. Government Printing Office, 1891;
5. Dr. Chris E., *The Wilmington Campaign: Last Rays of Departing Hope*, page 44; Robinson III, Charles M., *Hurricane of Fire*, Page 66; Ripley, Warren, *Artillery and Ammunition of the Civil War*, pages 140-141
6. Wilkinson, John, *Narrative of a Blockade-Runner*, page 152
7. Lamb, William, *Colonel Lamb's Story of Fort Fisher*, pages 4-5; Fonvielle Jr., Dr. Chris E., *The Wilmington Campaign: Last Rays of Departing Hope*, Page 45; Rod Gragg, *Confederate Goliath: The Battle of Fort Fisher*, page 19

Chapter 2 Wilmington Takes On New Importance

1. Mark A. Moore, *The Wilmington Campaign and the Battles for Fort Fisher*, page 14
2. Rod Gragg, *Confederate Goliath: The Battle of Fort Fisher*, page 39; Shelby Foote, *The Civil War: A Narrative, vol. I*, pp. 370, 533
3. Butler, Major General Benjamin, *Butler's Book*, pages 775-776, Rod Gragg, *Confederate Goliath: The Battle of Fort Fisher*, pages 39-40; Holzman Robert S., *Stormy Ben Butler*, pages 103-105, 147
4. Richard B. McCaslin, *The Last Stronghold: The Campaign for Fort Fisher*, page 52-53
5. Porter to Butler, December 13, 1864, *O.R.N., Series I, Vol 11*, page 191; Richard B. McCaslin, *The Last Stronghold: The Campaign for Fort Fisher*, page 42; Fonvielle Jr., Dr. Chris E., *The Wilmington Campaign: Last Rays of Departing Hope* Page 79;
6. Gragg, Rod *Confederate Goliath: The Battle of Fort Fisher*, page 49

Chapter 3 The First Attack

1. Fonvielle Jr., Dr. Chris E., *The Wilmington Campaign: Last Rays of Departing Hope*, Page 124; Report of A.C. Rhind, December 26, 1864, *ORN 11*, pages 226-227; Gragg, Rod, *Confederate Goliath*, p. 52
2. Fonvielle Jr., Dr. Chris E., *The Wilmington Campaign: Last Rays of Departing Hope*, Page 125; Lamb, William, *Lamb Diary*, December 24, 1864
3. Lamb, Colonel William, *Colonel Lamb's Story of Fort Fisher* page 14
4. Lamb, William, *Colonel Lamb's Story of Fort Fisher*, pages 15-16; Gragg, Rod, *Confederate Goliath*, page 63; Trotter, William R., *Ironclads and Columbiads*, page 358; Fonvielle Jr., Dr. Chris E., *The Wilmington Campaign: Last Rays of Departing Hope*, Page 119
5. Blair, B.F., letter *To Mother*, December 27, 1864, B.F. Blair Papers, Archives Division, U.S. Army Military History Institute
6. Gragg, Rod, *Confederate* Goliath, page 65, Robinson III, Charles M., *Hurricane of Fire*, P 123

7. Selfridge, Thomas, *Battles and Leaders of the Civil War*, Vol. 4, page 657

8. Simms, Joseph, *Personal Experience in the Volunteer Navy During the Civil War*, page 12

9. Lamb, William, *Colonel Lamb's Story of Fort Fisher*, page 15

10. Robinson III, Charles M., *Hurricane of Fire*, pages 124-125; Trotter, William R., *Ironclads and Columbiads*, page 360

11. *O.R.N,. Series I*, Vol. XI, pages 298-299

12. Fonvielle Jr., Dr. Chris E., *The Wilmington Campaign: Last Rays of Departing Hope*, Pages 137-138

13. Gragg, Rod, *Confederate Goliath*, page 69

14. Lamb, William, *Colonel Lamb's Story of Fort Fisher*, pages 16-17

15. *O.R.N,. Series I, Vol. 11*, page 253

16. Fonvielle Jr., Dr. Chris E., *The Wilmington Campaign: Last Rays of Departing Hope*, Page 141

17. Gragg, Rod, *Confederate Goliath: The Battle of Fort Fisher, page 77*; Turner, Henry M. *Civil War Times Illustrated*, 31 (October/November, 1980)

18. Longacre, Edward G., *Antietam to Fort Fisher*, page 223-224; Trotter, William R., *Ironclads and Columbiads*, page 369

19. Fonvielle Jr., Dr. Chris E., *The Wilmington Campaign: Last Rays of Departing Hope*, Page 143; Mark A. Moore, *The Wilmington Campaign and the Battles for Fort Fisher*, page 23

20. *O.R. Series I, Vol. XLII, part 1*, pages 985-986,

21. Robinson III, Charles M., *Hurricane of Fire*, Pages 133-134

22. *O.R. Series I, Vol. XLII, part 1*, pages 1020-1022

23. *O.R., Series I, Vol. XLII, part III*, page 1307; Gragg, Rod, *Confederate Goliath: The Battle of Fort Fisher*, pages 85-86;

24. Gragg, Rod, *Confederate Goliath: The Battle of Fort Fisher*, pages 83-84; Fonvielle Jr., Dr. Chris E., *The Wilmington Campaign: Last Rays of Departing Hope*, Pages 151-152; Walker, James L., *Rebel Gibraltar*, page 285

25. Fonvielle Jr., Dr. Chris E., *The Wilmington Campaign: Last Rays of Departing Hope*, Page 152; Gragg, Rod, *Confederate Goliath: The Battle of Fort Fisher*, page 85

26. Gragg, Rod, *Confederate Goliath: The Battle of Fort Fisher*, page 85; Fonvielle Jr., Dr. Chris E., *The Wilmington Campaign: Last Rays of Departing Hope*, Page 152

27. *O.R.N,. Series I, Vol. XI*, page 295

28. *O.R.N., Series I, Vol. XI*, pages 296-297

29. *O.R.N. Vol. XI*, pages 298-299

30. *O.R. Series I, Vol. XLII, part 1*, page 986

31. Edited by W. F. Beyer and O. F. Keydel, *Deeds of Valor: How America's Heroes Won the Medal of Honor, Volume I*, page 471

32. Fonvielle Jr., Dr. Chris E., *The Wilmington Campaign: Last Rays of Departing Hope*, Page 157; Lamb, William, *Colonel Lamb's Story of Fort Fisher*, page 18

33. Fonvielle Jr., Dr. Chris E., *The Wilmington Campaign: Last Rays of Departing Hope*, Pages 159-160; Gragg, Rod, *Confederate Goliath: The Battle of Fort Fisher*, page 87-90

34. Fonvielle Jr., Dr. Chris E., *The Wilmington Campaign: Last Rays of Departing Hope*, pages. 169-170; Gragg, Rod, *Confederate Goliath: The Battle of Fort Fisher*, page 95; Walker, James L., *Rebel Gibraltar*, pages 290-191; Mowris, Regimental Surgeon James A., *A History of the 117th Regiment, New York Volunteers,(Fourth Oneida)* page 157;

35. *O.R. Series I, Vol. XLII, part 1*, page 981; *O.R. Series I, XLII, part 1*, page 986; Gragg, Rod, *Confederate Goliath: The Battle of Fort Fisher*, pages 88-89;

36. Simpson, George, *Capture of Fort Fisher*, page 8, Curtis Collection, Chicago Historical Society

37. *O.R. Series I, Vol. XLII, part 1*, Pages 979 to 980; Lamb, William, *Colonel Lamb's Story of Fort Fisher*, page 21

38. *O.R.N., Series I, Vol. 11*, pages 261-262, 264; Whiting's reply to questions submitted by General Butler, *O.R. Series I, Vol. XLII, part 1*, page 981; Lamb, William, *Colonel Lamb's Story of Fort Fisher*, page 21; *O.R. Series I, Vol. XLII, part 1*, page 66

39. *O.R. Series I, Vol. XLII, part 3*, page 1087; Walker, James L., *Rebel Gibraltar*, page 298
40. Gragg, Rod, *Confederate Goliath: The Battle of Fort Fisher*, pages 105-107
41. Lamb, William, *Colonel Lamb's Story of Fort Fisher*, page 20
42. *Daily Journal*, January 6, 1865; Walker, James L., *Rebel Gibraltar*, pages 295-296
43. Gragg, Rod, *Confederate Goliath: The Battle of Fort Fisher*, pages 99-100
44. Fonvielle Jr., Dr. Chris E., *The Wilmington Campaign: Last Rays of Departing Hope*, page 178

Chapter 4 The Second Attack

1. *O.R.N.*, Series I, *Vol. 11*, page 391; Fonvielle Jr., Dr. Chris E., *The Wilmington Campaign: Last Rays of Departing Hope*, page 191; Mark A. Moore, *The Wilmington Campaign and the Battles for Fort Fisher*, page 35
2. Jones, Reverend J. William, *Personal Reminiscences, Anecdotes, and Letters of Gen. Robert E. Lee*, page 40
3. Lamb, William, *Colonel Lamb's Story of Fort Fisher*, page 35; *O.R Series I, Vol. XVIII*, Pages 818-819; Lee to Smith, January 4, 1863
4. *O.R. Series I, Vol. XLVI, part 2*, page 1023
5. Fonvielle Jr., Dr. Chris E., *The Wilmington Campaign: Last Rays of Departing Hope*, pages 204-205; Gragg, Rod, *Confederate Goliath: The Battle of Fort Fisher*, page 111; Lamb, William, *Colonel Lamb's Story of Fort Fisher*, page 22-23; Robinson III, Charles M., *Hurricane of Fire*, Page 152
6. Lamb, William, *Colonel Lamb's Story of Fort Fisher*, page 23; Fonvielle Jr., Dr. Chris E., *The Wilmington Campaign: Last Rays of Departing Hope*, page 218; Gragg, Rod, *Confederate Goliath: The Battle of Fort Fisher*, page 121,
7. *O.R. Series I, Vol. XLVI, part 2*, page 1048, 1056,
8. *O.R. Series I, Vol. XLVI, part 2*, pages 1056-1057, 1061-1062
9. Gragg, Rod, *Confederate Goliath: The Battle of Fort Fisher*, pages 112-113
10. Buell, Augustus, *The Cannoneer: Recollections Of Service In The Army of the Potomac*, Page 329
11. Deeds of Valor Volume 2, pages 85-86,
12. Longacre, Edward G., *Civil War Times Illustrated*, volume XXI, No. 10, February, 1983, *The Task Before Them*, page 38,
13. Fonvielle Jr., Dr. Chris E., *The Wilmington Campaign: Last Rays of Departing Hope*, page 210,
14. Little, Lieutenant Henry F., *The Seventh Regiment New Hampshire Volunteers in the War Of the Rebellion*, pages 358-359,
15. Fonvielle Jr., Dr. Chris E., *The Wilmington Campaign: Last Rays of Departing Hope*, page 210; *New York Tribune*, January 18, 1865; *National Tribune*, "Fort Fisher: The Part Taken by the 27th US Colored Troops*, July 17, 1865; *The Cannoneer: Recollections Of Service In The Army of the Potomac* Page 327; Gragg, Rod, *Confederate Goliath: The Battle of Fort Fisher*, pages 116-117; Little, Lieutenant Henry F., *The Seventh Regiment New Hampshire Volunteers in the War of the Rebellion*, pages 358-359;
16. Little, Lieutenant Henry F., *The Seventh Regiment New Hampshire Volunteers in the War Of the Rebellion*, pages 358-359,
17. *O.R. Series I, Vol. XLVI, part I*, page 397, Gragg, Rod, *Confederate Goliath: The Battle of Fort Fisher*, pages 123-124, Fonvielle Jr., Dr. Chris E., *The Wilmington Campaign: Last Rays of Departing Hope*, pages 219-220
18. Fonvielle Jr., Dr. Chris E., *The Wilmington Campaign: Last Rays of Departing Hope*, page 228
19. Fonvielle Jr., Dr. Chris E., *The Wilmington Campaign: Last Rays of Departing Hope*, page 214; Asa King Memoir, *Confederate Veterans' Talks*, Lower Cape Fear Historical Society, Wilmington, North Carolina; Gragg, Rod, *Confederate Goliath: The Battle of Fort Fisher*, page 117
20. *O.R. Series I, Vol. XLVI, part 2*, page 1047, Colonel William Lamb to Major Hill

Chapter 5 The Final Day of Battle

1.   Lamb, William, *Colonel Lamb's Story of Fort Fisher,* page 25

2. McNeill, Sergeant Thomas A., *Histories of Several Regiments and Battalions from North Carolina in the Great War 1861-65,* by Walter Clark, volume IV, page 308-309

3. Curtis, Colonel Newton Martin, *The Capture of Fort Fisher, Personal Recollections of the War of the Rebellion, Addresses Delivered Before the Commandery of the State of New York, Military Order of the Loyal Legion of the United States,* pages 47-48

4. Sand, Benjamin, *From Reefer to Rear Admiral,* page 263

5. Fonvielle Jr., Dr. Chris E., *The Wilmington Campaign: Last Rays of Departing Hope,* page 217; Gragg, Rod, *Confederate Goliath: The Battle of Fort Fisher,* pages 121-122; James Montgomery papers, Confederate Veterans' Talks, Lower Cape Fear Historical Society Archives; R.P.C. to "My Dearest Cousin," January 24, 1865, Lybrook Collection, N.C. Department of Archives and History; *North Carolina State Troops,* volume I page 214; Still, William N., Jr., ed., *The Yankees Are Landing Below Us: The Journal of Robert Watson, C.S.N., Civil War Times Illustrated,* Volume XV, No. 1, April 1976, page 15,

6. *O.R.N.,* Series I, *Vol. XI,* page 438, 477,

7. Longacre, Edward G., *The Task Before Them,* Letter from Captain Adrian Terry to his wife, page 41, *Civil War Times Illustrated,* February 1983, Volume XXI, Number 10,

8. McNeill, Sergeant Thomas A., *Histories of Several Regiments and Battalions from North Carolina in the Great War 1861-65,* by Walter Clark, volume IV, page 309,

9. *O.R. Series I, Vol. XLVI, part 2,* page 1053; Fonvielle Jr., Dr. Chris E., *The Wilmington Campaign: Last Rays of Departing Hope,* pages 234-235,

10. Terry, Major General Alfred H, *O.R.,* Series I, XLVI, part I, page 398; Fonvielle Jr., Dr. Chris E., *The Wilmington Campaign: Last Rays of Departing Hope,* page 242; Gragg, Rod, *Confederate Goliath: The Battle of Fort Fisher,* page 169;

11. Curtis, Colonel Newton Martin, *The Capture of Fort Fisher,* page 49, *Personal Recollections of the War of the Rebellion, Addresses Delivered Before the Commandery of the State of New York, Military Order of the Loyal Legion of the United States;* Little, Lieutenant Henry F.W., *New Hampshire Volunteers in the War of the Rebellion,* pages 391-392; Mark A. Moore, *The Wilmington Campaign and the Battles for Fort Fisher,* pages 49, 50,

12. Mowris, Regimental Surgeon James A., *A History of the 117th Regiment, New York Volunteers, (Fourth Oneida)* page 167-168; Walrath, Colonel E. L., *The Syracuse Daily Courier and Union,* February 3, 1865;

13. *O.R.N., Vol. XI,* page 427, Merrill, James M., ed. *The Fort Fisher and Wilmington Campaign: Letters From Rear Admiral David D. Porter, North Carolina Historical Review,* XXXV (October, 1958) page 467, Fonvielle Jr., Dr. Chris E., *The Wilmington Campaign: Last Rays of Departing Hope,* page 231; Gragg, Rod, *Confederate Goliath: The Battle of Fort Fisher,* page 134,

14. Letter from Admiral David D. Porter to Secretary of the Navy Gideon Wells, *O.R.N.,* Series I, *Vol. XI,* page 439; *O.R., Series I, Vol. XLVI,* part I, page 397,

15. Dawson, Captain Lucien L., *O.R.N., Series I, Vol. XI,* page 576

16. Dawson, Captain Lucien L., *O.R.N.,* Dawson, Lucien L. Captain, *ORN, Series I, Vol. XI,* page 576,

17. Simms, Lieutenant Commander Joseph, *Personal Experiences in the Volunteer Navy During the Civil War: War Papers Read Before the Military Order of the Loyal Legion, Commandery of the District of Columbia,* page 365, Parker, Lieutenant Commander James, *Personal Recollections of the War of the Rebellion: Addresses Delivered Before the Commandery of the State of New York, Military Order of the Loyal Legion of the United States,* page 112, Harris, Ensign Ira, *Military Essays and Recollections, Papers Read Before the Commandery of the State of Illinois: Military Order of the Loyal Legion of the United States,* Volume II, page 173,

18. Breese, Lieutenant Commander Randolph Kidder, *O.R.N.*, *Series I, Vol. XI*, page 446, Report of Captain Lucien L. Dawson, U.S. Marine Corps, answering criticisms of Rear-Admiral Porter, *O.R.N.*, *Series I, Vol. XI*, page 578; Little, Lieutenant Henry F.W., *New Hampshire Volunteers in the War of the Rebellion*, page 388,

19. Evans, Ensign Robley, *A Sailor's Log*, page 87,

20. Simms, Ensign Joseph, *Personal Experiences in the Volunteer Navy During the Civil War, War Papers Read Before the Military Order of the Loyal Legion, Commandery of the District of Columbia*, page 365, Gragg, Rod, *Confederate Goliath: The Battle of Fort Fisher*, page 154,

21. Breese, K. Randolph, *O.R.N.*, *Series I, Volume XI*, page 446, Fonvielle Jr., Dr. Chris E., *The Wilmington Campaign: Last Rays of Departing Hope*, page 254-255; Gragg, Rod, *Confederate Goliath: The Battle of Fort Fisher*, page 164, Grattan, John W., *Under the Blue Pennant*, pages 183-188, Mark A. Moore, *The Wilmington Campaign and the Battles for Fort Fisher*, page 45,

22. *O.R.N.*, *Series I, Vol. XI*, p 446-447, Sands, Francis, p. 20, Buel, Augustus, *Cannoneer*, p. 332, Grattan, "Under the Blue Pennant, page 168,

23. Lamb, Colonel William, *Colonel Lamb's Story of Fort Fisher*, page 26,

24. Evans, Robley, *A Sailor's Log*, pages 88-89,

25. Evans, Robley, *A Sailor's Log*, pages 86-87, Fonvielle Jr., Dr. Chris E., *The Wilmington Campaign: Last Rays of Departing Hope*, page 252, Gragg, Rod, *Confederate Goliath: The Battle of Fort Fisher*, page 156, Robinson III, Charles M., *Hurricane of Fire*, Page 156,

26. *O.R.N.*, *Series I, Vol. XI*, page 578, Letter of Lieutenant John Bartlett, U. S. Navy, to his sisters,

27. Lanman, Commodore Joseph, *O,R.N.*, *Series I, Vol. XI*, page 498,

28. Lamson, Lieutenant Roswell H., *O,R.N.*, *Series I, Vol. XI*, page 450,

29. Evans, Ensign Robley D., *A Sailor's Log*, page 95-96, Porter, Rear-Admiral David D., *O,R.N.*, *Series I, Volume XI*, page 448,

30. Lieutenant Commander William T. Truxton, *O,R.N.*, *Series I, Vol. XI*, page 471, Breese, Lieutenant Commander Randolph Kidder, *O,R.N.*, *Series I, Vol. XI*, page 446,

31. Lamb, Colonel William, Colonel Lamb's Story of Fort Fisher, page 27,

32. Harris, Ensign Ira, *Military Essays and Recollections, Papers Read Before the Commandery of the State of Illinois: Military Order of the Loyal Legion of the United States*, Volume II, page 172-173,

33. Cobb, Seaman William T. Papers, *Dear Father*, Fort Fisher State Historic Site

34. Fonvielle Jr., Dr. Chris E., *The Wilmington Campaign: Last Rays of Departing Hope*, page 256; Gragg, Rod, *Confederate Goliath: The Battle of Fort Fisher*, pages 166-167,

35. Lanman, Commodore Joseph, *ORN*, Series I, Volume XI, pages 498-499; Breese, Lieutenant Commander Randolph Kidder, *ORN*, Series I, Volume XI, pages 446-447; Selfridge, Lieutenant Commander Thomas O., Battles and Leaders, Volume IV, page 660; Robinson III, Charles M., *Hurricane of Fire*, Page 172; Walker, James L., *Rebel Gibraltar*, page 338; Letter of Lieutenant John Bartlett to his sisters, ORN, Series I, Volume XI, page 528,

36. Lanman, Commodore Joseph, *O,R.N.*, *Series I, Vol. XI*, page 499

37. Lanman, Commodore Joseph, *O,R.N.*, *Series I, Vol. XI*, page 499

38. Letter of Lieutenant John Barlett, U.S. Navy, to his sisters, *ORN*, Series I, Volume XI, page 528

39. Curtis, Colonel Newton Martin, *The Capture of Fort Fisher*, page 47, *Personal Recollections of the War of the Rebellion, Addresses Delivered Before the Commandery of the State of New York, Military Order of the Loyal Legion of the United States*; Dawson, Captain Lucien L., *ORN, Series I, Vol. XI*, pages 581-582; Fonvielle Jr., Dr. Chris E., *The Wilmington Campaign: Last Rays of Departing Hope*, page 258; Gragg, Rod, *Confederate Goliath: The Battle of Fort Fisher*, page 167,

40. Lamb, William, *Colonel Lamb's Story of Fort Fisher*, page 27; Fonvielle Jr., Dr. Chris E., *The Wilmington Campaign: Last Rays of Departing Hope*, pages 260-261; Gragg, Rod, *Confederate Goliath: The Battle of Fort Fisher*, page 168

41. Curtis, Colonel Newton Martin, *The Capture of Fort Fisher*, page 40, *Personal Recollections of the War of the Rebellion, Addresses Delivered Before the Commandery of the State of New York, Military Order of the Loyal Legion of the United States*; Lamb, William, *Colonel Lamb's Story of*

Fort Fisher, pages 27-28; Fonvielle Jr., Dr. Chris E., *The Wilmington Campaign: Last Rays of Departing Hope,* pages 260-261; Gragg, Rod, *Confederate Goliath: The Battle of Fort Fisher*, page 168, 191; Robinson III, Charles M., *Hurricane of Fire,* Page 172,

42. Fonvielle Jr., Dr. Chris E., *The Wilmington Campaign: Last Rays of Departing Hope,* page 243; Gragg, Rod, *Confederate Goliath: The Battle of Fort Fisher*, pages 176-177,

43. Terry, Major General Alfred H, *O.R.*, Series I, XLVI, Part I, Page 398, 407; Fonvielle Jr., Dr. Chris E., *The Wilmington Campaign: Last Rays of Departing Hope,* pages 243-244; Gragg, Rod, *Confederate Goliath: The Battle of Fort Fisher*, page 171; Robinson III, Charles M., *Hurricane of Fire,* Page 173,

44. Fonvielle Jr., Dr. Chris E., *The Wilmington Campaign: Last Rays of Departing Hope,* pages. 244-245; Gragg, Rod, *Confederate Goliath: The Battle of Fort Fisher*, page 172,

45. Towle, Captain George F., *Terry's Fort Fisher Expedition,* page 297, *Old and New,* Volume XI,

46. Terry, Major General Alfred H, *O.R.*, Series I, Vol. XLVI, part I, page 398; Ames, Colonel Adelbert, *The Capture of Fort Fisher, January 15, 1865, Personal Recollections of the Rebellion,* pages 11-12; Fonvielle Jr., Dr. Chris E., *The Wilmington Campaign: Last Rays of Departing Hope,* pages. 244, 261; Gragg, Rod, *Confederate Goliath: The Battle of Fort Fisher,* page 172-173; Curtis, Colonel Newton Martin, *The Capture of Fort Fisher, Personal Recollections of the Rebellion,* pages 38-39; Lockwood, Colonel Henry C., *The Maine Bugle, A True History of the Army At Fort Fisher,* page 45,

47. Curtis, Colonel Newton Martin, *The Capture of Fort Fisher, Personal Recollections of the Rebellion,* pages 38-39,

48. Longacre, Edward G., *The Task Before Them,* Letter from Captain Adrian Terry to his wife, page 42, *Civil War Times Illustrated,* February 1983, Volume XXI, Number 10,

49. Thomas, Leonard R., *Story of Fort Fisher, January 15, 1865,* page 19; Hyde, William L., *History of the 112th New York Volunteers,* pages 122-123; Mowris, Regimental Surgeon James A., *A History of the 117th Regiment, New York Volunteers,(Fourth Oneida)* page 175,

50. Ames, Colonel Adelbert, *O.R.*, Series I, Vol. XLVI, page 417; Fonvielle Jr., Dr. Chris E., *The Wilmington Campaign: Last Rays of Departing Hope,* page 265; Gragg, Rod, *Confederate Goliath: The Battle of Fort Fisher*, page 177,

51. Towle, Captain George F., *Terry's Fort Fisher Expedition,* page 298, *Old and New*, Vol. XI; N. M. Robinson in a letter dated February 27, 1865, Private collection of Dr. Chris E. Fonvielle, Jr.

52. Lamb, Colonel William, *The Battles of Fort Fisher, Southern Historical Society Papers*, Volume XXI, page 283,

53. Hyde, William L., *History of the 112th New York Volunteers,* pages 120, 123; Walker, James L., *Rebel Gibraltar,* page 339,

54. McNeill, Sergeant Thomas A., *Histories of Several Regiments and Battalions from North Carolina in the Great War 1861-65,* by Walter Clark, volume IV, page 310; Lockwood, Colonel Henry C., *The Maine Bugle, A True History of the Army At Fort Fisher,* page 48,

55. Fulmore, Judge Zachary F., in a letter to Colonel William Lamb, *Southern Historical Society Papers,* Volume XXI, page 283,

56. Simpson, 2nd Lieutenant George, *Capture of Fort Fisher,* page 12; Clements, 1st Lt. J. C., *History of Company B, Twenty-First Regiment (Infantry) South Carolina Volunteers,* page 115;

57. Curtis, Colonel Newton Martin, *The Capture of Fort Fisher, Personal Recollections of the Rebellion,* page 48; Fonvielle Jr., Dr. Chris E., *The Wilmington Campaign: Last Rays of Departing Hope,* page 265; Gragg, Rod, *Confederate Goliath: The Battle of Fort Fisher*, page 178; Walker, James L., *Rebel Gibraltar,* page 340,

58. Lamb, Colonel William, *The Battles of Fort Fisher, The Southern Historical Society Papers,* Volume XXI, page 284; Lamb, Colonel William, *Colonel Lamb's Story of Fort Fisher,* page 32, The Blockade Runner Museum, 1966

59. McQueen, Corporal Henry Clay, Henry Clay McQueen papers, *Confederate Veterans' Talks,* Lower Cape Fear Historical Society Archives; Fonvielle Jr., Dr. Chris E., *The Wilmington Campaign: Last*

Rays of Departing Hope, pages 265, 281; Gragg, Rod, *Confederate Goliath: The Battle of Fort Fisher,* page 186; Moore, Mark A., *The Wilmington Campaign and the Battles for Fort Fisher,* page 50,

60. Mowris, Regimental Surgeon James A., *History of the 117th Regiment New York Volunteers,* page 169,

61. Curtis, N. Martin, *Capture of Fort Fisher,* pages 39-40; Fonvielle Jr., Dr. Chris E., *The Wilmington Campaign: Last Rays of Departing Hope,* page 266; Gragg, Rod, *Confederate Goliath: The Battle of Fort Fisher,* page 186,

62. Ames, General Adelbert, *O.R., Series I, Vol. LVIII,* page 417; Lockwood, Colonel Henry C., *The Maine Bugle, A True History of the Army At Fort Fisher,* page 46; Gragg, Rod, *Confederate Goliath: The Battle of Fort Fisher,* page 184,

63. Lockwood, Colonel Henry C., *The Maine Bugle, A True History of the Army At Fort Fisher,* page 49; *O.R., Series I, Vol. XLVI* page 420; Fonvielle Jr., Dr. Chris E., *The Wilmington Campaign: Last Rays of Departing Hope,* page 268; Gragg, Rod, *Confederate Goliath: The Battle of Fort Fisher,* page 184,

64. Lockwood, Colonel Henry C., *The Maine Bugle, A True History of the Army At Fort Fisher,* page 49; *O.R., Series I, Vol. XLVI,* page 420; Fonvielle Jr., Dr. Chris E., *The Wilmington Campaign: Last Rays of Departing Hope,* page 268; Gragg, Rod, *Confederate Goliath: The Battle of Fort Fisher,* page 184; Fox, Lt Colonel William F., *Regimental Losses in the American Civil War 1861-1865,* pages 19, 459,

65. Price, Major Isaiah, *History of the Ninety-seventh Regiment, Pennsylvania Volunteer Infantry During the War of the Rebellion,* pages 355-356; Harding, Major Oliver P., *O.R. Series I, Vol. LVIII, part 1,* page 420; Gragg, Rod, *Confederate Goliath: The Battle of Fort Fisher,* page 186,

66. Fulmore, Zachariah T., *Wilmington Messenger,* June 27, 1897,

67. Braddy, Captain Kinchen, Kitchen Braddy letter to Z.T. Fulmore, March 25, 1901, misc. Civil War papers, Division of Archives and History, Raleigh, North Carolina; Fonvielle Jr., Dr. Chris E., *The Wilmington Campaign: Last Rays of Departing Hope,* page 273;

68. Pennypacker, General Galusha, to journalist Philip R. Dillon, *The Pittsburg Press,* November 16, 1911,

69. Colonel Curtis, *The Capture of Fort Fisher,* page 41, *Personal Recollections of the War of the Rebellion,* Fonvielle Jr., Dr. Chris E., *The Wilmington Campaign: Last Rays of Departing Hope,* page 281;

70. Bouton, John Bell, *A Memoir of General Louis Bell,* page 26-28; Gragg, Rod, *Confederate Goliath: The Battle of Fort Fisher,* pages 195-197;

71. Terry, Adrian's letter to his wife, *The Task Before Them,* page 43, Longacre, Edward G., *Civil War Times Illustrated,* volume XXI, No. 10, February, 1983;

72. Bouton, John Bell, *A Memoir of General Louis Bell,* pages 28-29; Fonvielle Jr., Dr. Chris E., *The Wilmington Campaign: Last Rays of Departing Hope,* pages 274-275; Gragg, Rod, *Confederate Goliath: The Battle of Fort Fisher,* page 197;

73. Bouton, John Bell, *A Memoir of General Louis Bell,* page 29; Gragg, Rod, *Confederate Goliath: The Battle of Fort Fisher,* page 198;

74. Lamb, William, *Colonel Lamb's Story of Fort Fisher,* page 34; Harkness, Edson J, *The Expeditions Against Fort Fisher and Wilmington,* page 174, *Military Essays and Recollections; Papers Read Before the Commandery of the State of Illinois, Military Order of the Loyal Legion of the United States,* Vol II; Gragg, Rod, *Confederate Goliath: The Battle of Fort Fisher,* pages 191-193;

75. Lamb, William, *Colonel Lamb's Story of Fort Fisher,* page 32-33; Towle, Captain George F., *Terry's Fort Fisher Expedition,* page 297, *Old and New,* Vol. XI;

76. *O.R. Series I, Vol. XLVI, part 2,* page 1062; Barefoot, Daniel W., *General Robert F. Hoke: Lee's Modest Warrior,* pages 258-259; Fonvielle Jr., Dr. Chris E., *The Wilmington Campaign: Last Rays of Departing Hope,* pages 278-279; Gragg, Rod, *Confederate Goliath: The Battle of Fort Fisher,* page 187-188;

77. Harkness, Edson J, *The Expeditions Against Fort Fisher and Wilmington,* pages 177-178, *Military Essays and Recollections; Papers Read Before the Commandery of the State of Illinois, Military Order of the Loyal Legion of the United States,* Vol. II,

78. Lamb, Colonel William, *The Defense of Fort Fisher,* page 229, Histories of Several Regiments and Battalions from North Carolina, Vol. 5, by Walter Clark;

79. Lamb, William, *Colonel Lamb's Story of Fort Fisher,* page 33-34;

80. Lamb, William, *Colonel Lamb's Story of Fort Fisher,* page 34; Fonvielle Jr., Dr. Chris E., *The Wilmington Campaign: Last Rays of Departing Hope,* page 284; Gragg, Rod, *Confederate Goliath: The Battle of Fort Fisher,* pages 201-202;

81. *O.R., Series I, Vol. XLVI,* Part 2, pages 1064-1065;

82. James Reilly's Account of Fort Fisher, W. L. DeRossett papers, North Carolina Department of Archives and History; Fonvielle Jr., Dr. Chris E., *The Wilmington Campaign: Last Rays of Departing Hope,* page 285; Gragg, Rod, *Confederate Goliath: The Battle of Fort Fisher,* page 203;

83. O.R., Series I, Vol. LVIII, Part 2, page 426;

84. Curtis, Colonel N. Martin, *The Capture of Fort Fisher, Personal Recollections of the War of the Rebellion, Addresses Delivered Before the Commandery of the State of New York, Military Order of the Loyal Legion of the United States,* page 41;

85. Curtis, N. Martin, *The Capture of Fort Fisher, Personal Recollections of the War of the Rebellion, Addresses Delivered Before the Commandery of the State of New York, Military Order of the Loyal Legion of the United States,* page 43; Fonvielle Jr., Dr. Chris E., *The Wilmington Campaign: Last Rays of Departing Hope,* page 287;

86. Curtis, N. Martin, *The Capture of Fort Fisher, Personal Recollections of the War of the Rebellion, Addresses Delivered Before the Commandery of the State of New York, Military Order of the Loyal Legion of the United States,* page 44;

87. Comstock, Lt Colonel Cyrus B., *The Diary of Cyrus B. Comstock,* pages 303-304, Gragg, Rod, *Confederate Goliath: The Battle of Fort Fisher,* page 212;

88. Gragg, Rod, *Confederate Goliath: The Battle of Fort Fisher,* pages 213-214; Fonvielle Jr., Dr. Chris E., *The Wilmington Campaign: Last Rays of Departing Hope,* pages 289-290

89. Ames, General Adelbert, *The Capture of Fort Fisher,* page 15, *Personal Recollections of the War of the Rebellion, Addresses Delivered Before the Commandery of the State of New York, Military Order of the Loyal Legion of the United States;*

90. Gragg, Rod, *Confederate Goliath: The Battle of Fort Fisher,* pages 214-215; Fonvielle Jr., Dr. Chris E., *The Wilmington Campaign: Last Rays of Departing Hope,* pages 289-290;

91. Lamb, Colonel William, *Colonel Lamb's Story of Fort Fisher,* pages 34-35; Gragg, Rod, *Confederate Goliath: The Battle of Fort Fisher,* pages 216-217; Fonvielle Jr., Dr. Chris E., *The Wilmington Campaign: Last Rays of Departing Hope,* pages 292-294;

92. Lamb, Colonel William, *Colonel Lamb's Story of Fort Fisher,* pages 34-35;

93. Lamb, Colonel William, *Colonel Lamb's Story of Fort Fisher,* pages 36-37; Fonvielle Jr., Dr. Chris E., *The Wilmington Campaign: Last Rays of Departing Hope,* page 293; Yearns and Barrett, *North Carolina Civil War Documentary,* pages 88-89;

94. Lamb, Colonel William, *Colonel Lamb's Story of Fort Fisher,* pages 4-5; Fonvielle Jr., Dr. Chris E., *The Wilmington Campaign: Last Rays of Departing Hope,* page 45;

95. Fonvielle Jr., Dr. Chris E., *The Wilmington Campaign: Last Rays of Departing Hope,* page 293-294; Gragg, Rod, *Confederate Goliath: The Battle of Fort Fisher,* page 218;

96. Reilly, Major James, *James Reilly's Account of the Battle of Fort Fisher,* W.L. DeRossett Papers, North Carolina Department of Archives and History;

97. Reilly, Major James, *James Reilly's Account of the Battle of Fort Fisher,* W.L. DeRossett Papers, North Carolina Department of Archives and History;

98. Watson, Seaman Robert, *Robert Watson's Diary, Yankees were landing below us,* page 16;

99. Yearns and Barrett, *North Carolina Civil War Documentary,* page 89;

100. Reilly, Major James, *James Reilly's Account of the Battle of Fort Fisher*, W.L. DeRossett Papers, North Carolina Department of Archives and History; Fonvielle Jr., Dr. Chris E., *The Wilmington Campaign: Last Rays of Departing Hope*, page 295;

101. *O.R. Series I, Vol. XLVI, part 2*, pages 442-447; Lamb, Colonel William, *Colonel Lamb's Story of Fort Fisher*, page 37; Fonvielle Jr., Dr. Chris E., *The Wilmington Campaign: Last Rays of Departing Hope*, page 295; Gragg, Rod, *Confederate Goliath: The Battle of Fort Fisher*, pages 224-225

102. Terry, Adrian's letter to his wife, *The Task Before Them*, page 43, Longacre, Edward G., *Civil War Times Illustrated*, volume XXI, No. 10, February, 1983; Fonvielle Jr., Dr. Chris E., *The Wilmington Campaign: Last Rays of Departing Hope*, page 296; Gragg, Rod, *Confederate Goliath: The Battle of Fort Fisher*, page 228;

103. Rockwell, Colonel Alfred P., *OR* LVIII, Series I, page 411;

104. Eldridge, Captain Daniel, *The Third New Hampshire and All About It, 1861-1865*, page 616;

105. Grattan, John W., *Under the Blue Pennant*, page 182;

106. Gragg, Rod, *Confederate Goliath: The Battle of Fort Fisher*, page 220;

107. *New York Herald-Tribune*, January 26, 1865;

108. Manarin, Louis H. and Weymouth T. Jordan, eds., *North Carolina Troops1861-1865: A Roster*, volume I, Artillery, page 263;

Chapter 6 The Aftermath

1. *New York Tribune*, January 17, 1865; Canning, Joseph, Joseph Canning's journal, McEachern and Williams Collection, UNCW; Fonvielle Jr., Dr. Chris E., *The Wilmington Campaign: Last Rays of Departing Hope*, pages 302-303;

2. Cleer, Seaman James J., James Cleer in a letter to his mother and father, January 17, 1865, James J. Cleer papers, Manuscript Department, William R. Perkins Library, Duke University; Gragg, Rod, *Confederate Goliath: The Battle of Fort Fisher*, pages 231-232;

3. Perrien, Joseph, *Historic Incidents From the fall of Fort Fisher*, page 473-474, *Deeds of Valor: How America's Heroes Won the Medal of Honor*;

4. Grattan, Acting Ensign John W., *Under the Blue Pennant or Notes of a Naval Officer 1863-1865*, page 176;

5. Rogers, Henry Munroe, *Memories of Ninety Years*, page 109-110;

6. Jones, Regimental Chaplain T.D., *Welshman in the Union Armies, Civil War History*, page 172, Published Quarterly by the State University of Iowa, Vol. 4, 1958

7. Turner, Reverend Henry M., *Rocked in the Cradle of Consternation*, page 79, *American Heritage Magazine*, October/November 1980;

8. *O.R., Series I, Vol. XLVI*, page 430; Turner, Reverend Henry M., *Rocked in the Cradle of Consternation*, page 78, *American Heritage Magazine*, October/November 1980; Walker Jr., James L., *Rebel Gibraltar*, page 363; Fonvielle Jr., Dr. Chris E., *The Wilmington Campaign: Last Rays of Departing Hope*, page 306; Gragg, Rod, *Confederate Goliath: The Battle of Fort Fisher*, pages 232-233;

9. Lamb, Colonel William, *Colonel Lamb's Story of Fort Fisher*, page 37-38; Clark, Lt James, *The Iron Hearted Regiment*, page 165;

10. Mowris, Regimental Surgeon James A., *A History of the 117th Regiment, New York Volunteers,(Fourth Oneida)* pages 179-180; Fonvielle Jr., Dr. Chris E., *The Wilmington Campaign: Last Rays of Departing Hope*, pages 304-305; Gragg, Rod, *Confederate Goliath: The Battle of Fort Fisher*, pages 233-234;

11. Mowris, Regimental Surgeon James A., *A History of the 117th Regiment, New York Volunteers,(Fourth Oneida)* page 182;

12. Clark, Lt James, *The Iron Hearted Regiment*, page 166;

13. *O.R. Series I, Vol. XLVI, part 1*, page 427; Fonvielle Jr., Dr. Chris E., *The Wilmington*

Campaign: Last Rays of Departing Hope, page 305; Gragg, Rod, *Confederate Goliath: The Battle of Fort Fisher,* page 234; Johnston, John M, *Personal Recollections,* pages 2-3, Collection of Bob Cook;

14. Turner, Reverend Henry M., *Rocked in the Cradle of Consternation,* page 79, *American Heritage Magazine,* October/November 1980;

15. *O.R. Series I, Vol. XLVI, part 1,* page 427; Fonvielle Jr., Dr. Chris E., *The Wilmington Campaign: Last Rays of Departing Hope,* page 305;

16. Quimby, First Lt. George, *OR, XLVI, Series I, part I,* page 430; Gragg, Rod, *Confederate Goliath: The Battle of Fort Fisher,* page 233;

17. *O.R. Vol. LVIII, Series I,* pages 399-401; Battles and Leaders, Volume IV, page 401; Fonvielle Jr., Dr. Chris E., *The Wilmington Campaign: Last Rays of Departing Hope,* page 393; Gragg, Rod, *Confederate Goliath: The Battle of Fort Fisher,* page 235; Mark A. Moore, *The Wilmington Campaign and the Battles for Fort Fisher,* page 80; Walker, James L., *Rebel Gibraltar,* page 362;

18. *O. R. Vol. XLVI,* pages 435-436; Lamb, William, *Colonel Lamb's Story of Fort Fisher,* pages 26-27;

19. Gragg, Rod, *Confederate Goliath: The Battle of Fort Fisher,* page 236;

20. Haigh, William H., *William H. Haigh Papers,* pages 2-3, Manuscripts Department, Wilson Library, University of North Carolina at Chapel Hill;

21. Haigh, William H., *William H. Haigh Papers,* pages 2-3, Manuscripts Department, Wilson Library, University of North Carolina at Chapel Hill;

22. Thomas, Leonard R., *The Story of Fort Fisher,* page 16, *The United Service: A Monthly Review of Military and Naval Affairs,* vol. X; Gragg, Rod, *Confederate Goliath: The Battle of Fort Fisher,* page 237;

23. Haigh, William H., *William H. Haigh Papers,* pages 2-3, Manuscripts Department, Wilson Library, University of North Carolina at Chapel Hill;

24. Haigh, William H., *William H. Haigh Papers,* pages 3-4, Manuscripts Department, Wilson Library, University of North Carolina at Chapel Hill;

25. Johnston, John M, *Personal Recollections,* pages 2-3, Collection of Bob Cook;

26. Gragg, Rod, *Confederate Goliath: The Battle of Fort Fisher,* pages 242-243;

27. *O.R., Series I, part II, Vol. XLVI,* page 1078;

28. *O.R., Series II, Vol. LVIII,* page 434;

29. *Wilmington Messenger* June 27, 1897;

30. *O.R., Series II, Vol. LVIII,* pages 440, 442;

31. Lamb, William, *Histories of the Several Regiments and Battalions From North Carolina In the Great War 1861-65,* volume I, edited by Walter Clark, pages 530-531;

Chapter 7 Regiment Placement Inside Fort Fisher During the Second Battle

1. McNeill, Thomas A., This book, page 114; Histories of several Regiments and Battalions from North Carolina, Volume IV, pages 308-309

2. Fulmore, Zachery T., This book, page 103; McNeill, Thomas A., Histories of several Regiments and Battalions from North Carolina, Volume IV, pages 309-310

3. Davis, Thaddeus, This book, page 99; Histories of several Regiments and Battalions from North Carolina, Volume II, page 760

4. *Wilmington Messenger,* July 2, 1898

5. Lamb, Colonel William, This book, page 91; The Southern Historical Society Papers, Volume XXI, page 284

6. Saunders, Major William J., This book, page 123; O. R. Volume VIL, Part 1, page 438

7. Watson, Robert, This book, page 128; *The Yankees Were Landing Below Us, Civil War Times Illustrated,* April 1976, page 15

8. Gordon, George T., This book, page 105; Lamb, William, This book, page 80

Bibliography

Articles and Periodicals:

Ames, Adelbert, "Capture of Fort Fisher, North Carolina, Jan. 15, 1865," page 1-24, Commandery of the Loyal Legion of the state of New York, 1897;

Ammen, Daniel, "Our Second Bombardment of Fort Fisher", Military Order of the Loyal Legion of the United States War Paper, 4, 1887;

Ashe, Samuel A., "Fort Fisher", Confederate Veteran, Volume XL, page 250;

Baldwin, Albert Marion, *Wilmington Morning Star News*, December 4, 1927;

Becker, Joseph, "Fort Fisher and Wilmington", Frank Leslie's Popular Illustrated Magazine, XXXVIII, August 1894;

Blackmore, Buckner Lanier, *Raleigh News & Observer*, August 30 1881;

Bouton, John Bell, *A Memoir of General Louis Bell, Massachusetts Historical Society,* December 14, 1866;

Buel, Augustus, *The Cannoneer*, pages 327-334, Washington, D. C., National Tribune, 1890;

Coffin, Charles Carleton, Chapter XII, *Freedom Triumphant, the Fourth Period of the War of the Rebellion*, pages 247-267;

Confederate States of America, Congress, *Joint Select Committee to Investigate the Condition and Treatment of Prisoners of War,* March, 1865;

Conway, Alan, *Welshmen In The Union Armies, Published Quarterly By the State University of Iowa,* pages 143-174, *Civil War History,* Vol. 4, Berkeley Square House, London, 1958;

Curtis, Newton Martin, *The Capture of Fort Fisher, Personal Recollections of the War of the Rebellion: Addresses Delivered Before the Military Order of the Loyal Legion of the United States, Commandery of Massachusetts,* Boston: Published by the Commandery, 1900;

Davis, Thaddeus C., *Confederate Veteran* Magazine, February, 1899, page 65, *Histories of Several Regiments and Battalions From North Carolina*, Volume II;

Davis, Mrs. Thaddeus C., *The Confederate Veteran Magazine*, March, 1905, Volume XIII, No. 3;

Dolan, Diane, editor, "A Yankee View of the Fall of Wilmington, 1865" *Lower Cape Fear Historical Society Bulletin,* XX, February 1977;

Elliott, Charles G., *Histories of Several Regiment and Battalions From North Carolina,* Volume IV, Pages 538-543;

Dillon, Philip R., *Great Moments In War, Told by Living Generals,* November 16, 1911, *The Pittsburg Press;*

Eldredge, Daniel, *The Third New Hampshire, 1861-1865,* Boston: Stillings & Co., 1893;

Finan, William J., *Major General Alfred Howe Terry: Hero of Fort Fisher*, Hartford, Connecticut, Civil War Centennial Commission, 1965;

Fulmore, Zachery T. Letter to Colonel Lamb, May, 1887;

Gordon, Colonel George T., O. R. Volume XLVI, Part I, pages 435-436;

Greer, William Robert, *"Recollection of a Private Soldier in the Army of the Confederate States."* Manuscript Department, William R. Perkins Library, Duke University;

Harkness, Edson J, *The Expeditions Against Fort Fisher and Wilmington,* pages 145-188, *Military Essays and Recollections; Papers Read Before the Commandery of the State of Illinois, Military Order of the Loyal Legion of the United States,* Vol. II;

Hunter, James B., *York Herald-Tribune, January 26, 1865;*

Izler, William V., *A Sketch of the War Record of the Edisto Rifles, 1861-1865,* Columbia, South Carolina, The State Company, 1914;

Johnston, John M., Papers From the Lower Cape Fear Historical Society;

Ketchum, Edgar, *Personal Reminiscences of the Capture of Fort Fisher and Wilmington, N. C., The United Service: A Monthly Review of Military and Naval Affairs,* XVI, 1896;

Lamb, Colonel William, *Colonel Lamb's Story of Fort Fisher, The Southern Historical Society Papers,* Volume XXI, page 257-290;

Lamb, Colonel William, *Colonel Lamb's Story of Fort Fisher*, The Blockade Runner Museum, 1966;

Lockwood, Henry Clay, "A True History of the Army at Fort Fisher", *The United States Service Magazine*, X, November, 1893, "The Capture of Fort Fisher", *Atlantic Monthly Magazine*, XXVII, May and June, 1871;

Longacre, Edward G., *The Task Before Them*, page 36-43, *Civil War Times Illustrated*, February, 1983;

Lossing, Benson J., "The First Attack on Fort Fisher", *Annals of War*, Dayton, Ohio, Morningside House, Inc., 1988;

McKethan, Augustus A., *Histories of Several Regiments and Battalions From North Carolina*, Volume 3, Walter Clark, page 215;

McNeill, Thomas A., *Histories of Several Regiments and Battalions From North Carolina*, Volume 3, Walter Clark, pages 306-311;

McQueen, Henry Clay, *The Veterans' Talks*, Lower Cape Fear Historical Society Archives;

Montgomery, James Alexander, *The Veterans' Talks*, Lower Cape Fear Historical Society Archives;

Mowris, J. A., *A History of the One Hundred Seventeenth Regiment N. Y. Volunteers (Fourth Oneida)*, Hartford, Connecticut, Case Lookwood and Company, 1866;

Palmer, Abraham J., *The History of the Forty-Eight Regiment New York State Volunteers in the War for the Union, 1861-1865*, Brooklyn, New York: Veterans Association of the Regiment, 1885;

Parker, Lieutenant Commander James, *Personal Recollections of the War of the Rebellion: Addresses Delivered Before the Commandery of the State of New York, Military Order of the Loyal Legion of the United States*, pages 104-117;

Pennypacker, General Galusha, "General Galusha Pennypacker at Fort Fisher", *The Pittsburg Press*, November 16, 1911;

Reilly, Major James, Manuscript Department, North Carolina State Archives;

Rose, George M., *Histories of Several Regiments and Battalions From North Carolina*, Volume 3, Walter Clark, pages 693-694;

Saunders, Major William J., O. R. Volume XLVI, Part I, pages 437-439;

Sims, Joseph M., "Personal Experiences in the Volunteer Navy During the Civil War", *War Papers Read Before the Military Order of the Loyal Legion, Commandery of the District of Columbia*, pages 356-370;

Stevenson, James Chapman, Document from Lower Cape Fear Historical Society;

Terry, Adrian's letter to his wife, *The Task Before Them*, page 43, Longacre, Edward G., *Civil War Times Illustrated*, volume XXI, No. 10, February, 1983;

Towle, Captain George F., "Terry's Fort Fisher Expedition*", Old and New*, Vol. XI, edited by Edward E. Hale, pages 290-304;

Turner, Reverend Henry M., "Rocked in the Cradle of Consternation", pages 70-79, *American Heritage Magazine*, October/November 1980;

Walrath, Colonel Ezra L., *The Syracuse Daily Courier*, February 3, 1865;

Watson, Robert, *The Yankees Were Landing Below Us: The Journal of Robert Watson, C.S.N.*, *Civil War Times Illustrated*, April, 1976, Edited by William N. Still, Jr.;

Wightman, S. K., "In Search of My Son, *American Heritage Magazine*, pages 64-78;

Books:

Abbott, Brigadier General Joseph C., O. R. A., Series I, Volume XLVI, pages 410-411; pages 426-431;

Ames, Brigader General Adelbert, O. R. A., Series I, Volume XLVI, pages 415-417;

Badeau, Adam, *Military History of Ulysses S. Grant, From April, 1861, To April, 1865.*, Vol. III, New York: D. Appleton and Company, 1885;

Barefoot, Daniel W., *General Robert F. Hoke: Lee's Modest Warrior*, John F. Blair Publisher, Winston-Salem, North Carolina, 1996;

Bartlett, Lieutenant John, O. R. N., Volume XI, pages 526-529;

Bates, Samuel P., *History of Pennsylvania Volunteers, 1861-65*, Volume 2, 945-949, Volume 3, pages 411-421, Volume 5, pages 338-383, pages 578-602;

Breese, Lieutenant Commander Kidder Randolph, O. R. N., Volume XI, pages 446-448;

Beyer, W. F. and Keydel, O. F., *Deeds of Valor from Records in the Archives of the United States Government,* Volume I, pages 469-474, Detroit, Perrien-Keydel Co. 1907;

Bouton, John Bell, *A Memoir of Colonel Louis Bell,* New York: s. n., 1865;

Butler, Benjamin F., *Butler's Book: Autobiography and Personal Reminiscences of Major-General Benjamin F. Butler,* A. M. Thayer & Co. Publishers, 1892;

Canney, Donald L., *The Old Steam Navy, Frigates, Sloops, and Gunboats, 1815-1885,* Vol. 1, Naval Institute Press, Annapolis, Maryland, 1990; *Lincoln's Navy, The Ships, Men and Organization, 1861-65,* Naval Institute Press, Annapolis, Maryland, 1998;

Carr, Dawson, *Gray Phantoms of the Cape Fear, Running the Civil War Blockade,* John F. Blair Publisher, Winston-Salem, North Carolina, 1998;

Chapman, Captain Robert T., Series I, Vol. XI, pages 372-373;

Chrisman, James A., editor, *76th Pennsylvania Volunteer Infantry, Keystone Zouaves: The Personal Recollections of John A. Porter,* Wilmington, North Carolina, Broadfoot Publishing Co., 1988;

Clark, James, *The Iron-Hearted Regiment: Being An Account of the Battles Marches and Gallant Deeds Performed by the 115th Regiment N. Y. Vols.,* pages 162-167, Albany, New York, J. Munsell Co., 1865;

Clark, Walter, editor, *Histories of Several Regiments and Battalions From North Carolina in the Great War 1861-65,* 5 volumes, Goldsboro, North Carolina, Nash Brothers, 1901;

Comstock, Cyrus B., *The Diary of Cyrus B. Comstock*, Edited by Merlin E. Sumner, Dayton: Morningside House, 1987; O. R. A., Series I, Volume XLVI, pages 405-409;

Current, Richard N., *The Lincoln Nobody Knows,* Hill and Wang, 1958;

Daggett, Colonel Rufus, O. R. A., Series I, Volume XLVI, pages 418-419;

Dawson, Captain Lucien L., O. R. N., Volume XI, pages 576-582;

Dubose, Henry Kershaw, *History of Company B, Twenty-first Regiment (Infantry) South Carolina Volunteers,* reprint of book published in 1909, The University of South Carolina Press;

Eldredge, Daniel, *The Third New Hampshire and All About It,* Boston, E. B. Stillings & Company 1893

Evans, Robley D, *A Sailor's Log: Recollections of Forty Years of Naval Life,* New York, Appleton and Co., 1901;

Fagan, Lieutenant Louis E., O. R. N., Volume XI, pages 514-516;

Fonvielle, Chris E., *The Wilmington Campaign: Last Rays of Departing Hope,* Savas Publishing, 1997; *Fort Fisher 1865, The Photographs of T. H. O'Sullivan,* SlapDash Publishing, LLC, Carolina Beach, North Carolina, 2011;

Fox, Lt. Colonel William F., *Regimental Losses In the American Civil War, 1861-1865,* page 19, Albany Publishing Company, 1889;

Gragg, Rod, *Confederate Goliath: The Battle of Fort Fisher,* Harper Collins, 1991;

Grattan, John W., *Under the Blue Pennant: Or Notes of a Naval Officer, 1863-1865, John Wiley and Sons, Inc.,* pages 162-173, New York, 1999;

Hallock, Judith Lee, *Braxton Bragg and Confederate Defeat*, Vol, II, University of Alabama Press, 1991;

Hagood, Johnson, *Memoirs of the War of Succession,* Columbia, South Carolina, The State Company, 1910;

Harding, Major Oliver P., O. R. A., Series I, Volume XLVI, pages 419-420;

Hyde, William L., *History of the One Hundred Twelfth N. Y. Volunteers,* pages 113-125, Fredonia, New York, W. McKinstry & Co., 1866;

Izler, William V., *A Sketch of the War Record of the Edisto Rifles, 1861-1865,* Columbia, South Carolina, The State Company, 1914;

Johnson, Lieutenant Colonel Nathan J., O. R. A., Series I, Volume XLVI, pages 421;

Johnson, Robert U. and Buel, Clarence C., editors, *Battles and Leaders of the Civil War,* New York, The Century Company, 1887;

Keith, H. J., *The Guns of Fort Fisher, A Pictorial Study of Ordinance,* Novus Development Corp., 2010;

Lamb, Colonel William, O,R.N., Series I, Vol. XI, pages 363-364, 366-369;

Lamb, William, *The Life and Times of Colonel William Lamb, 1835-1909*, Austin, Texas, 2000;

Lamson, Lieutenant Roswell H., *O,R.N., Series I, Vol. XI,* pages 450-451;

Little, Henry F. W., *The Seventh New Hampshire in the War of the Rebellion*, pages 353-421, Published by the Seventh New Hampshire Veteran's Association, Concord, N. H., 1896;

Lockwood, Colonel Henry C., *The Maine Bugle, A True History of the Army At Fort Fisher,* pages 29- 71;

Manarin, Louis H. and Weymouth T. Jordan, eds., *North Carolina Troops1861-1865: A Roster,* 13 volumes, Raleigh, North Carolina: Division of Archives and History, 1966-1993;

Mast, Greg, *State Troops and Volunteers, A Photographic Record Of North Carolina Civil War Soldiers,* North Carolina Department of Cultural Resources, Volume I, 1995;

McCaslin, Richard B., *The Last Stronghold: The Campaign For Fort Fisher,* McWhiney Foundation Press, 2003;

McNeill, Jim, *Masters of the Shoals, Tales of the Cape Fear Pilots Who Ran the Union Blockade,* Da Capo Press, 2003;

Moore, Mark A., *The Wilmington Campaign and the Battles For Fort Fisher,* Savas, 1999;

Mowris, Dr. J. A., A History of the One Hundred Seventeenth Regiment, N. Y. Volunteers, (Fourth Oneida), Case, Lockwood & Company Printers, Hartford, Conn., 1866;

Parker, Lieutenant Commander James, *O,R.N., Series I, Vol. XI,* pages 495-500;

Paine, Brigadier General Charles J., O. R. A., Series I, Volume XLVI, pages 423-424;

Phelps, Lieutenant Commander Thomas S., *O,R.N.,* Series I, Vol. XI, pages 537-538;

Phisterer, Frederick, *New York in the War of the Rebellion, 1861-1865,* Volume 2 pages 1523-1541, Volume 3, pages 1719-1738, 2337-2356, 2357-2377; Volume 4, 3320-3334, 3346-3358, 3371-3384, Volume 5, 3642-3656, 3936-3951, Albany, N. Y., Weed, Parsons & Company, 1890;

Poe, Clarence, *True Tales of the South At War, How Soldiers Fought and Families Lived, 1861-1865,*Dover Publications, 1995;

Porter, Rear Admiral David D., O,R.N., Series I, Vol. XI, pages 436-442; O,R.N., Series I, Vol. XI, General Order 70, pages 245-247; Series I, Vol. XI, General Order 73, page 248;

Pratt, Fletcher, *Stanton: Lincoln's Secretary of War,* W. W. Norton & Company Inc., 1953;

Price, Isaiah, *History of the Ninety Seventh Regiment Pennsylvania Volunteer Infantry During the War of the Rebellion 1861-65*, pages 338-367, Philadelphia, 1875:

Robinson, Charles M., *Hurricane of Fire, The Union Assault on Fort Fisher,* Naval Institute Press, Annapolis, Maryland, 1998;

Roby, First Lieutenant F. M., Series I, Vol. XI, pages 373-374;

Rockwell, Colonel Alfred P., O. R. A., Series I, Volume XLVI, pages 411-412;

Rogers, Henry Munroe, *Memories of Ninety Years,* Cambridge, Massachusetts: Houghton, Miflin, 1928;

Rollins, Lieutenant Augustus W., O. R. A., Series I, Volume XLVI, pages 414-415;

Sands, Benjamin Franklin, *From Reefer to Rear-Admiral,* pages 241-269, Frederick A. Stokes Company, New York, 1899;

Selfridge, Lieutenant Commander, Thomas O., O. R. N., Volume XI, pages 476-478;

Silverstone, Paul H., *Warships of the Civil War Navies,* Naval Institute Press, Annapolis, Maryland, 1989;

Southern Historical Society Papers, published 1876-1959, in Richmond, Virginia;

Stephens, Alexander H., *A Constitutional View of the Late War Between the States,* Vol. II, Chicago: National Publishing Co. 1868;

Terry, Major General Alfred H., O. R. A., Series I, Volume XLVI, pages 394-402;

Thomas, Leonard R., *The Story of Fort Fisher*, page 16, *The United Service: A Monthly Review of Military and Naval Affairs,* vol. X, Philadelphia: L.R. Hamersly & Co., 1893;

Travis, Colonel Black Jack, *Men of God, Angels of Death, History of the Rowan Artillery,* Travis Publishing Company, Wilmington, North Carolina, 2008;

Trickey, Captain William H., O. R. A., Series I, Volume XLVI, pages 413-414;

Triebe, Richard H., *Fort Fisher to Elmira: The Fatal Journey of 518 Confederate Soldiers,* Coastal Books, Wilmington, North Carolina, 2012;

Trotter, William R., *Silk Flags and Cold Steel,* John F. Blair, 1988; *Ironclads and Columbiads, The Civil War In North Carolina Volume III; The Coast,* Signal Research, Inc., 1989;

Truxtun, Lieutenant Commander W. T., Series I, Vol. XI, pages 471-472;

Walker, James L., *Rebel Gibraltar, Fort Fisher and Wilmington C. S. A.,* Dram Tree Books, Wilmington, North Carolina, 2005

Walrath, Major Ezra L., O. R. A., Series I, Volume XLVI, page 422;

Whiting, Major General William H. C., O,R.N., Series I, Vol. XI, pages 364-366;

Wideman, John C., *Civil War Chronicles: Naval Warfare, Courage and Combat on the Water,* MetroBooks, Michael Friedman Publishing Group, Inc., 1979;

Internet:

American Civil War Research Database, Historical Data Systems
Chemung Valley History Museum
Fold3.com

Manuscripts:

Alden, Alonzo Papers, Civil War Miscellaneous Collection, Archives Branch, U. S. Army Military History Institute;

Allen, Weld Noble Papers, Manuscript Department, William R. Perkins Library, Duke University

Ames, Adelbert Papers, Archives Branch, U. S. Army Military History Institute;

Bell, Louis Papers, Compiled Service Records of the 4th New Hampshire Infantry, National Archives;

Biggs, Asa Papers, Manuscript Department, William R. Perkins Library, Duke University;

Blair, B.F., letter *To Mother,* December 27, 1864, B.F. Blair Papers, Archives Division, U.S.;

Bland, Christopher Papers, Compiled Service Records of the 36th North Carolina Artillery, National Archives;

Boyd, Joseph Fulton Papers, Manuscript Department, William R. Perkins Library, Duke University;

Bragg, Braxton Collection, Archives Department, Rosenberg Library;

Braddy, Captain Kinchen, Kitchen Braddy letter to Z.T. Fulmore, March 25, 1901, misc. Civil War papers, Division of Archives and History, Raleigh, North Carolina;

Calder, William Diary, Manuscript Department, William R. Perkins Library, Duke University;

Cleer, Seaman James J., James Cleer in a letter to his mother and father, January 17, 1865, James J. Cleer papers, Manuscript Department, William R. Perkins Library, Duke University;

Cobb, Seaman William T. Papers, *Dear Father,* Fort Fisher State Historic Site;

Confederate Veterans' Talks, Lower Cape Fear Historical Society, Wilmington, North Carolina, McQueen, Corporal Henry Clay, Henry Clay McQueen papers, *Confederate Veterans' Talks,* Lower Cape Fear Historical Society Archives;

Fales, Robert, *First Visit to Fort Fisher,* Unpublished manuscript, N. C. Pamphlet File, New Hanover County Public Library;

Follet, Edward Diary, Manuscript Department, William R. Perkins Library, Duke University;

Haigh, William H. Papers, Southern Historical Collection, University of North Carolina;

Gratten, John W. Papers, Manuscript Division, Library of Congress;

Greer, William R. Papers, *Recollections of a Private Soldier of the Army of the Confederate States,* Manuscript Department, William R. Perkins Library, Duke University, North Carolina;

Izlar, James F. Diary, Manuscript Collection, South Carolina Library, University of South

Carolina;

Kelley, John H. Papers, Manuscript Department, William R. Perkins Library, Duke University;

King, Asa Papers, Confederate Veterans' Talks, Lower Cape Fear Historical Society Archives;

Kinton, John H. Papers, Manuscript Department, William R. Perkins Library, Duke University;

McClean, Alexander Torrey, "The Fort Fisher and Wilmington Campaign: 1864-1865",
     Master's Thesis, University of North Carolina, 1969;

McNeill, Hector H. Papers, Manuscript Department, William R. Perkins Library, Duke University;

McQueen, Henry Clay, "The Veterans' Talks", Lower Cape Fear Historical Society Archives;

Montgomery, James Alexander, "The Veterans' Talks", Lower Cape Fear Historical Society
     Archives;

Osborne, Joseph B. Papers, Manuscript Division, Library of Congress;

Pennypacker, Galusha Papers, The Historical Society of Pennsylvania;

Porter, Benjamin H. Papers, Records of the Bureau of Naval Personnel, National Archives;

Porter, David D. Papers, Manuscript Division, Library of Congress;

Preston, Samuel W. Papers, U. S. Navy Military Service Records, National Archives;

Read, William Jr. Papers, Manuscript Department, William R. Perkins Library, Duke University;

Regimental Correspondence, 1861-1865, Maine State Archives;

Reilly, James, James Reilly's Account of Fort Fisher, W. L. DeRossett papers, North Carolina
     Department of Archives and History;

Saunders, William J. Papers, Compiled Service Records of Confederate General and Staff
     Officers and Non-Regimental Enlisted Men, National Archives;

Scroggs, Joseph Diary, Civil War Collection, Archives Department, U. S. Army Military
     History Institute;

Shepard, Surgeon Joseph C., Letter to Wife received from Tom Morrison;

Singleton, Spiers Papers, Compiled Service Records of Confederate General and Staff
     Officers and Non-Regimental Enlisted Men, National Archives;

Tallentine, James Papers, U. S. Navy Military Service Records, Record Group 24, National
     Archives;

Taylor, John J. Papers, Manuscript Department, William R. Perkins Library, Duke University;

Terry, Adrian Papers, Terry Family Collection, Manuscripts and Archives Division,
     Sterling Memorial Library, Yale University;

Turrentine, Michael Papers, Manuscript Department, William R. Perkins Library, Duke University;

Watson, Robert Diary, Manuscript Department, Cornell University;

Westcoat, Joseph J. Papers, Manuscript Department, William R. Perkins Library, Duke University;

Whiting, Henry Chase Papers, Manuscript Department, William R. Perkins Library, Duke
     University,

Wightman, Edward K. Papers, Private Collection of Dr. Henry B. Wightman, Ithaca, N. Y.;

Newspapers:

New York Times
New York Tribune
New York World
The Pittsburg Press
The Syracuse Daily Courier and Union
Wilmington Daily Journal
Wilmington Messenger

Official Publications:

United States War Department, ed. *The War of the Rebellion: A Compilation of the Official Records of the Union and Confederate Armies,* 128 vols. Washington, D.C.: Government Printing Office;

Official Records of the Union and Confederate Navies In the War of the Rebellion 1861-65, Published Under the Direction Of the Honorable H.A. Herbert, Secretary of the Navy, by Lt. Commander Richard Rush, U.S. Navy;

Published Primary Sources:

"A Yankee Account of the Battle of Fort Fisher." *Our Living and Our Dead,* Vol. 1, No. 4, December, 1874;

Ames, Adelbert, "The Capture of Fort Fisher, North Carolina, January 15, 1865." Commandery of the Loyal Legion of the State of New York, 1897;

Ammen, Daniel, "Our Second Bombardment of Fort Fisher", Military Order of the Loyal Legion of the United States War Paper, 4, 1887;

Ashe, Samuel A., "Fort Fisher", Confederate Veteran, Volume XL, page 250;

Baldwin, Albert Marion, *Wilmington Morning Star News,* December 4, 1927;

Becker, Joseph, "Fort Fisher and Wilmington", Frank Leslie's Popular Illustrated Magazine, XXXVIII, August 1894;

Blackmore, Buckner Lanier, *Raleigh News & Observer,* August 30 1881;

Buel, Augustus, *The Cannoneer,* pages 327-334, Washington, D. C., National Tribune, 1890

Coffin, Charles Carleton, Chapter XII, *Freedom Triumphant, the Fourth Period of the War of the Rebellion,* pages 247-267;

Curtis, Newton Martin, *The Capture of Fort Fisher, Personal Recollections of the War of the Rebellion: Addresses Delivered Before the Military Order of the Loyal Legion of the United States, Commandery of Massachusetts,* Boston: Published by the Commandery, 1900;

Davis, Thaddeus C., *Confederate Veteran* Magazine, February, 1899, page 65, *Histories of Several Regiments and Battalions From North Carolina,* Volume II;

Davis, Mrs. Thaddeus C., *The Confederate Veteran Magazine,* March, 1905, Volume XIII, No. 3;

Dolan, Diane, editor, "A Yankee View of the Fall of Wilmington, 1865" *Lower Cape Fear Historical Society Bulletin,* XX, February 1977;

Elliott, Charles G., *Histories of Several Regiment and Battalions From North Carolina,* Volume IV, Pages 538-543;

Dillon, Philip R., *Great Moments In War, Told by Living Generals,* November 16, 1911, *The Pittsburg Press;*

Eldredge, Daniel, *The Third New Hampshire, 1861-1865,* Boston: Stillings & Co., 1893;

Fulmore, Zachery T. Letter to Colonel Lamb

Gordon, Colonel George T., O. R. Volume XLVI, Part I, pages 435-436

Greer, William Robert, *"Recollection of a Private Soldier in the Army of the Confederate States."* Manuscript Department, William R. Perkins Library, Duke University

Harkness, Edson J, *The Expeditions Against Fort Fisher and Wilmington,* pages 145-188, *Military Essays and Recollections; Papers Read Before the Commandery of the State of Illinois, Military Order of the Loyal Legion of the United States,* Vol II;

Hunter, James B., *York Herald-Tribune, January 26, 1865;*

Izler, William V., *A Sketch of the War Record of the Edisto Rifles, 1861-1865,* Columbia, South Carolina, The State Company, 1914;

Johnston, John M., Papers From the Lower Cape Fear Historical Society;

Ketchum, Edgar, *Personal Reminiscences of the Capture of Fort Fisher and Wilmington, N. C., The United Service: A Monthly Review of Military and Naval Affairs,* XVI, 1896;

Lamb, Colonel William, *Colonel Lamb's Story of Fort Fisher, The Southern Historical Society Papers,* Volume XXI, page 257-290;

Lamb, Colonel William, *Colonel Lamb's Story of Fort Fisher*, The Blockade Runner Museum, 1966;

Lockwood, Henry Clay, "A True History of the Army at Fort Fisher", *The United States Service Magazine*, X, November, 1893; "The Capture of Fort Fisher", *Atlantic Monthly Magazine*, XXVII, May and June, 1871;

McKethan, Augustus A., *Histories of Several Regiments and Battalions From North Carolina*, Volume 3, Walter Clark, page 215;

McNeill, Thomas A., *Histories of Several Regiments and Battalions From North Carolina*, Volume 3, Walter Clark, pages 306-311;

McQueen, Henry Clay, *The Veterans' Talks*, Lower Cape Fear Historical Society Archives;

Montgomery, James Alexander, *The Veterans' Talks*, Lower Cape Fear Historical Society Archives;

Mowris, J. A., *A History of the One Hundred Seventeenth Regiment N. Y. Volunteers (Fourth Oneida)*, Hartford, Connecticut, Case Lookwood and Company, 1866;

Parker, Lieutenant Commander James, *Personal Recollections of the War of the Rebellion: Addresses Delivered Before the Commandery of the State of New York, Military Order of the Loyal Legion of the United States*, pages 104-117;

Reilly, Major James, Manuscript Department, North Carolina State Archives;

Rose, George M., *Histories of Several Regiments and Battalions From North Carolina*, Volume 3, Walter Clark, pages 693-694;

Saunders, Major William J., O. R. Volume XLVI, Part I, pages 437-439;

Sims, Joseph M., "Personal Experiences in the Volunteer Navy During the Civil War", *War Papers Read Before the Military Order of the Loyal Legion, Commandery of the District of Columbia*, pages 356-370;

Stevenson, James Chapman, Document from Lower Cape Fear Historical Society;

Terry, Adrian's letter to his wife, *The Task Before Them*, page 43, Longacre, Edward G., *Civil War Times Illustrated*, volume XXI, No. 10, February, 1983;

Towle, Captain George F., "Terry's Fort Fisher Expedition*", Old and New*, Vol. XI, edited by Edward E. Hale, pages 290-304;

Turner, Reverend Henry M., "Rocked in the Cradle of Consternation", pages 70-79, *American Heritage Magazine*, October/November 1980;

Walrath, Colonel Ezra L., *The Syracuse Daily Courier*, February 3, 1865;

Watson, Robert, *The Yankees Were Landing Below Us: The Journal of Robert Watson, C.S.N.*, Civil War Times Illustrated, April, 1976, Edited by William N. Still, Jr.;

Index

D

About the author:

Richard H. Triebe is a freelance writer and historian published in multiple periodicals. He is the author of several historical novels and has done extensive research work regarding the Fort Fisher prisoners. His book *Fort Fisher to Elmira* was awarded the coveted Jefferson Davis Historical Gold Medal Award.

Richard has an Associate's Degree in Marine Technology. Richard is a former Chicago police officer and was a provost marshal investigator in the United States Army. He is a member of the Coastal Carolina Writers Guild, a Brunswick Writers Forum panelist, and has appeared as a guest on several television shows, including *The Artist's Craft* hosted by Stacy Cochran and WWAY TV's *Book Corner* with Marcy Cuevas. He is a member of the Cape Fear Civil War Round Table, and has presented historical overviews of the battles of Fort Fisher to many local organizations. He and his wife, Barbara, live in Wilmington, North Carolina.